VERANDAH OF VIOLENCE

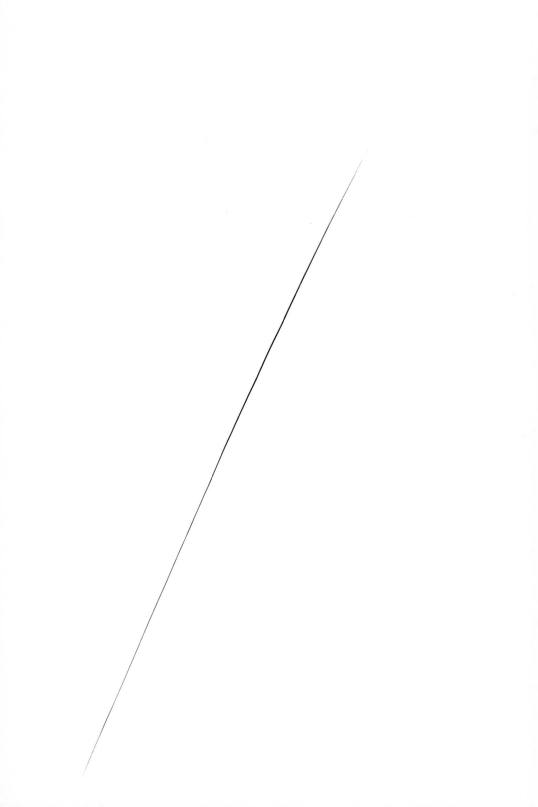

VERANDAH OF VIOLENCE

The Background to the Aceh Problem

Edited by

ANTHONY REID

SINGAPORE UNIVERSITY PRESS

in association with

UNIVERSITY OF WASHINGTON PRESS
Seattle

Published simultaneously in Singapore and the United States of America.

Singapore University Press, NUS Publishing
AS3-01-02. 3, Arts Link
Singapore 117569
www.nus.edu.sg/npu

ISBN 9971-69-331-3 (Paper)

University of Washington Press
P.O. Box 50096
Seattle, WA 98145-5096, U.S.A.
www.washington.edu/uwpress

Library of Congress Cataloging-in-Publication Data

Verandah of violence: the background to the Aceh problem / edited by Anthony Reid.
    p. cm.
  Includes bibliographical references and index.
  ISBN 0-295-98633-6 (pbk. : alk. paper)
  1. Aceh (Indonesia)—History. 2. Aceh (Indonesia)—History—Autonomy and independence movements. 3. Aceh (Indonesia) Politics and government.
4. Political violence—Indonesia—Aceh. 5. Gerakan Aceh Merdeka. I. Title: Background to the Aceh problem. II. Reid, Anthony.
  DS646.15.V47 2006
  959.8'1—dc22   2006008589

Printed in Singapore

In memory of

M. Isa Sulaiman
and all of Aceh's victims

Contents

Maps and Illustrations   ix

In Memoriam   xi

Preface   xiii

Acknowledgements   xiv

Spelling and Usage   xv

Contributors   xvi

Glossary and Abbreviations   xix

Chronology of Events   xxvii

1. Introduction   1
    Anthony Reid

2. Indian and Indonesian Elements in Early North Sumatra   22
    E. Edwards McKinnon

3. Aceh in the Sixteenth and Seventeenth Centuries:
    "*Serambi Mekkah*" and Identity   38
    Peter G. Riddell

4. The Pre-modern Sultanate's View of its Place in the World   52
    Anthony Reid

5. Aceh at the Time of the 1824 Treaty   72
    Lee Kam Hing

6. Colonial Transformation: A Bitter Legacy   96
    Anthony Reid

7. Aceh and the Holy War (*Prang Sabil*)   109
    Teuku Ibrahim Alfian

8. From Autonomy to Periphery: A Critical Evaluation of the
    Acehnese Nationalist Movement   121
    M. Isa Sulaiman

9. Violence and Identity Formation in Aceh under
    Indonesian Rule   149
    Edward Aspinall

10. Sentiments Made Visible: The Rise and Reason of
    Aceh's National Liberation Movement   177
    William Nessen

11. Military Business in Aceh   199
    Damien Kingsbury and Lesley McCulloch

12. Insurgency and Counter-Insurgency: Strategy and the
    Aceh Conflict, October 1976–May 2004   225
    Kirsten E. Schulze

13. Democratisation, the Indonesian Armed Forces and the
    Resolving of the Aceh Conflict   272
    Aleksius Jemadu

14. What's Special about Special Autonomy in Aceh?   292
    Michelle Ann Miller

15. Local Leadership and the Aceh Conflict   315
    Rodd McGibbon

Bibliography   360

Index   380

Maps and Illustrations

Maps

1. The Premodern Indian Ocean   21
2. North Sumatra, 18th–19th centuries   73
3. Aceh in the 1990s   150

Illustrations

1. Banda Aceh after the tsunami   1
2. Chinese bell of 1469, hanging in the Aceh citadel in 1874   11
3. Lokeśvara head recovered from Banda Aceh area during the Aceh-Dutch War   27
4. The Acehnese Ambassador to the Netherlands, Abdul Hamid, paying his respects to Prince Maurits in The Hague, 1602   59
5. Captain Thomas Forrest received by Sultan Mahmud Syah in 1764   80
6. The "Nine-fold seal" (*Cap Sikureuëng*) of Sultan Daud, giving the names of eight of his illustrious predecessors, surrounding his own   102
7. A version of the *Hikayat Perang Sabil*, copied out on modern paper and captured by the Dutch from the wife of Sultan Daud in 1902   112
8. Hasan Tiro standing on a river raft in Northeast Aceh during the DI revolt in 1958   137
9. Later GAM military commander Muzakkir Manaf saluting Hasan Tiro at Acehnese training camp in Libya, 1980s   138
10. Tgk. M. Daud Beureu'eh addressing a peace-making meeting, c. 1959   153
11. Poster of the Cease-fire (CoHA) period of 2002–3, reminding the TNI and GAM, in Indonesian and Acehnese, of offenses now forbidden to them — torturing, killing, plundering, bombing, burning, raping and so forth   155

12. Bullah, a GAM district commander, in front of Aceh's
    independence flag, 3 January 2003   178
13. GAM guerrillas on patrol in the forest near the
    massive Exxon-Mobil natural gas facilities, North Aceh,
    June 2001   192
14. GAM stealing arms from a TNI store   227
15. GAM and the ICRC negotiating the release of
    journalist Ferry Santoro, Lhok Jok, Peudawa, East Aceh,
    May 2004   229
16. Army Chief Ryamizard Ryacudu at closing ceremony
    of "Aceh" Raider battalion 300 in Cianjur,
    December 2003   246
17. A house targeted by the TNI as supporting a member
    of GAM   253
18. Acehnese woman demonstrating for a referendum on
    independence in mid-December 2002, days after the
    signing of a cease-fire between the Indonesian
    Government and the GAM guerrillas   299
19. GAM guerrillas on guard outside largest-ever meeting
    of GAM commanders, North Aceh, 4 January 2003   303
20. Local Aceh (NAD) Government poster on display in
    Banda Aceh, celebrating the cease-fire agreement (CoHA)
    of 9 December 2002   344

In Memoriam

M. Isa Sulaiman, 1951–2004

Only one contributor to this volume lived through the events described in it, as a home-grown Acehnese historian of his people. Tragically, he shared the fate of many thousands of his countrymen on 26 December 2004. His home was near the coast in the northern suburbs of Banda Aceh, and few residents there survived when the giant tsunami carried everything before it. This book is dedicated to him, and to the many thousands of his countrymen who died on that day.

Mohammad Isa Sulaiman was born on 30 June 1951 in remote Manggeng, Southern Aceh, and had all his early education in the province. He took his masters (S2) degree from the teacher training (IKIP) section of the state university of Aceh (Universitas Syiah Kuala or Unsyiah), in 1977, having joined its faculty the year before. In 1979 he was chosen to participate in the innovative field research training station funded by the Ford Foundation in Ujung Pandang (Makassar). There, under the direction of the French ethnologist and Bugis specialist Christian Pelras, he wrote an exceptionally interesting and much quoted report on the principal Bugis ironworking village of Massepe, in Sidenreng. This led to a scholarship to Paris, mastery of another language, and a doctorate under the supervision of historian Denys Lombard. The dissertation covered the crucial struggles for power in the 1940s, with the title "Les ulèebalang, les ulémas et les enseignants de madrasah: la lutte pour le pouvoir local en Aceh de 1942 à 1951" (EHESS, 1985).

Returning to Banda Aceh he continued to teach in his alma mater and became a model of the engaged historian of his people. In 1997 he published the first comprehensive professional history of twentieth century Aceh — *Sejarah Aceh: Sebuah Gugatan terhadap Tradisi*. Three years later he accomplished an outstandingly balanced survey of the independence movement (GAM) — *Aceh Merdeka: Ideologi, Kepimpinan dan Gerakan* (2000). His chapter in this book is his last completed work and the first substantial piece to appear in English. It demonstrates well his concern to show the continuities in the various Acehnese resistance movements of the twentieth century, and the roots of Hasan Tiro's movement in a much longer past.

His work reflected his roots in a rural Acehnese society far from the elite centres of power. He was interested always in the apparently marginal and the marginalised. His first (bachelors) thesis documented a pesantren in his native south Aceh district; and a later research project was on an even more remote community in Gunong Kong, West Aceh. The offer of a visiting position in Singapore caught him on another research project in Simeuleu island off the west coast. His newest project sought to recover the history of the left in Aceh, a vital element in all the conflicts of pre-1965 Aceh which was first suppressed in the 1965 bloodbath, and then expunged from national memory.

Although a quiet achiever who did not frequent the international conference circuit, he gradually built a reputation as the most reliable and knowledgeable of Aceh's historians. When the negotiations between GAM and Jakarta appeared to be facing breakdown in October 2002, he was one of six neutral Aceh intellectuals and NGO representatives flown to Geneva by the HDC intermediaries, to convince the two sides how strong was the popular demand for peace. In 2003 he was invited to Leiden to take part in a KITLV project on "Access and Identity in post-Suharto Indonesia". Between March and July 2004 he was a Visiting Fellow at the Asia Research Institute, National University of Singapore, writing his chapter for this book.

He was co-convenor of the May 2004 Conference which gave birth to this volume. All of those who knew him came to treasure his quiet dignity, erudition, and good sense. As with so many of Aceh's finest who died with him, his loss will be irreparable.

Selamat jalan, Pak Isa. *Poteu Allah peuseulamat, la'en handjeuët ma'nusia.*

Preface

This book originated in a Singapore conference on 28–29 May 2004, at a time when the prospects for a negotiated consensual solution to the long-standing problem of Aceh appeared particularly dark. The short-lived Cessation of Hostilities Agreement had broken down just a year earlier, a military solution was being attempted yet again, and plans for Acehnese autonomy were further than ever from being implemented.

As the book was being prepared following this conference, Aceh suffered an unimaginable tragedy. The giant earthquake and tsunami of 26 December 2004 made everybody in Aceh a victim, with colossal losses to all sides in the dispute. Some chapters were updated as peace talks were again being conducted, and final editing was taking place as the 15 August 2005 Memorandum of Understanding between the warring parties was signed. This set of events represents the best opportunity in decades for Aceh to be reconstructed in a peaceful atmosphere of democracy and reconciliation, but nobody should expect it to happen without heroic efforts from all sides.

Experience has made Acehnese deeply sceptical about paper agreements between civilians to which the men with the guns were not committed. A very small number of civilian leaders on each side was responsible for negotiating the Helsinki Agreement. Peace and democracy will only come to Aceh if the international community, now with a huge stake in tsunami reconstruction, uses the peace actively to support those people on the ground who are committed to democratic and consultative outcomes.

The deep distrust built up over decades will not readily be overcome, particularly when Acehnese society is on its knees from the brutalising effects of war and tsunami. Previous agreements for regional autonomy in 1950, 1959 and 2001 have never been effective in a climate of military dominance, bureaucratic centralisation and personal corruption. Can autonomy and democracy become realities after a devastating natural calamity when the local administration was weaker than ever? This book does not predict the future, nor offer a blueprint for peace. It represents a plea for listening to the people of Aceh and involving them democratically in the search for solutions.

Acknowledgements

We acknowledge in the first place the support of the Asia Research Institute (ARI) of the National University of Singapore in funding and coordinating the 2004 conference, and galvanising the authors into writing and rewriting their chapters. ARI's Lynn Tan was a tower of strength in organising the conference. Muhammad Nur Djuli and Wiryono Sastrohandoyo also wrote valuable papers for that conference, though they were not able to attend in person. The input of a number of discussants, including M.C. Ricklefs, K. Kesavapany, Jamie Davidson, Marcus Mietzner and Mark Hong, was also valuable to the authors.

In preparing the book for publication, a major role was taken by Jiang Yang, too briefly a research assistant at ARI before departing for Canberra to pursue her own academic career. She edited the chapters for consistency, formatted the book and prepared or collated the combined bibliography, maps and illustrations. Jiang Na took over for the last stage and coordinated the final shape of the volume.

An initial translation of Isa Sulaiman's conference paper was undertaken by Zuraidah Ehsan. Mok Ly Yng drew the elegant maps. Connie Teo Eng Sook contributed her efficiency to much of the correspondence. Billie Nessen provided many striking photos. Michelle Miller did an outstanding job on the index to a tight deadline. At Singapore University Press we thank Lena Qua for her copy-editing and Winnifred Wong for the cover design.

Spelling and Usage

Aceh has been spelled in numerous ways since the Portuguese introduced *Dachem* and the Arabs and Italians *Assi*. English usage was most commonly *Achin* before the twentieth century but thereafter usually *Acheh*, in deference to what Acehnese themselves call their country. The Dutch consistently romanised the same word as *Atjeh*, as did Indonesians in the first years of independence. In 1974, however, the common spelling agreement between Indonesia and Malaysia accepted the letter *c* to represent the English sound *ch* or Dutch *tj*, and *j* to represent Dutch *dj*. Since then Indonesia called its province *Aceh* and the world has in general followed suit. That is the usage followed in this book, as with all other place names such as *Calang*.

The older leadership of GAM, however, has rejected Bahasa Indonesia as the language of Aceh (though accepting the long-term use of Malay as lingua franca), and consequently rejected also the new spellings since 1974. In quotations from GAM statements, therefore, the older English usage *Acheh* continues to appear.

The capital of Aceh has been called Banda Aceh since 1962, and on the whole was called either that or simply "Aceh" before 1873. The Dutch, however, introduced the term Kota Radja or Kutaradja (the city or citadel of the king) for the fortified capital they captured in 1874, and this remained the name of the town until changed in 1962. This book accepts the usage Kutaradja during the period it was official (1874–1962), as it does Batavia for the capital of the Indies between 1619 and 1942. Before and after these dates we use Banda Aceh and Jakarta.

In order to capture the diphthongs of spoken Acehnese, Snouck Hurgronje and Hoesein Djajadiningrat (author of the first scholarly dictionary) introduced a complex pattern of diacritics on vowels. As this system has never been formally updated or overturned, we follow it for Acehnese words, but not for place names which now have a simpler orthography.

Contributors

Teuku Ibrahim Alfian is Professor of History at Gadjah Mada University. He is the author of *Hikayat Raja Pasai* (Yogyakarta, 1973), *Perang di Jalan Allah: Aceh 1873–1912* (Jakarta, 1985), *War Literature* (Jakarta, 1992), *The Face of Aceh in the Glimpse of History* (Banda Aceh, 1999), and *Contribution of Samudra Pasai towards Islamic Studies in Southeast Asia* (Yogyakarta, 2005).

Edward Aspinall is Fellow in the Department of Political and Social Change, Research School of Pacific and Asian Studies, Australian National University. He previously taught at the University of Sydney and University of New South Wales. His publications include *Opposing Suharto: Compromise, Resistance and Regime Change in Indonesia* (Stanford University Press, 2005) and (with Harold Crouch) *The Aceh Peace Process: Why It Failed* (East West Center, 2003).

Aleksius Jemadu has been Head of the Department of International Relations, Parahyangan Catholic University, Bandung, Indonesia since 2004. He obtained his PhD in Political Science from Leuven in 1996. His publications include: "Democratization and the Dilemma of Nation-Building in Post-Soeharto Indonesia: The Case of Aceh", *Asian Ethnicity* 5, 3 (October 2004) and "Seeking a More Participatory Approach in the Resolving of the Aceh Conflict", *Inter-Asia Cultural Studies* 5, 3 (2004).

Damien Kingsbury is Director of International and Community Development, Deakin University, Victoria, Australia. His books include *The Politics of Indonesia*, 3rd edition (Oxford University Press, 2005), *South-East Asia: A Political Profile*, 2nd edition (Oxford University Press, 2005), and *Power Politics and the Indonesian Military* (RoutledgeCurzon, 2003).

Lee Kam Hing studied at the University of Malaya and Monash University, Melbourne, and taught at the University of Malaya, eventually as professor of history. He is presently Research Editor at Star Publications in Kuala Lumpur. His publications include *The Sultanate of Aceh: Relations with the British 1760–1824* (Oxford University Press, 1995).

Lesley McCulloch collaborated with Damien Kingsbury, at the time their joint chapter was prepared, in a Research Project on the Indonesian military at Deakin University. Her publications include *Trifungsi: The Role of the Indonesian Military in Business* (Bonn, 2000).

Rodd McGibbon is Manager of the United Nations Humanitarian Information Center for Sumatra and has a PhD in political science from the Australian National University. His previous publications include *Plural Society in Peril: Migration, Economic Change and the Papua Conflict.* (Washington DC: East West Center, 2004) and *Secessionist Conflicts in Aceh and Papua: Is Special autonomy the Solution?* (Washington DC: East West Center, 2004).

E. Edwards McKinnon was Visiting Fellow at Asia Research Institute (2004/5) after a career in Indonesia for over 30 years in plantation agriculture and development work. His Ph.D. (Cornell) in Archaeology concerned the north Sumatra site of Kota Cina. His interests in Aceh stem from conversations with the late H. Mohammad Said (*Waspada*) and his publications include "Beyond Serandib, a Note on Lambri at the Northern Tip of Aceh" in *Indonesia* (1988).

Michelle Ann Miller is completing her PhD on Aceh at Charles Darwin University, where she also previously taught. She has tutored at Deakin University. Her publications include "The Nanggroe Aceh Darussalam Law: A Serious Response to Acehnese Separatism?", *Asian Ethnicity* 5, 3 (October 2004), and "From reform to repression: the post-New Order's shifting security policies in Aceh", *Review of Indonesian and Malaysian Affairs* 38, 2 (2004).

William Nessen is a freelance journalist, photographer and documentary film-maker. He has written for numerous publications in Europe, North America, Australia and Asia. He specialises in Indonesia and the South Pacific. His forthcoming film, *The Black Road*, is about the conflict in Aceh.

Anthony Reid is Foundation Director of the Asia Research Institute at the National University of Singapore. He was previously Professor of Southeast Asian History at the Australian National University (1989–99) and UCLA (1999–2002). His books include: *The Contest for North Sumatra: Atjeh, the Netherlands and Britain, 1858–1898* (1969); *The Indonesian National Revolution, 1945–1950* (1974); *The Blood of the*

People: Revolution and the End of Traditional Rule in Northern Sumatra (1979); *Southeast Asia in the Age of Commerce, 1450–1680,* 2 vols. (1988–93); *Charting the Shape of Early Modern Southeast Asia* (1999); *An Indonesian Frontier: Acehnese and other Histories of Sumatra* (2004).

Peter G. Riddell is Professor of Islamic Studies at the London School of Theology, and previously taught at the London School of Oriental and African Studies and the Australian National University. His publications include *Islam in Context* (with Peter Cotterell; Grand Rapids, 2003), *Islam and the Malay-Indonesian World* (London, 2001), and *Transferring a Tradition* (Berkeley, 1990).

Kirsten E. Schulze is senior lecturer in International History at the London School of Economics, and previously taught at the Queen's University of Belfast. She specialises in conflict and conflict management focusing particularly on Indonesia, the Middle East and Northern Ireland. Her publications include *The Free Aceh Movement (GAM): Anatomy of a Separatist Organisation* (East West Center, 2004), *The Jews of Lebanon: Between Conflict and Coexistence* (Sussex Academic Press, 2001), *The Arab-Israeli Conflict* (Longmans, 1999) and *Israel's Covert Diplomacy in Lebanon* (Macmillan, 1998).

M. Isa Sulaiman, victim of the tsunami, is described in the memorial tribute.

Glossary and Abbreviations

ABRI   *Angkatan Bersenjata Republik Indonesia*; The Armed Forces of the Republic of Indonesia

adat   customary law

ASNLF   Aceh-Sumatra National Liberation Front

bangsa   nation, race

BKI   *Bijdragen tot de Taal-, Land-, en Volkenkunde*, issued by KITLV

BPK   *Badan Pemeriksa Keuangan*; National Audit Agency

Brimob   (paramilitary police) Mobile Brigade

BSOAS   *Bulletin of the School of Oriental and African Studies*

bughat   revolt against a legal government; rebellion

bupati   district head

Bulog   *Badan Urusan Logistic*; State Logistics Agency

CoHA   Cessation of Hostilities [Framework] Agreement, signed by GAM and government, 9 December 2003

Daerah Istimewa   Special Region; status granted to Aceh in 1959

dakwah   preaching, proselytism

Darul Islam (Ar)   House of Islam; Indonesian Islamic rebellion of 1948–63

dayah (Ac)   Acehnese religious school of the highest level, boarding school

Dewan Repolusi   Revolutionary Council; Darul Islam Aceh leadership under Hasan Saleh

DI   *Darul Islam*

DOM	*Daerah Operasi Militer*; Military Operation Zone
DPA	*Dewan Perwakilan Aceh*; Aceh Representative Council
DPR	*Dewan Perwakilan Rakyat*; People's Representative Council
EMOI	ExxonMobil Oil Indonesia
Florin or guilder	pre-war currency
fardhu'ain (Ar)	religious obligation
fatwa (Ar)	legal ruling by a Muslim Jurist
firman (Turkish)	decree
GAM	*Gerakan Aceh Merdeka*; Free Aceh Movement
Golkar	*Golongan Karya*; Functional Group (Suharto-era government party)
hari raya	(great day), holiday
hari raya puasa	*idulfitri*; feast at end of fasting month
HDC	Henri Dunant Centre
HGU	*Hak Guna Usaha*; Land Concession
hikayat	chronicle; Acehnese verse epic
HPH	*Hak Pengusahaan Hutan*; Forestry Exploitation Concession
HPS	*Hikayat Perang Sabil*; Tales of Holy War
HRW	Human Rights Watch
HUDA	*Himpunan Ulama Dayah Aceh*; Association of (Traditional) Acehnese Ulama
IAIN	*Institut Agama Islam Indonesia*; State Islamic Institute
ICG	International Crisis Group
ICRC	International Committee of the Red Cross
IDP	Internally Displaced Persons
imam	leader of the Friday prayer, in Aceh head of *mukim*

infaq	war fees
Inpres	*Instruksi Presiden*; Presidential instruction
ISEAS	Institute of Southeast Asian Studies, Singapore
jihad (Ar)	struggle (popularly equated with holy war)
jihad fi sabilillah (Ar)	struggle in the way of God; holy war
jilbab (Ar)	Muslim women's headscarf, concealing hair
JMBRAS	*Journal of the Malaysian Branch, Royal Asiatic Society*
JRAS	*Journal of the Royal Asiatic Society*
JSBRAS	*Journal of the Straits Branch, Royal Asiatic Society*
JSC	Joint Security Committee (established under CoHA)
JSEAH	*Journal of Southeast Asian History*
kadi	religious official or judge
kafir / kaphé (Ac)	unbeliever; infidel
kapur Barus	*Dryobalanops aromatica*; camphor
keistimewaan	special-ness
Kepres	*Keputusan Presiden*; Presidential Decree
Khedive (Ar)	viceroy
Kodam	*Komando Daerah Militer;* Regional Military Command
Kolakops Jaring Merah	Operation Red Net (1989–98)
Komnas HAM	*Komisi Nasional Hak Azasi Manusia*; National Commission for Human Rights
Kontras	*Komite untuk Orang Hilang dan Korban Tindak Kekerasan*; National Commission for Missing Persons and Victims of Violence
Kopassandha	(predecessor of Kopassus)
Kopassus	*Komando Pasukan Khusus*; special forces

Korte Verklaring (D)	short agreement
Kostrad	*Komando Cadangan Strategis Angkatan Darat*; Army Strategic Reserve Command
KRA	*Kongres Rakyat Aceh*; Aceh People's Congress
Kraton (D/Javanese)	fortified citadel
Ksatria Unit Penegak Pancasila	Noble Warriors for Upholding Pancasila
KSBO	*Komando Sektor Barat dan Oetara*; West and North Sector Command (Medan Front)
kubah	dome
LBH	*Lembaga Bantuan Hukum*; Legal Aid Foundation
Linmas	*Perlindungan Masyarakat*; People's Protection
LIPI	*Lembaga Ilmu Pengetahuan Indonesia*; Indonesian Institute of Sciences
madrasah (Ar)	Islamic school
M.A.E.	Ministère des Affaires Etrangères (Paris)
Mahkamah Syari'ah (Ar)	Islamic court system
Majelis Penimbang	Advisory Council
Majelis Ulama	Council of Ulama
meunasah (Ac)	communal hall
MPR	*Majlis Permusyawaratan Rakyat*; the People's Consultative Assembly
MUI	*Majelis Ulama Indonesia*; Islamic Scholars Council
mujahidin (Ar)	warriors of God

mukim (Ar)	parish; in Aceh a territorial unit of a few villages
murtad (Ar)	apostasy
NAD	*Nanggroe Aceh Darussalam*; State of Aceh, Abode of Peace; name of Aceh province following Law No.18 of 2001
nanggroë (Ac)	state (cf Malay *negeri*); domain of an *uleëbalang*
Negara Islam Indonesia	Islamic State of Indonesia
NGO	Non-governmental Organisation
NKPM	*Nederland Koninklijk Petroleum Maatschappij*
OCHA	Office for the Coordination of Humanitarian Aid
OIC	Organisation of the Islamic Conference
oknum	rogue elements
OKPH	*Operasi Pemulihan Keamanan dan Penegakan Hukum*; Security Recovery Operation, 2001–2
Operasi Terpadu	Integrated Operation (of TNI from 19 May 2003)
ORPAD	*Organisasi Perempuan Aceh Demokratik*; Organization of Democratic Acehnese Women
OUP	Oxford University Press
panglima	war-leader; commander
panglima wilayah	regional commander
PDIP	*Partai Demokrasi Indonesia Perjuangan*; Indonesian Democratic Party of Struggle
PDMD	*Penguasa Darurat Militer Daerah*; Regional Military Emergency Authority

PDSD	*Penguasa Darurat Sipil Daerah*; Regional Civilian Emergency Authority
pembinaan	guidance
pemuda	youth
penghulu	head
Peperda	*Penguasa Perang Daerah*; Regional War Administrator
Perang Beulanda (Ac)	the Dutch War
perang sabil	holy war
perikatan	federation
perlawanan rakyat (wanra)	civil defence groups
Perusahaan Perkebunan Negara	state-owned plantations
Pesindo	Indonesian Socialist Youth
PKI	Indonesian Communist Party
PKPB	*Partai Karya Peduli Bangsa*; Concern for Nation Functional Party
PPN	*Perusahaan Perkebunan Negara*; state-owned plantations
PPP	*Partai Persatuan Pembangunan*; United Development Party
PPRC	*Pasukan Pemukul Reaksi Cepat*; Quick Reaction Strike Units
prahu	sailing vessel
PRI	*Pemuda Republik Indonesia*
PUSA	*Persatuan Ulama Seluruh Aceh;* all-Aceh union of Islamic Scholars
pungli (*pungutan liar*)	wild fees; extortion
Qanun (Ac)	Regional regulation

Qitāl (Ar)	fighting
raja	ruler
rakaat	act of prostration in ritual prayer
RPI	*Republik Persatuan Indonesia;* United Republic of Indonesia (rebel coalition 1960–1)
sagi	corner; district of Aceh Besar
santri	traditional Muslim students
satuan kerangka	stationary garrison, framework troops
sejarah	history
serambi Mekkah	verandah of Mecca
SIRA	*Sentral Informasi Referendum Aceh;* Aceh Referendum Information Center
SMI	*Sekolah Menengah Islam*; Islamic Secondary School
SMIA	*Sekolah Menengah Islam Atas*; Islamic Senior High School
SMUR	*Solidaritas Mahasiswa untuk Rakyat*; Student Solidarity for the People
Socfin	*Société Financière de Caoutchouc*; Rubber Finance Company
SRI	*Sekolah Rendah Islam*; Islamic Primary School
SSKAD	*Sekolah Staf Komando Angkatan Darat;* the Army Staff Command School
SSR	security sector reform
syahbandar	port official
syariah(Ar), *syariat* (Ind)	Islamic law
T.	Teuku (title of Acehnese *ulèëbalang*)
taslīm (Ac)	peace

TMSU	*Tambang Minyak Sumatra Utara*; North Sumatran Oil Wells
TNI; *Tentara Nasional Indonesia*	Indonesian Armed Forces
TPR	*Tentera Perjuangan Rakyat*; People's Army of Struggle
ulama (pl. of Ar. *'alim*)	Islamic scholar, religious teacher
ulèëbalang (Ac)	lit. war-leader (Malay *hulubalang*); Aceh territorial chief
umat	Islamic community
UNAMET	United Nations Mission in East Timor
UNHCR	United Nations High Commission for Refugees
VKI	*Verhandelingen van het Koninklik Instituut* (KITLV Proceedings)
VOC	*Verenigde Oost-Indische Compagnie*; [Dutch] United East India Company
Wali Nanggroë	Head/Guardian of State
wanra	*perlawanan rakyat*; civil defence
yayasan	foundation
zakat	Religious tithe paid by Muslims to the poor

Chronology of Events

1873	First (defeated) and second Dutch invasions of Aceh.
1874	Death of Sultan Mahmud Shah; Abolition of the sultanate by the Dutch.
1881–90	Resistance leadership by militant ulama Tgk. Chik di Tiro (Syech Saman).
1896	Teuku Umar defects from Dutch and leads resistance until killed 1898.
1898	J.B. van Heutsz, advised by C. Snouck Hurgronje, begins systematic conquest.
1903	Surrender of last sultan, Mohd Daud Syah, and Panglima Polem.
1912	Death in battle of the last "Tiro-Teungkus", family of Tgk Chik.
1939	Foundation of PUSA unites reformist ulama under Daud Buereu'eh.
1942	PUSA-inspired revolt (Feb) ahead of Japanese invasion (March).
Aug. 1945	Japanese surrender, leaving *ulèëbalang* establishment in charge. Independence of unitary Indonesian Republic proclaimed in Jakarta.
Jan. 1946	Violent "social revolution" ends *ulèëbalang* authority. PUSA popular leadership pro-Republic.
June 1948	Republican Sumatra formally divided into three Provinces, making Aceh nominally part of North Sumatra.
Dec.	Dutch advances leave Aceh the only Republican stronghold.
July 1949	UN restores Republican government in Yogyakarta.
17 Dec.	Vice Premier Sjafruddin Prawiranegara authorises Aceh Province.
27 Dec.	Transfer of Dutch Sovereignty to Indonesia. Sukarno as President.
Jan. 1951	Aceh again merged into North Sumatra Province.
Sept. 1953	Daud Beureueh rebels, proclaiming Aceh part of N.I.I.

Robust Government response drives rebels out of urban areas. Hasan di Tiro defects from Indonesian mission in NY.

1957   Aceh returned to status of Province, with Ali Hasjmy as first Governor.

1959   Negotiations lead to end of armed rebellion, in return for Daerah Istimewa status. Daud Beureueh refuses to submit until 1962.

Oct. 1965   Coup attempt against Army leadership; General Suharto seizes control in Jakarta; massacres of communists, including in Aceh.

1966   Suharto replaces Sukarno as President.

1971   Mobil discovers natural gas at Arun, near Lhokseumawe. Production begins 1977.

Dec. 1976   Hasan Tiro declares "independence of Acheh Sumatra" in Aceh with c.200 supporters.

1977   Beginning of counter-insurgency operations.

1979   Hasan di Tiro leaves Aceh, with most of leadership killed or fled to Malaysia.

1987–9   200–300 Tiro supporters obtain military training in Libya.

1989   GAM begins serious strikes against military in Aceh, prompting declaration of DOM and military launch of *Kolakops Jaring Merah* operation.

1990–91   6,000 Kopassus troops to Aceh; fierce military repression drives much of GAM leadership to Malaysia.

1998   Suharto forced to resign in favour of Vice-President Habibie, who frees press, ends DOM, and permits referendum in East Timor (Feb. 1999).

Feb. 1999   Formation of student group SIRA and campaign for referendum; mobilises mass rally Banda Aceh 8 November.

Oct.   Abdurrahman Wahid becomes President after May general elections, and attempts to curb military.

Nov.   Wahid suggests (but later denies) that Aceh could be allowed an East-Timor style referendum.

Jan. 2000   Henri Dunant Centre begins encouraging direct contacts between GAM and Jakarta

12 May   Geneva agreement for a "Humanitarian Pause" from 2 June, which lowers violence only marginally.

April 2001 Wahid decrees "comprehensive programme" for Aceh, of

	which only the TNI "Security Recovery Operation", OKPH, is implemented.
23 July	Megawati becomes President, with ex-Gen. Susilo Bambang Yudhoyono (SBY) as Coordinating Minister for Political and Security Affairs.
8 Aug.	Megawati signs Nanggroe Aceh Darussalam (NAD) autonomy law, to come into effect 2002.
19 Jan. 2002	TNI raid GAM HQ and kill its commander Abdullah Syafi'ie, 3 days after invited to talks by Aceh Governor.
Feb.	Peace talks resume in Geneva, with NAD law as starting point.
May	Agreement in Switzerland for a future "all-inclusive dialogue process" and mechanism to establish cessation of hostilities.
9 Dec.	HDC-brokered Cessation of Hostilities Agreement (CoHA) signed in Geneva, with monitoring teams from Philippines and Thailand quickly into place. Sharp drop in violence.
April 2003	International monitoring missions withdrawn after militia attacks on some of them.
18 May	Declaration of military emergency, followed by TNI offensive, *Operasi Terpadu.*
May 2004	Change from status of military to civil emergency, but troop level of 40,000 remains. Governor Abdullah Puteh indicted for corruption.
Oct.	SBY becomes President, after decisive electoral win.
26 Dec.	Earthquake and tsunami destroy much of Banda Aceh and western coast. Aceh opened to foreign aid workers.
28 Jan. 2005	Peace talks commence in Helsinki.
22 Feb.	At second round of talks GAM accept "self government" within Indonesia.
11 April	Aceh Governor Abdullah Puteh sentenced to ten years in prison for corruption.
20 May 2005	Civil Emergency is lifted. Authority returns to civilian officials, but 39,000 TNI personnel remain.
17 July	Peace agreement in Helsinki between GAM leadership and Indonesian Government delegation.
15 Aug.	Formal signature of Memorandum of Understanding two sides in Helsinki, with immediate placement of 350 international monitors from EU and ASEAN. Comprehensive agreement for self-government within Indonesia.

1

Introduction

Anthony Reid

A Tragic History

Acehnese have learned to be stoic in the face of suffering. Nothing, however, could have prepared them for the destruction of 26 December 2004. After being subjected to military occupation for most of the previous 130 years, they faced the brunt of the world's worst recorded earthquake and tsunami. Nobody was able to count or identify the dead accurately, but the death toll of that single day gradually rose to over 160,000 people, more than 4 per cent of Aceh's population. The elite urban population of Banda Aceh was disproportionately hit, and much of its administrative infrastructure destroyed (see Fig. 1).

Fig. 1   Banda Aceh after the tsunami

Aceh has long prided itself on being the "Verandah of Mecca" (*Serambi Mekkah*), an exemplary focus of religious practice and learning and a channel to the heartland of Islam. The title of this book, *Verandah of Violence*, was intended to convey the irony of Aceh's reality over the last 130 years, marked by almost continual war, rebellion and repression. The violence that men have inflicted on this beautiful landscape was dwarfed, however, by the sudden violence of nature on the morning after Christmas. Aceh's vulnerability then became cruelly exposed as another kind of verandah; a frontier of the Southeast Asian tectonic plate, undercut by the eastward lurch of the Indo-Australian plate. This verandah was not the place to be when the earth moved.

The international community came at last to Aceh's assistance. When Aceh suffered in the past from invasion and occupation, it suffered alone. The first strategic move of those who sought to rule Aceh from Batavia/Jakarta was to cut the region off from the countries which had been its trading partners before 1873. The international media was briefly interested when the Dutch invaded in 1873 and again when the Indonesian military did so in 2003, but it did not sustain that interest when the struggle became a guerrilla one and foreign journalists were not welcome.

This time international attention needs to be sustained. This book is dedicated to arguing that Aceh needs and deserves that attention. Aceh desperately requires international assistance to get back on its feet. It also needs creative international attention to solving its political problems so that the talents of its people can be directed to building a strong society and economy. The authors represented here hope that the new generation, both Indonesian and international, of aid workers and policy-makers now seeking to get Aceh on its feet, will learn from past mistakes. These mistakes are abundantly chronicled in the pages that follow.

An Understudied Region

Like most parts of Indonesia outside Java-Bali, Aceh has been poorly served by the literature. There are two exceptions to the general neglect, when Aceh was acknowledged as a "problem". Dozens of Dutch works were devoted to Aceh in the period 1873–1904, when it represented Holland's major colonial problem. Apart from several detailed works on the military and diplomatic history,[1] the best representative of this period was Snouck Hurgronje's comprehensive *De Atjehers* of 1895, a brilliant ethnography often marred by its overtly political purpose.[2] The second period to spawn a substantial amount of work was the democratic space after Suharto's fall in 1998, when numerous works in Indonesian and a few in English discussed the separatist issue.[3]

The earlier history of Aceh is particularly inaccessible for the general reader looking for an overview in English. For this reason we have attempted in Chapters 1–7 to provide the connected story lacking elsewhere. Useful specialist monographs do exist on particular episodes, by Amirul Hadi, Lee Kam Hing, Anthony Reid, Ibrahim Alfian, A.J. Piekaar, Eric Morris and Nazaruddin Sjamsuddin.[4] The current book, however, provides for the first time a comprehensive picture of the evolution of Aceh's connections with Indonesia and of her more extensive links (before 1873) with other places.

Serious fieldwork on Aceh's ethnography, archeology and linguistic pattern has been severely discouraged by the unstable conditions. Since Snouck Hurgronje and J. Kreemer[5] achieved ethnographic marvels under wartime conditions around the turn of the twentieth century, there have been only modest windows for research in the 1930s and the 1970s. These opportunities were seized by Raymond Kennedy in the 1930s,[6] and by James Siegel, who worked as an anthropologist in the Pidië region in the late 1960s, learning Acehnese with excellent results.[7] His only successor to publish substantial work based on village-level ethnographic fieldwork was John Bowen, working on the highland Gayo of Central Aceh in the 1980s.[8] The only linguist to spend substantial time in rural Aceh was Mark Durie in the 1970s, who drew attention to the substantial dialectical variations of Acehnese.[9] None of the potentially rich archaeological sites in Aceh has yet been systematically excavated.

An Earthquake Zone

The December 2004 tsunami took the world by surprise not only by its magnitude, its destructiveness, and the unprecedented extent of the casualties in countries around the Indian Ocean. It occurred in a part of Sumatra that had not previously made the world's headlines as a great earthquake zone. The occurrence of one of the worst quakes in a century, 9.0 on the Richter scale, was not expected in the way that Californian, Japanese and Turkish quakes had been.

It should have been. The Sumatran subduction zone, where the heavy material of the Indian Ocean floor presses under the lighter material of the Sumatran plate, is one of the world's most critical. The

Indo-Australian plate moves forward at a rate of more than 4 cm a year against the west coast of Aceh, and over decades enormous pressure is built up, which must be released in earthquakes. Many of these must have hit the west coast of Aceh and Nias over the centuries, but as one of the last places to have received the persistent attention of Europeans, these areas are poorly served by the historic record. European records are better in the more southerly parts of the zone, where major quakes were recorded. Heavy earthquakes caused much damage in Dutch-occupied Padang in 1691 and even more seriously in 1697.[10] The 1833 quake centred on the Mentawei Islands was calculated as 9.0 on the Richter scale, though the tsunami effects were much greater for the terrifying quake of 1797 which again hit Padang. Stamford Raffles took over the British Settlement of Bengkulen, in the south, at a time in 1818 when every major building was damaged by earthquakes, said to recur on a destructive scale every 5–6 years.[11] By contrast the century prior to 2004 does indeed appear to have been a quieter time, which should have given rise to some anxiety.

In the northern third of Sumatra we have records only for the last 150 years. The Nias quake of 1861 was calculated to be Richter 8.5. The 1907 Simeulue earthquake, and the subsequent giant tsunami which killed a large proportion, perhaps 1,800, of that west coast offshore island's inhabitants, have lived on in popular memory there, but was little noticed by historians.[12] A moderating factor was the Sumatran pattern of building light wood and thatch houses on wooden poles, so that even very large earthquakes caused relatively little loss of life before the twentieth-century urban transition to building in brick and concrete. William Marsden was able to describe astonishing changes in coastal land-forms as a result of a 1770 earthquake near Bengkulen, but the quakes were "but little formidable to the natives".[13] That changed as modern concrete buildings took over the urban landscapes.

Aceh's Population and Migration

The population of Aceh was 3.4 million in the 1990 census, and is presumed to be about 4 million today, after the terrible losses from the tsunami of December 2004.[14] The interior is relatively lightly populated, save for a few of the more fertile valleys (Aceh, Tangse) and the area around the upland lake, Laut Tawar. The latter is the home of Aceh's largest indigenous minority, the Gayo, about 200,000 strong or 5 per cent of Aceh's people. Their language is much closer to Karo-Batak than to Acehnese, but through Islamisation and affiliation to the Aceh sultanate since the seventeenth century they have come to identify with Aceh. Over 80 per cent of Aceh's population are ethnically Acehnese, and outside the cities they habitually speak Acehnese in one of its dialects, although educated in Indonesian as the national language. Most of them are rice cultivators spread along the fertile plain of the northern coast, though with also a strong tradition of cash cropping (pepper, betelnut, copra, coffee, rubber and tobacco) in the foothills.

The largest single minority in contemporary Aceh are Javanese, 275,000 strong (7 per cent) in 2000.[15] Some of these are officials, military personnel and petroleum industry employees, predominately in the cities. The majority, however, are transmigrants, introduced by the state as rice-growers in less-populated interior areas, in an attempt at once to relieve Java's population pressure and to help "Indonesianise" the peripheral parts of the Archipelago. A smaller number came to work on pre-war plantations, many of whom have since moved on to other kinds of work.

The great majority of Aceh's population consider themselves Acehnese by language, history and *adat* (custom). Observers have often noticed the physically heterogeneous nature of that population.[16] The unusual position of its language is discussed below. So dominant in Acehnese memory were stories of connections with Turkey and the Arab world that Teungku Kutakarang, one of the leading Acehnese *ulama* of the late nineteenth century, assured Snouck Hurgronje that the Acehnese population was a mix of Arab, Turkish and Persian elements.[17] In reality, however, the principal source of ethnic admixture with the Austronesians of Sumatra appears to be from southern India, even if it was a smaller Chamic input which gave rise to the language.

By contrast, Chinese migration has been less prominent in Aceh in the past five centuries than in other parts of Sumatra or Java. On at least two occasions, under Sultans Iskandar Thani (1636–41) and Ala'ud-din Mansur Syah (alias Ibrahim, 1838–70), Chinese residents were explicitly banned on religious grounds,[18] although they were certainly present at the most flourishing periods of Aceh's commerce. At least subsequent to Aceh's rise after 1500 as an explicitly Islamic polity, there appears to have been relatively little of the Chinese-Indonesian intermarriage here, which helped form elites in Java and elsewhere. Penang Chinese traders had extensive dealings with the pepper-exporting *ulèëbalang* of the 1840s to 1870s, but did not make Aceh the base of their operations.

The modern community of Chinese in Aceh began with the substantial needs of the Dutch occupation army for supplies from Penang in the 1870s and '80s. These were largely provided for by the Hakka magnate Thio Tiau Siat, which may explain the continuing Hakka dominance among Aceh's Chinese today. At the 1930 census Aceh numbered 22,000 Chinese, 40 per cent of them Hakka.[19] This Chinese urban population was well-integrated by the 1960s, but suffered heavily in the anti-communist violence of 1965. Many were killed and thousands fled to Medan. Since then the Chinese population has been closer to 10,000, about half of them in Banda Aceh. Nevertheless, the subsequent anti-Chinese and anti-Christian violence encouraged by elements of the Suharto government and reaching its peak in 1998, scarcely affected Aceh.

The close trade connection of Aceh with southern India has provided the major source of migrants over the past thousand years. In the late nineteenth century the inhabitants of Aceh Besar divided themselves into four tribes (*kaum*), the largest of which, dominating the XXII Mukims of the upriver Montasiek area, was remembered as descended from Islamised Hindu migrants.[20] Snouck Hurgronje recorded that there were, "within the memory of man", a large number of south Indian agriculturalists in upland Aceh Besar (XXII Mukims). He noted that some were still "manifestly of Hindu origin, since they wear their hair long and twist it into a top-knot (*sanggoy*) on the back of the head in the Hindu fashion".[21] This substantial migration is one clear cause of the visible differences in the Acehnese population in comparison with its Batak and Malay neighbours.

During Aceh's seventeenth-century prosperity there was a deliberate import of unfree labour from South India. The valley of the Aceh River, known as Aceh Besar, was little populated or cultivated except for the great metropolis of the capital at the time of Aceh's heyday in the early 1600s. Foreign observers noted the dependence of the port-capital on food imports from Pidie, the Peninsula, Java and South India.[22] By the end of the century, however, foreign visitors noticed a significant cultivation of rice in the Aceh river valley, initiated by Tamil migrants.

> There are many Indians of the Coromandel [Tamil] coast .... Slaves to the great men and Merchants .... To these the Acheenes owe the greatest part of their husbandry in managing their crops of Paddy, or Rice, which was hardly known on this part of the Island, till these were driven here by the famine from Fort St. David, and other places on the Coromandel Coast.[23]

Although this very deliberate introduction of a substantial Tamil agricultural population is an extreme case, a constant flow of traders and adventurers from southern India was a feature of most periods of Aceh's history. In Chapter 2 McKinnon shows some of these connections even before the rise of Aceh, while in Chapter 5 Lee demonstrates a continuing influx of Tamil traders (mostly Chuliah Muslims) and mercenaries through the eighteenth and early nineteenth centuries.

Language

In language, Acehnese is a single Austronesian (Malayo-Polynesian) language with much local dialect variation. It is not, however, part of the natural continuum of the Sumatran sub-set of Austronesian languages. As early as 1891, G.K. Niemann noted that the lexical and grammatical distinctiveness of Acehnese were such that its closest Austronesian relatives were not in Sumatra at all, but in the Cham area, of what is today Central Vietnam. Although some contrary views were voiced in the 1920s, "the issue has been conclusively put to rest" by the work of H.K.J. Cowan and others, in favour of a distinct Aceh-Chamic group of Austronesian languages.[24]

Graeme Thurgood has recently reconstructed proto-Chamic from the various Chamic languages of Indochina, compared it carefully with Acehnese, and concluded the following: "The distribution and patterning of the borrowed Mon-Khmer vowels by itself constitutes strong evidence that Acehnese is a Chamic language that migrated from the mainland to northern Sumatra, evidence only made stronger by the parallel innovations found in the inherited Austronesian vocabulary." He has fully endorsed Cowan's suggestion that Cham-speakers must have migrated to northern Sumatra subsequent to much borrowing of Mon-Khmer loan-words on the Indochina mainland.[25]

The historical basis for this would have to be the strong role of Austronesian-speakers, and particularly Chams, along with Arabs and Sinified Muslims, in the maritime trade route which linked the Middle East to southern China between the eighth and fourteenth centuries. Northern Sumatran ports such as Pasai, Pidië and Lamri were important links in this chain, as were the Cham ports, and these often came together to China in trade/tribute missions. The fall of the Champa capital to Vietnamese arms in 1471 is undoubtedly one likely moment for half-Islamised Chams and Sino-Chams to relocate to ports they knew in Sumatra. The Melaka chronicle is very specific about this, putting in legendary form what happened when the Champa kingdom fell.

> There were two sons of the King of Champa, one named Shah Indera and one named Shah Pau Ling. Both of them fled by boat with many people including their wives and children; Shah Pau Ling went to Aceh, and that is the origin of the kings of Aceh.... Meanwhile Shah Indera Berma went to Melaka, where Sultan Mansur Shah [r. 1459–77] rejoiced to see them all.[26]

This story must now be taken seriously in light of the linguistic evidence. But how can a small group of a few hundred Cham-speaking migrants have infiltrated their language along more than 1,000 km of coast? The answer can only be by gradual conquest, colonisation and the absorption of migrants over 400 years. The earlier linguistic diversity of the tiny port-states of northern Sumatra was noted by Marco Polo in 1292 — "each of the eight kingdoms has its own language".[27] The Cham-speaking commercial migrants may have become dominant initially in only one small port-state of what is today Aceh Besar. Aceh's conquests of the 1520s (see below) extended its reach to several other small port-states — Pidie, Pasai and Daya. Speakers of Batak and Gayo dialects appear to have been driven away from the coast insofar as they did not convert and assimilate over the following century. The forests of the east and west coasts of Aceh were only gradually opened by Acehnese pepper-growers, notably in the nineteenth century. However, the continuing diversity of Acehnese dialects must reflect other language underlays that interacted with this spreading of Acehnese, merging differently in each district.

Malay, however, remained a vital *lingua franca* and written medium at least for coastal traders and Islamic scholars, as well as the royal court. This role of Malay and later Indonesian as the "outer" language of formal and external exchanges may have preserved Acehnese as the intimate language of the village and family, and of poetic recitation. Written Acehnese appeared subsequent to written Malay (the oldest reference to Acehnese writing is 1658), and was always the written version of a poetic text meant for recitation. Even such poetic texts were always "framed" in Malay, as the appropriate formal language for introductory material in prose.[28] Acehnese was only written in prose by Dutch language purists in the 1930s, and more recently by some Aceh nationalist purists in the 1990s.

Religion and *Adat*

Like the Minangkabaus of West Sumatra, Acehnese are deeply committed to Islamic norms but are also embedded in a set of kinship structures and relations (*adat*) of older derivation. Until 1946 there were two elites responsible for upholding the two normative systems, which a variety of proverbs expressed in terms of complementarity. The *ulama* were expert in Islamic law and administered it when appropriate. *Adat* governed the system of landholding and inheritance, however, and in such matters the village head (*keucik*) and the hereditary chief of the district (*ulèëbalang*) held authority. The sultan's court in its seventeenth century heyday patronised the ulama as a means to increase its leverage against the *ulèëbalang*, though as its grip subsequently weakened it was often the victim of clerical criticism. Dutch abolition of the sultanate left *ulèëbalang* and ulama in more direct confrontation as rival authorities in defining Acehneseness. The *ulèëbalang* were swept from power in the social revolution of 1945–6, as described in Chapters 5 and 8 below. Although their descendents remained influential in Jakarta, they were no longer in a position to defend *adat* on the ground when it was criticised by reforming *ulama*. Nevertheless, the confidence of Acehnese in the appropriateness of their own institutions has allowed much of the system in rural areas to remain as it was observed by writers like Snouck Hurgronje, Kreemer, Kennedy and Siegel.

Inheritance is bilateral, but houses are exclusively passed to daughters, so that the wife is "the one who owns the house" (*njang po rumoh*).[29] Parents often pass the family house to the eldest daughter at her marriage, and build another house for themselves nearby. Hence villages often comprise clusters of houses owned by sisters and nieces. Rice-fields near the house are also passed to daughters. Hence it is mothers who provide for household and children through the revenue of their rice-fields and other household activities. After puberty sons do not sleep in their maternal house but in the communal hall and religious school (*meunasah*) of the village. The house is therefore female space in large measure, and men feel like "guests in the houses of their wives".[30] Young men and adolescents often leave home for religious studies, and mature men are frequently away trading, growing cash-crops in more distant and sparsely-settled areas, or in modern times serving in war or in government. The Islamic commitment, that all Acehnese feel is part of their identity, has never reduced the economic independence of women, and in turn their relative autonomy.

Aceh Identity

Nothing is known with certainty about Aceh before the conquests of its Sultan Ali Mughayat Syah (d. 1530) in the 1520s. The most reliable and matter-of-fact of its chronicles, by Raniri, simply declares that this was the first sultan to rule Aceh, and also the first to embrace and enforce Islam. Before that there were no rajas but only village communities.[31] Other chronicles provide some mythical antecedents, among which the *Hikayat Aceh* intriguingly begins with an incomplete story about one Raja Indera Syah (reminiscent of the name of the Cham king in the Sejarah Melayu story) being honoured at the court of China, and his progeny there being assured of a mighty destiny.[32] The relatively firm date of 1471 for the most important Cham migration as the foundation of the Aceh dynasty, fits well with the Chinese date (equivalent to late 1469 or January 1470) on the great bell with Chinese and Arabic/Persian inscriptions, which became one of the regalia of the Aceh kingdom (see Fig. 2).[33] This Chinese bell may well have been brought to the Aceh Besar area by the Sino-Cham Muslim refugees from Champa, avoiding older-established Pasai which appears to have lost direct contact with China during its mid-century civil wars.[34] New port-states could arise quickly whenever the international traders transferred their patronage from one port to another as a result of internal conflicts and upheavals, and earthquakes should also not be ruled out as a means of suddenly removing or creating a viable harbour. This dating also fits well with the gravestones of the Aceh Besar area, which, combined with chronicles, suggest that Ali Mughayat's father Moethaffar Syah united the two sides of the Aceh river and began the kingdom of Aceh Darussalam sometime in the late fifteenth century.[35]

The point of re-examining these origins is to underline the intense linguistic, religious and ethnic pluralities of the north Sumatra coast, and especially the northwestern corner of Sumatra now known as Aceh Besar, before and during the rise of the Aceh sultanate. European sources suggest there were still strong Hindu communities in sixteenth-century Banda Aceh, and that Malay was a lingua franca for a polyglot population.[36] Aceh was united by an aggressive new dynasty determined to eliminate foreign interference in the name of militant Islam. Aceh's rise was thus an exact counterpoint to Portugal's intrusion into the area in the period 1509–20. Pasai and Pidie already suffered from a pattern of instability, but Portuguese interference on the side opposed to the Indian and Arab Muslim traders worsened the situation, with three

Fig. 2 Chinese bell of 1469, hanging in the Aceh citadel in 1874 (*Illustrated London News*)

successive rulers of Pasai assassinated in 1516.[37] A Portuguese fleet under Jorge de Brito overreached itself in a raid on Aceh in 1518, hoping to seize a "temple of the heathen" (chettiars?) containing "much gold".[38] Aceh's defeat of this rash enterprise provided both the motivation and many of the Portuguese weapons for the vigorous new sultanate to begin its crusade to expel the Portuguese from Sumatra.

The Acehnese conquest of all the important ports of northern Sumatra was accomplished by the death of Ali Mughayat in 1530. This was the effective foundation of the Acehnese state and identity. The expulsion of the Portuguese was clearly popular among the international Muslim trading group who supported it. This motif of resisting foreign interference continued to provide a *raison d'etre* for the sultanate through the centuries that followed. It marked Aceh as sharply different, not only from the semi-stateless Batak and Minangkabau populations of the highlands, but also from the world of Malay rulers. A Malay raja typically occupied a single river-mouth or other strategic waterway, and presided very loosely over interior populations as a mediator between them and the outside world. His power was of a charismatic type, resting heavily on assertions of magical sanctity, but usually relying on other groups (the Bendahara house of Melaka, and later *orang laut*, Bugis, Indian, Chinese, Batak or European traders) to manage the practical affairs of state.

Aceh was geopolitically impossible to control in this way. Its people were strung out along 1,000km of coast containing dozens of rivers as important as the Krueng Aceh of Aceh Besar and the capital. Each of these rivers had its own raja or *ulèëbalang* who would pursue his own policies as far as a weak sultanate allowed him to. They almost never challenged the sultanate's sovereign rights over them, and would greatly value a royal decree (*sarakarta*) establishing their rights in their lands. But the sultan had constantly to impose his will by force if he wanted to preserve his rights to be the sole mediator of external trade. Only when fighting against outsiders in the name of Islam could he be sure that the whole country would unite behind him. As Chapters 3–6 below make clear, however, there were many such occasions. Until the disastrous Dutch invasion of 1873, no European power ever found it possible to establish a presence in Aceh, despite what appeared to be weakness and division internally.

If, therefore, Javanese society was created and maintained by a particular culture, and Minangkabau or Batak society by a particular set of kinship obligations, Aceh was held together by a state. The sultanate, a strong Islamic commitment, language and *adat*, and pride in Aceh's self-reliance were all part of what made up its identity. After the Dutch attempted to abolish the sultanate in 1874, and forced the sultan's acceptance of this in 1903, the sultanate was removed from this equation. Arguably, however, the resistance idea itself replaced the symbol of royal sovereignty with the longing for a restored national dignity.

Every part of the Indonesian archipelago has its own character. Reviewing the chapters that follow suggests that the argument that Aceh's distinctiveness is of a different order rests, historically, on the following factors:

–   Its independence was complete before 1873, largely because the passionate opposition to foreign bases on the part of many of its people discouraged such settlements.
–   Its people found their identity as Acehnese in their relationship to a state, in the form of the dynasty of Aceh Darussalam, to a degree not found elsewhere.
–   Aceh had virtually no connection with Java or Batavia/Jakarta before 1873, but many connections with the Peninsula and a variety of Indian Ocean ports, as well as with powers such as Britain, France and Turkey.
–   The identification with Turkey (see Chapters 3 and 4), embodied in the flag and sixteenth century cannons, was sufficiently revived in the nineteenth century to represent an alternative self-image of how to enter the modern world.
–   Aceh's resistance to incorporation into the Netherlands Indies/ Indonesia state project, while it had echoes elsewhere, was far more widespread, bitter, and enduring than that of any other region.

The Book

More than half of this book, comprising its eight final chapters, deals directly with the contemporary conflict over Aceh's uneasy place in Indonesia. They are written chiefly by political scientists concerned to understand the nature and conditions of separatism, ethnic nationalism and conflict. Each is forced to turn to the past in order to explain the pattern of events in Aceh, however. Several of these writers, notably Isa (Chapter 8), Aspinall (Chapter 9) and Nessen (Chapter 10), are concerned to show the continuities between the current independence movement and the rebellion of Daud Beureu'eh in the 1950s. They explicitly refute the argument that has been widely made elsewhere, that GAM (Aceh independence movement) was principally a response to the repressive actions of the Suharto government. McGibbon (Chapter 15), too, is sceptical about this argument and the ability of a grievance-based approach more generally to explain disaffection. He, however, looks particularly at internal Acehnese politics, and what he sees as the failure of local elites to mediate effectively between Jakarta and the Acehnese.

The conflict has grown out of a long history, and we make no apology that the first half of the book is written by historians taking an even longer view. The first four of the chapters that follow describe pre-colonial Aceh, before the 1873 invasion that began the process of turning it into a province of Indonesia. All demonstrate the ways in which Aceh was connected with the world of the Indian Ocean rather than that of the Java Sea. McKinnon goes further back before the establishment of the Aceh sultanate, to examine deeper Indian influences in the region. Chapters 3–5 tell the story of the sultanate itself, and seek to explain how successive European imperial powers were discouraged from attempting to control it. Aceh was unruly and sometimes troublesome, but those who knew it consistently warned of the certain costs of any direct intervention.

Riddell's Chapter 3 looks particularly at Aceh's self-image as a centre of Islamic civilisation below the winds. The abundant Malayo-Muslim literature produced there in the seventeenth century made it in one sense exemplary for the Islamic Archipelago; yet in another it was oriented outward, as "the verandah of Mecca". The following chapter also uses Aceh's literature to consider how the sultanate saw its place in the world. It takes up to the nineteenth century the story of Aceh's international relations, its long love affair with the Ottoman Turks, and its increasingly desperate attempts to find allies against the Dutch.

While Aceh's eighteenth and early nineteenth centuries are often seen as a period of uninteresting decline, Lee Kam Hing (Chapter 5) uses them to consider the question why Aceh was not Thailand. Aceh and Siam were the only two substantial Southeast Asian states to retain their integrity and sovereignty fully into the mid-nineteenth century. The question arises as to how close Aceh was to continuing its path into the modern world without direct colonial rule. One disadvantage Aceh suffered in relation to Thailand was its strategic maritime position inviting foreign adventurers; the other was internal conflict. Both factors helped to propel the Netherlands into the ill-conceived war of 1873–1903 described in Chapter 6. Aceh's passage into Indonesia was a uniquely bitter one, and only for a brief period of the 1930s did it approach colonial normalcy. Its long war of resistance foreshadowed Vietnam in its drawn-out guerrilla strategies, but prefigured al-Qaedah and Jamiat al Islamiah in some of its jihadist rhetoric. Ibrahim Alfian discusses this rhetoric in Chapter 7 on the holy war.

If Chapters 2–7 are primarily concerned to lay the foundation for understanding what Aceh is and how it has become so, the remaining chapters engage directly with the conflict between two contemporary visions for Aceh. Isa Sulaiman lived through the events while studying them, and all the other authors made frequent research visits to interview the leading actors on the side of the military, the independence movement, officials and NGOs. Their expertise on the facts of what happened does not make them of one view about where the blame falls, and most serious arguments on all sides of the debate are represented here. Kirsten Schulze (Chapter 12) has a sympathetic understanding of the position and strategies that the military (TNI) used, with all its flaws, in combating the resistance. On the other hand Kingsbury and McCulloch (Chapter 11) are convinced the TNI is an inherent part of the problem, and Jemadu portrays it sabotaging all the civilian peace initiatives. William Nessen, on the other hand, has extensively interviewed GAM personnel and gives a sympathetic picture of its goals and strategies, of which Schulze is much more critical. McGibbon and Miller have worked extensively with civil government authorities in Aceh and identify many of Aceh's problems arising from their shortcomings. Isa Sulaiman, while providing much new data on the political history of Aceh, is also particularly concerned to show economic exploitation and marginalisation as the most fundamental long-term cause of the problem.

What the authors all share is a commitment to understanding the basis of conflict in this tormented region. Nobody believes the issue has recent origins or shallow roots, or can be resolved by simple force or a clever legislative programme. Sulaiman, Aspinall and McGibbon all return to the 1940s and '50s to understand the roots of the Aceh independence movement. They join hands with the historians of the first half of the book in revealing separations of a much longer term. Jemadu shows that the democratisation of Indonesia has not achieved for Aceh what it did for East Timor; the economic and ideological interests of the military are even stronger at the western extremity of the Archipelago than the eastern, while the international community's interest in post-1975 East Timor was not paralleled in Aceh.

A New Peace

This book represents the first serious attempt in English to set out the problems that have led to conflict in Aceh, and to present informed if divergent views of how to move ahead towards a more peaceful future.

The chapters that follow often assume some knowledge of the sequence of events in Aceh and Indonesia as they seek to probe more fundamental causes. To aid the reader, therefore, an elementary sketch of war and peace follows, accompanied by a schematic chronology which may be used for reference.

Aceh's first bitter struggle with Jakarta, from 1873–1913, was resolved not by negotiation but by the imposition of the rigorous application of force. That "military solution", even while accompanied by a more far-sighted political strategy than has recently been on offer in Jakarta, ensured that the scars and bitterness would remain, and that force had to be unrelenting to prevent a new rebellion. The second phase ended with what felt like an Acehnese popular victory over the Dutch and their local allies, in 1946. The relatively orderly (by the standards of 1940s Indonesia) peace of 1946–50 was, however, based on a misunderstanding that Aceh had regained its ancient freedom in the name of "Indonesia", rather than a place in a new kind of Jakarta-centred polity.

After the rebellion of 1953–62 there was a solution that looked to be more genuinely contractual. In return for surrendering their arms, Aceh's militants received their own province and a large say in its governance, as well as a "special" status that appeared to allow Islam to have a more central place in Aceh than in the Archipelago as a whole.

That tentative peace itself unravelled in the terror of 1965–6, and the crucial role of a centralising military in all that followed. Aceh appeared relatively peaceful in the decade 1966–76, as in the 1930s, but it was again a peace backed up with a heavy threat of force, which some would call terror. Terror became overt in the so-called DOM period of emergency rule in Aceh, 1989–98. The initiatives that followed the fall of Suharto towards reaching a negotiated peace were, therefore, something novel. For the first time there was a quiet international element in the negotiations between Jakarta and GAM, leading to an internationally observed cessation of hostilities (CoHA) in November 2002. This, however, was a cease-fire, not a peace. Each side hoped to trick the other into abandoning its essential goals. In the six months the CoHA lasted, only a little progress was made towards dealing with Aceh's longer-term needs. It was ended with a new attempt at a military solution from May 2003, without any clear exit strategy.

The terrible destruction of 26 December 2004 appeared to change everything. It caused more terrible loss and suffering in one day than many decades of war could ever do. It brought unprecedented international attention and international resources to Aceh. Through the despair came glimmers of hope, that Aceh could be rebuilt on the basis of trust between people and government; between local, national and international communities. Both the new Jakarta government of Susilo Bambang Yudoyono, and the Aceh independence movement, expressed a desire for a new peace, though this did not stop the men on the ground from fighting. Finally, on the initiative of the former Finnish President Martti Ahtisaari, peace talks led to the signing of an agreement in Helsinki on 15 August 2005, on the basis of self-government rather than the old alternatives of independence or autonomy.

This book represents an argument for ensuring that the new attempts at both peace and reconstruction allow Acehnese to choose their leaders and their destiny, so that they have a stake in a peaceful and democratic order. Whatever their dissent on other matters, the authors here agree remarkably that previous strategies have failed because the Acehnese did not own them. They have never had a vote on their own destiny, nor on who they would trust to lead them. Since 1874, only the period 1945–50, definitive for both sides of the debate, gave them a sense of being in control of their own affairs.

Aceh's history indicates the need for some form of association with Indonesia and a high degree of self-government, but neither of these requirements in themselves will guarantee an open and democratic society. The authors hope that in the wake of the suffering caused by the tsunami, the debate will shift away from emotive and divisive issues of national sovereignty, and focus on how the Acehnese can be helped to rebuild the kind of society they need and want, with leaders they have chosen.

Notes

[1] Notably E.B. Kielstra, *Beschrijving van den Atjèh-oorlog*, 3 vols. (The Hague, 1883–5); E.S. de Klerck, *De Atjèh-oorlog* (The Hague: Nijhoff, 1912). A later overview is Paul van't Veer, *De Atjeh-oorlog* (Amsterdam: Arbeiderspers, 1969).

[2] Later translated as C. Snouck Hurgronje, *The Achehnese*, trans. A.W.S. O'Sullivan, 2 vols. (Leiden: E.J. Brill, 1906).

[3] The best of the Indonesian works is M. Isa Sulaiman, *Aceh Merdeka: Ideologi, Kepemimpinan dan Gerakan* (Jakarta: Al-Kautsar, 2000). The English material is more fully reviewed in Chapters 8–15 below, but includes Timothy Kell, *The Roots of Acehnese Rebellion 1989–1992* (Ithaca: Cornell Modern Indonesia Project, 1995); Geoffrey Robinson, "Rawan is as Rawan does: The Origins of Disorder in New Order Aceh, Indonesia", *Indonesia*, no. 66

(1998); Edward Aspinall and H. Crouch, *The Aceh Peace Process: Why it Failed*. Policy Studies, No.1 (Washington DC: East West Center, 2003).

[4]   See bibliography in this volume.

[5]   J. Kreemer, *Atjèh*, 2 vols. (Leiden: Brill, 1922).

[6]   Raymond Kennedy, "The Ethnology of the Greater Sunda Islands" (unpublished PhD dissertation, Yale University, 1935). Kennedy's ethnographic findings were extensively followed in Frank M. Lebar (ed.), *Ethnic Groups of Insular Southeast Asia*, Vol. I: *Indonesia, Andaman Islands and Madagascar* (New Haven: Human Relations Area Files, 1972).

[7]   James T. Siegel, *The Rope of God* (Berkeley: University of California Press, 1969); *Shadow and Sound: The Historical Thought of a Sumatran People* (Chicago: University of Chicago Press, 1979).

[8]   John R. Bowen, *Sumatran Politics and Poetics: Gayo History, 1900–1989* (New Haven: Yale University Press, 1991); *Muslims through Discourse: Religion and Ritual in Gayo Society* (Princeton: Princeton University Press, 1993).

[9]   Mark Durie, *A grammar of Acehnese on the basis of a dialect of North Aceh* (Leiden: Foris for KITLV, 1985). Another dissertation, Ira. V. Collins, *The Austro-Asiatic Substratum in Acehnese* (PhD dissertation, University of California, Berkeley, 1975), was not available to me.

[10] Peter Boomgaard, "Crisis Mortality in Seventeenth Century Indonesia", in *Asian Population History*, ed. Ts'ui-jung Liu *et al.* (New York: OUP, 2001), p. 213.

[11] *Memoir of the Life and Public Services of Sir Thomas Stamford Raffles, by his widow* (London: James Duncan, 1835), Vol. I, pp. 334–5.

[12] A website which contains some of this data is <http://www.techtonics. caltech.edu>.

[13] William Marsden, *The History of Sumatra* (3rd ed. 1811; reprinted Kuala Lumpur: OUP, 1966), p. 30.

[14] The 2000 census occurred at a time when the independence movement (GAM) controlled large sections of the population, so that only an estimated 44 per cent of its population could be surveyed. The "estimated" population in 2000 was 3.9 million. Leo Suryadinata, Evi Nurvidya Arifin and Aris Ananta, *Indonesia's Population: Ethnicity and Religion in a Changing Political Landscape* (Singapore: Institute of Southeast Asian Studies, 2003), pp. 2–3.

[15] Ibid., p. 15.

[16] LeBar, *Ethnic Groups*, p. 16.

[17] Snouck Hurgronje, *The Achehnese* I, p. 18.

[18] Anthony Reid, *An Indonesian Frontier: Acehnese and Other Histories of Sumatra* (Singapore: Singapore University Press, 2004), p. 195; Anthony Reid, *The Blood of the People: Revolution and the End of Traditional Rule in Northern Sumatra* (Kuala Lumpur: OUP, 1979), p. 6n7.

[19] Reid, *Indonesian Frontier*, p. 396.

20 K.F.H. van Langen, "De Inrichting van het Atjehsche Staatsbestuur onder het Sultanaat", *BKI* 34 (1888): 387: this was the Kaum Imampet, so called because after Islamisation they were represented by four imams.

21 Snouck Hurgronje, *The Achehnese* I, pp. 18–9.

22 *The voyage of Sir James Lancaster to Brazil and the East Indies*, ed. Sir William Foster (London: Hakluyt Society, 1940), p. 136. Ito Takeshi, "The World of the Adat Aceh: A Historical Study of the Sultanate of Aceh" (unpublished PhD dissertation, Australian National University, 1984), pp. 393–6. Denys Lombard, *Le sultanat d'Atjeh* (Paris: EFEO), p. 61, sees the insoluble problem of rice as a reason for the eventual decline of Aceh.

23 Charles Lockyer, *An Account of the Trade in India* (London, 1711), p. 54. William Dampier, *Voyages and Discoveries,* ed. C. Wilkinson (London: Argonaut Press, 1931), p. 91, had noted earlier that the wealthy elite of the city "have sown pretty large Fields of Rice" by putting to work there "the Slaves brought lately by the English and the Danes from the Coast of Coromandel".

24 Mark Durie, "Proto-Chamic and Acehnese mid Vowels: Towards Proto-Aceh-Chamic", *BSOAS* 53, no.1 (1990): 100. See also G.K. Niemann, "Bijdrage tot de kennis der verhouding van het Tjam tot de talen van Indonesie", *BKI* 40 (1891): 27–44; H.K.J. Cowan, "Acehnese dialects in connection with Chamic migrations", *VICAL 2: Western Austronesian and contact languages: papers of the fifth congress on Austronesian linguistics,* part I, ed. Ray Harlow (Auckland: Linguistics Society of New Zealand, 1991).

25 Graham Thurgood, *From Ancient Cham to Modern Dialects: Two Thousand Years of Language Contact and Change* (Honolulu: University of Hawaii Press, 1999), pp. 52 and 47–58 passim. An unpublished reaction to Thurgood by Paul Sidwell argues that the original connection of Aceh with Chamic languages may be much older, linked with similar patterns in Mon-Khmer languages of the Malayan Peninsula, while the particular features which led Thurgood to posit a late migration could be attributable to Chamic borrowings following the fifteenth-century migration described below; Paul Sidwell Seminar at Australian National University, Canberra, 5 November 2004, <www.clrc.anu.edu.au/seminars>.

26 *Sejarah Melayu* (*The Malay Annals*), ed. W.G. Shellabear (1909, 10th printing, Singapore: Malay Publishing House, 1961), p. 162 (section 21). The better-known Raffles text of the chronicle has a shorter version of the story, naming the prince who went to Aceh "Shah Palembang", without stating that he began the line of Aceh kings; "Sejarah Melayu or 'Malay Annals'", trans. C.C. Brown, *JMBRAS* 25, 2 & 3 (1952): 110.

27 *The Travels of Marco Polo*, trans. Ronald Latham (Harmondsworth: Penguin Books, 1958), p. 224.

28 P. Voorhoeve, *Catalogue of Acehnese Manuscripts in the Library of Leiden University and Other Collections outside Aceh* (Leiden: Leiden University

Library, 1994), pp. 13–9; Mark Durie, "Framing the Acehnese Text: Language Choice and Discourse Structures in Aceh", *Oceanic Linguistics* 35, no. 1 (June 1996).

29 Siegel, *Rope of God*, p. 51.

30 Snouck Hurgronje, *The Achehnese* I, p. 339; also Siegel, *Rope of God*, pp. 52–6.

31 Nuru'd-din ar-Raniri, *Bustanu's-Salatin, Bab II, Fasal 13*, ed. T. Iskandar (Kuala Lumpur: Dewan Bahasa dan Pustaka, 1966), p. 31. The first Portuguese mention of Aceh, about 1515, describes it as a warlike kingdom newly risen to power over neighbouring Lamri and "Biar" — *The Suma Oriental of Tomé Pires*, ed. Amando Cortesão (Cambridge: Hakluyt, 1944), pp. 138–9.

32 *De Hikajat Atjeh*, ed. T. Iskandar (The Hague: KITLV, 1958), p. 66.

33 T.J. Veltman, "Nota over de geschiedenis van het landschap Pidië", *TBG* 58 (1919): 46 began a false tradition with a misreading of the Chinese date as 1409, and the conclusion on that basis that since this was too early for Aceh the bell must have come to Pasai and been acquired by Aceh as war booty in 1524. Wolfgang Franke, *Chinese Epigraphic Materials in Indonesia*, Vol. 1 (Singapore: South Seas Society, 1988), p. 44 has confirmed the correct date as 1469–70.

34 C.C. Brown (ed.), "Sejarah Melayu or 'Malay Annals'", *JMBRAS* 25, 2 & 3 (1952): 104–8; Jorge Manuel dos Santos Alves, *O Dominio do Norte de Samatra: A historia dos sultanatos de Samudera-Pacem e de Achém, e das suas relações com os Portugueses (1500–1580)* (Lisbon: Sociedade Historica da Independência de Portugal, 1999), pp. 80–1.

35 Van Langen, "Nota", pp. 37–9. Lamri, probably modern Lamreh near Krueng Raya, 50 km east of Banda Aceh, was a small Muslim polity at least since Ma Huan's visits in the early 1400s, and perhaps since the oldest Arabic-inscribed tombstone there which appears to be dated 608 Hijrah or 1211 CE. Aceh must have incorporated this port, but did not claim descent from it. Suwedi Montana, "Nouvelles données sur les les royaumes de Lamuri et Barat", *Archipel* 53 (1997): 85–95.

36 Francois Martin, as translated in Anthony Reid, *Witnesses to Sumatra: A Travellers' Anthology* (Kuala Lumpur: Oxford University Press, 1995), pp. 61–3; and see Barros below.

37 Geneviève Bouchon, "Les premiers voyages Portugais à Pasai et à Pegou (1512–1520)", *Archipel* 18 (1979): 148–55.

38 João de Barros, *Da Asia* (Lisbon 1773, reprinted Lisbon: San Carlos, 1973), Decada III, Livro v, p. 538.

Map 1 The Premodern Indian Ocean

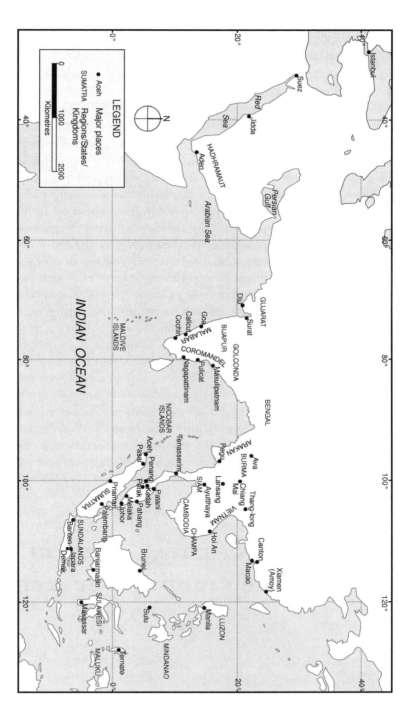

LEGEND

• Aceh   Major places

SUMATRA   Regions/States/
Kingdoms

N

Kilometres

0   1000   2000

Istanbul

Suez

Jidda

Red Sea

Aden

HADHRAMAUT

Persian Gulf

Arabian Sea

INDIAN OCEAN

MALDIVE ISLANDS

Diu

GUJARAT

Surat

BIJAPUR

Goa

Calicut

Cochin

MALABAR

COROMANDEL

GOLCONDA

Pulicat

Masulipatnam

Nagapattinam

BENGAL

NICOBAR ISLANDS

ARAKAN

Pegu

BURMA

Ava

Tenasserim

Thang-long

Chiang Mai

Lansang

SIAM

Ayutthaya

VIETNAM

CAMBODIA

Hoi An

CHAMPA

Canton

Macao

Xiamen (Amoy)

Aceh

Pasai

Penang

Kedah

Patani

Perak

Pahang

Priaman

Melaka

Johor

SUMATRA

Palembang

SUNDA LANDS

Banten

Japara

Demak

Banjarmasin

Brunei

Sulu

MINDANAO

Manila

LUZON

SULAWESI

Makassar

MALUKU

Ternate

0°

20°

40°

60°

60°

80°

100°

120°

20°

0°

40°

2

Indian and Indonesian Elements in Early North Sumatra[1]

E. Edwards McKinnon

Although geography appears to place Aceh squarely within Sumatra, and therefore within modern Indonesia, its "Indonesian" identity has been strongly challenged by proponents of Aceh's distinctiveness. Aceh itself did not exist before the early sixteenth century, but there is evidence from earlier periods that suggests both its strategic position and the strength of commercial links made this coast more open to Indian colonisation than other parts of the archipelago. This question needs to be examined in the light of archaeological evidence for external contacts, often recoverable in the form of domestic rubbish. The history of Aceh no doubt exists at many sites throughout the region, but still remains to be recognised. Some of this evidence may be hidden by the passage of time, but some, often associated with early burial complexes, such as those at Lhok Cut on the Ujung Bateë Kapal promontory overlooking the Krueng Raya in Aceh Besar and near Geudong, south of Lhoksuemawe, lies strewn across the surface of the land. The humble potsherd, in particular, whether it be earthenware from south India or higher-fired stoneware imported from China or elsewhere in Southeast Asia, plays an important role in identifying ancient settlement sites and provides important clues for the linkages of inter-regional trade and cross-cultural contacts of former eras.

Aceh: Early Inter-Regional Contacts

Early Routes around the Bay of Bengal

The discovery of long distance navigation by means of the monsoon winds which carried ships directly across the Indian Ocean in barely a month of sailing was made around the beginning of the Christian era. The nature of the monsoons meant, however, that it was not possible for mariners and merchants involved in longer-reach trade to make the return journey from the sub-continent to Southeast Asia and back or vice-versa in any one season. It was thus necessary for sailors and merchants to wait at some suitable point at either end of the voyage in order that they could prepare themselves to catch the winds for the return journey at an appropriate time.

Before the discovery of monsoon navigation, voyages from India eastwards or from Southeast Asia to Sri Lanka and southern India were made around the coast of the Bay of Bengal. Numerous anchorages that would have given access to a supply of potable water existed at points along the coast.

Whether the earliest initiatives for monsoon navigation came from the east or west is not yet known, but certainly by the beginning of the first millennium C.E., Indian and Indonesian spices were appearing in the markets of ancient Rome.[2] At about the same time, Romano-Indian pottery known as rouletted ware found its way eastwards and appears in the Buni complex of ancient sites in the Sundalands, on the northwest coast of Java[3] and at Sembiran on the north coast of Bali.[4]

By the mid/late first millennium C.E. there were two, possibly four ancient maritime sailing routes across the Indian Ocean from and to Southeast Asia: the more northerly route ran from the coast of Kedah, and the more southerly from the northern tip of Aceh, to Sri Lanka and Tamilnadu, and thence to Kerala on the west coast of India and on to the Persian Gulf and the Red Sea.[5] As the European demand for oriental spices and aromatics grew, Roman specie was drawn eastwards to India, creating a major problem for the economics of the Roman Empire. Probably about the same time, aromatic resins, including highly valued products such as frankincense and myrrh from the Arabian Peninsula were also carried eastwards. Arab and Persian traders appear to have played an important role in this inter-regional commerce, and possessed maritime knowledge which was later documented in Arabic sources.[6]

Although harbours undoubtedly existed on the northern coasts of Sumatra from the first millennium C.E., and indeed possibly well before Śrīvijayan expansion in the seventh century, it seems that the focus of early shipping on the eastern side of the Indian Ocean was for some considerable period of time at the Sungei Mas site in the Merbok estuary on the west coast of Kedah, where an inscription datable to the fifth century C.E. has been recovered.[7] Several sites with recognisable

Indianising influences are to be found in and around the Merbok estuary. Further south, the northwest coast of Aceh between Aceh Head and the Krueng Raya was thus one of two possible departure points and landfall destinations for ships leaving for, or arriving from southern India and Sri Lanka. Indeed, Lamri or Lamuri, (as Al-Ramni) is mentioned frequently along with Fansur and Kalah in Arab sources. From about the third century C.E., the Aceh region appears in ancient Chinese sources as a source of pine resin. Chinese sources also indicate that there was an established relationship between Aceh and Srivijaya in southeast Sumatra by the seventh century,[8] suggesting that this area was already part of an extended inter-regional trading scene by the early/mid-first millennium C.E. In the medieval period, Chou Ku-fei (1178) was the first Chinese to mention the toponym Lan-li (Lamri, located at the northern tip of Aceh) where Chinese ships wintered before proceeding across the Indian Ocean.[9] The voyage westwards to Sri Lanka thereafter took 20 days.[10] For the moment, however, tangible archaeological evidence for external connections during this earlier period has yet to be discovered.

Medieval Cōla Elements in Northern Sumatra

By about the end of the eighth or early ninth century Indian trading associations were being formed in southern and western India. Among the first of these was the Manigrāman in the Kerala region of southwest India who comprised a group of resident Christians from the Persian Gulf.[11] At about the same time further north, at Aihole, also known as Ayyāvole in Kanarese, and Āryapura in Sanskrit, another group known as the Ayyāvole after their place of origin or the Aiññūrruvar (The Five Hundred of the Thousand Directions) formed and rapidly rose to prominence in inter-regional trade, extending their activities from the Red Sea to South China.

By the early eleventh century, then, mariners from southern India would appear to have been quite familiar with the geography of Southeast Asia prior to the Cōla raids of the 1020s. Whether these raids were intended purely for plunder, or were punitive in the sense that they were intended to deter local Southeast Asian rulers from interfering with expanding Tamil trade initiatives in the region is, however, still not clear. The Tanjavur inscription of the Cōla monarch Rajēndra, dated to a year equivalent to 1033, the 22nd year of his reign, mentions several toponyms thought to be located in Southeast Asia.[12]

Of direct interest to the student of Tamil contacts with Sumatra is reference to "Ilamuridesam, whose fierce strength rose in war", thought to refer to Lamri, or Lambri, and "Pannai with water in its bathing ghats", which appears to refer to a polity located in the Padang Lawas region located in the middle or upper reaches of the Panai/Barumun river on the border between the east coast region and central Sumatra; Malaiyur, in all probability Melayu Jambi, on the Batang Hari river and "Śrivijaya, (Palembang) with a jewelled wicket gate adorned with great splendour".[13]

Kadaram (Kedah) on the isthmus, opposite Sumatra, where the raiders "caught Sangrama Vijayottungavarman, the King of Kadaram, together with the elephants in his glorious army" is also mentioned as Māppapālam, a term meaning betelnut (*pinang*), as "having abundant deep water as a defence" possibly indicating a contemporary harbour settlement on the island of Penang.

It is within a few decades of these raids that a Tamil inscription (actually one of two or possibly three, notices[14]) dated to an equivalent of 1088 C.E. was set up at Lobu Tua near Barus on the northwest coast of Sumatra. The ancient harbour settlement at Lobu Tua, located immediately to the south of the mouth of the Aek Sibusuk, to the northwest of modern Barus, was the source for camphor (Malay: *kapur barus*: Dryobalanops aromatics, *Gaertn*), an aromatic resin in great demand for medicinal purposes throughout Asia during the pre-modern period. The immediate hinterland of Barus was also the source of another aromatic resin important during early trade, benzoin or gum benjamin (Malay: *kemenyan*; Tamil *sambirani*, mentioned in Sanskrit medicine as *apakva*: Styrax benzoin, Dryander), that was used as a substitute for incense.

Another Tamil inscription, discovered lying in a mosque at Desa Neusu in Banda Aceh, is somewhat later and thought to date from about the thirteenth century.[15] The legible portion of the Neusu Tamil language inscription, written in Tamil Grantha script (one face has been very badly abraded), does not apparently mention any guild by name, but is clearly related to trading activity. The legible portion that survived on the reverse of the stone states that:

> [...] that [we] would not hold (*kaikkollakadavadlla*); for this decision. [If any violation comes or situation rises against it (?) ... those] who put the [royal] emblem (*ilachchinal*, Skt. *lañcana*) will come to take and go (seize?) [....] that [we] would not get or collect (*kolludal*)

interest [in kind] (*polisai*) [... even] afterwards our people (*makkal*)
would do in accordance with this inscription (*ikkalvettu kokka* [*okkal*]).
Let there be prosperity![16]

This provisional reading of the remaining text suggests that this
inscription was set up to regularise trading regulations covering losses
of goods, the waiving of collection of interest, and perhaps, fees or
royalties payable to the monarch. The term *makkal*, meaning "our
people", implies membership of a guild or association, again possibly the
Aiññūrruvar or Ayyāvole. As such inscriptions were often set up within
the precincts of a religious foundation, either a Visnu temple or a
Buddhist sanctuary, this announcement is clear evidence for an established
Tamil presence in Aceh.

By the time Tamil guilds established themselves on Sumatran soil,
it is likely that the power of Srîvijaya, or as it was known by the eleventh
century, Melayu in Jambi, was either refocused in the southern part of
the Strait of Melaka or had waned considerably.[17] This was thus a factor
in changing circumstances that allowed foreign traders to insert themselves
at strategic locations along both the northeast and northwest coasts of
Sumatra by the mid/late eleventh century.[18]

Tamil merchant guilds are known to have traded in a wide variety
of goods, over a wide area. The products from southern India at this time
included horses, cotton fabrics (with possibly also dye stuffs such as
indigo),[19] glass, iron, salt, spices including cardamom and pepper, and
possibly ivory, together with precious stones from Sri Lanka. Not
mentioned as an item of trade, but apparently often transported across
the oceans, were vessels of coarse red earthenware used for water jars and
cooking purposes that were necessary on the voyage. Such vessels may
conceivably also have been used as containers for salt, an item that would
have been in demand in Sumatra.

In the late nineteenth century, the head of a Lokeśvara image with
distinct Sri Lankan stylistic affinities,[20] now in the Museum Nasional,
Jakarta, was recovered from an unidentified site in Aceh (see Fig. 3).
Interestingly, it has been noted recently that Tamil Guild communities
tended to be involved in syncretic religious activity, involving Śaivite,
Vaisnavite and Buddhistic elements in the mercantile community.[21]
Where the head of the Lokeśvara or the Neusu inscription were originally
located we may never know, unless there was perhaps an early settlement
occupied by Tamil traders in or near what is now Desa Neusu. There
are, however, two, if not more other possible locations where these items

Fig. 3 Lokeśvara head recovered from Banda Aceh area during the Aceh-Dutch War (*National Museum, Jakarta*)

may have originated: one in or around Lambadeuk, on the bay of Lambaro, a short distance to the west of Banda Aceh and a second near Lamreh, a point on the coast around the Krueng Raya some 50 kilometres to the east where a distinctive type of south Indian pottery has been found. Tectonic subsidence has seemingly all but obliterated any sign of early coastal habitation in the Lambaro area, but the foundations of a now-submerged rectangular masonry structure are visible beneath the waters of the bay between the present shore line and Pulau Tuan (also known as Pulau Angkasa).

Chinese exports brought by Indian as well as other traders to India and Sri Lanka and to harbours in Southeast Asia included Chinese silk, gold, copper — in the form of strings of cash or ingots, porcelain and stoneware, iron blades and cast iron cooking vessels. Salt may also have been exported from China. There appear to have been regional preferences for certain items and different areas were recipients of different quality materials, although such differences could well relate to the relative value of whatever goods were available at these various harbours.

Tamil guild activity in northwest and northeast Sumatra between the eleventh and fourteenth century was essentially to gain access to the valuable and highly profitable aromatic resins that were available in the mountainous hinterlands of Barus and Kota Cina and to bring them into the mainstream of Sino-Indian trade. The camphor of Barus may initially have been exploited by Arab merchants from the Persian Gulf, though when exactly these products entered the trade network is not yet known. Gold was available, at least in modest quantities, as were other relatively valuable forest products such as aloes wood (*Aquilaria* spp.), ivory, and other items such as wax, honey, and foodstuffs, all of which are mentioned in later accounts of items of trade in northern Sumatra and Aceh,[22] and would have been exported from a strategically located coastal settlement or settlements in what is now Aceh Besar.

Christie has underlined the fact that by the twelfth century, there were numerous ethnic groups involved in trade between Southeast Asia and China.[23] But the Tamil merchants were perhaps the only foreign traders who actually appear to have ventured into the hinterland of the harbour settlements of the northern part of Sumatra, and to have left some tangible evidence of their activities in the interior. Evidence of a Tamil-speaking, South Indian presence appears in the form of inscriptions at two inland sites in northern central Sumatra. A Tamil and Javanese presence may also have been established in the Padang Lawas area in the upper reaches of the Panai River that stretches from the east coast deep into the heart of the island.[24] There are inferences of the presence of Tamil speakers in the interior of central and northern Sumatra in the form of place names such as Mappapalam in the Dairi/Pakpak region, in northern Minangkabau/Mandailing region and yet again further south in the name Kerinci, which may derive from a Tamil term *kurinchi* meaning "a mountainous region".

With established evidence for a Tamil-speaking mercantile presence on both the west and east coasts of northern Sumatra,[25] a Tamil presence in the interior is also reflected in the folk tales, vocabulary and sept names of the Sembiring and other Karo-Batak as well as among the Dairi Pakpak who lived in and around the resin-producing regions of the Bukit Barisan range. There also appears to be some vestige of Indianising community organisation among the Karo. Until the early years of the twentieth century, their villages were organised into loose federations known as *urung*, a term that seems to derive from the Tamil *ur*, meaning a village, and to a medieval term *urom*, meaning a federation of villages of the *sudra* class, those comprising the lowest element of south Indian Hindu society. There were no less than 18 *urung* still extent in the Karo and adjacent areas at the end of the nineteenth century, including those in the Dairi Pakpak region and others the lowlands of Deli, and two in Simalungun.

Although the guild activities in this part of northern Sumatra may not relate directly to early settler communities in Aceh itself, they are an integral part of evidence for much wider networks of trade and commercial activity which, due to its strategic location, influenced events in Aceh and Aceh's perceptions of itself. And although guild activity in Sumatra seems to have come to an end by about the beginning of the fourteenth century, or soon after, this was not the end of the story of south Indian involvement in Aceh and northern Sumatra. This direct and relatively long term involvement of Tamil merchants in Sumatran, or more particularly in Acehnese affairs, continued to have an important impact upon what came later.

Apart from the inscriptional evidence, ceramics, and earthenware in particular, also provide evidence of a long-established Indian presence in northern Sumatra and Aceh. Sherds of a medieval coarse red ware, similar to that found at Arikamedu and Kaveripattinam in southern India and in Polonnaruva in Sri Lanka, have come to light at two medieval sites in Aceh, namely Lhok Cut, just landward of the Ujung Batëe Kapal headland on the eastern side of the Krueng Raya and at Lambaro,[26] as well as at Kota Cina near Belawan in the Deli region of northeast Sumatra.[27] The presence of this earthenware, which appears to have been a shipboard export item from southern India, clearly links these areas to wide ranging medieval Tamil mercantile activity. Other ceramics, including southern Song, Yuan and Ming period porcelain and stoneware from south China, as well as stoneware from Burma, Thailand, Vietnam and sixteenth-century Karatsu ware from Japan,[28] emphasise the continuity of Aceh's links with other parts of Southeast and East Asia.

It seems unlikely that Śrîvijaya, based initially in Palembang and thereafter in Jambi in southern Sumatra, would have exerted much direct influence, either politically or culturally, over what happened in northern Sumatra and Aceh from about the late eleventh century on. Even though some of the small, early harbours in this region were in all probability linked into Śrîvijayan period networks of trade over an extended period of time, tangible evidence of long-lasting cultural impact from such interactions has still to be found.[29] East Javanese influences seem to be restricted to the Minangkabau region and the Padang Lawas.

Early Islamic Influences

Muslim tombstones (*Nisan*) discovered recently at Kuta Lubhok on the eastern side of the Ujung Bateë Kapal promontory, a short distance from the Lhok Cut site, suggest the existence of an Islamic community in Aceh Besar by about the beginning of the twelfth century.[30] Whether these people were Indian Muslim merchants who came from southern India, Gujarat or Bengal is not yet clear, but sherds of medieval south Indian red ware are to be found in this vicinity. It may be that some of those people who originally came as Hindu Tamil merchants were converted at a relatively early date in southern India and continued trading along the same routes,[31] fitting in to different circumstances with the rise of entrepots at Samudera Pasai and Melaka. Muslim, Jewish, Zoroastrian and Christian merchants were all present in Kerala by the eighth and ninth centuries C.E. and established themselves on the eastern coast of India soon afterwards. The influence of such communities who established themselves on the Aceh coast, with their westward-looking links, was eventually to have a profound influence on the fiercely-independent but indigenous way in which the Acehnese saw themselves.

What is quite clear is that there was a long and continuous intercourse between southern India in particular, and Aceh, that commenced long before the Islamisation of the region.

Certain Acehnese place names too, suggest early pre-Islamic Indian connections: those of Indrapuri, Indrapatra and Indrapurwa.[32] Interestingly, these locations were each the site of an ancient mosque founded under the seventeenth-century Sultanate at the centres of the three *sagi* or political divisions of Aceh Besar. They affirm strong Indianising influences in the area at the time of the formation of the Acehnese Sultanate. But by then, however, a strong "local" identity seems to have revealed itself in Acehnese society.[33]

Indrapuri (XXII Mukim) is located some distance inland in the Aceh valley. The mosque here, which has several archaic features, is thought to have been erected on the site of a former (Hindu?) temple. The other former great mosques of Indrapatra at Ladong (XXVI Mukim), and Indrapurwa at Lambaro (XXV Mukim), both located on the coast, had all but disappeared by the beginning of the twentieth century.[34] The foundations of this last-mentioned mosque at Lambaro have now sunk under the sea, but are still visible beneath the restless waters of the bay.

Trade had been following long-established sea routes, for by the seventh century, or possibly much earlier, Arab merchants knew of Barus and its valuable camphor.[35] They undoubtedly passed through the Selat Melaka and perhaps also the Selat Sunda, *en route* for South China.[36] Later they settled in Quanzhou and built mosques there. There have been numerous attempts to assert the presence of Islam well before the twelfth or thirteenth centuries but none of it is as yet convincing for tangible archaeological evidence is not forthcoming. Even so, Arab ships may well have waited at anchorages in Aceh for the monsoon to take them westwards as the Chinese were to do also by the Southern Song period.

With the establishment of the port of Samudera Pasai on the northeast coast in the late thirteenth century, merchants from all over the Asiatic world settled themselves there. The founder of the Islamic dynasty of Samudera, who may well have been Indian in origin, organised his court in an Indian manner and is said to have married a daughter of the Sultan of Peureulak.[37] Odoric of Pordenone, who visited this coast in 1323, says Samudera was at that time in a state of perpetual war with Lamuri (Lambri or Aceh), which at that time was still "pagan". Moreover, numerous merchants of Indian (probably Gujarati) origin were in evidence. Samudera was reputedly attacked and occupied by Javanese Majapahit forces circa 1350. Lambri was also attacked at the same time, and is listed in the Negarakrtagama as a dependency of Majapahit. This occupation would not appear, however, to have had any long-lasting cultural or political effect

By the late fifteenth century, Gujaratis appear to have largely replaced the Tamils, who until then had dominated trade in northern Sumatra. No doubt mirroring what had transpired earlier, goods bartered in Sumatra were taken eastwards and sold in Java.[38] But the Tamils did not entirely disappear from involvement in this region. Muslim Tamils appear to have been intimately involved in the affairs of the region long after the departure of the Guilds.

The most densely populated part of Aceh was, and is, the region known as Aceh Besar, an area that extends roughly from the western tip of the island eastwards to the Krueng Raya, and its immediate hinterland up into the Aceh river valley. By the early sixteenth century, the seat of the sultanate was established at Banda Aceh, some distance inland from the mouth of the Aceh River at Uleelheue.[39]

A map of Aceh as it was at the end of the sixteenth century, reconstructed from information contained in the Portuguese *O Roteiro das Couas do Achem*[40] shows four different *kampung* or villages spread along the west bank of the Aceh River: "Bengala", "Pegu", "Pedagang" and "Pedayung" which suggest that the Kampung Bengala was inhabited by Bengalis, Pegu by Burmese, Pedagang by traders of various ethnic groups and Pedayung, presumably by mariners,[41] who were all part of an "Indian Ocean", rather than an archipelagic community.

Indonesian Influences

Although Javanese Majapahit forces appear to have conquered and occupied Samudera Pasai[42] and also Lambri for a short period during the fourteenth century,[43] direct Javanese influence on Aceh as a whole appears rather limited. Javanese shipping did reach northern Sumatra and indeed appears to have reached as far as Aden. The cultural influence of the Javanese does not appear to have exerted anything like the same influence on Aceh or northern Sumatra as traders of Indian origin. Brakel has suggested that despite there being many underlying Indic elements in Acehnese culture, the Acehnese Sultanate was typically "Indonesian" rather than an Indic or Moghul concept.[44] This does suggest indigenous development, albeit strongly influenced by "Malay" perceptions of kingship, which were themselves often Indic in flavour. More recently, Laffan has suggested that both Samudera and Aceh were part of what he calls the influence of "Jâwîs in an Islamising Ocean",[45] Islamic cultural influences that also extended westward from Sumatra along with the export of the produce of the archipelago.

Evidence for an erstwhile Javanese presence at Samudera Pasai appears in the form of one of a pair of *nisan* or tombstones erected on the grave of a former Queen, Al-Alah, wife of Sultan Ahmad, whose antecedents seemingly ruled both Pasai and Kedah. Of the two *nisan*, located in a grave complex at Minyë Tujoh, one is inscribed in Arabic whilst the second is inscribed in Old Javanese, dated to 781 Hijrah [1379]. The stone with the Arabic inscription appears, inconsistently, to be dated 791 Hijrah.[46]

Mohammad Said has suggested that the existence of an inscription written in Old Javanese is due to the presence and influence of Javanese "advisors" who stayed in Samudera after it was conquered by Majapahit.[47]

Abundant archaeological evidence for overseas trade at Samudera Pasai appears also in the form of marble tombstones imported from

Gujarat and literally tons of broken potsherds relating to fourteenth- to sixteenth-century stoneware from the kilns of Burma, Thailand and Vietnam as well as from China, that litter the area around Geudong south of Lhokseumawe. Earthenwares of probable Middle Eastern provenance are also to be found here, but an organized study of the ceramic assemblage still needs to be undertaken.

Acehnese forces conquered Samudera Pasai in 1521 but Aceh allowed trading to continue there until about 1539, for until then Aceh itself had not yet developed as an entrepot.[48] After 1539, the year in which Pinto says the Acehnese conquered Aru, at that time in all probability centred on a Karo *dusun* settlement now known as Deli Tua, trade appears to have been moved to Aceh itself. The subjugation of these coastal areas may have had a marked impact upon indigenous peoples such as the Gayo and Karo in these areas. Karo folk tales, for example, portray vivid memories of the Acehnese incursions into Deli during the early sixteenth century. Numbers of Karo were carried off to Aceh where they became a distinct element of the population of the Aceh valley. The success of these conquests and the displacement of peoples may have engendered culturally unique internal images of the Acehnese themselves, but still strongly influenced by Indianising concepts.

Summary

Indianising influences, initially "Hindu" and "Buddhistic", and latterly Islamic appear therefore to have had direct and sustained impact upon developments in Aceh over a long period of time. With its strategic location at the very tip of Sumatra, from the beginning of the second millennium, if not rather earlier, it served as a landfall focus for shipping from the west as well as a focus for ships from Burma and from Indo-china. Western-oriented commercial, cultural and religious contacts strongly influenced Acehnese perceptions of themselves over a long period of time. With the rise of the Sultanate at the beginning of the sixteenth century, Aceh developed as a major entrepot where the continuing major cultural, economic, religious and trading horizons were essentially westward towards Sri Lanka, India, Burma and the Middle East and to the northeast, to China. This gave rise to a strong local sense of identity, that although Indonesian, and rooted in a Hindu past, was perhaps unique in the archipelago. Acehnese ties with the rest of Indonesia and with Java in particular, appear to have been far less strong.

Notes

[1]   I am most grateful to Dr Geoff Wade for reading an earlier draft of this chapter and for making several useful observations and suggestions.

[2]   J. Innes Miller, *Spice Trade of the Roman Empire* (Oxford: Oxford University Press, 1969), pp. 13, 14.

[3]   M.J. Walker and S. Santoso, "Romano-Indian Rouletted Ware in Indonesia", *Asian Perspectives*, no. 20 (2) (1977): 228–35.

[4]   I.W. Ardika and Peter Bellwood, "Sembiran: the Beginnings of Indian Contact with Bali", *Antiquity*, no. 65 (247) (1985): 221–32.

[5]   Ptak, quoting Ming Chinese and earlier sources suggests that there were actually three sailing routes westwards from the Straits of Melaka to South Asia, all of which commenced at the Nicobar Islands and one of which proceeded via the Andamans. R. Ptak, "Die Andamanen und Nikobaren nach chineische Quellen (Ende Sung bis Ming)", *Zeitschrift der Deutschen Morgenlandischen Gesellschaft* 140: 343–73; quoted by David Bulbeck, "Indigenous Traditions and Exogenous Influences in the Early History of Peninsular Malaysia", in *Southeast Asia: From Prehistory to History*, ed. Ian Glover and Peter Bellwood (London and New York: RoutledgeCurzon, 2004), pp. 314–36.

[6]   See G.R. Tibbetts, *A Study of the Arab Texts Containing Material on South-East Asia,* Oriental Translation Fund, New Series Vol. XLIV (Leiden: E.J. Brill, published for the Royal Asiatic Society, London, 1979).

[7]   The site at Sungei Mas extends to some 10 ha. It has been partially excavated revealing a wide range of early brick-built structures and evidence for a thriving entrepot that may have existed over a period of several centuries. Nik Hasan Shuhaimi Nik Abd. Rahman and Othman Mohd. Yatim, *Warisan Lembah Bujang* (Bangi: Universiti Kebangsaan Malaysia, 1992).

[8]   See O.W. Wolters, *Early Indonesian Commerce* (Ithaca, N.Y.: Cornell University Press, 1967), especially Chapter 7, pp. 107–10.

[9]   F. Hirth and W.W. Rockhill, *Chau Ju-kua: His work on the Chinese and Arab Trade in the Twelfth and Thirteenth Centuries Entitled Chu-fan-chi* (Taipei: Ch'eng-wen Publishing, 1967), pp. 72–5, especially n. 1.

[10] The time taken would no doubt have varied with the winds and the skills of the navigators.

[11] For a full discussion of the formation of the Indian trading guilds see: Meera Abraham, *Two Medieval Merchant Guilds of South India* (New Delhi: Manohar, 1988). But see also Jan Wisseman Christie, "The Medieval Tamil-language Inscriptions in Southeast Asia and China", *Journal of Southeast Asian Studies* 29, 2 (1998): 239–68.

[12] See K.A.N. Sastri, *History of Śrivijaya* (Madras: University of Madras, 1949), pp. 80, 81. Christie's "Inscriptions", p. 254 says, however, that it is

interesting to note that Rajendra's son later claimed on his father's behalf only the conquest of Kadaram (Kedah) (re: *Annual Report of South Indian Epigraphy* 1912–3: no. 961, no. 26).

13 Sastri, *History,* pp. 80, 81.

14 In addition to the Tamil inscription, Bronson *et al.* noted that there were remains of an Old Malay inscription in Javanese *kawi* script, of which one part is in Jakarta and another remains in Lobo Tua. Ben Bronson, M. Suhadi Basoeki and J. Wisseman, *Laporan Penelitian Arkeologi di Sumatera* (Jakarta: Pusat Penelitian Arkeologi Nasional, 1977). There may, however, be part of yet another inscription in Grantha characters at Lobu Tua. A Buddha image, now lost, was also recovered from this site.

15 The inscription was discovered lying in a mosque where the stone was used as a base for ritual ablutions and is consequently extremely abraded on one side.

16 Also quoted in Christie, "Inscriptions", p. 259.

17 Modern scholarship suggests that Śrivijayan power had not waned as much as was thought in the past. See Christie, "Inscriptions", pp. 254–6. Firth and Rockhill, *Chau Ju-kua,* p. 73, note, however, that Lambri "sends a yearly tribute to San-fo-ts'i". As long as adequate tribute was sent to the overlord, it is likely that whoever ruled in Lambri would remain undisturbed.

18 At Barus, for example, archaeological evidence suggests the presence of Arab, Javanese and Tamil traders in a settlement that may have existed for about a century. See Claude Guillot, ed., *Histoire de Barus: Le site de Lobu Tua II, Étude archéologique et Documents* (Paris: Cahiers d'Archipel, 2003), p. 28.

19 Christie, "Inscriptions". See also Ruth Barnes, *Indian Block-printed Cotton Fragments in the Kelsey Museum, the University of Michigan* (Ann Arbor: University of Michigan Press, 1993).

20 E. Edwards McKinnon, "Beyond Serandib: A Note on Lambri at the Northern Tip of Aceh", *Indonesia* 46 (1988): 114, n. 74.

21 See Peter Schalk, ed., *Buddhism among Tamils in Pre-Colonial Tamilakam and Ilam,* 2 (Uppsala: University of Uppsala Press, 2002), pp. 681, 780, 842.

22 McKinnon, "Beyond Serandib", pp. 111–3.

23 Christie, "Inscriptions", p. 267.

24 Rumbi Mulia noted what she considered to be eastern Javanese influences in this area during the eleventh to fourteenth century. Rumbi Mulia, "The Ancient Kingdom of Panai and the Ruins of the Padang Lawas", *Bulletin of the Research Centre of Archaeology,* no. 14 (Jakarta: The Research Centre of Archaeology, 1980).

25 E. Edwards McKinnon, "Medieval Tamil Involvement in Northern Sumatra, C. 11-14 (The Gold and Resin Trade)", *JMBRAS* 69, 1 (1998).

26 E. Edwards McKinnon, "Ceramic finds from Landfall sites at Krueng Raya, Kabupaten Aceh Besar", *HKI Newsletter* (1995).

27   E. Edwards McKinnon, *Kota Cina,* Cornell PhD dissertation (1984), currently being revised for publication during a visiting fellowship at the Asia Research Institute, National University of Singapore (May 2004).

28   E. Edwards McKinnon, "Ceramic Recoveries (Surface Finds) at Lambaro, Aceh", *Journal of East West Maritime Relations* 2 (1992): 63–73.

29   Christie suggests that there was a marked difference between South Indian influence in the "core" areas and the peripheral areas further west. Christie, "Inscriptions", p. 267.

30   Suwedi Montana, "Nouvelles données sur les royumes de Lamuri et Barat (Aceh)", *Archipel* 53 (1997): 85–95. Montana links this to the erstwhile sultanate of Lamri. The *nisan* are in a distinct style known locally as "plakpling". Mohd. Said describes Kota Lubhok as being located "on the Krueng Lamreh, close to the Krueng Raya". H. Mohammad Said, *Aceh Sepanjang Abad,* 2nd edition (Medan: Waspada, 1981), p. 144. This fort was the one seemingly captured by the Portuguese and retaken by Iskandar Muda in 1606.

31   Certain Buddhists and members of some Hindu communities who converted early on to Islam for economic reasons, appear to have retained names which reflected their original occupations or castes. Thus, the same families from Tamilnadu, who had traded to Sumatra as Buddhist or Hindu members of Guilds in the twelfth or thirteenth centuries, may have continued their activities as Muslims in virtually the same or similar roles. I am grateful to Torsten Tschacher for bringing this point to my notice.

32   Brakel suggests that these names reflect the notion that the king or sultan was an incarnation of Indra. L.F. Brakel, "State and Statecraft in 17th Century Aceh", in *Pre-colonial State Systems in Southeast Asia: the Malay Peninsula, Sumatra, Bali-Lombok, South Celebes. Monographs of the Malaysian Branch of the Royal Asiatic Society No. 6,* ed. Anthony Reid and Lance Castles (Kuala Lumpur: MBRAS), pp. 56–66.

33   Brakel suggests that the sultanate "can be best understood within the general context of the 'Hinduised States of Southeast Asia'". Ibid., p. 66.

34   C. Snouck Hurgronje, *The Achehnese* I (Leiden: Brill, 1906), p. 82.

35   This may have been the Barousai of Ptolemy. If so, it would suggest external contact with the region from the beginnings of the Christian era. Persian Arab merchants took (Sumatran) camphor to China in 724 C.E. O.W. Wolters, *The Fall of Śrivijaya in Malay History* (Kuala Lumpur: OUP, 1970), pp. 26, 39.

36   The earliest Arab written sources date to the ninth century, but maritime activities were already well-established by then and Arabs were resident in Guangzhou by the late seventh century.

37   R.A. Kern, "The First Muslim Kingdoms in North Sumatra", in *The Propagation of Islām in the Indonesian-Malay Archipelago,* ed. Alijah Gordon (Kuala Lumpur: Malaysian Sociological Research Institute, 2001), pp. 32, 33.

[38] This may well have been going on for some considerable time as the presence of Tamils is noted on early Javanese inscriptions.

[39] Arun Das Gupta, "Aceh in Indonesian Trade and Politics: 1600–1641" (PhD dissertation, Cornell University), p. 27.

[40] Jorge M. dos Santos Alves and P-Y Manguin, *O Roteiro das Cousas do Achem de D. João Ribeiro Gaio* (Lisbon: Commissão Nacional para as Comemorações dos Descobrimentos Portugueses), Map 2, p. 116.

[41] *Pedayung* translates literally as oarsmen, possibly those who rowed the galleys or *lancang* of the sultan.

[42] There were actually two settlements, Samudera, which stood on the left or west bank of the Kruëng Pasai was at some distance from the coast. Pasai is thought to have been probably centred around a low hill known as the *Cot Astana* (palace hill) near the modern village of Geudong. Alternatively, it may have been on the opposite bank of the river.

[43] The Negarakrtagama, a fourteenth-century Javanese epic dated 1365, claims that Majapahit conquered several polities in the northern part of Sumatra during the mid/late fourteenth century. See Th.G.Th. Pigeaud, *Java in the 14th Century: A Study in Cultural History*, 5 vols. (The Hague: M. Nijhoff, 1960–3).

[44] Brakel, "State and Statecraft", p. 66.

[45] Micheal Laffan, "Camphor, Ka'ba, Jâwa: Muslim Visions of Southeast Asia from Srîvijaya and on, 850–1885", a paper presented at the Conference of Northeast Asia in Maritime Perspective: a Dialogue with Southeast Asia, Okinawa, Japan, Nov. 2004.

[46] Mohd. Said, *Aceh*, p. 101.

[47] Mohd. Said discusses this in depth. Ibid., pp. 100–9.

[48] Jorge M. Dos Santos Alves, "The Foreign Trader's Management in the Sultanates of the Straits of Malacca", in *From the Mediterranean to the China Sea*, ed. Claude Guillot, Denys Lombard and Roderich Ptak (Wiesbaden: Harrassowitz, 1998), p. 137.

3

Aceh in the Sixteenth and Seventeenth Centuries: "*Serambi Mekkah*" and Identity

Peter G. Riddell

Introduction

The famous Dutch Orientalist Christian Snouck Hurgronje produced a pioneering study of Aceh in the latter years of the nineteenth century. In this work he recorded a term of reference that the Acehnese used for themselves, as follows:

> [B]efore sailing ships were replaced by steamers as a means of conveyance for visitants to Mekka, Acheh formed a great halting-place for almost all the pilgrims from the Eastern Archipelago. The Achehnese used to speak of their country with some pride as "the gate of the Holy Land" [*Serambi Mekkah*]. Many remained there a considerable time on their way to and fro, while some even settled in the country as traders or teachers for the remainder of their lives.[1]

Hurgronje goes on to suggest that Javanese could obtain a taste of Arabia while in Aceh by interacting with certain learned Malay scholars.[2]

The earliest surviving reference to this term can be found in Nur al-Din al-Raniri's famous *Bustan al-Salatin*. As the text explains the sumptuousness of the funeral arrangements for Acehnese Sultan Iskandar Thani in 1641, it has the observers exclaiming to each other:

> Banyak-lah negeri yang di-bawah angin dan atas angin kita melihat, di-istana segala raja2 yang besar2, tiada sa-orang jua pun saperti perentah menjelis Duli Hadharat tuan kita ini. Sa-suggoh-nya-lah negeri Acheh Daru's-Salam ini serambi Mekah Allah yang mahamulia.[3]

In all the states we see both above and below the wind, in the palaces of all the great kings, there is no-one who is equal in righteous authority to our noble Lord the King. Truly this state of Aceh Daru's-Salam is the very verandah of God's most honoured city of Mecca.

There are thus two dimensions to the term *Serambi Mekkah* evident in these quotations. Al-Raniri's use of this term is Aceh-focused, reflecting the Mecca-like splendour of Aceh, regarding it as a kind of "Mecca of the East". Hurgronje affirms this understanding, but also looks westwards, portraying Aceh as a door to Arabia for pilgrims from all over the archipelago.

This brief diachronic analysis may well have ramifications for the developing identity of the Acehnese. In order to explore this possibility, we will focus upon the period of Acehnese imperial greatness, the sixteenth and seventeenth centuries. We will consider the process of empire building and the literary arena in turn, and then draw the threads together in a re-evaluation of the significance for Acehnese identity of the term *Serambi Mekkah*.

Conflict Without: The Rise and Decline of Islamic Aceh

At the beginning of the sixteenth century, Aceh was just one of several minor coastal settlements of North Sumatra. However, in 1511 the great Muslim state of Melaka, which had dominated the Malay world during the fifteenth century, fell to the Portuguese. This was a watershed event that was to lead to the reshaping of the Southeast Asian region. It opened the way for a struggle for regional hegemony among various North Sumatran Muslim ports in order to capture the lucrative trading activities which had hitherto been dominated by Melaka.

During the 1520s, the Acehnese Sultan Ali Mughayat Syah (d. 1530) undertook successful military campaigns against the neighbouring cities of Deli, Pidie, Pasai, and Daya, the last of which was not fully Islamised around this time.[4] Acehnese domains in Sumatra continued to expand relentlessly thereafter.

Melaka did not disappear as a state, but henceforth it was to project a Portuguese profile in the region, threatening Acehnese expansion. Sultan Ali Mughayat Syah defeated a Portuguese fleet in a sea battle in 1521. During the reign of Sultan Alau'd-Din Ri'ayat Shah al-Kahar (1537/9–71) there were unsuccessful attacks on Melaka in 1537, 1547, 1568, 1573 and 1575, and consolidated contacts with the heart of the Islamic world, particularly, the Ottoman Turks as detailed in the following chapter.

The enmity between Aceh and Portuguese Melaka was paralleled by a developing rivalry between Aceh and the Kingdom of Johor, which had been established in 1518 by the son of the last sultan of Melaka. In 1564 the Acehnese sacked the capital of Johor, and carried the Johor sultan to Aceh where he was killed. Four years later, when the Acehnese unsuccessfully attacked Melaka, Johor provided assistance to the Portuguese.

In 1575 Aceh attacked and conquered Perak, killing the sultan who was a kinsman of the Johor house and carrying off the dead sultan's widow and children. Through conquest and subsequent marriages, Perak became a vassal of Aceh. Acehnese campaigns against Johor and its allies continued in 1582, when an attack on Johor was beaten off with assistance from Portugal.

The 34-year reign of Sultan Alau'd-Din Ri'ayat Shah al-Kahar was followed by a period of instability in Aceh, with eight sultans occupying the Acehnese throne during the next 36 years. The strongest of them was Sultan 'Ala u'd-Din Ri'ayat Shah Sayyid al-Mukammil (r. 1589–1604) who changed the direction of Acehnese policies. He slowed down Acehnese imperial expansion, sought rapprochement with the Portuguese and diminished the struggle with Johor. If French visitors of the time can be trusted, he radically centralised the administration and disarmed the great lords.[5]

Aceh's position as a significant political power in the region was accompanied by a growing reputation in the spiritual realm. Syed M. Naguib Al-Attas describes Aceh in 1590 as "the intellectual and spiritual centre of Islam in the Malay world at that time".[6] This position was to be cemented during the seventeenth century.

The greater Acehnese openness towards the Portuguese was accompanied by developing contacts with other European powers. The turn of the seventeenth century witnessed the opening of official contacts between Aceh and both England and Holland. In 1602 Sir James Lancaster led the first expedition of the newly constituted English East India Company with letters and gifts for the Kings of Aceh and Bantam.[7] Similarly, 1602 saw the formation of the Dutch East India Company (VOC), leading to expeditions in 1603, 1605, 1606 and 1607.

Revolts by Aceh's vassal states had never been far away. When Sultan Iskandar Muda came to the throne in 1607, the supremacy of the

Acehnese sultanate was somewhat tenuous. There was considerable room for consolidation of power and further expansion throughout the region.

The push for Empire was resumed from 1612. Deli and Aru to the east were subjugated once again, and in 1613 the capital of the Kingdom of Johor was overcome, with the Sultan of Johor and his family carried back to Aceh as prisoners. The following year the Portuguese suffered heavy losses to the Acehnese at Baning. In 1617 Pahang was attacked. Iskandar Muda adopted Raja Sulung, the seven-year-old son of the sultan of Pahang, as his own son in an attempt to win "the hearts and minds" of the defeated population. Kedah was overcome in 1619, and 7,000 inhabitants were transported back to Aceh as slaves; Kedah itself, a rival producer of pepper, was destroyed.

This first phase of expansion under Iskandar Muda was followed by several years of consolidation in preparation for the big push against the ultimate prize on the Malay Peninsula, Portuguese Melaka. However, the 1629 siege of Melaka by a massive Acehnese expeditionary force ended in disaster, with the Acehnese routed, suffering enormous losses in men and equipment.[8]

After 17 years of external military adventure, with associated losses, such a military disaster must have had a profound impact on Acehnese society. In subsequent years both external policy and internal theological doctrine were to undergo great changes, no doubt reflecting a society in deep turmoil.

In 1636 Sultan Iskandar Muda died. His successor was his adopted son who had been brought back from Pahang aged seven in 1617. The new sultan took the title Iskandar Thani, but only ruled for five years, dying prematurely at the age of 31 in 1641. His rule was characterised by religious turmoil and dispute. Politico-religious events during this period were driven not by Iskandar Thani himself but by his appointee to the position of chief religious authority, Nur al-Din al-Raniri, a migrant of Hadhrami descent from Gujarat.

Iskandar Thani's widow succeeded to the Acehnese throne, initiating a period of almost 60 years of rule by women in the Sultanate. The new sultana, Taj al-'Alam Safiyat al-Din Shah (1641–75), was the daughter of Iskandar Muda. She did not share her father's appetite for empire building, which probably reflected the mood of her society after the disaster in Melaka in 1629. During her 34 years on the throne, the area under Acehnese control shrank to the point where it consisted only of the northern part of Sumatra.

Safiyat al-Din was succeeded by another female sovereign, of uncertain ancestry. Sri Sultan Nur al-'Alam Nakiyat al-Din Shah reigned for only three years. It was during her rule that the Bayt al-Rahman mosque and the Sultan's palace, both built by Iskandar Muda, were destroyed by fire.

The next two rulers were also women. Sultana 'Inayat Shah Zakiyat al-Din Shah reigned from 1678 to 1688 and Sultana Kamalat Shah from 1688 to 1699. In the latter year Kamalat Shah was expelled from power as a result of a *fatwa* issued by the Sheriff of Mecca ruling that it was unIslamic for a woman to serve as Sultan.[9]

Aceh's decline was now terminal, a fact marked by a gradual erosion of control at the leadership level, with Aceh's supreme position of leadership over the next 239 years being filled by "eleven inconsequential Sultans, including three Arabs (1699–1726), two Malays (both in 1726) and six Bugis (1727–1838)".[10]

Conflict Within: Shaping Islamic Identity in Aceh

Law in Aceh: Islamic, Adapted Islamic and Local

During his first three years in power, Iskandar Muda amplified and strengthened the legal system, which was based on Shafi'ite law and centred upon the ruler as the head of an Islamic state. There were four separate courts in operation during Iskandar Muda's reign: a civil court, located in the Bayt al-Rahman mosque; a criminal court; a religious court with the Chief Judge of the Sultan (*Qadi al-Malik al-'adil*) as the presiding judge; and a court at the customs house which settled disputes among merchants, both foreign and local.

The Chief Judge played a dominant role in the religious life of the Sultanate of Aceh, although this role changed somewhat during the course of the seventeenth century. During the reign of Iskandar Muda, the Chief Judge, Shams al-Din al-Sumatra'i, was powerful in the religious sphere but political power rested clearly in the hands of the Sultan, who also served as overall head of all areas, be they religious or political. The dominant religious figure during the reign of Iskandar Thani, Nur al-Din al-Raniri, exerted a significant influence in the political sphere as well, and this continued during the early part of the rule of Safiyat al-Din. The blurring of the lines between religious and political authority peaked during the tenure of the Minangkabau Sayf al-Rijal as Chief Judge from 1644–53. His involvement in political intrigue led to his downfall after an unsuccessful plot to enthrone him. This was probably linked with an ongoing internal struggle between the established sultans and those who were opposed to female tenure of the office of sultan. The role of Chief Judge reverted to an essentially religious one from the time of 'Abd al-Ra'uf's appointment in the early 1660s, leading to increased political stability.

Cases and Punishment

The available evidence of legal cases and the resulting punishment show some variation between reported punishments laid down by the Acehnese religious authorities and the prescriptions for punishment by Shafi'ite law.

In Aceh death by strangulation was the standard punishment meted out to convicted adulterers, whereas under Shafi'ite law stoning was the prescribed punishment for adultery. Likewise, penalties for drinking alcohol appear to have been at variance with Shafi'ite prescriptions, and were somewhat more severe, including amputation of hands, and pouring molten lead down the throats of those adjudged as guilty. Punishment for theft appears to have been considerably more severe in Aceh than was the case under Shafi'ite law. In 1636 four royal concubines in the Acehnese court were executed for stealing silver plates from the palace.

In the case of penal law, as we have seen with criminal law above, there appears to have been a composite practice in Aceh. Debtors were liable to enslavement in case of failure to pay debts,[11] and this too was at variance with Qur'anic injunctions.

In certain areas, Acehnese practice appears to have closely followed Islamic prescriptions, as applied to marriage, divorce and inheritance.

There was also a set of judicial practices under the direction of the rulers, which drew on traditional local practice and was known as *Hukum Adat*. The use of this term varied from the use in other locations in the Malay-Indonesian world, because it was driven not by the community but by the rulers, and supplemented Islamic law. Some offences were judged according to Islamic law, others according to the *Hukum Adat*. At the village level, life apparently tended to be administered by an indigenous unwritten *adat* under strong Islamic influence.[12]

Islamic Literature and Doctrinal Conflict in Aceh

Acehnese literary activity in this period occurred within a dynamic and changing social environment. Sultan Iskandar Muda gave priority to the strengthening of the Islamic faith both within and without the territory of Aceh. The famous Bayt al-Rahman mosque in Aceh was just one of many mosques built during this period.

Acehnese pilgrims visited Arabia in increasing numbers during this time, and Acehnese religious scholars increasingly travelled to Arabia to study at various centres of Islamic learning. Hamzah Fansuri, the great mystic of the late sixteenth century, is the first such scholar whom we can identify, yet he was probably preceded by others whose names have disappeared from the pages of history.

The Monistic School

Hamzah came from the prosperous West Sumatran trading port of Fansur, also known as Barus. He lived most, and possibly all, of his life in the sixteenth century. His writings suggest that Hamzah travelled to the Malay Peninsula, Siam and various points in Arabia. His time in Arabia was spent studying with several mystical orders, leading to a formal initiation of the Qadiriyya order.[13] He may have studied Persian in Siam, and come into contact there with doctrines of a heterodox nature, possibly through the substantial Siamese Muslim community which was influenced by Indian Islam.[14]

Shams al-Din al-Sumatra'i was born before 1575 and died on 25 February 1630.[15] His primary work, the *Mir'at al-Mu'minin*, presents his monistic teachings within a framework of seven grades of being. Its date of composition in 1601 suggests it may have been sponsored by Sultan 'Ala al-Din Ri'ayat Shah al-Mukammil.[16] Shams al-Din received the direct patronage of Sultan Iskandar Muda and served as the supreme spiritual guide in the Sultanate. Furthermore, Shams al-Din initiated the Sultan into the Naqshbandiyya order.[17] This points to Islamic monistic theosophy enjoying pride of place during Aceh's golden years under Iskandar Muda. These doctrines were initially expounded by Hamzah, consolidated by Shams al-Din and his followers, and were later to be condemned as heretical. However, we should note the arguments of Al-Attas, who considers that later accusations of heresy against Hamzah were undeserved. He claims that eager disciples took Hamzah's monistic teachings much further than the great writer himself would have agreed to.

Reformist Awakenings

The first possible evidence of reformist thinking from the region is provided by the Malay translation of the 'Aqa'id (Creed) of al-Nasafi

(d. 1142). The surviving manuscript that contains this text was copied in 1590,[18] and Aceh is the likely place where it was produced. Al-Attas speculates that the Malay translation may have been produced by one of the students of Muhammad al-Hamid, the paternal uncle of Nur al-Din al-Raniri, who taught Islamic sciences at Aceh between 1580–3 and again from 1589–1604.[19] Of particular interest is the "orthodoxy" of this text, in contrast to what Al-Attas points to as the adaptations of Hamzah's teachings by pseudo-Sufis in Aceh at the time. The introduction of a standard, uncontroversial text such as al-Nasafi's Creed may well have had as its purpose to serve as a corrective to the excesses of certain Sufis. It includes an accessible, yet sufficiently comprehensive statement of key Ash'arite doctrines. It may have represented an opening shot in an emerging war of words between competing schools in Aceh, which was to reach its peak in the late 1630s.

Shortly after Iskandar Thani's succession to power, Nur al-Din al-Raniri arrived in Aceh. Al-Raniri's rapid appointment as Chief Judge by Sultan Iskandar Thani enabled him to place his stamp on the theological life of the kingdom. Over the next seven years he wrote a total of 14 works in various fields,[20] mostly aimed at refuting what he considered to be the heretical teachings of Hamzah and Shams al-Din.

Al-Raniri was forced to leave Aceh in disgrace in 1644, in favour of the new Minangkabau scholar named Sayf al-Rijal.[21] Al-Raniri returned to India where he died on 21 September 1658.[22] In spite of spending barely seven years in the Sultanate of Aceh, al-Raniri left a lasting legacy. He ignited a doctrinal dispute, and stimulated a process of reform, which was to have a significant impact on Acehnese religious circles and, indeed, on the whole region.

The other great Islamic reformer of the seventeenth century was 'Abd al-Ra'uf b. Ali al-Fansuri al-Singkili (c. 1615–93). Born in the West Sumatran coastal town of Singkil, a vassal state of Aceh, 'Abd al-Ra'uf's early years were spent studying the Islamic sciences during the period of predominance of the monistic Sufis. 'Abd al-Ra'uf's childhood coincided with the years of great external expansion of the Sultanate.

In 1642, 'Abd al-Ra'uf followed the footsteps of Hamzah Fansuri by travelling to Arabia to study. His study programme is recorded in a codicil to his work 'Umdat al-muhtajin (The Support of the Needy).[23] 'Abd al-Ra'uf lists teachers and other scholars and students with whom he had contact in Mecca, Jeddah, Bayt al-Faqih, Zabid, and Medina during his 19 years' stay in Arabia. Key teachers were Ahmad al-Qushashi

(d. 1660) of Medina, the spiritual father of many seventeenth-century Indian mystics, and his successor Ibrahim al-Kurani (d. 1690). The latter authorised 'Abd al-Ra'uf to establish a school of the Shattariyya Sufi Order in Aceh, which was to trigger the spread of the Order throughout the archipelago.[24]

This codicil identifies the priorities for such visits to Arabia by Malay scholars. The key priority was a wide-ranging study of the Islamic sciences, including law, dogma, the prophetic traditions, history, Qur'anic recitation, Sufism, and other subjects. Furthermore, visiting scholars needed to be mobile, progressing from location to location. Moreover, there needed to be recognisable output; Ibrahim al-Kurani awarded 'Abd al-Ra'uf a licence which authorised him to propagate the mystical teachings he had acquired. Finally, scholars typically attached themselves to a variety of Sufi orders; 'Abd al-Ra'uf studied with teachers following the systems of the Shattariyya, Qadiriyya, Habashiyya, Firdawsiyya, Tinuriyya, Khalwatiyya, Hamadaniyya and the famous Naqshbandiyya Orders.

'Abd al-Ra'uf returned to Aceh in 1661. He was soon commissioned by the Sultana Safiyat al-Din Shah (1641–75) to write Mir'at al-Tullab, a work on jurisprudence, and completed it in 1663.[25] A further work commissioned by Sultana Zakiyat al-Din Shah was a commentary upon the famous Arba'ina Hadith by al-Nawawi (d. 1277).[26] This work is based on 40 Hadith accounts addressing fundamental but key issues in Islamic belief and practice. Abd al-Ra'uf's selection of this work as a focus provides a window into his reforming motives, as it emphasises the place of the shari'a after its perceived neglect during the long period of dominance of Hamzah and Shams al-Din.

Little is known about the details of 'Abd al-Ra'uf's life between his return to Aceh and his death around 1693, except that he wrote prolifically under the patronage of successive sultans.

"*Serambi Mekkah*" and Acehnese Identity Formation

We will now return to the term Serambi Mekkah, which serves as an important key in understanding Acehnese self-perceptions in the sixteenth and seventeenth centuries. This period is crucial for identity formation, as at the outset of the sixteenth century Aceh was merely a footnote in Southeast Asia, with its identity yet to be formed.

The first feature to note is the pervasive theme of conflict and violence during the period under examination, in the form of outward imperial expansion and inward doctrinal struggles. It should be remembered that violent assertiveness is an effective catalyst in identity formation.

Initially Aceh sought to develop a Malay-focused political identity, striving to become the imperial ruler of states on both sides of the Straits of Melaka. In this context the understanding of Serambi Mekkah was essentially inward-looking, with a vision for Malay hegemony overriding pan-Islamic notions. However, as Aceh encountered problems in this quest, especially from the Portuguese, they looked west for "superpower" support. We considered earlier the contacts with the Ottoman Turkish authorities under Sultan Alau'd-Din Ri'ayat Shah al-Kahar, which led to the acquisition by Aceh of significant material assistance. Aceh sent various envoys to Sulayman the Great in Constantinople from 1563, requesting help against the Portuguese in the following pan-Islamic terms:

> The Sultan [of Aceh] says that he is left alone to face the unbelievers. They have seized some islands, and have taken Muslims captive. Merchants and pilgrim ships going from these islands towards Mecca were captured one night [by the Portuguese] and the ships that were not captured were fired upon and sunk, causing many Muslims to drown.[27]

Further evidence for an emerging sense of pan-Islamic authority overriding pan-Malay sentiment is found in the developing perception of final authority lying not with Acehnese but with significant people in the Muslim heartlands. For example, the last of the four female sultanahs of Aceh, Kamalat Shah, was stripped of her office as a result of a 1699 fatwa by the Sheriff of Mecca, to the effect that it was unIslamic for a woman to rule.

This trend towards a more westward oriented identity is also seen if we examine religious issues. We saw evidence of emerging identity in the domestic legal operations of the Acehnese state. *Hukum Adat* continued to play a role in decisions in diverse areas of law, but Shafi'ite law had also come to be a significant point of reference. It had not, however, managed to completely displace *Hukum Adat* in the period under examination in this chapter.

Furthermore, Aceh had gained a flourishing reputation for Islamic scholarly excellence, which transcended parochial Sumatran or even Malay boundaries. A key factor was Aceh's function as a channel for scholarly visits in both directions. Late sixteenth-century visits by Muslim scholars to Aceh from elsewhere are well attested. During the rule of Acehnese Sultan ʿAli Riʿayat Shah (1571–9), Islamic sciences in the Sultanate were taught by the Meccan scholar Muhammad Azhari.[28] In the 1580s two more Arab scholars, Abu al-Kahyr ibn Shaykh ibn Hajar and Muhammad al-Yamani, came to play significant roles as Islamic teachers in Aceh, while Muhammad al-Hamid, the paternal uncle of Nur al-Din al-Raniri, also taught Islamic sciences at Aceh between 1580–3 and again from 1589–1604.

In the opposite direction, we saw how Hamzah Fansuri and ʿAbd al-Raʾuf were pioneers in undertaking visits to Arabia to study the Islamic sciences, for the purpose of returning to Aceh to transmit what they had learnt. We are fortunate in having the surviving testimony of the ʿUmdat al-muhtajin, which provides an invaluable window into what was to become a common practice among subsequent generations of young Islamic scholars from different parts of the Malay world.

The movement of people was mirrored in the movement of ideas between Arabia and the Indonesian archipelago, with the two processes closely intertwined. Major works by Arab and Indian scholars were translated into Malay by Hamzah Fansuri, Shams al-Din al-Sumatraʾi and ʿAbd al-Raʾuf. Furthermore, there was evidence of Acehnese scholars looking west for authoritative theological decisions to supplement the political decisions mentioned above. For example, Ibrahim al-Kurani wrote to Ithaf al-dhaki, probably in response to a request from ʿAbd al-Raʾuf, to provide guidance to Acehnese in dealing with the polemic between the followers of the early monists and al-Raniri.

However, Aceh did not merely serve as a telecommunications control point for the inhabitants of the Indonesian archipelago to contact Arabia. Rather, Aceh was a conduit for the dynamic processes of change taking place throughout the archipelago. At one level this took the form of empire building, via Acehnese efforts to establish supremacy in the Malay world in the sixteenth century as we have seen. But perhaps more significant was Aceh's role as the catalyst for much of the Islamisation which was taking place throughout the archipelago. The early monistic Sufis embraced and transmitted doctrines which were to reappear, in locally adapted forms, throughout the region in subsequent centuries. Similarly, reformist pulses that made themselves first felt in Aceh were subsequently in evidence in other parts of the archipelago. For example, ʿAbd al-Raʾuf's school of Sufism led to the spread of the Shattariyya Order throughout the archipelago, carrying with it its reformist tendencies.

Conclusion

In the early period of Indonesian Islamic history, Aceh played a crucial role in defining the newly emerging faith identity of the whole region. In doing so, it drew on elements from other Islamic areas in India and Arabia, adapted them to local contexts, and transmitted them to different parts of the Indonesian archipelago.

In the sixteenth and seventeenth centuries under examination in this chapter, Aceh itself was in quest of its own identity. This search was resolved by the formation of a society that viewed itself as pre-eminent among the Malays, but more importantly achieved a status that mirrored the great core city of Islam, Mecca. Hence for the Acehnese, Serambi Mecca came to serve as a statement which moved Aceh well beyond its own Malay region to assume a prominent role on the world Islamic stage. In such circumstances, any later efforts to "clip Aceh's wings", by way of squeezing it into an exclusively Malay-world box dependent upon neighbouring Malay-Indonesian communities, were bound to encounter significant resistance from the inhabitants of "the verandah of Mecca".

Notes

1. C. Snouck Hurgronje, *The Achehnese II* (Leiden: E.J. Brill, 1906), p. 19.
2. "Thus many Javanese may on their journey through, or in the course of a still longer visit, have imbibed the instruction of the Malay teacher ['Abd al-Ra'uf]." Ibid., p. 19.
3. T. Iskandar, ed., *Bustanu's-salatin: bab II, fasal 13* (Kuala Lumpur: Dewan Bahasa dan Pustaka, 1966), p. 68. With thanks to Lance Castles and Anthony Reid for this information.
4. M.C. Ricklefs, *A History of Modern Indonesia since c. 1300*, 2nd ed. (Basingstoke: Macmillan Press, 1993), p. 33, citing Tome Pires.
5. See Francois Martin and Augustin de Beaulieu, as translated in *Witnesses to Sumatra: A Travellers' Anthology* (Kuala Lumpur: Oxford University Press, 1995), pp. 57, 60, 76–8.
6. S.M. Naguib Al-Attas, *The Oldest Known Malay Manuscript: A Sixteenth Century Malay Translation of the 'Aqa'id of al-Nasafi* (Kuala Lumpur: University of Malaya, 1988), p. 33.
7. For a copy of the authority to trade given by the King of Aceh to the first East India Company expedition, see, W.G. Shellabear, "An Account of Some of the Oldest Malay MSS Now Extant", *JSBRAS* 31 (1898): 113–20.

8   For detailed accounts contemporaneous with the event, refer to D. Lombard, *Le Sultanat d'Atjèh au temps d'Iskandar Muda 1607–1636* (Paris: Ecole Française d'Extrême Orient, 1967), pp. 247–8. See also C.R. Boxer, "The Acehnese Attack on Malacca in 1629, as described in contemporary Portuguese sources", in *Malayan and Indonesian Studies: Essays Presented to Sir Richard Winstedt on His Eighty-fifth Birthday*, ed. J. Bastin and R. Roolvink (Oxford, 1964), pp.108ff.

9   H. Djajadiningrat, "Critisch Overzicht Van de in Maleische Werken vervatte gegevens over de Geschiedenis van het Soeltanaat Van Atjeh", *BKI* 65 (1911): 191.

10 Ricklefs, *A History of Modern Indonesia Since c. 1300*, p. 36. But note the more positive views in the following two chapters.

11 Anthony Reid, *Southeast Asia in the Age of Commerce 1450–1680*. Volume One, *The Lands Below the Winds* (New Haven and London: Yale University Press, 1988), pp. 140–3.

12 For a comprehensive discussion of the Islamic legal system in the Sultanate of Aceh, see T. Ito, *The World of the Adat Aceh: A Historical Study of the Sultanate of Aceh* (unpublished doctoral dissertation, Australian National University, 1984).

13 See R.O. Winstedt, "Some Malay Mystics, Heretical and Orthodox", *JMBRAS* 1 (1923): 312. S.M. Naguib Al-Attas, *Some Aspects of Sufism as Understood and Practised among the Malays* (Singapore: Malaysian Sociological Research Institute, 1963), p. 22. A. Vakily, "Sufism, Power Politics and Reform: Al-Raniri's Opposition to Hamzah al-Fansuri's Teachings Reconsidered", *Studia Islamika* 4, 1 (1997): 119. Vakily claims that this initiation took place in Baghdad, while Winstedt implies that it occurred at Mecca or Medina.

14 G.W.J. Drewes and L.F. Brakel, *The Poems of Hamzah Fansuri* (Dordrecht: Foris Publications, 1986), p. 5. Vakily, "Sufism, Power Politics and Reform", p. 119.

15 A. H. Johns, "Shams al-Din al-Samatrani", in *The Encyclopaedia of Islam*, 2nd ed., vol. 9 (Leiden: E.J. Brill Johns, 1997), p. 296.

16 Djajadiningrat, "Critisch Overzicht Van de in Maleische Werken vervatte gegevens over de Geschiedenis van het Soeltanaat Van Atjeh", p. 182.

17 Johns, "Shams al-Din al-Samatrani", p. 296.

18 Al-Attas, *The Oldest Known Malay Manuscript*, pp. 6ff.

19 Ibid., p. 34.

20 T. Iskandar, "Nuruddin ar-Raniri Pengarang Abad ke-17", *Dewan Bahasa* 8, 10 (1964): 440.

21 T. Ito, "Why Did Nuruddin ar-Raniri Leave Aceh in 1054 AH?", *BKI* 134 (1978): 491. A. Azra, *The Transmission of Islamic Reformism to Indonesia: Networks of Middle Eastern and Malay-Indonesian 'Ulama' in the Seventeenth and Eighteenth Centuries* (PhD dissertation, Columbia University, 1992), pp. 362–5.

22 P. Voorhoeve, "Short Note: Nuruddin ar-Raniri", *BKI* 115 (1959): 91.

23 For the Malay transliterated text and an English translation of this codicil, see P.G. Riddell, *Transferring a Tradition: 'Abd al-Ra'uf al-Singkili's Rendering into Malay of the Jalalayn Commentary* (Berkeley, CA: Centres for South and Southeast Asian Studies, University of California, 1990), pp. 223–38.

24 J.S. Trimingham, *The Sufi Orders in Islam* (Oxford: Oxford University Press, 1971), p. 130.

25 T.S. Abdurrauf, *Mir'at At-Tullab* (Banda Atjeh: Universitas Sjiah Kuala, 1971), Foreword.

26 P. Voorhoeve, "Bajan Tadjalli", *TBG* 23, 1 (1952): 111.

27 Cited in Anthony Reid, *Southeast Asia in the Age of Commerce 1450–1680. Volume Two: Expansion and Crisis* (New Haven and London: Yale University Press, 1993), p. 147. See also the following chapter.

28 S.M. Naguib Al-Attas, *The Oldest Known Malay Manuscript*, p. 32, citing the *Bustan al-Salatin*.

4

The Pre-modern Sultanate's View of its Place in the World

Anthony Reid

"Sumatra" was not a meaningful unit to most Sumatrans of the early nineteenth century, but to European imperial strategists studying their maps, its unity seemed obvious. To avoid clashes between English and Dutch agents in the east, and the messiness of land boundaries, they sought to consign whole islands to one side or the other. The London Treaty of 1824, therefore, created the future countries of Malaysia and Indonesia by drawing the line between English and Dutch spheres along the Straits of Melaka and Singapore. The Peninsula would be British/Malaysian, and Sumatra would be Dutch/Indonesian.

The same logic eventually propelled the Netherlands to make good on this stroke of the pen a half century later, at a time when the whole non-western world was being divided between colonial powers, and paper claims were no longer enough to keep rivals at bay. The story of the Dutch conquest and its consequences is told later in this volume. Here we wish to try to establish where pre-colonial Aceh saw its place in the world, before being forced into the dichotomy of part, or not part, of Indonesia.

The World of the Chronicles

To begin on the negative side, Java seems almost absent from the world-view of the Aceh chronicles, in marked contrast to the centrality of Java in chronicles from Banjarmasin, Bali, Makassar or even Melaka. Of the texts originating from North Sumatra, only one is aware of the reality of Java as a rich and powerful factor in Nusantara. This is the *Hikayat*

Raja-Raja Pasai, and the reason is that the sole text we have of it was evidently written in Java, and very likely for a Javanese patron, not very long after its author or his forebears had been brought captive to Majapahit by the conquering fleet of Gajah Mada in the 1350s. The latter part of the text gives a glittering account of the Majapahit court and its conquest of Pasai.[1] At one point it lists Java alongside China and India (Keling) as examples of strong states.[2]

However, the older part of the text, presumably written in Sumatra, has no mention of Java, and it was only this part representing an older text that was borrowed by subsequent Aceh chroniclers and by the *Sejarah Melayu* of Melaka. In this section it is South Indian terms, and references to Keling and the Arab world, which abound. Various remarkable figures from South India make their entrance in this part of the text, including an ingenious yogi credited with "naming" one of the Muslim sultans Perumudal Perumal, in evocation of the ancient kings of Malabar.[3] To add to the Indian connections, Tomé Pires believed that the first Muslim king of Pasai was a Bengali, and that Pasai subsequently had a special relation with Bengal.[4]

After that extraordinary mid-fourteenth-century interlude, Java had very little contact with Pasai or its Acehnese successor. Pires noted that traders from Java did not proceed beyond Melaka, leaving Pasai and later Aceh as predominately Indian Ocean ports. "The merchants who trade in Pasai are Gujaratis, Klings, Bengalis, men of Pegu, Siamese, men of Kedah and Bruas .... They do not trade in Pasai from the east, only with the populous city of Melaka."[5]

The chronicles written at the Acehnese court in the seventeenth and eighteenth centuries were very well aware of Acehnese wars, alliances and interactions with Peninsula and Sumatran ports such as Melaka, Pahang, Perak, Johor, Deli and Siak. But they mention Java only in lists of the kind of performances that embellish great festivals at the Aceh court.[6] There is no mention of commercial or political contacts. Where places beyond the Melaka Straits area impinge on the narratives, these are China, India and the Middle East as the source of technologies and entertainments, Gujarat, Bengal, South India and the Arab world as the origin of traders and learned men (*ulama*), Siam, India and Turkey (often *Rum*), as places of diplomatic relations, and of course the Peringgi (Portuguese) as constant antagonists.

For both the *Hikayat Aceh* and the *Bustan al-Salatin,* written in honour of Sultans Iskandar Muda (1607–36) and Iskandar Thani

(1636–41) respectively, relations with Turkey are the most important. The latter matter-of-factly and accurately ascribes the crucial links to the reign of Sultan Alau'd-Din Ri'ayat Shah al-Kahar (1537–71), who "sent a mission to Sultan Rum, to the state of Istanbul, in order to strengthen the Muslim religion. The Sultan Rum sent various craftsmen and experts who knew how to make guns."[7] The *Hikayat Aceh* has a more literary and hagiographic form, and epitomises the extensive diplomatic dealings of Iskandar Muda through stories of embassies to Aceh from Siam and Turkey. The Siam story has a definite basis in the realities of Iskandar Muda's reign, at which time, a Dutch factor in Ayutthaya reported, Aceh and Siam "have never been vassal or tributary to each other. To maintain the friendship they often send to each other their ambassadors with letters full of exaggerated titles and compliments and with presents."[8] The Turkey story on the other hand appears to conflate the undoubted commercial embassies that came to Iskandar Muda from the Red Sea ports under Ottoman authority, with the high-level contacts of the previous century.

As the chronicle tells it, the King of Siam (*Sharnawi*) sent an embassy to Aceh, which was astonished at the splendour of the court and especially the supernatural skills of the young Iskandar Muda in riding horses and elephants. When the envoys returned to Siam, bringing with them three Acehnese reciprocal ambassadors, the Siamese king was in turn amazed to hear of the powers of Iskandar Muda. He summoned to his court the kings of Cambodia, Chiang Mai, Lansang (Laos) and "Paslula", as well as ambassadors from the rulers of China and Champa, who all declared that they had never heard of such amazing feats. The King of Siam summoned two astrologers, who prophesied that Iskandar Muda was destined to be a great ruler over all other kings. The Siamese king then asked the Aceh ambassadors whether Iskandar Muda could be sent to Ayutthaya to inherit his own throne and rule over all the Siamese dependencies, but of course the answer was in the negative. This was how Iskandar Muda "became famous among all the kings of the East (*Mashrik*)".[9]

The following story relates that the Sultan of Rum was sick, and his doctors explained that he could be cured by application of camphor and naptha (petroleum), which could only be found in Aceh. Envoys were dispatched with a hundred men and all kinds of armaments. Their instructions were initially to the Pasha of Yemen, who passed the task of equipping a ship for the mission to Mir Haidar of Mocha. The envoys arrived in the Acehnese capital at a time when Iskandar Muda was away conquering Deli. Once he returned, royal entertainments were laid on for the envoys.

The chronicler devotes several pages here describing the marvels of Aceh they witnessed, including the water of the Aceh River, which "traders from the Arab world, Persia, Turkey, the Mughal empire and all India" had found to be the best in the world.[10] The Great Mosque of Aceh was so vast and splendidly decorated with gold, silver and jewels that it had no equal in the world, "except for the mosque al Haram in Mecca which is also beautiful". There were hundreds of other Friday mosques. The fame of Aceh had reached as far as Mecca and Medina, and Iskandar Muda was "the master of two lands and two seas, that is the lands and seas of east and west".[11] When the envoys of Rum related these marvels to their sultan, and to various great men of the Turkish, Arab, Persian, and Mughal domains who were present, the Sultan Rum declared that just as in former times Solomon and Alexander were the great kings in the world, "Now in our time also in the providence of God there are two great kings in the world. In the west we are the great king, and in the east Sri Sultan Perkasa Alam [Iskandar Muda] is the king who is great and who upholds the religion of God and his Prophet."[12] The various envoys went home to the various Arab, Persian and Mughal countries with this news, so that the fame of Iskandar Muda was eventually known throughout the whole world.

A third text, the epic poem *Hikayat Meukota Alam*,[13] also begins with an account of relations with Turkey. In this case the story takes the form of the popular oral tradition attaching to the large Turkish cannon, *Lada secupak* (one measure of pepper), preserved at the Acehnese citadel until taken to the Netherlands as a war trophy in 1874.[14] A sultan sent an envoy to Istanbul with ships laden with a gift of pepper, but the voyage was so difficult that only one measure of pepper remained at its end. Nevertheless, the Turkish Sultan was magnanimous, and sent the envoys back with the great cannon named in honour of this token tribute, as well as various skilled warriors and gunsmiths.

The Sixteenth Century: Islamic Alliances

Aceh's self-image in the sixteenth century was bound up with two issues — its Islamic struggle against the Portuguese, and its role in the international pepper trade. Before the Portuguese most of Sumatra's pepper had been shipped to China, often through the Melaka entrepot. The aggressive Portuguese stance both in Melaka, on the normal route to China, and in southwest India, which had been the next trans-shipment point after Aceh in the Islamic trading route westward, caused much disruption and eventual relocation.

When the Islamic trading route from Southeast Asia revived in the 1530s, it was along a new direct route from Aceh via the Maldives to the Red Sea ports, avoiding the centres of Portuguese power. Henceforth Aceh's pepper went to the west, locking the sultanate further into an Indian Ocean network of exchange. Boxer documents the first Acehnese pepper-shipment to the Red Sea in 1534.[15] By the 1560s five large shiploads of pepper were reported by Venetian sources to be arriving from Aceh each year in Jidda, and Jesuit letters complained that "the Turks merchandise with this king, who, every year, sends them many loaded vessels to Mecca".[16]

By this period, Aceh under the powerful Sultan Alau'd-Din Ri'ayat Shah al-Kahar was the Southeast Asian pivot of a revived Islamic trading system, which succeeded in shipping as much pepper, and nearly as much clove and nutmeg, to the Mediterranean, as the Portuguese did to Lisbon.[17] Commercially as well as ideologically Aceh was the rival of Portuguese Melaka, and its interests allied it with the other key nodes on the Muslim route from Maluku to Suez — Bijapur and Golconda in India, Japara in Java, and above all the Ottoman empire that controlled the Red Sea and Egypt. From this period dates the Acehnese vision of itself as a vassal of the Ottomans and the "verandah of Mecca" (*serambi Mekka*) for Southeast Asia.

All the direct relations with Turkey can be attributed to the Acehnese Sultan al-Kahar. Profiting from his pepper-trade to the Red Sea, he must first have made contact with Turkish officials around the time of the first, abortive Ottoman naval expedition against the Portuguese in the Indian Ocean in 1537–8, under Sulaiman Pasha, which reached only as far as Diu. A little help in the form of Turkish soldiers and materiel reached Aceh at that time, and assisted al-Kahar's campaigns against the Portuguese and their local friends, such as Aru and the Batak kingdom.

Around 1561–2 there are better-documented missions from Aceh to Istanbul to procure supplies and men for a major operation against the Portuguese. These efforts succeeded, to the extent that Turkish gunners were sent to Aceh at least by 1564, and gratefully acknowledged in an Acehnese letter still in Ottoman archives. An Acehnese embassy led by an envoy called Husain, which probably covered the years 1565–8, came close to achieving a more spectacular success. After a delay caused by the death of Sulaiman the Magnificent in 1566, his successor Selim II energetically took up the project of extending Turkish power into the Indian Ocean. In a series of decrees in the autumn of 1567 he not only ordered a fleet of 15 galleys and 2 barks to be sent to assist Aceh, but also instructed the Governor of Egypt to construct a canal at Suez so that his warships could go back and forth to the Indian Ocean on a regular basis. In the event a serious revolt in Yemen interrupted these plans, the designated fleet was diverted to suppressing it, and only a few guns and gunsmiths appear to have reached Aceh.[18]

Among the documents in Ottoman archives from the time of this alliance is an appeal of January 1566 from Sultan al-Kahar, probably the oldest surviving Acehnese diplomatic document. It addresses the Turkish Sultan as Khalifa of Islam, and thereby bound to aid oppressed Muslims throughout the world. The Aceh ruler acknowledges the safe arrival of eight Turkish gunners sent in response to an earlier request. He appeals repeatedly to the Turkish sultan to come to the aid of Muslim pilgrims and merchants being attacked by the infidel Portuguese as they travel to the Hejaz. The Muslims of Calicut and Ceylon, who are also harassed by the Portuguese, promise that the non-Muslim rulers of their states will be willing to fight the Franks if the Ottoman sultan leads the campaign. "If Your Majesty's aid is not forthcoming, the wretched unbelievers will continue to massacre the innocent Muslims."[19]

For at least as long as al-Kahar lived, Aceh retained this strong sense of solidarity with other ports of the Muslim network to destroy the threat posed by the Portuguese. He seems to have taken the first militant step on behalf of the alliance by laying siege to Portuguese Melaka in early 1568. The attack was repeated in 1570 in apparent coordination with the four southern Indian Muslim sultans — Bijapur, Golconda, Bidar and Ahmadnagar — who briefly buried their differences to attack Portuguese Goa.[20] This was certainly the time when the Portuguese experienced the heaviest Muslim pressure on all fronts.

In this late sixteenth century period, pre-eminently, Aceh saw itself as part of an Indian Ocean Islamic network. The commercial links with the Red Sea ports made it possible to make the pilgrimage in a single ship and a couple of months' voyage. From Raniri we know that renowned *ulama* from "above the winds" came to teach in Aceh in this period — the Egyptian Sheikh Nuru'd-Din in the 1570s, Sheikh Abu al-Kahyr ibn Shaykh ibn Hajar and Sheikh Muhammad al-Yamani from Mecca in the 1580s, and the Gujarati Sheikh Muhammad Jailani ibn Hassan ibn Muhammad a little later.[21]

Seventeenth-century Apogee of Absolutism: Europeans and Others

Aceh was a major target of the first English, Dutch and French expeditions to the Indian Ocean, who knew that the Sultanate was anti-Portuguese and the major non-Portuguese source of pepper for Europe. Beginning with the authoritarian Sultan Ala'ud-din Ri'ayat Shah al-Mukammil (r.1589–1604), therefore, Acehnese rulers found themselves courted by rulers from near and far. For the first time they now made alliances with non-Muslim rulers and traders, beginning with the Portuguese, who made overtures for a peaceful relationship with the new Sultan. The first Dutch mission under the brothers de Houtman was a disaster, perhaps because Portuguese warnings against these dangerous "pirates" and republicans had hit the mark. After a quarrel which remains mysterious, the elder brother Cornelis was killed and the younger Frederick was held captive for two years (1599–1601), while their English pilot John Davis managed to get the remnants of the fleet back to Holland. Frederick was repeatedly threatened with death if he did not convert to Islam.[22]

Nevertheless, opinion in Holland was inclined to blame the de Houtman brothers for their own misfortunes, and a second mission was sent from Zeeland in 1601 with the wise precaution of a personal letter from the Stadhouder, Prince Maurits. This was well received, and al-Mukammil decided even to send an embassy back to the Netherlands with the Zeeland ships (Fig. 4). Two Acehnese, their Luxemburg-born interpreter, and a couple of Arab merchants travelled safely to the Netherlands, where the elder quickly died, but the younger met Prince Maurits in a grand ceremony, and returned eventually to Aceh.[23]

James Lancaster arrived in 1602 at the same time as envoys from Siam and Portugal, and just before one from France. He was well received because he too carried a personal letter from Queen Elizabeth to the Sultan, "our loving Brother". In contrast with the religious pressure Frederick de Houtman had experienced, Lancaster had excellent relations with the leading *ulama*, probably Sheikh Shamsuddin of Pasai, "a man very wise and temperate".[24] The Sultan gave Lancaster in return a Malay document granting most of the privileges of free trade and legal security that the Englishman had requested. The sultan's letter positioned him as a mighty Southeast Asian ruler, seeking peace with all the world's powers.

> I am the reigning monarch who is below the winds,[25] holding the
> throne of the kingdom of Aceh and Samudra, and of all the countries

Fig. 4 The Acehnese Ambassador to the Netherlands, Abdul Hamid, paying his respects to Prince Maurits in The Hague, 1602 (reproduced from Ibrahim Alfian *et al.*, eds., *Wajah Aceh dalam Lintasan Sejarah,* Banda Aceh: The Documentation and Information Centre of Aceh, 1999)

> subject to Aceh .... I have made friends with the English ruler [*raja Inglitir*], and you [readers of the letter in the west coast pepper districts] shall be friends with all that ruler's people, as you are friends with all the rest of humanity in this world: and you shall do good to those people, as you do good to all other people.[26]

By the time the most powerful of Aceh's sultans, Iskandar Muda came to the throne in 1607, the court was familiar with a variety of European envoys, with the Siamese missions, and with traders from various parts of Asia. The importance of Aceh's port in the first decade of the seventeenth century was at a peak. Lancaster found in the harbour 16–18 large ships, from Gujarat, Bengal, Malabar, Pegu and Patani.[27] Davis, travelling with the Dutch vessels two years earlier, noted that there was a particular quarter of the city for the Chinese merchants, and others for the Gujaratis, the Arabs, the Portuguese, the Bengalis and the people of Pegu.[28] Javanese traders were not significant or distinctive enough to be noted by European accounts, but we know from other sources that Javanese did bring foodstuffs to Aceh in exchange for Indian cloth, and that there was a *Kampung Jawa* (though probably more Malay in the broad sense than Javanese) near the river.

The reign of Iskandar Muda, though remembered much later as exemplary of Aceh's power, was an exceptional period of megalomania, with no fixed external relationships. With Siam the relationship was most consistent and equal, though poisoned at the end of the reign by Iskandar Muda's pursuit of a Thai princess to wife.[29] He was extremely pragmatic in his temporary alliances, using the English and Dutch to squeeze the Gujaratis and his own subjects out of the pepper trade. After 1622 the Europeans in turn were driven away by his determination to dominate the market himself. Although he attempted to keep up the direct trade to the Red Sea, building his own exceptionally large ship for the trade in 1620, the direct link was broken in the following few years. The greater efficiency of the direct Cape route and of the dozens of ships of the Dutch, English and Portuguese proved too strong. The king's own shipping now focused on Coromandel, where he sent a large vessel every year exchanging pepper for cloth. Iskandar Muda made war on his Malay neighbours from Deli to Johor and Pahang, and terrorised his own subjects. But as the French Admiral Beaulieu noted with a mixture of admiration and horror, all his policies were "carried out with mature consideration, after making very clear and practical calculations".[30]

An effect of his 30-year reign was, however, to leave Aceh in many respects more like a coastal Malay state than he found it. In part this was by bringing in captured Malays on a large scale. Beaulieu explained, "He tried to repopulate his city by conquests, ... because after he ruined the kingdoms of Johor, Deli, Pahang, Kedah and Perak ... he took about twenty-two thousand people."[31] One of these captives was a seven-year-old Pahang prince who eventually succeeded him as Iskandar Thani (r. 1637–41), introducing what may reasonably be seen as a more Malay style of kingship. A "Princess of Pahang" (*Putroe Phang*) is linked to Iskandar Muda in the semi-historical epic poem *Hikayat Malem Dagang*, and is also rhetorically celebrated as the origin of Acehnese customary law.

Iskandar Thani was celebrated in the *Bustan al-Salatin* as the builder of a beautiful palace garden including the *gunungan* meditation centre, widely seen as a representation of Mount Meru. In this Lode Brakel saw evidence of similarities with Hindu-Javanese and Malay ideas of sacral kingship, suggesting there had been a shift here towards a more Nusantara pattern once the link with the Red Sea was weakened.[32] The reign of

Iskandar Thani and that of his widow Taj al-Alam which followed, roughly the middle two decades of the century, also marked the highest point of Aceh's relations with the VOC, arguably another key feature of Nusantara-ness. Dutch envoys succeeded one another in Aceh. In return Iskandar Thani sent a formal embassy to the Governor-General in Batavia in 1640, with a letter establishing his centrality largely in terms of his supernaturally powerful elephants.[33]

If the first half of the seventeenth century made Aceh more Southeast Asian, the second half may have made it more Acehnese. The key pepper-producing areas of West Sumatra, as well as the tin-producing centres of the Peninsula, were lost to Dutch commercial hegemony in the 1650s and '60s. The port of Banda Aceh thereby became less interesting to foreign traders, and weaker in its conflict with agrarian dependencies. Land grants given by Iskandar Muda and some of his predecessors to reward and retain loyalty were transformed into hereditary fiefs, giving rise to the territorial aristocracy of *ulèëbalang* which marked nineteenth-century Aceh. The hereditary Panglima Polem dynasty at Gle Yeung up the Aceh river, reputedly sprung from an illegitimate son of Iskandar Muda, emerged as an alternative locus of power from the port-capital, adding to the difficulties of the port-Sultans.[34]

During this period (1641–99) when four successive queens ruled in Aceh, the Acehnese language began to be used for written communication as well as speech. The earliest evidence of an Acehnese *hikayat* being committed to writing is in 1658. In the next generation Islamic texts also began to be translated into Acehnese rather than Malay. One translator wrote in 1679 that because "few people now know the Malay (*Jawoe*) language", he would give the text "a form after our own manner".[35]

The Turkish connection became in the seventeenth century only a memory, kept alive by the cannons, flags and popular traditions. It was, however, not replaced by any patron closer to hand. Aceh's own remaining exports were now predominately gold, live elephants, betelnut and forest products, all destined chiefly for India.[36] It remained important to traders anxious to avoid Dutch domination of other Nusantara ports, and notably to Chulia and Gujarati merchants, English and French country traders, Arabs and other adventurers of all kinds.

The Pepper Revival, 1790–1840

As the leading independent port of Nusantara, strategically near the entrance to the Melaka Straits, Aceh was bound to be of interest to ambitious powers, particularly the French and English. Both parties contemplated making it the major base of their Southeast Asian activities, but were deterred by the unruly and independent spirit of the Acehnese.[37] The English East India Company sent a mission to Aceh in 1684, after losing their base in Banten two years earlier. It was discouraged by Acehnese popular distrust of foreign motives, and decided to establish a pepper-collecting base at Bengkahulu (Bengkulen) instead. The French sometimes used Aceh as a naval base for "wintering" their fleet during campaigns against the English in India, particularly in the 1780s. Throughout the eighteenth century, these two were the powers with whom Aceh had most to deal with. There were occasional individual Dutchmen among the variety of Europeans, Arabs, Jews, Armenians and Indians who saw the sultanate as an open frontier. However, the official Dutch Company, the VOC, despite its somnolent bases in Padang (Sumatra) and Melaka, had virtually nothing to do with Aceh.

The British were the most persistent foreign factor, as explained in Chapter 5 below. Those in charge of the Company in London considered taking over or extending the operation of the Madras Association in Aceh, and frequent official missions were sent there. The quest for a British base in the Straits led them instead, however, to Penang (1786) and later Singapore (1819). In explaining why Penang was preferable, Francis Light made the usual case against Aceh:

> The Country is fertile beyond description and very populous. The inhabitants are rigid and superstitious Mahometans, sullen, fickle and treacherous. To form a settlement there of safety and advantage, a force sufficient to subdue all the chiefs would be necessary.[38]

The legendary fertility of Aceh would continue to be developed by Acehnese, not Europeans. Pepper-production boomed after 1790, drawing pepper-traders from Europe and the U.S. (see next chapter). But the additional wealth and power did not now go to the sultan and his court, but to local *ulèëbalang* who controlled particular ports. While they acknowledged successive sultans, sometimes paid him a little tribute, and sought his confirmation of their status, they did not necessarily obey him. Even less did the pepper traders heed the sultan's pleas to deal only through the capital and pay their duties to him. The US Navy sent gunboats to the coast twice to punish villages where attacks on Americans had taken place, in 1826 and 1838, with no reference at all to the sultan. The French navy did the same in 1839 and 1840.

The British continued to be the power most interested in relations with the sultanate. Indeed, during the Aceh civil war of 1805–23, one contestant was a Penang shipping tycoon, while the other spoke fluent English as a result of serving in his youth in an East India Company ship. It was this conflict into which Stamford Raffles intervened in support of the latter contestant, Jauhar al-Alam, signing with him in 1819 a treaty which offered British military support in return for the right to trade in all Aceh's ports, to appoint an agent to the sultan's court, and to retain a veto against any other European entanglements. The treaty was never enforced since Jauhar never regained his capital and Penang saw no interest in reinforcing royal power over the dozens of open ports. It did however continue to be appealed to by both sides. Tuanku Ibrahim, brother of the king and future sultan, produced the original text in Malay and English in 1833, to clinch his claim that a Penang vessel was violating its provisions by shipping arms to "rebel" Acehnese.[39] Straits Governor Butterworth in turn reminded Ibrahim in 1844 that the treaty gave "the trade of all Achehnese ports to the British".[40] Its main importance however was in European calculations, as discussed below.

Up until the 1830s, therefore, Aceh was open to a great variety of foreign contacts, often friendly but sometimes hostile. Relations with governments were almost exclusively European and American, with the Dutch the notable absentees. The chief foreign advisers of the court were European and Chulia merchants, in contrast to the Turkish, Arab and Gujarati *ulama* and traders of earlier periods. It was a highly cosmopolitan court, but an unstable and divided one, with no individual able to speak confidently on behalf of the country as a whole.

Seeking Friends Against Dutch Expansion, c. 1840–73

A new era began for Aceh when the able Tuanku Ibrahim took control of the court on the death of his ineffective brother in 1838, initially as guardian of the young heir, but from 1857 as uncontested Sultan with the reign title Ali Ala'ud-din Mansur Shah. His long reign (1838–70) saw the most effective assertion of royal power for more than a century, and its theme was resistance to the growing power of the Dutch on both west and east coasts. After concluding the Padri War in 1838, giving them control of Minangkabau, the Dutch took Inderagiri on the east coast (1838) and Singkil and Barus on the west (1839–40). Ibrahim's tactics to combat these threats was to renew Acehnese authority in the

Deli-Serdang area of the east coast for the first time in two centuries, in 1854, and to pursue alliances with any European powers who would assist — Turkey seemingly being the preferred option. There seems no evidence of seeking friends "below the winds".

The first initiative, in 1840, was to the French King Louis-Philippe, "who rules with justice the city of Marseilles". Ibrahim's letter was stimulated by the leading French pepper-trader François Martin, who had visited the court to try to overcome Ibrahim's anger over the unilateral actions of the two French gunboats in the previous years. The Sultan appealed to an alliance with France, which he had heard dated from the time of Admiral de Suffren's visits in the 1780s. Now he needed help against the Dutch.

> We will have to fight the Dutch because they want to occupy our Kingdom. Nevertheless, with the help of God, we will yield them no part of it. What concerns us particularly in this matter is the ability of the Dutch on the sea, whereas we do not know how to fight there. We therefore come to ask help of our friend…. If he helps us to gain the victory, we will give him a base wherever it suits him.[41]

In addition, he promised to protect French trading vessels, provided they first called at the capital.

This letter inaugurated a period of official contacts with France, culminating in a gracious letter from Louis-Philippe himself in January 1843, expressing his desire for closer official relations and for the Sultan's protection of French pepper-traders.[42] It did reflect a short-lived interest in the Malay world in Paris, including the establishment of the world's first chair of Malay, though the Quai d'Orsay had already decided against seeking a naval station in Aceh. Nevertheless it was the first letter from a European head of state to reach Aceh since the seventeenth century, and was sufficiently treasured to be one of the few foreign documents preserved in the Acehnese palace until the Dutch conquest of 1874. Ibrahim resolved to try to send a mission in reply, though the opportunity arose only in 1849.

Sultan Ibrahim then made use of the pilgrimage to Mecca of a wealthy pepper-trader, Muhammad Ghauth, to carry royal appeals for support not only to France but more importantly to Turkey. Enough memory evidently remained of the sixteenth-century connection, stimulated by a growing flow of pilgrims to Mecca in the nineteenth century, to make crucial Acehnese believe that they might escape Dutch designs by becoming again a vassal province of the Ottoman Empire.[43]

The embassy of Muhammad Ghauth was a brilliant success in Istanbul, where Sultan Abdul Mejid issued two decrees (*firman*) in 1850, one renewing Turkish protection over Aceh, the other confirming Ibrahim in his royal status.[44] Ghauth was sent back to Aceh in style, with a recommendation to the Viceroy (*Khedive*) in Egypt, and instructions to the Turkish Governor of Yemen to send the envoy safely home. The Turkish connection returned to the centre of Acehnese thinking. When the Crimean war began in 1853 Ibrahim sent a contribution of $10,000 to his Turkish counterpart to show his loyalty and solidarity against the Russians. He received in return confirmation of the right to fly the Turkish flag, and an imperial decoration (the *Mejidie*), which he made a point of wearing when receiving Dutch envoys in 1855.[45] The Crimean war, generously covered in the Penang press, aroused considerable pro-Turkish enthusiasm in Aceh and the Malay world, as evidenced by a number of surviving poetic celebrations.[46]

This success in Istanbul must have made the French connection seem unnecessary as well as very difficult. While in Cairo on his return journey in 1852, therefore, Muhammad Ghauth entrusted Sultan Ibrahim's letter to the French Consul, along with his own apology for his "inability to come in person".[47] The sultan's letter to Louis Napoleon was primarily concerned to obtain from France a warship or two, on favourable credit terms, and if possible French assistance to throw the Dutch out of their west coast conquests.[48] For Louis Napoleon, however, the idea of receiving exotic oriental envoys was attractive, and he authorised Ghauth's coming to Paris as a guest of the government.[49]

It was not Muhammad Ghauth who was eventually received by the Prince-President in Paris on 31 October 1852, but his young writer Teuku Nyak Adum, who became known in France as Sidi Muhammad. He and another Acehnese were hosted by the French Government for several months before being sent back to Aceh in January 1853 with a polite letter and a fine sword of honour as a present to Sultan Ibrahim, but no warship.

In the 1850s and '60s, most of Aceh's trade shifted to Penang, as the closest entrepot on the regular steamer routes serving China, India, and points beyond. British governors (generally unsympathetic) and Penang traders (fitfully enthusiastic to keep their Aceh pepper suppliers out of Dutch hands) became in practice the chief links with the wider world. It was often in the Straits Settlements that connections with other powers now occurred. Crucially, the Straits connection continued to make Batavia remote, and of interest only as a dark threat. The positive elements of the western presence in the region — modernity, technology, and profitable trade — were for Acehnese represented only by Penang and Singapore.

Naturally, Sultan Ibrahim first appealed to the British Governor of the Straits Settlements when the Dutch continued their forward movement on Sumatra's east coast in the 1860s. Ibrahim wrote to Governor Cavenagh to protest each major advance at his expense, but Cavenagh could offer nothing but words in response. Whatever the feelings in Penang, Whitehall was convinced that the only logical policy for Britain was to support Dutch claims over the remainder of Sumatra, rather than see some potentially hostile European power become established there as an alternative. In 1871 the Foreign Office formally abandoned its guarantee of Aceh independence. In its last years of independence, therefore, Aceh became more desperate in appealing to a wider circle of potential allies.

The sentimental favourite was always Turkey, to which another appeal was carried in 1868, almost certainly by Habib Abdurrahman az-Zahir. This letter came not from the ageing Sultan, with whom the ambitious Hadhrami Sayyid had fallen out of favour, but from 65 notables whose signatures were appended. They appealed to Turkey's former rule, "as proof of which splendid tokens still exist, namely various cannons". Since the Dutch have been able to dominate some parts of Aceh, and if not stopped, will come to dominate the whole country, the people of Aceh "have decided to be subjects of the Sublime Porte and to enjoy the protection of the Imperial Government". They requested Turkey to tell "all foreign peoples" that Aceh was under its protection.[50]

Habib Abdurrahman returned to Aceh with a letter of recommendation from the Turkish Governor-General of the Hejaz, to whom this appeal had been directed.[51] He took charge of the country for a time as regent for the young Sultan Mahmud in 1870, but in December 1872 left again for Istanbul, in an atmosphere of mounting threats of a Dutch invasion. This time he carried a letter from the sultan which put the argument for Turkish sovereignty over Aceh in the strongest terms. The letter claimed that Acehnese had considered themselves subjects of the Ottomans since the time of Selim II (the 1560s relationship).

> We acknowledge also that the August Emperor of Turkey is the Sovereign of Muslim Sovereigns, and that he is the sole Khalif and ruler of the Muslim nation.... Moreover our attachment and submission to the Ottoman Government is proved by the fact that we have always

laboured to conform to his orders, and that our flag, where the crescent shines forth, and which is none other than the flag of the Ottoman empire, flies above and protects us by sea and by land ... [our ambassador will express] the keen desire we all have to be forever your subjects, to belong to you, and to submit the whole country to your laws, for you to dispose of according to your good pleasure, promising moreover to conform to the wishes of whoever you send to us to govern us.[52]

This letter, and the presence of the extremely persuasive Habib in Istanbul at the time of the Dutch invasion in March 1873, gave rise to a great deal of interest in the plight of this plucky and loyal "vassal" of the Ottomans. Given its habitual weakness and dependence on the European powers, however, the most the Turkish government would actually do was present a diplomatically worded offer of mediation to its Dutch counterpart.[53]

While the Habib was pursuing the Turkish option, his rivals at the Acehnese court dealt with the Europeans in Singapore. Essentially they tried to delay Dutch attempts to impose a lopsided treaty on them, while exploring what support they might receive elsewhere. Sultan Mahmud wrote to Governor Ord in Singapore in October 1871, but getting no response, sent envoys to Singapore in 1872 to appeal directly. The surprising development for these envoys was the degree of interest shown by the U.S. consul, Major Studer, in a defensive treaty with Aceh. It was in fact the conversations of the Acehnese envoy with Studer that were used as the pretext for war by the Dutch in March 1873.

Once war had been declared and the invasion begun, the sultan wrote again to both British and American representatives, reminding the former of the 1819 treaty in which Britain had promised to defend Aceh. Again the British were unsympathetic, but Studer encouraging. Eventually Acehnese representatives formally submitted to Studer a proposed treaty in October 1873, whereby Aceh would cede Pulau We (Sabang) in perpetuity to the US in return for American protection by sea against any force that attacked Aceh. Interestingly, the first two clauses, however, set out Aceh's older foreign relationships. The Turkish one was to be retained, as the US was asked to acknowledge that Aceh "has received from His Highness the Sultan of Turkey a banner which has long been used and is now and will hereafter be used by the Government of Achin". The British relationship of 1819, on the other hand, "was cancelled in the year 1871 by the British Government; as no notice was given of this act, it was silently acquiesced in by the Achin Government".[54]

In short, Aceh's ruling elite saw itself positioned between various powers in the Indian Ocean, of which Turkey was always the sentimental favourite. The national hostility to Portugal, which gave rise to the sultanate of Aceh, was transferred to the next great threat to Acehnese independence, Holland. While Acehnese outside the immediate reach of the rulers paid little heed to their command, they placed a high price on the independence of the sultan from outside forces.

Notes

[1]   "Hikayat Raja-Raja Pasai", romanised and translated by A.H. Hill, *JMBRAS* 33, 2 (1961): 93–101.

[2]   Ibid., p. 99.

[3]   Ibid., pp. 117, 123, 134, 136. Perumal was the title of the royal lineage of Hindu middle Kerala, up to the point when legend has the last king converting to Islam sometime in the ninth to thirteenth centuries: Roland E. Miller, *Mappila Muslims of Kerala: A Study in Islamic Trends* (New Delhi: Orient Longman, 1976), pp. 46–51.

[4]   *The Suma Oriental of Tomé Pires*, ed. A. Cortesão (Cambridge: Hakluyt, 1944), pp. 143–4. This Bengali Muslim, Pires alleged, was placed on the throne by the predominately Bengali Muslim merchants, but "on condition that anyone who could kill the king should become king". The Bengalis who had established this rule so appreciated its unruly consequences that they later adopted it also in Bengal, so that "there is no country where this practice exists and lasts except in Bengal and Pasai".

[5]   Cortesão (ed.), *The Suma Oriental of Tomé Pires*, p. 144.

[6]   Nuru'd-din ar-Raniri, *Bustanu's-Salatin, Bab II, Fasal 13*, ed. T. Iskandar, pp. 65, 68. T. Iskandar (ed.), *De Hikajat Atjeh* (The Hague: KITLV, 1958), p. 97.

[7]   *Bustanu's-Salatin*, pp. 31–2.

[8]   Jeremias van Vliet, "Description of the Kingdom of Siam" [1636], trans. L.F. van Ravenswaay, *Journal of the Siam Society* 7, 1 (1910): 43–6; Anthony Reid, *Southeast Asia in the Age of Commerce, c.1450–1680*, vol. II (New Haven: Yale University Press, 1993), p. 239. The Ayutthaya chronicles, not noted for much interest in the southern countries, make no mention of Aceh. But there are two curious references in the chronicle of Nakhon Sithammarat that appear to claim "Muang Acè" as a tributary; *The Crystal Sands: The Chronicles of Nagara Sri Dharrmaraja*, trans. David Wyatt (Ithaca: Cornell University Southeast Asia Program, 1975), pp. 109, 115.

[9]   *Hikajat Atjeh*, pp. 157–61.

10 Ibid., p. 165.

11 Ibid., p. 166.

12 *Hikayat Atjeh*, p. 167.

13 This has been published only in the form of a shortened Malay prose translation by T. Mohamad Sabil, entitled *Hikajat Soeltan Atjeh Marhoem (Soeltan Iskandar Moeda)* (Batavia, 1932). H.K.J. Cowan believes the Acehnese original to be a reworking of the better-known Acehnese verse epic *Hikayat Malem Dagang*, with the addition at the beginning of this Turkish incident — *De "Hikajat Malem Dagang"* (The Hague,1937), pp. 12–3.

14 The cannon is described in K.C. Krucq, "Beschrijving der kanonnen afkomstig uit Atjeh, thans in het Koninklijk Militair Invalidenhuis Bronbeek", *TBG* 81: 545–6.

15 Charles Boxer, "A Note on Portuguese Reactions to the Revival of the Red Sea Spice Trade and the Rise of Aceh, 1540–1600", *JSEAH* 10, 3 (1969): 416.

16 Letter of L Peres, Malacca, 2 December 1566, in J. Wicki, ed., *Documenta Indica* VII (MHSI 89, Rome, 1962), p. 88.

17 David Bulbeck, Anthony Reid, Tan Lay Cheng and Wu Yiqi, *Southeast Asian Exports since the 14th Century: Cloves, Pepper, Coffee and Sugar* (Singapore: Institute of Southeast Asian Studies, 1998), pp. 32, 72–3.

18 Anthony Reid, *An Indonesian Frontier: Acehnese and other Histories of Sumatra* (Singapore: Singapore University Press, 2004), pp. 78–86. Also Reid, *Age of Commerce* II: 146–7, and Riddell in this volume.

19 Naimur Rahman Farooqi, "Mughal-Ottoman Relations: A Study of Political and Diplomatic Relations between Mughal India and the Ottoman Empire, 1556–1748" (PhD dissertation, University of Wisconsin, 1986), pp. 267–8.

20 Vincent Smith, *The Oxford History of India* (Oxford: Clarendon Press, 1958), 3rd ed., pp. 298–9; Richard Eaton, *Sufis of Bijapur, 1300–1700: Social Roles of Sufis in Medieval India* (Princeton: Princeton University Press, 1978), pp. 83–5.

21 Raniri, *Bustanu's-Salatin*, pp. 32–3.

22 Part of de Houtman's narrative of his captivity is translated in *Witnesses to Sumatra: A Travellers' Anthology*, ed. Anthony Reid (Kuala Lumpur: OUP, 1995), pp. 43–9.

23 Dr Wap, *De Gezantschap van den Sultan van Achin, Anno 1602, aan Prins Maurits van Nassau en de Oud-Nederlandsche Republiek* (Rotterdam: H. Nigh, 1862).

24 Ibid., p. 96.

25 "Aku raja yang kuasa yang dibawah angin ini".

26 Jawi, romanised and translated texts are in W.G. Shellabear, "An Account of Some of the Oldest Malay MSS Now Extant", *JSBRAS* 31 (1898):

113–20. I have used the romanised text to modify Shellabear's translation, which imposes a male vocabulary not in the original, to the extent of calling Elizabeth "King of England"! A contemporary translation of the same document in "The Grant of Privileges by the King of Achin", in *The Voyages of James Lancaster to Brazil and the East Indies 1591–1603*, ed. Sir William Foster (London: Hakluyt, 1940), pp. 155–60.

27   Foster (ed.), *The Voyages of James Lancaster*, p. 90.

28   Reid (ed.), *Witnesses to Sumatra*, p. 20.

29   Reid, *Age of Commerce* II: 239.

30   Beaulieu, 1621, in ibid., p. 80.

31   Ibid., p. 80.

32   L.F. Brakel, "State and Statecraft in 17th Century Aceh", in *Pre-colonial State Systems in Southeast Asia*, ed. Anthony Reid and Lance Castles (Kuala Lumpur: MBRAS monograph no.6, 1979), pp. 67–76.

33   Analysed in Reid, *An Indonesian Frontier*, pp. 114–5.

34   Ibid., pp. 145–7.

35   *Catalogue of Acehnese Manuscripts in the Library of Leiden University and other collections outside Aceh*, compiled by P. Voorhoeve, trans. and ed. M. Durie (Leiden: Leiden University Library, 1994), pp. 14–5.

36   Ito Takeshi, "The World of the Adat Aceh: A Historical Study of the Sultanate of Aceh" (unpublished dissertation, Australian National University, 1984), pp. 391–427.

37   The English interest is documented in Chapter 5 below, and French connections are discussed in Reid, *An Indonesian Frontier*, pp. 151–75.

38   Francis Light to Governor-General, 15 February 1786, cited Lee Kam Hing, *The Sultanate of Aceh: Relations with the British, 1760-1824* (Kuala Lumpur: Oxford University Press, 1995), p. 80.

39   George Bennett, *Wanderings in New South Wales, Batavia, Pedir Coast, Singapore and China*, 2 vols. (London: Richard Bentley, 1834), II: 8.

40   Butterworth to Sultan of Acheh, 20 Jan. 1844, cited in Nicholas Tarling, "British Policy in the Malay Peninsula and Archipelago, 1824–1871", *JMBRAS* 30, 3 (1957): 137.

41   Sultan Mansur Shah to King Louis-Philippe 15 Jumadi II, 1256H (14 Aug. 1840). Dulaurier's French translation of 24 April 1841, from which this extract is taken, is in M.A.E. *Mémoires et Documents*, Hollande 152, ff.159-60. I was unable to locate the Malay original.

42   King Louis-Philippe to Sultan of Aceh, 2 January 1843, reproduced in E.S.de Klerck, *De Atjèh-oorlog* (The Hague, 1912), p. 435.

43   Reid, *An Indonesian Frontier*, pp. 172–3.

44   Heldewier to Gericke, 19 and 26 June 1873, Buitenlandse Zaken Dossier Atjeh.

45   Anthony Reid, *The Contest for North Sumatra* (Kuala Lumpur: University of Malaya Press/Oxford University Press, 1969), p.84. J. Woltring, ed.,

Bescheiden Betreffende de Buitenlandse Politiek van Nederland Tweede Periode, 1871–98, I (The Hague, 1962), pp. 612–3. E.S. de Klerck, *De Atjeh-oorlog* (The Hague: Nijhoff, 1912), pp. 216–7.

46 Voorhoeve, *Catalogue of Acehnese Manuscripts,* pp. 54–9.

47 Mohammad Ghauth to Louis Napoleon 21 Jumadi 1, 1268H (12 March 1852), French translation in M.A.E. *Mémoires et Documents,* Hollande 132, f.167.

48 The original Arabic and Malay versions of Ibrahim's letter are in M.A.E. *Mémoires et Documents,* Hollande 152, ff.161–5, together with very free French translation from the Arabic by Alix Desgranges, Professor of Turkish at the Collège de France. I have romanised the Malay version in *An Indonesian Frontier,* pp. 191–3.

49 Affaires Etrangères to Lemoyne 20 April 1852, M.A.E., Egypte, Depêches Politiques des Consuls, Alexandria, 24, f. 69.

50 My English translation (from the Dutch) of this appeal is in Anthony Reid, "Indonesian Diplomacy: A Documentary Study of Atjehnese Foreign Policy in the Reign of Sultan Mahmud, 1870–4", *JMBRAS* 42, 2 (1969): 75–6.

51 The appeal must at least have been forwarded to Istanbul, since in December 1868 a Turkish official enquired of the Dutch whether Aceh was under their sovereignty; Reid, "Indonesian Diplomacy", p. 75.

52 My translation in ibid., pp. 80–1.

53 Reid, *The Contest for North Sumatra,* pp. 119–29.

54 Draft Treaty of Alliance, enclosed in Studer to Davis 4 October 1873, US Consular Despatches, Singapore, reproduced in Reid, "Indonesian Diplomacy", pp. 97–100.

5

Aceh at the Time of the 1824 Treaty

Lee Kam Hing

How close did Aceh come to surviving the colonial era as an independent state, buffered between Britain and the Netherlands as Siam was between Britain and France? If at least a semi-colonial status was inevitable, could it have been drawn into the British-influenced world of the Straits Settlements entrepôts, rather than falling under the Dutch at Batavia? While Aceh's historiography has naturally been influenced by its current status as part of Indonesia, could pre-colonial Aceh be more usefully compared to the stronger independent states of Mainland Southeast Asia?

The last of the dynasties in Aceh came to power in 1727. Founded by Sultan Ala'ad-din Ahmad Syah the ruling house came to an end when the Dutch invaded the sultanate in 1873. Of Bugis descent, this dynasty ruled at a time of the Konbaung Dynasty in Burma (1752–1886), the Nguyen (1782–1945) in Vietnam, and Chakri (since 1782) in Thailand.[1]

Right up to 1871, the independent status of Aceh was tolerated by the two main Western powers in the region, Britain and the Netherlands. There was little reason for either to absorb the sultanate. Recovering from the Napoleonic wars in Europe, the two powers were too preoccupied elsewhere. Still, there was a brief period just before the 1824 Treaty that offered a chance to the British to establish a stronger presence in the sultanate. But that did not happen, and this chapter therefore looks at conditions in Aceh that long attracted British interest and yet evoked a view of the place as risky that for a time Western advance into the sultanate was deterred.

The Acehnese during this period were aware of the forces of change around them. There were new foreign powers in the region such as the British, the Dutch, the French, and the Americans.[2] Foreign enclaves

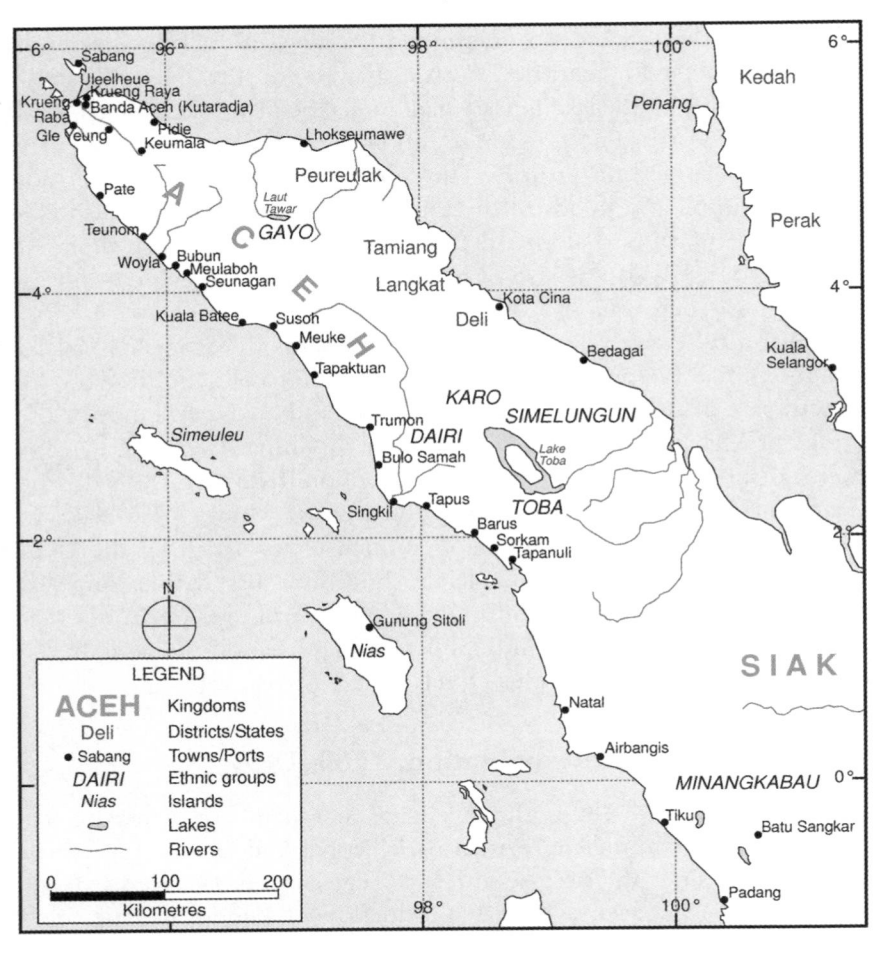

Map 2 North Sumatra, 18th–19th centuries

including Bengkulen and Padang on Sumatra's west coast and Penang and Singapore in the Straits of Melaka were close by and exerting some economic and political pull. There were new trading communities, such as the Chulias from India and the Bugis from Sulawesi, integrating into the local commercial networks. World demand for pepper spurred the opening of new pepper plantations and bringing change within Aceh. There was a shift of population from Aceh Besar to the distant coasts. New pepper and betelnut wealth along the west and Pidie coasts created powerful and independent-minded coastal *ulèëbalang*.

Despite these changes, sometimes disruptive, in the late eighteenth and early nineteenth centuries, Aceh displayed considerable resilience.[3] The eight rulers of the last dynasty had long, albeit troubled, reigns. And although they struggled to exercise influence over distant regions, they lost no major tracts of territory. The sultanate remained important not only as a supplier of goods to the expanding British trade but also as a convenient transit port along the India-China route for British ships. At the same time, Aceh was also of great strategic value as evident during the Anglo-French wars.

Historically, Aceh was more oriented towards the Straits of Melaka and the Indian Ocean. It was a frequented trading centre located on the eastern side of the important Indian Ocean and at the entrance of the Straits of Melaka, and linking the West with China. Eventually, Aceh's political future was set out under the London Treaty of 1824. In the treaty Britain and the Netherlands accepted the Straits of Melaka to demarcate their respective sphere of influence. An article in the 1824 treaty affirmed Aceh's independence, but once the delineation was accepted, the two powers steadily extended control over territories that in subsequent years evolved into modern Malaysia and Indonesia. In the process, Aceh came under the Dutch sphere of control.

Aceh's Commercial Revitalisation, 1760–1824

Between 1760 and 1824, the Acehnese sultanate experienced a re-vitalising of its commercial agricultural. Pepper had been cultivated in the sultanate since the early seventeenth century and had been a major export. However, over the years, production of pepper had declined because of soil exhaustion. Then, in the mid-eighteenth century new pepper vines were introduced from the Malabar coast. These grew well in the sloping and well-drained coastal plans and river valleys of Aceh, particularly a stretch from Meulaboh in the north to Singkil in the south. This replanting marked a new phase of growth, and in response to world demand production of pepper rose from an estimated 2.13 million pounds in 1797 to some 18.6 million pounds in 1822. In this period, the sultanate produced an estimated half of the world's supply of pepper.[4]

The opening of new pepper plantations was undertaken by immigrants from Aceh Proper (Aceh Besar) led by enterprising territorial chiefs or *ulèëbalang*.[5] The most important of these entrepreneurial chiefs was Lebai Dappah. Lebai Dappah had held a position in Aceh Besar but moved to Singkil where he became the ruling *ulèëbalang*. Family members opened up pepper land in neighbouring districts and of these Susu was the most important. He also encouraged planters from nearby regions to sell through Singkil. Coastal chief such as Lebai Dappah, by their position and role, created a safe and stable environment conducive to the cultivation and trade in pepper.

Susu became the principal Acehnese port from which pepper was exported. The place attracted foreign traders of whom the most important were the Americans. The first of the American ships turned up in Sumatra in 1790. From then until 1860, American ships made an estimated 967 voyages to Sumatra. They carried away more than 370 million pounds of pepper worth about 17 million dollars. This represented almost half of all pepper produced in Aceh in the period. The pepper was shipped to Salem and Boston, and from there exported to the Caribbean, Europe, and the Mediterranean. With carrying rates lower than those of the British, the American ships made gross profits of several hundred per cent.[6]

Commercial agriculture also developed in the Pidie (Pedir) districts. The Pidie coast in north-eastern Sumatra was once a pepper-producing area until soil exhaustion forced many of the planters to move to the west coast. Those remaining continued to grow betelnut and turned it into a lucrative export crop. There was demand for betelnut, both locally and on the Indian coast, and Chulias were the main buyers. In Southeast Asia betel chewing was a widespread habit that was popular at all levels of society.[7]

Indeed, betelnut became a vital part of the Aceh-Penang trading network at the beginning of the nineteenth century. So important was the betelnut trade that when in 1814 a Penang company, Dunbar and McGee, secured from the sultan of Aceh a monopoly, strong objections were voiced in the Penang Council. Governor W. Petrie warned during Council proceedings in July 1814 that the monopoly could adversely affect the Chulia-Penang trade.[8] Furthermore, according to Governor Petrie, thousands of traders, boat owners and crew members were involved in the collecting, transporting, and selling of betel nut in Pidie and in Penang. Hundreds of Acehnese traders arriving in Penang used the proceeds from sale of pepper and betelnut to purchase opium and piece goods for the return trip. While pepper was the most valuable of the Acehnese imports into Penang, the contribution of betel-nut trade to the island's economy was still of significance. In 1813/4 the value of betelnut imports into Penang from Aceh was 76,840 Spanish dollars while that of pepper was 78,563 dollars.[9]

Expanding Acehnese Trade

During this period of Aceh's history, new trading groups were active in the expanding Acehnese trade. Reference has been made of the Chulias who were important in the network of Acehnese trade. In the eighteenth century Aceh was one of two key ports in Southeast Asia for traders from India. From the Coromandel coast Indian ships sailed to Aceh and bringing textiles in exchange for pepper, betel-nut, benzoin, tin, and gold.[10]

Aceh was vital to Indian traders especially during periods when the Dutch imposed trade monopoly in the Straits of Melaka region. During such times, Indian traders disposed off their piece-goods in Aceh and from there took away tin collected by local boats from neighbouring Malay states. Under normal conditions, the Chuliah network extended to Kuala Kedah and later Penang, Kuala Selangor, and Riau. In Aceh, the Chulias usually stayed for several months awaiting favourable wind to take them back. Many owned residences there and they used the long stay to sell goods on credit and build close ties with local merchants and *ulèëbalang*. They became even more influential when Acehnese rulers appointed them as advisors, *syahbandars*, and royal traders. Through this, the Chulias came to dominate the trade in benzoin and betel-nut, which they exchanged for Indian textiles, opium, and salt.

The Bugis were another group whose influence was in this period extending into the Straits of Melaka region. The Bugis had left south Sulawesi following protracted civil wars there. By the middle of the eighteenth century they had established trade and political ascendancy in Riau and in Kuala Selangor where in those two places, the Bugis became actively involved in the tin trade. Close links developed between the Bugis and the Acehnese as their ships traded in one another's ports. Through Riau, Aceh's trade was linked to the eastern part of the Malay Archipelago.[11]

Ties also developed between the ruling Acehnese class and leading Bugis merchants. Indeed, according to Acehnese tradition a Bugis trader was made Maharaja Lela by Jemal al-Alam (1703–26) and, following an uprising against the sultan was appointed ruler. The Maharaja Lela as Sultan Ala'ad-din Syah started the Bugis line in Aceh. The new sultan and subsequent rulers developed close ties with the Bugis rulers of Selangor. More than just trade, there were political links. Aceh supported Selangor against Dutch invasion in 1784 and later, Sultan Ala'ad-din Muhammed Syah when facing an *ulèëbalang* uprising received assistance from Sultan Ibrahim Syah of Selangor.[12]

Acehnese trade with Sumatran and Peninsular Malaya ports also grew with expanding pepper and betel-nut production. Acehnese boats became an important component of the developing commerce in the region. In the Sumatran west coast they went as far south as Padang and Bengkulen. Acehnese traders also traded in Kedah, Selangor and Melaka. From the Pidie coast many Acehnese crossed over the Straits to avoid the Acehnese capital where duties on all goods were demanded by the sultan.[13] Figures compiled from the Dutch Melaka shipping lists of the late eighteenth century indicated that there had also been a steady traffic between Aceh and Melaka. And Acehnese boats were probably the first trading vessels to sail up to Penang when Francis Light took over the island for the British: "several Acheen naquedah from Taloo [sic] have offered to contract with me for Beetlenut, pepper and all the produce of the east coast of Sumatra and demand passes for the praws [prahus]".[14]

Acehnese Presence in the Coasts

The expansion of the Acehnese along the west coast of northern Sumatra proceeded along fairly peacefully. Trade was likewise orderly carried out as a large number of ships arrived to buy pepper. Still, given the fact that Acehnese immigrants were moving into regions where large number of non-Acehnese had long settled in and where there was no clear demarcation of boundaries, there were bound to be friction and clashes. The fertile Susu and Singkil areas, for instance, bordered territories that were then occupied by non-Acehnese. Furthermore, the arrival of large number of ships along the long coasts of Aceh made some of them easy targets for plunder. Incidents of piracy occurred along the long coast-line of Aceh. Those carrying out these attacks ranged from purely criminal elements to small traders and ousted ruling groups resorting to occasional robbery on the high sea to supplement their income. Others could not be termed as acts of piracy. Some of the seizures were carried out by rulers or local chiefs following non-payment of port duties. Others had arisen from trade disputes or from misunderstanding because of different cultures, particularly between foreign and local traders.[15]

All these contributed to an impression that the Acehnese coasts were unsafe, and Acehnese expansion into the west coast was therefore viewed with great concern by the Dutch and the British. In the mid-eighteenth century Dutch and British officials at Padang and Bengkulen frequently reported incidents of Acehnese piracy off the west of Sumatra and of Acehnese incursions and encroachment into territories they controlled.

There were also occasional sightings of a Panglima Laut or commander of an Acehnese fleet on the west coast exacting taxes and port duties.[16]

Then in February 1760 the British settlements of Natal and Tapanuli came under attack from two French warships. The Acehnese Panglima Laut reportedly assisted the attacks. The settlements were captured. Natal was given to the Dutch while Tapanuli was handed over to the Panglima Laut. Soon after the attack, the Panglima Laut withdrew to Tapus, a short distance to the north of Barus.[17]

Later, in June 1771, the Dutch resident at Barus reported to Padang that increased Acehnese military activity was observed in the surrounding districts. Shortly afterwards several hundred armed Acehnese attacked Barus. One Dutch and three Bugis soldiers were killed. The Acehnese withdrew soon afterwards to Tapus while Padang, on being notified, immediately sent military reinforcements and supplies to Barus.[18]

For the British the most serious incident was in early 1786 when some 200 Acehnese attacked Tapanuli, the northernmost outpost of Bengkulen. The Acehnese burned the factory, seized a few sepoys as hostages, and took some Company goods. Bengkulen responded immediately by sending troops against the Acehnese attackers. The Acehnese attackers had by then retreated across the Singkil River. Lebai Dappah in neighbouring Singkil was suspected of being involved in the attack as he appeared keen to control all the pepper trade in the region. Tapanuli was targeted because by taking pepper from surrounding regions, including Sorkam, it became a competitor to Singkil. Sorkam was a new pepper area settled recently by some Acehnese and probably eyed by Singkil.[19]

There was also a case in 1803 when a British-registered ship, the *Crescent,* claimed that it was attacked in Muki. Muki, some distance north of Singkil, was frequented then by American ships. In the incident, the *Crescent* had run aground off the Muki coast. The Muki people gave assistance to the stricken ship, but kept part of the salvaged goods, which they claimed was a right under their maritime laws. But the crew saw this differently and complained to the authorities in Bengal. The Supreme Government on learning of this instructed Bengkulen to investigate. In April 1804 Bengkulen sent a detachment of troops. An attack was launched on Muki and a few of the *ulèëbalang* there detained.

Clearly, the growing pepper trade and the expansion of Acehnese presence created some problems in the region, mostly arising from trade competition and piracy. After the Tapanuli attack, the British entered into an agreement in 1786 with Lebai Dappah, whereby the Singkil

River marked the limit beyond which Acehnese were not allowed to settle. This was to safeguard Sorkam and Tapanuli by preventing large numbers of Acehnese settling in the surrounding areas. The agreement was not always strictly enforced, and Acehnese from Singkil continued to migrate to Susu and Tapus, areas south of the Singkil River, where new pepper plantations were opened. But the British saw the agreement as a step towards keeping the Acehnese within their own territories. Once an understanding was reached, trade developed between Singkil and Tapanuli. Increasingly, Singkil looked towards the British for support, especially when it felt threatened by the sultan.

Reports of incidents in Aceh created an impression of the sultanate as a source of danger to traders as well as to British interest in northern Sumatra. Stamford Raffles took a similar view. However, he argued that this situation was due to weak central authority, and he therefore called for a treaty with the sultan of Aceh. The treaty was to provide British support to the Acehnese ruler. As secretary to the Penang council between 1805 and 1810, Raffles would have come across reports about how Aceh and its surrounding waters were unsafe for traders. In 1810 he wrote to Lord Minto advocating the establishment of British presence in Aceh:[20]

> The King upon a proper agreement being made would I have every reason to think assent to the measure and by this means should equally preserve the tranquillity of the country, prevent it from becoming a nest of pirates and cut off a vast source of illicit trade which after our acquiring the domination of the eastern isles is more likely to be increased than impaired.[21]

Troubled Centre

The opening of pepper ports along Aceh's west coast took place at a time of weakened rulers. The sultans were too preoccupied at the capital dealing with troublesome *ulèëbalang*, and in such circumstances the coastal settlements found the freedom to develop pepper production and trade. At the capital, the power of the royal court was then seriously limited by the powerful *ulèëbalang* and the three Panglima Sagis. Contemporary accounts of the late eighteenth and early nineteenth century suggest a capital beset with political uncertainties, with the rulers often vulnerable to attacks from rebellious *ulèëbalang*.

Such a situation of conflict and civil wars is captured in one of the most celebrated of Acehnese *syair*, the *Hikayat Potjut Muhamat*. This epic poem is a narrative of a civil war during the reign of Sultan Ala'ad-

Fig. 5   Captain Thomas Forrest received by Sultan Mahmud Syah in 1764
(*Forrest*)

din Jehan Syah (1735–60).[22] Although Sultan Ala'addin and his brother
prevailed, the situation did not change vastly under his son and successor
Sultan Mahmud Syah (1760–81) who was overthrown three times by
the *ulèëbalang*. Mahmud Syah regained his power on each occasion. A
Westerner who met him was Charles Desvouex, sent by the East India
Company to Aceh in 1772. In the meeting, the sultan allowed the British
to set up a trading factory and work was started. But when the *ulèëbalang*
gathered in opposition to the construction of fortifications, Sultan
Mahmud was forced to withdraw permission. Desvouex decided that

the *ulèëbalang*'s hostility to the British and the Sultan's weakness had created a situation that was too dangerous, and he thereupon withdrew from Aceh.[23]

Mahmud's successor, Muhammed Syah reportedly could not quite trust his own Acehnese guards. Thomas Forrest visiting Aceh in 1784 recorded that the sultan employed sepoys and Indian mercenaries to guard the palace. Under such conditions it was difficult for the British to consider having a factory in Aceh. Botham, in Aceh earlier to negotiate a British factory, wrote in his report that the *ulèëbalang*, instigated by the Chulias, opposed a British presence. He believed that the British would require a military force of 300 troops to secure a base in Aceh.

Francis Light wrote in August 1788 that, "The King of Acheen afraid to confide in any of his own People, has procured from the Coast a thousand Sepoys to guard his person and expects a further supply daily by his vessels which are sent to Vijagapatem and other ports on the coast of Coromandel."[24]

When Muhammed Syah died, his son, Jauhar, was only nine. From 1790 till 1805, the brother of the queen, Tuanku Raja, was regent. In 1802 the young prince, however, claimed the throne. For the next 15 years, Jauhar had to battle strong opposition, and the young ruler was too distracted by civil war and the divided capital to pay attention to the outlying settlements.

In 1805 Penang commented on the Acehnese situation: "Although a very considerable trade is carried on, we are of opinion that to establish and to maintain a permanent post there would require a very considerable body of European as well as native troops in force sufficient to overawe if necessary a populous and turbulent city [Banda Aceh] ...."[25]

Right down to the time of Raffles, the British painted a similar picture of the weakened position of the Acehnese ruler and of rebellious *ulèëbalang*. Raffles in 1818 wrote: "I have recently received information that about three years since the King of Acheen, offended at the measure of the Government of Prince of Wales, was advised to address a Letter to the Emperor of Russia offering to that Country a settlement in his dominions with such privileges as might be required on condition of the Emperor assisting him to maintain his authority at Acheen."[26]

Of the territorial chiefs, the most powerful were the Panglima Sagis, each of whom headed a federation of mukims. The Panglima Sagis especially the head of the 22 mukims in the interior were generally suspicious of foreigners. Over the years, Panglima Sagis and the *ulèëbalang* became involved in trade and they connected to merchants and foreign traders.[27] They therefore joined in resisting what they regarded as heavy imposition of taxes and royal trade monopolies. It is possible that declining pepper production and trade in Aceh Besar led to more intense competition among the various power groups. This was perhaps worsened by the rise of the coastal ports along the west coast in the late eighteenth century when a significant portion of trade shifted away from the Acehnese capital.

By the nature of its geography Aceh did not allow for a politically compact system. It has very long coastlines that made administrative control very difficult. Ships proceeded directly to the coastal ports and the sultans were often helpless in enforcing duties or taxes on goods. With declining revenue the sultan had consequently less patronage to win over the *ulèëbalang*. Furthermore, nearby settlements established by Western powers drew some trade away from Aceh and the ties they built with outlying settlements further weakened the sultan's ability to maintain a cohesive state.

Yet although rulers were weak, the *ulèëbalang* and the Panglima Sagis were not always able to unite. Rivalry among them led to struggles for territories and trade. The sultans were able to exploit the division among them. Furthermore, within the Acehnese political tradition it was the ruler who conferred privileges, granted economic concessions, rights to revenue collection and, theoretically at least, confirmed all succession or appointments in Aceh. And where there were disputes among the *ulèëbalang* it was the ruler who mediated. There were also marriage and blood ties among the *ulèëbalang* and between them and the royal families. For example, Tuanku Packie of Pidie's sister was married to Jauhar while Lebai Dappah in Singkil was said to be father-in-law of Tuanku Raja, Jauhar's maternal uncle and briefly a regent.[28]

During the last dynasty, successive sultans tried to exercise more effective power at the capital and along the coasts. Against the coastal chiefs, rulers decreed that all trade be conducted through the capital port in Banda Aceh. Early in his reign, Sultan Mahmud Syah appointed a Panglima Laut to enforce surveillance of the coast and collect revenue from the outlying settlements. Foreign ships were allowed in the west and Pidie coast only after paying duties. But Aceh's long coastline posed a major problem to the sultan's efforts. Many of the coastal ports such as Singkil and Barus on the west coast were located several sailing days from Banda Aceh. Foreign traders therefore were able to evade the payment of duties and traded directly with the coastal ports.

To be effective, a much larger naval force was required, and this was quite beyond the resources of the Acehnese rulers then. Furthermore, rulers also had difficulties in overseeing discipline of their armed fleets. Some of the cases of Acehnese piracy reported off the west coast of Sumatra could have been committed by such revenue fleets. Botham, while in Aceh, reported that a Panglima Laut had been arrested and was being brought back to the capital. It was likely that the commander had exceeded his instructions and carried out excesses against ships and Acehnese settlements; or that such naval commanders were getting too powerful and therefore posing a threat to the rulers.[29]

But more than any other ruler, Jauhar was aware of the nature of changing economic and political order in the region. As with earlier sultans, he took steps to reassert control over the coastal districts when he came to power. He directed that all ships proceed to Banda Aceh or to ports where permits were issued. Where he was different was the more active role he took to impose his authority. On several occasions he headed a small fleet of armed vessels to the west and Pidie coasts.

Above all, Jauhar wanted British support in his efforts to regulate trade in his domain. He wrote to British officials in Penang and India offering to sign a commercial treaty and to have a British commercial agent at the Acehnese capital. He wanted improved trade and above all military support especially of arms. Thus when Raffles wrote to him in 1810 in connection with British preparations for the Java invasion, Jauhar was delighted at the warm tone from an important British official. Probably in appreciation of this message, he conferred an Acehnese award on Raffles.[30]

When Jauhar later found no response from the British to his overtures, he turned increasingly to a number of foreigners, mostly adventurers and traders, who joined him as advisers. They prepared his correspondence especially with Western governments, made contact with Penang and Bengal merchants, and entered into commercial contracts with private traders on behalf of the sultan. Some of the advisers also acted as the sultan's merchants. However, these Western advisers, mostly of questionable character and motives, eventually damaged the sultan's standing within Aceh and in his relations with the British.

British Interest in Aceh

Jauhar's period of rule presented the best chance for the British to establish a base in Aceh. And indeed a treaty of friendship between Aceh and the East India Company was signed in 1819. There had long been British interest in Aceh following an expansion of British commercial activities in Southeast Asia. The global economic recovery in the middle of the eighteenth century resulted in a general upturn in British trade to Southeast Asia.[31] Important in this was the China trade where tea, silk and porcelain were bought by British traders for the European market. In exchange for China goods, Southeast Asian products such as tin and pepper were offered. The EIC's trade position with China was boosted when opium was found in India sometime around 1760. As its China trade developed, the EIC was keen to have a base and transit stop somewhere along the Straits of Melaka. Aceh was thought of as suitable since British country traders were already using it.

The British in India also recognised Aceh's strategic importance. This became evident during the Anglo-French conflict in the eighteenth century when warships of the two powers fought for dominance in the Bay of Bengal. In the days of sailing ships, French and British navies operating in the Indian Ocean had to seek shelter during the monsoons. In 1760, French warships under Admiral D'Ache using Aceh could return early to threaten Madras and other British possessions along the Coromandel coast. British warships, in the meanwhile, were forced to take the longer trip to Bombay. In 1778, Lawrence Sullivan and William James, the chairman and deputy chairman respectively of the EIC, wrote to Lord Hillsborough, the Secretary of Trade, arguing that Aceh should be acquired to safeguard British interests in the area. To rationalise operations in the region, it was proposed that the civil and military establishment of Bengkulen be transferred to Aceh.[32]

There was also concern about the French presence. Beyond the fact that French trading and naval ships were using Aceh, the worry was that the rulers there could be friendly to the French. Sultan Muhammed Syah, in particular, was thought to be close to the French. It was said that he had stayed briefly in French Mauritius after his ship was wrecked there on his pilgrimage to Mecca, and while on the island, developed an interest in the French language.

The newly-established British base in Penang was also watchful over possible French threats from Aceh. In 1810 there was some alarm on the island over reports of French naval presence in Aceh. The news was particularly disturbing at a time when the British were preparing an invasion against the French in Java. So seriously did they take the news that the Supreme Government at Calcutta sent its own official, David Campbell, to check on the reports. As it turned out, Campbell learnt that the foreigners consisted of only a few Europeans including French adventurers. Jauhar's subsequent letter to Raffles in 1810 also calmed British concern. However, British officials did not follow up the sultan's overtures of treaty arrangement.[33]

This non-response to Jauhar had, to an extent, to do with the success of the Java expedition. With the occupation of Java and the end of the Anglo-French war in 1815, the strategic urgency of a British base in Aceh receded. There was now no fear of a hostile power using Aceh. Aceh's ports continued to be accessible and the trade between Aceh and Penang was growing. Nevertheless, events within Aceh continued to draw British attention to the sultanate. At the Acehnese capital there were continued political uncertainties and growing unrest against the new sultan. At the coastal settlements, there were reports of Acehnese encroachment into neighbouring territories. All these threatened orderly trade in the region and became a matter of some worry to the British.

Civil War, 1814–9

Efforts by Jauhar to exercise some control over trade in Aceh drew disapproving reaction from the British. Officials and merchants in Penang were opposed to such Acehnese moves and saw these as the sultan's attempt to monopolise trade. Complying with the Acehnese commercial regulations could result in higher prices for commodities, increased costs, and additional inconvenience. Ships would have to travel all the way to Banda Aceh to trade. There was anticipation that the regulations would have a disruptive effect on trade. Soon reports came of trading vessels being stopped by the sultan's revenue boats.

In 1813, a British-registered ship, the *Annapoorny*, was detained. A complaint was made by the ship's owners to the Supreme Government in Calcutta and to Penang. The Penang government in response sent a British warship that happened to be in the port to investigate. Arriving at Banda Aceh and having located the *Annapoorny*, the warship simply towed the ship back to Penang. The sultan of Aceh protested, and sent an embassy to Calcutta to bring the matter up with the Governor-General. The sultan of Aceh insisted that the *Annapoorny*, owned and manned by Chulias, had traded in Susu without a permit and had not paid duties. The captain of the ship, in his defence, contended that he had traded in areas he believed did not come under Aceh and therefore was not liable to duties.[34]

In 1814, the Governor-General in Bengal sent Capt. John Canning on a mission to Aceh to find out the circumstances surrounding the *Annapoorny*'s detention.[35] One of Canning's tasks was to ascertain the extent of Aceh's borders and how far the sultan's powers reached. It was argued that once the limits were established a decision could be made as to whether or not the detention of the *Annapoorny* by the sultan was within his sovereign rights. Intended or not, Canning was to define the borders of Aceh.

In all, Canning spent nearly six months in Aceh, travelling first to the west coast where he met with coastal chiefs, including those of Singkil, Barus, as well as John Prince of Natal. He retraced his route towards the capital but did not visit the sultan. Canning decided not to meet the sultan, contending that the ruler had already given his side of the story in the exchange of correspondence with Penang and India. The mission continued on to Penang and then to the Pidie coast. At the end of his mission, Canning submitted a lengthy report where he concluded that the *Annapoorny* was not in Acehnese waters when she was detained. In his recommendations he called for the destruction of the sultan's armed fleet, stationing of British cruisers to force the opening up of the Pidie trade to all British merchants, the temporary occupation of Telok Samoy (Lhokseumawe) to extract compensation from the sultan, and the removal of foreign advisers. He also advised that Tapus marked the limits of Aceh's influence and Barus' independence recognised. On 26 July Canning had signed a treaty of friendship with Barus which granted British protection to the port-state.[36] The Supreme Government did not act on Canning's recommendations, realising that it would be impractical to carry these out.

But the immediate impact of the *Annapoorny* incident and Capt. Canning's visit was to worsen the already uncertain political situation in Aceh for the sultan and encourage renewed unrest among the *uleebalang*. British action, in forcibly releasing the *Annapoorny* in Acehnese waters, damaged the standing of the sultan. If there was anger among the Acehnese population over the *Annapoorny* incident, it was directed at the sultan. Resentment had been building up in Aceh against the rulers' trade regulations, the actions of his armed boats, and his motley band of adventurers. The *Annapoorny* incident and Canning's visit were viewed as a consequence of the sultan's own doing.

On 10 October 1814 the powerful Panglima Sagis met at the capital to depose Jauhar.[37] They cited his non-observance of Islamic practices as grounds for his removal, but also complained about the presence of foreign advisers. Opposition had been gathering against the advisers who by acting also as the sultan's merchants, were seen as rivals to some of the powerful *ulèëbalang*.

A few months later the *ulèëbalang* invited Syed Hussein Aidit, a wealthy Penang merchant, to become the new ruler. Syed Hussein was a formidable challenger to Jauhar. Not only did he claim descent from a former sultan, he was an Arab with considerable influence. He was also a wealthy merchant and had commercial links to British merchants in Penang and Calcutta. Syed Hussein was part of a network of commercial relations involving British merchants, *ulèëbalang*, and coastal chiefs. Among them were Lebai Dappah, John Prince of Natal, John Palmer of Calcutta and number of Penang merchants and officials. Lebai Dappah had over the years traded with John Prince, while the latter himself had commercial links with influential officials in Calcutta and Penang. These merchants, like the Acehnese *ulèëbalang*, were clearly opposed to any move that could strengthen the sultan and his control of trade. They had generally been cool towards the idea of a British treaty with Jauhar. Syed Hussein was installed sultan, but abdicated a few days later in favour of his son, who took the title Saiful Alam Syah.

Meanwhile, Jauhar was able to rally some support within Aceh against the challenge of Syed Hussein and opposing *ulèëbalang*. The result, then, was a protracted civil war. Saiful held on to Banda Aceh while Jauhar used Lhokseumawe as his base. Direct military encounters were few and the combatants mostly confined themselves to exacting duties from ships and from coastal chiefs. Trade was consequently affected. Figures showed that trade between Aceh and Penang fell during the period of conflict.[38] It became clear that Saiful was just as determined to regulate trade as Jauhar Alam had been.

Raffles in Bengkulen backed Jauhar Alam Syah. He had followed events in Aceh since he arrived as secretary to the Penang Government in 1805 and he was familiar with developments there. In 1814 when he wrote to William Petrie, Governor of Penang on affairs in the region, he was likely to have had Aceh in mind:

> The principles of my suggestions on this subject have been that nothing can tend so effectually to the suppression of piracy, to the encouragement and extension of lawful commerce, and to the civilization of the inhabitants of the Eastern Islands, as affording a steady support to the established native sovereigns and assisting them in the maintenance of their just rights and authority over their several chiefs and along the shores dependent upon their dominions.[39]

In 1818 Raffles was invited to Calcutta to explain his case on the urgency of settling the civil war in Aceh and the situation in the Archipelago. Raffles saw Aceh as important in his plans to advance British interest — both strategic and commercial — in the region. His earlier fears had been that Aceh might be used as a base by other Western powers. In 1810 it was the French he was anxious about. Now it was the Dutch. With the end of the Napoleonic wars, Java and other possessions were returned to the Dutch. Raffles had served as governor of Java and he now saw Aceh as important to regain a strong British presence in the Malay Archipelago. To him, Aceh in the north, together with Bengkulen, could check Dutch expansion in the Straits. Raffles also wanted the British to occupy an island south of Melaka, either Bangka or Riau, to ensure British access to the important markets in that region. Penang was too far up north to be of any use. He argued that Aceh was strategic, and warned that the fragmentation of political power there as in other states in the Malay world could lead to disorder and piracy. All these harmed British trade.[40]

The Supreme Government agreed and Raffles, along with Capt. J. Coombs who had led an earlier mission, were sent to Aceh to help end the conflict and to secure a British base. Raffles, as it turned out, had an amended plan. From Penang he proceeded southwards, and on January 1819 he claimed the island of Singapore for the EIC.

Only after Singapore did Raffles go to Aceh. It was clear that by this time the *ulèëbalang* in Aceh Besar and along the coasts were too politically divided. The capital, however, was more anti-Jauhar and there was hostility among the *ulèëbalang* as the British party arrived. Already news had reached the capital that the mission favoured Jauhar. Even Raffles sensed the hostility, especially from the tone of the Panglima Sagis' message to the British mission and decided not to disembark. Soon afterwards, Raffles as the senior of the two commissioners voted to recognise Jauhar as the sultan. They then proceeded to Jauhar's base and there signed a treaty with him. The treaty provided for the setting up of a British factory in Aceh and the exclusion of other European and American permanent presence. In return, the British offered military supplies and a loan to the sultan.[41]

The civil war showed what a difficult place Aceh was. There were too many powerful *ulèëbalang* in Aceh Besar and along the coasts. No one side could gain enough support from among the *ulèëbalang* to prevail — not even Saiful who had the backing of the Panglima Sagis and support from his father and reportedly from some British merchants.

The period also revealed that while the Acehnese were open to trade, there were forces within Aceh that were distrustful and even hostile to any strong British commercial or political presence. These forces included the *ulèëbalang*, divided as they were, and the influential Chulias who were commercial rivals of the British. In such a situation, even the rulers turned cautious.

The 1819 treaty underlined the fact that agreements with politically weak rulers in the region served little purpose. For while Jauhar gained British recognition he had difficulties winning back enough support of the *ulèëbalang*. Unable to bring the territorial chiefs with him, Jauhar no more than past rulers of Aceh could use the prosperity of the pepper trade to transform his state. Nor was he in a position to deal effectively with Western powers at a juncture when the map of the region was being redrawn.

The British did little to follow up the Raffles mission and seemed in fact to have forgotten about the treaty for a while. Only in August 1820 was W. Sartorius sent to find out how the sultan was doing and to hand over a ratified copy of the treaty. Sartorius met the sultan and his armed men who were camped outside the capital.[42] Penang supplied some arms to Jauhar. But Jauhar died without ever recovering the capital. Meanwhile Saiful Alam was pensioned off by the British. After that, there was little reason for Britain to involve itself directly in Acehnese affairs. With the end of the civil war, trade with Aceh and its coastal ports returned to previous levels. There was little interference from the sultan. And following Canning's mission there was now some understanding of the territorial limits of Aceh, at least from the British perspective.

The 1824 Treaty and After

Raffles' founding of Singapore led to strong protests from the Dutch and this set off an exchange of correspondence that eventually led to negotiation of the 1824 London Treaty. A major concern of London then was the security of Britain through the maintenance of a power balance in Europe. This required a strong Netherlands able to recover quickly from the aftermath of the Napoleonic wars, and London had therefore decided to return to the Dutch all their former territories in the Malay Archipelago. The 1824 treaty formally divided the Malay Archipelago into the British and the Dutch spheres of influence. Under the treaty Aceh fell within the Dutch sphere. Clearly then Aceh was subordinated to larger British interests elsewhere.

Nevertheless, British negotiators for the 1824 treaty sought to ensure that the return of territories to the Dutch should not be at the expense of British commercial interests. British trade in Southeast Asia and China was vital to British interests in India. The newly founded Singapore was therefore retained.[43] For the Dutch, the only other major power in the Straits of Melaka area, the attention was on Java where their concern was to rebuild the export economy following the collapse of the VOC. Still, the British insisted on a provision in the 1824 London Treaty that took note of the 1819 treaty and Aceh's independence.[44]

The 1824 treaty marked the end of a British search for a permanent presence in Aceh. However, commercial relations with the sultanate was continued and in fact Aceh was linked for most of the nineteenth century to a thriving trading network that included Penang, southern Thailand and southern Burma. Trade figures also showed growing pepper exports from Aceh to Penang. Aceh, in return, imported the bulk of its textiles through Penang. In Penang, Acehnese traders and settlers created an urban enclave in Acheen Street. Within this was Gedung Aceh, which was once Syed Hussein's office and pepper godown. This area was the centre of Penang's pepper trade and a number of merchants and *ulèëbalang* from Aceh bought properties in this area.[45]

The sultans after Jauhar enjoyed relatively less troubled rule. The rulers placed few hindrances to the growing commerce with Penang and Singapore. In fact under Sultan Muhammad Syah (1823–38), there was a second phase in the revitalising of pepper production. Yield from the old pepper region had begun to decline. New plantations were opened further to the north such as Pate, Rigas, Teunom, and Meulaboh. Production of pepper there reached 13 million pounds (5,800 tons) in 1839.

A third phase of pepper production began in 1850 with the opening of new plantations along the north eastern tip between Lhokseumawe and Tamiang. Political stability and the granting of a degree of autonomy by Sultan Ali Ala'ad-din Mansur Syah (1838–70) encouraged *ulèëbalang* to expand pepper production. At its peak, this region also produced some 13 million pounds annually. The population in the eastern region of Aceh swelled to an estimated 100,000 in 1873 through arrival of workers from other parts of Aceh. Pepper enriched many *ulèëbalang* who benefited from taxes, trade participation, and ownership of pepper plantations.[46] Rivalries among territorial chiefs persisted and rulers had still to contend with aristocratic resistant to strong central authority.[47] The Acehnese sultan granted land and trading rights to those *ulèëbalang* who were his strong supporters.

Pepper became less important in the Acehnese economy towards the last quarter of the nineteenth century. Falling world prices and production decline owing to soil exhaustion were the reasons. But the east coast of Aceh was able to shift first to tobacco and later more successfully to rubber and palm oil cultivation. Thus, the decline of the pepper industry ended an important phase of economic activity sustained largely by the enterprise of Acehnese coastal *ulèëbalang*, American traders, Chuliah and Country traders, and private merchants from Natal, Penang and Singapore.

Conclusion

In a period of growing Western power in the region, Aceh remained until 1873 both economically vibrant and territorially resilient. This was against a background where of all the sultanates in the Archipelago, Aceh had had more extensive and regular encounters with foreign powers. It was a contact that was mostly one of peaceful trade with merchants of many nationalities. Its own boats ventured into regional and international commerce. It was producing some of the most highly sought commodities in the world market. Throughout, its rulers and people demonstrated alertness to economic opportunities and change.

Aceh's trade oriented towards the Indian Ocean and to Penang, Riau and Singapore. Its historical ties had been closer with the Malay states of west Peninsular Malaysia. Its rulers established contact with British officials in India and in Penang. This relationship and Aceh's ties with the Malay Peninsula continued to encourage Acehnese rulers to look across the Straits to safeguard their commercial and political interests.

Looking back, it was during Jauhar's rule that Aceh appeared likely to have been drawn into the British sphere of influence. There were foreign advisers in the court, American traders in the west coast, boat seizures by both the sultan and the British, British missions to Aceh, and a civil war where foreign merchants and residents had a stake. And indeed, the civil war ended only through intervention of the British.

However, there was a persistent view in the British records during this period of an Aceh posing security and military risks to British interest in India and in the Straits of Melaka. Aceh was seen as a source of marauding pirates and encroaching settlers. There were also fears that powers hostile to the British could use Aceh as a naval base. But once the French threat in the region receded, British authorities were less willing to pursue the idea of a permanent commercial or naval base in Aceh. They saw it as a place with weak rulers unable to control rebellious *ulèëbalang*.

Certainly, the Acehnese rulers always had to contend with powerful and independent-minded *ulèëbalang* bent on safeguarding their own commercial interests. But the *ulèëbalang* themselves were divided by political and economic rivalry. They also responded differently to external forces with some enjoying close commercial ties with foreign traders while others were always cautious to outside powers. Thus while its trade flourished, a disunited Aceh found its future course largely decided by outside forces.

Following the 1824 treaty and the founding of Singapore, Aceh became less vital in the scheme of British strategic and commercial interest in the region. British needs were now better served by Singapore while British merchants continued to have access to Aceh's ports. And with Aceh within the sphere of Dutch influence, there was also less fear that the sultanate could be used by other powers hostile to British interest. This arrangement remained until new factors subsequently emerged.

Notes

[1]   Nicholas Tarling, ed., *The Cambridge History of Southeast Asia,* Vol. 1 (Cambridge: Cambridge University Press, 1992), pp. 572–617; David J. Steinberg *et al., In Search of Southeast Asia: A Modern History* (Kuala Lumpur: Oxford University Press, 1971), pp. 95–6.

[2]   Dianne Lewis, *Jan Compagnie in the Straits of Malacca 1641–1795* (Athens, Ohio: Ohio University Monographs in International Studies, 1995), pp. 81–110.

[3]   Anthony Reid, *The Last Stand of Asian Autonomies: Response to Modernity in the Diverse States of Southeast Asia and Korea, 1750–1900* (New York: St. Martin's Press, 1997).

[4]   James Gould, "Sumatra — America's Pepperpot 1784–1873", *Essex Institute Historical Collections* 92 (1956): 100–4.

[5]   The experience of immigrant Acehnese in the west coast was captured in *Hikajat Ranto*. G.W.J. Drewes, ed. and trans., *Two Achehnese Poems: Hikajat Ranto and Hikajat Teungku Di Meuke* (The Hague: Martinus Nijhoff, 1980).

[6]   John Bastin, *The Changing Balance of the Early Southeast Asian Pepper Trade*, Papers on Southeast Asian Subjects, No. 1 (Kuala Lumpur: Department of History, University of Malaya, 1960).

[7]   Dawn F. Rooney, *Betel Chewing Traditions in South-east Asia* (Kuala Lumpur: Oxford University Press, 1993), pp. 1–15.

8   Lee Kam Hing, *The Sultanate of Aceh* (Kuala Lumpur: Oxford University Press, 1995), pp. 200–1.

9   John Anderson, *Acheen and the Ports on the North and East Coasts of Sumatra* (Kuala Lumpur: Oxford in Asia Historical Reprints, 1970), p. 222.

10   S. Arasaratnam, *Merchants, Companies and Commerce on the Coromandel Coast 1650–1740* (Delhi: Oxford University Press, 1986).

11   Lee Kam Hing, "The Shipping Lists of Dutch Melaka: A Source for the Study of Coastal Trade and Shipping in the Malay Peninsula during the Seventeenth and Eighteenth Centuries", *Kapal dan Harta Karam: Ships and Sunken Treasure*, ed. Muhammad Yusoff Hashim (Kuala Lumpur: Persatuan Muzium Malaysia, 1986), pp. 53–76.

12   Raja Hj Ali ibn Ahmad, *Tuhfat al-Nafis (The Precious Gift)*, trans. V. Matheson and B.W. Andaya (Kuala Lumpur: Oxford University Press, 1982), p. 379 fn.4.

13   Report of Capt. J. Canning, 24 Nov. 1814, *Sumatra Factory Record*, Vol. 27 (India Office Library).

14   Francis Light to Bengal, 25 November 1786, *Straits Settlements Factory Records* (hereafter *SSFR*), Vol. 1 (IOL).

15   Elsbeth Locher-Scholten, *Sumatran Sultanate and Colonial State: Jambi and the Rise of Dutch Imperialism, 1830–1907* (Ithaca: Cornell Southeast Asia Program, 2004), pp. 56–8; A.P. Rubin, *The International Personality of the Malay Peninsula: A Study of the International Law of Imperialism* (Kuala Lumpur: University of Malaya Press, 1974), pp. 58–165.

16   J. Kathirithamby-Wells, *The British West Sumatran Presidency (1760–85): Problems of Early Colonial Enterprise* (Kuala Lumpur: University of Malaya Press, 1977), pp. 167–9.

17   R.J. Young, *The English East India Company and Trade on the West Coast of Sumatra, 1730–1760* (PhD thesis, University of Pennsylvania, 1970), pp. 235–8.

18   Resident at Barus to Padang, 14 March 1771, 27 July 1771, 26 October 1771, KB 3361 OB 1771, Rijsarchief, The Hague.

19   Fort Marlborough Consultations, 30 April 1786, *Sumatra Factory Records*, British Library.

20   Lee Kam Hing and Ahmat Adam, "Raffles and the Order of the Golden Sword", *JMBRAS* 63, 2 (1990): 77–89.

21   T.S. Raffles to Lord Minto, 11 June 1810, *Raffles-Minto Collection*, British Library.

22   G.W.J. Drewes, *Hikajat Potjut Muhamat: An Achehnese Epic* (The Hague: Martinus Nijhoff, 1979).

23   Charles Desvoeux to Select Committee, 9 December 1772, *Fort St. George Council Proceedings* (hereafter *FSGCP*); *FSGCP*, 29 December 1772; Fort St. George to C. Desvoeux, undated (*FSGCP* 7 January 1773); C. Desvoeux

to Select Committee, 7 January (*FSGCP* 7 January 1773) all found in *Sumatra Factory Record*, Vol. 15, British Library; Fort St. George Consultations, 23 July 1773, *Madras Public Department Consultations*, Range 240, Vol. 36, British Library.

24 Francis Light to Governor-General, Bengal, 25 August 1788, *SSFR*, Vol. 3.

25 Penang to London, 12 November 1805, *SSFR*, Vol. 179 (IOL).

26 T. S. Raffles to the Secret Committee, London, 5 August 1818, *Sumatra*, Vol. 47.

27 James Siegel, *The Rope of God* (Berkeley and Los Angeles: University of California Press, 1969), pp. 11–34.

28 Siegel, *The Rope of God*, pp. 11–34; Lee, *The Sultanate of Acheh*, pp. 7–12.

29 Report of H. Botham to Bengal, 17 December 1782 (Fort William Council Proceedings [hereafter FWCP], 19 January 1784), *Sumatra*, Vol. 23.

30 Lee Kam Hing and Ahmat Adam, "Raffles and the Order of the Golden Sword", *JMBRAS* 43, 1 (1970): 64–86.

31 Anthony Webster, *Gentlemen Capitalists: British Imperialism in South East Asia, 1770–1890* (London, New York: Tauris Academic Studies, 1998), pp. 27–48.

32 L. Sullivan and W. James to Lord Hillsborough, 16 November 1781, *Home Miscellaneous Series*, 155 (3); L. Sullivan, "Plans with Reasons and Observations Suggested for Reducing our Settlement at Bencoolen to a Contracted Subordinate and Making our Principal Establishment at Acheen", 20 December 1778, *Sumatra*, Vol. 30.

33 First report of D. Campbell on his mission to Aceh, 14 July 1810, encl. 1 in letter from Bengal to Penang, 31 July 1810 (Fort Cornwallis Council Proceedings [hereafter FCCP], 18 June 1811), *SSFR*, Vol. 31; second report of D. Campbell on his mission to Aceh, 24 July 1810, encl. 2 in letter from Bengal to Penang, 31 May 1811 (FCCP, 18 July 1811), *SSFR*, vol. 31.

34 Deposition of the supercargo made on 28 July 1813 at Prince of Wales Island; Deposition of Coomba Toomby and Noor Mahomed, 24 July 1813 (24 August 1813), *SSFR*, Vol. 40.

35 Capt. Canning led missions to the court of Ava in Burma in 1803, 1809, and 1811.

36 Court of Directors, London, to Bengal, 25 October 1820, Abstract of Despatches to India, Vol. 1, para. 4, British Library.

37 Report of Capt. J. Canning to the Secretary to Supreme Government, Bengal, on his mission to Aceh, 24 November 1814, *Sumatra*, Vol. 27, para. 105; Panglima Polim to Tuanku Pakeh Hussein, undated but probably 10 October 1814, cited in report of Capt. J. Canning, 24 November 1814, para. 109.

38 J. Anderson, *Acheen*, pp. 220–7.

39 T.S. Raffles to W. Petrie, 18 February 1814, in "Raffles and the Indian Archipelago", *Journal of the Indian Archipelago and East Asia* (1856): 266–7.

40 T.S. Raffles to Bengal, 24 April 1818 (FWCP 26 June 1818), *Bengal Secret and Political Consultations*, P/Ben/Sec/305; C.E. Wurtzburg, *Raffles of the Eastern Isles* (London: Hodder and Stoughton, 1954), p. 453.

41 Report of T.S. Raffles and J. Coombs on their proceedings in Aceh, 18 May 1819 (FWCP 10 July 1819), *Bengal Secret and Political Consultations*, P/Ben/Sec/309.

42 Instructions to W. Sartorius, 5 August 1820 (FCCP, 10 August 1820), *SSFR*, Vol. 75; Diary of W. Sartorius proceedings in Aceh, 1 September 1820 (FCCP 3 November 1820), *SSFR*, Vol. 76.

43 N. Tarling, *Anglo-Dutch Rivalry in the Malay World, 1780–1824* (Cambridge: Cambridge University Press, 1962); Harry Marks, *The First Contest for Singapore, 1819–1824*, Verhandelingen van het Koninklijk Institutut voor Taal-, land- en Volkenkunde, No. 27 (The Hague: Martinus Nijhoff, 1959).

44 Anthony Reid, *The Contest for North Sumatra: Atjeh, the Netherlands and Britain 1858–1898* (Kuala Lumpur: Oxford University Press, 1969), pp. 1–24; Elsbeth Locher-Scholten, *Sumatran Sultanate and Colonial State: Jambi and the Rise of Dutch Imperialism, 1830–1907* (Ithaca: Cornell Southeast Asia Program, 2004), pp. 59–63.

45 Neil Khor, *Glimpses of Old Penang* (Petaling Jaya: Star Publications, 2002), pp. 120–4.

46 The two principal pepper producers in this district were Simpang Ulim and Idi Rayeuk, each exporting an estimated 4.6 million pounds (35,000 pikuls) per annum. The other areas were Julok Rayeuk, Perureulak and Peudawa Rayeuk. Lee Kam Hing, "Pepper and the Revival of Aceh", in *Indonesian Heritage Series,* Vol. 3: *Early Modern History,* ed. Anthony Reid (Singapore: Archipelago Press, 1999), pp. 110–1.

47 Sultan Alauddin Mansur Syah appointed Teuku Muda Nyak Malim from Tungkok of the XXVI Mukim to open new pepper land at Simpang Ulim which became a major pepper centre. Peudawa Payeuk was opened in 1850 by Sayid Yusof who in 1855 was appointed *ulèëbalang* of the district. Salina Hj Zainol, "Hubungan perdangan antara Aceh, Sumatera Ttimur dan Pulau Pinang, 1819–1871" (unpublished MA thesis, University of Malaya, 1995).

6

Colonial Transformation: A Bitter Legacy

Anthony Reid

The Dutch occupation of Aceh was a military one from start to finish. It is important to realise that this was exceptional in Indonesia (as in most colonies), even if it accorded better than most with some nationalist readings of the nature of colonialism. Dutch influence penetrated other parts of the Archipelago gradually, with moments of bitter warfare but much longer periods of political accommodation and economic pragmatism. Monarchies were won over through the economic and status advantages to elites of the *pax Neerlandica*; stateless areas, accustomed to a "freedom bordering on anarchy", found unprecedented opportunities in a colonial world where they did not have to fear their neighbours. Aceh experienced neither of these routes into Netherlands India, but rather a bitter, humiliating conquest.

As the foregoing chapters have made clear, Aceh was never part of the Batavia-centred orbit of Dutch commercial influence. Initially oriented to the Indian Ocean, it gradually fell under the commercial influence of the British ports of Penang (1786) and Singapore (1819). Stamford Raffles organised a Britain-Aceh treaty in 1819, whereby Aceh promised to make no foreign alliances without British consent, and Britain to support the Sultan militarily. The Anglo-Dutch Treaty, which partitioned the Archipelago only five years later, was incompatible with this agreement in allocating all of Sumatra to the Dutch sphere. The problem was dealt with through a secret exchange of notes, the Dutch promising to deal with Aceh so that, "without losing anything of its independence", the sultanate would accept "the moderate exercise of European influence" that would guarantee security of trade.[1]

In practice the Dutch continued to have only token relations with Aceh, which remained within the commercial orbit of the British Straits Settlements. After a half-century of Anglo-Dutch wrangling over Dutch advances on the east coast of Sumatra, Britain agreed in 1871 to abandon its "guarantee" of Aceh's independence in return for trade concessions and the acquisition of Holland's Elmina fort on the Gold Coast (Ghana). Aceh was not consulted, but its agents quickly became aware of the increased belligerence on the Dutch side. Both sides moved quickly after 1871 — Holland to put pressure on Aceh to sign an unequal treaty; Aceh to look for alternative allies such as Turkey, France and America. It was the discussions of the Acehnese syahbandar, Panglima Tibang, with the US consul in Singapore at the beginning of 1873 that enabled the war party in Batavia to get The Hague's approval for a reckless war.[2]

Thirty Years of War

In February 1873 Governor-General James Loudon sent his deputy to Aceh with 3,000 men, and the instructions to issue "an ultimatum to recognize us as sovereign or war". There was to be no negotiation. This precipitate belligerence proved the gravest Dutch strategic mistake of the century. It is explained in part by Loudon's belief that war with Aceh was inevitable, and should be launched as quickly as possible. A more normal Dutch strategy of using its naval power to pressure and divide the opponent was ruled out lest Aceh succeed in obtaining the support of the Penang merchants and of other European powers. Loudon and the Dutch consul in Singapore played up Aceh's negotiations with consuls there as a means to force the hand of a more prudent government in The Hague.

The Dutch fleet began to bombard the capital, Banda Aceh, on 26 March, as a sign that war had been declared. In view of the dangers of foreign involvement, a formal declaration of war was communicated to the European powers. The force landed on 8 April, in appalling ignorance of what they might expect. Its commander, General Köhler, was killed in the first week. With 80 men dead and nearly 400 wounded within the first three weeks, without having gained any strategic objective, the demoralised "First Expedition" withdrew. Holland had suffered its most humiliating defeat ever at Indonesian hands.

This setback ruled out any talk of compromise until Dutch honour had been restored. By November 1873 the Dutch had put together the largest force they had ever assembled, including many mercenaries recruited in Europe. They landed 13,000 men in December, and advanced slowly until they seized the "kraton" (the Javanese term the Dutch used for the fortified citadel) on 24 January 1874. Cholera had spread from the Dutch troops to the defending Acehnese, who abandoned the pestilential citadel the night before the Dutch attack. They carried with them the ailing young sultan, Mahmud, who also died of cholera two days later. Since there was no obvious replacement, the Dutch commander saw no way to carry out the original policy of seeking to rule indirectly. He now declared that Netherlands India had replaced the sultanate, which was thereby abolished.

With this second mistake the Dutch made a peaceful outcome impossible. They refused all attempts at mediation from Britain, Turkey and the former Aceh Prime Minister Habib Abd ar-Rahman. While Dutch forces only occupied the citadel and the three kilometre strip that united it to the sea, they hoped in vain that substantial numbers of Acehnese would come voluntarily to submit. On the contrary the Dutch positions were under a kind of siege from fighters who came from around the country to try their hand at warfare. Outside the capital the Dutch imposed an ineffective blockade, handicapped by both Aceh's long coastline and their own need to placate the Penang traders. Already the fundamentals of Aceh's uniquely difficult passage into Netherlands India were clear. Because of Aceh's proud history and the blundered invasion, neither a peaceful nor an aggressive strategy would now work.

After failing with peace in the months following the capture of the empty citadel, Dutch troops were again reinforced to undertake the conquest, in 1875–7, of the coastal part of Aceh Besar (or "Aceh Proper"), the heartland of the old sultanate around the Aceh River. Acehnese resistance was led in this period by Habib Abd ar-Rahman az-Zahir, a charismatic and capable Arab who had returned to Aceh in 1876 after failing to arrange a diplomatic solution in Istanbul, Singapore or Penang. His strategy was to unite the Acehnese forces sufficiently either to win a decisive battle or to arrange an honourable truce. During a renewed Dutch attempt at a pacific policy, in mid-1878, he led an offensive that laid siege to the Dutch post in Krueng Raba. This provoked another Dutch offensive to occupy the whole of the Aceh River valley. Failing to persuade the Acehnese *ulèëbalang* elite to negotiate a submission, the Habib accepted a Dutch offer of a comfortable exile in Jidda. This left nobody strong enough either to negotiate for peace or unite for war.[3]

For their part, the Dutch were desperate to declare the war over and to hope that a more passive strategy would bear fruit after the ruinous costs of the offensive. More than 7,000 were dead on the Dutch side alone by the end of 1878, chiefly of cholera and other diseases. A civil government was declared, the great mosque was rebuilt in Moorish style as a symbol of goodwill, and no further attempt was made to pursue the resistance leaders as they moved into the hilly area between Aceh Besar and Pidie. The troops were expected to hold the line of advance reached in 1880, but without retaliating beyond the line for attacks. The result was that throughout the 1980s the initiative was with the Acehnese resistance, which developed Southeast Asia's first successful guerrilla strategy against modern European arms.

In 1879 some key survivors of the royal lineage established a new royal capital at Keumala, just on the Pidie side of the watershed, and proclaimed the young grandson of the penultimate ruler as the new Sultan Mohammad Daud. The most determined opponents of the Dutch soon made Keumala their capital, whence they drew increasing support, funds, and fighters from the whole country. Religious inspiration was provided pre-eminently by Teungku Sheikh Saman di Tiro (1836–91), one of the most influential Pidie *ulama* as doyen of the important religious school of Tiro. He popularised the *Hikayat Perang Sabil*, an Acehnese epic poem exhorting the youth to exchange their earthly lot for the instant rewards of martyrdom, and turned the resistance into a holy war for the faith. Those *ulèëbalang*, who had sided with the Dutch during the military offensives, were now obliged to demonstrate their loyalty to the resistance.

During the 1880s raids were mounted virtually every week on the Dutch positions, and the morale of their defenders sank to a pathetic low. European soldiers began to defect to the Acehnese side, usually accepting Islam as the price of acquiring an Acehnese wife. In total there were 70 such desertions in the period 1882–92, 48 of them Europeans and 5 Eurasians.[4] Teungku di Tiro confidently replied to the Dutch governor's overtures for peace by writing, "As soon as you accept Islam by pronouncing the two articles of faith, then we can conclude a treaty."[5]

The war was so deeply unpopular in Holland that no government could send more troops and resources to pursue it. Some favoured abandoning Aceh altogether, but this was ruled out by considerations of Dutch prestige in the Indies more generally. Others sought to negotiate the restoration of the Sultan under Dutch protection, but the war party was not interested. Instead the Dutch tried to batten down the hatches in an impregnable, if entirely useless, fortress. In 1885 the troops were pulled back to a *concentratie* of about 40 square kilometres around Banda Aceh (Kutaradja) and the port at Uleelheue (Olehleh), and the land cleared for a kilometre along the whole fortified perimeter. The attacks declined, but the resistance party could reasonably claim that it had won. The party of holy war against the invader, led by Teungku di Tiro, was able to raise funds throughout Aceh, to train armed bands along strict religious lines, and to undermine the authority of *ulèëbalang* local rulers.[6]

The Dutch were more strongly placed by sea, and could persuade many of the coastal *ulèëbalang* to raise the Dutch flag as the price for being allowed to trade. But more systematic use of the trade weapon to enforce obedience was considered too costly both in warships and in already tattered goodwill from the British Straits Settlements. This always-tense relationship was vastly complicated when the British steamer *Nisero* was wrecked off the West Aceh coast in November 1883, and the local Acehnese *ulèëbalang*, Teuku Imam of Teunom, took hostage the 29 mostly British crew. The Dutch government went to extraordinary lengths to avoid a threat of unilateral British intervention to free them. The eventual package of measures that brought about their release 10 months later included not only a large reward for Teuku Imam, but the freeing of trade throughout Aceh after a short blockade intended to look punitive.

By the 1890s, however, Aceh's wealth and commerce had been sadly eroded by years of war, and it was no longer the most important arm of Penang's trade. Dutch strategists found to their surprise that they could impose a systematic control of Aceh's trade in 1892 with only token protests from the British. When the free port of Sabang was developed in 1903 on an island just off the Aceh capital, the Netherlands finally removed much of the fatal disadvantage of trying to control an area in the economic orbit of British ports.[7]

This was one factor that made possible a gradual Dutch conquest of Aceh after 1893. Another was the death of Teungku Sheikh Saman di Tiro in 1891, and the conflict between his unpopular sons and local leaders elsewhere who resented their attempts to centralise the money-raising for the struggle. One of these was the West Coast *ulèëbalang* Teuku Uma, whose ambivalent relations with the war party led him to fight on the Dutch side briefly in 1884, and again in 1893–6, when Dutch guns and money made him the most powerful of the *ulèëbalang*. His attempts to play both sides inevitably broke down, and in 1893 his well-armed force changed sides for the last time and laid siege to the

Dutch posts established in his areas. Holland was obliged to dismiss its Aceh Governor and send new troops to rescue the situation.

The third factor was Christiaan Snouck Hurgronje, a brilliant and intensely committed Dutch Islamist who took it upon himself to devise a solution based on a realistic assessment of Aceh. After first achieving celebrity status by his first-hand observation of Mecca, he spent eight months gathering information in the Acehnese capital in 1891–2.[8] His incisive report, a controversial classic of engaged colonial ethnology, made very clear how and why the Dutch were hated throughout Aceh, and poured scorn on the wishful thinking behind attempts to negotiate. Instead there must be a ruthless pursuit of the war party especially including the hostile *ulama*, combined with concrete measures to give other Acehnese a stake in peace. In 1898 Snouck was named Adviser for Native affairs with particular responsibility for Aceh, and his choice of a military counterpart, Col. J.B. van Heutsz, was named military governor. Together they masterminded the relentless pursuit of the Acehnese resistance, which killed over 20,000 Acehnese in the ensuing ten years.[9]

Holland's "Aceh Policy" Trusting the *ulèëbalang*

The alternate capital at Keumala was taken in June 1898. Teuku Uma was killed eight months later, though his heroically defiant widow Cut Nyak Dien was not captured until 1905. In 1903 the two leading symbols of secular resistance, Sultan Daud and Panglima Polem, submitted formally, the former being exiled and the latter accepting a place within the colonial administration. Until 1913 resistance remained very strong in the interior on the part of *ulama*-led guerrillas who came to be known to the Dutch as *jahats* (baddies), but to the Acehnese simply as *muslimin* (Muslims). The annual death toll of war only dropped below 100 after the leading heirs of Teungku di Tiro in the Pidie region were killed in 1910–2.[10] All Teungku di Tiro's seven sons died in this period, including Teungku Mahyuddin, the maternal grandfather of Hasan Tiro, eventual prophet of Acehnese independence.[11]

Snouck Hurgronje particularly insisted that the territorial *ulèëbalang* of Aceh be treated with respect, and their views heeded whenever possible. After Snouck's rival Van Daalen had alienated many by his aggressive policy as Governor in 1905–8, the Snouck policy of relying on the *ulèëbalang* became something of a dogma. In 1909 a government commissioner appointed to redress the mistakes of Van Daalen enunciated the central principle "to make the broadest possible use of the services

Fig. 6 The "Nine-fold seal" (*Cap Sikureuëng*) of Sultan Daud, giving the names of eight of his illustrious predecessors, surrounding his own

of the native chiefs, and to entrust them with the principal responsibility for the way things are done .... The more that can be left to them, the better it is."[12] Each of the 102 self-governing *ulëëbalang* recognised by the Dutch was given a substantial fixed allowance, sometimes worth as much as half of the income of their district.

Later Aceh governors often rejected calls for reform of the system, or the modest democratic advances favoured in Batavia, on the basis of this policy. The *ulëëbalang* were transformed by it into something like feudal potentates with sometimes arbitrary powers over land and judicial matters, whereas their pre-Dutch role had been primarily that of entrepreneurs and financiers who opened up a new area, and of leaders who mobilised the population in the event of crisis or war. Their entrepreneurial role continued, however, by virtually monopolising the new economic opportunities of the colonial era, like rice-milling and the planting of new cash-crops like coffee and rubber. These factors widened the gulf between rulers and ruled to a degree even greater than elsewhere in Indonesia.[13]

The most hated aspect of the Dutch administration was the tax system, and especially the obligation to labour for 24 days a year to help build the roads, bridges and irrigation canals the colonial system required. Although the Dutch justified this system in terms of tradition as "service to the feudal lord" (*herendienst*), it was even less part of Sumatran tradition than of Javanese. Many of those who left Aceh for the Peninsula in the period 1890–1920 identified the absence of this practice as the major advantage of British-style colonialism. Only in the 1920s did it become possible for the more prosperous peasantry to buy out of the hated system.

The ferocity of the struggle in Aceh, the substantial proportion of the population who died in it (4 per cent killed in the decade 1899–1909 alone,[14] perhaps 20 per cent dead overall if the resulting disease is included); and the bitterness of having nothing but defeat and humiliation to show for this sacrifice, undoubtedly produced traumatic consequences in the Acehnese population. Dutch officials were correct in judging that only the presence of superior force dissuaded Acehnese from seeking to reverse the humiliation. Many did attempt to end it for themselves through a suicidal attack on a Dutchman. At least once a week on average until the early thirties there was an individual attack of this kind, the so-called *Aceh-moord*.[15]

New Forms of Resistance

At least before 1930, Aceh remained exceptional in Indonesia in these and other ways. Violent attacks against the Dutch system were more common, notably in the period 1925–7 when the Bakongan revolt on the West coast produced over a hundred deaths on both sides. The positive sides of the Dutch regime, education and social services were also less appreciated. The Dutch spent more on modern schools in Aceh than in other provinces in the hope of winning the population around, but up until the 1920s the village schools were distrusted, and traditional Islamic schools preferred. Force had to be used by the *ulèëbalang* to fill the schools provided in their districts. At the 1930 census only 1.1 per cent of Acehnese were literate in the Roman alphabet, one of the lowest proportions in Indonesia.[16]

Yet gradually a change did come over Acehnese society, and became palpable in the last five years of the Dutch regime. Education was the key to it. By 1935 Aceh had caught up with and even surpassed the national average for school attendance, with 33,000 children in the village schools. The conviction of living in an era of astonishing progress, which had energised other Indonesians two decades earlier, began also to sweep through Aceh in the 1930s. With it came the idea that modern forms of organisation through Islamic movements and even parties, were the new key to reversing the humiliation of conquest.

While the children of *ulèëbalang* were well-supported to enrol in Dutch-medium secondary schools in Java, ambitious non-*ulèëbalang* parents sent their children to a new kind of modernised Islamic school. Muhammadiah was the pioneer of such schools in Aceh as elsewhere, but it was so strongly dominated by Minangkabaus and other outsiders that it drew negligible support from Acehnese. In the late 1920s, however, some Acehnese who had studied in modern ways in West Sumatra, Java, Egypt or Mecca began to open a new kind of Islamic school for Acehnese. These schools accepted students who had already acquired basic literacy and numeracy in the village schools, and incorporated some modern knowledge alongside training in *Quran, hadith, fikh* and *tassawuf.*

The most charismatic of the young *ulama* to respond to this challenge was Teungku Mohammad Daud Beureu'eh (1899–1987). Although educated entirely in Acehnese Islamic schools, he was receptive to the new ideas, and extremely persuasive in preaching them. Where other modern Islamic schools were supported by an *ulèëbalang* patron, the Jamiatul Diniyah organisation he established in 1930 raised its money from the people through the popularity of his *tabligh* (preaching). His movement established a number of schools in the Pidie (Sigli) area, training a new generation who became the revolutionaries of the next decade — including the young Hasan Tiro.

While Java-based organisations like Muhammadiah gained a few adherents in the towns, the first genuinely Acehnese movement arose in 1939 from among the founders and activists of these modern-style Islamic schools. The all-Aceh Association of Ulama (PUSA) was in fact strongest in Pidie and the north coast. Daud Beureu'eh was elected its President. In the next two years it became something approaching an Acehnese popular movement under *ulama* leadership, the very thing the Dutch had most feared. Although some *ulèëbalang* had initially patronised it, they quickly withdrew as it became a vehicle for anti-*ulèëbalang* campaigns. That the Dutch allowed it reveals how far they had moved in the previous decade, towards seeing Indonesian nationalism as the principal threat to their regime as a whole, and the *ulèëbalang*, who were the only real supporters of nationalism as no longer essential. Several

Dutch officials quietly encouraged PUSA to keep non-Acehnese out of its membership.[17]

The Revolution of the 1940s

The 1940s marked a complete turnaround, in which the popular leadership galvanised by PUSA moved from being a purely Acehnese movement suspicious of *ulèëbalang* cosmopolitanism, to itself embracing Indonesian nationalism. An explanation needs to be given here.

The Japanese invasion of 1941–2 once again placed Aceh in a situation very different from other parts of Indonesia. The Japanese occupied Penang and northern Malaya on mid-December 1941, and began immediately broadcasting propaganda from there to Sumatra. They did not cross the Strait to invade northern Sumatra, however, until 12 March. There were three months for rival parties in Aceh to contact the Japanese and try to secure a better place in the rising sun.

PUSA was more active in advancing its anti-Dutch credentials, and one of its *ulama* members, Said Abu Bakar, agreed with Japanese fifth-column specialist Col. Fujiwara Iwaichi to support the coming Japanese invasion. He told Fujiwara, "the people of Aceh were extremely hostile to the Dutch Government, but also to the *ulèëbalang* because they also oppress the people, even more than the Dutch".[18] Back in Aceh, Abu Bakar found enthusiastic support for a rebellion from many PUSA activists. However, the rebellion that began on 19 February 1942 was only successful in areas such as Aceh Besar and West Aceh, where PUSA-*ulèëbalang* relations were least polarised and some *ulèëbalang* also supported the uprising.

Because it was the Acehnese rather than the Japanese who drove the Dutch from Aceh, Japanese troops were faced with a delicate task. Said Abu Bakar and PUSA were the first to use the Japanese to destroy their enemies, having two West Aceh *ulèëbalang* who had obstructed the rebellion executed by the Japanese. But the more politically experienced *ulèëbalang* struck back viciously, readily convincing the Japanese administrators that PUSA was a populist threat to stability, including to the Japanese themselves. Daud Beureu'eh and the other PUSA leaders were arrested for questioning, a few PUSA activists were executed, and PUSA was prevented from operating throughout the occupation.

Both sides were now embittered against each other. The subsequent shifts of Japanese policy, as they prepared after 1943 for the possibility of needing popular Acehnese support against an Allied counter-attack, exacerbated this tension. In 1944 both secular and religious legal authority was transferred from the *ulèëbalang* to a new court staffed by PUSA sympathisers. Several outspoken *ulèëbalang* who had most vigorously opposed these steps were executed. Although the Japanese tried to keep both rival elites in play in a series of representative bodies, the distrust remained profound in many areas at the time the Japanese Emperor unexpectedly surrendered in August 1945.[19]

This sudden surrender left a power vacuum in Aceh as elsewhere, and most appear to have assumed the Dutch order would return. A few of the *ulèëbalang* who were most likely to be targets of PUSA-led revenge attacks were particularly inclined to contact Dutch officials who returned to Medan. But both the Dutch and Japanese assumed that Aceh was the least likely corner of the Archipelago to accept a Dutch return, and so it indeed transpired. Despite an escalating series of attacks against the Japanese during 1945, Japanese die-hards made Aceh, one of their targets, as a last refuge. When Japanese troops were evacuated from an increasingly hostile Aceh on 18–20 December, most of their arms and about a hundred defectors remained behind in Acehnese hands.

As elsewhere, the youths who had enjoyed military or semi-military training from the Japanese, were the first to mobilise effectively. They put increasing pressure on the *ulèëbalang* left in control by the Japanese to support Republican Indonesia rather than the Dutch. Most of them compromised, and many genuinely supported Indonesian independence. The Pidie *ulèëbalang* with most to fear from it, however, made a recklessly defiant stand against the rising republican pressure. They were led by T. Mohammad Daud, *ulèëbalang* of Cumbok and official in charge of Lammeulo, one of the three major districts of Pidie.

Cumbok's defiance made it clearer to the PUSA generation educated in modern Islamic schools that they should side with the Republic to defeat their major enemy. They mobilised during October in a youth movement known initially as BPI, but later as PRI and then Pesindo. They helped galvanise the leading *ulama*, including their own charismatic hero Daud Beureu'eh but also traditionalist teachers, to declare that the fight for Indonesian independence was a holy war and "a continuation of the former struggle in Aceh which was led by the late Tgk. Chik di Tiro".[20] At a series of meetings in mosques throughout Aceh, Islamic students and *ulama* were effectively mobilised in a series of quasi-military groups dedicated to holy war on Indonesia's behalf, and generally dominated by former PUSA activists.

In January 1946 the best-armed of these forces, strengthened with Japanese arms and Japanese-trained officers, destroyed the formidable defences of the defiant *ulèëbalang* in Lammeulo and throughout Pidie. All but two of the 25 ruling *ulèëbalang* of Pidie were killed, along with most of their families. These events polarised the rest of Aceh, with the result that the most aggressive *ulèëbalang* elsewhere were killed and the remainder arrested, including the leading government official, Resident T. Nyak Arif. In the place of these officials, senior PUSA figures or those sympathetic to them were "elected" as government leaders everywhere.[21] This was the most profound social revolution anywhere in the Archipelago, overthrowing forever a hated pattern of oppression, and giving the leading authority for the rest of the 1940s to *ulama* of relatively modern type.

All of this was achieved without help or interference of any kind from republican authorities elsewhere in Indonesia. The Acehnese revolution followed its own logic, and its own leadership, albeit in the name of Indonesia. Since Aceh was the only area the returning Dutch troops never sought to enter (save for the island and port of Sabang), it became the exemplary bastion of the struggle. The Republic needed Aceh far more than Aceh needed the Republic. All this changed once the Dutch threat was removed in 1950, as is described in the following chapters.

Notes

[1] The full treaty and appended notes are in Harry Marks, "The First Contest for Singapore, 1819–1824", *VKI* 27 (1959): 252–62, and in W.G. Maxwell and W.S. Gibson, eds., *Treaties and Engagements Affecting the Malay States and Borneo* (London: Truscott, 1924), pp. 8–16.

[2] Anthony Reid, *The Contest for North Sumatra: Atjeh, the Netherlands and Britain 1858–1898* (Kuala Lumpur: University of Malaya Press/OUP, 1969), pp. 52–75 and 83–97. The text of the 1871 Sumatra Treaty is in ibid., pp. 291–2.

[3] The detailed military history of this phase of the war is E.B. Kielstra, *Beschrijving van den Atjeh-oorlog*, 3 vols. (The Hague, 1883–5). Critical modern accounts are in Reid, *The Contest*, pp. 108–17 and 187–207; and Paul van't Veer, *De Atjeh-oorlog* (Amsterdam: Arbeiderspers, 1969), pp. 57–125. Acehnese diplomatic attempts at a way out are covered in Reid, *The Contest*, pp. 119–85, and Anthony Reid, "Indonesian Diplomacy: A Documentary Study of Atjehnese Foreign Policy in the Reign of Sultan Mahmud, 1870–1874", *JMBRAS* 42, 2: 74–114.

4 Reid, *The Contest*, p. 207.

5 Letter from Teungku Sheikh Saman di Tiro to Resident K.F.H. van Langen, September 1885, in H.C. Zentgraaff, *Atjeh* (Batavia: De Unie, 1938), pp. 18–9 (my translation).

6 The ideology of Teungku di Tiro and the holy war, which gained dominance in this period, is well described in the following chapter.

7 Reid, *The Contest*, pp. 237–70.

8 His two original Dutch reports on these visits (*Mekka*, 1889, *De Atjehers*, 1895) were later translated as C. Snouck Hurgronje, *Mekka in the Latter Part of the 19th Century*, trans. J. Monahan (The Hague, 1889); *The Achehnese*, trans. A.W.S. O'Sullivan, 2 vols. (Leiden/London: Brill, 1906).

9 Reid, *The Contest*, pp. 270–83.

10 For the resistance see Chapter 7 below, and for the last stage of the war more generally, see Paul van't Veer, *De Atjeh-oorlog*, pp. 209–82.

11 M. Isa Sulaiman, *Aceh Merdeka, Ideologi, Kepemimpinan dan Gerakan* (Jakarta: Pustaka Al Kautsar, 2000), pp. 11–2.

12 Liefrink report 31 July 1909, translated in Anthony Reid, *The Blood of the People: Revolution and the End of Traditional Rule in Northern Sumatra* (Kuala Lumpur: Oxford University Press, 1979), p. 12.

13 Reid, *Blood of the People*, pp. 11–5; James Siegel, *The Rope of God* (Berkeley: University of California Press, 1969), pp. 14–29; M. Isa Sulaiman, *Sejarah Aceh: Sebuah Gugatan Terhadap Tradisi* (Jakarta: Sinar Harapan, 1997), pp. 18–31.

14 van't Veer, *De Atjeh-oorlog*, p. 260.

15 See Alfian in the following chapter, and Reid, *Blood of the People*, p. 11.

16 Reid, *Blood of the People*, pp. 21, 34.

17 See Chapter 8 below, and Reid, *Blood of the People*, pp. 25–31.

18 Fujiwara Iwaichi, *F-kikan* (Tokyo: Hara Shobo, 1966), pp. 200–1; Joenoes Djamil, *Riwajat Barisan F (Fudjiwara Kikan) di Atjeh* (1943; reissued in Banda Aceh, 1975), p. 17.

19 The Japanese occupation is discussed in detail in A.J. Piekaar, *Atjèh en de Oorlog met Japan* (The Hague: Van Hoeve, 1949); Reid, *Blood of the People*, pp. 84–147; Isa Sulaiman, *Sejarah Aceh*, pp. 74–113.

20 The declaration is discussed in more detail in Reid, *Blood of the People*, pp. 187–91, and in Chapter 8 below.

21 A contemporary account of the struggle is Abdullah Arif, *Disekitar Peristiwa Pengchianat Tjoembok* (Kutaradja, 1946), translated by Anthony Reid as "The Affair of the Tjoembok Traitors", *Review of Indonesian and Malayan Affairs* 4/5 (1970–1): 36–57. For the background and the revolution more generally see Reid, *Blood of the People*, pp. 195–211; Isa Sulaiman, *Sejarah Aceh*, pp. 114–214. Isa, pp. 484–6 gives a list of 98 *ulèëbalang* and their family members killed as a direct result of the January 1946 violence in Pidie.

7

Aceh and the Holy War (*Prang Sabil*)

Teuku Ibrahim Alfian

Jihad in Islam

The idea of *Perang Sabil* or Holy War is considered in many writings to be the same as a struggle in the path of Allah or *jihād fī sabilillah*, or in Indonesian *perang sabil*. The basic meaning of the word *jihād*, derived from the verb "*jāhada*", is "to exert oneself as much as one can"[1] or "to struggle to the utmost of one's capacity".[2] Such a meaning is found in the *Qur'an* Surah S. 29 (al-'Ankabut: 6, 69) and S. 22 (al-Hajj: 78).

A Muslim is also under an obligation to be engaged in jihad with all his or her soul as stated in S. 61 (al-Saff: 10, 11, 12).

Particularly for the term "war", the Qur'an applies the term *qitāl* (fighting), as in:

> Lo! Allah has bought from the believers their lives and their wealth because the Garden will be theirs: they shall fight in the way of Allah and shall slay and be slain. It is a promise which is binding on Him in the Torah and the Gospel and the Qur'an. Who fulfils His covenant better that Allah? Rejoice then in your bargain that ye have made, for that is the supreme triumph. (S. 9 [al-Taubah]: 111)

In Western languages *jihād* is often understood as Holy War. As a matter of fact the word *jihād* has other meanings, such as *jihād al-nafs* (the struggle against oneself, also called The "Greater *Jihād*", *jihād al-akbar*) and *jihād al-syaiṭān* (the struggle against the devil). These concepts were aptly articulated by The Prophet Muhammad when he returned from a battle, "We have now returned from the Smaller *Jihād* to the Greater *Jihād*".[3] The "Smaller *Jihād*" is *jihad* with the sword. There are also other kinds of *jihād*, such as *jihād al-tarbiyah* (educational *jihād*) and *jihād al-da'wah* (spreading Islam amongst the unbelievers by peaceful means). Sometimes the latter is also termed *jihād al-lisan* (*jihad* of the tongue) or *jihād al-qalam* (*jihad* of the pen).[4] It is founded on *al-Qur'an* S. 16 (al-Nahl: 125): "Call unto the way of thy Lord with wisdom and fair exhortation, and reason with them in the better way". Therefore, the translation of *jihād* exclusively as "Holy War" is incorrect or at best incomplete, for it refers only to the restricted meaning of the word in the language of the *Shari'ah*.

Theoretically the idea of the Holy War has existed in Indonesia since Islam took a firm hold in this part of Southeast Asia. Throughout Indonesian history four contexts could be found in the application of the idea by Indonesians against their opponents, namely: conversion of people to Islam; battles against foreign aggressors in self-defense or to protect the interests of the nation; movements to resist Dutch colonialism after the Dutch subdued Indonesian rulers and occupied their territories; and adoption by Republican supporters after the Proclamation of Independence in 1945.

This chapter will investigate "the Smaller *Jihād*" or *jihād al-asghar*, such as the wars against the Portuguese in Melaka waged by the Acehnese Sultans in the sixteenth and seventeenth centuries and the Dutch-Aceh War in the nineteenth and early twentieth centuries. The doctrine of Holy War could also be seen during the Japanese Occupation and in the Indonesian War of Independence.

Holy War in Aceh

The *Hikayat Raja-raja Pasai* (The Pasai Chronicles), which was written around the mid-fourteenth century, as well as the Maghribi traveller Ibn Battuta, mentioned that the Sultan of Samudera Pasai in the Northeast of Aceh waged war against his infidel neighbours in the fifteenth century.[5] Although early Acehnese chronicles of this period do not greatly emphasise the *jihad* theme, Raniri does say of Sultan Alau'd-Din Ri'ayat Shah al-Kahar (±1537–68), "he it was who first fought victoriously (*ghazi*) with all the unbelievers, to the point of going to attack Melaka himself".[6] All sources agree that he made war against Melaka in 1537 and 1568, and more successfully against non-Muslim Bataks. It was one of his enemies, Ferdinand Mendez Pinto, who most graphically portrayed Sultan al-Kahar, whom he called the Tyrant of Aceh, as a holy warrior in alliance with the Turks.[7] It is assumed that such wars to convert the neighbours to Islam were based on al-Qur'an S. 9 (al-Taubah): 29, that is, "Fight against such of those who have been given the Scripture as believe not in Allah nor the Last Day, and forbid not that which Allah hath forbidden by His messenger, and follow not the religion of truth, until they pay the tribute readily, being brought low."

After Portugal occupied Melaka in 1511, rivalry existed between the sultanate of Aceh and the Portuguese over the hegemony of the Straits of Melaka. The great Acehnese Sultan Iskandar Muda (±1585–1636), like Sultan al-Qahhar as mentioned above, waged war against the Portuguese. Iskandar Muda launched a campaign using a navy of heavy galleys and several hundred ships, but failed to seize Melaka in 1629. In the *Hikayat Malém Dagang* (Tales of Malém Dagang) written in the seventeenth century one can find an account of that war that calls it "war in the path of Allah" (*sabilillah*).[8] There are verses in the *Hikayat* which could be translated as follows.

> Why are you afraid of going to war against the Jews [sic!]
> Such a war originally was from the Prophet
> Why are you afraid of going to war in the way of Allah
> Our Master Ali is in command
> Today the King [Iskandar Muda] is waging war
> Malém Dagang has been appointed as commander

The implication is that the war against the Portuguese was considered *jihad fi sabilillah*.

In April 1873 shortly after the declaration of war, the first Dutch force of 3,000 men landed on the Aceh shore under the command of Maj. Gen. J.H.R. Köhler. A month later the Dutch retreated to Batavia having lost their commander in the fighting. Then they returned to Aceh in November 1873 with 13,000 troops under the command of Lieutenant General J. Van Swieten to conquer Aceh.[9]

The Dutch-Aceh War lasted for more than 40 years and cost more lives, money and social dislocation than any other Dutch colonial war. According to Paul van't Veer, up to 1914 only, no less than 17,500 people were killed on the Dutch side, and about 70,000 on Aceh's side.[10]

The Acehnese called this war the "Dutch War" (*Prang Beulanda*) or "Infidel War" (*Prang Kaphé*). The Acehnese people's fighting spirit was heightened through poetic tales called *Hikayat Perang Sabil* (*HPS*), Tales of Holy War (Fig. 7). In one of the *Hikayat* preserved in Leiden University, the Netherlands,[11] it is mentioned that those who participate in the Holy War will undoubtedly be granted rewards: (a) their sins will be

Fig. 7 A version of the *Hikayat Perang Sabil*, copied out on modern paper and captured by the Dutch from the wife of Sultan Daud in 1902 (reproduced from Ibrahim Alfian *et al.*, eds., *The Dutch Colonial War in Acheh*, Banda Aceh: The Documentation and Information Centre of Aceh, 1999)

forgiven by God, *Allah Taala*; (b) seats are reserved, and bliss as well as enjoyment are provided for them in Heaven; (c) they will be safe and sound and the tomb will be comfortable; (d) they will be protected from destruction in the doomsday; (e) they will be granted luxurious dresses with emeralds in Heaven; (f) they will be married to beautiful angels and living with 72 of them in a palace; (g) all sins of 70 persons in the family of the martyr will be forgiven by God. In addition to that, those who support the war with money will be allowed to enter Heaven. One *Hikayat* composed by Tgk. Nya' Ahmad is translated as follows.[12]

> Those who give their support
> Will be granted rewards many times
>
> No matter that you give just one piece
> Many pieces God will pay you back

> One *dirham* you give
> Seven hundred when it is returned
>
> Repayment is seven-hundred times
> God mentions it in the Qur'an

The Holy War is a deed of *fardhu'ain,* which means it is compulsory for men and women, old and young, including children. One text from the year 1710 runs as follows.[13]

> When the unbelievers occupy this land
> We must go to war
>
> Don't keep silent and be idle
> Let alone making merry ....
>
> To do fasting and having prayer service are not sufficient
> Unless you go to the war

Two couplets seem to be considered important. They are:

> The unbelievers who attack our country
> Must be fought soon
>
> It is a sin to run away
> Because of the law of *fardhu'ain,* fighting them is a must

The *Hikayat* appears to have been effective in stimulating men, women and children to go to war, even against overwhelmingly superior weapons. Dutch sources reveal that in 1904 alone, 95 women and children were killed by the Dutch in a battle in Penosan; 51 in Tumpeng; 248 in Kuto Reh; 316 in Kuta Lengat Baru.[14] They thought they would be happy in heaven because they died in the *jihad fi sabilillah.*

The *HPS* was usually read just before people went to the battlefield. It is comparable to the story in the Melaka royal chronicle, the *Sejarah Melayu,* when Melaka's warriors asked for the stories of the legendary Arab warrior, the *Hikayat Muhammad Hanafiyah,* to be read before the Portuguese attacked in 1511.[15] During the war against the Dutch, people in Aceh recited the *Hikayat* in *dayah* (Acehnese religious school of the highest level), in *meunasah* (communal hall) and in any other place where people got together to make preparations for the battle. In some places already occupied by the Dutch, people read the *Hikayat* secretly so as not to be caught by the police.

The Dutch military authorities regarded the *HPS* as extremely dangerous and burned all the copies they confiscated. Some copies survived for scholarship only because a Dutch government official and Aceh expert, H.T. Damsté, took the initiative to rescue texts of the *HPS* in order to understand the mentality of the Acehnese. Now copies of the *HPS* are most readily consulted in Leiden University Library.

In the Dutch colonial war in Aceh, the Dutch and the Acehnese put forth brave fighters who fought to defend their respective beliefs. However, as the fighting continued through the first decade of the twentieth century, three prominent resistance leaders, namely Tuanku Mahmud, Tuanku Raja Kumala, and Teuku Panglima Polem, had to rethink their world view concerning the holy war. On 5 August 1909, they appealed to the descendants of Teungku Chik di Tiro Muhammad Saman and other religious leaders, in a letter arguing that if the utmost efforts to resist had proved unsuccessful, and the ability to continue the resistance had become very weak, it was not a mistake to make peace (*taslīm*) with the Dutch, since further resistance would only destroy the country, its people and its religion. Furthermore, the Dutch did not forbid Islam. The Muslims in British India had already made *taslīm*, on the grounds that the British allowed Muslims to practise their faith freely.[16]

Even after the Dutch regarded the Dutch-Aceh War as over, attacks on them continued, launched by individual Acehnese men and women in cities assumed to be safe and peaceful. This was so disturbing that the colonial government in Batavia sent R.A. Kern, adviser for native affairs, in 1921 to Aceh to investigate the phenomena of killing the unbelievers — *poh kaphé* in Acehnese, *Atjehmoord* in Dutch. In the period 1910–21, 99 Dutchmen were attacked in this way. Twelve of them died and the remainder were seriously wounded. Kern in his report put forward the argument that the killers were inspired by hatred toward unbelievers and basically stimulated by the spirit of the Holy War.[17]

The Acehnese *Hikayat Perang Sabil*

The ultimate source for the Holy War idea is naturally the *Holy Qur'an*. This inspired works such as *Mukhtasar Muthiri'l-gharam* (A Brief Account Which Stimulates Passionate Love), copied in 1710 and circulated in Aceh.[18] Another important treatise was *Nasihat al-Muslimin* (Advice to Muslims), written by Syaikh Abdussamad of Palembang (±1704–88).[19] This famous saint emphasised that going to the Holy War is compulsory, and listed all the benefits given by Allah in the hereafter to those who go to fight the infidels. These two main sources were intertextually reproduced Acehnese writings on the subject. In one of the *Hikayat* composed in Acehnese in 1834, long before the Dutch-Aceh War began in 1873, the author acknowledged that his source in writing it was the *Nasihat al-Muslimin* of Syaikh Abdussamad.

A prominent Acehnese *ulama* (religious scholar), Syaikh Abbas ibn Muhammad alias Tgk. Chik Kutakarang, in his 1889 treatise *Tazkirat al-Rakidin* (exhortation to the inactive), presents stories, quoted from *Mukhtasar* mentioned above, of robbers who repented and confessed their sins, turning away from the dark world to the ways of God by participating in the Holy War.[20] He enunciated the central doctrine that Aceh was *Dar-al-Islam* except for the small area controlled by the Dutch which had become *Dar-al-Harb*. Like Syaikh Abdussamad al-Falimbani, Syaikh Abbas also emphasised that it was compulsory (*fardhu 'ain*) for all Muslims, including women and children, to fight to recover the infidel-ruled land for the Darul Islam.

Written indigenous sources concerning the ideology of the Holy War were present in Aceh as early as the seventeenth century, but were revitalised by religious teachers through *HPS*, pamphlets, and letters at times of crisis. One of the *HPS* found in the collection of Leiden University belonged to Tengku Putroë, the first lady of Sultan Muhammad Daud Syah, last ruler of Aceh Darussalam, who was exiled by the Dutch authorities to Ambon in December 1907. This *HPS* was completed on Tuesday, 27 Muharram of 1320 H (1902 AD). At the end of this *HPS* the writer prayed to God that the Sultan be restored to his previous position. Elsewhere in the text he encouraged people to go to the holy war and to donate funds to win the war. He criticised religious scholars who did nothing to win the *perang sabil*.

In this key text of the *HPS*, four stories were presented as parables to inspire the Muslims to voluntarily and sincerely go to *perang sabil*. The first story contained a narrative of Abdul Wahid, a saint who sat in a discussion with some of the elders concerning the holy war against the Dutch [sic]. Others joined the discussion, while somebody read verses of the Qur'an. When verse 111 ("Lo! Allah has bought from the believers their lives and their wealth because the Garden will be theirs" S. 9 al-Taubah) was being read, a young orphan stood up before it was finished. The verse affected his heart so deeply that he asked Abdul Wahid for permission to trade his life for paradise through the holy war. He went home immediately to get clothes, not just for himself but also for all of his friends. He spent all that he had to buy horses and weapons, which were distributed to his comrades, and set off with them and with Abdul Wahid to the holy war. In a dream during the journey, the young man saw an indescribable Heaven, full of gold and pearls, lavishly described in the text. He met beautiful angels, and got into intimate conversations with the most beautiful one, Ainul Mardiyah. When he woke, remembering the wonders of Heaven, he tearfully told Abdul Wahid about his dream, and conveyed his longing for Ainul Mardiyah. Abdul Wahid urged him to go to battle immediately in order to meet the angel without delay. He jumped on his horse, killed many infidels with great spirit, and died in the battle as a martyr.

The angels welcomed him and took him to his heart's desire, Ainul Mardiyah. More than 20 pages of text were taken up with the beauty of Heaven, and of Ainul Mardiyah. The beauty of her yellowish white skin could not be compared with that of any woman in the world. Her calf shone under seven layers of cloth, her legs were like pure gold, and one could not gaze at her face for long without arousing desire. Her voice was as beautiful as the sound of a Persian violin and like melodies produced by a mythical flute, irresistible to men. Other versions of the *HPS* contained the same story in different forms.

A second story in the same text was about a very virtuous king from Bani Israil, whom God endowed with a thousand handsome sons, all of whom died as martyrs in the holy war. A third was also set in the Mecca of the time of the Prophet, but named as Dutch some of the enemy infidels to be defeated and Islamised. The hero of the story lost his precious son while fighting the holy war, but through divine intervention was able to see him again. The fourth story was about Sa'id Salmi, a disciple of the Prophet who was too ugly to attract a woman. Nevertheless the Prophet appreciated his willingness to fight the holy war, and arranged for him to marry the beautiful and virtuous daughter of Umar bin Khattab. Suddenly the Jewish infidels attacked the Muslims, the Prophet declared the *perang sabil*, and Sa'id forgot his desire for a wife in his longing for eternity. Sa'id killed many infidels before meeting his own death in the victorious battle. Sa'id Salmi's body was found by the Prophet, who cried, but then looked to the right and left, and smiled. He explained to his disciples that he was sad because Sa'id's desire in the world did not come true, and he smiled because he saw beautiful angels from heaven competing to have Sa'id. God gave him 70 angels in heaven, delicious food and everlasting happiness.

Besides these four stories and other rewards from God to participants in the holy war, the writer of this *Hikayat* used his pen to show how God helped Muslim troops fighting the infidels. He repeated the pre-Islamic Arab story of *Ashabil fiil*, mentioned in *al-Qur'an*, in which Allah sent birds to throw rocks on an elephant troop which was going to attack the Ka'batullah, killing them all and saving the Ka'bah. Similarly, the writer claimed, the Acehnese were helped by Allah. During the *Perang Sabil* against the Dutch in Idi, east coast of Aceh, he claimed that many infidels died from being struck with knives, whereas the Acehnese fighters had stayed behind in the fort. In other words the writer was aware of what God has predestined. This could be seen in Surah 8 al-Anfal verse 17: "You (Muslims) slew them not, but Allah slew them. And You (Muhammad) threw not when you did throw, but Allah threw, that He might test the believers by a fair test from Him."

The writer reminded his readers that the Prophet once talked about three kinds of eyes that would not shed tears during the doomsday — eyes loyal to God, eyes shut towards prohibited things, and eyes aware of the infidel enemy that would come. If praying a thousand *rakaat* (verse of ritual prayer) in one's own country equals one *rakaat* in Mekkah, he claimed that a thousand in Mekkah equals one before the *perang sabil.*

Holy War in the Era of Independence

During the turbulent 1940s the *HPS* re-emerged as a motif of resistance. Acehnese read the *HPS* and prepared for a martyr's death during the last months of the Japanese occupation, as a resistance to intolerable conditions.[21]

During the war of independence many armed groups emerged in Java, Sumatra and other parts of Indonesia to resist the Dutch, organised by local Muslim leaders with the Holy War idea, *jihād fi sabilillah.* Some of them used the name *Hizbullah* which means the "Army of God". In Aceh, the Muslims organised one army division named Divisi Teungku Chik di Tiro after the most prominent religious leader of the Dutch-Aceh War.

One declaration made by Tgk. Haji Hasan Krueng Kale, Tgk. M. Daud Beureu'eh, Tgk. Haji Ja'far Sidik Lamjabat, and Tgk. Haji Ahmad Hasballah Indrapuri on behalf of the *ulama* of Aceh was acknowledged by the Republican-appointed Resident of Aceh, Teuku Nyak Arif, a former territorial chieftain (*ulèëbalang*). It was approved by Tuanku Mahmud, Chairman of the Regional National Committee and descendant of the sultan of Aceh, on 15 October 1945, a few months after the Declaration of Independence by Soekarno and Hatta. Part of the Declaration reads in translation as follows:

> All the people have united to stand up for the great leader Ir. Soekarno, and are waiting for his orders and the responsibilities they should carry out. It is our conviction that this is a struggle in the way of Allah called "the Holy War".[22]

In 1976 the Free Aceh Movement (GAM), was launched by Tgk. Hasan Tiro. Systematic military repression from the Indonesian government began in 1989 and continued until 1998. After the fall of Suharto a movement for self-determination began to grow rapidly among Acehnese students through organisations such as Aceh Referendum Information Center (Sentral Informasi Referendum Aceh, SIRA). A series of pro-referendum demonstrations occurred in the provincial capital Banda Aceh on 8 November 1999.

In that rally demonstrators recited lyrics from the *HPS*,[23] just as during the war against Dutch colonialism. Despite the interaction with newer ideologies, they persisted with the tradition and rhetoric of Holy War, the belief that had been deeply rooted among the Acehnese people. The propaganda machinery of the Free Aceh Movement tried hard to influence the Acehnese people to view Indonesian rule as colonialist. Edward Aspinall commented in relation to GAM, but also student-led groups like SIRA:

> In materials produced by such groups, the Indonesian government is routinely characterized as the "Javanese colonial government" (*pemerintah penjajah Jawa*: this or some close equivalent tends to be the favored choice for GAM), or the "neo-colonial Indonesian government" (such terms being more commonly used by younger activists).[24]

In a visit to Pidie, one student activist from Gadjah Mada University saw many leaflets distributed especially in the evacuation camps mentioning Indonesia as a colonial state like the Dutch. He added that Acehnese parents had already taught the lyrics of *HPS* in those camps to children of the victims of the Indonesian military operations.[25]

Below are some of the lyrics sung by the students in translation.

> Rather than dying in a bridal room
> I would sooner be killed by the enemy

Rather than dying on a mattress
Let me become a martyr in the battle[26]

Another one runs as follows:

Both heaven and earth are the same
Strong to carry on the rewards
The smell of the track during the *sabil* war
The smell of musk in heaven
My sweetheart, don't be prejudiced
Those who use a gun
Against the infidels, God's enemy
Whether you return or not
You get the rewards and are alive

In short, this theme remains a potent one for Acehnese today.

Notes

[1]   M. Yunan Nasution, *Djihad* (Jakarta: Publicita, 1970), p. 6. Cf. H. Th. Obbink, *De Heilige Oorlog volgens den Koran* (1901), pp. 24–5. See also Rudolph Peters, *Islam and Colonialism: The Doctrine of Jihad in Modern History* (Den Haag: Mouton, 1979), p. 118.

[2]   Abul 'A'la Maududi, *Toward Understanding Islam* (Nairobi: The Islamic Foundation, 1973), p. 107.

[3]   Abduh, *Djihad* (Bandung: Penerbit Peladjar, 1968), p. 7. See also Peters, *Islam and Colonialism.*

[4]   Peters, *Islam and Colonialism,* pp. 118–9.

[5]   A.H. Hill, "Hikayat Raja-raja Pasai", *JMBRAS* 33, 2 (1960): 14.

[6]   Nuru'd-din ar-Raniri, *Bustanu's-Salatin, Bab II, Fasal 13*, ed. T. Iskandar (Kuala Lumpur: Dewan Bahasa dan Pustaka, 1966), pp. 31–2.

[7]   Fernão Mendes Pinto, *The Travels of Mendez Pinto*, trans. Rebecca Catz (Chicago: University of Chicago Press, 1989), pp. 21, 30, 48.

[8]   H.K.J. Cowan, *De Hikayat Malém Dagang* (The Hague: KITLV, 1937), p. 38.

[9]   On the Dutch-Aceh War, see Ibrahim Alfian, *Perang di Jalan Allah* (Jakarta: Sinar Harapan, 1987). See also Ibrahim Alfian *et al.,* ed., *The Dutch Colonial War in Acheh* (Banda Aceh: The Documentation and Information Center of Aceh, 1999), 3rd ed.

[10]   Paul van't Veer, *De Atjeh-Oorlog* (Amsterdam: de Arbeiderspers, 1969).

[11]   *Hikayat Perang Sabil* (*HPS*), Ms. Cod. Or. 8667 (Leiden University Library), pp. 37–8.

[12]   *HPS*, Ms. Cod. Or. 8035 (Leiden University Library), p. 21.

[13]   *HPS*, Ms. Cod. Or. 8163 B (Leiden University Library), pp. 7 and 123–30.

[14]   Ibrahim Alfian, *Perang di Jalan Allah* (Jakarta: Sinar Harapan, 1987), p. 210

[15]   C.C. Brown (ed.), "Sejarah Melayu or Malay Annals", *JMBRAS* 25, 2 & 3 (1952): 168.

[16]   Letter from three prominent resistance leaders to the Tiro Teungkus, 18 Rajab 1327 (5 August 1909), in M. H. du Croo, *De Maréchaussée in Atjeh* (Maastricht: Leiter Nypels, 1943), p. 134. Sayyid Ahmad Khan, an Indian intellectual, was of the opinion "that jihad is only allowed in case of positive oppression or obstruction of the Muslims in the exercise of their faith, impairing the foundation of some of the pillars of Islam". See Rudolf Peters, *Islam and Colonialism: The Doctrine of Jihad in Modern History* (The Hague: Morton, 1979), p. 51.

[17]   R.A. Kern, "Onderzoek Atjeh-moorden", Report to the Governor General in Batavia, 16 December 1921, *Kernpapieren* No. H 797/559 KITLV Leiden.

[18]   *HPS*, Ms. Cod. Or. 8163 B (Leiden University Library).

[19]   G.W.J. Drewes, *Directions for Travelers on the Mystic Path* (The Hague: Martinus Nijhoff, 1977), p. 223.

[20]   *HPS*, Ms. Cod. Or. 8038 (Leiden University Library), p. 186.

[21]   Anthony Reid, *The Blood of the People: Revolution and the End of Traditional Rule in Northern Sumatra* (Kuala Lumpur, New York: OUP, 1979), p. 137.

[22]   See the copy of the Declaration, in Teuku Ibrahim Alfian, *Wajah Aceh dalam Lintasan Sejarah* (Banda Aceh: The Documentation and Information Center of Aceh, 1999), p. 236.

[23]   *Kompas*, Pustakaloka, 24 January 2004.

[24]   Aspinall, "Sovereignty, the Successor State and Universal Human Rights", *Indonesia* 73 (2002): 10.

[25]   See Ulyati Retno Sari, "Song as the Resistance Language against Domination: A Case Study on 'Hikayat Perang Sabil' in Aceh and 'Oh freedom' in the Black American Society" (unpublished MA Thesis, Gadjah Mada University, Graduate Study Program, 2004), p. 62.

[26]   Ibid., pp. 60–1.

8

From Autonomy to Periphery: A Critical Evaluation of the Acehnese Nationalist Movement[1]

M. Isa Sulaiman

The leading question of this chapter is why the Acehnese nationalist movement, *Gerakan Aceh Merdeka* (GAM, or Free Aceh Movement) under the leadership of Hasan Muhammad di Tiro, has been revolting against Indonesia since 1976. The phenomenon has attracted the attention of experts, including Kell, Robinson, Aspinall, and Siapno, to find out the causes.[2] Basically, they think the root causes of the separatist movement are the New Order Regime, which exploited natural resources but brought loss to the province, as well as the doctrine or actions of the military in suppressing the revolt. On the other hand, Sukma holds that the rise of GAM at the beginning of the reform era resulted from the fall of the authoritarian government, which had been in power for over 30 years, the ambivalence of the government in handling it, and the economic crisis.[3] To find an external factor for the intensification of the revolt among Acehnese seems justified because Aceh is a part the national political environment with Jakarta as its centre. However, the question remains why intransigent revolts have occurred repeatedly only in Aceh? In other regions, opposition to the central government was either absent, or declined in scale once political concessions were granted. For example, Riau suffered greater exploitation of its natural resources by the government, yet the movement for autonomy led by Tabrani Rab, which appeared at the beginning of the Reform era, did not turn to armed rebellion. Violent actions by the army occurred in many parts of the Archipelago, but did not provoke the same response as in Aceh.

Even so, it cannot be denied that this revolt grew from a very complex situation. Besides economic and political analysis, we will have difficulties in understanding the cause of the conflict until the political biography of Hasan di Tiro is analysed because Hasan himself formulated the concept of nationalism, proclaimed the movement and has been leading it. He not only played an important role in the Darul Islam revolt from 1954, but also initiated the "social revolution" in Aceh in 1946.

The first part of this chapter will discuss the economic exploitation of Aceh since the colonial era. Colonial policies made Aceh a producer of raw materials for the national economy, and resulted in the emergence of deprived groups among the peripheral communities. The second part will present the emergence of young Hasan di Tiro in the struggle to topple the colonial-feudal power, which was accompanied by the autonomy enjoyed by the PUSA (*Persatuan Ulama Seluruh Aceh,* or All Acehnese Religious Scholars) elites. The third part will analyse the role of Hasan di Tiro in the Darul Islam revolt and his efforts with a group of hardliners in demanding the status of a federal state for the region of Aceh. The fourth part is about the nationalism concept of Hasan di Tiro and his struggles to achieve it. In the conclusion I make a comparison between GAM and a similar movement, the Moro nationalist movement in southern Philippines.

Colonial Legacy, Marginalisation and the Emergence of Relative Deprivation

The exploitation of natural resources in Aceh began a century ago when the Dutch integrated Aceh into the Netherlands East Indies. The colonial government constructed an economic and communications infrastructure, initially to serve military purposes but later to meet economic needs. However, the infrastructure was developed for new growth centres in Medan and Batavia. This brought about double consequences: on the one hand Aceh was integrated with the rest of the Indonesian Archipelago; on the other it became a peripheral region. The economic infrastructure naturally encouraged capitalists, generally from outside Aceh, to come and exploit this area of 57,635 sq. km. That situation was clearly seen in the early 1900s when a Dutch oil company, NKPM (*Nederland Koninklijk Petroleum Maatschappij*) with its main office in Pangkalan Brandan, East Sumatra, explored Peureulak and expanded to Tamiang, East Aceh after 1928. Oil from that area was piped to Pangkalan

Brandan for distillation or export. In 1908, a Belgian Company based in East Sumatra, Socfin (*Societe Financière des Cautchouc*), also set up palm and rubber plantations in East Aceh. Commercial agriculture developed rapidly and expanded into many areas. There were 150 estates at the end of the colonial period.[4] In short, the economic policy caused Aceh to become a producer of raw materials to support the national economy and world market; at the same time, it was the capitalists from outside the region who benefited from it.

Economic development also attracted migrants. They arrived in Aceh in huge numbers, which changed the demographic balance. According to the census of 1930, about 12 per cent of the 1,003,063 residents in Aceh were migrants. The biggest group were Javanese, who numbered 60,236; the Chinese numbered 21,775.[5] The flow of migrants to Aceh was not a new phenomenon. However, in contrast to previous periods, migration was now on a large scale. The migrants generally settled down in cities, plantations or mining areas run by capitalists, and no integration with local residents took place, as a result of the Dutch segregation policy.

The natives of Aceh were mostly multi-lingual. The dominant group was Acehnese who comprised 85 per cent of the population and spread throughout the area.[6] Six other minority groups lived either in the hinterland or border areas. The biggest of these were Gayo, who numbered around six per cent. The minority groups had been integrated with the Acehnese through Islam and through long-term subordination to the Sultanate of Aceh. Besides, socio-economic networks, especially marriage alliances, integrated the various groups.

When the world economy with segregationist policies entered the villages, it seemed that only the nobility were ready to benefit from the changes. With their high socio-economic status as territorial chiefs, *ulèëbalang*, or as officials in the colonial bureaucracy, they were generally able to obtain Western education. With capital in their hands, the *ulèëbalang* tended to control the land under their jurisdiction, especially paddy fields. Some villagers were forced to mortgage or sell their land to satisfy the capitalists' needs which were increasingly becoming consumerist. At the same time, the villagers had to meet tax requirements: the poorest paid F1 per head, as well as forced labour of 15 days a year for a male adult, or substituted for F5-6. In rice-growing areas like Pidie, the *ulèëbalang* controlled hundreds of hectares of land.[7]

The control of production undoubtedly had political implication in the framework of strengthening patron-client relationship between territorial chiefs and farmers. However, that relationship brought about greater disparity between their lives. Mr T. Hanafiah, an Acehnese lawyer practicing in Medan, pointed out that a farmer who worked on a 0.25-hectare paddy field in Pidie in 1939 earned F80 a year, which was far lower than a labourer's income. The situation was made worse by the tax and forced labour as well as the increase in consumption as the world economy crept into the villages. In a speech to the PUSA Congress on 24 April 1940, T. Hanafiah called on the government to reconsider the tax and labour imposed upon the people because most Acehnese were living in utter poverty.[8] Hamka, former Editor of *Pedoman Masjarakat* in Medan, described the living conditions of the poor villagers as "sinking in ignorance, lack of education and utter poverty", while the *ulèëbalang* lived in extravagance.[9]

However, this does not mean all villagers lived in poverty. Some switched jobs to trade, or increased their income by growing commercial crops. Piekaar shows that in 1939, the export of Aceh besides rice included 1,300 tons of rubber, 25,000 tons of areca-nut, 12,150 tons copra, 158 tons patchouli oil, and 833 tons pepper.[10]

A dualistic economic pattern persisted into the independence era. However, the wars and the revolts between 1942 and 1962 heavily damaged the economic infrastructure. Moreover, the economic policies of the central government after 1950 disadvantaged Acehnese traders and had an adverse impact on the local economy. They included the abolition of barter trade between Aceh and the Malay Peninsula, the implementation of codes for trade, and the designation of Belawan as the export port for North Sumatra.[11]

The wars and revolts also affected the oil industry, which provided the main natural resource of Aceh, with its refineries being successively burnt down in 1942 and 1947. After being repaired, the oilfields were managed by the Japanese military and later transferred to the TMSU (*Tambang Minyak Sumatra Utara*, or North Sumatra State Oilfield Enterprise) in 1946. Until 1953 the TMSU, headed by Tgk. A Husin Al Mujahid (1910–83), had its office in Langsa. After he joined in the Darul Islam rebellion on 21 September 1953, its main office was moved back to Pangkalan Brandan. But on 10 December 1957, the TMSU became Permina (*Perusahaan Minyak Nasional*, or State Oilfield Enterprise; then on 20 August 1968, *Pertamina*) headed by Maj. Gen. Ibnu Sutowo with its head office in Jakarta. In the early 1960s the Permina cooperated with the Kobayashi Group, a Japanese oil consortium, and Asamera Inc. of Canada to explore oil in East Aceh. In the early 1970s

Pertamina cooperated with Mobil Oil to explore natural gas in North Aceh.[12] In 1973, they formed PT Arun NGL, a joint venture enterprise, to exploit natural gas of the area. Such efforts made Aceh a large producer of natural gas for the national economy, as at its peak, between the mid-1980s and the mid-1990s, the gas export from Aceh reached more than US$2 billion per annum.[13]

Damaged in the wars, commercial plantations decreased to 52 estates in 1968, covering 131,000 ha resin, 88,850 ha rubber/palm oil, and 376 ha Arabica coffee. The estates were no longer owned by foreigners. After the sovereignty recognition, only 30 estates were restored to their former owners, while the others were appropriated by the government to become *Perusahaan Perkebunan Negara* (PPN, State-owned Plantations) and Indonesian businessmen. Most European capitalists sold them immediately due to the Darul Islam rebellion. In 1968, only 7 out of 52 estates were owned by joint-venture companies, and the rest were owned by the government or Indonesian businessmen.[14] In 1987, when Governor Ibrahim Hasan (1986–93) launched the programme "the Agricultural Zone" to make use of the former felling area of companies enjoying *Hak Pengusahaan Hutan* (HPH, or License to Exploit the Woods), investors from outside the region, often in collaboration with local bureaucrats or contractors, came to open up plantation estates especially palm oil. By the end of the New Order Era, nearly one million hectares of land had received *Hak Guna Usaha* (HGU, or Land Concession) permits, with 350,000 hectares of oil palm owned by 121 companies.[15]

Moreover, the need for foreign exchange to support national development for growth encouraged the New Order government to invite investors to exploit the jungle of Aceh, which had comprised 3.4 million hectares. In 1975 alone, 20 HPH companies obtained permits for tree felling from the Ministry of Forestry, in an area covering 1,095,500 ha. The total number of enterprises and the area of felling rose steadily, from the mid-1970s to early 1990s, until Aceh's timber export reached US$450 million per year.[16] However, the profits were only enjoyed by the capitalists, who generally came from outside of the region especially Medan and Jakarta, and who received support from the government.

The extensive exploitation of land for gas, timber and large plantations caused various adverse economic and ecologic impact on the people. The problem was that the procedure to determine the site of concessions was through a top-down mechanism without considering the customs of the area concerned. As a result, a clash of interests occurred between the HPH/HGU usage and local customary practices, especially in traditional felling and livestock areas. Various incidents occurred between HPH/HGU holders and local residents, including between PT Alas Helau and the people of Central Aceh, between PT Indonusa and the people of Aceh Besar/Pidie, between PT Karya Subur and the people of Kaway XVI (West Aceh), as well as between PT Cemerlang Abadi and the people of Kuala Bate (South Aceh). In every case, the capitalists obtained the services of the security apparatus to protect their interests from the protestors.[17] On the other hand, the release of the land for industrial use had made proletarians out of the people, because they received little compensation from their agricultural lands.

Hence, the economic policy orientated towards growth brought little benefit to the local economy. The high GDP of Aceh, as a result of its contribution of gas since the 1980s, did not immediately elevate the local standard of living. One comparative analysis by Booth found that in 1987 the consumption per capita per year in Aceh was US$168, compared to the high GDP per capita of US$1,021.[18] However, on a closer observation, poverty struck more in Pidie and North Aceh with their high population density and reliance on a rice-based economy, despite sharing the area with gas exploitation. The indication could be clearly seen from the proportion of poor villages, 64 per cent and 52 per cent respectively, in these two areas in 1994.[19] Major Heros Paddupai, Commander of Satgassus Tribuana III, who carried out an order resto-ration operation in North Aceh in 1998, expressed worry that the high poverty level in North Aceh was making the people restless.[20] In short, the conditions of the poor in Aceh at the time of the New Order did not experience any qualitative improvement when compared to the conditions during the colonial period.

Hasan di Tiro, The Fall of Colonial-feudal Power and Autonomy

Hasan di Tiro was born in 1923 in the village of Tanjong Bungong, in the *ulèëbalang* jurisdiction of V Mukim Cumbok, Lameulo, Pidie, into the colonial-feudal society described above. He was the great-grandson in the maternal line of Tgk Chik di Tiro M. Saman. The latter, who died in 1891, was an *ulama* and leader fighting the Dutch during the Acehnese War; so were his children and grandchildren.[21] Hasan di Tiro's father was an ordinary person but respected in his village. Like most young Acehnese of his generation, Hasan di Tiro attended a religious school.

He frequented the *Madrasah Saadah al Abadiyah* which was headed by Daud Beureu'eh, 1899–1987, and afterwards *Perguruan Normal Islam,* the religious teachers' school that was set up by PUSA on 27 December 1939, under Nur El Ibrahimy (f. 1914). It was there that he initially participated in the PUSA organisation as a scout activist.[22]

Hasan di Tiro apparently received Indonesia's independence with much enthusiasm. In Aceh itself, independence was marked by the appointment of T. Nyak Arif, *Panglima Sagi XXVI Mukim* (one of the three prominent nobles in Great Aceh) and former head of the Aceh Council, as the First Resident by the Government of the Republic of Indonesia on 3 October 1945. In the eyes of Hasan di Tiro, the Dutch were not able to suppress the determination of the Indonesian people for independence or a martyr's death.[23] He and his associates enthusiastically formed the PRI (*Pemuda Republik Indonesia,* which later became *Pesindo* — Indonesian Socialist Youth). He was head of the PRI Lameulo branch for a short while in early November 1945. However, the organisation was formed in an atmosphere of tension between the nobles and the militant group in their respective areas of jurisdiction, which had been going on since the period of Japanese occupation.[24] The *ulèëbalang* were suspicious about the competing movements. The most aggressive of them was T. Daud Cumbok (1910–46), head of the Lameulo district, who formed armed militia to protect *ulèëbalang* against the radicals.[25]

The existence of the two competing militia groups caused various incidents as both strove to protect their own interests. The Aceh Residency Government of T. Nyak Arif was still too weak to act as a mediator and was busy with the Japanese evacuation and the arrival of the Allied Forces (including the Dutch who wanted to re-establish power). The *ulèëbalang*-militia conflict went out of the government's control. Believing that they were defenders of the Republic against *ulèëbalangs* who sided with the Dutch, the people's militia declared holy war against the nobles.[26] As a result, the Cumbok War was fought between 22 December 1945 and 13 January 1946 in Lameulo, Pidie. This was followed a month later by an expedition by the TPR (*Tentera Perjuangan Rakyat* — The People Struggle Army) led by Husin al Mujahid. Around 150 nobles were killed in battle or executed, and around 60 more were imprisoned. Only underage men, women and those who were capable of establishing good relations with the militia escaped the violence. Following that, the properties of the nobles who were involved in the Cumbok War were confiscated on the grounds of repaying the losses caused by the war. However, confiscation of property extended to other *ulèëbalang.*[27]

The positions vacated by the *ulèëbalang* were filled immediately by the leaders of the militia affiliated to PUSA. Hasan di Tiro chose to move to Yogyakarta to continue his education at the Law Faculty of University Islam Indonesia. The Provincial Government of Sumatra could only acquiesce in what had been done by the militia. It became even weaker after its capital Pematang Siantar was occupied by the Dutch on 29 July 1947, beginning the Second Aggression. Vice-President Hatta, who was at that time making a working visit to Sumatra, had to organise a government which made Daud Beureu'eh, Aceh's strongman, military governor on 26 August 1947. With that, the domination of PUSA in the political arena of Aceh was complete.

With that domination, the finance of Aceh's *madrasahs* was taken over by a local government office headed by Nur El Ibrahimy (later Ismail Yakub). They also formed the *Mahkamah Syariah* (Syariah Court) in each district, which was headed by Tgk Hasballah Indrapuri (1888– 1958) at the Residency level, until the Religious Office of Aceh headed by Daud Beureu'eh (later Nur El Ibrahimy and Wahab Seulimeum) emerged with an extensive power base. From this position, they issued various regulations to put religious life into order, including the fixing of the fasting month *Ramadhan*, a ban on various practices that they regarded as superstitious, a ban on gambling, theft and adultery, and also a ban on *seudati* (an Acehnese traditional dance).[28] An associate of Daud Beureu'eh, Husin Al Mujahid, was entrusted to manage the oil fields, and Said Abu Bakar (1916–77) managed the plantation estates in East Aceh to supply funds for their struggle. In short, the PUSA leadership controlled political and economic life in Aceh during the War of Independence. The confiscated properties of the *ulèëbalang* were managed by an Advisory Council (*Majelis Penimbang*), which was formed on the basis of a Local regulation of Aceh Residency (*Perda* No. 1) on 24 June 1946.[29] This Board with almost absolute power not only managed the properties, but also returned some to rightful owners or traded others to third parties.[30]

Having such practical autonomy, the PUSA leaders gave full support to the central government. They sent hundreds of soldiers to Langkat, under command of Major Hasballah Haji and later Major M. Nazir, to confront Dutch forces in the Medan area, constituting a KSBO (*Komando Sektor Barat dan Oetara Medan*). They gave constant financial support to the central government, purchasing national bonds in mid-1946 and buying two aircraft in mid-1948.[31] It was a recognition of Acehnese reliability that Vice Premier Sjafruddin Prawiranegara had his office in

Kutaradja from August till December 1949, to be prepared for the likely failure of the Round Table Conference in Den Haag.

The intervention by the leadership of PUSA in the management of natural resources and of *ulèëbalang* property earned a reaction from those who had suffered politically. They protested at what was done by Said Ali in Kutaradja (Banda Aceh) in the second half of 1948 and the operations by the labour group led by Riphat Senikentra, former editor of *Sinar Deli Medan*, in Langsa in early May in 1949.[32] However, the protests were easily overcome by Daud Beureu'eh, and the leaders imprisoned. Dissatisfaction remained latent among the group.

Hasan di Tiro returned to Aceh in this tense situation on the personal staff of Vice Premier Syafruddin Prawiranegara, who opened his office in Kutaradja.[33] Solving the increasingly complicated problem of the *ulèëbalangs* became the most urgent priority in anticipation of the end of the Dutch-Indonesian conflict following the recognition of sovereignty. With his experience in the Cumbok War, Hasan di Tiro issued a white paper entitled *Repolusi Desember '45: Pembasmian Peng-khianat Tanah Air* (December Revolution '45: Eradication of Traitors).[34] He and his associates lobbied Syafrudin Prawinegara, already a Masyumi figure sympathetic with PUSA, both on the detained *ulèëbalangs* and on making Aceh a separate province instead of part of North Sumatra as prescribed in Law No. 10/1948.[35] After obtaining verbal consent from Hatta as Premier and Vice-President, Syafrudin issued two decrees directed to the former military governors of Aceh and of Tapanuli-East Sumatra. The first on 17 December 1949 concerned the formation of the Province of Aceh with effect from 1 January 1950. The second on 21 December ordered the release of the imprisoned *ulèëbalangs*.

Hasan di Tiro returned to Yogyakarta and soon thereafter went to New York to study at Colombia University. His associates in Aceh formed the Provincial Council with 26 seats on 21 January 1950. It was dominated by PUSA as 24 seats were occupied by its national-level vehicle, *Masyumi*, one by PSII and one by a minority Chinese. This composition paved the way for Daud Beureu'eh to become the governor of Aceh.

Darul Islam Rebellion, Hasan di Tiro and the Struggle for a Federated State

During Hasan di Tiro's stay in New York, his associates were extremely disappointed with a series of measures carried out by Jakarta towards

Aceh, which culminated in the abolition of Aceh Province on 25 January 1951. The initial impact of the abolition of autonomy was that 199 religious schools and the Syariah Court went into disarray financially because their finance had been the responsibility of the province. Those schools consisted of SRI (*Sekolah Rendah Islam* — Islamic Primary School, a conversion from primary *madrasahs*), SMI (*Sekolah Menengah Islam* — Islamic Secondary School) and SMIA (*Sekolah Menengah Islam Atas* — Islamic Senior High School). The abolition of the province, including the military demobilisation earlier, caused much dissatisfaction among the Acehnese because they were no longer able to enjoy the revenue from the local government. At the same time, the *ulèëbalangs* used the political situation to claim their properties from the Advisory Council, which continued to claim that what it did was only to fulfil the local government regulation No.1/1946.[36] The disgruntled *ulèëbalang* families attempted to take back their paddy fields and plantation estates directly, whether from the authority of the Advisory Council or from the third parties to which they had been transferred. This resulted in sporadic incidents between the aristocrats and those controlling the lands.[37]

These conditions were immediately politicised and exploited by Daud Beureu'eh to mobilise his followers to resist the government. He announced on 21 September 1953 that the whole region of Aceh was declared part of *Negara Islam Indonesia* (NII Indonesia Islamic State) which was proclaimed by Kartosuwiryo on 8 August 1949.[38] His armed units began attacks on security posts and government offices to seize arms and to take over power. The aristocrats who had claimed their property also became initial targets. In the early days of the rebellion, around 390 *ulèëbalang* and their followers in Pidie district became victims of abduction or murder.[39] Understandably those who managed to escape immediately took up the position of fighting against the rebellion.

Regarding his struggle as a holy war (*yuqtal au yaghlib*) to uphold the law of religion, Daud Beureu'eh immediately imposed tithe, the duty of paying *infaq* (war fees) on those who were not fighting, and a death sentence to whomever he felt was harming the struggle, like the followers of the nobles.[40] However, the violent actions of Daud Beureu'eh in his struggle for the Negara Islam were opposed by the traditional *ulama* and the *tarekat* leaders who had been out of power before this. For example Tgk. Mudawali Al Khalidy (1917–61), the leader of the Darussalam *pesantren* and Naqshabandiah *tarekat* in Labuhan Haji, attacked the *modus operandi* of Daud Beureu'eh. On the basis of scriptural evidence, Mudawali issued a *fatwa* (legal ruling by a Muslim Jurist) stating that the movement of Daud Beureu'eh was *bughat* (a revolt towards a legal government) and as such forbidden, as the position of President Sukarno was now legal as *Sultanah* with *istila* (the power of arms and army).[41]

The difference in opinion among the people of Aceh regarding the rebellion proved to be an advantage for the government in its attempt to restore order. By the end of November 1953, it had driven the rebels into the hinterlands. Yet the operation did not succeed in suppressing them as the rebels adopted guerrilla tactics. Moreover, the political complexies at the national level due to the clash among the elites caused the government to act intermittently in its attempt to suppress the rebellion.[42]

Prime Minister Ali Sastroamijoyo stressed armed suppression more than dialogue, and caused much anxiety for Hasan di Tiro, who was at that time working at the Information Department in the Indonesian Embassy at the United Nations in New York. The problem was that his associates and relations were actively involved as leaders of the rebellion. On 1 September 1954, he sent an ultimatum to the Premier to demand that he change his policy of restoring order by force to one of dialogue by 20 September 1954, otherwise Tiro would begin to act as a representative of DI (Darul Islam) in the international forum. Enraged, Ali Sastroamijoyo ordered the return of Hasan di Tiro to Indonesia by 22 September 1954, under threat of having him deported.[43]

With that, Hasan di Tiro became an important overseas force for Daud Beureu'eh in forging alliances with other separatist groups. He made frequent visits to the Malayan Peninsula to meet with other Indonesian dissidents, particularly envoys of Kahar Muzakkar.[44] He also corresponded with ten Islamic countries in South Asia and the Middle East and appealed to them to boycott the Afro-Asia Conference which was being held in Bandung in 1955 as the government had been massacring Islamic people in Indonesia. However, his calls were ignored by those countries.[45]

At the same time, Hasan di Tiro was reflecting on the foundation or the shape of nationhood that would fit Indonesia best with its heterogeneous population. He thought the problem was that the form of a unitary state and the democracy of "one man one vote" did not bring justice to minority groups.[46] He felt the ideal nationhood for the multi-ethnic population of Indonesia was federation with Islam as its base.[47] His idea of nationhood apparently obtained support from his associates in Aceh, as on 23 September 1955 Daud Beureu'eh changed the military *Komandemen V NII* to *NBA-NII* (*Negara Bagian Aceh* or State of Aceh).[48]

Tiro also tried to convince other separatist groups of the federal idea during their meetings in Geneva in mid-December 1958, where he joined Hasan Ali, the *NBA-NII* Premier, as its representative. He sought to insert these same ideas into the *Republik Persatuan Indonesia* (RPI), formed on 8 February 1960 under his former boss Sjafruddin Prawira-negara. He became the international envoy for this RPI.[49]

The religious slogans of the rebels were answered by the government's own religious approach. This was seen in the early days of the rebellion, when the Minister of Religious Affairs KH Masykur accompanied governor Amin around Aceh in early November 1954. His speeches to the people would include verses from the *Qur'an* intended to show God's condemnation of the rebels — "God will punish those who destroy those who destroy unity among the *ummat* and those who create disturbances on earth" (verse *Al-Maidah*). They also approached the *ulamas* who were not on the side of Daud Beureu'eh. In 1957, the Department of Religion took over financial responsibility for religious schools and the Syariah Court. To add to that, the Syariah Faculty in Kutaradja that became the embryo of *IAIN Araniry* (the State Islamic Institute) was opened in early 1960. The Great Mosque in Kutaradja was declared a national one and expanded from three domes to five. In short, the government policy increased the number of religious elites in the administration, which in turn made them into government spokespersons.

The rebels' demand for an Aceh Province was also revisited by the government, which on 29 November 1956 issued Law No. 24 concerning the formation of the Province of Aceh on 1 January 1957. The governor-ship was entrusted to a PUSA activist and also former rebel, Ali Hasjmy. The status of the Aceh military was elevated from Regiment to *Kodam Iskandar Muda* (Regional Military Commando), whose commander-in-chief was Lt. Col. (later Colonel) Syamaun Gaharu. Acehnese military units that had been on duty outside Aceh were brought back to restore order. These actions automatically increased the number of Acehnese in the government administration. At the same time, Syamaun Gaharu requested permission from the army commander-in-chief A.H. Nasution to revive barter trade between Aceh and the Malay Peninsula from mid-1957.[50] This paved the way for traders to deal in import and export, and provided income for the area. In short, these government policies won over more and more Acehnese elites to their side.

With the authority they now held, Ali Hasjmy and Syamaun Gaharu began a personal approach towards the rebel leaders. The contacts resulted in the *Lamteh* Charter on 8 April 1957 which contained an agreement for a truce until negotiations could take place. However, the negotiations got into difficulty on the issue of the final status of Aceh. The problem was precisely that Daud Beureu'eh had adopted the federated state as the status of Aceh. Only when the government agreed to give that status to Aceh on the basis of Islam could peace be achieved.[51]

It appeared that disagreement on this issue caused a rift among the rebel leaders. Those led by Daud Beureu'eh stood firm on the federated state, as did Hasan di Tiro when he returned home to meet with his comrades during the truce in 1959. He convinced them that he was cooperating with other regional movements to establish a federal state. The moderate ones led by Hasan Saleh (1922–97), an ex-Captain who deserted the Army in September 1953, separated from Daud Beureu'eh and named their group the Revolutionary Council on 15 March 1959.[52] It was the latter group who negotiated with Vice Premier Hardi in Kutaradja from 25–26 March 1959. They eventually reached an agreement whereby the government would grant amnesty to the rebels, provide rehabilitation to those from the officers or police, and accommodate their armed units into the regular military and provide jobs for those not accommodated. Most important was the willingness of Hardi to issue a decree stating that the status of the province of Aceh would be changed to the Special Region Of Aceh, which would control religion, custom, tradition and education so long as they would not contradict with Law No. 1/1957 with regard to the basis of the provincial government.[53]

The internal rift in Darul Islam and the increasing number of leaders whose needs were now fulfilled by the government inevitably weakened the position of Daud Beureu'eh. Moreover, the RPI under which they had taken shelter was thrown into disorder by the government in mid-1961. Daud Beureu'eh was left with no choice but to return to his homeland on 7 May 1962.[54] Hasan di Tiro did not surrender to the government and remained abroad.

Hasan di Tiro and GAM

The special region status issued by Vice Premier Hardi was never reinforced by any higher legislation and the details were not implemented either. The only body formed as a manifestation of the special region status was the *Majelis Ulama* (Council of Ulama) in 1966. However, since 1975, its functions became only an extension of the *Majelis Ulama Indonesia* at the provincial level.[55] The *Majelis Ulama* was made into an advisory board to the Governor on religious issues, and was headed by

Tgk. Abdullah Ujung Rimba (1900–82), the former Head of *Syariah* Court. The board was a hierarchical organisation whose members comprised local *ulamas*. With operational funds coming from the local government, it could be noted that its position was inclined towards becoming an instrument of the local government.

Even if the Special Region status had been implemented, there would have been a problem with finance. Since the early 1950s, Aceh's income had depended heavily on the central government. Law No. 32/1956, concerning the financial balance between the centre and the regions, in fact strengthened the financial hold of the central government in the region because a large portion of revenue from taxes and leases went into the coffers of Jakarta.[56] The barter trade with the Peninsula which was revived by Syamaun Gaharu in 1958 was abolished by the government in early 1960 to coincide with the opening of the free port in Sabang. However, Sabang at the far western end of Sumatra was never more than an entry point for some imported goods, and lacked even a significant hinterland for that purpose. With the opening of a free port in Batam, the free port in Sabang was closed in 1985. Eventually, all of Aceh's produce during the New Order except natural gas and fertiliser was exported through Belawan, reducing local income.[57] The main natural resources in Aceh, oil and natural gas, did not contribute much to the local economy, since these industries were directly controlled by the central government. The local government and elite from 1957 until 1966 repeatedly sent out petitions and lobbied the government to return ten per cent of the revenue from oil production from the region for its development.[58] However, the government remained evasive regarding this request and just provided aid that appeared to be incidental and an act of charity.

The New Order government was obsessed with national integration, imposing various assimilation policies which tended to promote Javanese culture. This could be seen through the implementation of *Pancasila* as the sole basis of organisation, homogenisation of village administration (Law No. 5/1979), and the centralised planning of school curricula. These policies gave rise to anxiety in areas like Aceh with their own longstanding cultural traditions.

The anger over Aceh's subordination to the central government, as stated above, did not emerge from within the established elites whose needs were already met, nor did it originate from the poorest sector who were generally resigned to their fate, but came from the educated who, nonetheless, had a major obsession to improve their region. It was Hasan di Tiro who had yet to make peace with the government. With the fall of RPI in mid-1961, as mentioned earlier, Hasan di Tiro was at a loss for ideas to create the federate state in Indonesia like what he had hoped for. His anger was increased by his failure to obtain the contract for the *PT Arun* development project for the exploitation of natural gas in North Aceh in the mid-1970s.[59]

The experience of previous movements being classified as "separatists" by the government and the UN Declaration regarding rights of self-determination inspired Hasan di Tiro to reformulate his goal.[60] He depicted it not as an action to break away from the Indonesian State, but to restore the sovereignty of Aceh as it was before the Aceh War on 26 March 1873.[61] Because of that, Hasan di Tiro condemned the Dutch annexation of Aceh and also its transfer to Indonesia at the Round Table Conference in 1949 as illegal. He also claimed that the Sultan (Muhammad Daud Syah, 1878–1903) had given power to one of his ancestors, Tgk M. Saman di Tiro, to lead the struggle against the Dutch aggressors, and that authority was then passed to his descendent Tgk Maad di Tiro, who died on 4 December 1911. The short Agreement (*Korte Verklaring*), that the chiefs (*ulèëbalang*) signed with the Dutch was regarded as illegal by him, because only the Sultan had the right to sign agreements with foreign powers.[62]

With this logic, Hasan di Tiro claimed that *Negara Aceh Sumatra*, which he proclaimed on 4 December 1976 was a "Successor State" freed from Dutch colonisation, and was transferred on 27 December 1949 to Indonesia, which he pictured as "neo-colonialist".[63] Anticipating the Islam-phobia of the West, he did not declare Islam as the basis of the Acehnese national state he was struggling for. However, this did not mean that Hasan di Tiro was denying Islam. In his many speeches and pamphlets through which he communicated with the people, including also *de facto* members' pledge (*baiat*), it was always stressed that GAM would always uphold Islam as the religion that is the pride of the Acehnese.[64] Because of that, it is not surprising that the GAM fighters regarded their struggle as a holy war (*udep sare mate syahid*) although they were fighting against the Indonesian government whose majority were Muslims.

However, the Islamic slogans of GAM apparently were not enough to attract the *ulamas* to their side. Their needs had been largely met through the bureaucratisation of the religious board, which was started as early as 1957. The Ulama Council led by Tgk. Abdullah Ujung Rimba, and later Ali Hasjmy, called on the rebels to settle the dispute with the government peacefully and persuaded the people not to side with the nationalist movement in June 1978 and June 1990.[65] The traditional *ulamas* and the *tarekat* leaders had a moderate interpretation of religion in its relation with the state. When GAM committed violent acts, *ulamas* such as Tgk. Usman Ali Kutakrueng, Tgk. Ali Irsyad and Tgk. Amin Blang Bladeh in 1990–91 repeatedly reminded the people that violent actions that destroy the unity of the people are forbidden by the religion.[66] Furthermore, traditional *ulamas* of Pengurus Dayah Inshafudin led by Tgk. Daud Zamzam (f. 1938), and Ahlussunnah Waljamaah led by Tgk. Abu Bakar Sabil (f. 1938), issued *fatwas* in 1997 and 2002 which stated that fighting a legal government is *bughat* as in the *fatwa* issued by Mudawali against the Darul Islam previously.[67]

Hasan di Tiro tried to eliminate cross-ethnic national loyalty that was already formed in the post Aceh War generation as it could make the younger generations forget about their identity as Acehnese. He introduced new national symbols of Aceh taking inspirations from myths of past glory and the heroism of the people in fighting the Dutch. It was reflected in the national symbol, national flag, national calendar and also language. The polarisation between the *ulamas* and the nobles since 1945 apparently preoccupied Hasan di Tiro. Therefore he called on them to reconcile by symbolizing it through the letter "T" (short for *Teungku, Tuwanku and Teuku*) in the "State" symbol.[68] It seems Hasan di Tiro did not realise how much the social structure of Acehnese society had changed, so that the nobles were no longer as dominant as they had been.

The backward-looking concept of nationalism in Aceh sparked off by Hasan di Tiro was sometimes interpreted as the "classic" concept, "undemocratic", because it could lead to the rise of ethnic sentiments with claims that the Sultanate of Aceh had previously extended beyond the present administrative territory and pressure to evacuate thousands of Javanese settlers to other areas through intimidation.[69] Such a worry was understandable. However, the "anti-Java attitude" which surrounded the movement was caused more by political-economic factors than racial/ethnic ones because national politics was dominated by the Javanese and the Javanese settlers of Gayo Highland were employed as militias by the military.[70] Hasan di Tiro and his associates moved in 2002 to clarify their stand on territory, state characteristics and the basis of Acehnese citizenship. They stated that their state territory was that of Aceh at the beginning of the colonial war, or more precisely the present administrative territory of Aceh. Their Successor State was based on

Fig. 8 Hasan Tiro standing on a river raft in Northeast Aceh during the DI revolt in 1958 (*courtesy William Nessen and Hassan Di Tiro*)

democracy while the citizenship of Aceh was based on "*ius sanguinis*" for the definition of race, but should be implemented on the basis of "*ius soli*" especially for those who had resided in Aceh before the proclamation in 1976.[71]

The structural condition of Aceh had undergone profound changes from the time when Daud Beureu'eh started the rebellion. The development process and bureaucratisation had given rise to a larger middle-class group in Aceh, comprised of the intelligentsia, officials and politicians absorbed into the local government as well as businessmen who worked as government contractors and suppliers. The government, including its security apparatus, was in a more solid position compared to the 1950s. Another important factor is that Hasan di Tiro had been away for such a long time that his ties with the people were almost broken.

So, it was understandable that Hasan di Tiro initially tried to persuade his former teacher to lead the struggle he planned. However, his advanced age prevented Daud Beureu'eh from coming forward as a

Fig. 9   Later GAM military commander Muzakkir Manaf saluting Hasan Tiro at Acehnese training camp in Libya, 1980s (*courtesy William Nessen and Hassan Di Tiro/GAM*)

leader, which forced Hasan di Tiro to take on that role himself. However, in the early days of the movement Daud Beureu'eh used his influence to support the struggle of Hasan di Tiro. This was why the military brought Daud Beureu'eh by force to Jakarta on 1 May 1978 so that he was separated from the Acehnese.[72] The dissemination of Tiro's ideology to the people had to be carried out secretly during three short visits to Aceh from 1974 to 1976. His message gained support especially in Medan, from his relations and a number of young intellectuals frustrated by the way Aceh had developed under the hegemony of Jakarta.[73] Through them, Hasan di Tiro spread his influence to the people. Although his independence proclamation was issued on 4 December 1976, the movement only went public a few months later when his followers numbered about three hundred with limited arms and logistics.

Hasan di Tiro's experience in leading the guerrilla for two years and four months boosted his confidence that the Aceh State he dreamed of could be achieved through a combination of armed struggle and diplomacy. During 1986–9 he recruited around 300 youths to be trained with military skills in Libya (see Fig. 9). They were then smuggled back to their homeland via Malaysia to form armed cells against the government.

With his residence in Sweden, he forged alliances with other separatist movements and lobbied various overseas bodies for international support. The fighting accelerated after 1990 with followers coming from the unemployed. The freedom of expression after the fall of Suharto (1998), and the collapse of the security authority enabled GAM to conduct widespread propaganda in Aceh. As a result, by the time of the military emergency in 2003, they already had around 5,326 armed personnel.[74] More importantly, the nationalism idea that GAM was struggling for attracted sympathy from NGO activists and university student activists who wanted political change in Aceh.

In accordance with their mission, the GAM militia targeted the security apparatus with guerrilla tactics. They also attempted to paralyse the local government by appointing their personnel to execute government functions in the areas concerned. Believing that their struggle, like that of Darul Islam, was to uphold religion and to free their region (*nanggroe*), they set up a struggle fund and collected money by imposing tithes and taxes on those not bearing arms, who were traders, officials, government officials or politicians. In carrying out this task, the GAM militia used intimidation and violence against whoever they saw as obstructing to their cause. This happened to Hasan Saleh in January 1978, when he was wounded and two of his associates were killed.[75] However, the intimidation and the acts of terror upon their opponents only caused widespread hatred among the community towards their movement. The victims naturally sided with the government.

Conclusion

This brief analysis shows clearly that the nationalist movement started by Hasan di Tiro did not emerge suddenly in 1976 or the 1980s, but developed gradually. The root cause was economic and political, but this was combined with aspiration, ideology, disappointment, ambition and vested interests. The suffering of Aceh from economic and political exploitation was not solely caused by the New Order government but had been going on ever since the colonial government integrated the Sultanate into the new national political environment with its centre in Jakarta at the turn of the twentieth century. This made the region a production base for the national and global economy. These conditions continued, except for the period of the independence revolution, and were intensified during the New Order period when only the capitalists, who generally came from outside the region but with government support, reaped the benefits. On the other hand, Aceh remained poor, backward and subordinated, which created a relatively deprived group.

Eventually a leader emerged to articulate local interests. The leadership did not emerge from the middle class whose needs were already met. Neither did it emerge from the lower class who were resigned to their fate before there was someone to speak up for them. The leadership came from the intelligentsia who were not co-opted by the bureaucratic power and were angry at the hegemony of central government. Among them, only Hasan di Tiro had a generic relationship to the *ulama* Tiro, the family of fighters during the Dutch–Aceh War. Because he grew up in a generation whose loyalty was national and inter-cultural, Hasan di Tiro initially, at least until 1962, was fighting for Aceh as a state of the Federation of States of Indonesia, because he felt that peripheral Aceh could obtain justice only through that structure. The failure to realise the federation and various other disappointments forced Hasan di Tiro to change his inter-cultural nationalism to an ethno-regional one.

It would be wrong to either overrate or to deny altogether the role of religious ideology as the basis of their movement.[76] The Islamic tradition in Aceh went back several hundred years and it is only natural that the religious ideology at a certain level could be a motivation for the nationalist fighters. On the other hand, *ulamas* whose needs were satisfied by the government had a different interpretation of the relationship between religion and the state. Some, like the Persatuan Dayah Inshafuddin and Ahlusunnah Waljamaah, felt that religion was not threatened in the national political environment, and regarded the movement as *bughat* (rebellion) against the legal government. In general, the ambition of the Aceh nationalists was shared by elites whose needs were not met by the government or who lost their jobs or agricultural lands as a result of development.

GAM had a number of similarities with the Moro nationalist movement in the Southern Philippines in its causes and patterns.[77] The two differences in the Moro nationalist movement were that it fought against a national government dominated by a Christian population, and that a rift within the leadership along ethnic lines obstructed the consolidation of the organisation. By contrast the Aceh that GAM wanted to free was part of what Reid calls the Malayo-Muslim civilisation.[78] This brought a double handicap to the nationalists. Firstly religious solidarity put the *ulamas* more on the side of the government than on that of GAM; and secondly GAM, unlike the Moro movement since the early 1970s, was unable to rally Islamic countries including

Malaysia, with the single exception of the military training in Libya, later withdrawn.[79]

Reacting to the religious slogan of GAM, the government countered the movement by employing a religious approach from the beginning. That action is understandable in their effort to co-opt the religious elite as government spokespersons. However, when the policy imposed was excessive and exclusive, this had long-run implications for the national integration process, because Indonesian nationalism is multi-cultural, and Indonesian society is plural.

The question now is how Aceh's relations with Jakarta can be reconstructed to make the region more prosperous and peaceful, more democratic and able to govern itself. Special autonomy has brought several advantages but not substantial changes to the relations that were created a century ago. On the other hand, the Islamic responsibility to uphold *jihad* (holy war) needs to be interpreted by both sides, as that concept has repeatedly been interpreted rigidly by the leaders of the fighting groups to mobilise their followers for political purposes.

Notes

[1]   The author wishes to express thanks to Prof. Anthony Reid, who gave constructive comments on my earlier version of this chapter. However, I am myself responsible for any errors in data or writing.

[2]   See Timothy Kell, *The Roots of Acehnese Rebellion 1989–1992* (Ithaca, New York: Cornell University Press, 1995). Geoffrey Robinson, "Rawan is as Rawan Does: The Origins of Disorder in New Order Aceh", *Indonesia* 66 (Oct. 1998): 127–56. Edward Aspinall, "Modernity, History and Ethnicity: Indonesian and Acehnese Nationalism in Conflict", *RIMA* 36, 1 (2002): 3–33. Jacqueline Aquino Siapno, *Gender, Islam, Nationalism and the State in Aceh: The Paradox of Power, Cooptation and Resistance* (London: RoutledgeCurzon, 2002), pp. 196–7.

[3]   See Rizal Sukma, "Aceh in Post-Suharto Indonesia: Protracted Conflict amid Democratisation", in *Autonomy and Disintegration in Indonesia*, ed. Damien Kingsbury and Harry Aveling (London: RoutledgeCurzon, 2003), pp. 152–65.

[4]   Regarding estate and mine, see J. Jongejans, *Land en Volk van Atjeh: Vroeger en Nu* (Kutaradja-S'Gravenhage: NV Barns, 1938), pp. 158–63. A.J. Piekaar, *Atjeh en de Oorlog met Japan* (S'Gravenhage-Bandung: W. Van Hoeve, 1949), p. 27.

[5]   See *Volkstelling 1930. Inheemsche Bevolking van Sumatra*, Vol. IV (Batavia: Departement van Economische Zaken, 1934), pp. 116–23.

6   The ethnic composition at that time comprised 775,760 Acehnese, 52,419 Gayo, 17,997 Simeulue, 15,448 Singkel, 13,621 Alas and 11,408 Tamiang. Ibid., pp. 20, 21 and 112.

7   As an illustration, T.P. Umar Keumangan had 820 ha of paddy field, T. Panglima H. Mae Trienggadeng 180 ha, T. Muda Dalam Bambi 107 ha and T. Bentara Ibrahim Pineung 100 ha. The numbers do not include estates and fish farms they owned. The data are based on the letters of claim by the descendents of the territorial chiefs concerned to the *Majelis Penimbang* in 1951–2 in typed script. The personal collection of T. Abdurarahman Muli and the Archives Bureau of Aceh Region.

8   See T. Hanafiah, "The Poverty of Acehnese People and How to Eradicate It", *Sinar Deli*, 27 April 1940.

9   See Hamka, *Kenang-Kenangan Hidup* (Kuala Lumpur: Antara, 1966), p. 96.

10 Piekaar, *Atjeh en de Oorlog met Japan*, p. 27.

11 See *Semangat Merdeka*, 19 and 30 May 1950; or, *Tegas*, 25 and 28 June 1951. Before the Darul Islam Rebellion, exports from Aceh to the Malay Peninsula amounted to Straits $1 million per month, *Antara*, 21 December 1953. Though less than pre-war, Aceh's exports in 1951 still comprised, besides palm oil and rubber, 10,000 tons of copra, 13,000 tons of areca nut, and 185 tons of patchouli. See *Propinsi Sumatera Utara* (Jakarta: Kempen R.I, 1953), pp. 576–7.

12 See M. Isa Sulaiman, "One hundred years of the Petrol industry in Aceh", in *Pertamina Peduli Pembangunan Daerah Istimewa Aceh*, ed. Jamaludin Ahmad (Jakarta: Hupmas Pertamina, 2001), pp. 13–21.

13 See *Aceh Dalam Angka 1985–1996* (Banda Aceh: Local Bureau of Statistics in cooperation with the Bappeda Aceh, 1996), pp. 185–90.

14 See *Atjeh Dalam Angka*, 1970, pp. 100–3.

15 See *Serambi Indonesia*, 6 Dec. 2001 and 20 Mar. 2003.

16 See *Waspada*, 15 March 1978. After 1997, the export of timber decreased and in 1999 only US$228 million in the total export US$1.5 billion. See *Aceh Dalam Angka,* 1999, p. 295.

17 See *Serambi Indonesia,* 11 February 1991 and 6 October 1999.

18 See Anne Booth, "Can Indonesia Survive as a Unitary State?", *Indonesia Circle*, SOAS, 58 (June 1992): 40–1.

19 See the annual report of local office for village affairs (Banda Aceh, 1994), p. 3.

20 See *Serambi Indonesia,* 30 March 1998.

21 Regarding the role of Tiro, see T. Ibrahim Alfian, *Perang di Jalan Allah: Perang Aceh 1873–1912* (Jakarta: Pustaka Sinar Harapan, 1987), pp. 73–82 and 205–9.

22 PUSA was formed on 5 May 1939 under the leadership of Tgk. Daud Beureu'eh. It emerged as the largest organisation in Aceh whose membership

numbered around 150,000 people by the Japanese invasion. For a description, see Anthony Reid, *The Blood of the People: Revolution and the End of Traditional Rule in Northern Sumatra* (Kuala Lumpur: Oxford University Press, 1979), pp. 25–7; and M. Isa Sulaiman, *Sejarah Aceh: Sebuah Gugatan Terhadap Tradisi* (Jakarta: Pustaka Sinar Harapan, 1997), pp. 45–53.

23   See Hasan M, "Where is our victory located?" in *Semangat Merdeka*, 23 July 1946. Besides that in early November 1945 Hasan di Tiro and his uncle Tgk. Umar Tiro (1904–80) sent a telegram to President Sukarno to say that the Tiro family of *ulamas* supported the Republic.

24   PUSA' s activists joined in the fifth column of F. Kikan (Fujiwara F. Kikan) before the Japanese invasion. Although they revolted against the Dutch from February till March 1942, the actions certainly affected the *uleëbalang* who were the mediators of colonial power in Aceh. *F. Kikan* conducted outrageous actions during the transition period. The conflict between the *uleëbalang* and the militant group intensified during the Japanese occupation. See Reid, *The Blood of the People*, pp. 87–90, and Sulaiman, *Sejarah Aceh*, pp. 75–86.

25   Some territorial chiefs, such as T. Daud Cumbok, T. Muhamad Keumangan, T. Laksamana Umar, T. Chik Mahmud Meureudu and T. Cik Abdullatif Geudong, formed militia groups. See Sulaiman, *Sejarah Aceh*, pp. 122–5.

26   On 17 November 1945, Daud Beureu'eh and Tgk. Umar Tiro at the Tiro mosque issued a *fatwa* that to fight the Dutch was part of *fardhu ain* (religious duty). On 19 December 1945 when the conflict with the chiefs and the militia almost reached its climax, Daud Beureu'eh, in Kutaradja, sent a letter to Hasan Ali to mobilise the people to fight the chiefs by quoting the *Qur'an* that Allah will not change the fate of the people if the people do not strive to change it themselves (*Surat Ali Imran: 19, al Anfal: 53 and Ar Raad: 11*), see ibid., p. 134.

27   Ibid., pp. 140–1 and 160–8.

28   The resolution was systematically contended at *Badan Pekerja Dewan Perwakilan Aceh* (DPA) meetings since July 1946, during the DPA plenary conference from 31 December 1946 to 1 January 1947, and *Maklumat Bersama Ulama* on 15 May 1948 or *Maklumat Gubernur Militer*. Ibid., pp. 180–7.

29   See *Peraturan Daerah No.1 Keresidenan Aceh*, 24 June 1946 regarding the management and ownership of the properties left by those who had committed treason. In a 1993 interview with the author, Hasan Ali admitted to being the compiler of the regulations.

30   Before Darul Islam erupted, about 310 ha and 60 estates belonging to the chiefs were sold by the *Majelis Penimbang*. See the letter from M.A. Ismail Baus in *Seksi Penyelesaian Revolusi 46 Musyawarah Kerukunan Rakyat Aceh* (typed edition), Sigli 21 October 1962.

31   See Sulaiman, *Sejarah Aceh*, pp. 69–79.

32   Ibid., pp. 203–14.

33   On his return from Dutc detention, President Sukarno appointed Hatta as premier and Sjafruddin Prawiranegara as vice premier on 4 August 1949. However, Syafrudin was given the specific task of handling the government in Sumatra while Hatta led the Indonesian delegation in the Round Table Conference.

34   The white paper brochure was published anonymously and funded by the government of the Aceh Region.

35   The Province of North Sumatra was made official through the appointment of the lawyer SM Amin, a fellow PUSA activist, as governor by President Sukarno in Kutaradja on 17 June 1948. However, because East Sumatra and Tapanuli were under Dutch rule, he could not govern effectively and was renamed Government Commissioner on 16 May 1949.

36   Application letters from the chiefs' heirs included that from Pocut Khairiah dated 10 April 1951 to the Supreme Court Medan; from Pocut Khatijah, 25 June 1951 to the Attorney General Jakarta; from T. Abdullah, 1 January 1952 to the Governor of North Sumatra; and from Tgk. Husin to the Minister of Interior, 27 April 1953. The government requested that matters outside the competency of the *Majelis Penimbang* be handed over to the court; letter of Minister of Interior No. 75/21/19 to the Governor of North Sumatra, 16 February 1953 and that of the latter to the regent of Pidie No. 55263/2/12, 12 January 1953. Also see the letter of Tgk Nyak Umar, Head of *Majelis Penimbang* Pidie No. 3/35, 20 January 1953.

37   Regarding conflict or land incident, see for example the complaint letter of Nyak Amat Comis Cs, Beureunun, Sigli 25 February 1953 to Head of Police Sigli Area.

38   In fact, two days before the *Proklamasi* was announced, associates of Daud Beureu'eh in Idi, East Aceh seized the government office in the area concerned. See Sulaiman, *Sejarah Aceh*, pp. 287–8.

39   The number did not include some others killed in the Takengon district. The data were based on the Parliament Commission Report RI in January 1954 and *Harian Rakyat,* 23 November 1953.

40   In his speeches, letters and appeals, Daud Beureu'eh always quoted *Qur'an* regarding the responsibility to uphold the laws of Islam, to participate or support the holy war and not to cooperate with the non-believers. See for example *Keterangan Politik,* 21 September 1953; Notice to Celebrate *Nisfu Syakban 1373H* on 5 April 1954; *Seruan Dakwah,* 15 April 1954; the letter of Daud Beureu'eh to Tgk Daud Tangse dated 18 May 1956; and his notice to the *Dewan Repolusi* on 15 March 1959 "*Bekerjasama dengan musyrik untuk menghancurkan Islam adalah musyrik*" (To ally with the polythesists to destroy Islam is itself polytheistic).

41   See H.M. Wali, *Tiang selamat bagi segala lapisan pemerintah dan rakyat*

(typescript), (Darusalam Labuhan Haji: 19 Rabiul Awal 1377). Besides that Tgk Hasan Krueng Kale on 30 November 1953 distributed "*Seruan dan Nasehat*", which also criticised the Darul Islam rebellion.

42 From 28 October 1953 to August 1954, there was a long debate in the National Parliament concerning the problem of Aceh. The debate reflected the split in the national elites between the *Masyumi-PSI* who were inclined towards dialogue and granting autonomy, and *PNI-PKI* who regarded the restoration of order as the government's priority.

43 See *Fikiran Rakyat*, 4 September 1954, *Keng Po*, 8 September 1954 and *Lembaga*, 18 December 1954.

44 In an interview by Muchtar Lubis in New York at the end of 1954, Hasan Tiro admitted that he got money from Daud Beureu'eh and Kahar Muzakkar. See *Lembaga*, 20 December 1954. In 1956 he met with Kaso Gani, Kahar Muzakkar's envoy in Kuala Lumpur, and in 1959 travelled to several countries together with A. Razak Mattaliu, Kahar Muzakkar's envoy, to get support for their movement. See *Antara*, 30 November 1959.

45 See "Djangan hadiri Konferensi AA", *Peristiwa*, 12 February 1955. "Teriakan Hasan Tiro dibawa angin lalu", *Bijaksana*, 16 February 1955.

46 See Hasan Muhammad Tiro, *Demokrasi Untuk Indonesia* (Aceh: Publisher Seulawah, 1958), pp. 98, 103–4.

47 Ibid., pp 150–3.

48 The formation was based on the Batee Kureng Congress on 23 September 1953. Before this, DI Aceh was given the military status of *Komandemen V TII-NII* with Daud Beureu'eh as its military governor with the rank of Colonel *TII*. Since then, Daud Beureu'eh became the Head of State *NBA-NII*.

49 Hasan Tiro also met foreign dignitaries for the interests of the *Darul Islam* struggle from 1958 to 1960. Author's interviews with Hasan Ali in 1993 and with Hasan di Tiro in 2002.

50 See the letter of Lt. Col. Syamaun Gaharu, *Komandan KDMA* dated 18 October 1957 No. PM-11067/57 to *PM/Menteri Pertahanan RI* and *KSAD/Penguasa Militer* regarding *TMSU* (*Tambang Minyak Sumatera Utara* = Oil Wells of North Sumatra) and barter trade.

51 See *Notulen Sidang Peperda I Aceh* with the community figures in Kutaradja on 16 March 1958, pp. 3–4.

52 See Sulaiman, *Sejarah Aceh*, pp. 409–19.

53 See *Keputusan Perdana Menteri RI No 1/Misi/1959 tentang Perubahan Propinsi Aceh Menjadi Propinsi Daerah Istimewa Aceh*.

54 See Sulaiman, *Sejarah Aceh*, pp. 455–6.

55 See *Perda Prop. D.I Aceh No.1 tahun 1966 tentang pembentukan Majelis Permusyawaratan Ulama*.

56 The proportion of local revenue or *PAD* (*Pendapatan asli daerah*) in the local budget has been less than 10 per cent. As an illustration, in 1965 the

local revenue was around 7 per cent which was equivalent to Rp 52,310,175, out of the total of provincial budget Rp 710,982,334. *Memori Serah Terima Jabatan Gubernur KDH Istimewa Aceh Brig.Jen. Nyak Adam Kamil tgl 7 Juli 1967* (Banda Aceh, 7 July 1967), p. 86.

[57]   It is difficult to obtain the exact figure of the export production of Aceh through Belawan. One estimate by the East Aceh Chamber of Commerce stated that 40 per cent of the export through Belawan came from Aceh. *Serambi Indonesia,* 16 December 2002.

[58]   See *Memorandum DPRDGR I Aceh,* 12 October 1966 No. 13-7/DPRDGR/ 1966 regarding the restoration of the railway and wider autonomy.

[59]   In 1974 Hasan di Tiro met with Governor A. Muzakir Walad to discuss the possibility of his company, Doral Inc, taking part in constructing the gas project in Northern Aceh. Muzakir Walad told him that he was not in a position to approve such an offer. He advised Hasan di Tiro to get in touch with *Pertamina.* We do not know whether Hasan di Tiro made contact with *Pertamina.* It was Bechtel Inc. that constructed the gas plant in the area. Author's interview with A. Muzakir Walad, 1996.

[60]   In his various writings, Hasan di Tiro often referred to the UN Declaration on 14 December 1960 regarding the granting of independence to colonised countries and the decision of the UN General Assembly on 12 and 14 October 1970.

[61]   For that opinion, see Hasan M. di Tiro, "The Political Future of Malay Archipelago" (New York, 3 January 1965), "Atjeh Bak Mata Donya" (New York, 15 March 1968), and "One Hundred Years Anniversary of the Battle of Bandar Acheh, April 23rd 1873–April 23rd 1973" (New York: Institute of Aceh in America, 1973).

[62]   Tiro, "Atjeh Bak Mata Donya", p. 3. For an analysis of his national concept, see M. Isa Sulaiman, *Aceh Merdeka, Ideologi, Kepemimpinan dan Gerakan* (Jakarta: Pustaka Al Kautsar, 2000), pp. 11–8.

[63]   Tiro, "Atjeh Bak Mata Donya", p. 2. See also Hasan M di Tiro, *The Case and the Cause of the National Liberation Front of Acheh Sumatra* (London: NLFAS, 1985).

[64]   Regarding their mission in upholding Islam, see the pamphlets *Perjuangan Aceh Merdeka* (Wilayah Berdaulat, 14 August 1977), and their pledge with quotations from *Surat an Nisa*: 59, *al Maidah*: 1, *ar Ra'd*: 25 and *Bani Israel*: 34.

[65]   See the statements of *Majelis Ulama Aceh* successively issued on 21 June 1978 and 26 June 1990 quoting *al Qur'an* verses *al Hujarat*: 10 and *Ali Imran*: 103.

[66]   See *Serambi Indonesia,* 21 May, 13 and 28 June 1991, 21 April 1993 and 22 May 1995.

[67]   See *Serambi Indonesia,* 26 and 27 April 1997; or *Waspada,* 18 October 2002.

[68] It is interesting to note that the flag and symbol of GAM were appropriated to fulfil current needs and were not the same as those of Darul Islam and the Sultanate of Aceh.

[69] See, for example, Edward Aspinall, "Sovereignty, the Successor State and Universal Human Rights: History and the International Structuring of Acehnese Nationalism", in *Indonesia,* no. 73 (April 2002): 1–24, reprinted in Aspinall, *Modernity, History and Ethnicity,* pp. 14–22.

[70] Three GAM leaders, namely Zaini Abdullah, Husani Hasan and Yusuf Daud, contested categorically the accusation of racial attitudes against their movement. See *Gamma,* No. 26 (22 August 1999): 35, and *Waspada,* 26 July 1999. Briggen Bambang Darmono, Commander of Operations based in Lhokseumawe stated that the military confiscated 1,436 hand-made weapons from Javanese settlers in 2003. See *Kompas,* 13 June 2003. The militias were headed by Marseto Mertoyo (1934–). See *Tempo,* 30 June to 6 July 2003, pp. 32–3.

[71] *Stavanger Declaration* 21 July 2002, *Kontras,* No. 202, 7–13 August 2002.

[72] The matter was communicated by Hasan di Tiro to Daud Beureu'eh when he visited the United States in mid-1970. See the statement of A. Wahab Umar Tiro in Court of first instance Banda Aceh, 28 April 1980. *Berkas No 47/14/79/T and Berkas case of M. Harun Mahmud No.83/1978/T.PN Banda Aceh or Tgk H. Nurdin Amin No 5/1980/T.PN Banda Aceh.* This casts doubt on claims that Daud Beureu'eh did not support the Movement, because it was not based on Islam. See Nazarudin Syamsuddin, "Issues and Politics of Regionalism in Indonesia", in *Armed Separatism in Southeast Asia,* ed. Lim Joo-Jock and Vani S. (Singapore: Institute of Southeast Asian Studies, 1984), p. 125.

[73] Of the 11 ministers appointed by Hasan di Tiro, only three resided in Aceh as traders, while six others were intellectuals in Medan and the remaining two were Singaporeans of Acehnese descent.

[74] The figure was based on the *Kodam Iskandar Muda* sources, see *Kontras,* No. 235 (2–8 April 2003) or *Republika,* 20 May 2003.

[75] See Hasan Saleh, *Mengapa Aceh Bergolak* (Jakarta: Grafiti, 1992), pp. 384–94.

[76] An example of the latter is Robinson, "Rawan is as Rawan Does", p. 127; and of the former, Syamsudin, "Issues and Politics of Regionalism", p. 126.

[77] See Eliseo R Mercado, "Culture Economics and Revolt in Mindanao: The Origins of MNLF and Politics of Moro", in *Armed Separatism in Southeast Asia,* ed. Lim Joo-Jock and Vani. S (Singapore: Institute of Southeast Asian Studies, 1984), pp. 151–75. Nagasara T. Madale, "The Future of the MNLF as a Separatist Movement in Southern Philippines", ibid., pp. 176–89.

[78] See Anthony Reid, "Aceh and Indonesia: A Stormy Marriage", Prosea Research Paper No. 42, Taipei: Academia Sinica, 2001, pp. 3–4.

79 The Moro had the support of Malaysia and were able to attend the Islamic
    state forum OIC (Organisation of Islamic Conference) since 1974. Malaysia's
    Foreign Minister Abdullah A. Badawi in early 1991 stated that GAM was
    regarded as Indonesia's internal issue. See *Serambi Indonesia,* 24 April 1991
    and 6 August 2003.

9

Violence and Identity Formation in Aceh under Indonesian Rule

Edward Aspinall[1]

During a visit to Malaysia in early 2004, I had the opportunity to ask about two dozen Acehnese refugees and GAM sympathisers why they supported independence. With the exception of two persons, who were university lecturers, all of those with whom I spoke began by relating instances of violence by the Indonesian security forces. They talked about personal experiences of violence, violence they had seen perpetrated against relatives, friends, or people from the same village, or stories of violence they had heard about but not witnessed directly. The stories ranged from the relatively trivial (for instance, farmers getting a beating if they failed to hand over money to troops at check points as they returned from their fields) to the far more severe (torture, sexual assault and murder). In some cases, especially when accompanied by the display of scars, the stories had a shocking immediacy to them. Others had the air of having been long passed from mouth to mouth.

In most cases, the speakers would proceed from re-telling these instances of violence to locating their stories within a broader narrative of Acehnese national suffering. They would explain that their personal experiences illustrated the historical victimisation of the Acehnese and the lowly position that Aceh had come to occupy in the Indonesian state. Indonesia (or Java) was oppressor and colonialist, they said, and this was why the Acehnese should be independent.

These comments are in line with what we might expect from the scholarly literature on Aceh, as well as from more popular accounts. In the years that followed the resignation of President Suharto in May 1998, it became almost a truism in discussions of the Aceh conflict that human rights abuses by the military have played a — if not *the* — major

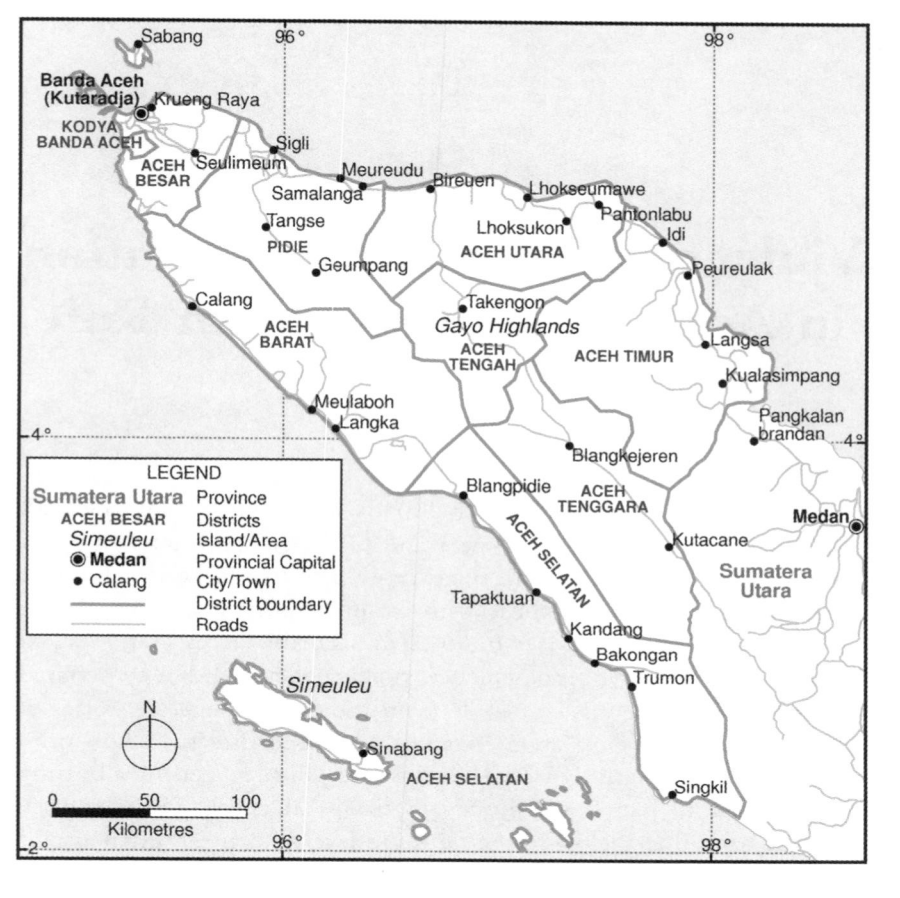

Map 3 Aceh in the 1990s

role in deepening Acehnese alienation with the central government. This view has been expressed by scholars from outside Indonesia, as well as by many activists and writers in Aceh and elsewhere in Indonesia.[2] Those who make this argument usually focus on President Suharto's New Order regime (1966–98), especially the notorious so-called "DOM" (*Daerah Operasi Militer* or Military Operations Zone) period of 1989 to 1998. As Robinson, for instance, put it in explaining disorder in Aceh during the last decade of the New Order: "… far from being the last bastion against national disunity and instability all these years, the New Order regime itself was largely responsible for the serious and protracted violence in Aceh".[3] It was under the New Order, so many analysts agreed, that political centralisation, natural resource exploitation, and militarism reached its apogee. Little wonder, then, that some Acehnese supported separatism.

My aim in this essay is to re-examine the relationship between violence and Acehnese resistance. I do this not only by looking at state violence and its effects in the recent, post-Suharto period, but also by extending the analysis back to the first major violent confrontation between the Acehnese and the Indonesian state. This was the Darul Islam (Abode of Islam) revolt that swept through large parts of rural Aceh in the mid-1950s.

When analysts compare the Darul Islam movement to more recent resistance to Indonesian rule, they often stress *discontinuity*. This is largely because the goal of the Acehnese Darul Islam leaders was different from that of today's secessionist rebels. Darul Islam leaders aimed for an autonomous Aceh within an Islamic Indonesia. They acknowledged the leadership of Kartosuwiryo in West Java, and declared Aceh to be part of his *Negara Islam Indonesia* (Islamic State of Indonesia). Even though they were disillusioned with aspects of the Indonesian Republic, they still had a commitment to the idea of Indonesian unity. Today, the goal of GAM (*Gerakan Aceh Merdeka*, or Free Aceh Movement) and allied groups is complete independence. GAM supporters argue for this goal not by stressing Islam but by emphasising that the Acehnese represent a distinct nation with an historic right to self-determination.[4]

In the following pages, I agree that state violence has been crucial in deepening Acehnese alienation and in helping to construct a sense of distinct Acehnese ethnic identity defined against that of Indonesia. Yet the analysis presented here also suggests that there was *continuity* between the two periods. During the 1950s, many of the patterns of behaviour for which the Indonesian military became notorious during the Suharto years were already visible. There was already, for instance, much arbitrary brutality against civilians. This violence in the two periods also had similar effects on how Acehnese rebels thought about their cause and their identity. Early on in the 1950s, Darul Islam leaders justified violence by describing their enemies as *kafir* and saying that fighting them was a religious duty. But abuses by Indonesian troops encouraged them to stress the ethnic unity of Acehnese against outsiders. Even in the 1950s, therefore, we see the first signs of the process which decades later gave rise to full-blown ethnic separatism.

However, in the 1950s the wider political context within which violent acts occurred — and the networks which Acehnese drew upon

— were very different from those that we see in the more recent period. In the 1950s, the reaction of the Acehnese to state violence, while in the long run reinforcing a discrete sense of Acehnese identity, also bound them to Indonesian national institutions and wider Islamic networks. By the late 1990s, Acehnese civilians faced an environment of escalating rather than receding violence, had longer historical experience of state violence, and could draw upon a ready-made alternative nationalist ideology, propagated by GAM, that stressed Aceh's violent victimisation by the Indonesian state. This background set the scene for the dramatic explosion of nationalist sentiment after 1999.

Darul Islam and Holy Violence in Aceh

A complex combination of causes gave rise to the Darul Islam revolt in Aceh.[5] They included regionalist sentiment and religious factors, as well as an internal struggle for control within Acehnese society. During the Indonesian revolution (1945–9), leading *ulama* and their allies had seized control of the apparatus of government in Aceh. They had decisively defeated their local enemies, the aristocratic caste or *uleebalang*, in a bloody social revolution and attained virtually unfettered control over local administration (see Chapters 6 and 8 above). The ulama also saw Islam as the natural foundation for the new Indonesian state and society they sought to create. They were thus greatly disappointed by the failure of central government leaders to share their Islamic goals and support implementation of Islamic law. Acehnese leaders were also disappointed by the abolition of Aceh's provincial status in early 1951, a decision which transferred considerable authority to non-Acehnese administrators in Medan and had wide-ranging economic and other implications.

The Darul Islam revolt in Aceh, therefore, took place after a period of obvious mounting political tension (by May 1953 one local newspaper already referred to a "Cold War" in the territory).[6] These tensions included some acts of repression, including a series of raids by security forces and arrests of supporters of the ulama in the second half of 1951. There were also signs of deteriorating relations between TNI units and local communities.[7] Beginning in 1950, military units in Aceh were re-organised. The Hatta cabinet's rationalisation programme led to the abolition of the Acehnese tenth division and the reduction of its size to that of a brigade. At the same time, "in order to attain control over the regional military forces, the central government pulled the

Fig. 10   Tgk M. Daud Beureu'eh addressing a peace-making meeting, c. 1959
(*courtesy William Nessen and Iqlil Tengku Ilyas Leubeu*)

Acehnese military units out of the region and replaced them with non-Acehnese units".[8]

But violent incidents had been relatively minor and sporadic. The Darul Islam revolt did not begin, in other words, as a response to serious violent repression by the Indonesian state. Instead, it was designed as an *offensive* action and took the form of a surprise and large scale-attack on government positions. It came after months of conspirational planning among leading *ulama* and their allies, many of whom still held positions of influence in the local administration. Hence, several *bupati*, a small number of army troops and police (most Acehnese soldiers were by then stationed outside of Aceh), and many junior bureaucrats joined the revolt.

The rebels initially justified violence in almost entirely Islamic terms. The declaration of the revolt, for instance, issued in the name of its leader Daud Beureu'eh in September 1953, justifies it primarily in terms of the obligation for all Muslims to create a government based on God's law. Declaring the "feelings of sadness and annoyance" held by the Acehnese in response to the adoption of a secular basis for the new republic, Beureu'eh notes that the Acehnese had from the start desired a state based on Islam. The declaration does appeal for autonomy for Aceh, but includes few passages that justify the revolt in specifically regionalist, let alone ethnic, terms.[9]

Darul Islam leaders justified their revolt as a *jihad* not only by referring to the desired goal of an Islamic state, but also by demonising their enemies as *kafir* and apostates. The declaration of the revolt itself notes that "Our God says: '... whoever does not carry out the laws determined by God, they are included among the *kafir*'." In an appeal released about seven months later, in April 1954, Daud Beureu'eh is even more explicit. He depicts Darul Islam's opponents as people who reject the *Qur'an* and Hadiths:

> The Government of the Republic of Indonesia that now exists is not the Government we fought for in 1945. The Government of the Republic of Indonesia of 1945 has been buried and replaced by a new Government as a mask. What it really is now is a *Hindu Government wearing a Nationalist shirt and very much resembling Communism.* It is patently anti-Islam, anti-God and largely run by the lackeys of the Dutch. As well as being anti-Islam and anti-God, they also hold as their enemies those Indonesians who are Muslims, especially the Acehnese, because the Acehnese defended the Indonesian lands from being colonized by the Dutch Government. [italics in original][10]

Similar remarks can be found in a 1956 book ("The Islamic Revolution in Indonesia") written by Hasan Saleh, another key Acehnese Darul Islam leader. He explains that even government troops who performed Islamic rituals should be considered *kafir*. This was because, "By resisting and challenging the Islamic soldiers who wish to carry out Islamic laws, they have fallen under the law of apostasy *(murtad)*."[11]

Their primarily religious understanding of their struggle had an impact on the rebels' choice of military tactics. As Sulaiman notes, the Darul Islam leaders believed in the slogan of "martyrdom or victory" (*Yuqtal atau Yaghlib*).[12] In the first phase of the revolt, therefore, they engaged in a type of conflict which has not recurred during the more recent GAM insurgency: massed frontal attacks by poorly armed crowds on military installations. Indonesian military accounts from this period give an impression of very one-sided combat. One description, of the initial Darul Islam assault in Lhokseumawe on 21 September 1953, describes several thousand rebels, armed with machetes, daggers and "several" rifles, carrying a flag with a crescent moon and star symbol, engaging in a "mass and fanatical attack" on the military barracks:

> A bitter battle took place, where the enemy showed they had an extraordinary contempt for death, but were greeted by our troops under the command of Company V Commander, Second Lieutenant

A. Simatupang with prideworthy perseverance and resoluteness. Although our troops in defending themselves spewed bullets, using all the weapons at their disposal, the rebels did not care about the number of victims on their side and kept advancing while shouting and crying for our troops to give themselves up along with their weapons.[13]

In the end, it went to "close combat", with the TNI forces using hand grenades to repel their assailants. Another assault by about seven thousand attackers the next day ended after three hours, with the Darul Islam forces retreating and leaving many corpses of their comrades on the battlefield.

This style of attack was also in accordance with the initial military strategy of the rebels. They aimed to seize control rapidly of not only the major population centres, but the entirety of Acehnese territory, and then defend it along the border with East Sumatra.[14] Essentially, they planned a kind of coup. However, they did not reckon with the capacity of TNI units to resist and to receive reinforcements and supplies by

Fig. 11   Poster of the Cease-fire (CoHA) period of 2002–3, reminding the TNI and GAM, in Indonesian and Acehnese, of offenses now forbidden to them — torturing, killing, plundering, bombing, burning, raping and so forth (*courtesy Rodd McGibbon*)

both air and sea. Within weeks, the army had mounted a successful counter-offensive and by late November, Takengon, the only district capital long in rebel hands, fell to government forces. The conflict then changed in character. It became a grinding guerrilla insurgency very similar to the GAM campaign of recent years. Darul Islam forces transformed into small armed bands and held large parts of the countryside, retreating into mountainous and forested areas when necessary. From there, they launched occasional surprise attacks on their enemies, and on transportation and other infrastructure.

State Violence in the 1950s

As noted above, there is a frequent tendency in both academic and more popular literature to view the New Order government as chiefly responsible for fanning the separatist conflict in Aceh. In this view, the militarisation of state responses to regional discontent eventually encouraged the victims to seek to break away from the Indonesian state altogether, rather than to reform or remold it, as most regional rebels had attempted in the 1950s. There is much to be said for this interpretation. However, it is important also not to downplay the extent or impact of state violence in the 1950s. Many of the basic patterns of state violence later used against civilians during the New Order were already visible in the 1950s.

One useful source in this regard, admittedly a highly partisan one, is a 1956 book by one of the Acehnese leaders of Darul Islam, "A. H. Gelanggang" (according to Sulaiman a pseudonym for the former *bupati* of Pidie, T. A. Hasan).[15] In this book, the author describes in sometimes graphic detail violence perpetrated against the local population by military and police units. Much of his criticism is reserved for the day-to-day arbitrary and predatory behaviour of troops, especially their thieving from locals. He also details other violent acts, including the burning of homes of villagers accused of assisting rebels, rape, kidnap for ransom, electric shock and other torture against suspects, abduction and execution of people suspected of assisting rebels, public torture to death of suspects, and massacres of villagers who do not cooperate in pursuing Darul Islam forces. In many cases, he lists the names of both victims and perpetrators, and he also describes what he claims to be the actions and taunts made by the troops as they commit their acts.

From Gelanggang's book and other contemporary descriptions, it is already possible to observe two causes of violence by the security forces which remain central to the Aceh conflict today. First, both Gelanggang and Hasan Saleh (whose book also contains accounts of violence) emphasise the "ordinary" criminality of the security forces. They describe troops who loot residents' homes when they carry out sweeping operations through villages and strip travellers of their possessions at check points on main roads. In the words of Gelanggang:

> Since the beginning of the outbreak of the rebellion in Aceh, we see here and there throughout Aceh, the state apparatus on operations, on patrol, pillaging the people's possessions, in the form of jewelry, gold, *suasa* (pinchbeck, a kind of false gold), silver, money, unhulled and hulled rice, cloth, furniture, bicycles, animals and so on. In short, from the most expensive to the cheapest of goods. From diamonds to chicken eggs.
>
> Whichever of these goods can be sold, they sell. Whatever they can wear or use as part of their own riches they set aside and take home when they leave. In this way, they obtain money and wealth. Whether this is best called robbery (or extortion) in war time is best answered by those who have the right.[16]

As an illustration, Gelanggang notes that those who wished to travel from Medan to Aceh by car would have to pay out at least one thousand rupiah per day. As a result of such exactions, "tens of chiefs of police and heads of other parts of the state apparatus have become fantastically rich and have been able to build stone houses in Medan and elsewhere, without being reprimanded by anyone".[17]

Hasan Saleh ascribes such behaviour to the general poverty and economic disarray of the armed forces and the government generally. He gives what purports to be a quotation from Colonel Simbolon, the chief military commander in Northern Sumatra, speaking before his troops: "My children! We are now suffering from a shortage of money to buy vegetables, we are suffering from a shortage of medicine, we are suffering from a shortage of vehicles for transportation, with most of them damaged and irreparable. We now have a shortage of dormitories, the dormitories we have are in ruins and are falling down. We are suffering from shortages of everything, all because the treasury in Jakarta is empty."[18] Is it any wonder, Saleh asks, that the troops "seize and steal the possessions of the people by force wherever they are on duty"?[19]

Second, as with so many counter-insurgency campaigns, much of the arbitrary violence against civilians occurred because troops were unable to distinguish between the general population and the combatants. They encountered a generally uncooperative population, which continued to shelter and feed the rebels, often refusing to reveal their whereabouts. Many of the acts of greatest violence catalogued by Gelanggang begin with unsuccessful sweeping operations against the rebels or with rebel ambushes, after which government troops retaliate against local people.

These factors came together in a series of massacres in Aceh Besar in early 1955. These massacres took place in and around villages called Pulot Leupung and Cot Jeumpa in late February, and remain well-known today because they were documented extensively in the local and national press.[20] They occurred after an ambush in which rebels fired on a military truck, hitting a fuel container and causing it to explode, so that almost all on board were killed. Unable to find the attackers, troops carried out reprisals against local villagers over the following days. According to the initial reports, by "Acha", the editor of the local newspaper, *Peristiwa*, the massacres began when troops appeared in the village of Cot Jeumpa on 26 February and rounded up all the men they could find, took them to a nearby beach and, in the words of one witness, "without being interrogated, they were straight away bren-gunned or shot, so that all collapsed flat on the ground as corpses".[21] Two days later, another 64 people were seized from their homes or when they were fishing or going about other business, taken to the beach and shot. In all, over 100 people were killed.

These events and the response they elicited bear many similarities to more recent patterns of military violence in Aceh. The scale of the killings was as great as any single massacre of civilians perpetrated by army troops in recent times; indeed, it was probably greater. The motive was collective punishment for an attack on troops in which locals were suspected of sympathising with the rebels. The calculated nature of the killings and the preponderance of force on the government side anticipate many recent cases of mass murder. In some respects, the response from government officials and opinion leaders in other parts of Indonesia was also similar. In the flurry of national press coverage that followed the initial reports by *Peristiwa*, for instance, it is striking that among the chorus of condemnation, some newspapers, especially those representing the secular left and nationalist forces, like *Merdeka*, struck a tone of sympathy with the central government and the troops, accusing those who were complaining about the events of giving aid to the rebels and besmirching the reputation of the military.[22] Some members of the national political elite justified the violence and, at least initially, decried compromise with the rebels. Prime Minister Ali Sastroamidjojo and his allies were especially in favour of a hard line. Strikingly similar, though perhaps not surprisingly so, to recent patterns was the response of the local military commanders themselves, who variously tried to deny the killings had taken place at all or described them as being the product of a fire-fight with rebels. Acha, the journalist who interviewed the victims directly and was responsible for breaking the story, was threatened and beaten up, and attempts were made to bribe him. Although the troops allegedly responsible for the killings were almost immediately transferred out of Aceh and various investigations were held, they were never punished for the killings.

Violence and Identity Formation in the 1950s

Nazaruddin Sjamsuddin argues that this series of massacres and the government's reluctance to investigate it had important consequences for the development of the conflict and of an Acehnese identity. In particular, he argues, "... it drove them [the Acehnese] further towards a deeper parochialism that cemented their ethnic sentiments".[23]

At the start of their revolt, as noted above, Darul Islam leaders generally described their aims and motivations in universalist Islamic terms. They said their movement aimed to uphold God's law and create an Indonesia-wide Islamic state. Such Islamic themes remained prominent throughout the revolt, but within months, Darul Islam leaders also began to make more open ethnic appeals. In his appeal to Acehnese soldiers on the government side seven months after the beginning of the revolt, Daud Beureu'eh calls on them not only to defend religion, but also to respect Acehnese solidarity:

> If you are really descendants of the heroes and martyrs of Aceh, who were martyred defending the Islamic religion and their *bangsa* [group or nation] .... Let us together defend the religion of Allah. Let us together defend the religion of Allah and the Land of Aceh.[24]
>
> Now the traitors to the *Bangsa* in the Government of the Republic of Indonesia have reversed their attitude and tactics. In the past they sent soldiers who were Bataks and the like to kill the Acehnese *Bangsa*. Now those traitors are sending you back home, my children, youths of Aceh to kill your own *bangsa*, the people of Aceh. Setting *Bangsa* Aceh against *Bangsa* Aceh.[25]

Such growing emphasis on ethnicity in the language in which the conflict was expressed was partly linked to the fact that, especially early on, most government troops in the territory were non-Acehnese. As the quotation from Daud Beureu'eh suggests, the government soon brought more Acehnese troops back to the province. However, TNI leaders apparently remained suspicious of their loyalties[26], and most front-line forces were non-Acehnese. The outsider status of most government troops meant that the violence they perpetrated against the civilian population could readily be interpreted in ethnic terms. A. H. Gelanggang is most graphic on this score:

> Before they electrocute someone or shoot them dead, those Pancasila butchers always preface their cruelty with the statement: "We are sons of Padang, wake your father from his grave to help you."
>
> How cruel and despicable such acts are, and the pride they take in their own ancestry, we feel it is unnecessary to make lengthy comment on such matters here, because all this has happened, is still happening and will continue to happen. These acts are attempts by one or several of the ethnic groups that make up the Indonesian nation [*suku Bangsa Indonesia*] to create splits and cracks within their own *bangsa*.
>
> Whether consciously or not, the Acehnese community (*ummat Atjeh*) has written a history in the depths of its heart that a majority of the Minangkabau and Batak ethnic groups [*suku*] are *suku* who are cruel, savage and ferocious. They are more savage than the *suku* Ambon at the time of the Aceh War with the Dutch. Their children and grandchildren should be told about this so that they don't take them as a model of how to live amongst civilized human beings.[27]

It is not only Gelanggang's acute consciousness of the ethnic identity of Darul Islam's adversaries that is striking here. Equally arresting is the way that he links that identity to consciousness of ancestry and the alleged heritability of traits. This is further confirmed by Gelanggang's reference to "the ferocity (*kebuasan*: a word suggesting the ferocity of predatory animals) of these instruments of the Pancasila state who are from the *suku* Batak who in olden days liked to eat people", a reference to the cannibalism practised in previous times among some Batak groups.[28]

Among these responses, we see the beginnings of a genuinely nationalist sentiment, as when Gelanggang makes an early comparison between the behaviour of the Indonesian state and Dutch colonialists:

> ... in this book, it needs to be explained briefly that the cruelties now occurring and being perpetrated by the state apparatus against the people of Aceh, both the TII (Indonesian Islamic Army) and the

general population, are truly extraordinary. They are extraordinary because it is as though this civil war is a war against colonialism. It is as though it is the Dutch who have landed and launched a war against Aceh.[29]

Such characterisations are the basic stuff of contemporary GAM discourse, by which the Indonesian state is depicted as an agent of alien Javanese oppression, and as heir to Dutch colonialism. In the 1950s, however, such conceptualisations remained halting and incomplete. There was as yet no all-encompassing nationalist ideological framework. No Darul Islam leader depicted the Acehnese as an entirely distinct national community. Instead, their statements had a parochial, almost earthy, immediacy. They condemned as ethnic enemies their immediate rivals in the field of battle: Batak, Minangkabau and, to a lesser extent, Javanese troops. No attempt is made to link the ethnic identity of these troops with the "ethnicity" of the state. Indeed, rather than positing fundamental enmity, Darul Islam leaders blame their enemies for undermining the true bonds that should link them: hence in the preceding quotation Gelanggang suggests Batak and Minangkabau savagery is driving a wedge into the Indonesian nation. Elsewhere, Daud Beureu'eh suggests that Javanese troops would not oppress the Acehnese if they "recognized the blood of Diponegoro that had flowed to defend the Islamic religion ...."[30] In short, this is still a response based on religion and ethnicity, not nationality. Darul Islam leaders still recognised common religious and national bonds with a wider Indonesia.

There was also evidence that Acehnese ethnic bonds were strengthening beyond Darul Islam ranks, including in the domain of what would today be called "civil society". The chief evidence that Sjamsuddin cites for his contention that the Pulot Leupung and Cot Jeumpa affairs and similar acts of state violence strengthened Acehnese ethnic sentiments was the "enthusiastic response to the establishment of the Front Pemuda Aceh [Acehnese Youth Front] which extended its branches in a mushrooming fashion all over the region during 1955. Wide support given to an ethnic and regional-based organisation such as the Front Pemuda Aceh widened the gap between the Acehnese and the central government."[31] Press reports indicate that this group took a very strong public line against the massacres, in a way which in some respects anticipates more recent human rights activism. For instance, shortly after the killings, the Front Pemuda Aceh held an emergency meeting in Kutarajda where it demanded the government hold satisfactory investigations into the killings. If not, the group continued, it would take its grievances to the United Nations.[32]

The growth of the Front Pemuda Aceh was not the only public response by Acehnese to the Pulot Leupung–Cot Jeumpa killings. In the weeks that followed the initial reports, Acehnese students, youth and others in Jakarta, Yogyakarta, Semarang, Medan, Bandung and other Indonesian cities organised many public gatherings, prayer meetings, and conferences to condemn the massacres and the government's approach to the conflict.[33] In these events we see more indications that some Acehnese were beginning to equate the behaviour of the Indonesian government and its army with the Dutch colonialists. As one Acehnese member of Indonesia's national parliament, Amelz put it, there were fears among the Acehnese that the government was simply continuing the policy of Van Heutz's "company war" (*perang kompeni*), by which if an armed rebel was found in a village, then all its inhabitants would be killed and their goods destroyed.[34]

There is another element of this public reaction to these massacres which bears consideration, however: the participation of many non-Acehnese sympathisers. For instance, in Semarang a "Committee in Defence of the Victims of the Cot Jeumpa and Leupong Affairs" was formed, with leaders representing a variety of Indonesian ethnic groups. The committee passed a resolution condemning the deaths of "Indonesian sons" in Aceh.[35] Leaders and ordinary members of Islamic groups who broadly sympathised with the Acehnese rebels because of their Islamic goals also loudly condemned the killings. Taking place early in Indonesia's passage to independence, large scale military violence against civilians was still relatively novel and therefore shocking. It was thus not only Acehnese who compared the actions of the troops to actions by the colonialists, many other commentators did the same (it was especially common in the press coverage for the comparison to be made with Captain Paul "Turk" Westerling, a notorious perpetrator of atrocities against Indonesian civilians during the independence struggle).

In sum, if these killings and other state violence did prompt some Acehnese, including those in far-flung parts of Indonesia, to emphasise their ethnic identity, another effect was also visible. The killings reinforced bonds of solidarity between the Acehnese and their supporters elsewhere. Many in the broader political public, and even within the government, were distressed that fratricidal killing could have reached such depths. Most of the public protest meetings and prayer gatherings thus concluded by calling for reconciliation. For example, a "lightning congress" attended by some 600 Acehnese youth in Jakarta ended, not by suggesting that Aceh should break free of Indonesia, but with a call for the government to abandon its security policy in Aceh, make contact with the rebels and seek peace.[36] Even the Front Pemuda Aceh, the organisation that Sjamsuddin cites as an example of the ethnic backlash taking place among the Acehnese, aimed to find a compromise solution between the Darul Islam and the government, including by restoring administrative autonomy to Aceh and involving Acehnese in the resolution of the conflict.[37] In other words, the reaction to state violence eventually contributed to the peaceful resolution of the conflict.

State Violence in Contemporary Aceh

The record of the Indonesian security forces in pursuing counter-insurgency operations in Aceh since the late Suharto period is well known, and need not detain us long here. A large number of reports produced by international human rights NGOs and, after 1998, local organisations and official government fact-finding teams have documented in considerable detail the routine use of torture, arbitrary killing, sexual assault, burning of homes and other forms of collective punishment by Indonesian forces. During the so-called "DOM" period, most estimates put the number of civilians killed at between one and three thousand.[38] To take a more recent example, according to one Acehnese human rights organisation, 534 people were killed and 144 went missing between the repeal of DOM in August 1998 and the beginning of December 1999. This was a little less than half of the group's estimate of deaths during the whole DOM period, 1989–98.[39] The loss of civilian life during 1999, the very year when the central government promised that there would be a new approach to the Aceh problem, included several well-publicised massacres. These included the "Simpang KKA" massacre in North Aceh in May 1999 in which, according to an official investigation, some 46 were killed and several dozens went missing. In the village of Beutong Ateuh in Central Aceh in July 1999, troops shot dead the *ulama* Tgk. Bantaqiah and 56 of his followers.[40]

When we compare the recent pattern of state violence with that which occurred in the 1950s, we can see many similarities. First, much of the seemingly indiscriminate violence of the security forces, just like that described in Gelanggang's 1956 book, is neither random nor arbitrary. Instead, it reflects attempts by troops to destroy the insurgency in conditions where they enjoy little sympathy from the local population.

Of course, troops murder and torture many Acehnese whom they specifically suspect of aiding the rebels (hence, for instance, the common reports of abduction and torture of known relatives of GAM members). Many casualties, however, are also caused by a generalised mentality on the part of troops that they are operating amidst a hostile population. Thus, there are numerous reports of troops shooting residents who flee when they enter their villages, or beating and even killing people who profess ignorance of the whereabouts of local GAM fighters. As in the Pulot Leupung–Cot Jeumpa affair, many of the worst instances of military violence against civilians occur when troops act out of vengeance shortly after being ambushed by guerillas who melt away into the landscape.

Second, the petty, day-to-day exactions described in sources from the 1950s have also become routine. Indeed, it is arguable that daily extortion by police and soldiers has been an even greater source of popular antipathy than the more spectacular cases of gross violations. It is certainly more widespread. Since 1998, many reports have detailed the various ways by which soldiers and police, both ordinary troops and officers, have extracted money from the local population. Theft from homes when troops conduct raids is common, but the more widespread technique has been the extortion of money and goods at check-points, especially on main roads, but also in or near villages and other settlements. The practice of extortion (*pungli*) on the main Medan-Banda Aceh highway has been a major cause of public concern since 1999, so much so that on some occasions truck drivers have gone on strike or demanded that they be accompanied by military convoys to guarantee free passage. Such practices have given rise to a form of grim humor, expressed in the widely-shared joke that "Indonesian soldiers come to Aceh carrying an M-16, but they leave with 16-M", by which is meant 16 *milyar* (billion) rupiah.

However, elements of continuity in military behaviour should not blind us to the differences. Two distinctions stand out. Firstly, the extractive activities of the armed forces are more institutionalised and routinised than they were in the 1950s. Indeed, they arguably have become not merely an accompaniment to, but a motivator for, state violence. Money-making activities include not merely petty theft and extortion by ordinary soldiers as they go about their daily duties (as was the case in the 1950s), but also a much wider range of income-generating activity, including involvement in both legal (such as forestry, palm oil plantations, etc.) and illegal (smuggling, illegal timber, marijuana, etc.) activities, as well as the levying of substantial fees for "security" from the major resource industries and other businesses in the province.[41]

In the accounts from the 1950s, Darul Islam writers suggested only that soldiers stole from the local population because of their meagre incomes, brutality, greed and lack of discipline, or because of their general impiety and immorality as representatives of the "Pancasila" government. Such accusations continued to be levelled against troops from late 1998 onward. But many intellectuals, NGO activists and other commentators also began to suggest that deeper and more structural factors motivated military violence. In this perspective, the Aceh conflict is a "*proyek*" (project) that allows individual officers and the military as an institution to extract substantial profits. These profits are crucial for the continued viability of the security forces in conditions when (as is often estimated) only approximately 30 per cent of their funding is derived from budgetary sources. It thus became common to accuse security forces of deliberately fomenting violence in the province after 1998, including by provoking or tolerating violence ostensibly committed by GAM. In short, in this view the military is not merely profiting opportunistically from the conflict, but generating and perpetuating the conflict for financial gain. Such accusations were not made in the 1950s.

Secondly, despite the occurrence of severe abuses against civilians in the 1950s, it does appear that there was a significant escalation in scale and ferocity by the 1990s. This is virtually impossible to measure quantitatively, although most Acehnese I have interviewed who remember the early period suggest that DOM marked the decisive turning point. It was at this time that they first saw phenomena like the deliberate display of corpses on roadsides as a warning to the local population, as well as the secret operations and deliberate targeting of individuals in the dead of night. Such behaviours were different from the angry reprisals in the heat of battle or shortly thereafter that first became common in the 1950s. Reports from the 1950s also contain none of the stories of mutilation of corpses or drinking of blood of victims that one hears more recently.[42] Another largely new phenomenon is the targeting in covert operations of civilian activists: while the Front Pemuda Aceh activists were able to conduct their activities with relatively little harassment (some were arrested or beaten), more recently, civilian human rights and pro-referendum activists have been detained, tortured, and, in some cases, killed by security forces. As Robinson puts it, "institutionalization of terror as a method for dealing with perceived threats to national security" distinguished military behaviour in Aceh from the late New Order period from that in the 1950s.[43] Such institutionalisation of terror must in turn be viewed as a product of the long transformation of the Indonesian army after the 1950s, flowing from its entrenchment in the political system and its role in defending an authoritarian regime for so long. A full account of this dynamic, not possible here, would need also to note factors like the growth of the intelligence services and of a counter-insurgency machinery, as well as the brutalisation produced by events like the 1965 massacres of communists and the occupation of East Timor.

Violence and Identity Formation after Suharto

In the years that followed the collapse of the New Order regime in 1998, the independence movement mounted its first truly serious challenge to Jakarta's control. In particular, in 1999, a massive movement in favour of a referendum on self-determination was organised by Acehnese youth and students. During the same year, as noted above, there was an escalation of violence in the territory, including a series of dramatic massacres of civilians by troops. In the explosion of anti-Jakarta activism and resistance that swept through Aceh, it is possible to witness both a visceral rejection of the Indonesian state's violent methods for maintaining its control, as well as tremendous recourse to ethnic, indeed nationalist, appeals. In short, there was a process of "ethnic consolidation" reminiscent of that which Sjamsuddin observed in the 1950s, but far outstripping it.

Space does not permit a comprehensive investigation here of the ways by which state violence contributed to the dramatic growth of ethno-nationalism. Nevertheless, even a superficial comparison with the 1950s is instructive. As in the Pulot Leupung–Cot Jeumpa killings of 1955, many of the best-publicised acts of military violence in 1999 were against unarmed civilians. Once again, it was relatively easy to identify the perpetrators (indeed, in the case of the Simpang KKA massacre, video footage of troops firing on a crowd of civilians was aired on Indonesian television). As in 1955, killings of civilians generated substantial media coverage and many expressions of sympathy and outrage beyond Aceh. And, crucially for our purposes, just as with the various congresses and prayer-meetings in 1955, the killings encouraged considerable protest and networking by a new generation of Acehnese youth. In both cases, a process of "ethnic consolidation" resulted from military violence. In 1955, however, the massacres also evoked wider expressions of sympathy and helped to reconnect Acehnese activists to Indonesia-wide networks, adding impetus to attempts to reconcile the rebels to the Indonesian state. This effect was visible in 1999, but it was much weaker and was rapidly overtaken by more negative reactions. As a result, the massacres helped to drive a wedge between younger Acehnese activists and the wider Indonesian community, and to strengthen and consolidate Acehnese nationalist beliefs among them.

The first demonstrations in which Acehnese students stated publicly that that they desired a referendum on Acehnese statehood were those demanding punishment for DOM-era violations. This demand was then formalised at a large meeting in Banda Aceh in February 1999, which involved representatives of over one hundred Acehnese youth and student groups from around the country. A new organisation, in some ways reminiscent of the earlier Front Pemuda Aceh, was established. This was SIRA (*Sentral Informasi Referendum Aceh,* the Aceh Referendum Information Centre). As its name suggested, SIRA's chief aim was to "socialise" the referendum goal. Its formation set off a snowballing series of mobilisations throughout Aceh, culminating in huge referendum rallies in October and November of 1999.

This flurry of organisational activity within Aceh was matched by Acehnese students, youth and others elsewhere in Indonesia. Partly drawing upon existing networks of Acehnese "expatriates", as in the 1950s, they held many seminars and conferences, organised demonstrations and lobbied national politicians. But a much more rapid nationalist radicalisation was visible in their ranks than had been the case in the 1950s. By late 2000, SIRA's Jakarta "consulate" was organising large demonstrations, in which protestors signaled their lack of faith in Jakarta by calling for the United Nations and United States to intervene to stop "war crimes" in Aceh and to enable a process of self-determination.[44] Leaders of the organisation also protested at the Dutch embassy, calling on Holland to "cancel" its 1949 transfer of Acehnese sovereignty to Indonesia.[45]

The most obvious difference between the Acehnese youth and student activism of the late 1990s and that of the 1950s was thus that the new generation demanded self-determination and independence, rather than autonomy and reconciliation. Context here was undoubtedly key. It was not simply that the new activism took place against a backdrop of a longer history of more extensive human rights abuses. It was also that there was already available an alternative ideological framework for understanding such abuses. This was the nationalist outlook propagated by GAM. During the period when the young activists were organising their referendum campaign, GAM was simultaneously experiencing a period of dramatic growth in rural areas. GAM spokespersons had a new confidence and, importantly, greatly expanded access to the local media. They also offered a ready-made explanation for violent actions by the Indonesian state. Among the thousands of comments by GAM field commanders and spokespeople recorded in the Acehnese and North Sumatran press between 1999 and 2003, a majority start with allegations of abuses carried out by Indonesian security forces. These descriptions of arrests, killings, house burnings or the like are typically concluded by remarks outlining to the audience what lesson should be drawn from such violence. One typical example, taken almost at random, is a comment made by Darwis Djeunib, GAM armed forces commander for Batee Iliek:

> the troops always propagandize that they come to Aceh to protect the people, but the reality is that they kill the people .... They kidnap and kill the Bangsa Atjeh without any sense of humanity. The GAM armed forces will continue to pursue these troops who harm and kill the Bangsa Atjeh ... the GAM armed forces are ready to die to defend their bangsa.[46]

Of course, there is much that is formulaic in such comments. They are arguably even disingenuous, because GAM guerrilla activity often led to military reprisals against civilians, rather than protecting them. The formulaic character, however, is part of the point. If, in the 1950s, Darul Islam leaders used only rather inchoate and immediate ethnic codes to depict their enemies (hence the attacks on the rival troops as Minangkabau and Bataks), by the 1990s GAM had positioned stories of human rights violations and state violence at the centre of a fully elaborated nationalist ideology. In this view, the Acehnese are an entirely separate national community from that of Indonesia. Indonesia, in turn, not only behaves *like* a colonial power in Aceh, it *is* a colonial power. State violence is the clearest evidence of this colonial relationship, hence GAM writers and spokespersons elaborate it at great length. Such arguments were appealing to many in the newer generation of activists, and though a few were repelled by the violence of GAM, many of them looked to it with a mixture of romanticism, awe and hope.

Almost without exception, leaders of SIRA and similar Acehnese youth and student organisations (including many who now describe themselves as committed Acehnese nationalists) look back at this period and say that the referendum demand did not initially stem from a strong desire for independence. Instead, most of them recollect that they initially viewed the referendum demand as a bargaining chip to pressure the government to curb human rights abuses and put military officers responsible for past abuses on trial. At first, many of them were barely aware of the aims of Acehnese nationalism. It was the massacres committed by the military in 1999 and afterwards, many of these young activists now say, that compounded their disillusionment with the Indonesian state and completed their transition from human rights activists to hardened Acehnese nationalists.

As in the 1950s, in 1999 there was a widespread reaction of shock in Jakarta and elsewhere to revelations of human rights abuse in Aceh, as well as sympathy for the Acehnese. The brutalities of the DOM period, as well as massacres that took place afterwards, received extensive press coverage and prompted many protests. Those who condemned military behaviour included Indonesia's formidable array of human rights non-governmental organisations (a spectrum of associational life that barely existed in the 1950s), prominent national political leaders and parties and, as in the 1950s, many Islamic organisations. Some groups went very far in expressing their sympathy: for example, a national congress of the Islamic Students Association (*Himpunan Mahasiswa Islam*) in late 1999 even said it would endorse a self-determination referendum in Aceh if the government did not properly investigate human rights abuses and punish the perpetrators.[47]

However, this mood of broad public sympathy did not last long. In the 1950s, revelations of military abuses had horrified many Indonesian nationalists, causing them to ask how their own armed forces had come so quickly to resemble those of the colonial power they had just defeated. By the 1990s, comparisons between the Indonesian state and Dutch colonialism in Aceh generated deep unease among Indonesian nationalists about potential "national disintegration", the most elemental threat imaginable to the legacy of the 1945–9 independence struggle.[48] In the 1950s, Acehnese Islamic and regionalist demands could, notionally at least, be accommodated within the institutions of the Indonesian state. Compromise with the rebels was not simply a matter of romantic principle. It was also realistic policy. After 1999, the growth of GAM, an avowedly and aggressively secessionist organisation, plus the spread of the referendum movement, posed a much more direct challenge to the Indonesian nation-state. But it was also a challenge which could be more readily dismissed by means of an established "discourse on separatists" which dehumanised supporters of separatist demands, distanced them from the Indonesian mainstream, and denigrated them as misguided or selfish.[49] There was thus a shift in the terms of public debate about the Aceh conflict, with public expressions of sympathy for the Acehnese rapidly becoming displaced by demands for stern action against separatism. By mid-2000, Acehnese human rights activists began to complain about growing public apathy about human rights abuses in Aceh. By early 2003, there was widespread public support for resumption of military operations.

Conclusion

It is not the intention to argue here that state violence was the *only* factor prompting ethno-nationalism in Aceh. Many other important factors have fallen outside the scope of this essay (the natural resource issue is an obvious example). Yet I hope to have demonstrated that state violence has played an important, even a crucial, role. Even in the 1950s, violence by government troops deepened Acehnese alienation with the centre and encouraged a greater emphasis on ethnic identity by Acehnese rebels. In the 1990s, state violence prompted many younger Acehnese activists to adopt an openly ethno-nationalist position.

Yet, for all the similarities, there were differences in the Acehnese response to state violence in the two periods. In the earlier decade, widespread outrage at military abuses paradoxically helped to *strengthen* links between Acehnese and other parts of the Indonesian community. This was especially evident in the activities of Acehnese youth activists who mobilised in Jakarta and other Indonesian towns. Revelations of military abuses contributed powerfully to the search for a negotiated resolution to the conflict. Ultimately, this did not happen in the 1990s. Most of the young activists in groups like SIRA continued much further along an ethno-nationalist trajectory than was imaginable in the 1950s. Far from searching for new forms of compromise between Aceh and Indonesia, many of them concluded that the Acehnese were a separate nation, which would be better off independent. Many of them speak with bitterness about the indifference and condescension of other Indonesians toward the Acehnese.

These different effects of state violence in the two periods demand explanation. An easy road would be to argue that state violence was simply far worse in the 1990s. As noted at the start of the chapter, it is common in analyses of Indonesian politics to suggest that separatism was primarily a response to the militarism of Suharto's New Order. In this view, the normalisation and institutionalisation of violence as a response to regional dissatisfaction compounded popular alienation and laid the ground for separatism. I have tried to suggest in this essay, however, that a comparison of patterns of military behaviour in Aceh in the 1950s and 1990s should make us question this interpretation. I do not deny that state violence may have become more institutionalised and, arguably, more sadistic in certain respects under the New Order. But the continuities are also striking. The patterns of petty and day-to-day military abuses, often with an economic motive, were similar. Gross abuses, including torture and rape, were already common in the 1950s. There were also large massacres of civilians, as well as the same military denials, impunity and obfuscation that we associate with the New Order and post-New Order periods.

All of this does not suggest that state violence has not had crucial effects on the Aceh conflict; quite the reverse. Perhaps it does suggest, however, that rather than focusing simply on particular violent acts or even patterns of violence, we should turn our attention to the wider context in which violence occurs and is interpreted. We should also think about how memories of violence accumulate and become fixed in ideological systems, and about how violence is represented, interpreted and justified. In the 1950s, those Acehnese who reacted against state violence described their adversaries in rather fluid ethnic terms, reflecting their daily lived experience. They also retained many links with other Indonesians, especially fellow Islamic activists. The political context of the early 1950s meant that comparisons between the behaviour of Indonesian and Dutch troops could still shock the wider Indonesian public. By the late 1990s, by contrast, massacres and other violence occurred against the backdrop of longer historical familiarity. They could be interpreted within nationalist ideological frames on both sides, in ways that did not disrupt nationalist ideologies, but rather reinforced them.

Notes

[1]   My thanks to Sally White and Wasmi Alhaziri for invaluable research assistance which helped me write this essay. Funding for the research was provided by the Australian Research Council.

[2]   See for example Geoffrey Robinson, "Rawan is as Rawan Does: The Origins of Disorder in New Order Aceh", *Indonesia*, no. 66 (1998): 127–56; Edward Aspinall and Mark T. Berger, "The Breakup of Indonesia?

Nationalism and the Contradictions of Modernity in Post-Cold War Southeast Asia", *Third World Quarterly: Journal of Emerging Areas* 22, 6 (2001): 1003–24; Jacques Bertrand, *Nationalism and Ethnic Conflict in Indonesia* (Cambridge: Cambridge University Press, 2004), pp. 161–83; Al Chaidar, Sayed Mudhahar Ahmad and Yarmen Dinamika, *Aceh Bersimbah Darah: Mengungkap Penerapan Status Daerah Operasi Militer (DOM) di Aceh 1989–1998*, 4th ed. (Jakarta: Pustaka Al Kautsar, 1999); Tulus Widjanarko and Asep S. Sambodja (eds.), *Aceh Merdeka Dalam Perdebatan* (Jakarta: Cita Putra Bangsa, 1999); Fikar W. Eda and S. Satya Dharma (eds.), *Sebuah Kesaksian: Aceh Menggugat* (Jakarta: Pustaka Sinar Harapan, 1999).

3   Robinson, "Rawan is as Rawan Does", p. 128.

4   On GAM ideology, see Edward Aspinall, "Modernity, History and Ethnicity: Indonesian and Acehnese nationalism in conflict", *Review of Indonesian and Malaysian Affairs* 36, 1 (2002): 3–33; "Sovereignty, the successor state and universal human rights: history and the international structuring of Acehnese nationalism", *Indonesia*, no. 73 (April 2002): 1–24; Kirsten E. Schulze, *The Free Aceh Movement (GAM): Anatomy of a Separatist Organisation* (Washington: East-West Center, 2004).

5   Several excellent studies are available: Cees van Dijk, *Rebellion under the Banner of Islam: The Darul Islam in Indonesia* (The Hague: M. Nijhoff, 1981), pp. 269–339; Eric Eugene Morris, *Islam and Politics in Aceh: A Study of Center-Periphery Relations in Indonesia* (PhD thesis, Cornell University, 1983); Nazaruddin Sjamsuddin, *The Republican Revolt: A Study of the Acehnese Rebellion* (Singapore: Institute of Southeast Asian Studies, 1985); M. Isa Sulaiman, *Sejarah Aceh: Sebuah Gugatan Terhadap Tradisi* (Jakarta: Pustaka Sinar Harapan, 1997); Clive J. Christie, *A Modern History of Southeast Asia: Decolonisation, Nationalism and Separatism* (London: Tauris Academic Studies, 1996), pp. 140–60.

6   "Perang dingin timbul di Atjeh. Mana jg benar dan mana jg salah ...?" *Tegas*, 22 May 1953.

7   For example, in May 1953 a mass brawl broke out when about 40 soldiers chased and beat a local man in Lho' Nga, whom one soldier accused of committing adultery with his wife. In response, residents held a large demonstration in front of the local police station, asking for the army company involved to be transferred: "Insiden di Lho' Nga: Tentera Pukul Rakjat", *Tegas*, 2 June 1953. The incident made local junior military commanders anxious. As one Captain Sumarhadi from the Territorial Bureau put it at a press conference: "... that beating has given rise to a sense of being degraded that could change into hate. Not only toward that one soldier, but toward all soldiers in uniform": "Sekitar Peristiwa Lho 'Nga: Perskonperensi dgn Biro Teritorial. Kedua Belah Pihak Harus Disalahkan, Kata Kapten Sumarhadi", *Tegas*, 10 June 1953.

8   Sjamsuddin, *The Republican Revolt*, p. 54.

9   A copy of this declaration can be found in Tk. Alibasjah Talsya (n.d.), *Sedjarah dan Dokumen-Dokumen Pemberontakan di Atjeh.* Penerbit Kesuma, Djakarta, pp. 66–71.

10 He made a similar statement at a public meeting some five months before the outbreak of the revolt, describing those who punish others according to other than God's law as *kafir*, godless (*fasic*) and tyrannical (*dhalim*): "Islam Mendjamin Kemerdekaan agama; seluruh ummat Islam djangan ketinggalan dalam pemilihan umum; Rapat Umum di Samalanga", *Tegas*, 4 May 1953.

11 Hasan Saleh, *Revolusi Islam di Indonesia* (Darussalam: Pustaka Djihad, 1956), pp. 21–2.

12 Sulaiman, *Sejarah Aceh*, p. 299.

13 Komando Tentara dan Territorium I Bukit Barisan (n.d.), *Memorandum Tentang Peristiwa Pemberontakan DI-TII di Atjeh.* Pertjetakan Madju, Medan, p. 34.

14 Sulaiman, *Sejarah Aceh*, p. 282 fn. 3.

15 Sulaiman, *Sejarah Aceh*, p. 286. A. H. Gelanggang, *Rahasia Pemberontakan Atjeh dan Kegagalan Politik Mr. S. M. Amin* (Kutaradja: Pustaka Murnihati, 1956), pp. 73–112.

16 Ibid, pp. 73–5.

17 Ibid., p. 77.

18 Saleh, *Revolusi Islam di Indonesia*, p. 38. A government source is Interior Minister Soenarjo who, on his return from Aceh in early 1955, stated that the situation faced by the army in the field was very difficult. Troops were frequently not paid their wages (at the time they were three months late). If they did not get paid, he said, "one could imagine" what their attitude to the people would be: "Bagaimana mentjegah peristiwa2 Tjot Djeumpa", *Keng Po*, 24 March 1955

19 Saleh, *Revolusi Islam di Indonesia*, p. 39. It is of interest that Saleh (p. 69) suggests that the police mobile brigades (then known as Mobbrig) were especially prone to such behaviour: "Then they gathered all the pick-pockets, all the thieves, all the robbers and all the former members of bands of brigands into one new force and they gave it the name of '*mobbrig*'." Mobile brigade forces (now known as brimob) have been accused of being especially unprofessional and brutal in their pursuit of counter-insurgency activities in contemporary Aceh.

20 Summaries of these killings and the responses they elicited are also available in Sjamsuddin, *The Republican Revolt*, pp. 140–4 and Sulaiman, *Sejarah Aceh*, pp. 314–5 and 332–6. These summaries, like my own in this paper, are in turn primarily based on the compilation of press reports presented in Kementerian Penerangan, Bagian Dokumentasi, *Kronik Kementerian Penerangan No. 20, Sekitar Peristiwa Daud Beureuéh III*, Djakarta, 1955 (hereafter abbreviated as Kempen 1955).

21 "Berita Peristiwa", *Abadi*, 8 March 1955.
22 See for example, "Peringatan Penting", *Merdeka*, 26 March 1955 in Kempen 1955, pp. 345–6.
23 Sjamsuddin, *The Republican Revolt*, p. 144.
24 Gelanggang, *Rahasia Pemberontakan Atjeh*, p. 59. The use of the word *bangsa* here deserves comment. Today, this word is typically translated into English as "nation", but as Laffan notes, it has a long heritage and over the twentieth century gradually evolved from an earlier, looser meaning of "grouping" into its more restrictive contemporary meaning: Michael Francis Laffan, *Islamic Nationhood and Colonial Indonesia: The Umma Below the Winds* (London: RoutledgeCurzon, 2003), p. 98. In the Acehnese Darul Islam writings cited in this chapter, usage is still in a state of flux. Most authors tend to use *bangsa* to describe the Acehnese, although they sometimes use other terms, such as *ummat Aceh* (*ummat* or "community" is usually reserved for the Islamic community of believers). Their writings also indicate that they still viewed the Acehnese *bangsa* as part of an over-arching Indonesian one. Interestingly, however, they relatively rarely use the terms "*suku*" or "*suku bangsa*" (usually glossed as "ethnic group", in the sense of being a constituent component of a larger *bangsa*) for the Acehnese, preferring to use them to describe other groups like the Minangkabau, Javanese, Bataks and Ambonese, perhaps suggesting that even linguistically we see here the beginnings of the slow emergence of modern Acehnese nationalism.
25 Ibid, p. 61.
26 Internal army documents suggest that there was distrust of the loyalty of Acehnese troops, with one document referring to the "security risks" that would follow from using members of the "A" ethnic group (*anggota-anggota suku "A"*) in front-line capacities: Komando Tentara dan Territorium I Bukit Barisan n.d., p. 85.
27 Gelanggang, *Rahasia Pemberontakan Atjeh*, pp. 89–90. The reference to Ambonese is to those who fought on the Dutch side. My thanks to Keith Foulcher for help in translating this passage.
28 Ibid., p. 86.
29 Gelanggang, *Rahasia Pemberontakan Atjeh*, p. 73.
30 Ibid., p. 58.
31 Sjamsuddin, *The Republican Revolt*, p. 144.
32 "Protes Front Pemuda Atjeh di Kutaradja terhadap peristiwa di Pulot Leupon dan Tjot Djeumpa", *Antara*, 9 March 1955 (Kempen 1955, p. 281).
33 These reports can be found in Kempen 1955, pp. 272–330.
34 "Keterangan Amelz mengenai Atjeh", *Aneta*, 8 March 1955 (in Kempen 1955, pp. 306–7). That this link was one which concerned the government is revealed by a report of a visit by Interior Minister Sunarjo to the graves of those killed in the massacres, in which he reportedly gathered residents

together and assured them that his was not a colonial government: "Menteri Dalam Negeri tentang peristiwa Atjeh", *Aneta*, 23 March 1955 (Kempen 1955, pp. 319–20).

35 "Panitia pembela korban Atjeh Besar", *Aneta*, 16 March 1955 (Kempen 1955, p. 290).

36 "Kongres kilat pemuda2 Atjeh berachir", *Aneta*, 20 March 1955 (Kempen 1955, pp. 296–7).

37 Sulaiman, *Sejarah Aceh*, p. 332.

38 International Crisis Group, *Aceh: Why Military Force Won't Bring Lasting Peace*. Asia Report 17 (Jakarta/Brussels: ICG), p. 3. The major report on violence during DOM is Amnesty International, *Indonesia: 'Shock Therapy' — Restoring Order in Aceh, 1989–1993* (London: Amnesty International, 1993).

39 "Kapolri: Banyak Preman Medan Menyamar Jadi Anggota GAM; Pasca-DOM 534 Tewas", *Kompas*, 24 December 1999.

40 A more detailed discussion of this series of massacres and the surrounding political context is found in Bertrand, *Nationalism and Ethnic Conflict*, pp. 173–81. Other discussions of violence in the post-Suharto period include: Amran Zamzami, *Tragedi Anak Bangsa: Pembantaian Teungku Bantaqiah dan Santri-santrinya* (Jakarta: Bina Rena Pariwara, 2001); Human Rights Watch, *Indonesia: Accountability for Human Rights Violations in Aceh*, Vol. 14, No. 1 (C) (New York. Human Rights Watch/Asia Division, 2002).

41 Lesley McCulloch, "Greed: The Silent Force of the Conflict in Aceh" <http://www.preventconflict.org/portal/main/greed.pdf>, 2003.

42 Such stories are common in Aceh: while those about the consumption of bodily parts are not verifiable, many people attest to having witnessed corpses of their friends with genitals, hearts or other organs removed.

43 Robinson, "Rawan is as Rawan Does", p. 140. Even so, it should be noted that most of the techniques described by Robinson (on p. 141 he mentions troops, probably from the Army's Strategic Reserve, Kostrad, under the command of Colonel Prabowo Subianto, engaging in "armed night-time raids, house-to-house searches, arbitrary arrest, routine torture of detainees, the rape of women believed to be associated with the movement, and public execution") were also practised in the 1950s. Only some, such as targeted killings and public display of corpses, were genuinely innovative.

44 "Warga Aceh Demo di PBB dan Kedubes AS", *Serambi Indonesia*, 9 November 2000.

45 "Jajak Pendapat di Aceh tidak Sah", *Media Indonesia Online*, 11 November 2000.

46 "AGAM Berondong Rombongan TNI:1 Tewas, 4 Luka, 30 Ruko Dibakar", *Waspada*, 2 November 1999.

47 "HMI Kembali ke Asas Islam", *Kompas*, 7 December 1999.

48   For one discussion of how historical discourses affected the way Indonesian nationalists viewed the Aceh conflict in the post-Suharto period, see Edward Aspinall, "History and separatism in Aceh: ethnic atavism versus civic voluntarism?" in *Political Fragmentation in Southeast Asia: Alternative nations in the making,* ed. Vivienne Wee (RoutledgeCurzon, forthcoming).

49   Dave McRae, "A discourse on separatists", *Indonesia,* no. 74 (2002): 37–58.

10

Sentiments Made Visible: The Rise and Reason of Aceh's National Liberation Movement

William Nessen

This chapter is dedicated to the memory of my friend Abu Kliet, the delightful Darul Islam and GAM fighter and village scholar. In mid-2003 in Krueng Sabe, West Aceh, Indonesian troops captured Kliet, slit his throat and tossed him in a nearby river. His body was never found.

This chapter examines the development of the Free Aceh Movement (Aceh Merdeka, AM, before 1998; and Gerakan Aceh Merdeka, GAM, since then). It questions the orthodox analysis of how, why and when the Free Aceh Movement and independence ideas developed.

My broader aim is to challenge the view that denies legitimacy to the Free Aceh Movement and its goal of Acehnese political sovereignty. That view — offered by scholars, human rights activists and journalists — is based in part on two intertwined historical arguments: First, large numbers of Acehnese have only recently supported independence; second, that popularity is largely the product of historical contingencies, unnecessary repression and other "mistakes" by the Indonesian government.[1]

The Orthodox View: The New Order and the Rise of Aceh Merdeka

Scholars and other Aceh analysts have pointed to the brutal repression of Suharto's New Order as the central explanation for the popularity of Aceh's independence movement.[2] The New Order and the level and

Fig. 12   Bullah, a GAM district commander, in front of Aceh's independence flag, 3 January 2003 (*photo by William Nessen*)

type of repression unleashed in Aceh was new and unparalleled in that province, we are told; the "ferocious and indiscriminate" violence of the late New Order (the 1990s) was an even more fundamental break with the province's past.[3] This brutality was an *overreaction* to just a few hundred guerrillas.

This view also serves (sometimes unintentionally) as the key argument against the very legitimacy of Aceh's national liberation movement. Aspinall, the leading English-language scholar of the current conflict, writes that the movement's reliance on repression for its popularity is "the essential contingency at the heart of the new Acehnese nationalism".[4] Because Acehnese nationalism is contingent, because it didn't *have* to be, the implication is that solutions beside independence are more reasonable. Because political sovereignty is therefore not a primordial need, it can't *really* be what the Acehnese want.[5]

In addition, the orthodox view stresses the discontinuity of Acehnese history and has several — sometimes contradictory — ways of dividing that history. First, when looking at Aceh, there is a tendency to portray the 30 years of New Order rule as an anomalous, avoidable period of Indonesian history, rather than one natural evolutionary form of Jakarta's and the military's deep domination of a vast and highly unequal archipelago. In this view, the New Order violence in Aceh should never have occurred and neither should the Free Aceh Movement. Second, the years that the Acehnese were not openly fighting to change their political status — from the end of Aceh's Darul Islam (DI) rebellion in 1961 to the founding of the Free Aceh Movement in 1976 (or to the second wave of guerrilla activity in 1989) — is what Aceh *really* is.[6] Third, orthodoxy draws a sharp historical line between Aceh before the Free Aceh Movement and after it.

The economic policies of Suharto's New Order 'produced' Aceh Merdeka in 1976, we are told. Here the argument is structural or would appear to be: the direct and indirect effects of the New Order's pillage of Aceh's natural gas and the associated enclave development around Lhokseumawe led to visible inequalities and to frustration and disappointment among Acehnese.[7] A structural argument means widespread impact and would suggest at least widespread sympathy and support for independence ideas. But the orthodox view says the Free Aceh Movement had few supporters back then. Meanwhile, what might seem a classic pattern of internal colonialism to a generalist is offered by these specialists as something that could have been — should have been — avoided.

The unusual life of Free Aceh Movement founder Hasan di Tiro adds to the movement's purported illegitimacy. Living in New York City for a quarter century and "circulating in the eddies and backwaters of international diplomacy", conservative businessman di Tiro picked up the secular, radical national liberation rhetoric of the 1960s and '70s and brought it back to traditional, Islamic Aceh. He also married a Jew. Later he turned to Libyan socialist leader Muammar Qaddafi to provide hundreds of Acehnese with guerrilla training. Much of the writing portrays di Tiro as a quixotic, self-promoting political dabbler prone to hysterics and exaggeration.[8,9]

An Alternative View: Subterranean Legacies

But this is only one possible way to read the history. Instead of something odd, alien or avoidable, independence sentiment might be the reasonable result of a steadily deepening and widening perception among Acehnese that they would never attain physical security, dependable economic welfare, reasonable moral standards in government, and justice for grave human rights abuses if Aceh remained *inside* Indonesia. Despite the end of dictatorship, the government's continuing failure to prosecute soldiers and military officers anywhere in Indonesia for decades of terrible crimes seems to confirm Acehnese perceptions. Their own *Meurdeka*, the Acehnese have learned, is perhaps the surest solution to what a GAM commander in West Aceh termed not the usual "*Masalah Aceh*" — the Aceh Problem — but "*Masalah Indonesia di Aceh*" — the Problem of Indonesia in Aceh.

Political opportunity theory also suggests recasting the timing and shape of independence sentiment. That theory makes a critical distinction between public emergence of mass action and long-held sentiment.[10] People with grievances often act only when new opportunities provide greater expectation of success. Suharto's fall provided that opportunity. As de Tocqueville wrote, "the most perilous moment for a bad government is one when it seeks to mend its ways".[11]

This alternative view therefore pays as much attention to the subterranean legacy of each phase of acute conflict as to obvious New Order changes. It stresses continuity. My evidence of such continuity comes mostly from GAM sources. But these sources find agreement with key details and conclusions of the work of Edward Aspinall and the late Acehnese historian M. Isa Sulaiman in this volume.

'Independence' Inside Indonesia: The 1940s and 1950s

From the 1930s through the 1940s, increasing numbers of Acehnese who were thinking about Aceh's future believed it was bound up in a promising way with 'Indonesia' own. Few if any Acehnese perceived a contradiction between their liberation from the Dutch and that of the tens of millions of others across the Archipelago living under Dutch rule. Perhaps they should have. More than anyone else in those islands, the Acehnese had resisted colonial rule. In any case, the Acehnese were "fired up" by a common spirit of Indonesian nationalism.[12] From the 1950s on, however, that spirit would grow cold as disappointments and distrust fed one upon the other.

The transformations of Hasan di Tiro — from pro-Indonesia fighter in Java against the Dutch, to overseas spokesperson and arms procurer for Aceh's Darul Islam (DI), and finally to Aceh independence leader — mark steps in an evolution of thinking and experience that a significant number of other Acehnese underwent.[13] The fight for the Republic around Medan involved a large number of Acehnese who later fought for DI. Acehnese who found themselves elsewhere in the East Indies also fought the Dutch. DI veterans would start and lead the Free Aceh Movement.

Jacoub Djuly, a life-long Acehnese friend of di Tiro, recalls how the transformation began:

> We didn't know anything about politics in 1946. I fought in Malang for the Republic and Hasan was with another fighting unit in Jogjakarta. We thought joining Indonesia meant Aceh independence also. Aceh would be independent but part of a larger Indonesian structure. We never thought Java would take from Aceh the way they have.[14]

Commentators differ over di Tiro's exact relationship to the Acehnese royal family and to heroes of the anti-Dutch struggle. In any case, he was from a highly respected family with a well-known history of anti-colonial struggle. He was also among an elite group of Acehnese who studied in Java before Indonesian independence; he was one of the first Acehnese to study in the West. "Only a few Acehnese were going off to school, so we were all famous," recalls Djuly. "Going to Europe or America was like going to the moon." Starting sometime in 1948, di Tiro was an assistant secretary to Indonesian leader Sjafruddin Prawiranegara, who by January 1949 headed Indonesia's Emergency Government based in Dutch-free Aceh.[15] Concludes Djuly: "Nobody did not know Hasan di Tiro in Aceh."

According to Djuly, di Tiro seems to have quickly begun doubting what Aceh had achieved by the joint fight against the Dutch. "Six months after Indonesian independence, we realised it was bad. The Javanese were taking all the power for themselves. Hasan and I and others were thinking more clearly about Aceh *meurdeka*, but we had no means to do anything about it."[16]

The 1950s Darul Islam rebellion in Aceh was, among other things, one of the most important regional reactions to Jakarta's early efforts at political centralisation. It was arguably the most "political" of the three DI rebellions in Indonesia. Di Tiro's star among Acehnese rose further with his prominent role.[17] In mid-1954, di Tiro, living in New York City, quit his part-time job with the Department of Information at the Indonesia consulate to the UN, and publicly demanded Indonesia stop military operations in Aceh. He tried to bring Indonesia's action to the UN itself. Indonesia withdrew his passport and demanded that the US deport him. Di Tiro's name was in Indonesian newspapers again when he criticised two massacres by Indonesian soldiers in early 1955.

By 1955, di Tiro and DI Aceh leader Daud Beureu'eh's public stance on the most viable relation between Aceh and the rest of Indonesia was some sort of federalism. This stance was embodied in the *Negara Bahagian*

Aceh-Negara Islam Indonesia (NBA-NII), and later, among the hold-out Beureu'eh wing of DI, in the short-lived *Republik Islam Aceh-Republik Persatuan Indonesia* (RIA-RPI).[18]

After 1957, from his home in New York, di Tiro travelled around the United States and to Southeast Asia, and Europe (including Holland, Switzerland and Germany) to advocate for, finance, and arm DI.[19] Di Tiro helped Aceh DI secure secret assistance from the United States. The US and its anti-communist allies — Taiwan, South Korea, South Vietnam, the Philippines, Thailand, Malaya, Britain and Australia were involved in covertly arming, training and otherwise assisting anti-Jakarta rebellions in the 1950s.[20] Most of the help went to the PRRI/Permesta military-led rebellions in Sulawesi and Sumatra.

Sulaiman reports that the Acehnese received weapons from the United States during 1958–9; the first shipment of 616 American guns came through the PRRI.[21] Amir Rasyid Mahmud, a DI courier based in Singapore (and the older brother of future GAM leader Malik Mahmud), says di Tiro's long friendship with Sjafruddin Prawiranegara, who became the civilian leader of the PRRI, strengthened ties between the two insurgent forces toward the end of the 1950s.[22] Sulaiman believes di Tiro and Sjafruddin were among those who put DI in contact with the US.[23]

Abu Kliet, aka Ramon Bazooka, a DI fighter during the late 1950s, said he and other Acehnese combatants received American uniforms, medicine packaged in wax, and weapons including bazookas and heavy machine guns from the United States.[24]

In the late 1950s, di Tiro sent Rasyid to South Vietnam to organise a load of guns and ammunition.[25] His contact was a Belgian priest (and ex-French Army officer) with close ties to top people in Diem's US-backed anti-communist government. Rasyid hired a floatplane to take the materiel to the east coast of Aceh. Rasyid is not certain, but he thinks this connection came through di Tiro's "friends" at the CIA, including Edward Lansdale. Citing a 1960 letter from di Tiro, Sjamsuddin says airplane drops coming from third countries were found to be prohibitively expensive, however.[26]

According to the Kahins, some of the PRRI men who were brought out by the United States for training at American bases and in several East Asian countries returned to instruct the PRRI and the DI forces in Aceh.[27] Kliet goes further: he says an American named Scott trained at least two DI battalions (his from West Aceh and another from South Aceh) in the forest near Banda in the late 1950s.

Meanwhile, overseas, di Tiro "was already going around talking independence. Independence inside or outside Indonesia — we didn't think about it," says Djuly.[28] Between 1959 and 1962, Djuly often lived with DI leader Daud Beureu'eh in the East Aceh forest: "Ordinary DI soldiers were always asking 'Why not Aceh meurdeka?' One DI soldier said to me, 'Why do we always fight for Indonesia?'"[29]

Beureu'eh and the last DI men left the forest in mid-1962, having attained, according to a leading historian of DI Aceh, "more than they had originally sought".[30] However, Djuly, di Tiro and at least some other DI veterans soon came to believe their achievement meant little.[31] "It seemed Indonesia had given us what we wanted," says Kliet, who eventually joined GAM and whose father had died in a final uprising against the Dutch in 1942. "[But] we learned if we didn't fight to become sovereign, Aceh could not be sovereign again."[32] DI's lessons passed to the next generation. "He taught me DI's mistake was to give up our guns," a GAM village head near Lhokseumawe told me about his uncle, a DI fighter. "He said it took him many years to understand how Indonesia worked, to understand we hadn't won anything at all."

Such realisations seem part of an incremental reawakening of Acehnese nationalism. The alliances of Beureu'eh with the two other DI rebellions and PRRI/Permesta were more tactical than they were ideological and also suggest a much stronger strictly political concern for Aceh even among the 'religious' side of Aceh DI than normally stated.[33] That concern prefigures the re-crystallisation of Acehnese nationalism in the independence demands of Aceh Merdeka.[34]

Throughout the 1960s, di Tiro lived in New York City. While he might not have understood certain changes going on in his homeland,[35] he maintained contact with various grassroots leaders in Aceh.[36] He also travelled often to Singapore to meet with future AM cabinet minister Amir Rasyid Mahmud and his younger brother, future GAM Prime Minister Malik Mahmud. According to the brothers, their many political discussions centred on DI's shortcomings and how to achieve independence from Indonesia.[37]

But after the ten-year DI rebellion, "ordinary people were tired of fighting," says Djuly. "What was the use of fighting if we cannot win?"

Independence *outside* Indonesia: Aceh Merdeka in the 1970s and 1980s

Time's passage brought hope and new energy to Acehnese dissatisfied with Indonesian rule. Confidence came first, as it often does, to men with the time and training to think and talk about 'what might be'. Even before he met di Tiro in 1973, Dr. Zaini Abdullah, a future AM cabinet minister, recalls conversations about independence among intellectuals, including AM's first Prime Minister, Muchtar Hasbi, and another future AM cabinet minister, Husaini M. Hasan.[38]

In several trips to Aceh from 1973–5, di Tiro was apparently viewed as the natural leader of the next effort at Acehnese self-determination. Zaini accompanied di Tiro to meetings in Pidie with hundreds of Acehnese leaders, including *ulama*, DI veterans, intellectuals and government officials. The next year, despite a police tail, di Tiro and Mahmud met with dozens of local leaders in small groups. Many of them, Mahmud says, endorsed a new effort to "gain Aceh's freedom".[39]

In October 1976, di Tiro returned without Indonesia's knowledge to begin an independence campaign. Mahmud recalls:

> There was already infrastructure, an organization ready for Teungku [di Tiro] .... DI combatants had been in communication with one another and di Tiro. Some of the DI people agreed with Teungku's ideas. Sons and younger brothers of DI were assigned by fathers and older brothers to help and to join AM. They were the ones who organized the villages. They would come to see Teungku.[40]

DI men served as the first political and military leaders in Aceh Merdeka.[41] The core of AM at its start were DI veterans, including hunter-trackers (*pawang*) and village heads (*geuchik*), and the younger family members of DI men, including 30-something intellectuals and doctors (both so often noted because they held the first AM cabinet positions). The first four AM military leaders were DI men in their 40s and 50s — di Tiro, Daud Paneuk (David the Short), 'Geuchik' Umar, 'Pawang' Rasyid. AM's second Prime Minister, Ilyas Leube, was a DI officer from Central Aceh. The fifth military chief, Abdullah Syafi'ie, had been a youthful DI supporter.[42]

There has always been some question whether Daud Beureu'eh — DI Aceh's pre-eminent political, military and spiritual leader — supported Aceh Merdeka, and whether the Free Aceh Movement should be seen as the legitimate successor to DI. The best available evidence suggests that Beureu'eh did support the new effort. According to Amir Rasyid, Beureu'eh felt he was too old to do much, but endorsed di Tiro to "take his place at the head" of a new struggle.[43] When di Tiro travelled to Aceh in 1974 and 1975, he met Beureu'eh. "I give everything to you,"

Djuly recalls Beureu'eh saying to di Tiro. "Aceh is in your hands now. Do it. I will help you."

The involvement of Pawang Rasyid, one of Beureu'eh's personal guards, and Leube, a DI officer very close to Beureu'eh, also suggests Beureu'eh's likely support. So do the personal ties between Beureu'eh and di Tiro. "Beureu'eh was very close to the di Tiro family and Hasan was like a son to him," recalls Djuly. "Hasballah, the oldest son of Daud [Beureu'eh], was close to Hasan." Di Tiro's older brother, Zainal Abidin di Tiro, had been a top Beureu'eh lieutenant and DI Aceh's Minister of Justice.

The strongest evidence of Beureu'eh's endorsement has recently come to light: the post-tsunami discovery of a written call from Beureu'eh to support the Free Aceh Movement. Dated 29 April 1977, six months after di Tiro re-declared Aceh's independence and national sovereignty, Beureu'eh penned a "Letter to the Achehnese Nation/People":[44]

> I herewith would like to tell the people of Acheh that we are now legitimately independent as we were in the past. From this day on, the only legitimate government on Achehnese soil is the independent and sovereign Government of the State of Acheh. This is the state and government that we all must abide by and defend. All religious treasuries, the portion set aside for *sabil*, and personal alms in Acheh must be delivered to our own Government of Acheh.

In mid-1978, the military drugged Beureu'eh and spirited him off to house arrest in Jakarta.

Aceh Merdeka did not have the support of all DI veterans. For and against seem to have fallen largely along the old lines of the DI *zuama-ulama* split. Hasan Saleh, DI Aceh's Minister of War and Beureu'eh's powerful *zuama* rival "fiercely opposed" AM.[45] Interestingly, Aceh Merdeka, a movement with secular aims, and di Tiro, a relatively secular man, drew not from DI's political *zuama* but from its ideological *ulama*.[46] In part, that may be because the *zuama* tended to be in the new political establishment. But other reasons should be entertained. Earlier, I wrote that DI could be seen as one step in the revival of Acehnese nationalism. Here, I suggest that Aceh Merdeka needs to be understood as a product of longer-standing historical sentiments that stretch back to the fight against the Dutch and of even deeper, centuries-old feelings that the Acehnese have about their unique place in the world.

Looking at the wider sweep of anti-colonial movements, di Tiro is hardly unique, of course. He fits a pattern of Third World insurgents–

to-be, including Indonesia's own first Vice-President Mohammad Hatta and other early nationalist leaders, who journeyed to the West for education or work of various kinds and came home to lead fresh challenges to the *status quo*.

But why did the movement emerge in 1976? Was it the development of natural gas and related facilities in the early and mid-1970s? To some extent, probably. As scholars have noted, di Tiro was directly affected by the gas projects. He failed to secure a multi-million dollar contract. It seems unlikely, despite his past, that di Tiro would have launched an independence struggle that could have hurt his own economic interests.

But in separate interviews in 2004, both di Tiro and Malik Mahmud were adamant that the timing of Aceh Merdeka resulted from things that had little to do with developments in Aceh or Indonesia. In his 1982 *The Price of Freedom: The Unfinished Diary of Tengku Hasan di Tiro*, di Tiro explains that in mid-1975 he was in a private jet whose engines had died. He promised himself that if God saved him, he would return to his duty and his destiny: leading his people, the Acehnese, and his country, Aceh, to freedom. About his decision, di Tiro told me he felt at the time that he "had lived long enough" — he was approaching 50, with 15 years in various businesses, a wife and a 6-year-old-son. It was "time to do what I was long supposed to do." A mid-life crisis of sorts. If we recall his family background, his extraordinary education and international experience, his relationship with Beureu'eh and his role during DI, such a grandiose vision of himself is not far-fetched. History has also proved him at least partly right.[47]

Why was Aceh Merdeka centred in the north and east? The standard response is that that was where New Order economic development and its problems were. That AM and GAM grew up there is thus used to bolster the explanatory power of the New Order economic argument about why AM emerged at all. But another explanation is possible. The north and east were historically the heart (not the entire body) of Acehnese resistance from Dutch times through the PUSA-led post-war social revolution and DI.[48] Economic development in Aceh long centred on that coast.[49] Pidie was also the home turf of di Tiro, Beureu'eh and other key DI leaders. In other words, the uneven impact of New Order changes could have played some role in AM's 'geography', but not a necessary one.[50]

New Order violence is the fulcrum of the orthodox view. In order to show the primacy of the New Order in explaining AM, analysts contrast the New Order's unforgiving response to the small AM insurgency with the Old Order's less violent response to the far larger Aceh DI.[51] Yet a number of reasons, besides the nature of the New Order, might explain why an earlier regime responded more flexibly to DI Aceh. Most obviously, Sukarno's Old Order could meet the political part of DI Aceh's demands without real harm to Indonesian unity. DI also enjoyed great sympathy among at least one of the largest political parties, Masyumi.[52] For a while, the government was battling several large, well-armed rebellions at once (the very weakness of the centre allowed the rebellions in the first place).[53] The army worried they would not be able to defeat DI Aceh:[54] Compared to the PRRI, DI Aceh enjoyed much greater support among the local population, operated in better guerrilla terrain, and had easier access to Malaysia.[55] Many Indonesian soldiers (both Acehnese and non-Acehnese) had also recently fought shoulder to shoulder against the Dutch with men who were now DI. The central military command wanted to turn its attention to dealing with the PKI, which was getting stronger and gaining Sukarno's support. Sukarno believed a settlement in Aceh would help him weaken the military; martial law and armed conflicts had increased its power relative to his.[56]

Moreover, in two respects, the contrast between New and Old Order responses is also overdrawn. First, even during the 20-plus years of Suharto's repression of Aceh Merdeka, the Indonesian government always had at least a *two-track* approach of brutal violence and non-violent persuasion (including what Indonesia called "mental upgrading"). In a variety of 'civic programmes', the government organised local *ulama*, village leaders and local Acehnese government officials to urge Aceh Merdeka to end its activities. The government also launched development projects.[57]

Second, the difference in government violence against DI and AM might not have been as great as the published record presumes. During the first several years of DI Aceh, there were worse massacres than under DOM, a similar display of brutalised dead bodies, and the rest.[58] Moreover, government violence against the Acehnese has been greater after the fall of the New Order, which makes clear other causal factors (and dynamics) are at work beside the nature of the regime.

It is also worth noting that by the late 1950s, Sukarno's Old Order prefigured the New Order in crucial ways: the dictatorial strength of the executive; the pervasive power of the military; the lack of elections; the dissolution or gutting of parliament, and periods of martial law; the banning and emasculation of political parties, and the key role of 'functional groups'.[59]

Perhaps surprisingly, Indonesian repression of Aceh Merdeka appears
to have caught di Tiro off-guard; he apparently believed AM could wage
its initial effort with words. Things first turned violent when the
government discovered AM's informational activities.[60] Mahmud, a
member of AM's first cabinet, recalls:

> Teungku [di Tiro] was not prepared for armed struggle. He said educate,
> develop the economy, etc. Others disagreed with him, argued with
> him and said, 'We need guns.' 'How many?' Teungku asked. The
> answer we gave was, 'If you don't have 10,000 guns you can't talk with
> your enemy.' When Teungku left Aceh, he knew we had to use armed
> struggle.

During the next few years, more than half of AM's first cabinet was killed
(including the first Prime Minister, Hasbi, in 1980 and the second,
Leube, in 1982). Other ministers fell into Indonesian hands or fled into
exile. At least 700 people (an extraordinarily high number for a supposedly
tiny movement) were imprisoned by 1980.[61] Indonesia believed they
had wiped out AM.[62] Appearances deceive, says Mahmud:

> By the numbers, there were only 50 in the jungle and it appeared to
> Indonesia we were finished. If you think like that, we can do more,
> we thought. It lulled the Indonesians ... and allowed us to rebuild
> without interference. We were working even harder to reorganize. The
> general public was supporting us even more; they were angry about
> the repression. All the while, the idea of independence was spreading.
> We had more people in 1982, but no means, no money, no arms.[63]

Other early Free Aceh members also claim more enthusiastic reception
of their ideas than usually noted. Two historians of the period summarise
that there was "widespread attention and sympathy" in the province.[64]
A young intellectual, Nurdin Abdul Rahman, was one of at least several
AM activists who worked for Bechtel at the LNG refinery project in
Lhokseumawe from 1975–6.[65] Rahman was arrested for circulating
informational leaflets. Upon release four years later, he was surprised at
the respect accorded him: "I thought people might treat me as ... a
pariah. [But] wherever I went in Aceh, people were happy to meet me.
I could see that the ideas had spread."

After 1979, AM's central command remained in Pidie, but AM had
already established groups of some sort in all the districts along the
coast between East Aceh and the capital, at the northernmost tip, as
well as in West Aceh.[66] After di Tiro fled Aceh in late 1979 (Indonesia
reported later they had killed him), Geuchik Umar, Daud Paneuk,

Pawang Rasyid and Abdullah Syafi'ie formed a four-person military-political leadership. After the departure of Daud Paneuk and an organisational restructuring, Umar became the top AM military commander in 1983. (He led until December 1992, when he was killed at the age of 70 in an ambush. Rasyid took over until he was killed in 1993. Syafi'ie was the top man in Aceh for a decade until he died in a firefight in February 2002.[67])

In the early 1980s, independence ideas quietly spread outside its northeast centre, recalls Rahman: "[S]tudents from around Aceh at the university where I was teaching English in Banda heard from students coming from Pidie and Lhokseumawe and went home to their villages with these ideas and news of what had happened."[68] Throughout the 1980s, there were constant arrests of AM "sympathisers", mostly farmers in their 30s and 40s.[69]

At the same time, di Tiro and his lieutenants on the outside were trying to make things happen anew. Mahmud, who lived in Singapore, recalls:

> We had a committee in KL [Kuala Lumpur] to pick people for training; it was made up of people from all areas [of Aceh]. People contacted me on the outside. They said, 'We are ready to do whatever.' They wanted to come out for training. We told people in Pidie, and suddenly 40 people were ready. They had sold their property, motor scooters and other things in anticipation. They said, 'We have the money for passports.' We told them to be patient. They were ready before we were.

As he had for DI, di Tiro sought training and other forms of assistance from the United States first.[70] He told this interviewer in 2004, "We have always been friends of the West." But his former friends, including legendary CIA operative Edward Lansdale, had either died or long before lost their pull. More importantly, well before Suharto's New Order, the United States had forsaken its strategy of supporting regional rebellion to achieve its economic and anti-Communist aims in Indonesia.

Indeed, just as the New Order had continuity with Sukarno's Old Order, the New Order also did not mark the decisive change in United States policy toward Jakarta. That change had already come by 1959.[71] At the end of 1958, the Eisenhower administration believed Sukarno was someone, as a National Security Council paper said, "to work with — not against" to combat the several million-strong PKI, the largest communist party outside the Soviet/Chinese bloc. The US ended large arms support of the rebellions in that year. Competition with the Soviets had also led the Americans to begin huge arms sales to Indonesia in November 1958 (unbeknownst to their DI and PRRI/Permesta allies).[72] By 1959, the power of the two biggest rebel supporters — the brothers Dulles, CIA Director Allan and Secretary of State John Foster (who died of cancer in the middle of the year) — declined within the US government.[73]

But if America would not help, there were new options for AM, less strategic to be sure, but useful in the short term. One possibility was Iran, says Mahmud, which offered to train Acehnese fighters:

> But they wanted us involved in an Islamic revolution. We had already tried that with DI. We were interested in independence, not religion; Islam was part of our lives, our culture. Another possibility was to fight in Afghanistan against the Soviets. That could have been useful experience. Again, we saw ourselves getting involved in something that didn't concern us. Syria [and] Libya were giving training. We chose Libya; we could just do what we had to do. The Libyans were surprised [in 1986] that when they said yes, we said we are ready. They wanted 50. Only 50? I had hundreds who wanted to go!

From 1986 to 1990, with few strings attached, more than 1000 men received military training in Qaddafi's Libya. Most came from Aceh's eastern and northern districts, but there was a conscious and successful effort to draw men from all over Aceh.[74]

"No More Time to Wait": The 1990s and the Post-Suharto Years

To explain why the Free Aceh guerrilla movement re-emerged in 1989, scholars have pointed to economic and political developments of the New Order in Aceh and Indonesia.[75] Yet, once again, AM's timing seems tied much more to the movement's internal processes, in this case, successfully solving one of the major shortcomings of 1976–9 and making sure that solution was not in vain. Mahmud recalls:

> Our fear was that Malaysia [where trainees returned] and Indonesia would find out about Libya. We also didn't want to wait too long: the boys were eager and ready. Some of the boys were waiting for two years .... When we began [in 1989], we still lacked guns. [But] [w]e believed we could get the guns from Indonesia if the boys did things properly.[76]

Mahmud says that he and others outside Aceh were "quite pleased with the performance of the 'boys'," who captured or bought a few hundred guns from the Indonesian military in late 1989 and early 1990.[77] But, by the middle of the next year, Indonesia's willingness to torture and kill anyone with the slightest connection to the guerrillas "put the 'boys' on the defensive".[78] Rather than responding carefully to AM's reemergence, what occurred, experts say, was the brutally violent reflex — an overreaction — of an unsparing New Order.[79]

Yet, if we look at the available evidence, the repression of the early 1990s appears less an overreaction than a necessary response to the extensive covert support and protection that Aceh Merdeka fighters say they received. The late AM (and GAM) commander Ishak Daud said he and his men were able to elude the military because "everywhere we went, people hid us and told us where the Indonesians were patrolling".[80] Civilians were tortured for information about his whereabouts, then killed and left in public places to "terrify Acehnese so that they wouldn't help me and my men". GAM leaders today imply independence sentiment was not something that had to develop even back then; they assumed it already existed. They simply needed to school and harvest it. However counter-productive the military's measures might appear in the long term to scholars and human rights activists,[81] the military might have correctly understood the urgent needs of that moment.

Kell has gathered a variety of evidence of extensive support for AM in the 1990s. Typically, experts have used that evidence to show support came principally as a *result* of repression. But on closer examination, it appears cause and effect should be reversed. Support came *before* the effects of New Order repression. Repression was the response.[82] A November 1990 report by Indonesian lawyers stated that the majority of Acehnese "agree with" Aceh Merdeka, but don't *openly* show their support: they hide the guerrillas and support them "silently".[83] In early 1991, *ulama* working with the government printed 100,000 booklets urging AM and its sympathisers to end the movement.[84] (A lot of paper to battle a tiny movement that the Indonesians claimed to have already defeated!) The regional Indonesian army commander, Maj. Gen. H.R. Pramono believed, in mid-1990, that the guerrillas were actually "running loose" and were "everywhere" among the people and had the support of "the masses" numbering in the "hundreds of thousands .... [T]here was no more time to wait."[85]

The then-governor said later that troops had to be brought in "before it snowballed and got bigger and bigger".[86] In other words, the troops were not causing the snowballing but responding to the already dangerous momentum of existing sentiment and support. AM had "active assistance" from village administrators, Acehnese in the urban bureaucracy and, more dangerously, from Acehnese in the army and police, including senior police officials.[87] Indeed, from DI to the present, Acehnese in the Indonesian security forces have not been reliable when fighting fellow Acehnese. A worrying number of Acehnese have always gone over to the rebels. According to Djuly, in the late 1950s, most of DI's guns came from Acehnese soldiers in the Indonesian ranks.[88] Non-Acehnese troops were brought in during the heaviest DI fighting, again to fight AM in 1976 (when an estimated half of all local troops were still DI veterans), and then again in 1990. These elite troops were not just better trained — they were not Acehnese.

In 1990, the threat of greater guerrilla activity and even perhaps of some kind of popular uprising seems to have been on the minds of Indonesian military and civilian leaders in Aceh. In other words, if there had not been such brutal repression — if there had been a 'political opportunity' — the huge independence movement of the post-Suharto years might instead have erupted back then (Fig. 13).

Instead, the military acted with sufficient ferocity to cut such possibilities short. While Aceh Merdeka was not crushed under Suharto,

Fig. 13 GAM guerrillas on patrol in the forest near the massive Exxon-Mobil natural gas facilities, North Aceh, June 2001 (*photo by William Nessen*)

it was largely pushed from the field. Initially excited by their success at capturing weapons, leaders on the outside, like Mahmud, admit they were "stunned" by Indonesian success against the first few hundred Libya trainees. The organisation survived because leaders were safe overseas and did not send other Libya men in. Perhaps less than a quarter of the Libyan-trained fighters were killed under DOM; some escaped back to Malaysia; some remained inside Aceh, and the largest number never left Malaysia (and many of them never did).[89] They had also drawn new recruits.

The Southeast Asian monetary crisis and the ensuing political changes in Indonesia would give the Acehnese a real 'opportunity'. In 1997, AM fighters began returning secretly to Aceh from Malaysia, in large part to avoid the large number of arrests of Acehnese by Malaysian police and the kidnapping of known AM men (Ishak Daud, most famously) by Indonesian intelligence agents. The Free Aceh Movement already had a large number of trained men in place when Suharto fell and reform swept Indonesia.[90]

GAM and independence sentiment in Aceh went 'public'. It is impossible to know whether a more drastic "mending" of government ways could have stemmed the independence tide. For example, in the angry and optimistic climate in Aceh, trials of Indonesian military personnel for past abuses would probably have swelled the independence movement, not deflated it (as foreign human rights groups contended).[91]

As an armed, hierarchical organisation, GAM naturally survived far better than the civilian referendum movement when *systematic* repression began in late 2000. It is tougher to kill people who can kill you back. In addition, the traditions of bold opposition to outside rule in Aceh have been largely martial. GAM had the only meaningful political network and remains the only organisation capable of coordinating large numbers of Acehnese for political action of any kind. To be sure, repression alone did not silence the referendum movement: a lack of organisation and tactical thinking helped too. International sympathy has been scant for Muslim Aceh, and once-optimistic referendum activists have learned a painful lesson about the West.[92] In 2002, an American Embassy official told Acehnese activists that he would not meet with them about Indonesian atrocities if they did not provide information of GAM violations.

With the massive military offensive from May 2003 to September 2005, the government and its security forces largely closed the political opportunity that came with Suharto's fall. Yet, the alternative view I have sketched should make clear that repression will not end Acehnese desire for independence.

This brief alternative reprise of Acehnese history should also warn outsiders that failing to distinguish between sentiment and its expression will lead again to the erroneous conclusion that most Acehnese do not want full independence from Indonesia.[93]

Postscript: The Two Tsunamis

The 26 December 2004 tsunami allowed an unprecedented international presence in Aceh. It put enormous pressure on GAM and especially the Indonesian government to find a peaceful way to resolve the conflict.

But more than the December tsunami, the two-year tsunami of the TNI (*TsuNamI*) has forced a change in GAM strategy. All of Aceh was inundated and terrorised. In large areas of Aceh, military and mobile police posts were established in every village. GAM's extensive logistics, intelligence and political networks in the villages and the towns broke down considerably. Thousands of people associated with GAM were killed. GAM has lost many of its guns and perhaps one-quarter of its fighters. While brave villagers kept other fighters alive and informed and a new cohort of Acehnese youth joined the fighters' ranks, guerrilla units were no longer properly equipped. The security forces knew they have made enormous progress.

In the face of this sustained and successful onslaught, GAM appears to recognise that establishing a new political space was probably the only way to continue the struggle for independence. GAM has proffered a radicalised version of the current special autonomy, what they called self-government. But it is not yet clear whether the Indian Ocean tsunami has created enough 'political opportunity' for GAM's self-government to be much more than special autonomy. In that sense, the effects of the two tsunamis are at war with each other.

Notes

[1]   Timothy Kell, *The Roots of Acehnese Rebellion 1989-1992* (Cornell University, Modern Indonesia Project 1995); Geoffrey Robinson, "Rawan is as Rawan Does: The Origins of Disorder in New Order Aceh", *Indonesia*, no. 66 (1998); Edward Aspinall, "Modernity, History and Ethnicity: Indonesian and Acehnese Nationalism in Conflict", in *Autonomy and Disintegration in Indonesia*, ed. Damien Kingsbury and Harry Aveling (New York; London:

RoutledgeCurzon, 2003), pp. 128–47; Human Rights Watch (HRW), "Indonesia: Why is Aceh Exploding", 1999; Sidney Jones, "Aceh: Why the Military Option Still Won't Work", *ICG Indonesia Briefing*, 9 May 2003; ICG, "Aceh: A Slim Chance for Peace", *ICG Indonesia Briefing*, 27 March 2002; ICG, "Aceh: Can Autonomy Stem The Conflict", *ICG Executive Summary*, 12 June 2001.

2   The key text is Robinson, "Rawan is as Rawan Does", p. 128.

3   HRW, "Indonesia: Why Aceh is Exploding"; Robinson, "Rawan", p. 140.

4   Aspinall, "Modernity, History and Ethnicity", p. 135.

5   Aspinall, "Modernity, History and Ethnicity", p. 135.

6   Robinson, "Rawan", p. 130.

7   The seminal text here is Kell, *The Roots of Acehnese Rebellion*, esp. pp. 52–60. See also Robinson, "Rawan", p. 139, and McGibbon, this volume.

8   Robinson, "Rawan", p. 133.

9   Anthony Reid, "War, Peace and the Burden of History in Aceh", *Working Paper Series*, No. 1 (Singapore: Asia Research Institute, 2003), <http://www.ari.nus.edu.sg/pub/wps.htm>.

10 Sidney Tarrow *et al.*, *Power in Movements: Social Movements, Collective Action and Politics* (Cambridge: Cambridge University Press, 1994), p. 81.

11 Alexis de Tocqueville, *Old Regime and the French Revolution* (New York: Doubleday, 1955), pp. 176–7, cited in Tarrow, *Power in Movements*, p. 81.

12 Reid, "War, Peace and the Burden of History in Aceh", p. 5.

13 See Nazaruddin Sjamsuddin, *The Republican Revolt: A Study of the Acehnese Rebellion* (hereafter *Republican*) (Singapore: Institute of Southeast Asian Studies, 1985), pp. 234–9.

14 Interview with Jacoub Djuly, May 2004, Kuala Lumpur.

15 According to Djuly, with the Dutch on their heels, during the last days of 1948 and into 1949, di Tiro and his contacts apparently guided Sjafruddin on his dangerous journey from West Sumatra to Aceh. However, Audrey Kahin, *Rebellion to Integration: West Sumatra and the Indonesian Polity 1926–1998* (Amsterdam: Amsterdam University Press, 1999), p. 141, and personal communication December 2004, leaves Sjafruddin in West Sumatra in late 1948.

16 Djuly interview. Djuly visited di Tiro in New York in February 1950.

17 On di Tiro: Reid, "Burden of History", p. 6; M. Isa Sulaiman, this volume; and for di Tiro's role in DI, Nazaruddin Sjamsuddin, "Issues and Politics of Regionalism in Indonesia: Evaluating the Acehnese Experience", in *Armed Separatism in Southeast Asia*, ed. Lim Joo-Jock and Vani S. (Singapore: Institute of Southeast Asian Studies, 1984), pp. 112–5; C. van Dijk, *Rebellion Under The Banner of Islam: The Darul Islam in Indonesia* (Dissertation, The Hague: Martinus Nijhoff, 1981), pp. 318–20. Interview with Hasan di Tiro, February 2004, Norsborg, Sweden; interview with Amir Rasyid Mahmud, May 2004, Singapore (Rasyid).

18 For di Tiro's federalism, see his 1958 book, *Demokrasi untuk Indonesia* (Penerbit Seulawah Aceh, 1958); and Kell, *The Roots of Acehnese Rebellion*, pp. 61–3; on DI federalism: Sjamsuddin, *Republican*, ch. 6 and pp. 295–7; Sulaiman, this volume.

19 Djuly interview, Rasyid interview.

20 See index in Audrey R. Kahin and George McT. Kahin, *Subversion as Foreign Policy* (New York: The New Press, 1995).

21 Personal communication, April 2003.

22 Rasyid interview.

23 Personal communication, May 2004; Sjamsuddin, in "Issues and Politics", p. 115.

24 Interview, August 2002, West Aceh.

25 Rasyid interview.

26 Sjamsuddin, *Republican*, pp. 211–2 and p. 239 fn. 37.

27 Kahin and Kahin, *Subversion,* p. 158, and Audrey Kahin, *Rebellion*.

28 Djuly interview.

29 Di Tiro joined Beureu'eh and Djuly for a few weeks during a 1959 cease-fire, ibid.

30 Sjamsuddin, *Republican*, p. 330.

31 See McGibbon, Miller and Sulaiman's chapters in this volume on how the governments of Sukarno and Suharto undermined the achievement of special regional autonomy.

32 Interview Abu Kliet, 2002.

33 Kahin and Kahin, *Subversion*, pp. 44, 202; Sjamsuddin, *Republican*, pp. 230–47.

34 Sjamsuddin, *Republican*, pp. 144–5, 152–3; Aspinall, this volume.

35 Sulaiman, this volume.

36 Interview with GAM Prime Minister Malik Mahmud, Norsborg, Sweden, February 2004.

37 Rasyid interview, Mahmud interview.

38 Interview with GAM Foreign Minister Zaini Abdullah, Norsborg, Sweden, February 2004.

39 For the whole paragraph: Zaini Abdullah and Mahmud interviews.

40 Mahmud interview; Zaini Abdullah interview.

41 For an example of those that mistakenly see little connection between DI and Free Aceh, see Anthony Smith, "Conflict in Aceh: The Consequences of a Broken Social Contract", *Harvard Asia Quarterly* 6, 1 (Winter 2002). Also Robinson, "Rawan", pp. 132–3.

42 Interviews with some dozen former DI fighters in mid-2002 in rural West Aceh who were GAM men; group interview with Malik Mahmud, Zaini Abdullah, and GAM Information Officer Bakhtiar Abdullah, February 2004, Norsborg, Sweden; interview with Munawar Zainal, September 2004, New York City. Also, see Hasan di Tiro, *The Price of Freedom: The Unfinished Diary of Tengku Hasan di Tiro* (Sweden: ASNLF Information Department, 1981).

43 Rasyid interview. See also Nazaruddin Sjamsuddin, *Integrasi Politik di Indonesia* (Jakarta: PT Gramedia, 1989), pp. 85–6. Hasan Saleh, *Mengapa Aceh Bergolak* (Jakarta: Pustaka Utama Grafiti, 1992), pp. 375, 384, 386.

44 Digital scanned copy in author's possession. The letter was among the personal papers of late GAM negotiator Teungku Sofyan Ibrahim Tiba, who died in the Banda Acheh prison when the tsunami hit. The letter was found in Tiba's home after the tsunami. Beureu'eh wrote the letter by hand in Achehnese using the *jawi* (adapted Arabic) script. This is the only known copy of the letter, and it is not clear how widely it was ever circulated.

45 Kell, *The Roots of Acehnese Rebellion*, p. 65 fn. 32.

46 See Kell, *The Roots of Acehnese Rebellion*, pp. 64–5, 70–1; Sulaiman, this volume; and a series of interviews with di Tiro entitled, "National Liberation Front of Acheh", in a Tehran newspaper *Kayhan International*, pp. 3, 10, 17 October 1982.

47 See Reid, "Burden of History", p. 9.

48 Eric Morris, "Aceh: Social Revolution and the Islamic Vision", in *Regional Dynamics of the Indonesian Revolution: Unity from Diversity*, ed. Audrey R. Kahin (Honolulu: University of Hawaii Press, 1985).

49 See Sulaiman, this volume.

50 See Robinson, "Rawan", pp. 130, 133.

51 Ibid., p. 140.

52 Kahin and Kahin, *Subversion*, pp. 44–5; Sjamsuddin, *Republican*, p. 145.

53 Sjamsuddin, *Republican*, p. 322.

54 Michelle Miller, this volume.

55 Sjamsuddin, *Republican*, pp. 145, 288–9.

56 For the political reasons: Sjamsuddin, *Republican*, pp. 286–90.

57 On 1976: Sjamsuddin, "Issues and Politics", p. 114; 1990: Kell, *The Roots of Acehnese Rebellion*, pp. 75–81.

58 Sjamsuddin, *Republican*, pp. 126–7; see Aspinall, this volume, on the massacres and government violence generally.

59 Sjamsuddin, *Republican*, pp. 217–20; Marcus Mietzner, "Business as Usual? The Indonesian Armed Forces and Local Politics in the Post-Soeharto Era", in *Local Power and Politics in Indonesia: Decentralization and Democratization*, ed. Edward Aspinall and Greg Fealy (Singapore: Institute of Southeast Asian Studies, 2003), p. 247; Daniel Lev, *The Transition to Guided Democracy* (Ithaca: Cornell Modern Indonesia Project, 1966), p. 286.

60 Sjamsuddin, "Issues and Politics", p. 113.

61 "Repression in Aceh", *Tapol Bulletin*, No. 45, May 1981.

62 Zaini Abdullah interview.

63 Mahmud interview.

64 Kell, *The Roots of Acehnese Rebellion*, p. 65, citing Eugene Morris, "Islam and Politics in Aceh: A Study of Centre-Periphery Relations in Indonesia" (PhD Thesis, Cornell University, 1985), p. 300.

65 Interview with Nurdin Abdul Rahman, November 2003, Sydney; Kell, *The Roots of Acehnese Rebellion*, p. 69, fn. 55.

66 Mahmud interview.
67 Interview with Umar's son-in-law, GAM spokesperson Bakhtiar Abdullah, February 2004, Norsborg, Sweden.
68 Rahman interview, November 2003.
69 See Amnesty International, *Urgent Action Report for Indonesia*, 4 November 1983.
70 di Tiro interview.
71 Kahin and Kahin, *Subversion*, pp. 209–16, 220–30.
72 Ibid., p. 206.
73 Ibid., pp. 208–9.
74 Mahmud interview
75 McGibbon, this volume; Robinson, "Rawan", p. 138; Kell, *The Roots of Acehnese Rebellion*, p. 71.
76 Mahmud interview.
77 Mahmud says that he and others outside Aceh were "quite pleased with the performance of the boys", ibid.
78 Bakhtiar Abdullah interview.
79 Robinson, "Rawan".
80 Interview with Ishak Daud, Alue Dua, Aceh, Jan. 2003.
81 Robinson, "Rawan".
82 Kell, *Roots of Acehnese Rebellion,* pp. 66–7.
83 YLBHI, "Observasi Lanjutan Kasus 'Aceh Merdeka'", p. 10, cited in Kell, *Roots of Acehnese Rebellion*, p. 70.
84 Kell, *Roots of Acehnese Rebellion*, p. 70.
85 Cited in Kell, *Roots of Acehnese Rebellion*, pp. 66–7.
86 Ibid., p. 74.
87 Ibid., p. 68.
88 Djuly interview. See also Sjamsuddin, *Republican*, pp. 54, 255–6, 308.
89 Mahmud interview.
90 Mahmud interview; interview with Sofyan Daud, North Aceh, December 2002; Ishak Daud, January 2003, and other GAM fighters.
91 HRW, "Why is Aceh Exploding". Two Acehnese human rights activists with ties to GAM, Rahman (interview) and Musliadi (interview, November 2003) said such trials would have just increased Acehnese anger. Security forces kidnapped, tortured and murdered Musliadi only days after my last interview with him.
92 Interviews and discussions with numerous members of SIRA since 2001.
93 Ironically, the Acehnese have long aided such a conclusion. To protect the referendum movement and human rights groups, both GAM and civilian activists have pretended there are no substantial connections or mutual support between them.

11

Military Business in Aceh

Damien Kingsbury and Lesley McCulloch[1]

Introduction

The Indonesian military (TNI) has in part predicated its existence and its political role in containing instability and disaffection: it has promoted itself and become established as the guarantor of the state. This role has, however, played a significant part in perpetuating instability and disaffection that has challenged the state. In some areas the TNI has — by design rather than default — contributed to maintaining this disequilibrium, thus creating the very conditions that justify its role. Both parallel to and overlapping this self-perpetuating function is the TNI's need to finance up to three-quarters of all its operational and readiness costs, which are not met by the state (on-line) budget. According to a range of sources, the TNI does this by its involvement in business activities in almost all sectors and at all levels of the Indonesian economy: at the formal, grey (informal), and even at the criminal level.

Not only do these business activities make a significant contribution to the shortfall in funding of the TNI, such profiteering also contributes to the length and intensity of violent conflict in several areas within the archipelago. Rather than being a force for unity, the military has become in part responsible for much of the internal conflict that threatens Indonesia's stability.[2] Moreover, much of the profit derived from these businesses often accrue to medium and senior level officers, providing further incentives for the TNI to perpetuate its inter-linked roles.

This chapter studies the above situation as it has related to Aceh, placing it within the context of military business throughout the state. It also discusses the problematic economic activities of the TNI within the broader framework of security sector reform (SSR). The SSR approach recognises the various structural, cultural and economic obstacles to military reform, which has been characterised as "pulling the military back to the barracks".

SSR Agenda in Indonesia

The complex and entrenched problematic nature of some of the less acceptable behaviour of the Indonesian security forces has been the focus of analysis for many years. The prescribed solutions have, however, tended to be of a traditional, military approach and have resulted in little, if any, real progress toward a more accountable and professional military in Indonesia.

The security sector comprises the following categories:

- groups with a mandate to wield instruments of violence including military and police forces, paramilitaries and intelligence services;
- institutions with a role in managing and monitoring the security sector; ministerial offices, civilian ministries, legislative mechanisms and civil society organisations;
- bodies responsible for guaranteeing the rule of law including the judiciary, the penal system, human rights ombudsmen, customary and traditional authorities and, where these bodies are particularly weak, the international community.

This chapter is not about the SSR agenda as such, but rather a study of the problems of only one group from the first of these three sub-sections, the military; while the analysis, however, benefits from widening the field of vision to include broader structural, political and economic influences and constraints. Viewed in this way, it becomes clear that the economic activities of the military are part of the wider issue of governance within Indonesia. Two of the seven challenges for security sector reform are relevant to this discussion: the formation of professional security forces, and the establishment of capable and responsible civil authorities.[3]

To achieve the first, the professionalisation of the security forces, a programme of doctrinal and skill development, technical modernisation, an understanding of and a commitment to the importance of accountability and the rule of law, and the effective "de-militarisation" of political culture must be implemented. To achieve the second, capable and responsible civil authorities, the executive and legislative branches of government must have access to independent information and expertise for consultation to enable them to achieve the capacity to develop security policy and to manage and oversee the security sector.[4] They must also have the capacity to assert authority over the security sector, rather than being reliant on and influenced by the self-serving agenda of the security sector, especially that of the military.

The specific concern of this chapter is the financing of the TNI. It is widely accepted that the official defence budget in Indonesian falls far short of what is actually required by the military for its operational, readiness and developmental costs. In fact, the central budget provides only around 25 to 30 per cent of what is actually required.[5] To compensate for this shortfall, the TNI undertakes its own economic activities. Initially to pay for troop welfare, these funds are now an integral part of the military's funding, for purchase of small weapons, spares, repairs and other costs. Moreover, there has been a burgeoning of the military's profit-making activities in the informal and criminal economy as many officers seek personal enrichment, often earning many times their official salary from these "businesses" endeavours.[6]

The term "off-budget" includes any contributions that lie outside the official defence budget, such as expenditures that might fall within the health, education or other line items in a national budget, including "hidden" contributions. It has been argued that such funding has come at a price, with a negative effect on transparency and accountability as well as levels of professionalism within the armed forces.

The focus of this chapter is the off-budget contributions that are derived from the business, informal and criminal activities. These activities have eroded the already low level of professionalism, which has in turn led to a decrease in the capacity of the military to carry out its prescribed function of defending the state with integrity. In addition, there is a direct relationship between the military's pursuit of profit and the level of human rights abuses, for which the Indonesian military is infamous.

Every Indonesian president, including Suharto, has felt the need to secure the military's support; compromise and accommodation have been the hallmarks of each administration. The notable exception was the impeached former president Abdurrahman Wahid. President Wahid tried to legislate for reform of the military, which was regarded by the military as too far-reaching and too fast in pace. Several powerful military officers, together with many in the political elite, were able to conduct manoeuvres that led eventually to his downfall.[7]

In Indonesia, the SSR agenda has thus fallen victim to power politics and a high level of military resistance. The security sector is influenced by and responds to a range of informal norms and practices that are closely shaped by national political, cultural and social circumstances. That is, as Kingsbury identifies: "the civil state continues to be so fundamentally weak, and the military relatively so strong, that the continued existence of the state without the active intervention of the military is at least improbable and perhaps impossible".[8] That is to say, an active (and actively compromised) role for the military is implicit in the structure of the Indonesian state, and this allows the TNI to remain to a large degree autonomous from the civilian authority.

The Budget

The TNI's on-line or formal budget fluctuates from year to year, reflecting the requirements of the military, its influence on, and economic and political capacities of the Jakarta administration. In 1998–99, the defence budget was Rp 10,349 billion (US$1,535 million).[9] In 1999–2000 this figure decreased to Rp 10,254 billion, and increased significantly the following year to Rp 13,945 billion. This increase continued in 2001 to Rp 16,416 billion (US$1,748 million). Such a large increase at a time when the economy was still struggling with the aftershocks of the economic crisis reflects the fact that the TNI was already reclaiming some of the political influence lost with the downfall of Suharto.[10] Of this budget, a little more than half was intended for paying salaries, about 30 per cent for purchasing equipment, about 8 per cent for maintenance and around 6 per cent for construction.

In 2002 the military saw its official budget cut to Rp 11,000 billion; some of the loss was compensated by a commitment of Rp 13,900 billion the following year. And in 2004, the official defence budget was Rp 13,200 billion. The fluctuations in the official military budget, however, do not reflect the total amount dedicated to the TNI by the government. For example, "contributions" to the security forces also come from the natural disaster fund, and health and education budgets. Often not appearing as a line item of expenditure in these budgets, such contributions are part of the military's "hidden" income.

During the period 1991–6, the defence budget was a steady 1.6 or 1.7 per cent in GDP. In the climate of the 1997 economic crisis this fell to 1.3 per cent and has not yet fully recovered, hovering around 1 per cent. That is, the increase in the defence budget has not kept pace with Indonesia's GDP, hence the diminishing burden. Budgetary changes in 2000 saw the rupiah value of on-line TNI income lift by more than 30 per cent, following a request from the Defence Minister Juwono Sudarsono for a 62 per cent increase.[11] Juwono pointed out at that time that the only way to remove the TNI from business activities was to fund it properly. However, the 32 per cent increase did not alter the level or style of the TNI's financial activities.

In 2004, the official defence budget of Rp 13.2 trillion continued to fail to meet the operational and readiness costs of the military. TNI headquarter has said that from this total, it will struggle to meet the salary obligations of Rp 11.5 trillion.[12] The shortfall will be met from businesses and substantial subsidies from other budgets. Furthermore, since autonomy laws gave regions increased budgets and control of their own expenditure, the military has been lobbying for and receiving financial contributions from these local authorities.[13]

Apart from on-line budgeting and its legal and illegal businesses, to demonstrate how desperately short of cash the military was and remains (in large part due to some funds being siphoned off), the TNI also raises income from a range of official sources. In its budget papers for 2001, the Department of Defence noted that the TNI's on-line budgeted costs were Rp 8,553,529,870,000 (a little less than US$ one billion[14]), of which Rp 9,295,500,000 (US$ one million) was raised through official departmental means.[15]

The contribution from the TNI official business activities, mostly run through *yayasan*[16], or non-taxable charitable foundations, has been small but significant. When they were audited for the first time in 2000, the National Audit Agency (BPK) found that internal control and supervision did not effectively exist within these *yayasan*. Moreover, there was evidence that finances were mismanaged, that the relationship between the foundations, their businesses and the military units that operated the *yayasan* was unclear and that most funds were not used for the purposes for which the *yayasan* were established (which was troop welfare).[17] These *yayasan* in turn ran their own businesses, as well as receiving donations of funds from unspecified and unaccountable sources. Despite their capacity to generate off-line income, the International Crisis Group claimed that *yayasan* only accounted for a fraction of off-line budget income.[18]

According to Juwono Sudarsono, the TNI owned or had interests in around 250 businesses,[19] but about two-thirds of these business profits were siphoned off before reaching the coffers of the TNI's respective forces.[20] Military business originated with the first military formation during the revolution of 1945–9, when it needed to be a self-sufficient guerrilla army, and then in the early days of the Republic when funding for the military was limited by the government's general lack of discretionary spending power. As noted in a Dutch intelligence report from that time, Republican officers operating in the Yogyakarta region engaged not only in business activities but in opium smuggling. It was also from this time that young Sino-Indonesian businessmen, such as Liem Sioe Liong, began what was to become an enormously lucrative business association with army officers.[21] With moves to reduce and "professionalise" the army in the early 1950s, many units found they could avoid much of this reductionist pressure by providing for themselves, hence avoiding the central budget. Indeed, the ability to be self-providing was often seen as a responsibility of local commanders.[22] Some commanders, such as then Colonel Suharto, appeared to take up this responsibility with considerable enthusiasm. Indeed, Suharto's enthusiastic involvement in business — including barter trade, "levies" on goods and services, industry and shipping, primarily via two *yayasan* (the model for the later development of military *yayasan*) — made him the subject of a corruption investigation. He was transferred from the command of the Diponegoro Division in October 1959 to redeem himself through a stint at the Army Staff Command School (*Sekolah Staf Komando Angkatan Darat* — SSKAD).[23] Therefore, the practice of siphoning off funds dates back to at least the 1950s and has continued as a standard operation. This lack of accountability meant that commanding officers retained the capacity to fund networks of patronage, that there was scope for the financing of independent or unofficial military, intelligence and political activities, and that officers were able to supplement their official incomes.

The Use of Off-line Income

The TNI's off-line or informal income is used for a range of purposes, although because most income is hidden in various ways, the exact level of income and its use are not known. Even within the TNI there is genuine vagueness up at the highest level about precisely how much the military earns from its businesses and what this is used for, reflecting the often very localised nature of much income generation and expenditure. One investigation, by the Indonesian Institute of Sciences (LIPI), estimated that TNI businesses had assets worth US$8 billion in 1998, across the range of activities.[24] And of course, activities that fall outside even Indonesia's own flexible legal parameters are never discussed or acknowledged in public. As with its manpower allocation, the TNI's business activities are spread across the archipelago, although tending to be concentrated in and around Jakarta and in the wealthier commodity producing provinces.

The off-line income derived by the branches of the TNI was used in three primary ways. The first was to buy capital goods and equipment for the TNI and its personnel, including the so-called "welfare" function; the second was for reinvestment into businesses; and the third was by way of cash payments primarily to senior officers, although TNI members of all ranks could benefit where they have access to business activity or through patronage networks. Salaries for junior TNI personnel do not adequately cover their living costs, especially for those with families, so there is a "top-up" function for their income through direct cash payment or, more usually, free or subsidised goods, education, health benefits and housing. Officers receive a higher income, but as a consequence of ingrained notions and requirements of patronage, they are expected to display a level of wealth as well as to disburse such wealth, which is well beyond their formal income. So, they too receive cash payments from various sources, usually through military *yayasan* (from which they skimmed profit),[25] from their own private businesses (which have TNI business directed towards them and which can place undue pressure on existing competition), and from percentage pay-offs from businesses under their "protection".[26]

The territorial structure is the primary institutional linkage by which wealth is created and distributed within the TNI. Members of the TNI who can manipulate their positions, which basically means ranks of non-commissioned officers and above, undertake "favours" for more senior officers and are in turn "looked after". Such "services rendered" can include quite conventional or mundane military duties, as well as special favours.[27] In this sense, there is little distinction between official and non-official military duties, especially in the Army. Being "looked after" frequently means having education provided for a soldier's children, but can also mean cash payment or granting opportunities through which easy money can be earned, such as establishing legal or black businesses, paying commissions on or directing purchases to such business or encouraging non-military businesses to deal with such military-linked businesses. According to Bob Lowry, in the mid-1990s, just prior to their retirement, officers were usually posted to areas where they wanted to retire, and given the time and opportunity to set up local business activities.[28] Kammen and Chandra[29] confirmed this was the case for non-commissioned officers. Rutherford also claimed (with considerable evidence) that "Military officers have a stake in the designation of certain areas as 'unstable'. Former commanders often live out their retirement in East Timor or Irian Jaya so they can reap the harvest of profitable business deals made in the areas under their command."[30]

Patron-clientism

In what amounts to a patron-client relationship — referred to by some outsiders as "bapakism"[31] — junior officers may owe allegiance directly to officers several rungs up their own command structure, or to officers outside their own direct command structure. Such a patron-client relationship might initially be established when junior and senior officers work in the same command and then separate, but retain their mutual obligation. Or it may somewhat less frequently originate through association with officers already established in such a separated patron-client relationship, i.e. a captain who owes allegiance to a brigadier-general in a separate line of command might bring in a colleague for a particular purpose, who would then also join that particular patron-client network (although usually at a lower level). Such patron-client relationships are, according to a confidential intelligence assessment, "totally endemic" in the TNI.[32]

Beyond cash payments and free or subsidised goods to military personnel, the various sources of income are also used for "professional" purposes, from the purchase and maintenance of military goods and equipment as basic as petrol to vehicle, ship and aircraft spare parts, to bullet-proof vests and vehicles, to large capital items such as ships, planes and other major military purchases, and extending as far as paying for covert or otherwise formally unauthorised military operations, such as for the training, armaments and salaries of militia.

Sources of Income

Income for these purposes is derived from three revenue streams. The first is businesses owned and operated by the branches of the TNI, usually through (still tax exempted but now theoretically auditable) *yayasan* and co-operatives, including natural resources and agricultural business, finance, real estate, manufacturing and construction. The second is from the "grey economy" such as the leasing out (or imposition) of military services and surcharges imposed on purchases, along with mixing private and military business interests. The third and most lucrative source of income is through the black market, in particular smuggling of oil or oil products, illegal mining and logging. In the latter case, one study shows that in Aceh's Bukit Tigapuluh National Park, 13 of the 25 illegal sawmills operating just south of the park were connected to the military.[33] Such black market trade began as barter trade and minor smuggling to directly finance the TNI, but quickly turned into personal enrichment for many senior officers. Apart from the black market, there was also a range of other illegal activities such as protection rackets, organised prostitution, drug production, distribution and dealing, gambling and even piracy and gun running.

Not surprisingly, with so much of Indonesia's wealth located in the commodity-rich provinces, the Army also has a close association with key income producing businesses. These associations are multi-faceted, in part being in response to separatist violence in Aceh and West Papua, to protect key installations from attack or threat of attack — which the TNI can manipulate or create in order to enhance the need for its protection — and in part as a form of rent-seeking behaviour rationalised under the Army's informal but lucrative "protection" policy, in which a percentage of the profits are siphoned off as "protection" payments. It is not surprising, therefore, that the Army has a significant presence in the vicinity of both the ExxonMobil sites near Lhokseumawe in Aceh. The creation of enclave industries imposed without the agreement of local communities, has, to date, bred high levels of conflict.[34]

In such circumstances, local TNI battalions are well entrenched in the business of "protecting" foreign-owned companies. Besides making direct cash payments to the local battalions, and in at least one case, buying them equipment (armoured four-wheel drives), the companies provide numerous perks, such as free air travel, holidays, housing and cash to regional officers. Government agencies, such as Pertamina and the State Logistics Agency (Bulog),[35] founded in 1966 and initially dominated by the Army, as well as private companies, also "donated" funds to the TNI.[36] This was especially the case where companies were involved in natural resource extraction and were located in a site of potential or actual conflict. These funds were donated by way of cash payments or gifts to senior officers to help ensure uninterrupted operations. In some cases this amounted to "protection" payments, in which the TNI not only demanded payment but would fulfil threats if payments were not made. In other cases, payment was intended to buy political leverage or goodwill.[37]

Reform?

The conventional view of Indonesian politics and the TNI in the period following May 1998 was that the state was undergoing a process of democratic transition and that the military was itself undergoing reform.[38] Elaboration of this view holds that, after 40 years of authoritarian military-backed government, Indonesia was following the Latin American example of shedding military intervention in civil affairs through military "professionalisation",[39] corresponding to what Huntington refers to as "The Third Wave".[40] However, fundamental aspects of Indonesia's political and economic history, ethnic composition and its geographic characteristics all contributed to a different context from that of Latin America. The TNI was compromised by its reliance on private and often illegal businesses, hence contributing to a different outcome from the successful moves away from military domination in Latin America. And even in Latin America, the success of bringing the military under civilian control was sometimes limited.[41]

The authors suggest that Indonesia's process of *reformasi* halted around the time when the elected president Abdurrahman Wahid was deposed from office in a constitutional coup in July 2001, to be replaced by his more conservative vice-president Megawati Sukarnoputri. The senior echelons of the TNI were opposed to Wahid's continuing presidential tenure and helped undermine his presidency. Further, after Megawati became president, the TNI assumed greater political authority and autonomy in cabinet, constitutional affairs and security matters. That is, Indonesian politics moved back towards a type of militarisation that had characterised it during the New Order era. The TNI's own process of "professionalisation" has removed it from being a personal tool of the president, but at the same time removed it from being accountable to the president. Where it has behaved "unprofessionally", most senior officers attribute this to "rogue elements" or *oknum* (military gangsters[42]), rather than acknowledging it as conventional operation.

Military Business in Aceh

In Aceh, there is very little formal military business, with most of the economic activities being in the informal, predominately illegal economy. Unlike in East Timor, where military business was often a spin-off from the "legal" businesses, in Aceh, such activities are largely independent of any legal structure. Without doubt, some of the benefits are used to supplement the meagre operational and readiness budget given by the central government; but significant sums accrue to military entrepreneurs who have become reliant on such "off-salary" sources of income. From May 2003, such activities took place against a backdrop of martial law. But even before this, Aceh was heavily militarised; the initial withdrawal of troops after the period 1989–98, when Aceh was a special militarised area (DOM), was not sustained. As the military has regained some political muscle, an increasing number of troops have been deployed in the province, and Aceh has become renowned for being a lucrative military posting. There is a common joke among the troops: "if you go to Aceh, you will come back either dead or very rich". It has even been suggested that such profiteering has become one of the motivating factors in the perpetuation of the conflict, and that "greed" is in fact "the silent force of the conflict in Aceh".[43]

Aceh has a long history of resistance and unrest; the violent conflict in concern here is, however, only that of the most recent past, since the establishment of the separatist movement GAM (*Gerekan Aceh Merdeka*) in 1976. From a very small rebellion in the 1970s, the conflict waxed and waned in level of intensity; so did the level of militarisation in the province. By 1998, Aceh had been under the status of DOM for almost ten years, which was only lifted by Suharto's successor Habibie. At the same time, the press was also given more freedom: public information about gross and systematic violations of human rights in the province during the DOM period began to emerge, leading to an increasing anger among the Acehnese. Perhaps not surprisingly, the support for, and the strength of the GAM, has grown since the end of DOM.

In early 1999, a group of Acehnese intellectuals and politicians met to discuss the political future of the province. The majority supported a referendum on the future status of Aceh. At the same time, a coalition of student organisations was coming together to form the Information Centre for an Aceh Referendum (SIRA). This new movement, led by SIRA, was responsible for organising a rally to express popular support for the right of the Acehnese to vote on whether to remain within the Republic, or to establish an independent state.

After a decade of effective military rule and in a background of the withdrawal of some troops after the lifting of DOM, it did look as if the military was losing its grip in Aceh. Not only did a popular civil society movement begin to emerge, the GAM was also enjoying increasing support, and began to make itself a more cohesive and structured organisation. So impressive and rapid was the development of GAM that Anthony Reid suggested that "the Free Aceh Movement (*Gerakan Aceh Merdeka* or GAM) began to look more and more like a government in waiting".[44] The civilian momentum encouraged by SIRA and other groups, together with the more organised independence movement and a more democratically-inclined President Abdurrahman Wahid in power, resulted in dialogue between the government and GAM.

The military was never comfortable with the pursuit of a peaceful, political solution to the conflict. For some time, powerful hard-line elements within the TNI had been pressing to be allowed to pursue a full-scale military solution in response to the increasingly volatile situation in Aceh. In the months before his impeachment in July 2001, President Wahid, in a vain attempt to appease his political opponents and garner military support, signed Presidential Instruction No. 4, 2001 on Aceh. It was, in theory at least, a new policy on Aceh, consisting of six points including political dialogue and special autonomy. In fact the decree was no more than "the provision of a political and legal umbrella for a new military operation".[45] With the downfall of Wahid and his replacement by Megawati Sukarnoputri, there was mounting pressure from the TNI for a military solution to the irritating conflict in the northwest of the archipelago.[46]

The negotiation for peace spanned four years, with its foundation in the presidency of Abdurrahman Wahid, before it finally collapsed in May 2003, leading to the imposition of martial law. At times it did appear that progress was being made in the negotiation between the Indonesian government and GAM towards finding at least a temporary cessation to the conflict. But the process was characterised by distrust, with each side making frequent threats to withdraw from the negotiation. The events leading to the eventual collapse of the peace process were in fact more than simply a manifested lack of compromise — the military had finally lost patience and asserted their political influence.

In the months before the collapse of the talks, some in the military and government had begun to make public statements that unless GAM renounced its push for independence and fully accept the special autonomy status already given to the province, there would be no further negotiation. As the level of violence in Aceh increased with attacks on the personnel and infrastructure of the Joint Security Committee (JSC), the institution whose job was to monitor violations of the then existing Cessation of Hostilities Agreement (CoHA), the fragile peace process was in imminent danger of collapse. The attacks were carried out by militia groups, generally thought to be supported by the TNI. Reid argues that this "strongly suggests that those elements of the military which most strongly opposed the CoHA were able to use tactics familiar from East Timor to wreck it at the local level".[47]

Eventually, bowing to pressure from these hardliners, the Megawati administration adopted the ultimatum as government policy. This demand that GAM effectively surrender, together with a second prerequisite that the latter lay down its weapons, was rejected by the movement's negotiators and the peace process ended. A fundamental obstacle in the now collapsed process was that "leaders in Jakarta were determined to maintain Indonesia's territorial integrity and prevent 'national disintegration', while GAM leaders were equally adamant that Aceh had an incontrovertible right to independence".[48] On this crucial point, the political future of Aceh, neither common ground nor compromise could be found.

The crackdown that the government had promised was the largest military operation since Indonesia invaded East Timor in 1975; with just under 60,000 troops and police being deployed in Aceh.[49] The motives behind this military manoeuvring have been increasingly questioned. There is a growing acceptance of the view that the economic interests of the military explain, at least in part, the government's reluctance to pursue a political solution to the problems in Aceh. Traditionally the conflict was viewed with the belief that the Acehnese felt they were legally entitled to be an independent state as they had never been legally colonised; that there was a general sense that the riches of the province were being plundered by companies such as ExxonMobil with little in return, and that those responsible for the gross and systematic human rights abuses in Aceh over years should be brought to justice.

Owing to the argument that a fairer share of the revenue from Aceh's vast natural wealth should remain in the province, in January 2002 Aceh was granted "special autonomy".[50] Much of the revenue from local oil, timber and other natural resources would remain in the province. The benefits have, however, yet to be seen by the people. In most parts of the province, the local economy remains stagnant; many schools and health care clinics wait to be rebuilt or repaired; and local irrigation and development projects to be funded by the autonomy windfall have yet to begin. There has been much media attention to local financial mismanagement; the Governor, Abdullah Puteh was convicted of corruption and embezzlement.[51] Moreover, a Central Bank study in 2001 concluded that Aceh was the most corrupt province in Indonesia.[52]

There is one aspect of the economic argument that is not addressed by the new status of special autonomy, the perception that Aceh's wealth is also being plundered by the military posted there; that "Aceh is simply too lucrative a place for military officers who rely so heavily on non-budgetary sources of income."[53] Not only does the pursuit of profit by the military affect the longevity and intensity of the conflict, but it is causing impoverishment of the local population, 40 per cent of whom live in poverty.[54] To facilitate such profiteering and enrichment, the military now have a vested interest in maintaining a level of conflict that justifies their presence.

The argument that the pursuit of profit is necessitated by the inadequate military budget has continued under martial law. Initially, a budget of Rp 1.3 trillion (US$153 million) was allocated for the first six months of the military operation in Aceh. But after only three months, armed forces commander Gen. Endriartono Sutarto was heard lamenting the inadequacies of the budget allocation. It has been estimated that the operation costs Rp 8.5 billion per day.[55] This includes all operational and running costs, as well as the Rp 21,000 daily allowance paid to each military personnel during their tour of duty in Aceh.[56] When martial law was extended for a further six months in November, an additional Rp 1.7 trillion was approved.

TNI "Business" Activities in Aceh

Aceh is rich in natural resources, and also has high manufacturing and agricultural capacity. The importance of its oil reserves has dwindled, but liquid natural gas (LNG) has become particularly profitable. The forests contain vast quantities of valuable wood; the coastal waters are rich fishing grounds; fertiliser and cement plants make significant contributions to the national economy; commercial crops, such as rubber, coffee, palm oil and coconuts, are grown with ease. Most people in Aceh can grow enough food from the fertile land when the conflict does not prevent them from farming.

The military is funded not only by abundant natural resources, but also by its wide involvement in the economy. For many years it has been an open secret that elements within the military are involved in illegal fishing, logging, trade of wildlife, drugs, and commercial plantations such as coffee, palm oil and other plantations. The security forces have actually become an integral part of the functioning economy and society. Troops are also known to provide "protection" to ExxonMobil, the

American oil giant with lucrative operations in the north of the province. In brief, the TNI is "monopolising local production, extraction, transport and processing of some natural resources; price controlling; appropriating land for themselves and on behalf of other parties; and many other commercial activities".[57] Such "criminal opportunism" is not confined to "lootable" commodities, but extends to collecting illegal fees from military checkpoints along the roads, "helping themselves" in restaurants and shops, and imposing fees for the release of those arrested or even dead bodies. Pursuing financial gains in every conceivable opportunity has become an integral part of the military's culture in Aceh.

The military is even supporting a drug economy in Aceh. There had long been suspicion of military involvement in the production, harvesting and transportation of grade-A marijuana, but this was difficult to verify due to lack of information during the DOM period. With more information available after DOM, this military business came to light. In one case, five serving soldiers were found by police to be transporting 60kg of the drug from Aceh to Medan.[58] From Medan, it would be split into smaller packages and sent, probably through a continuing military network, all over the archipelago.[59]

The following is a profile of the level and type of (TNI's) involvement in criminal opportunist activities that have flourished in Aceh in recent years.

Drugs

The military is less involved in the drugs economy now than in the past due to efforts by the police to limit this illegal trade, but it is still significant. The security forces "encourage" locals to grow and harvest the crop for what remains a predominantly military market, and pay them with a price far below the market value. As a result, the majority of profits accrue to armed forces, while the farmers live in both poverty and fear.[60]

In early 2001, a police helicopter pilot was arrested by the air force for drug trafficking. He flew 40kg of marijuana from Aceh and admitted that it belonged to Aceh Besar Police Chief, Lt. Col. Ali Hussein.[61]

In September 2002, police caught an army truck transporting 1,350 kg of marijuana near the town of Binjai, North Sumatra, on its way from Aceh. Army soldiers attempted to take back the truck and their arrested colleagues, attacking the Binjai police post on 29 September. In the ensuing nine hours' melee, soldiers used automatic rifles, grenades and mortars, resulting in six policemen, one soldier and one bystander killed, and 23 bystanders wounded.[62] Such incidents are not unusual, contributing to increasing levels of tension between the TNI and the police. A journalist from the Aceh daily paper *Serambi* said: "There are many incidents such as these, but we are afraid to report the details."[63]

Again, in late November 2002, a haul of 675 kg of marijuana was seized and sent to the Polda police station in Banda Aceh. A senior officer said, "it [the marijuana] came from Pulau Aceh where the military supervises its cultivation. We got information that the truck was carrying drugs, and also that the local military commander in Pulau Aceh paid the truck driver and his four companions."[64] There were many other clashes between the police and military in Aceh for what was widely believed to be the control of illegal activities.

Arms

Another "open secret" in Aceh is that the military has been supplying weapons to GAM. This supply chain operates on two levels. First, individual military men often sell their weapons to the separatist movement, reporting them as "seized in battle" to their commanding officers. Second, on a more problematic level, certain key military personnel have provided a supply chain of specific weapons. A spokesperson for GAM said: "Yes, it is true; we do receive weapons from the military — ammunition too. It is a very reliable source. But recently the cost of these weapons has increased, so we may be looking for alternative avenues."[65] A district GAM commander told one of the authors in September 2001 that via a senior general in Jakarta, GAM had purchased weapons directly from the P.T. Pindad arms factory in Bandung.[66]

Throughout Aceh, villagers tell stories of the military passing weapons to GAM, with local commanders justifying it in terms of raising local military slush funds. The Navy is also believed to be involved in allowing weapons consignments to arrive by boat. The fee for such "safe passage" can be as much as Rp 20 million.[67]

Logging

The military's involvement in illegal logging is extensive. Companies — many are foreign owned — pay the military and police to "look the other way" as they log out of their permitted area. The security authorities also commonly provide false documentation for export. *Ad hoc* logging by locals also finds armed forces personnel an insatiable market. The illegally felled timber is then often processed by unlicensed sawmills.

The Leuser Development Project, which was based in Medan and funded by the European Union from the mid-1990s, was puzzled by the increasing rate of logging within the protected area. Project staff eventually realised that the police and military — the very people they were relying on to prevent illegal logging — were in fact facilitating, and in some cases, initiating logging. A member of the project staff commented: "The forest cover is decreasing in the more easily accessible areas, and this is where much of the wildlife is. We know that the military and police are involved as they have threatened several of our [Indonesian] staff."[68]

On the island Simeulue to Aceh's west, the wholesale destruction of forests is due in large part to the collusion of the local government, the police, and to a lesser degree, the military. There is strong evidence to suggest that the local police and military provide "protection" for the companies, being paid to ignore illegal logging and facilitating shipping.[69]

In June 2001, in response to concerns about flooding and other environmental damages, the local *bupati* issued an order that all logging should cease until further permission was granted. However, police continued to accept payments from the Thai company PT Panto Teungku Abadi to continue operation.[70] There has also been an illegal trade related to logging — that of wildlife to other parts of Indonesia.

Protection

The military has been involved in "protecting" — for a "fee" — companies such as ExxonMobil, PT Arun, palm oil, coffee and rubber plantations, etc. The relationship is similar to that of other large multinationals involved in the extractive industries. In the early relationship between Exxon and the Indonesian government, provision was made for the military to protect the company's operations. Exxon was not alone in "contracting" the services of the Indonesian military for security. In what is now West Papua, Freeport signed a Contract of Work (CoW) in 1967 with the government which locked them into what has essentially become a "protection racket" by TNI.

A source previously involved in the "negotiations" between ExxonMobil and the authorities disclosed that not only does the company pay the military officially for its security services, but the company also began very early on to pay "small sums of money 'here and there' to local military commanders for their cooperation".[71] Investigations by *Kontras* in 2001 found that the company paid the military deployed to guard the facilities at Lhoksukon a daily allowance of around Rp 40,000.[72] The same report also suggests that ExxonMobil paid a substantial monthly allowance to the local military command, and provided transportation facilities, offices, posts, barracks, radios, telephones, dormitories and other equipment.

Via the territorial structure, the local military is able to come to its own local arrangement with these companies. It is common practice for the local military to demand increasing amounts of money, often laying an "unspoken" security threat on the negotiation table: the company has little choice but to pay.

ExxonMobil has established a "mutually beneficial relationship" with the military. But in fact, in this relationship, the weight of benefit lies with the military. The military command of Aceh, Kodam Iskandar Muda, has come to rely on the financial and logistic "support" of the company. No doubt, benefits gained in the military's local operation — such as cash, food, the use of buildings and equipment and other "services" — are the "incentives" to maintain a presence there. The commanding officers also accrued personal wealth from payments to the military.

In addition to "protecting" Exxon, the military often seize plantation lands for companies, killing or injuring many locals to prevent them from reclaiming their land. The Medan office of human rights NGO, the Legal Aid Foundation or *Yayasan Lembaga Bantuan Hukum Indonesia* (LBH) reported that land disputes (in particular involving the military) was the fastest rising case load.

Fishing

Local fishermen are forced to engage in a military market that "offers" them a price far below real market value for their catch. These armed middlemen then normally sell to local businesses at a vastly inflated price.

At sea, the Indonesian Navy often board vessels for "inspection", and the captain has to pay for the freedom of his vessel. A fisherman from Lampulo, Banda Aceh, told a story common in Aceh: "The Navy signalled they wanted to board our boat for inspection, so we had no choice but to allow them to. They seized all our fish and siphoned off our fuel. They had been tailing us all day, so they knew we had good fish on board. We tried to get to land, but the fuel ran out before then and we drifted for five hours. Another fishing boat from our village [Lampulo] saw our boat in trouble and helped us ashore."

In addition, many fishermen say they must pay the local police or military a regular amount for "protecting" their boats. The amount varies, but is usually between Rp 50,000–Rp 100,000 every two weeks.

Coffee

The situation in coffee is similar to fishing and logging. Coffee farmers have been forced to sell their coffee to the military at almost half the market rate (following a similar arrangement in East Timor between 1976 and 1999, though in the latter case enforced through a military controlled monopoly). In Central Aceh, the military-backed militia has forced some locals to leave their plantations. These plantations now have a dual use —both as training camps and source of production revenue. In the villages of Pondok Gajah and Sidodadi, the locals tried to resist the militia and the military's pursuit of profit, with a high price — disappearances and deaths of people.

Martial law presented new opportunities to financial benefit. A new red and white KTP (*Kartu Tanda Penduduk*) residency card was introduced in the province. Officially, this new KTP is issued free of charge. But in reality, sums ranging from Rp 50,000 to 300,000 (occasionally more) have been demanded. Anyone found without the new KTP was assumed to be a member of GAM and was immediately arrested. As one refugee noted, "we must obtain that card, at any price".[73] According to villagers in Lhoknga district, close to Banda Aceh, the TNI were charging relatives of GAM members Rp 1 million in January 2003 not to be taken to the local military posts for interrogation. There has also been an increase in the categories and amounts of fees demanded for the release of relatives arrested, even for the collection of dead bodies from the military and police posts in Aceh.

Similarities and Differences

The Indonesian military's involvement in businesses in Aceh is similar in many respects to their businesses elsewhere, but retains differences, in particular, from the previously heavily militarised territory, East Timor. In East Timor between 1976 and 1999, there was a greater use of large "legal" businesses to control the territory's economy, usually through monopolistic or nearly monopolistic practices, often trading directly overseas, primarily with Singapore but also with Macao, Hong Kong and other regional economic centres. This practice followed that of existing businesses under previous Portuguese rule, predominantly owned by ethnic Chinese. The Suharto clan and its crony network came to dominate East Timor's economy to enhance their own economic status.

Key similarities, however, can also be found throughout the archipelago, and occur in the lower orders of the economy, particularly in the "grey" and "black" areas, including smuggling, gambling, prostitution, extortion (in particular from prisoners and transportation) and so on. The military not only controlled these activities, but also took a share of profits from private legal enterprises, including the importation and distribution of petrol products. Similarly, a share of profits earned by the lower ranks was distributed up the chain of command, and finally many soldiers and officers either ran small local businesses through local men, or engaged in extortion for a regular income.

The most important similarity between military businesses in Aceh and elsewhere throughout Indonesia was that the military would not have been able to function without access to various levels of business and criminal activities. This partly echoed the practice of the army during the revolution, when its units were required to fend for themselves economically. However, in both East Timor and Aceh, such practice led to a high degree of lawlessness (and to a lesser extent in less militarised areas), subverted the military's security function, in effect turned much of the military into little more than a uniformed mafia, and alienated them from most of the local population.

The TNI Without Business?

Bridging the gap between the TNI's spending and its on-line budget is widely regarded as crucial to the reform of the TNI and a key factor in the SSR agenda. This involves stopping officers and troops from illegal and corrupt activities, removing their capacity of private profiteering, and breaking the nexus between the TNI's business interests and the management of the state. The International Crisis Group (ICG) outlined three options for resolving the TNI's budget gap. They included cutting the size of the TNI to fit the budget, increasing the budget to fit the

TNI, and a middle way combined with efficiency measures. As the ICG noted, the first option would mean that Indonesia would be unable to confront separatist and communal conflicts, and hence unable to maintain the unity of the state. It could also create problems with discharged soldiers seeking alternative income sources (or indeed illegal sources) as well as further instability. The second option "would be a waste of money because of endemic corruption and inefficiency", and also exceed the current capacity of the state. McCulloch has noted that "no discussion of the Indonesian military in business would be complete without attention being drawn to the inefficiency, mismanagement, and rampant corruption which have all become hallmarks of ABRI's (*Angkatan Bersenjata Republik Indonesia*, or Armed Forces of the Republic of Indonesia) commercial activities".[74] The ICG also suggested that the TNI assisted this process by selling "some of its large land holdings scattered all over Indonesia, including in the major cities".[75]

There is a significant question whether the TNI could function without its extensive business interests and other sources of off-budget income. The answer is almost certainly negative if the TNI remains largely unreformed. There is also a view that the TNI continues to pursue business and criminal activities not just to support itself and enrich some members, but also to maintain its political autonomy from the civilian authority. In other words, if the TNI remains largely self-funded, it will be less beholden to the civilian authority as primary provider of its economic and hence military capacity.

However, TNI's existing form is so problematic that altering its structure and size does not seem able to stop it from getting off-budget income, or to bring it under greater civilian authority. Indeed, one scenario for the TNI would be that it reduce itself to an essentially "professional" — disciplined, ordered and under civilian control — presence, and that its internal security functions are taken over by a retrained national police and overseen by a functioning, non-corrupt judiciary working with clear and equitable laws.

The basic problem, however, lies only in part with the TNI and its business activities. According to TNI, Indonesia's size and fragmented nature requires an internally active military, but the state cannot afford such a military and hence TNI must have its own off-budget sources of income. Off-budget sources of income, by definition and especially within Indonesia's historical context, naturally lead to corruption and other illegal activities. The problem, then, comes back to the nature of the Indonesian state. Assuming that the state does have significant internal legitimacy and logic, it should not require an organisation like the TNI to sustain it. Perhaps the return of equitable and consistent rule of law and a genuine distribution of economic benefits, which were largely lost during the New Order period, would ensure a degree of state cohesion. But it is illogical to suggest that cohesion can be legitimised at the point of a gun, or that to express concern with the way the state governance has lost the "national spirit" is hence disrespectful, as the TNI suggested.

The argument that the state cannot afford to finance its (necessary) military apparatus is the dominant theme in all discussions on military funding in Indonesia. Undoubtedly, the pursuit of economic profits has had a detrimental effect on the efficiency of the military and has also led to low levels of professionalism. But this argument ignores the fact that between 50–60 per cent of the official budget is lost to mismanagement and corruption. A report by the Supreme Audit Agency (BPK) found that more than US$450 million had been lost to military expenditure during 1994–2001.[76] If measures were taken to stop this leakage, and to maximise the usefulness of the existing budget, the shortfall between the military budget and the actual demand would be much less.

Regardless of the logic or lack thereof in state construction, or even the related logic of the TNI, the military's role in business, grey income earning and criminal activities is much more of a problem than a benefit to the state. Not only does it institutionalise corruption and crime, subvert legitimate businesses which could aid development, but it also institutionalises a structure with a self-referential logic that no longer requires the security of the state as its justification. The TNI may argue that it must engage in business to support itself as an organisation, but in fact many officers are intent on accruing personal wealth through the military's businesses. It is more relevant to say that the TNI must keep a major role in the running of the state, by perpetrating the problems of the state, in order to stay in business.

Notes

[1]   This chapter is presented as a part of Drs. Kingsbury and McCulloch's Australia Research Council project on the political economy of the TNI and security sector reform.

[2]   D. Rutherford, "Waiting for the end in Biak", in *Violence and the States in Suharto's Indonesia*, ed. Benedict Anderson (Ithaca, NY: Cornell University Press, 2001).

[3]   Ibid.

4   For a complete list of challenges of SSR, see ibid., p. 4.

5   This common assessment has been endorsed officially by the Indonesian Defence Minister, Juwono Sudarsono, as quoted in "Govt to take over TNI businesses", *The Jakarta Post*, 9 December 2004. See also A. Widjojo, "Indonesia's Changing Security Structure and its Implications for US Policy", Paper to United States-Indonesia Society, Washington DC, 21 February 2002.

6   International Crisis Group, *Indonesia: Next Steps in Military Reform*, ICG Asia report No. 24, Jakarta/Brussels, 2001, p. 13.

7   This group was known as Poros Indonesia (indicating its secular orientation, as opposed to the earlier Poros Tenggah), according to an Indonesian journalist close to one of the group's key actors at that time (personal communication).

8   Damien Kingsbury, *Power Politics and the Indonesian Military* (London: RoutledgeCurzon, 2003), p. 6.

9   SIPRI military expenditure database. All annual military spending data 1998–2001 are from the SIPRI database based on a calendar year. The dollar figure is based on constant 2000 prices and exchange rates.

10 This was a pro-rata budget based on changing budgetary dates, and was therefore less than that expected for this year.

11 *Jakarta Post*, 23 November 1999.

12 *Jakarta Post*, 14 March 2004.

13 Confidential interviews with members of Aceh and West Papua Dewan Perwakilan Rakyat Daerah, December 2003.

14 Based on the exchange rate in 2001.

15 Department of Defence, Republic of Indonesia, 2001.

16 Such *yayasan* were initially developed by Suharto in the early 1950s as a means of generating income to support the troops under his command, although he also personally benefited from such business activities.

17 A. Fatcurrahman, "Governance Yayasan Militer", BPK, 2001.

18 International Crisis Group, *Indonesia: Next Steps in Military Reform*, ICG Asia Report No. 24, Jakarta/Brussels, 2001, p. 13.

19 Ibid.

20 S. Weiss, "Indonesia: The Military Can Shape up if Washington Helps", *International Herald Tribune*, 20 August 2001.

21 Robert E. Elson, *Suharto: A Political Biography* (Melbourne: Cambridge University Press, 2001), pp. 1–2.

22 See Abdul H. Nasution, *Fundamentals of Guerilla Warfare*, 2nd ed. (Jakarta: Seruling Masa, 1970), pp. 59, 137.

23 Elson, *Suharto*, pp. 60–5.

24 C. Barber and K. Talbott, "The Chainsaw and the Gun: The Role of the Military in Deforesting Indonesia", *Journal of Sustainable Forestry* 16, 2/4 (June 2003).

25 According to confidential interviews conducted in Jakarta with individuals close to the TNI.

26 According to confidential interviews with Papuan NGO representatives, February 2002, and Acehnese NGO representatives, May 2005.

27 These can range from personal conveniences to undertaking highly illegal tasks. This information is based on a series of interviews with low ranking TNI officers in Maluku, March 2002, and West Timor, January 2000.

28 Robert Lowry, *The Armed Forces of Indonesia* (Sydney: Allen and Unwin, 1996), p. 129.

29 Douglas Kammen and Siddharth Chandra, *A Tour of Duty: Changing Patterns of Military Politics in Indonesia in the 1990s,* Cornell Modern Indonesian Project (Ithaca: Cornell University Press, 1999), p. 74.

30 D. Rutherford, "Waiting for the End in Biak", in *Violence and the State in Suharto's Indonesia,* ed. Benedict Anderson (Ithaca: Cornell University Press, 2001), p. 193.

31 "Bapakism" derives from the term *bapak* (father), which is frequently used as an honorific to denote respect, or to a male of superior status.

32 This source, from Australian military intelligence, cannot be identified.

33 McCulloch, *Trifungsi,* p. 26.

34 This is based on observations from Aceh and Papua in 2001 and 2002.

35 Bulog was the site of extensive corruption investigations from 1999 onwards, primarily over funds siphoned off for political purposes, in particular by the former government party, Golkar.

36 Angel Rabasa and John Haseman, *The Military and Democracy in Indonesia: Challenges, Poltiics and Power* (Santa Monica: Rand Corporation, 2002), Chapter 7.

37 AFP, "Police say Indonesian army behind Papua ambush: report", 26 December 2002.

38 See B. Singh, *Civil-military Relations in Democratising Indonesia: The Potentials and Limits to Change* (Canberra: Strategic Defence Studies Centre, Australian National University, 2001).

39 See A. Stepan, "The New Professionalism of Internal Warfare and Military Role Expansion", in *Armies and Politics in Latin America,* ed. Abraham F. Lowenthal (New York, London: Jolmes and Meier Publishers, 1976).

40 Samuel P. Huntington, *The Third Wave: Democratisation in the Late 20th Century* (Norman: University of Oklahoma Press, 1991).

41 See Bruce W. Farcau, *The Transition to Democracy in Latin America* (Westport, Connecticut; London: Praeger, 1996), Chapter 5.

42 Some observers translate *oknum* as "rogues" or "rogue elements", both of which are incorrect. The term "rogue elements" derives from the TNI's attempts to deny its formal involvement in illegal or otherwise doubtful activities, allocating responsibility to such "elements" outside the formal command structure. In fact, such "elements" are a part of the formal

command structure, as well as a result of the TNI's public acceptance of the necessity of both business activities and the use of militias.

43 Lesley McCulloch, "Greed: The Silent Force of the Conflict in Aceh", Paper presented at Asian Studies Association of Australia, 1–3 July 2002.

44 Anthony Reid, "War, Peace and the Burden of History in Aceh", *Asia Ethnicity* 5, 3 (October 2004): 309.

45 Jacques Bertrand, *Nationalism and Ethnic Conflict in Indonesia* (Cambridge: Cambridge University Press, 2004), p. 181.

46 Munir, "The Stagnation of Reforms in the Indonesian Armed Forces", *INFID*, 2003.

47 Reid, "War, Peace and the Burden", p. 313.

48 E. Aspinall and H. Crouch, *The Aceh Peace Process: Why it Failed*, Policy Studies, No. 1 (Washington: The East-West Centre, 2003), p. x.

49 M. Davies, unpublished open-source intelligence assessment of TNI and Polri troop numbers in Aceh, August 2003.

50 See Miller in this volume.

51 *Tempo*, 6–12 May 2004.

52 *Sinar Haripan*, 31 March 2003.

53 ICG, *Indonesia: Next Steps in Military Reform*, p. 7.

54 NAD (Nanggroe Aceh Darrulsalam) data, October 2003.

55 Munir, "The Stagnation of Reforms in the Indonesian Armed Forces", *INFID*, 2003.

56 In December 2003, a parliamentary team monitoring the situation in Aceh recommended that this allowance be increased to Rp 35,000. This increase has not yet been approved.

57 McCulloch, "Greed: The Silent Force of the Conflict in Aceh", p. 18.

58 *Suara Pembaruan*, September 1999.

59 For further examples of military involvement in this trade, see McCulloch, "Greed".

60 Interviews with local farmers involved in the drugs trade in Greater and North Aceh in December 2001 highlighted a common fear that the military will intimidate them if they refuse to participate, as one major reason local people are involved in what they know to be an illegal trade.

61 "Indonesia: The War in Aceh", *Human Rights Watch* 13, no. 4 (August 2001).

62 "Anggota Linud 100 Granat Markas Brimob", *Kompas*, 30 September 2002; K. Yamin, "Indonesian Forces' Corruption Exposed", *Asia Times On-line*, 14 October 2002.

63 Interview, Banda Aceh, May 2002.

64 Interview, Polda, Banda Aceh, 23 November 2002.

65 Interview, Banda Aceh, April 2002.

66 Interview with GAM deputy spokesman and District Commander, Teuku Jamaika, near Lhokseumawe, September 2001.

67   Interview with crew members who travel regularly to Sumatra, Kuala Lumpur, February 2004.

68   Interview, Medan, November 2000.

69   PT Panto Teungku Abadi, a company with logging concessions on the island, makes regular payments to the military to protect the concession area, but has paid nothing to the local villagers for road access.

70   Interview with PT Panto employees, November 2001.

71   Such "cooperation" may be simply paying officers to keep them happy, or may require the performance of particular services, including resolving any local disputes which could affect the company's operations.

72   *Kontras* 11(2001).

73   Interview with Acehnese man who fled to Kuala Lumpur, 17 February 2004.

74   McCulloch, *Trifungsi*, p. 3.

75   ICG, *Indonesia: Next Steps in Military Reform*.

76   Infid, "Transparency, Accountability and Control in Military Expenditure: Problems and Recommendations". <http://66.102.7.104/search?q=cache: gTeBa_13QN0J:www.infid.be/millitary%2520reforms.pdf++site: www.infid.be+tni+budget+corruption&hl=en&start=2&client=firefox-a> [6 June 2005].

12

Insurgency and Counter-Insurgency: Strategy and the Aceh Conflict, October 1976–May 2004

Kirsten E. Schulze

Since 1976 the province of Aceh has been wracked by protracted low-intensity warfare between the guerrillas of the Free Aceh Movement or *Gerakan Aceh Merdeka* (GAM) and the Indonesian security forces or *Angkatan Bersenjata Republik Indonesia* (ABRI), which in 1999 split into the military or *Tentara Nasional Indonesia* (TNI) and the police. GAM's challenge to the Indonesian state came in the form of a rural insurgency and it was met by a series of often ruthless counter-insurgency operations. The armed conflict between the two was fundamentally asymmetrical in terms of personnel numbers, equipment, strategy and tactics. The Indonesian security forces at all times significantly outnumbered GAM. Moreover, they were better equipped and trained. Yet it was GAM that held the advantage on the ground as it benefited from local support and superior knowledge of the terrain, allowing it to determine the timing of much of the engagement.

Throughout the New Order the conflict was primarily fought by military means. Only after the fall of Indonesian President Suharto in 1998 did both GAM and the Indonesian government fully develop the hitherto rudimentary political, diplomatic and legal aspects of their respective insurgency and counter-insurgency strategies. This chapter seeks to analyse GAM's insurgency strategy since 1976 and Indonesia's counter-insurgency strategy since 1977. It looks at GAM's guerrilla warfare, tactics and targets as well as the movement's political strategy, notably the East Timor blueprint, the negotiations and internationalisation. This is followed by a discussion of Indonesia's security operations, tactics and targets as well as its political, diplomatic and legal strategy, notably its efforts at compelling GAM to agree to an internal settlement and at prosecuting the exiled GAM leadership.

It is argued here that GAM's strategy benefited greatly from the peace process 2000–3, raising the movement's profile within Aceh and internationally. However, it fell short of attracting a single foreign government's support for Acehnese independence. One difficulty was the exiled leadership's inability to compromise, but the movement's greatest weakness was the increasing criminalisation of some of its rank and file as well as its ethnically and politically motivated targeting of civilians. In comparison, Indonesia largely failed to harness the negotiations to its advantage, in the end returning to the military option. Yet, while having secured the full backing of the international community for the unity and integrity of the Republic, Indonesia's counter-insurgency efforts since 1977 all suffered from the same difficulties: the lack of an exit strategy, the inability to implement the non-military aspects of its comprehensive operations, and until May 2003, flawed tactics. Its greatest weakness, however, was its failure to address successfully the root causes of the conflict as well as the human rights abuses perpetrated by the security forces. Both served to further alienate the Acehnese population.

GAM's Insurgency Strategy, 1976–2004[1]

GAM's insurgency strategy from 1976 until 2004 consisted of two components: guerrilla warfare and a political strategy of internationalisation. Both were rudimentary when GAM was first established and when GAM leader Hasan di Tiro himself was fighting in the jungles of Aceh. The movement's guerrilla strategy only started to develop properly in 1986–9 when GAM fighters received training in Libya. The organisation's political strategy took even longer to mature, not coming into its own until after the fall of Suharto.

Guerrilla Warfare

When GAM was established in 1976 it comprised 70 guerrilla fighters. It has since grown considerably. In 2002 GAM Minister of State Malik Mahmud claimed GAM had an active guerrilla army of 30,000 and a reserve of almost the whole population of Aceh.[2] Both observers and

Fig. 14 GAM stealing arms from a TNI store (*courtesy William Nessen and GAM*)

the TNI believed the number to be lower, estimating the size of GAM troops to be between 3,000[3] and 8,000.[4] The fighting capacity of GAM was somewhat smaller. In 2001, most observers estimated that GAM had between 1,000 and 1,500 modern firearms, a few grenade launchers, even fewer rocket-propelled grenade launchers, and perhaps one or two 60 mm mortars.[5] According to Indonesian military intelligence, GAM increased its arsenal during the 2002–3 Cessation of Hostilities Agreement (CoHA) to 2,134 weapons.[6] These weapons were unevenly spread, showing the heaviest concentration in the traditional GAM areas of Pidie, North Aceh and East Aceh. GAM's weapons were a mixture of *rakitan* (home-made) and standard firearms. Standard firearms were obtained both from domestic and foreign sources. Domestically, arms were captured, stolen or purchased from the TNI and the police (see Fig. 14).[7] Internationally, weapons were widely available from Cambodia, Vietnam and Thailand.

GAM's strategy was one of attrition, using guerrilla warfare and making use of its superior knowledge of the terrain and the population to counter-balance its lack of real military capacity. It relied upon the civilian population — sometimes using force — to provide it with information, food, shelter, and money to buy weapons. During the martial law period May 2003–May 2004, the movement also appropriated people's identity cards[8] to increase its own freedom of movement as well as forcing villagers to obstruct the mobility of the TNI by, for example, digging holes in roads.[9] Since 1999, GAM boasted a battalion of female fighters known as *Inong Bale* whose main function was logistics, communications and intelligence. It also used children as spies or *cukoi* to gather information on the position and activities of the Indonesian security forces.[10]

GAM's tactics were primarily those of hit-and-run ambushes followed by withdrawal into the mountains or dispersal among the civilian population. As one GAM operational commander explained: "When they advance, we retreat; when they leave, we return. When they grow tired or weak or careless, we attack."[11] Another guerrilla fighter added: "We don't have to win the war; we only have to stop them from winning."[12] Or in the words of the GAM negotiators in 2001:

> We mainly resort to ambush and hit-and-run. We can't fight a frontal war. They have better equipment and more ammunition .... From a military perspective there is no way for us to defeat them and for them to defeat us. We want to tie down as many of their troops as possible in Aceh. We want them to spend more money on this operation. We want to exhaust them financially.[13]

GAM tactics further included general strikes in order to paralyse the province and bombings using home-made explosives. The latter were generally against highly symbolic targets. For instance on 17 August 2002, GAM claimed responsibility for a series of Indonesian Independence Day bombings.[14] The Indonesian government also attributed a series of bombings in Medan and Jakarta to GAM.[15] GAM, however, stated that it does not operate outside Aceh.[16]

The period of martial law saw an upsurge in both piracy and kidnappings for which GAM was deemed responsible. Piracy in the Melaka Strait was carried out by GAM "navy" operating from Jambu Air Cape, Aceh, and the waters around Berhala, near Belawan, North Sumatra.[17] Kidnappings, which GAM considered as the taking of prisoners of war, rose to over 300. They were held for ransom in the case of businessmen, for "re-education" in the case of village heads, young women dating soldiers and journalists for biased reporting (see Fig. 15), or for punishment in the case of civil servants and teachers who were seen as working for the enemy. The increase in kidnappings, piracy and more generally extortion and taxation since 1999, was seen as an indication

Fig. 15   GAM and the ICRC negotiating the release of journalist Ferry Santoro, Lhok Jok, Peudawa, East Aceh, May 2004 (*courtesy Tempo*)

that GAM had undergone a process of criminalisation coinciding with, and arguably resultant from, its increase in membership.[18]

The aim of GAM's strategy was to weaken Indonesia's hold on Aceh by destroying the state's provincial infrastructure, civil government, and education institutions. This was coupled with efforts to establish GAM control over Aceh's territory and population. With respect to the Indonesian military, the guerrillas sought to extract the highest price possible for the "occupation". Moreover, the movement's bellicose rhetoric and attacks on vital industries, Javanese migrants, and populated areas "were designed to provoke the most hostile possible reaction from the Indonesian armed forces".[19]

GAM consciously raised the level of violence so that the international community would feel compelled to intervene and thereby "deliver" independence. It calculated that the counter-violence by the security forces against the civilian population would drive the latter into GAM's camp and alienate Aceh even further from Jakarta, confirming independence as the only viable solution and the validity of GAM's narrative of the conflict.[20]

In May 1977, when GAM was still in its "educational phase" or "in the political and preparatory stage of the armed struggle", di Tiro's strategy was as follows:

(a) The Acehnese army should always keep to the hills. This will nullify Javanese superiority in armoured vehicles, naval and air power.
(b) The Acehnese army should always hover in the enemy's neighbour-hood, preventing him from gaining any permanent base, becoming an elusive but powerful shadow on the horizon, diminishing the "glamour" of the Javanese colonialist troops.
(c) Time and surprise are the most vital elements: understand all lines of expectations and lines of surprises. NO attack without surprise!
(d) Engagement must be done at the place and time of our choosing despite enemy provocations.
(e) When [the] enemy advances, we retreat, and harass him when he returns.
(f) Engagement with the enemy should only be done when we are sure of winning, that is of having superior force at the point of engagement.
(g) Our present objectives are to cripple [the] enemy's communications and economy and to destroy his foreign backers' confidence.
(h) Our safety lies in the secrecy of our movement at all times and in the mobility of our forces. The enemy should never know where our forces are.
(i) Our strategy is defensive; our tactic is swift offensive action against the enemy whenever an opportunity presents itself.[21]

GAM's military strategy and targets did not change significantly between 1977 and 2004. Its operations focused on five distinct targets in Aceh:

1. *The Indonesian Political Structures*

GAM aimed at paralysing the local government structure. This was achieved through attacks on public buildings,[22] the intimidation of civil servants at all levels, and the recruitment of as many as possible into GAM's parallel civilian government.

In this context, civil servants, judges, members of the regional parliaments, and village heads were intimidated, kidnapped or shot. In 2000–1, such actions caused the virtual collapse of Aceh's legal system. In several districts courthouses were destroyed and many judges, prosecutors and lawyers were subject to repeated intimidation.[23] Most judges fled.[24] Local legislators, especially those who criticised GAM,[25] as well as the governor and deputy governor, were also targeted because they were all seen as the lackeys of Jakarta. Governor Abdullah Puteh, in particular, was blamed for the death of GAM commander Abdullah Syafi'i in January 2002, for the re-establishment of the regional military command or *kodam* in 2002[26] and for lobbying for a military solution in 2003. GAM went as far as stating that with these acts Puteh "lost his civilian rights in the war".[27] Other examples include the June 2003 shooting of the city secretary of Lhokseumawe, Bachtiar, as he was travelling to Banda Aceh.[28] Later that month GAM kidnapped 23 village heads in Bireuen.[29] Langsa city councillor Budiman Samaun was also taken hostage.

According to GAM Tiro field commander, Amri bin Abdul Wahab, establishing a parallel government was one of the most important elements of GAM's strategy.

> The crucial element is how to establish a GAM government so we can exercise control and society does not have to deal with the Indonesian structure. That strengthens our relationship with society and we can spread our ideology.[30]

He estimated that in April 2003 about 70 per cent of Acehnese society used GAM's civil government offices as opposed to Indonesian ones. This take-over was seen as one of GAM's successes since 1999. As GAM Minister of State Malik Mahmud explained in February 2002:

> In two years we took over 60–80 per cent of the administration of the Indonesian government in Aceh. We make use of Indonesian officials. We know they have a job with Indonesia but now we are in power in Aceh and we want them to change so what you see is positive. They just change sides and now work for *Negara Aceh*.[31]

Indeed, when martial law was declared in May 2003, 99 out of 228 districts and 4,750 out of 5,947 villages did not have a functioning local government.[32]

2. *The State Education System*

GAM also systematically targeted Indonesia's state education system. This included the burning of schools as well as the intimidation and killing of teachers. Between 1998 and 2002 some 60 teachers were killed, and 200 others physically assaulted.[33] Some 170 were seriously injured or tortured.[34] Many were kidnapped. Between the beginning of 1989 and June 2002, 527 schools, 89 official houses for teachers, and 33 official houses for principals were burnt down.[35] In May–June 2002 alone 27 schools were destroyed. In the first two days of the military emergency in May 2003 an estimated 185 schools went up in flames. By the next day the number had risen to 248 and by the first week of June to 448,[36] a number which eventually rose to over 600.

While there remains considerable scepticism as to whether GAM was responsible for all of these burnings, it was clearly responsible for a large part of them. Religion teacher Rusli Abdullah believed GAM was responsible because "this is something that GAM has done in the past. The rebels target schools because they think these are where Indonesia brainwashes Acehnese children."[37] Similarly Sidney Jones of the International Crisis Group stated that there was "evidence that GAM was responsible for some of the initial burnings".[38] In June 2003, two teenagers were caught setting a school on fire. One of them, Samsul, who had joined GAM in 1999, admitted that he and Zulkifli received Rp 200,000 for each school they burned down. The two teenagers had burnt down 60 schools over the previous three years.[39]

The underlying motivations for the destruction of the Indonesian education system in Aceh were primarily ideological. According to GAM, the Indonesian syllabus actively destroyed Acehnese history and culture while promoting "the glorification of Javanese history".[40] Already in the late 1970s, di Tiro recorded in his diary that "for the last 35 years they have used our schools and the mass media to destroy every aspect of our nationality, culture, polity and national consciousness".[41] The destruction of state schools can thus be seen as a direct attack on the curriculum which teaches that Aceh joined the Republic of Indonesia voluntarily and has been an integral part of the state ever since. One way of countering this was the tailoring of school curricula in GAM strongholds to include a local view of history.[42] Another way was the burning of the schools so "that they were not used to turn Acehnese children into Indonesians".[43]

The burning of schools also had more "practical" aspects. It drove many of the children into the rural Islamic boarding schools or *dayah*, most of which were under GAM control. Moreover, it deprived the Indonesian security forces of the use of school buildings as night shelter for troops on patrol. During martial law in particular it prevented schools "from being used as billets for troops" and "from housing the displaced so that the humanitarian problem got more international attention".[44] And finally, according to the TNI, GAM also torched the schools to try to divert troops away from offensive operations to guard duties.[45]

3. *The Energy Infrastructure*

Closely connected with the dismantling of Indonesia's political and educational structures was the targeting of the Acehnese energy infrastructure. This had two main components, first electricity and second, natural gas. Since 1999, GAM repeatedly targeted electricity pylons with the result of causing black-outs in Aceh's urban areas. This served to slow down the local economy, to make life more difficult for the Indonesian security forces, and to instil a general feeling of fear among the population. During the martial law period three electricity pylons were taken down by GAM[46] and two electricity relay stations in East Aceh were damaged by arson attack. Indonesia's national electricity company, PLN, blamed GAM.[47] Blackouts also occurred in some villages. According to a resident of Lhok Jok, GAM cut electricity to the village for security reasons.[48]

However, GAM's focus was on the oil industry in the greater Lhokseumawe area. Employees of both domestic and foreign companies lived under the threat of intimidation, kidnapping or death since the early days of GAM. Di Tiro himself in 1974 had lost out in a bid for building a pipeline for Mobil Oil (MOI)[49] to the US construction company Bechtel. So when GAM was established two years later, it was not "a mere coincidence that expatriate employees were among the first targets of rebel attacks".[50] GAM actions, according to di Tiro's diary, aimed at closing "down foreign oil companies ... to prevent them from further stealing our oil and gas".[51] They started with a GAM Cabinet decision on 16 October 1977 to safeguard Aceh's natural resources, "especially our oil and gas".[52] Four days later, on 20 October, GAM leafleted the Lhokseumawe industrial complex calling upon all Americans, Australians and Japanese employees of MOI and Bechtel "to pack and leave this country immediately, for the time being, for we cannot guarantee the safety of your life and limbs"; the reason being that "your employers, Mobil and Bechtel, have made themselves co-conspirators with Javanese colonialist thieves in robbing our unrenewable gas resources".[53]

Just over a month later, in early December 1977, three foreign contractors for Bechtel, an American and two Koreans, who were involved in the construction of Arun Field Cluster III, came under attack. The

American was killed by what di Tiro in his diary described as "stray bullets"[54] and Bechtel's doctor at the time recalled as an armed attack on the unarmed foreign civilians.

GAM's grievances grew with the expansion of the industrial zone. In 1999, GAM stepped up attacks on the vulnerable oil and gas production facilities and pipelines operated by ExxonMobil Indonesia (EMOI) in Aceh. In March 2001, EMOI was forced to close production from the four onshore gas fields and to evacuate workers. GAM was also believed to have been responsible for firing at aircraft transporting ExxonMobil workers, hijacking the company's vehicles, as well as stopping and burning buses and planting landmines along roads to blow them up.[55] As EMOI Public Affairs Manager Bill Cummings described the security situation:

> Between May 1999 and the onshore shutdown in March 2001, acts of vandalism increased and over 50 vehicles were hijacked from public roads. In 2000, two chartered airplanes carrying ExxonMobil workers were hit by ground fire. In one case in March 2000, a gunman on the back of a motorcycle fired at the plane as it was taxiing to the terminal in Point A, the Arun Field control centre, wounding two passengers. Through a news story in a local newspaper a few days later, GAM claimed responsibility for the attack. Also in 2000, there was an increase in small arms fire directed at the facilities.[56]

In addition to di Tiro's initial personal grievance, GAM's problem with the oil industry was twofold: first, it was seen as exploiting Aceh's resources and second, it was perceived as collaborating with the Indonesian military because the latter was securing their premises and receiving funds for this service from Pertamina. This allowed GAM to regard these corporations as legitimate targets. As GAM spokesman Isnander al-Pasè explained in April 2003:

> ExxonMobil is a legitimate target in war. Why? Because it helps the opponent's military and now Exxon is housing a military base within its complex. And the people living next to Exxon tell us that they do not get anything from Exxon while Exxon takes our oil.[57]

4. *The Javanese*

One of the most controversial objectives of GAM's guerrilla strategy was the systematic attempt to cleanse Aceh of all Javanese presence. GAM saw Javanese migrants as colonial settlers who demographically shored up Jakarta's claim to Aceh and as potential collaborators with the

Indonesian security forces. In fact, in April 2001, following Presidential Instruction (*Inpres*) 4 which initiated a security recovery operation, GAM field commanders called upon the Javanese transmigrants to leave[58] as "these people can be forced to become military informers. The military can even turn them into militiamen."[59] While GAM denied that it specifically targeted Javanese, the evidence on the ground was to the contrary.

In mid-1990, GAM went on an offensive against Javanese settlers and transmigrants in North Aceh.[60] According to Amnesty International, thousands of Javanese transmigrants were intimidated into leaving their homes.[61] This scenario repeated itself in September 1999. *The Jakarta Post* reported that thousands of Javanese transmigrants were fleeing North Aceh following harassment by GAM including terrorisation, extortion, and arson.[62] Ahead of GAM's anniversary on 4 December 1999 more Javanese settlers and transmigrants began to flee Aceh amidst fears of violence.[63] The Central Java transmigration office said that since July that year 1,006 had returned with their families from Aceh. GAM also started routine inspections of vehicles travelling through their areas, often claiming to be looking for Javanese passengers.[64]

In early 2001, GAM harassment of ethnic Javanese began to escalate. GAM used a combination of terror tactics including arson and murder to force the Javanese out. On 19 May 2001, GAM burned six Javanese houses in Lhoksari village, Pante Cermin, West Aceh. "They ordered all Javanese working at PT Telaga Sari Indah plantation to leave within three days or they would be killed, one by one. Some 200 families fled into Meulaboh town."[65] Similarly in May–June 2001, GAM guerrillas and local sympathisers staged a number of attacks on the ethnically mixed Aceh-Gayo-Javanese areas of Central Aceh in which people were killed, houses looted and burned.[66] One of the villages attacked by GAM was Kresek in Kecamatan Bandar. In this village ten houses were burnt and five people were killed on the night of 5 June 2001. One resident recalled the night:

> It was between 10 pm and midnight. We were attacked while sleeping. We heard bangs.
>
> Some were asleep and some were guarding. They came. They shot and burnt. My two-year-old daughter was shot in the head and killed. She was sleeping. They broke in and sprayed my house with bullets. My mother was also hurt. Her leg had to be amputated. My father was killed. The house was burnt. And while they were shooting they shouted "Javanese neo-colonialists get out of Aceh". Then on the houses they

could not burn because they were made of cement they wrote in blood "the Javanese people must go home".[67]

An estimated 64 people were killed over that May–June two-week period, of whom 50 were Javanese. Some 1,000 houses were burnt. One source interviewed by the International Crisis Group stated that "GAM told its supporters, who included Acehnese and Gayo, that they could take the lands if the Javanese were forced out." [68] According to Staffan Bodemar, who worked in Aceh for the UNDP in 2001, "the expansion of GAM in 1999 most likely was the trigger for ethnic conflict in Central Aceh, which then led to the exodus of some 120,000–176,000, mostly Javanese, to North Sumatra".[69]

5. *The Indonesian Security Forces*

Since its establishment GAM has targeted both Indonesian military and police as "occupation forces". In the late 1970s this ranged from "attacking the enemy posts that are obnoxious to us",[70] ambushing troops, planting bombs and launching grenades near military installations, to executing off-duty security personnel and disrupting "enemy communication lines", as well as intercepting and destroying Indonesian military vehicles.[71] While between 1976 and 1979 GAM's attacks were sporadic and not particularly effective, in 1989, after their troops returned from Libya, they had become better organised, more systematic and forced the Indonesian security forces onto the defensive.[72]

After 1998 GAM attacks on the security forces rose again. According to police figures, 53 policemen were killed from July to December 1999, and many more were injured. A police spokesman stated that casualties for the month preceding 12 April 2001 included 33 military personnel and 36 police killed as well as 128 military personnel and 132 police injured.[73] According to the TNI, between June 2000 and April 2001 some 50 soldiers were killed, while 206 were injured and 8 were listed as missing.[74]

GAM's Political Strategy

GAM's guerrilla strategy was accompanied by a political strategy centred on the idea of internationalisation. Since 1979, when the top GAM leadership was forced into exile, internationalisation was seen as the only way to level the playing field with Indonesia, and eventually to swing the pendulum in favour of an independent Aceh. Internationalisation as a fully formulated policy, however, did not develop until 1999.

Until then GAM's political efforts were haphazard, uncritical, without direction, and largely based on di Tiro's previous business contacts. GAM lobbied for support in the United States, Europe and Australia without making much of an impact. GAM set up offices in Singapore and Malaysia but generally attracted diaspora Acehnese rather than locals. GAM also tried to gain support from the Islamic world. Only Libya, in 1985, was receptive. From 1986 until 1989 GAM guerrillas received training in Libya and lessons on Acehnese nationalism by di Tiro, who joined them there.[75]

In the 1990s, GAM focused on lobbying the United Nations. In 1991 di Tiro made the case for an independent Aceh at the 44th Session of the UN Sub-Commission on Prevention of Discrimination and Protection. He also made a submission to the 48th Session of the Human Rights Commission on 29 January 1992. While the conflict in Aceh started to attract some attention from human rights organisations, GAM failed to gain broader support.

The situation changed substantially with the fall of Suharto in May 1998. The Indonesian government under B.J. Habibie started to re-evaluate its approach toward conflict areas such as Aceh, East Timor and Irian Jaya. This aided GAM's political strategy of internationalisation in two important ways: First, East Timor's successful bid for independence in 1999 provided GAM with a "blueprint" for its struggle. Second, in 2000 GAM and the Indonesian government embarked upon negotiations.

The East Timor Blueprint

Since East Timor's successful bid for independence in 1999, its struggle served as an inspiration. GAM used East Timor as a blueprint but also as a key element in its public relations, calculating that the international sympathy for East Timor could be transferred to Aceh. Playing upon the East Timor scenario, GAM first incorporated the idea of referendum into its political vocabulary. It also called for international peace negotiations under the auspices of the United Nations. At the same time the organisation stepped up political and military activities in order to provoke the Indonesian security forces into a violent overreaction. GAM openly approached the people, held gatherings in mosques, spread its ideology and recruited. Attacks on the security forces increased in 1999 and continued to rise even during the 2000 Humanitarian Pause and the 2001 Moratorium on Violence. Not only did attacks on the Indonesian security forces increase, but they increased in populated areas. Only during the CoHA did the overall violence in Aceh drop.

GAM's calculations were simple. Its enemy's greatest weakness was lack of discipline and professionalism. Turning Indonesia's weakness into GAM's strength, it sought to destabilise the general situation in Aceh to such an extent that a security response became unavoidable. This would raise the spectre of a second East Timor and the international community would feel compelled to intervene and thereby "deliver" independence.

GAM also contributed significantly to the creation of a refugee population, which it, in turn, politicised. For instance, in the run-up to the June 1999 general elections, GAM "organised" the flight of villagers from Bandar Dua, Pidie, North and East Aceh. As one foreign observer noted, "GAM hoped that its exodus operation would attract the attention of the world and that its cause of an independent Aceh would be received."[76] In 2001, there were repeated reports that GAM had encouraged people to leave their villages and asked refugees to stay in camps rather than move in with relatives. In these camps they were visible and accessible by the foreign media and open to GAM propaganda. There was also evidence that refugees were paid by GAM to leave their villages.

Following the "blueprint", GAM actively cultivated relations with human rights organisations, in particular, foreign NGOs. In fact, with the 2002 Stavanger Declaration GAM adopted an official "foreign policy" aimed at building "cooperation with friendly and neutral NGOs worldwide".[77]

GAM also drew direct comparisons with East Timor. A June 2001 press release stated that the "Indonesian government has been committing gross human rights violations in Aceh, in a degree much worse than they did in East Timor."[78] Militias were emphasised to evoke images of the militia destruction of Dili in the wake of the 1999 referendum. For instance in June 2001 GAM explained that:

> The Indonesian authorities were very successful in establishing pro Indonesia (pro integration) militias in East Timor and [in using] them against [the] East Timorese freedom movement. Similar attempts [have] been made by [the] Indonesian government in Aceh by means of recruiting and arming indigenous Acehnese to form pro Indonesia militias, but [with] little success. However, [the] Indonesian military has recruited several hundreds of militias among Javanese transmigrants and [has] used them as combat aides.[79]

In March 2003, GAM blamed the demonstrations against the Joint Security Committee (JSC) and destruction of its offices on TNI-sponsored militias.

> The demonstration carried out by a few dozens [sic] people against the JSC in Sigli was definitely masterminded by the TNI .... The demonstration carried out by a score of people in Bireuen also presented the marks of TNI's handy work. The same with the mass riots perpetrated in Takengon (Central Aceh) and in Langsa (East Aceh) last week; they all pointed to the TNI's created militias.[80]

Negotiations

In January 2000, GAM and the Indonesian government under President Abdurrahman Wahid entered into negotiations aimed at finding an end to the conflict in Aceh. The dialogue, which was facilitated by a Swiss-based NGO, the Henry Dunant Center (HDC), continued until 18 May 2003. It became the cornerstone of GAM's political strategy of internationalisation. It was used to gain international legitimacy and to obtain outside support for GAM's struggle. From the beginning GAM's participation in the dialog was motivated less by what GAM could receive from Indonesia than by what it could receive from the international community. GAM displayed little interest in the Indonesian delegation and its position and on occasion used the dialogue to voice its contempt towards Indonesia on the one hand, while courting the international community on the other. For instance, di Tiro in his "opening statement" in January 2000 in Geneva stated that Aceh "should never have been subjected to the rule of those idiots [Indonesia]", that the Netherlands should be condemned for "failing to exercise her responsibilities towards Acehnese independence" and that the US Government and members of the EU should "review their policies towards Indonesia and to help Aceh gain back its rightful independence".[81]

According to GAM, the international community had a moral obligation to support Acehnese self-determination as it had "colluded" in the illegal transfer of sovereignty. As di Tiro stated in 1995, "the western colonial powers responsible for setting up 'Indonesia' in the first place, have a moral, political and legal obligation to effect an internationally supervised election".[82] Not surprisingly, GAM believed that internationalisation of the conflict would result in an East Timor-like solution. Only the international community, in particular the US and UN, could put pressure on Jakarta. According to GAM negotiator

Amni bin Marzuki, international pressure had been crucial in getting Indonesia to the negotiating table and only "thanks to international pressure on the Indonesian government they agreed in Geneva to a moratorium on violence and now there is peace through dialog".[83]

The US, in particular, captured GAM's imagination. Bin Marzuki explained, "we can internationalise our cause to reach the US Senate".[84] In February 2002, Malik Mahmud pointed out that Jakarta had to grant what the Americans asked, "because they depend on the Americans".[85] Di Tiro went even further: "We don't expect to get anything from Indonesia. But we hope to get something from the US and UN. I depend on the UN and the US and EU .... We will get everything."[86]

When the "wise men" joined the dialogue process, GAM singled out the American, retired Marine General Anthony Zinni, and Thailand's former foreign minister, Dr. Surin Pitsuwan. While each of the wise men was participating in a purely personal capacity, this was not GAM's interpretation:

> As is well-known, General Zinni is President Bush's special mediator for the Israeli-Palestinian conflict, while Dr. Pitsuwan is former Minister of Foreign Affairs of Thailand. The latter's participation was at the special request of the UN Secretary-General, Mr. Kofi Annan.[87]

In February 2002, di Tiro elaborated further, saying that "Zinni is the representative of the US in these talks. The wise men support Acehnese independence, and the members of the UN will follow."[88]

Not surprisingly, internationalisation became the key element of GAM's negotiating strategy. Senior GAM negotiator Sofyan Ibrahim Tiba explained it as follows:

> It is based on three pillars: First, the Acehnese people, second, the Indonesians, and third the international community .... But at the moment we only have the first pillar and the third .... Regarding the third — we give information to the international community about the situation here. Also the dialog is part of this. Everything needs to be conducted outside of Aceh and Indonesia![89]

For GAM the mere initiation of official negotiations already constituted a victory as negotiations were tantamount to recognition by Jakarta. The fact that the meetings took place outside of Indonesia further provided the movement with domestic and international legitimacy, casting it in the role of the sole legitimate representative of the Acehnese people. Dialogue in Geneva was also a way to raise international awareness and to draw in foreign players, encouraging the Western world in particular to put pressure on Indonesia. The location of the negotiations in Switzerland, the HDC as facilitator, and the inclusion of the foreign wise men all aided GAM's strategy. The CoHA itself sanctioned "foreign intervention" through the international monitors, which Malik Mahmud likened to a UN presence. "The operation had UN backing because individual governments sending monitors would not support it otherwise."[90] UN Secretary General Kofi Annan's statement welcoming the CoHA, the international commitment to resolving the conflict in Aceh peacefully and the development assistance pledged at the Tokyo conference further underlined GAM's strategy of drawing in the international community. On the ground, GAM used the space created by the peace zones to tell the Acehnese population not only that independence was imminent but that GAM's aspirations had the backing of the UN.

By March GAM's misinformation campaign had reached such heights that the head of the UN Office for the Coordination of Humanitarian Aid (OCHA), Michael Elmquist, issued a public statement that "we are deeply concerned to read statements by the spokesperson of GAM implying that GAM is expecting the United Nations to assist them in their quest for independence".[91] The UN fully supported the territorial integrity of the Republic of Indonesia. This did not, however, make much of an impression on GAM. In April 2003, when the CoHA had already collapsed in all but name, GAM negotiator Amni bin Marzuki re-emphasised the importance of the international dimension.

> What is important is the international context. Even without the COHA we still have Tokyo. The Thai commander, the Thai army and the Philippine army all know what happened in Takengon.[92] [a reference to TNI involvement in the systematic dismantling of the JSC monitoring mechanism]

After the Tokyo talks collapsed on 18 May, GAM condemned Jakarta "for destroying all prospects for peace", but expressed its "deepest gratitude to the international community ... for their tireless efforts towards realising peace in Aceh", and appealed to the UN "for its immediate involvement in the resolution of the Aceh conflict, and for an international fact-finding mission to be sent to Aceh to investigate the crimes against humanity that have been and are being committed in Aceh".[93]

GAM's Strategy: Evolution, Strengths and Weaknesses

GAM evolved from a small vanguard force of 70 in 1976 to a movement which at the time of the collapse of the peace process in May 2003 was estimated to have a membership of 8,000. Along with the expansion of the organisation both in terms of membership and territory, GAM's insurgency strategy evolved from a purely military strategy focused on guerrilla warfare into a politico-military strategy since 1999.

GAM's primary strength was its superior knowledge of the terrain as well as a considerable support base within the population. The former allowed GAM to choose the place and timing of armed contact with the Indonesian security forces. It also provided the guerrillas with a large number of hiding places, safe-guarding its regional commanders and protecting the overall command structure. The latter provided GAM with intelligence on Indonesian troop movements and logistical support.

GAM successfully tailored its ideology to appeal to the largest number of Acehnese. Key to this was a strong emphasis on Acehnese culture and identity, emphasising the differences with Indonesian nationalism. At the same time GAM allowed a degree of flexibility and ambiguity in other aspects of its ideology, which preserved the existence of the movement. For instance, GAM's anti-capitalist and anti-Western sentiments of the 1970s and early 1980s have all but disappeared. By shifting from the "world revolutionary" vocabulary of its early days to the "democratic" vocabulary of the 1990s GAM was able to survive the transition from the Cold War environment into the post-Cold War world. Similarly, its ambiguity on Islam — emphasising Aceh's devoutness and leaving it up to individual GAM commanders to enforce aspects of Syariah while at the same time changing their model of state from that of an Islamic Sultanate to a democracy — kept internal challenges under control in an era when many other Muslim national liberation movements factionalised over the role of religion. It also prevented the West from becoming alienated.

And finally, GAM successfully harnessed the peace process — until its collapse — turning its strategy from a military one into a well-coordinated politico-military one. GAM was able to shape the negotiations to its internationalisation agenda by demanding and receiving talks outside of Indonesia, a foreign facilitator, and the involvement of foreign advisers, and ultimately foreign monitors on the ground. Through the internationalisation strategy and the peace process GAM achieved a maximum amount of international focus on Aceh. Involvement in the dialogue also provided GAM with recognition by the Indonesian government, the people of Aceh, and foreign countries and organisations. Arguably the success of GAM's strategy of internationalisation was one of the key reasons why the Indonesian security forces moved to undermine the CoHA.

While the negotiations constituted one of the biggest successes in the evolution of GAM's strategy, they also revealed some of the movement's greatest limitations and constituted one of the factors for the failure of the peace process. At an individual level GAM negotiators lacked capacity and sophistication; at an ideological and political level GAM proved inflexible and unimaginative. For instance, the movement did not even attempt to develop a political wing or party as a vehicle to pursue its struggle in a more non-violent fashion or indeed as a way of including the people of Aceh in the process. In fact, the political decision-making was almost exclusively restricted to the aging GAM leadership in exile. This undermined GAM's self-proclaimed democratic credentials as well as its claim that it truly represented the people of Aceh.

It was also not interested in engaging with Indonesia other than discussing independence. Rather than seizing the opportunity to shape autonomy proposals to its liking and to use autonomy as a spring-broad toward eventual independence, GAM rejected everything on offer by Indonesia, ultimately closing the door to further negotiations.

GAM's inflexibility in the negotiations was partially related to another one of its weaknesses, namely misjudging and misreading the political situation in Indonesia as well as internationally. With respect to Indonesia GAM believed that the Republic after the fall of Suharto was on the verge of collapse and territorial disintegration. Time was on GAM's side and all the movement needed to do was to sit back and wait. With respect to the international community it failed to detect the shift from a post-Cold War, pro-human rights mood to the post-September 11th loss of sympathy for Muslim national liberation movements and the reinforcement of the notion of state boundaries and territorial integrity.

GAM's weaknesses at the political level were compounded by weaknesses in the field. Here the main problem was GAM's lack of real military capacity. GAM was no match for the Indonesian security forces who were larger in number, better trained, better equipped, regularly rotated, and generally better supported logistically. GAM did not have a military option in the sense of being able to liberate Aceh. It had the capacity to make life difficult for the Indonesian government and to tie down troops and resources. It could try to use violence as a means to achieve policy-change by either directly pressuring the government, by terrorising the population into demanding a change from the government, or by trying to make the situation so unbearable on the ground that the international community would feel compelled to intervene. However, there was no evidence that Indonesia came to the negotiating table because of GAM's use of force, nor that GAM was interested in a policy-change short of letting Aceh go. Similarly the international community did not feel compelled to intervene in Aceh once martial law was declared on 19 May 2003. In fact, every state as well as the UN reaffirmed Indonesia's territorial integrity.

By far the greatest weaknesses of GAM were the ethnically and politically motivated attacks on civilians and the criminalisation of the movement since 1999. GAM's targeting of the Javanese, the forced taxation of the Acehnese people and even foreign humanitarian NGOs especially during the CoHA, the burning of schools, the intimidation, torture, killing, and kidnapping of civilians, and the piracy in the Melaka Strait undermined GAM's strategy. The upsurge in kidnappings — some 300 during martial law — at a time when brutal abductions in Iraq were in the media, alienated some international sympathy. The kidnappings of journalists Ferry Santoro and Ersa Siregar eroded the sympathy of the press. The taxation/extortion strained GAM relations with the ordinary Acehnese. Not surprisingly, many of the GAM members denounced to the security forces once martial law began were "tax collectors".

Indonesia's Counter-Insurgency Strategy, 1977–2004

Since the emergence of GAM's separatist challenge, Aceh saw numerous security operations. These included four major military campaigns since 1977, two during the New Order and two since the fall of Suharto.

Security Operations

During the New Order Indonesian counter-insurgency efforts were primarily of a military and intelligence nature. The key operations were the *Nanggala* intelligence operations 1977–9 and the *Jaring Merah* (Red Net) operations 1989–98, which are commonly referred to as *Daerah Operasi Militer* (DOM). Both operations relied heavily upon what the Indonesian military refers to as the "security approach" whereby more often than not the ends justified the means and the use of force was prevalent. The security operations dealt with the symptoms of the conflict but made few if any attempts to address its root causes. Dialogue with the people, political negotiations or talking to separatists were unthinkable. Efforts to address the economic and political grievances ran up against economic centralisation policies, wide-spread corruption, civilian incompetence, and the belief that any form of regional autonomy would lead to federalism and then disintegration.

After the fall of Suharto in 1998, and the 1999 loss of East Timor amidst international condemnation over human rights abuses, the Indonesian government changed its approach toward counter-insurgency in three important ways. First, there was a change in attitude on the part of the government and most of the TNI hierarchy in that insti-tutionalised human rights abuse was neither encouraged nor condoned. This was a major departure from New Order policies. It was reflected in the establishment of a national human rights commission, Komnas HAM and a special commission to investigate past abuses in Aceh. Moreover, in 2003–4 soldiers for the first time were court-martialled during an on-going operation. Second, a distinctly political dimension was added to Indonesia's strategy by offering both regional autonomy and negotiations with GAM. Third, the Indonesian military made concerted efforts at professionalisation. Starting in early 2001 new combat reconnaissance platoons (*tontaipur*) were established. This was followed by the re-instatement of the *Rajawali* training to prepare army units for counter-insurgency. This training course focused on combat effectiveness and discipline, including rules of engagement and human rights. Human rights training was given by the International Committee of the Red Cross (ICRC) and the United Nations High Commission for Refugees (UNHCR). The use of Quick Reaction Strike Units or *Pasukan Pemukul Reaksi Cepat* (PPRC) was also expanded. In 2003, the army's Raider battalions were reorganised (see Fig. 16), creating 8 territorial and 2 Kostrad battalions which underwent an intensive 6-month training and were equipped with the newest weapons, the locally produced SS1-V5, and technology — global positioning systems and night vision goggles.

These changes were reflected in the Security Recovery Operation or *Operasi Pemulihan Keamanan dan Penegakan Hukum* (OKPH) 2001–2 and the Integrated Operation or *Operasi Terpadu* 2003–4. Unlike the New Order security approach both OKPH and *Operasi Terpadu* had a comprehensive "classical" counter-insurgency approach. Such an approach comprises military and non-military aspects aimed at reducing the capacity of the insurgents by isolating them from their bases of support, destroying their physical structure, diluting their political message, mitigating popular

Fig. 16 Army Chief Ryamizard Ryacudu at closing ceremony of "Aceh" Raider battalion 300 in Cianjur, December 2003 (*courtesy Kirsten E. Schulze*)

grievances, operating within a legal framework, and above all, winning the hearts and minds of the people.[94] At the village level such classical counter-insurgency usually involves technical assistance, economic aid and propaganda plus the use of small independent infantry forces in small-scale action against guerrilla forces. At the national level it provides economic aid and technical assistance plus the use of conventional forces in large-scale operations.[95]

OKPH, which was launched in April 2001, a year after the beginning of the peace process, and which was concurrent with intermittent negotiations, was based on a six-point plan. Security operations would be combined with the restoration of the rule of law, economic recovery, new autonomy legislation for Aceh, the promotion of Acehnese culture, and social recovery. The aim of OKPH was twofold: First, to move the stalled talks forward by pressurising GAM toward a compromise by eliminating or at least weakening its military option; second, to restore security and create the space for putting in place a package of special autonomy for Aceh. Moreover, it was also a response to the deterioration of the security situation as exemplified by the increase in casualties during the so-called Humanitarian Pause from 2 July 2000 to 10 March 2001 and the failed cease-fire arrangements in Pidie and North Aceh between 22 March and 3 April 2001.

Similarly, *Operasi Terpadu* which followed the collapse of the peace process and the placing of Aceh under martial law on 19 May 2003 comprised four aspects: first, the military operation; second, law enforcement; third, humanitarian aid; and fourth, restoring local government. With the second martial law period in November 2003 economic recovery was added as a fifth aspect. All aspects together aimed at reducing, if not eliminating GAM's political, civilian and military capacity, at restoring local government services, at securing the Lhokseumawe industrial complex, and at curbing Acehnese support for independence by "winning the hearts and minds" of the people.

Operasi Terpadu made up for some of the tactical shortcomings of OKPH. The re-establishment of *Kodam* Iskandar Muda together with the operational headquarters in Lhokseumawe meant that the counter-insurgency operations were run from within the area of conflict — Aceh — rather than from outside — Medan — in the neighbouring province of North Sumatra. The Indonesian navy instituted a more effective cordon to interdict weapons smuggling and the army drew upon more accurate intelligence for ground operations. As a whole *Operasi Terpadu* had better trained troops and better equipment. The large number of stationary garrison or framework troops, *satuan kerangka,* prevented GAM from creeping in behind the lines which had been a particular problem during OKPH. But most importantly, the Raider battalions took the fight to GAM. Aggressive patrolling together with cordon and sweep operations pushed GAM away from population centres, allowing for the return of normal economic activity. Together with the non-military aspects of the operation, it enabled the pacification of many GAM controlled areas. Finally it destroyed much of GAM's fighting ability. GAM was forced to revert to embryonic guerrilla tactics.

Strategy, Tactics and Targets

Indonesia's overall counter-insurgency strategy evolved from a security only to a comprehensive approach, and the presence of the Indonesian security forces in Aceh increased with each operation from the few dozen *Kopassandha* (now *Kopassus*) special forces of the *Nanggala* operations in the late 1970s to an estimated 30,000 TNI and 13,000–15,000 police and *Brimob* during *Operasi Terpadu* in 2003. Yet all security operations had a similar strategy, tactics, and targets.

The military strategy sought first, to separate GAM from the people and loosen its grip over them; second, to isolate GAM by severing its logistical and communications lines; and third to destroy GAM's military command and civilian infrastructure.[96] The main challenge for the Indonesian security forces in all operations from 1977 to 2004 was to separate the insurgents from the population and to win the hearts and minds of the people. The former was complicated by the fact that GAM guerrillas virtually disappeared into the local population, not wearing uniforms or carrying weapons. The latter was undermined by the security forces' brutal treatment of the local population, the destruction and theft of people's property during searches, and above all by the failure to implement the non-military aspects: revitalising the local economy, rebuilding the education and healthcare infrastructure, reducing unemployment, and restoring the rule of law.

One of the key elements of Indonesian military strategy was the raising of civil defence groups or *perlawanan rakyat (wanra)* in line with standard counter-insurgency strategy as well as Indonesia's Total People's Defence doctrine (*sistem pertahanan keamanan rakyat semesta* or *sishankamrata*). In 1977 *Nanggala* 21 was tasked with this job.[97] During *Jaring Merah* from 1989 to 1998 a number of different groups were raised such as *Laskar Rakyat* (People's Troops), which was established in East Aceh, given basic military training, traditional weapons — knives, machetes, and spears — and told to hunt GAM.[98] Another organisation, *Ksatria Unit Penegak Pancasila* (Noble Warriors for Upholding Pancasila), was based in North Aceh and reportedly helped the army flush out some 300 rebels.[99] During OKPH self-defence groups emerged in Central Aceh and South Aceh in response to GAM's brutal entry into those areas. These groups were not only tolerated by the TNI but nurtured, supported, organised and, according to some locals, trained in basic defence skills. During *Operasi Terpadu, wanra* were systematically raised in December 2003 and January 2004. In Central and South Aceh existing organisations were brought under unified command, in all other districts new groups were set up. Some *wanra* claimed that they received rudimentary paramilitary training.[100] According to TNI spokesman Maj. Gen. Sjafrie Sjamsoedin, the military had been asked by the local government to train and organise them.[101] The *wanra* were formally under the *bupati* (regent). They did not, however, receive weapons. They were also not formally part of any tactical operations. However, most *wanra* members possessed traditional arms like everyone else in Aceh — machetes, knives, and spears.

Looking at *Operasi Terpadu* the *wanra* had three key functions: First, to gather information on GAM; second, to increase Acehnese resistance to GAM ideology by raising their educational level, exposing GAM's lies, and reducing the fear factor by creating a community;[102] and third, to relieve the TNI of some of the more routine security duties such as guarding villages at night, building sandbag barricades, and patrolling.[103]

Indonesia's security operations since 1977 focused on seven key targets.

1. *GAM's military command structure and civilian leadership*

The most obvious target was GAM's military command structure, in particular the Tiro Central Command and the 17 regional commanders or *panglima wilayah*. They were targeted since 1977 in an attempt to break GAM in the belief that without its leaders GAM will implode or disintegrate and its directionless supporters could be brought under control more easily. During the 1977–9 *Nanggala* operations *Kopassandha* teams pursued di Tiro and his men into the jungle. By the end of 1979, the first GAM Cabinet had effectively been deactivated. Its members had been killed, captured, or, like di Tiro himself, forced into exile. GAM's command structure was again the main target during the *Jaring Merah* operations, especially from 1990–2. By the end of 1991, observers believed that GAM had again been largely crushed, its field commanders captured or killed.[104] The killing of GAM *panglima wilayah* Samudra-Pase Yusuf Ali and the subsequent capture of his wife Mariani Ali — a modern day Cut Nyak Dien — who had led the guerrillas after her husband's death, brought to an end organised GAM resistance in the stronghold of North Aceh. The movement's remnants in Aceh were driven underground; the remaining command structure joined scores of Acehnese refugees in Malaysia.[105] It was only after the fall of Suharto that the GAM commanders returned to rebuild their military and civilian structures.

During OKPH, the security forces conducted low-intensity operations against GAM's military leaders. In an almost unprecedented feat TNI troops killed GAM's Commander-in-chief Abdullah Syafi'i in January 2002. However, contrary to Indonesian expectations this did not result in the implosion of GAM. Neither did it sever the link between GAM in Aceh and their political leadership in Sweden, for two reasons: First,

GAM had a triangular structure in which the GAM leadership was not only in contact with the Aceh commander, but also directly with the 17 regional commanders. Second, internal dissention between Syafi'i and Sweden had already resulted in the side-lining of Syafi'i and his *de facto* replacement with Muzakkir Manaf. In addition to Syafi'i, a number of low-level GAM commanders were also eliminated.

After the collapse of the peace process in May 2003, *Operasi Terpadu* targeted not only GAM's military command structure and civilian leadership but also GAM's negotiators. During the first week of martial law Amni bin Marzuki, Teungku Kamaruzzaman, Sofyan Ibrahim Tiba, Nashiruddin Ahmad and Teungku Muhamed bin Usman Lampoh Awe were arrested. They were charged with treason and terrorism and sentenced to between 12 and 16 years.

Pressure was also exerted upon high-ranking GAM personnel to give themselves up. Those who surrendered included West Aceh district commander Teuku Ali Said, Tamiang governor Zulfauzi, Sabang governor Abdul Muthalib, Bireuen district commander Dedi, and Tiro field operations commander Amri bin Abdul Wahab. Many more GAM personalities were captured or killed. Those captured included spokesman and campaigner Irwandi Yusuf, North Aceh subdistrict commander Efendi Saputra, GAM adviser Abdul Wahab bin Daud, North Aceh Muaradua subdistrict deputy commander Mustafa bin Ibrahim, Central Aceh governor Dailami, East Aceh district commander Hamdan, tax collector Heri Hurmansyah, South Aceh district commander Awaluddin, and Aceh Besar district commander Teungku Djohan. Those killed included Pase deputy commander Teungku Ibrahim, Pase deputy commander Teungku Ramli Basyah, North Aceh GAM police Nurdin, operational commander Batee Iliek Herizal, operational commander Lhok Tapak Tuan Fajri, Gaja Keng commander Udin, governor Samudra Pase Said Adnan, deputy district commander Bireuen Ayi, and Peureulak spokesman Mansur. Peureulak operational commander Ishak Daud, who baited the TNI throughout martial law with high profile operations and kidnappings, was shot dead after the end of martial law on 8 September 2004.

2.   *GAM members*

In addition to the GAM command structure and civilian leaders, GAM members of all ranks were targeted. Here the aim was to reduce the overall strength of GAM as an organisation as well as GAM's territorial control. In the 1970s, when GAM was still a small organisation of some 70 men, targeting the leadership virtually overlapped with targeting members. This changed with the *Jaring Merah* operations, during which houses of suspected GAM members were systematically burnt down[106] and GAM members were hunted. Similarly during OKPH, operations commander Maj. Gen. Djali Yusuf stated that the operation specifically targeted GAM concentrations and training camps.[107] The TNI deemed the operation successful, as it reduced GAM's strength from 3,000 to 2,000[108] as well as GAM's control over the province from 60–70 per cent to 30–40 per cent.[109]

When *Operasi Terpadu* was launched, TNI Commander-in-chief General Sutarto ordered his troops to "destroy GAM forces down to their roots" by "finishing off, killing, those who still engage in armed resistance".[110] This was made easier since the TNI's intelligence capacity had improved as the Indonesian army had used the peace process to identify previously secret leaders of GAM.[111] In fact, according to Martial Law administrator Maj. Gen. Endang Suwarya intelligence was so good that "we have a list of targets that we want killed or captured".[112] A common tactic of the Indonesian security forces was house-to-house searches for GAM members, weapons and ammunition, and information about any young men who had left the village.[113] These were generally assumed to be GAM.

According to TNI commander-in-chief Gen. Endriartono Sutarto, during the first martial law period 1,165 GAM members were killed, 1,403 captured, and 799 surrendered. During the second martial law period 798 GAM members were killed, 697 were captured and 477 surrendered. Overall 1,963 GAM were killed, 2,100 were captured and 1,276 surrendered totalling 5,339 GAM from an organisation that in May was estimated to have had a strength of 5,251.[114]

GAM members who surrendered also became the target of a different kind of "operation", namely re-education and rehabilitation or *pembinaan*. They received classes on Indonesian nationalism and religion, but also basic education such as reading and writing. These were further complimented with vocational training in areas such as farming, fish farming, animal husbandry, mechanics, tailoring and carpentry as well as a Rp 2 million stipend each.[115] During martial law a total of 1,681 former GAM members underwent "re-education" in camps in Aceh Besar, North Aceh and West Aceh. The majority of them, however, were GAM supporters who provided the guerrillas with food, or civilian GAM rather than GAM fighters.[116]

3.   GAM logistics and communications

Severing GAM's logistics and communications was another important aspect of Indonesia's counter-insurgency strategy. This aimed at isolating GAM by cutting its communication links within Aceh as well as with the exiled leadership in Sweden. It also sought to sever "internal" logistics such as food supplied by villagers and "external" logistics such as weapons smuggled in from Thailand, Malaysia, and Cambodia. In an attempt to achieve the former, the TNI during *Operasi Terpadu* pushed GAM away from urban areas in order "to force them out of the reach of Telkom".[117] That did not, however, affect GAM's main means of communication with Sweden, namely satellite phones. With respect to weapons, the TNI relied on naval blockades. During OKPH the navy and air force were tasked with the surveillance and the interception of unauthorised movement across the Melaka Strait. This was stepped up during *Operasi Terpadu*. Twelve warships guarded Indonesia's sea borders around the province.[118]

4.   GAM families

One of the most controversial targets was the families of GAM members. Parents, wives, siblings, and children of key GAM leaders were routinely interrogated in order to obtain information. During the *Nanggala* Operations female family members in particular were detained as hostages in order to get their male relatives to surrender.[119] During the *Jaring Merah* Operations, family members of GAM were tortured, and many of the women suffered humiliation, sexual abuse, and rape at the hands of the security forces.[120]

During *Operasi Terpadu*, the houses of the families of GAM members were marked with a red "X" by the military (Fig. 17).[121] This made them easy to identify and keep under surveillance by the security forces. However, it also turned them and their occupants into outcasts within their own communities. Their businesses were boycotted and sometimes these families became the victims of popular vengeance in response to a GAM kidnapping of local villagers.

In August 2003, known GAM wives were registered with the security forces. Family members were asked to locate the guerrillas.[122] Many GAM wives were obliged to report to the security forces twice a day. Some GAM wives, including Jamilah, the wife of GAM Aceh Rayeuk governor Teungku Achyar, were even forced to divorce their husbands.[123]

Fig. 17 A house targeted by the TNI as supporting a member of GAM (*courtesy Acehkita*)

GAM family members were repeatedly arrested and sometimes disappeared. On 7 April 2004, TNI troops reportedly arrested Aisyah Usman, wife of GAM commander-in-chief Muzakkir Manaf, and her young children, and detained them first at a TNI post and then in a controlled village.[124] On 30 April, members of GAM Aceh Rayeuk commander Tengku Muharram Idris' extensive family were arrested and detained in order to force him to surrender. On 23 April 2004 all GAM families in the Keude Bieng area were called to the *Kopassus* post in Lhokgna, and told that if their GAM relatives did not surrender within the next 20 days, their identification cards would be revoked and their houses marked.[125]

5. *Human rights activists and NGOs*

The fifth group targeted by the TNI and the police was human rights activists and non-governmental organisations (NGOs). This was partially a broader response to the negative NGO-security forces dynamic since the fall of Suharto and partially a more direct response to GAM's strategy of drawing in and building "alliances" with NGOs. From 2000 onwards security forces' pressure on local and foreign NGOs in Aceh increased significantly. Some NGOs such as the Aceh Referendum Information Center (SIRA) and Student Solidarity for the People (SMUR) were seen as particularly close to GAM. On 19 September, two leading SIRA activists, Mohammed A. Saleh and Muzzakir were abducted by out-of-uniform *Brimob*. They were interrogated, beaten, and released.[126] In November, SIRA's office was raided by the police, and its chairman Mohamad Nazar, was later arrested.

> I was accused of separatism. Also SIRA members in Jakarta were arrested. I was not arrested because I was part of GAM but because I organised people power. SIRA has no institutional relations with GAM, but we do not reject GAM's struggle.[127]

Other NGOs, both foreign and local, were also subjected to repeated harassment and intimidation. One of the most brutal incidents occurred on 6 December 2000, when four volunteers from RATA, a local organisation for the rehabilitation of torture victims, were abducted and three of them killed, outside of Lhokseumawe.[128]

With OKPH the targeting of activists and NGOs was stepped up and SIRA again headed the list because, as *Korem* spokesman Maj. Edi Sulistiadi stated in June 2001, "GAM and SIRA are the same. SIRA is the political wing of GAM."[129] During this period, according to one member of an international NGO, "*Brimob* has broken into NGO offices and has forced staff at gunpoint to access the computer and download data and pictures of the missing. The NGOs are not safe."[130]

The then *Korem* commander Col. Endang Suwarya complained that the NGOs did not just give support to the people, "but they also give money to GAM".[131] They were also seen as a tool for foreign intervention, as foreign spies, and as agents of conflict. Gen. Ryamizard Ryacudu asserted in April 2003, a month before the declaration of martial law, that the problem with NGOs was that "they get money only when there is conflict so they don't want the conflict to end".[132]

Not surprisingly, during the first week of *Operasi Terpadu*, military authorities started to arrest activists and NGO personnel systematically. Between 19 and 27 May, 45 students and activists were apprehended on suspicion of links with GAM.[133] According to Amnesty International 21 activists were charged and brought to trial during the martial law period. These included SIRA chairman, Muhammad Nazar, sentenced to two years jail for campaigning for a referendum; Cut Nur Asikin of *Srikandi* Aceh women's rights organisation, who was accused of being the commander of GAM's *Inong Bale*; Husni Abdullah and Mahyeddin, members of the People's Crisis Centre, a humanitarian organisation that helped Acehnese IDPs;[134] Daun, a university student and volunteer for the local Monitoring Committee for Peace and Democracy in Aceh;[135] Mohamed Yusuf Puteh the head of *Forum Peduli HAM*; Reza Fahlevi of *Himpunan Aktivis Anti Militer;* Nursyamsyiah and Nadaria of *Pemberdayaan Harkat Inong Aceh;* Nuraini, a member of Kontras;[136] and Sabela and Hurriah of *Himpunan Mahasiswa Kabupaten Aceh Tamiang* as well as four members of the Center for Human Rights and two volunteers with the Indonesian Red Cross.[137]

The clamp-down on local NGOs was followed by government restrictions on foreign NGOs. Letters were sent asking them not to come to Aceh and to those already in Aceh to leave. Even civilian politicians worried that the presence of foreign NGOs would facilitate the cause of GAM. Then Minister for People's Welfare Yusuf Kalla argued that GAM might claim the foreigners were representatives of the UN. "Such propaganda is extremely dangerous."[138] Foreign Minister Hassan Wirayuda said that the government should be extra cautious about the activities of international agencies in Aceh as "there are questions about the sincerity of these organisations in helping the Acehnese, especially non-governmental organisations, which could have other motives or might support GAM".[139]

6.   *GAM's support base*

In order to weaken and ultimately isolate the GAM commanders and troops it was essential to cut GAM off from its support base. During the *Jaring Merah* operations villagers were placed under tight control and some were relocated. During *Operasi Terpadu* efforts were made to prevent GAM blending with the population, and to deny them access to food and information.[140] "We are mounting pressure on the rebel strongholds to narrow their room for movement and trying to separate the rebels from civilians."[141]

In 2003, GAM was first pushed out of the urban areas and away from the main transport routes. The next move into rural areas saw the TNI's more controversial tactics of relocating entire villages suspected of supporting insurgents. According to senior officials, interning whole villages enabled the soldiers to pick through emptied areas thoroughly in search of GAM members or sympathisers.[142] They claimed it was restricted to "areas where GAM has a particularly strong influence".[143]

A TNI spokesman explained:

> In the first two weeks we started to separate GAM from the people. There were some problems. Some villages were physically under GAM control and GAM was using the people. So we decided to remove the people from the villages to camps and to sweep and clear the village of all GAM. We did this right from the beginning but we had some problems. Many of the people were unhappy but to improve the situation we had to do it. We had to regain control over the territory.[144]

7.   *The people of Aceh*

Partly because of the difficulties the security forces faced in distinguishing GAM from the Acehnese people, the people as a whole were targeted. They were also terrorised in order to deter them from supporting GAM. Above all, the Acehnese population was targeted because of the widespread perception that they were intrinsically disloyal. This resulted in punishment for disloyalty on the one hand and efforts to compel loyalty on the other.

Systematic terrorising to discourage the people from supporting GAM was the preferred approach during the *Jaring Merah* operations. This was pursued through heavy-handed military reprisals against villages believed to provide logistical help or sanctuary to the insurgents. Common tactics included the burning of the homes of suspected independence supporters or sometimes their entire village. This "shock therapy" was described as a "campaign of terror designed to strike fear in the population and make them withdraw their support from GAM"[145] and "state-sanctioned terror" in the form of "targeted killings and public executions".[146]

> In an effort to undercut the civilian support base of the guerrilla resistance, Indonesian forces carried out armed raids and house-to-house searches in suspected rebel areas. The houses of villagers suspected of providing shelter or support to the rebels were burned to the ground. Anyone suspected of contact with *Aceh Merdeka* was vulnerable to arbitrary arrest and detention, torture, "disappearance" or summary execution.[147]

The people were also forced to assist the security forces in intelligence and security operations. The Aceh Governor estimated that 60,000 people were mobilised for such assistance, including "fence of legs" operations or *operasi pagar betis* in which villagers were forced into a rebel area ahead of armed troops.[148]

During the first four years of *Jaring Merah* scores of guerrillas and civilians were killed, tortured and disappeared. Kidnap victims spoke of being forced to bury people shot by the military; women related accounts of sexual assault and rape. Subsequent investigations revealed that in the period of 1989–98 between 1,258[149] and 2,000[150] people were killed and 3,439 tortured.[151] Human Rights Watch put the number of disappeared at 500 while the Aceh Regional Assembly estimated it at between 1,000–5,000, Kontras at 1,958,[152] and the NGO Forum Aceh believed the number to be as high as 39,000. A total of 625 cases of rape and torture of women were recorded.[153] An estimated 16,375 children were orphaned[154] and 3,000 women widowed. Some 597 houses were burnt by the Indonesian security forces.[155] After DOM 7,000 cases of human rights violations were documented[156] and at least 12 mass graves were investigated.[157]

Security operations post-Suharto placed more emphasis on rules of engagement, international humanitarian law, and human rights. The TNI perception of the Acehnese, however, did not change. They continued to see them as disloyal and tried to tackle this disloyalty, above all, through "loyalisation". For instance, during OKPH over 6,000 villages were compelled to declare their loyalty.[158] During *Operasi Terpadu* "loyalisation" was multi-layered. During the second month of martial law, in July, the military began mobilising the people to attend loyalty ceremonies and to swear allegiance to the Republic of Indonesia. Mass participation in the recitation of oaths of loyalty to the Indonesian state or *ikrar kesetiaan* was even broadcast on television.[159] The population was encouraged to show allegiance to Indonesia's red and white flag as, "flying the flag is an indication of whether they are really Indonesian or not", as an Army spokesman put it.[160]

"Loyalisation" further included the introduction of "loyalty tests". According to Governor Puteh, 67,000 civil servants were to be screened due to suspicion that many were supporting or providing funds to GAM.[161] In this context 13 district heads or *camats* were replaced by military officers. Two Acehnese councillors, one from Aceh Besar (Golkar) and one from Sabang (PPP) were also detained for collecting funds for GAM.[162]

Another administrative measure was the issuing of new "red and white" identity cards in efforts to distinguish civilians from GAM.[163] These new ID cards needed to be produced at checkpoints and people unable to produce them fell under the suspicion of being GAM.

The other side of "loyalisation" was punishment for disloyalty. This
continued post-Suharto albeit to a lesser extent. During the police
operations *Wibawa* 99, *Sadar Recong* I, II and III and *Cinta Meunasah*
I and II whole villages were "punished as retaliation for GAM attacks".[164]
One of the most prominent examples is the collective punishment of the
residents of the East Aceh town of Idi Rayeuk in March 2001. This
followed the 28 February GAM occupation of the town, during which
GAM burnt down the police barracks and the jail as well as bombing
the police station. After the Indonesian security forces had recaptured
Idi Rayeuk, they burnt down the centre of the town. They also torched
six surrounding villages.[165]

Another example is the security forces' response to the killing of
Mak Pri, the wife of the TNI sub-district commander who had disappeared
during a visit to the village of Simpang Mamplan in May 2001. After
her body was recovered, security forces burnt down the house of the
village head, local businesses, and killed three male villagers.[166]

During *Operasi Terpadu* punishment for disloyalty in the form of
beatings, summary killings, and torture of unarmed civilians was still
occurring despite efforts to curb human rights abuses.[167] Many of
these came at the hands of frustrated soldiers who felt that they were
being lied to by the people and who suspected that the people sympathised with GAM. For instance, on 27 May 2003, soldiers from
battalion 144 entered the village of Lawang, Bireuen, in search of GAM.
They shot dead one man suspected of being GAM and beat up another
three in search of further information.[168] In the subsequent court-
martial, the soldiers testified that they felt they had been lied to, that
the villagers were protecting GAM, and that they got emotional so they
hit them.[169] Lawang was not an isolated incident. In fact, as interviews
with Acehnese refugees in Malaysia by Human Rights Watch revealed,
beating villagers seemed to be the standard response by the security
forces to non-cooperative, "disloyal" villagers.[170] Beyond the frustration
of the individual soldier, the conviction that all Acehnese supported
GAM continued to pervade the mindset of Indonesia's military on the
ground. This often translated into indiscriminate use of force, especially
against young men.[171]

Indonesia's Political Strategy

Like GAM's, Indonesia's military strategy after 2000 was accompanied
by a political strategy. This was the direct outcome of a series of post-

Suharto policy shifts on resolving the conflict in Aceh, starting with President B.J. Habibie's decision to withdraw non-organic military forces from the province and declaring an end to DOM. This was followed by a public apology by Commander-in-Chief Gen. Wiranto for the trauma experienced at the hands of the security forces. When Habibie was succeeded by Abdurrahman Wahid in 1999 the new president took Habibie's position one step further by committing himself to resolving the Aceh conflict through negotiations. Together with his Foreign Minister Hassan Wirayuda and Coordinating Minister for Security and Political Affairs Susilo Bambang Yudhoyono, Wahid embarked upon dialogue with GAM in the hope that the violence in Aceh could be brought to an end and that Acehnese grievances could be addressed. This step was almost unprecedented in Indonesia's history and marks the most significant change since the New Order.

The negotiations became the key element in Indonesia's new comprehensive approach to Aceh. In 2001, special autonomy was added. When the peace process collapsed in May 2003, Indonesia's focus shifted to countering GAM militarily and legally within Aceh, to improving the implementation of special autonomy, and to diplomatic and legal efforts to deal with the exiled GAM leadership.

Negotiations

Indonesia's main interest in the political dialogue was the reduction of violence in Aceh. At the core of its negotiating strategy was "forcing" GAM to give up the armed struggle and to accept autonomy. It was not uncommon for Indonesian politicians to believe that GAM's acceptance of a cease-fire had ended the conflict. Both the 2000 Humanitarian Pause and the 2002/3 CoHA were initially celebrated as peace agreements, despite the fact that neither touched upon substantive political issues.

Indonesia tried to exert pressure upon GAM through the very elements of the international community whom GAM looked to for support. As far as Indonesia was concerned the primary function of the wise men was to talk sense into GAM, making the movement see that it could not win a guerrilla war and that independence was an unrealistic goal. Similarly, Indonesia turned toward the EU and US to pressure GAM, most notably in the run-up to the CoHA when international incentives in the form of economic rehabilitation of Aceh by the US, EU, Japan, Canada and the World Bank aimed at enticing GAM into an agreement. (For more details on the CoHA see Chapter 10.)

While GAM successfully harnessed the peace process, Indonesia's negotiating position was undermined from the beginning by President Abdurrahman Wahid's erratic behaviour such as first promising a referendum then rescinding this promise, and by internal discord. Wahid supported negotiations while the military did not believe in talking to rebels. Many parliamentarians feared that an official, bilateral dialog with GAM afforded the separatists recognition, legitimacy, and a status equal to that of the Indonesian Republic. They were also worried that negotiations would lead to the break-away of Aceh. Thus, like much of the military, they maintained that negotiations on an internal issue should not be conducted outside Indonesia yet Wahid agreed to Geneva as the venue. Indonesia's aim of an internal solution by getting GAM to agree to autonomy was fundamentally at odds with the structure of the negotiations.

Furthermore, Indonesia's negotiating position was damaged by the disconnection between the dialogue and the autonomy process. The Indonesian government saw regional autonomy for Aceh as a way of addressing Aceh's economic, political and cultural grievances, as explained fully in Chapter 14.

There is no doubt that the autonomy legislation was a historic shift in comparison to the New Order and its focus on unity and uniformity. GAM, however, was not interested in any form of autonomy and had no part in the autonomy process. This was not the only problem. Special autonomy had been enacted in isolation from civil society and thus had little public support. It was a product of the provincial elites and the national parliament. The lack of ownership by the Acehnese people was exacerbated by failure to implement the autonomy provisions. Indeed, for the majority of Acehnese nothing changed. Life under special autonomy did not differ significantly from life under centralisation. Popular concerns over the growing violence and over past human rights abuses remained unaddressed. Economic grievances increased as the local political and business elites scrambled for the newly devolved resources. Apart from the introduction of *Syariah*, arguably the only other change was Aceh's transition from a province governed by technocrats to one governed by kleptocrats (see Chapter 10). This failure to deliver effective and accountable regional government fundamentally undermined both the prospects of resolving the conflict through negotiation and managing it through counter-insurgency operations.

Diplomatic and Legal Efforts

In tandem with the declaration of martial law and *Operasi Terpadu*, a third element of the political strategy aimed at isolating GAM in an attempt to counteract GAM's strategy of internationalisation. The Indonesian government solicited both Malaysia's and Thailand's support in clamping down on arms smuggling to Aceh. In June 2003, police chief Gen. Da'i Bachtiar announced that the government planned to ask the UN to put GAM on the list of terrorist groups as "GAM has been involved in several bombings of public places, which can be considered indiscriminate acts of violence and therefore an act of terror".[172] In the end, however, Indonesia refrained from going down this road.

In the same month, the Indonesian police issued a "red notice" to Interpol in an effort to arrest seven GAM leaders: Hasan di Tiro, Armea, Malik Mahmud, Zaini Abdullah, Tgk Muhamad Syafi'i, Zakaria Zaman, and Muhammad Nur Djuli bin Ibrahim.[173] This was followed by visits of an Indonesian police team to Thailand to find Zakaria and of a government team to Stockholm. The Indonesian Government asserted that the exiled GAM leadership in Sweden had "been sending instructions to their forces in Aceh, including orders to burn schools, kidnap village chiefs and carry out bomb attacks".[174] It asked the Swedish government to initiate legal proceedings against Hasan di Tiro, Zaini Abdullah and Malik Mahmud on charges of directing a rebellion in a foreign country and involvement in terrorism.

On 15 March 2004, a team from the Swedish prosecutor's office came to Indonesia and interviewed 19 witnesses in Jakarta, Medan, and Aceh. In April, the Swedish government announced that it would investigate the GAM leaders residing in Stockholm. This investigation focused on "the involvement of Tiro and associates in the Senen Atrium, Jakarta Stock Exchange, and Cijantung mall bombings as well as the killings of Teungku Nazaruddin Daud and Professor Dayan Daud, the kidnapping of 243 civilians, along with the burning of at least six schools".[175] At the end of June, the Swedish prosecutors took Zaini Abdullah and Malik Mahmud into temporary custody on suspicion of violating international law.

Three days later Mahmud and Abdullah were released for lack of sufficient evidence. However, in August 2004, following the confiscation of documents, a laptop, seven cellular phones, and $10,000 cash as well as pictures and video cassettes of GAM military training from the residence of Tiro, Mahmud, and Abdullah, the head of the Swedish Prosecutors Office announced that Mahmud and Abdullah would stand trial in December.[176]

Indonesia's Strategy: Evolution, Strengths and Weaknesses

Indonesia's counter-insurgency strategy evolved significantly between 1977 and 2004. In terms of size, the efforts to deal with the separatist challenge grew from the sole reliance upon small, 18–20 persons, intelligence units to *Operasi Terpadu* comprising some 30,000 TNI and 13,000–15,000 police. But more importantly, the strategy shifted from the military option or "security approach" to a more comprehensive approach which included a political component. Despite the breakdown of the peace process and the declaration of martial law in 2003, Indonesia's political leadership, as well as many in the TNI, recognised that Aceh's conflict required a political solution.

Indonesia's greatest strength was that according to international law, it had legal recognition both of its sovereignty and its right to defend the unity and integrity of its territory. While the international community did not always agree with the means deployed for this defence, every state as well as the UN supported Indonesia's right to do so. Thus, any future secession of Aceh required the consent of Indonesia.

Indonesia's decision in 2003 to pursue GAM legally in Sweden, Malaysia and Thailand strengthened this international position. For the first time since di Tiro fled Aceh in 1979 Indonesia had found a way of addressing the dilemma of an exiled leadership. Indonesia was able to hold GAM's activities up to international scrutiny but also to get the international community to curb GAM's overseas activities by initiating legal proceedings. At the same time Indonesia gained respect as a new democracy which followed the diplomatic rules of the game. The more rights and regional autonomy the Acehnese were afforded, the less "legitimacy" GAM had in pursuing its aims by violence — and the greater Indonesia's legitimacy in the eyes of the international community.

These political strengths were accompanied by a number of military strengths. First, the TNI had a greater military capacity than GAM. The TNI comprises some 300,000 troops. While the majority were either tied up in training establishments and the territorial structure, or were deployed to other conflict areas such as Maluku or Papua, the TNI still had significantly more troops at its disposal than GAM. Moreover, these troops were better equipped, better trained, frequently rotated, and better supported than GAM's guerrilla army. Indonesia's security forces in a narrow sense had to do no more than hold the territory. GAM simply did not have the capacity to take Aceh by force. Second, the TNI's process of professionalisation increased Indonesia's counter-insurgency capacity. Third, Indonesia changed its strategy to a comprehensive one and the TNI brought its tactics in line with classic counter-insurgency operations, getting out into the field with the ten Raider battalions. Indeed, foreign military observers in Jakarta saw *Operasi Terpadu*'s military aspects as a success because the military campaign combined "the right tactics, with properly trained and much better disciplined soldiers, with an effective hearts and minds campaign, with government support, and much improved intelligence collection and targeting operations".[177]

While Indonesia's security forces made considerable progress on the road to professionalisation between 1999 and May 2004, discipline remained one of the greatest challenges. All of Indonesia's counter-insurgency operations since 1977 were plagued by differing degrees of lack of discipline of the security forces. By far the lowest level of professionalism was during the ten years of *Kolakops Jaring Merah*, which was characterised by wide-spread and systematic abuses including humiliation, torture, kidnapping, rape, disappearances, extra-judicial killings, and collective punishment. These abuses were compounded by the propensity of the TNI and the police for road-side extortion, theft and the destruction of property. As a result the security forces alienated the population whose hearts and minds it was necessary to win.

Another weakness on the military side was the reliance on civil defence organisations. These were an integral part of Indonesian military doctrine and it was standard procedure to encourage them but they were problematic for three main reasons. First, they were less well trained than soldiers, less disciplined, less accountable, and could easily get out of control, undermining the operation. Second, the "franchising" of violence blurred the line between combatants and non-combatants, turning the civilian population into targets and actors. This, in turn, made the conflict more difficult to resolve. And third, since GAM's information warfare revolved around the comparison with East Timor, the raising of civil defence organisations in Aceh played into GAM's hands.

Military weaknesses were exacerbated by political weaknesses. Every single operation since 1977 suffered from the failure to implement the non-military aspects. This was partly an "attitude" problem among the civilian leadership, who expected the military to do everything. The local officials were either unable or unwilling to assume responsibility for providing meaningful development and effective governance. Greed and corruption ironically increased with the post-Suharto decentralisation and special autonomy for Aceh. The Acehnese provincial legislature and above all the governor and his wife mismanaged and embezzled the provincial budget, humanitarian aid and development funds, as well as money allocated for the humanitarian operation during the martial law period. The unresponsiveness of the civilian leadership to the local needs of the Acehnese undermined counter-insurgency efforts as much as the lack of discipline by the security forces.

The failure to integrate counter-insurgency operations into a broader political strategy can most clearly be seen during the period of the peace process from 2000 to 2003, which overlapped with OKPH. There was no obvious connection between the two. OKPH was almost exclusively a response to the deteriorating security situation in Aceh rather than a carefully designed means to pressure GAM into being more flexible at the negotiating table. Similarly, the autonomy legislation which was passed during this period was disconnected from both the peace process and OKPH. It was unilaterally decided in Jakarta with input from the Aceh provincial legislature, but without consultation of the people of Aceh. In fact, the people of Aceh neither featured in the peace process nor in the changes to the governance of the province.

Even in periods where there were no negotiations, before and after the peace process, there was no broad political exit strategy. *Kolakops Jaring Merah* lasted for ten years. It was concluded not because the operation had achieved its aims but because of the fall of Suharto. Similarly, it was unclear whether *Operasi Terpadu* fitted into any greater political strategy for resolving the conflict in Aceh.

Finally, between 1977 and 2004 there was not one successful attempt at addressing the primary causes of the conflict — economic and social inequalities, the feelings of exploitation, and the loss of dignity and of the space for political, cultural and social expression with the effective removal of *daerah istimewa* status. These not only remained unresolved, but were compounded by secondary causes and grievances such as the brutality by the security forces, injustice, and the decline into poverty of many parts of Aceh.

Conclusion

The conflict between GAM and the Indonesian state between 1976 and 2004 evolved from one fought primarily by military means to one fought militarily, politically, legally and diplomatically. Both GAM and Indonesia benefited from the broadening of their respective strategies. Yet, both also saw their strategies undermined on the ground in Aceh. GAM used the peace process 2000–3 to obtain international recognition and to propel itself into the position of representative of the Acehnese people. GAM's achievements, however, were limited as it failed to attract the support of a single government. The changing international climate after September 11 looked unsympathetically on Muslim national liberation movements. But GAM was also weakened by the increasing criminalisation of some of its rank and file as well as the ethnically and politically motivated targeting of civilians. Extortion, the kidnapping of civil servants, teachers and journalists, the shooting of local politicians, as well as the terror tactics against Javanese migrants undermined the movement's political strategy.

Indonesia did not manage to harness the peace process to its advantage. It did, however, benefit from the adoption of a comprehensive classical counter-insurgency strategy which allowed it virtually to destroy GAM's civilian infrastructure, to damage GAM's fighting ability, and to limit the freedom of movement of GAM's exiled leadership. While the Indonesian military during the martial law period clearly achieved a tactical victory, a strategic victory for the Indonesian government remained elusive. Indonesia was unable to compel GAM to accept autonomy and to give up armed resistance. Moreover, its counter-insurgency strategy was repeatedly undermined by the failure to implement the non-military aspects of any of its comprehensive operations as well as the failure to address the root causes of the Aceh conflict.

Notes

[1] This section draws heavily upon Kirsten E. Schulze, *The Free Aceh Movement (GAM): Anatomy of a Separatist Organization*, Policy Studies 2 (Washington DC: East West Center, 2004) and Kirsten E. Schulze, "The Struggle for an Independent Aceh: The Ideology, Capacity, and Strategy of GAM", *Studies in Conflict and Terrorism* 26, no. 4 (July–August 2003).

[2] Interview with Malik Mahmud, GAM Minister of State, Norsborg, 22 February 2002.

[3] International Crisis Group (ICG), *Aceh: Why Military Force Won't Bring Lasting Peace*, Asia Report 17, 2001, p. 3.

[4] Gen. Endriartono Sutarto, press conference, TNI headquarters, Cilangkap, 5 May 2004.

5   ICG, *Why Military Force Won't Bring Lasting Peace*, p. 7.

6   Data obtained from SGI Lhokseumawe, April 2003.

7   ICG, *Why Military Force Won't Bring Lasting Peace*, p. 8.

8   *Acehkita*, 15 November 2003, p. 4.

9   Ibid.

10 *BBC*, 9 June 2003.

11 As quoted by William Nessen in the *San Francisco Chronicle Magazine*, 2 November 2003.

12 Ibid.

13 Interview with Kamaruzzaman and Amni bin Marzuki, GAM negotiators, Banda Aceh, 25 December 2001.

14 Human Rights Watch (HRW), *World Report 2003: Asia: Indonesia* <http://www.hrw.org>.

15 *Tempo*, 16 June 2003.

16 *CNN.com*, 9 July 2002.

17 *Tempo*, 28 June–5 July 2004.

18 For details see Schulze, *The Free Aceh Movement* (*GAM*).

19 Geoffrey Robinson, "Rawan is as Rawan Does: The Origins of Disorder in New Order Aceh", in *Violence and the State in Suharto's Indonesia*, ed. Benedict R.O'G. Anderson (Ithaca, NY: Southeast Asia Program Publications, Cornell University, 2001), p. 225.

20 Schulze, *The Free Aceh Movement (GAM)*, p. 41.

21 Hasan di Tiro, *The Price of Freedom: The Unfinished Diary of Tengku Hasan di Tiro* (Ministry of Education and Information, State of Acheh-Sumatra, 1982), p. 70.

22 *The Jakarta Post*, 3 June 2003.

23 Testimony of Sidney Jones, Indonesia Project Director, International Crisis Group before the Subcommittee on East Asia and the Pacific, House International Relations Committee, Hearing on Recent Developments in Southeast Asia, US House of Representatives, 10 June 2003.

24 *Agence France Presse*, 5 June 2001.

25 Press Statement, ASNLF Military Spokesman, 26 January 2002.

26 Press Release, ASNLF Central Military Command, 23 January 2002.

27 Press Statement issued by Tgk. Sofyan Dawod, Military Spokesman of the Aceh-Sumatra National Liberation Front, 4 January 2002.

28 *The Jakarta Post*, 1 June 2003.

29 *Agence France Presse*, 10 June 2003.

30 Interview with Amri bin Abdul Wahab, GAM Tiro field commander, Banda Aceh, 22 April 2003.

31 Interview with Malik Mahmud, GAM Minister of State, Norsborg, 23 February 2002.

32 Gen. Endriartono Sutarto, press conference, TNI headquarters, Cilangkap, 5 May 2004.

33 *The Jakarta Post*, 13 and 16 September 2002.

34 *The Jakarta Post*, 4 May 2004.

35 *Kompas*, 19 June 2002.

36 *The Jakarta Post*, 21 and 22 May 2003; *Media Indonesia*, 5 June 2003.

37 *The Straits Times*, 31 May 2003.

38 Testimony of Sidney Jones, Indonesia Project Director, International Crisis Group before the Subcommittee on East Asia and the Pacific, House International Relations Committee, Hearing on Recent Developments in Southeast Asia, US House of Representatives, 10 June 2003.

39 *The Jakarta Post*, 8 June 2003.

40 Interview with Malik Mahmud, GAM Minister of State, Norsborg, 23 February 2002.

41 di Tiro, *The Price of Freedom*, p. 29.

42 *The Jakarta Post*, 29 October 2002.

43 ICG, *Aceh: How To Lose Hearts And Minds*, Indonesia Briefing, 23 July 2003, p. 1.

44 Ibid.

45 *Agence France Presse*, 21 May 2003

46 OCHA Daily Sitrep Aceh No. 31, 17 June 2003.

47 *The Jakarta Post*, 8 June 2003.

48 *The Jakarta Post*, 28 May 2003.

49 Robinson, "Rawan is as Rawan Does", p. 223.

50 Ibid., p. 224.

51 di Tiro, *The Price of Freedom*, p. 78.

52 Ibid., p.107.

53 GAM leaflet quoted in di Tiro, *The Price of Freedom*, pp. 108–9.

54 di Tiro, *The Price of Freedom*, pp. 125–6.

55 *Sydney Morning Herald*, 3 April 2001.

56 Interview with Bill Cummings, Public Affairs Manager, ExxonMobil Oil Indonesia, Jakarta, 19 March 2003.

57 Interview with Isnander al-Pase, GAM spokesman, Nisam, North Aceh, 19 April 2003.

58 *Waspada*, 23 April 2001.

59 *The Jakarta Post*, 24 April 2001.

60 Richard Barber (ed.), *Aceh: The Untold Story* (Bangkok: Asian Forum for Human Rights and Development, 2000), p. 32.

61 Amnesty International, *'Shock Therapy' Restoring Order in Aceh, 1989–1993*, August 1993, p. 5.

62 *The Jakarta Post*, 9 September 1999.

63 Barber, *Aceh: The Untold Story*, p. 101.

64 Anthony L. Smith, "Aceh: Democratic Times, Authoritarian Solutions", *New Zealand Journal of Asian Studies* 4, 2 (December 2002): 76.

65 HRW, *Indonesia: The War in Aceh* 13, no. 4 (August 2002): 23.

66 ICG, *Aceh: A Slim Chance for Peace*, Asia Briefing Paper, 30 January 2002, p. 7.

67 Interview with resident, Kresek, Kecamatan Bandar, 20 August 2002.

68 ICG, *A Slim Chance for Peace*, p. 7.

69 Staffan Bodemar, "Conflict in Aceh, Indonesia: Background, Current Situation and Future Prospects", Unpublished Paper, March 2004, p. 24.

70 di Tiro, *The Price of Freedom*, p. 162.

71 Ibid., p. 114.

72 Barber, *Aceh: The Untold Story*, p. 32.

73 Police Inspector-Gen. Didi Widayadi, *The Indonesian Observer*, 25 April 2001.

74 *The Jakarta Post*, 3 September 2002.

75 Interview with Malik Mahmud, GAM Minister of State, Norsborg, 22 February 2002.

76 Interview with humanitarian aid worker, Banda Aceh, 29 June 2001.

77 Stavanger Declaration, Stavanger, Norway, 21 July 2002.

78 Press Release, ASNLF, Central Bureau for Information, 4 June 2001, p. 1.

79 Ibid., p. 2.

80 Press Release, Aceh National Armed Forces, Military Information Centre, 18/19 March 2003.

81 Hasan di Tiro, Head of State of Acheh-Sumatra, President of Acheh-Sumatra National Liberation Front in the meeting at Henry Dunant Centre, Geneva, 27 January 2000.

82 Hasan di Tiro, *Denominated Indonesians*, Address delivered to UNPO General Assembly, The Hague, 20 January 1995, p. 7.

83 Interview with Amni Ahmad bin Marzuki, GAM negotiator, Banda Aceh, 24 June 2001.

84 Ibid.

85 Interview with Malik Mahmud, GAM Minister of State, Norsborg, 22 February 2002.

86 Interview with Hassan di Tiro, GAM Wali Negara and President, Norsborg, 22 February 2002.

87 Press Statement, ASNLF/GAM from Stockholm, 30 January 2002.

88 Interview with Hassan di Tiro, GAM Wali Negara and President, Norsborg, 22 February 2002.

89 Interview with Sofyan Ibrahim Tiba, GAM senior negotiator, Banda Aceh, 21 April 2003.

90 Malik Mahmud interview, "Aceh rebels want UN help, more monitors", *Reuters*, 5 December 2002.

91 Statement by OCHA at the Workshop on "Aceh — Peace and Development" held at Hotel Indonesia, 12 March 2003.

92 Interview with Amni bin Marzuki, GAM negotiator, Banda Aceh, 17 April 2003.

93 ASNLF, "Official Statement on the Failure of the Joint Council Meeting of CoHA in Tokyo on May 18, 2003 and the Declaration of War by Indonesia on Aceh", released by Malik Mahmud, Stockholm, 20 May 2003.

94 John Baylis, James Wirtz, Eliot Cohen and Colin S. Gray, *Strategy in the Contemporary World: An Introduction to Strategic Studies* (Oxford: Oxford University Press, 2002), pp. 224–5.

95 Edward Luttwak, *A Dictionary of Modern War* (London: Penguin Press, 1971), p. 61.

96 Interview with Maj. Gen. Bambang Dharmono, Commander *Operasi Terpadu*, Lhokseumawe, via telephone, 19 October 2003. See also Rizal Sukma, *Security Operations in Aceh: Goals, Consequences, and Lessons*, Policy Paper 3 (Washington: East-West Center, 2004), p. 6 and Isa Sulaiman, *Aceh Merdeka: Ideologi, Kepimpinan dan Gerakan* (Jakarta: Al-Kautsar, 2000), pp. 79–80.

97 Ken Conboy, *Kopassus: Inside Indonesia's Special Forces* (Jakarta: Equinox Publishing, 2003), p. 263.

98 Amnesty International, *'Shock Therapy'*, p. 6.

99 Ibid., p. 7.

100 *Tempo*, 7 July 2003.

101 *The Jakarta Post*, 23 April 2004.

102 Interview with Sofian Ali, leader of Front Perlawanan Separtis GAM (FPSG), Bireuen, 20 February 2004. Interview with Satria, leader of Berantas, Lhokseumawe, 21 February 2004. Interview with Tengku Hasyim, leader of Front Perlawanan dan Pembela Rakyat Bumi Teuki Umar (FRONT-TUM), Meulaboh, 24 February 2004. Interview with Tengku Hafid, leader of Front Perlawanan Separatis GAM (FPSG), Tapak Tuan, 24 February 2004.

103 *Tempo*, 7 July 2003.

104 Robinson, "Rawan is as Rawan Does", p. 217; Michael Ross, "Resources and Rebellion in Aceh, Indonesia", Yale World Bank Project on "The Economics of Political Violence", Unpublished manuscript, 5 June 2003, p. 18.

105 Interview with Lt. Gen. (ret), Sofian Effendi, former Nanggala unit commander, Jakarta, 25 September 2003.

106 Robinson, "Rawan is as Rawan Does", p. 226.

107 Interview with Maj. Gen. Djali Yusuf, Pangdam Iskandar Muda, Banda Aceh, 18 April 2003.

108 *Koran Tempo*, 16 February 2002.

109 ICG, *Aceh: A Slim Chance for Peace*, p. 2.

110 *Kompas*, 20 May 2003.

111 *Business Week*, 22 May 2003.

112 *The Financial Times*, 22 May 2003.

[113] HRW, *Aceh Under Martial Law: Inside the secret war* 15, no. 10 (December 2003): 16.

[114] Gen. Endriartono Sutarto, press conference, TNI headquarters, Cilangkap, 5 May 2004.

[115] *Tempo*, 26 August–1 September 2003.

[116] *The Jakarta Post*, 7 July 2004.

[117] *Detik.com* 9 June 2003.

[118] *The Jakarta Post*, 23 May 2003.

[119] Ross, "Resources and Rebellion in Aceh, Indonesia", p. 13.

[120] Robinson, "Rawan is as Rawan Does", p. 227.

[121] *Acehkita*, 16 July 2004.

[122] *The Jakarta Post*, 19 January 2004.

[123] *Acehkita*, 16 July 2004. Reports from Aceh, Acehnese Community of Australia, 14 July 2004.

[124] Ibid.

[125] GAM families targeted May/April, AHRO, 27 July 2004.

[126] HRW, *Indonesia: The war in Aceh*, p. 20.

[127] Interview with Mohamad Nazar, SIRA chairman, Banda Aceh, 26 December 2001.

[128] HRW, *Indonesia: The war in Aceh*, p. 33.

[129] Interview with Maj. Edi Sulistiadi, Satgaspen, Korem 012, Banda Aceh, 26 June 2001.

[130] Interview with member of an international NGO, Banda Aceh, 28 June 2001.

[131] Interview with Col. Endang Suwarya, Danrem Teuku Umar 012, Banda Aceh, 28 June 2001.

[132] Interview with Gen. Ryamizard Ryacudu, Army Chief-of-Staff, Jakarta, 5 April 2003.

[133] *The Jakarta Post*, 27 May 2003.

[134] *Agence France Presse*, 26 January 2004.

[135] *World Press Review*, 9 February 2004.

[136] Ibid.

[137] *The Jakarta Post*, 9 June 2003.

[138] *Tempo*, 3–9 June 2003.

[139] *The Jakarta Post*, 27 May 2003.

[140] *The Times*, 22 May 2003; *The Los Angeles Times*, 31 May 2003.

[141] TNI Aceh operations spokesman Lt. Col. Yani Basuki, cited *Agence France Presse*, 30 May 2003.

[142] *The Straits Times*, 23 May 2003.

[143] *Far Eastern Economic Review*, 5 June 2003.

[144] Interview with Maj.-Gen. Sjafrie Sjamsoedin, TNI spokesman, Cilangkap, 4 September 2003.

[145] Smith, *Aceh: Democratic Times, Authoritarian Solutions*, p. 77. Also Tim

Kell, *The Roots of Acehnese Rebellion, 1989–1992* (Ithaca: Cornell Modern Indonesia Project, 1995), p. 74.

146 Robinson, "Rawan is as Rawan Does", p. 227.

147 Amnesty International, *'Shock Therapy'*, p. 6.

148 Ibrahim Hassan, in *Editor*, 20 July 1991, p. 28; Amnesty International, *'Shock Therapy'*, p. 6.

149 HRW, *Indonesia: The War in Aceh*, p. 8.

150 Amnesty International, *'Shock Therapy'*, p. 8.

151 Barber (ed.), *Aceh: The Untold Story*, p. 47.

152 Kontras data cited in Samsul Bahri, "Aceh: A land of silenced and marginalized voices", Paper published at the World Social Forum, Mumbai, India, January 2004, p. 3.

153 Banda Aceh Legal Aid Foundation as cited by *The Straits Times*, 29 July 1998.

154 *Far Eastern Economic Review*, 19 November 1998.

155 Kontras data cited in Samsul Bahri, "Aceh: A land of silenced and marginalized voices", Paper published at the World Social Forum, Mumbai, India, January 2004, p. 3.

156 *Suara Pembaruan*, 26 November 1999.

157 Data gathered by Forum Peduli HAM as cited in Barber (ed.), *Aceh: The Untold Story*, p. 47.

158 Interview with Col. Endang Suwarya, Danrem Teuku Umar 012, Banda Aceh, 26 December 2001.

159 ICG, *Aceh: How to lose Hearts and Minds*, p. 4.

160 Col. Ditya Soedarsono, *The Straits Times*, 31 May 2003.

161 Indonesia Consolidated Situation Report No 132, OCHA, 7–13 June 2003.

162 *The Jakarta Post*, 13 June 2003.

163 Ibid., 28 May 2003.

164 HRW, *Aceh Under Martial Law*, p. 9.

165 *Time*, 23 April 2001; HRW, *Indonesia: The war in Aceh*, p. 18.

166 Ibid., pp. 12–3.

167 *The Jakarta Post*, 3 June 2003 and *The Jakarta Post*, 11 June 2003.

168 *Tempo*, 29 May 2003.

169 *Tempo*, 10–16 June 2003.

170 HRW, *Aceh Under Martial Law*, p. 15.

171 Ibid., p. 5.

172 *The Jakarta Post*, 3 June 2003; also *The Straits Times*, 22 May 2003.

173 *Tempo*, 10–16 June 2003

174 *Far Eastern Economic Review*, 1 July 2004.

175 Ibid.

176 *Tempointeractive*, 27 August 2004.

177 Interview with a foreign military observer, Jakarta, 10 April 2004.

13

Democratisation, the Indonesian Armed Forces and the Resolving of the Aceh Conflict

Aleksius Jemadu

Introduction

If democratisation is understood as the subjection of the use of military force to the will of the people and the rule of law, such political process should facilitate the superiority of the use of peaceful means and the primacy of human rights in dealing with political groups who aspire to secede from a nation-state. However, the political reality of a democratising country like Indonesia always presents a more complicated picture than what might be plausible in theory. The fact that the democratically elected governments since the fall of Suharto have readily resorted to a military approach in dealing with the separatist movement in Aceh indicates that the departure of a military-dominated government may not necessarily lead to the abandonment of the use of repressive measures against the secessionist movement. Indeed, after six years of struggling to democratise the political system there remain uncertainties and paradoxes concerning the integration of the Indonesian Armed Forces (TNI) into the democratic state. What is the appropriate place of TNI within the democratic framework of the Indonesian political system? Will the TNI be willing to develop a new mindset that it should subordinate itself to the democratically elected civilian government? How can we understand the re-emergence of militarism in Aceh from the perspective of the progress (or setbacks?) of the democratisation process?

After seven years of democratisation since the collapse of Suharto's authoritarian regime in May 1998, political analysts have tried to make an assessment of the real progress of democracy in Indonesia, especially with regard to the way the government deals with the issue of separatist movements in Aceh and Papua. One way of looking at democratisation in Indonesia is to follow the path of the democratic transition theorists who optimistically assume a linear process of democratisation. However, there is a growing awareness among Indonesian political scientists that this approach underestimates the impact of the contestation of political and economic interests among various social and political groups, which can undermine the democratisation process itself.

In a recent article, Vedi Hadiz uses case studies of North Sumatra and Yogyakarta to provide evidence of the inadequacies of democratic transition theories which seem to envision a mechanistic political change toward democracy. By referring to Eva Bellin's work[1], Hadiz emphasises, instead, the importance of looking at the apparent manifestation of democratisation as primarily the product of competition among social forces and interests.[2] This alternative way of understanding the current political change in Indonesia should be of great use for analysis that tries to establish linkages between democratisation, the TNI and the resolving of the Aceh conflict. It is naive to assume that political actors engaged in the Aceh problem would value their respective interests as less important and urgent than their concern for democracy and human rights. Paradoxes, inconsistencies and discontinuities in government policies in dealing with the conflict in Aceh stem from the fact that at one time the use of peaceful means is endorsed by Jakarta but at another time military force is employed to its full strength. People may wonder what can explain the fact that a democratising country like Indonesia could produce totally different approaches in dealing with its intra-state conflict. I would argue that the politics of policy making and implementation regarding the Aceh conflict need to be thoroughly investigated during the era of democratisation in which opportunities for political manoeuvres are relatively dispersed.

Many studies have been conducted on how the Indonesian government has been dealing with the separatist movement in Aceh. Rizal Sukma, for instance, focuses on the failure of the Indonesian government in the post-Suharto era to address issues of justice and welfare of the Acehnese people. He argues that perpetual peace in Aceh will very much depend on a satisfactory accomplishment of the government's tasks of ensuring justice and promoting people's economic welfare.[3] In another article Sukma analyses the implications of the security operations in Aceh, in which he emphasises the necessity of winning the hearts and minds of the Acehnese by carrying out a clear military exit strategy and socio-economic reconstruction. On top of that, security operations aiming at crushing the Free Aceh Movement (GAM) may not necessarily lead to the resolving of the Aceh conflict once and for all.[4] Edward Aspinall and Harold Crouch conduct a deep investigation into the peace process in Aceh and conclude that the peace process aimed at determining the final political status of Aceh may take a long time, on the basis of precedents for similar types of intra-state conflicts in other parts of the world.[5] The International Crisis Group (ICG) warned that the military solution would not bring lasting peace due to the multi-dimensionality of the conflict. It is argued that the Aceh case is not only a conflict of two diametrically opposed political visions regarding the political status of Aceh, but a competition over control of resources that has led the Acehnese people into an endless agony.[6]

While acknowledging the validity of these observations, my argument puts more emphasis on the importance of the context of democratisation which opens the way for various political actors to accomplish their respective interests by exploring and manipulating ample opportunities within the main arenas of democratisation, as suggested by Juan J. Linz and Alfred Stephan.[7] According to the authors there are five interacting and reinforcing arenas within which various political actors struggle for their respective interests. These arenas include civil society, political society, establishment of the rule of law, the state apparatus or bureaucracy, and economic society. The contestation among the actors within these arenas may not lead to an easy jump from democratic transition into democratic consolidation. As far as the argument of this chapter is concerned, the identification of these arenas should be useful in the specification of five different variables in explaining the inter-linkages between democratisation, the TNI and the resolving of the Aceh conflict. Those variables include the de-civilisation of the state by giving primacy to its coercive power, the existence of a political society in which political parties (civilian leaders) and the military are competing for state resources, the politicisation of the new legal framework (with the manipulation of the judiciary leading inevitably to the practice of impunity) to ensure institutional and individual interests, the competition for bureaucratic positions and the struggle for economic benefits from the conflict.

By using the theoretical framework mentioned above, this chapter will try to explain the peculiarity of the relationship between democratisation and the resolving of an intra-state conflict. According to an empirical study, out of 47 new member states recognised by the United Nations between 1974 and 1997, 26 countries or 57 per cent managed to proceed to a successful secession within the first years of democratisation in the parent country.[8] As it turns out, the case of Aceh contradicts this research finding in that democratisation of the national political system goes hand in hand with the tightening of the state control over the troubled region. This chapter seeks to explain this "deviation" by focusing on four important points. First, after the 1999 election the Indonesian national parliament was dominated by the nationalist parties especially the Indonesian Democratic Party of Struggle (PDIP) whose main constituents were in Java.[9] President Habibie's decision to allow the East Timorese to have a referendum was taken before that election. Thus, as the Acehnese enthusiasm for referendum managed to attract popular support especially among young people and students, their "window of opportunity" had passed. It should also be noted that the position of the Ministry of Domestic Affairs, which controls the regions both in Abdurrahman Wahid and Megawati's periods, was held by military generals. Thus, the Aceh case indicates the importance of the configuration of power in the national parliament and the basis of support of the winning party in the parliament. Second, over the six years since the collapse of Suharto's authoritarian regime, under each of the three different presidents, the Indonesian military has maintained its traditional privilege of portraying itself as the only force capable of keeping the nation from disintegration. Third, it is too simplistic to depict the Aceh problem as a conflict between a sovereign state and a separatist movement. The Indonesian civilian and military elite have transformed the process of democratisation into arenas of contestation for political and economic interests. Therefore, political freedom in those arenas has not led to the consolidation of democracy but the hollowing out of the process. Fourth, related to the second, the grassroots or the majority of the Acehnese people have been alienated from the whole process in such a way that they just became powerless victims of the conflict regardless of which side had an upper hand. This process of disempowerment was further exacerbated by the de-civilisation of the state during the one-year implementation of the martial law.

Habibie's Ambiguity

If democratisation is the promotion of popular control and political equality, it must result in the emergence of civil society groups who share the public sphere with the state. In other words, democratisation involves the civilisation of the state in its actions towards its citizens. If the state or its agencies use coercive power only for perpetuating control or power, such a state is in the process of de-civilising itself. According to Robert W. Hefner, the state and the civil society may not exclude each other. They should, instead, strengthen each other for they depend on each other in accomplishing their respective tasks in social life.[10] Hefner also suggests that to make democracy work, "the creation of a civilized state and self-limiting state" is essential.[11] A civilised state gives high priority to human security for each individual citizen, whereas a de-civilised one promotes state or national security even at the expense of human security.

Soon after President Habibie took power, General Wiranto as the TNI Commander made a public announcement that the military would support the new government, but would also protect Suharto and his family. Many perceived the announcement as the insistence of the military to defend its political role against marginalisation by the civilian leaders. As a transition leader, President Habibie faced a tremendous challenge of striking a balance between the old forces including the military, who wanted to defend their political and economic privileges, and the new forces of civil society who demanded radical change in the political system. The main target of people's demand for accountability was obviously the TNI, which was involved in many cases of violation of human rights in the past. As a civilian leader, President Habibie seemed to be quite reluctant to take effective control of the TNI. This might be because the survival of his government depended largely on support from generals like Wiranto and Faisal Tanjung.

Facing sharp criticisms from society, the TNI took the initiative to respond in a way that would not undermine its dominant position in society. The military leaders also wanted to prevent the civilian leaders from forcing the military to return to their barracks in responce to democratic demands. Hence, in August 1998 General Wiranto went to Aceh and apologized for what the TNI had done to the people of Aceh in the past, especially during the period of the enactment of *Daerah Operasi Militer* (DOM) or Military Operations Zone. The fact that the TNI itself revoked Aceh's DOM status indicated the unwillingness or un-readiness of the military to subordinate itself to the civilian authority. Although some generals appeared before the parliament to account for the atrocities committed by the military in Aceh, the investigation did not go beyond a formal and normative explanation as there was no clear follow-up. It was evident that Habibie's project of democratisation failed to create an independent judiciary as a crucial element for such a project to have some credibility.

President Habibie's policy on Aceh was dictated by his own political calculation, seeking to consolidate his power base in the lead-up to the presidential election in October 1999. The first thing he tried to do was to distance himself from the authoritarian image of his predecessor. He introduced some democratic measures like press freedom, the establishment of independent political parties, endorsement of the formulation of the new regional autonomy law, the release of political prisoners and a democratic general election in 1999. Habibie's policy on Aceh was based on a belief that socio-economic policies might be effective in persuading the Acehnese to remain part of the Indonesian unitary state. Habibie was also aware that the previous government made mistakes in committing human rights violations and exploiting the natural resources of Aceh. Before his visit to Aceh at the end of March 1999, Habibie made a sympathetic political gesture by declaring amnesty for 39 GAM political prisoners. He also made a promise that the central government would build railways in Aceh in order to boost economic development in that region. He convinced the Acehnese people that his government would focus more on economic development and dialogue than on using military means.[12]

Unfortunately, Habibie's ambivalence between democratic measures on the one hand and the fear of losing military support on the other brought him total failure in implementating these policies. Although he managed to prevent the TNI from imposing martial law in Aceh, he did not really have control of the situation in Aceh. To be sure, the introduction of some democratic measures led to the strengthening of local civil society groups in Aceh which began to prepare a campaign for referendum. These groups were also inspired by Habibie's approval of a referendum for East Timor. While Habibie's reconciliatory policy on Aceh can be regarded as his contribution to the civilisation of the state, he did not realize that this process was sabotaged by the military's continuing use of military means in eliminating the rebel groups. For instance, the democratic image and conciliatory approach of President Habibie was undermined by the incident of Beuteng Ateuh on 23 July 1999 when Indonesian soldiers massacred 57 students and a teacher of an Islamic school. What was more painful for the Acehnese was that the military officer who was responsible for this massacre mysteriously vanished during the trial process.[13]

A Rocky Way to a Civilian Control over the TNI

When Abdurrahman Wahid replaced Habibie as the new president there was much hope that his government would promote a more human face in the form of conciliatory policies related to the issue of separatism in Aceh and Papua. Such expectations were based on the fact that before being elected as a president, Wahid was a top figure in the largest Islamic mass organisation, Nahdlatul Ulama. Unlike Habibie, who tended to capitalise on the support of some generals, Wahid was a man of his own and had an independent vision of what to do with his job. For instance, in the 1990s Wahid took the initiative to establish the *Forum Demokrasi* with the aim of promoting democratisation as a counter-movement against Suharto's authoritarianism.

As far as the resolving of the Aceh conflict is concerned, the period of Abdurrahman Wahid can be seen as one of tough competition between the president who wanted to use peaceful means and the military that preferred military means. This indicated the difficulty for Indonesian civilian leaders to make the TNI obedient to their policies. There were at least four instances in which we can see the competition between the president and the TNI in securing their respective positions. First, Wahid dismissed General Wiranto from his position as Coordinating Minister for Political and Security Affairs on the grounds that Wiranto was held responsible for gross violations of human rights by the TNI after the pro-independence group won the referendum in East Timor in September 1999. This move was also seen as Wahid's strategy to cut the ties between the general and his supporters within the TNI. Second, Wahid made a political move to put his own man in a strategic position in the military. Despite strong opposition by many generals, Wahid appointed Lt. Gen. Agus Wirahadikusumah, known as the most reform-minded general, as the Kostrad Commander replacing Lt. Gen. Djadja Suparman, who was close to Wiranto.[14] Third, without asking the consent of the local military commander, Wahid took the initiative of sending his Acting State Secretary, Bondan Gunawan, to talk with GAM military commander Abdullah Syafi'ie. Almost two years later, on 22 January 2002, Abdullah Syafi'ie was killed by the military in a "routine patrol".[15] From this we can see the contrast between the willingness of the civilian government to conduct dialogues with the rebel groups and the insistence of the military to eliminate them. On top of that, lack of policy coordination on the government side allowed the security forces to respond to what they saw as pragmatic requirements. In fact, both the police and TNI soldiers sent to Aceh had only one thing in mind: that they had to prevent the independence of Aceh at any cost.[16] Fourth, when President Abdurrahman Wahid made a statement that the Indonesian government would allow the Acehnese to have a referendum like Indonesia did in East Timor, some military officials were upset and openly resisted such a move.[17]

Learning from the bitter lesson of East Timor where the internationalisation of the conflict led to its separation from Indonesia, the TNI would never accept the involvement of any foreign actor in the resolving of the Aceh conflict. However, as a civilian leader President Abdurrahman Wahid had a task of restoring Indonesian image abroad that had been shattered in East Timor, by showing to the international community that it had the capacity to resolve its intra-state conflict by peaceful and democratic means. This was probably the reason why Wahid made an initiative to invite the Henry Dunant Centre to facilitate and mediate the negotiations between the Indonesian government and GAM. In the eyes of some senior military leaders, such an initiative would be tantamount to the recognition of the international status of GAM.[18] Thus, from the very beginning the civilian government could not secure genuine support from the military for direct talks with GAM.

Despite the unwillingness of the military to support Wahid's initiative, the president continued with his conciliatory approach by conducting dialogues with GAM. The result of this dialogue was the establishment of "Joint Understanding on Humanitarian Pause for Aceh" on 12 May 2000 signed by Hassan Wirayuda as Indonesia's Permanent Representative to the United Nations in Geneva and GAM's "Minister of Health" Zaini Abdullah.[19] This was the first formal agreement achieved by the Indonesian government and GAM. It was also the first time the Indonesian government presented a more human and civilised face in dealing with the Aceh separatist movement. The "civil" spirit of the agreement emerges from the way the agreement gave priority to consensus of humanity above the standard demands of the two sides. Unfortunately, what was good on paper was not necessarily so in the field. The diplomats and the soldiers apparently lived in totally different worlds, and the agreement was ineffective and temporary. Escalation of the conflict in the battle field could not be prevented especially when the military officers were convinced that the humanitarian transition had been used by the rebel group to consolidate its military strength. What started out as a foundation for building a mutual trust for both sides, in a relatively short period of time turned into even more mutual suspicion and hatred.

The climax of the contestation between the enthusiasm of the civilian government to solve the Aceh conflict by peaceful means and the insistence of the TNI to solve it by military force took place in April 2001, when President Wahid had to issue a Presidential Instruction No. 4/2001 called *Operasi Keamanan dan Penegakan Hukum* (Operation for the Restoration of Security and Upholding of Law). It was the tragic end of the Humanitarian Pause and the beginning of yet another escalation of violence in Aceh. According to a report made by the ICG, the failure of the agreement was not surprising for it was extremely difficult to guarantee that the soldiers in the field could restrain themselves from using their arms when they felt threatened. Moreover, some elements in the military provoked the use of violence in order to derail the agreement.[20] When Wahid was facing an impeachment threat by parliament, the TNI refused to defend him, preferring his vice president Megawati Sukarnoputri who appeared to be indifferent on the issue of civilian supremacy.

Megawati's Pragmatism and the Declaration of Martial Law in Aceh

Unlike her predecessor, Megawati had no significant argument with the military. While Habibie and Wahid had prevented the military from re-establishing the regional military command (*kodam*) in Aceh, Megawati allowed the TNI to do this in February 2002. Once the military is authorised to institutionalise its presence in a region, it will be difficult for the government to revoke the decision in the future. This was a kind of foreshadowing of a smooth path to the enactment of martial law more than one year later. The departure of Wahid brought an end to the hope of many that reform-minded generals would take over the leadership of TNI. More conservative "security first" generals like Gen. Ryamizard Ryacudu (Army Chief of Staff), Lt. Gen. Bibit Waluyo (Kostrad Commander), and Maj. Gen. Sjafrie Sjamsoedin (Military Spokesman) came to prominence under the government of Megawati, who had a very strong nationalist view and allowed no compromise on the unitary form of the Indonesian state. Megawati was similar to Habibie in her dependence on the support of the TNI. From a democratic point of view, a feeling of gratitude to the military may create an obstacle to any civilian leader to push for substantive reform within the TNI. At the same time, the generals may capitalise on the weaknesses of the civilian leaders to strengthen their position in policy making or in securing their access to politics since the collapse of Suharto's regime. Very rarely, if ever, did Megawati advance any standpoint with regard to the ideal form of civil-military relationship in a democratising country like Indonesia. On the contrary, Megawati relied heavily on the TNI to accomplish her passion for defending the territorial integrity of the Indonesian unitary state.

Notwithstanding her close relationship with the military, President Megawati tried to keep her democratic credentials in resolving the Aceh conflict. Soon after she became president, she signed the Special Autonomy Law No. 18/2001 for the province of Nanggroe Aceh Darussalam. However, six months later in February 2002 the TNI managed to convince Megawati's government that a special military command was indeed necessary for Aceh. According to some analyses of how the TNI advanced its interests, the re-establishment of a TNI regional military command was important for security building, but equally important for securing TNI's access to Aceh's development resources during the implementation of the new autonomy law. If this speculation is correct, this is just another indication that contestation for state resources among the civilian and military leaders in the resolving of the Aceh conflict took place not only in the political arena but also in the economic one. The regional military command in Aceh made it possible to secure badly needed additional income, as Damien Kingsbury and Lesley McCulloch explain extensively in Chapter 11.

Law No. 18/2001 on Aceh's special autonomy can be regarded as the bottom line for the government of President Megawati in its negotiations with GAM. But it should be noted that the actual implementation of this policy reflects the accommodation made by the president to various actors, including the Acehnese delegates to the DPR and the conservative generals within TNI. The TNI gave its consent to the autonomy law with an assumption that GAM would accept it as a final solution to the conflict and abandon its claim for independence. Thus, under the government of Megawati there was again a tug of war between the enthusiasm of the government to endorse negotiations with GAM on the basis of the autonomy law, and the seeming impatience of the military leaders to solve the problem by force. For instance, the then Kostrad Commander Lt. Gen. Ryamizard Ryacudu expressed his disappointment with the fact that negotiations with GAM had paralysed his forces so that GAM could easily kill them. For Ryacudu there was no need to open new negotiations with GAM.[21] No wonder the course of events in the battlefield proceeded independently from what the government was doing in the diplomatic arena. A case in point was the encirclement of GAM by the TNI forces in late October 2002 near the village of Cot Trieng.[22] By such military manoeuvres the TNI wanted not only to pressure GAM but to convince the Indonesian civilian leaders that the military could do things their own way if the circumstances in the battlefield forced them to do so. At the same time, however, Megawati's cabinet ministers, like Coordinating Minister for Political and Security Affairs Susilo Bambang Yudhoyono and Minister for Foreign Affairs Hassan Wirayuda, continued to find ways to revive the peace process by dialogue and negotiations. The simultaneous application of peaceful means and the increasing intensity of military pressure indicate that it was hard for Indonesian civilian leaders to prevent the TNI from claiming its traditional self-assigned task of maintaining the territorial integrity of the nation. Thus, in the eyes of the TNI leaders, military reform must never change, let alone eliminate, their commitment to the territorial integrity of the Indonesian unitary state. The TNI has put this vision in the book released in October 1998 on the redefinition, reposition and re-actualisation of the role of ABRI in the twenty-first century.[23]

Thanks to the effectiveness of the mediation conducted by the Henry Dunant Centre, the representatives of the Indonesian government and GAM eventually managed to sign the Cessation of Hostilities Agreement (CoHA) on 9 December 2002. It should be admitted that compared to previous agreements, this one was considered by many to constitute substantial progress towards a more comprehensive solution to the conflict.[24] However, GAM entered into this agreement without abandoning its claim for total independence. Nor was it willing to undertake unilateral disarmament. On the other hand, from the very beginning the TNI was not happy with the interference by international actors in this process. Some military leaders expressed suspicion of the real mission of international actors. Taking into account the predispositions of GAM and the TNI towards this agreement, it makes perfect sense to say that the signing of CoHA "significantly increased the stakes of failure".[25] Notwithstanding its significance as a stepping stone towards a more comprehensive peace agreement, from a democratic point of view CoHA still contains many unanswered questions and the possibility of conflicting interpretations by both sides. For instance, it was not immediately clear how the agreement would implement the so-called "All Inclusive Dialogue". While GAM understood the dialogue as a mechanism towards the revision of the autonomy law and the execution of a referendum, the Indonesian government insisted that dialogue was never meant to lead to a referendum.

When it became apparent to the TNI that GAM was not genuinely committed to implementing the agreement, especially with regard to the issue of disarmament according to the consented timetable, the TNI leaders began to doubt whether peaceful resolution to the conflict was still relevant. Mutual distrust and suspicion increased and each side tried to consolidate its military power. Under pressure of this uncertainty, the TNI took the initiative to design a contingency plan by which it would urge the government to impose martial law in Aceh. The reluctance of GAM to disarm was a long-awaited justification for the TNI to launch an all out attack to eliminate the separatist movement. The statements of the military leaders indicated their impatience with the implementation of CoHA.[26]

Although CoHA mentions explicitly the recognition of the importance of civil society groups in the peace process, there was little evidence of sincere acceptance of their contribution to conflict resolution. The preoccupation with the use of military force and the reduction of the problem into an oversimplified clash between the sovereign state and the separatist movement had marginalised the role of the Acehnese grassroots and civil society groups in general. No matter which side had the upper hand in the military conflict, the majority of the Acehnese were just abandoned and forced into becoming refugees under constant fear and misery. When the leader of a pro-referendum organisation, *Sentral Informasi Referendum Aceh* (SIRA), Mohammad Nazar, again organised rallies as he had done in 1999, he was arrested by the security authorities. Nazar's arrest was only the beginning of a continuing series of arrests and imprisonment of many civil activists and students between the beginning of February 2003 and the enactment of martial law on 19 May 2003. This was further evidence of the ironical process of de-civilisation of the state at the local level, despite the democratisation of the political system since the 1999 general election.

Nor was the military friendly with international civil society organisations. Having experienced their nightmare with the involvement of the United Nations Mission in East Timor (UNAMET), which the military accused of supporting the pro-independence group, some military officers did not hide their suspicion of the role of HDC officials in the peace process. In the midst of increasing tension and uncertainty, series of mass demonstrations against the role of HDC in the peace process took place in various places in Aceh. Many accused the military of being behind the demonstration or at least they deliberately let it happen in order to show to the public that the Acehnese would prefer a martial law to the mediation by international NGOs. The hostility toward the HDC climaxed on 6 April 2003 when the demonstrators burnt down the office of HDC in Langsa.[27] With the forced termination of the role of HDC, the door was wide open for the imposing of martial law that had been impatiently sought by the military.

Martial Law and the 2004 Election

The enactment of Presidential Decree No. 28/2003 on the Declaration of a State Emergency with the Status of Martial Law in Nanggroe Aceh Darussalam Province on 19 May 2003 can be regarded as the victory of a military to resolving the Aceh conflict in the midst of the Indonesian democratisation process. According to Munir, a well-known human rights activist, the government's decision on Aceh was largely determined by the military.[28] Although it was meant to be an integrated operation consisting of the restoration of security and order through military operation, humanitarian operation, law enforcement and the restoration of government and bureaucratic functions, in reality it was very much dominated by the first element. Under this legal umbrella the military had a free hand to resolve the conflict in its own way. Article 3 (1) of the Presidential Decree appointed the Commander of the Iskandar Muda Military Command as the regional martial authority (*Penguasa Darurat Militer Daerah* or PDMD). In order to control the flow of information to "independent and counterproductive" evaluation of the implementation of martial law, President Megawati also issued Presidential Decree No. 43/2003 which authorised the regional martial authority to ban all the activities of foreigners, domestic and international NGOs and students deemed not in line with the spirit and objective of martial law. There is little wonder that after six months of implementation of martial law, the evaluation of its success was measured solely by military indicators such as the number of GAM soldiers killed or captured, the confiscation of weapons, and the occupation of GAM strongholds. There was no explanation to how this military achievement had reduced the popularity of the idea of independence among the Acehnese people.

Despite mounting protests and criticisms raised by human rights activists and political analysts, the government of Megawati insisted on extending the enactment of martial law for another six months until

19 May 2004. After a field trip to Aceh from 29 September until 4 October 2003, the Ad Hoc Team of the National Commission on Human Rights (Komnas HAM) urged the government to terminate martial law in Aceh on the grounds that its extension could undermine the freedom of the Acehnese people in giving their votes during the election. The head of the team M.M. Billah also reported rampant violations of human rights by the TNI during the implementation of martial law.[29] The TNI Chief Gen. Endriartono Sutarto admitted the wrongdoings of his soldiers in Aceh during the implementation of martial law.[30]

President Megawati's extension of martial law for another six months in November 2003 may have been based on her nationalist and conservative standpoint that only the military could guarantee peace and stability in Aceh. The continuation of the military presence in Aceh could ensure that the conflict would not create unnecessary trouble to her government as she concentrated on preparation for the 2004 legislative and presidential elections. As far as the TNI is concerned, the extension of martial law had an important meaning. The endorsement of the extension by the parliament was considered as formal recognition that the use of military force in Aceh was indeed necessary and politically justified. Less resistance against martial law or the indifference of the political parties in this matter might be related to their political calculation that direct confrontation with the TNI prior to the 2004 election might cost them the support and protection of the military during the election campaign period in the conflict areas. The political parties were aware that PDMD had an extensive authority over the conduct of the election in the whole province of NAD. Certain political parties capitalized on their proximity to the military authorities enough to arouse NGO protests. Various NGOs in Aceh and Jakarta reported to the media that some political parties like the Democratic Party, whose top figure was the then Coordinator Minister for Political and Security Affairs, Susilo Bambang Yudhoyono, and the Concern for the Nation Functional Party (PKPB) did collaborate with the PDMD in Aceh. The facility given by PDMD included allowing a party member card to substitute for the official identity card (known as the red and white identity card). Pointing out the political consequences of that kind of collaboration, the chairperson of the Organization of Democratic Acehnese Women (ORPAD), Raihana Diani, told the press that the assistance given by members of the military to the Democratic Party could be seen as pressure by the TNI to vote for the party in the election.[31]

Theoretically, a general election is meant to be an opportunity for the people to ask the legislative candidates to attend to the fundamental social and political problems they are facing. Unfortunately, the 2004 legislative election seemed to have only little, if any, relevance for the most fundamental issue of conflict resolution in Aceh. The political parties in the campaign seemed quite reluctant to talk about violations of human rights, conflict resolution, accountability of the military budget during the martial law period and the importance of human security for each citizen. Since independence the Indonesian state had allowed only one national election. Like the issue of federalism, discussion of local elections was viewed by the central government as a threat to the existence of the unitary state. This is probably why in the CoHA the Indonesian government insisted on the national election as the only general election. Taking into account the diversity of Indonesian society both at the national and regional levels, it might be good for the development of local democracy to have a local election in addition to a national one. The weakness of Indonesian political parties in resolving the Aceh conflict is a clear indication that a party system that is too centralistic is unreliable as a mechanism to channel the grievances of the people in a troubled region like Aceh.

Nor were the local media critical and objective enough in providing information regarding the quality of the election process. A critical and widely quoted website on the Aceh conflict, <www.acehkita.com>, conducted a small survey on media coverage of the election in Aceh. It found that the dominant angle of their coverage was to confirm the government's public announcement of the smoothness of the election process. No question was raised about the feeling of voters when they went to the ballot box. There was no exploration of the peculiarity of an election under martial law. Monitoring of the media coverage from 3 March until 9 March indicated that the three local print media: *Serambi Indonesia, Waspada,* and *Analisa* (the latter two are based in Medan, North Sumatra, but routinely run substantial coverage on the Aceh conflict) produced 133 (82.71 per cent) news reports on the election and only 23 news reports on security matters.[32] The indifference of the local media to issues of greater importance for the Acehnese people reflected the powerlessness of the civil society elements to counterbalance the process of the de-civilisation of the state during the martial law period. It also indicated the effectiveness of the military's repressive measures imposed upon the media people in presenting the Aceh conflict to the public. According to a noted NGO activist from Aceh, Saifuddin

Bantasyam, sometimes the journalists had difficulties in exposing the voice of the victims of a military attack for fear of being seen as taking side in the conflict.[33]

Another source of growing concern among civil society activists in Aceh was related to the fact that during the implementation of the martial law the regional martial law authority initiated and supported the establishment of a paramilitary group, *Linmas* (*Perlindungan Masyarakat* or People's Protection). Although the TNI spokesman, Maj. Gen. Sjafrie Sjamsoedin, argued that these groups were not militias but a form of people's resistance in a situation of emergency,[34] there was fear that this could provoke an endless cycle of violence between the militias and GAM. On top of that the establishment of paramilitary groups like this might only lead to permanent dependence of the Acehnese upon the presence of the military.

If Acehnese society was alienated by the primacy of the coercive nature of the state, this was exacerbated by rampant corruption in the bureaucracies of the provincial government. The chapters of Michelle Miller and Rodd McGibbon explain at length the alleged involvement of Governor Abdullah Puteh in various corruption cases. What I need to underline here is that regardless of the motives of the civilian and military leaders in their competition against each other, the Acehnese grassroots are systematically alienated from the governing process.

It remains to be seen how the events following the tsunami that killed hundreds of thousands of people in Aceh on 26 December 2004 may create new opportunities for peace. Signs of good will on both sides to resolve the conflict through dialogue and negotiation can be seen from the progress that has been achieved in a series of informal talks in Helsinki during 2005, mediated by the Crisis Management Initiative (CMI) led by Finland's former president, Marti Attisari. New optimism for a peaceful resolution also arises from the fact that President Susilo Bambang Yudhoyono insists on distancing himself from the traditional security approach. However, the road to a permanent solution to the conflict remains rocky and fragile. For instance, will the military accept the condition that it has to pull out all its forces from Aceh as an exchange for GAM's total disarmament? Will GAM accept the special autonomy law as the legal framework of their political participation in the local election? Will the nationalist political parties seek to sabotage any peace deal with GAM? How much of the current tendency towards peaceful conflict resolution is based on the pragmatism of some Indonesian political leaders and businessmen whose main interest is the lucrative business of Aceh's post-tsunami reconstruction projects? In the final analysis much depends on the leadership of President Susilo Bambang Yudhoyono to ensure that the movement towards peace in Aceh will benefit the Acehnese themselves rather than those interested in exploiting Aceh politically and economically.

Concluding Remarks

This chapter started with the question why the democratisation of the Indonesian political system has not led to a peaceful and permanent resolution to the conflict in Aceh like many cases of the same nature in other parts of the world. Four interrelated explanations have been offered. First, the peculiarity of the relationship between democratisation and the resolving of the Aceh conflict can be explained by the fact that the rise of popular support for referendum in Aceh coincided with the victory of the nationalist parties in the parliament after the 1999 general election. Megawati's PDIP would surely oppose the move of any region to separate from the Indonesian unitary state. Second, in each of the three post-Suharto governments, the same policy pattern took place with regard to conflict resolution in Aceh. President Habibie started with a promise to focus on economic development in Aceh but was unable to prevent the military from conducting one of the bloodiest military attacks so far in the incident of Beuteng Ateuh. Nor was Habibie's leadership effective enough to ensure that the perpetrators of this human tragedy were brought to justice.

Being a man of his own with a rich background in civil society organisation, Abdurrahman Wahid tried to control the military and establish effective civilian supremacy. Without the consent of the military, he promised a referendum for the Acehnese, and sent his Acting State Secretary to have discussions with the GAM commander Abdullah Sjafi'ie. But then on April 2001 he was forced to sign a presidential decree for yet another security operation in Aceh. A few months later the collaboration between the military and his Vice President Megawati led to his impeachment. Under President Megawati the same pattern recurred. Although Megawati's government got the credit of being able to produce CoHA with GAM on 9 December 2002, about six months later she had no other choice but to sign the enactment of the martial law in Aceh, which authorized a massive military offensive against GAM. This explanation is quite similar to what Angel Rabasa and John Haseman call the "muddling through" scenario by which Indonesia continues to go through a democratic path but at the same time fails to avoid the primacy of security approach in dealing with the separatist movements. Such failure in turn leads to overreaction by the military and to human rights violations.[35] The third explanation of the peculiarity of the Aceh case is related to the fact that the Indonesian civilian and military elite both at the central and regional levels have transformed the process of democratisation into arenas of contestation of their political and economic interests. From this analysis we learn that it is too simplistic to depict the problem in Aceh as merely a conflict between a sovereign state and a separatist movement. The fourth explanation is understood as the consequence of the second and the third explanation. The exclusion of the Acehnese grassroots from the political and economic processes, which was related to the primacy of the military approach to conflict resolution and to the de-civilisation of the state, explains why it has been so difficult to achieve a sustainable peace in Aceh. The current process of conflict resolution through informal talks, mediated by the CMI in Finland, and the interplay of political and economic interests in the post-tsunami reconstruction of Aceh, give rise to cautious optimism. The need for security and stability in the reconstruction of Aceh should convince the conflicting parties that man-made disasters, unlike natural ones, can be prevented by the primacy of respect for human life over the inclination for violence.

Notes

1   Eva Bellin uses the concept of "stalled democracy" to explain how the dominant social forces "are eager to push the state to be responsive to their own interests, but once this has been achieved, they are not eager to generalize such responsiveness to society as a whole through the creation of democratic institutions". See Eva Bellin, *Stalled Democracy: Capital, Labor, and the Paradox of State-Sponsored Development* (Ithaca and London: Cornell University Press, 2002), p. 4; See also her article "Contingent Democrats: Industrialists, Labor and Democratization in Late-Developing Countries", *World Politics* 52 (January 2000): 175–205.

2   See Vedi R. Hadiz, "Reorganizing Political Power in Indonesia: A Reconsideration of so-called 'Democratic Transitions'", *The Pacific Review* 16, 4 (2003): 592.

3   Rizal Sukma, "The Acehnese Rebellion: Secessionist Movement in Post-Suharto Indonesia", in *Non-Traditional Security Issues in Southeast Asia*, ed. Andrew T.H. Tan and J. D. Kenneth (Singapore: Select Publishing, 2001), p. 403.

4   See Rizal Sukma, "Security Operations in Aceh: Goals, Consequences and Lessons", *Policy Studies* 3 (Washington: East-West Center, 2004), pp. 36–7.

5   See Edward Aspinall and Harold Crouch, "The Peace Process in Aceh", *Policy Studies* 2 (Washington: East-West Center, 2004).

6   International Crisis Group (ICG) Asia Report, *Aceh: Why Military Force Won't Bring Lasting Peace* (Jakarta: ICG, 12 June 2001).

7   See Juan J. Linz and Alfred Stephan, *Problems of Democratic Transition and Consolidation: Southern Europe, South America, and Post-Communist Europe* (Baltimore: The John Hopkins University Press, 1996).

8   See Baogang He, "Democratization and the National Identity Question in East Asia", in *New Challenges for Development and Modernization: Hong Kong and the Asia-Pacific Region in the New Millenium*, ed. Yeung Yue Man (Hong Kong: Chinese University Press, 2002), pp. 245–73.

9   It is important to note that GAM explicitly demonises Javanese domination and imperialism in justifying its struggle for an independent state. This is one of the reasons why Aceh's struggle of independence is not really popular in Java.

10   See Robert W. Hefner, "Introduction: Multiculturalism and Citizenship in Malaysia, Singapore and Indonesia", in *The Politics of Multiculturalism: Pluralism and Citizenship in Malaysia, Singapore, and Malaysia*, ed. Robert W. Hefner (Honolulu: University of Hawaii Press, 2001), p. 43.

11   See Robert W. Hefner, *Civil Islam: Muslims and Democratization in Indonesia* (Princeton, NJ: Princeton University Press, 2000), p. 215.

12   *Kompas*, 27 March 1999.

13   See Dyah Rahmany P., *Matinya Bantaqiah: Menguak Tragedi Beutong Ateuh* (Banda Aceh: Cordova, 2001).

14   See Jun Honna, *Military Politics and Democratisation in Indonesia* (London: RoutledgeCurzon, 2003), p. 180.

15   See *The Jakarta Post*, 25 January 2002.

16   See ICG, *Aceh: Why Military Won't Bring Lasting Peace*, p. 4.

17   See *Republika*, 17 November 1999.

18   See ICG Indonesia Briefing, *Aceh: Escalating Tension* (Banda Aceh, Jakarta, Brussels, 7 December 2000).

19   The content of the agreement emphasised the objective of halting violence, facilitating humanitarian assistance for the refugees, and the building of mutual trust. It was to cover the period from 2 June 2000 until 2 September 2000. It was then extended until 15 September 2001. For the content of the agreement see "Joint Understanding on Humanitarian Pause for Aceh", <www.deplu.go.id> [3 July 2003].

20   See ICG, *Indonesia: Keeping the Military Under Control*, September 2000, p. 18.

21   See *Kompas*, 25 August 2001.

22   See *The Jakarta Post*, 7 November 2002.

23   See Mabes ABRI, *ABRI Abad XXI: Redefinisi, Reposisi, dan Reaktualisasi Peran ABRI dalam Kehidupan Bangsa*, Jakarta, 1998.

24   Rizal Sukma, for instance, mentioned three reasons why this agreement provides some optimism. They include: the function of a Joint Security Committee (JSC) to monitor the implementation of the agreement, second, the establishment of "peace zones", and third, the guarantee of international support from donor countries such as Japan, the European Union and the United States. See Rizal Sukma, "Security Operations in Aceh", p. 20.

25   See ICG, *Aceh: A Fragile Peace*, Asia Report No. 47, 27 February 2003, p. 8.

26   TNI's Commander-in-Chief Gen. Endriartono Sutarto and Aceh Military Commander Maj. Gen. Djali Yusuf, for instance, made an open threat against GAM should it fail to disarm its forces. See *Kompas*, 4 February 2003 and *Serambi Indonesia*, 31 January 2003.

27   See *Kompas*, 7 April 2003.

28   See Tempo Interaktif, "*Munir: Keputusan Pemerintah Soal Aceh Ditentukan oleh TNI*", <www.tempo.co.id/news/2003/5/15>.

29   See *Kompas*, 11 October 2003.

30   See *The Jakarta Post*, 6 May 2004.

31   See *Kompas*, 19 February 2004.

32   See <www.acehkita.com> [20 April 2004].

33   See Saifuddin Bantasyam, "Peran Media dalam Proses Damai di Aceh" (The Role of the Media in the Aceh Peace Process), Paper presented in the International Seminar on Conflict and Media Analysis and Conflict De-escalating Radio Programming in Indonesia, organised by Conflict Studies Network, UNESCO Local Radio Network, International Media Support and Finnish Embassy, at Parahyangan Catholic University, Bandung, 6–14 April 2003.

34   See *The Jakarta Post*, 21 April 2004.

35   See Angel Rabasa and John Haseman, *The Military and Democracy in Indonesia* (Santa Monica: RAND's National Security Research Division, 2002), pp. 123–4.

14

What's Special about Special Autonomy in Aceh?

Michelle Ann Miller

Decentralisation has become an important dimension of post-Suharto politics. Since Indonesia began its unpredictable and complex journey of regime transformation in 1998, regional autonomy initiatives have been incorporated into a national reform process (*reformasi*) that has aimed to restore national stability by moving toward democratic governance. There have also been offers of "special autonomy" that have sought to find negotiated solutions to the armed separatist conflicts in Aceh, West Papua (formerly Irian Jaya) and East Timor. Despite these government concessions, however, East Timor successfully seceded in 1999 and the wars in Aceh and West Papua have continued unabated.

This chapter looks at the historically uneasy relationship between Jakarta and Aceh from a "special autonomy" perspective. The focus is the three offers of special autonomy that have been made to Aceh — the 1959 *Daerah Istimewa* (Special Region) formula, Law No. 44 of 1999 on the "Special Status of the Province of Aceh" and Law No. 18 of 2001 about "Special Autonomy for the Special Region of Aceh as Nanggroe Aceh Darussalam". It is argued that the failure to resolve Aceh's conflict through these political strategies can be largely explained by four interrelated factors. First, there has been a lack of commitment by successive national governments toward properly enforcing Aceh's special status, which has eroded Acehnese confidence in, and expectations of the Indonesian state. Second, human rights violations that have accompanied security operations against the armed separatist Free Aceh Movement (*Gerakan Aceh Merdeka*, GAM) — which have been at the heart of Acehnese grievances in recent years — have not been addressed through special autonomy. Third, GAM has consistently rejected autonomy as a compromise to Acehnese independence. Fourth, the protracted conflict has produced numerous systemic obstacles to the implementation of autonomy, such as a thriving war economy, dysfunctional state infrastructure and corrupt political culture.

The Origins of Aceh's Special Status

When Aceh agreed to join the newly independent Indonesian State in 1945, it was based on the twin assumptions that Aceh's important contribution to the nationalist struggle against the Dutch would entitle it to an equal stake in the Republic's future, and that Indonesia would be founded on, and strive to uphold, the principles of Islam.[1] As Isa Sulaiman points out in Chapter 8, governmental authority was still weak in Aceh during this period and central government leaders were largely concerned with the task of securing international support to prevent the reassertion of colonial rule.

It was only in 1950, when the Netherlands formally transferred sovereignty to the "Republic of the United States of Indonesia", that the almost complete autonomy that Aceh had enjoyed since independence came to an end. Earlier in December 1949, the Deputy Prime Minister, Sjafruddin Prawiranegara, at the request of Acehnese leaders, passed a government decree that dissolved the military region of Aceh in North Sumatra and created a separate "Province of Aceh". After the handover of sovereignty, however, government leaders queried the constitutionality of Sjafruddin's decision, which was made three days after the administration in which he had served was dissolved.[2] Responding to rising resentment in North Sumatra over the separate Aceh province, the Home Affairs Ministry argued that the decree had violated an earlier decision to only divide the island of Sumatra into north, south and central administrative components.[3] Sulaiman describes how this dispute came to a head in August 1950, when Aceh was incorporated into North Sumatra as part of the government's reorganisation of the Republic into just ten provinces. The strong sense of betrayal in Aceh that resulted from this decision was exacerbated by the subsequent influx of non-Muslim, non-Acehnese workers and military troops into the region, as well as declining local socioeconomic conditions after Aceh's special foreign exchange agreement with the national government was terminated and a greater portion of the national budget began to be allocated to Java than to the outer islands.

In September 1953, this resentment gave rise to rebellion when Acehnese insurgents, under the leadership of Aceh's most prominent *ulama*, Teungku M. Daud Beureu'eh, joined the broader Darul Islam (House of Islam) revolt that had began in West Java and sought to transform the Indonesian Republic into an Islamic federation of states.[4] As Edward Aspinall points out above when describing the relationship between violence and Acehnese identity during this period, the Acehnese leaders of the Darul Islam revolt justified violence by portraying their enemies as *kafir* (infidels) and emphasising the un-Islamic character of the Indonesian state and its "anti-Islamic" activities. It was only after January 1957, when the Sukarno government re-established the "Province of Aceh" — which raised hope amongst some Darul Islam leaders that Aceh would be granted greater autonomy over its religious affairs — that Acehnese participation in the Darul Islam movement gradually subsided.[5]

Aceh first won *Daerah Istimewa* status on 26 May 1959, when President Sukarno agreed in principle to grant the province special autonomy over its religious, educational and customary law affairs.[6] This compromise offer was made in response to an earlier proposal by the former Darul Islam Army Chief-of-Staff and founding leader of the movement's Revolutionary Council (*Dewan Repolusi*), Hasan Saleh, who had sought to enhance Aceh's self-governing power by creating a "Federal State of Aceh" (*Negara Bagian Aceh*) within an "Islamic State of Indonesia". Unlike Teungku M. Daud Beureu'eh, who vowed to continue the Darul Islam struggle, Hasan Saleh pragmatically realised that the only way to win concessions for Aceh was by regionalising the rebellion's Islamic goals.[7] Another factor in Saleh's reluctant acceptance of special autonomy was that Jakarta had made it clear that it considered federalism to be tantamount to returning to the discredited Dutch colonial system.

The biggest difficulty concerning the implementation of the *Daerah Istimewa* formula was that the parameters of Aceh's special status were not clearly specified. At first, former Darul Islam Revolutionary Council leaders (who dominated Aceh's new provincial government) attempted to establish linkages between Aceh's religious autonomy and the controversial 1945 Jakarta Charter, which contained a clause obliging Muslims to adhere to Islamic law (*Syari'ah*).[8] This apparent bid to reintegrate Acehnese Islamic goals into the broader national debate about Indonesia's ideological foundations did not sit comfortably with Jakarta, however, which deemed that Aceh's special status did not exempt it from adhering to the same rules and regulations that applied to the other provinces.

Amidst these unresolved tensions, Teungku M. Daud Beureu'eh continued to wage his Darul Islam struggle from the mountains. Beureu'eh's campaign had lost much of its momentum by the early 1960s, however, which was demonstrated through his changing demands of the government. From his initial proclamation of a *Negara Islam Indonesia* (Islamic State of Indonesia) in 1953, Beureu'eh was forced to modify his goal in September 1961 to the implementation of "Islamic law in Aceh, in particular, and in Indonesia, in general".[9] Acting on Beureu'eh's compromised military capacity and softer ideological stance, the government decided to reopen negotiations with the Acehnese rebels. In early 1962, these talks culminated in a "spiritual settlement" between Jakarta and Aceh, in which the latter was allowed to enforce Islamic law for Muslims within its territory.[10]

After almost a decade of peaceful centre-periphery relations, Acehnese discontent resurfaced in the early 1970s. At issue was the increasing centralisation of state power under General Suharto's New Order regime, which did not accommodate Acehnese aspirations to restore Islam as a dominant socio-political force. Nor did the New Order's modernising and nation-building projects result in any marked improvement to Aceh's economy. Although parts of Java and eastern Indonesia experienced worse poverty than Aceh under the New Order, the 1971 discovery of vast oil and natural gas reserves in North Aceh by ExxonMobil Oil Indonesia, and the subsequent meteoric growth of North Aceh's Lhokseumawe district as a major Industrial Development Zone (*Zona Industri Lhokseumawe*, ZILS), fuelled regional resentment as virtually all of the profits were siphoned out of Aceh. Acehnese anger was compounded by the forced resettlement of villagers to make way for the expansion of ZILS, as well as the arrival of non-Acehnese, non-Muslim skilled workers to operate oil and gas industries and the increased armed forces presence to defend the lucrative national asset.[11]

The New Order also expanded its authority by introducing major structural changes, including the reorganisation of Indonesian society. In Aceh, the armed forces established a permanent presence to defend strategic state assets and enforce social and political order. Suharto also nurtured the growth of a class of indigenous Acehnese technocrats to promote and implement national development programmes and counteract the influence of the ulama. Rodd McGibbon, discussing the rise of the technocrats in the final chapter, points out that the competitive nature of the vertical New Order power structure did not encourage local elite unification. Acehnese technocrats saw the *ulama*'s religious ideals as a deterrent to foreign investment, just as the *ulama* viewed the state's development-oriented policies as a threat to the moral fabric of Acehnese society.[12]

As the sociopolitical influence of the Acehnese *ulama* became increasingly marginalised under the New Order, so did their calls for the *Daerah Istimewa* formula to be meaningfully implemented. An early indication of the growing centralisation of state power and the national government's shifting priorities came in November 1968, when Aceh's representative assembly attempted to enforce the province's religious autonomy by passing Regional Regulation No. 6 of 1968 on the implementation of aspects of *Syari'ah*. This regulation required Acehnese Muslims to observe Islamic rituals and obligations, particularly those pertaining to the "Five Pillars of Islam" — to pray five times daily, pay *zakat* (religious tithe to the poor), profess the Islamic faith, adhere to the Muslim fasting month of *Ramadhan* and, if physically and financially capable, undertake a pilgrimage to Mecca. Conspicuously absent from the regulation, however, were provisions to create new institutions for the promotion and enforcement of *Syari'ah*. Nor did Jakarta ever formally approve the regulation so that it could be legally implemented.[13] In another unsuccessful attempt to validate Aceh's *Daerah Istimewa* status, Acehnese leaders sought to improve the quality of Islamic education for primary school students. This initiative stemmed from provincial concerns that the religious education curriculum in state schools was far less comprehensive than that provided by traditional *madrasah* schools. Although Aceh's two leading tertiary institutions, the State Islamic Institute (*Institut Agama Islam Negara*, IAIN) and the more secular Syiah Kuala University, presented the Departments of Education and Religion with proposals to integrate the two education curricula, neither department ever issued a response. Instead, Jakarta demonstrated its disapproval by allocating far more funding to secular education.[14]

The final disappointment concerning Aceh's *Daerah Istimewa* status came in 1974, when the New Order issued Law No. 5 on "The Principles of Regional Government Administration".[15] At first glance, this legislation appeared to reconfirm Aceh's autonomy over its religious, educational and customary law affairs. The provision for regional autonomy in the law was effectively nullified, however, by other sections that increased Jakarta's control over regional administrations. In particular, Law No. 5/1974 restricted the power of the provincial parliament by making the President the final authority on gubernatorial appointments, and the governor became responsible for managing provincial government affairs on behalf of the President. Toward the end of the New Order in 1991, the Home Affairs Minister, General (ret.) Rudini, explained that the reference to autonomy in Law No. 5/1974 was actually about "administrative and development affairs" and not "politics, defence and security".[16] Phrased differently, the law only granted the province autonomy over those administrative and developmental policy directives that had initially been approved by Jakarta.

Special Autonomy in the Post-authoritarian Order

The collapse of the New Order in 1998 ushered in some major changes to Acehnese society, which rapidly mobilised in a national climate of political openness to present Jakarta with wide-ranging reform demands. In a departure from the New Order's heavy-handed security approach, Suharto's successor, President B. J. Habibie, decided to pursue a negotiated solution to Aceh's conflict by ending the decade-long counterinsurgency campaign against GAM, withdrawing non-organic military troops from the province, launching human rights investigations and releasing hundreds of Acehnese political prisoners.

It was also within the context of Indonesia's regime transition that Habibie made the first moves to reform centre-periphery relations by decentralising state power. These reforms aimed to restore national stability and promote economic recovery amidst the wave of organised demonstrations and unorganised dissidence that had erupted across the archipelago following the 1997 national economic crisis. Habibie instigated the decentralisation process by ordering a review of those laws and regulations that had limited regional authority under the New Order.[17] His government then introduced three new autonomy laws. Law No. 22 of 1999 on "Regional Government" and Law No. 25 of 1999 on "Fiscal Balance Between the Central Government and the Regions", which were passed by the national parliament on 23 April 1999 and came into effect on 1 January 2001, devolved political, administrative and economic powers to all district-level governments.[18] Law No. 44 of 1999, which only applied to Aceh, was passed one month before the end of Habibie's presidency on 22 September 1999 and formally recognised the "Special Status of the Province of Aceh Special Region".

Law No. 44 of 1999 was based on the 1959 *Daerah Istimewa* formula in that it granted Aceh autonomy over its religious, cultural and educational affairs within guidelines set by the national government.[19] As Rodd McGibbon points out in his chapter, Law No. 44/1999 was premised on the assumption that Aceh's contemporary conflict stemmed from the government's failure to implement its first promise of special autonomy. McGibbon stresses that the dominant view in Jakarta at that time was that GAM's influence would be reduced if the *ulama* were restored to their pre-New Order position of predominance over Acehnese society. It was this rationale that informed the decision to allow Aceh to "implement Islamic law in all aspects of life".[20] The legislation also envisaged the creation of an independent *ulama* council with the same status and decision-making powers as the provincial legislative council.[21] Although Aceh's education system was to remain part of the national education system, Law No. 44/1999 authorised the provincial government to provide supplementary religious material in the Aceh curriculum and to establish an "Islamic Education Organisation". In cultural matters, the legislation authorised the provincial government to encourage Acehnese society to adhere to Islamic law by promoting regional customs, traditions and cultural values based on Islam.[22]

Whereas those Acehnese who had fought in the Darul Islam rebellion would have welcomed the opportunity to implement *Syari'ah*, the structure and expectations of Acehnese society had undergone a major trans-formation since the 1950s. Most Acehnese ulama, who had survived the New Order by becoming integrated into its institutional framework, had been unable to establish an influential independent political base in the post-authoritarian regime. And the majority of Acehnese, who were traumatised after the decade of military operations in the province and angered by the government's diffidence in relation to past and ongoing human rights abuses, "preferred to listen to students and NGOs than to government officials and ulama".[23] Capitalising on the widespread lack of grassroots support for Law No. 44/1999, GAM's political leadership in Sweden announced that it "firmly rejects the autonomy solution for Acheh as it is not in accordance with the true aspiration of the majority of Acehnese", and condemned the government for pursuing "deplorable 'stick and carrot' methods to solve the Acheh problem".[24]

The almost unanimous rejection of Law No. 44/1999 in Aceh was also strongly linked to Habibie's handling of East Timor. The President's famous pronouncement in February 1999 that the East Timorese could elect to "separate [from Indonesia] in a peaceful manner" if they were incapable of sharing the "spirit of our program of struggle" prompted the rapid growth of Aceh's student-led referendum movement and its umbrella organisation, SIRA.[25] Comprising 104 student, religious, social and human rights organisations at the time of its inauguration, SIRA

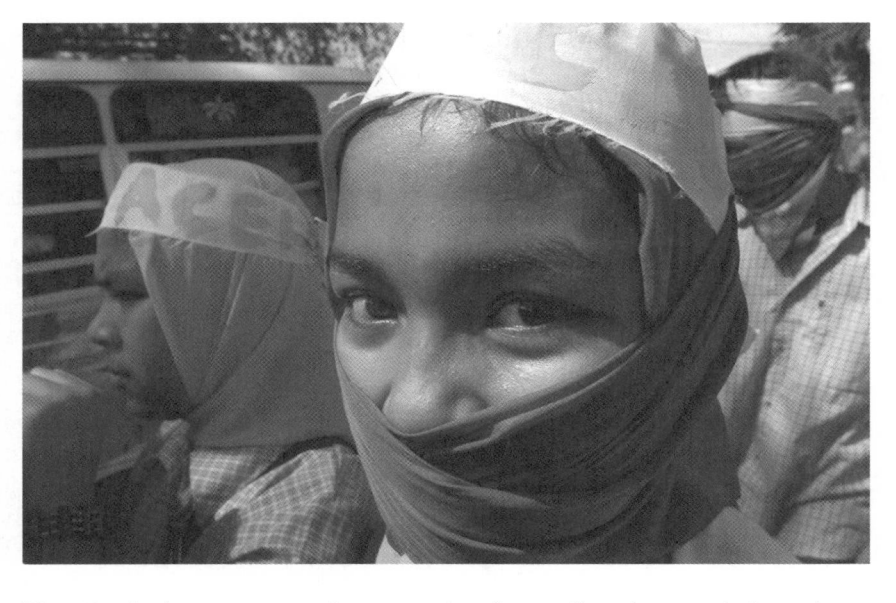

Fig. 18 Acehnese woman demonstrating for a referendum on independence in mid-December 2002, days after the signing of a cease-fire between the Indonesian Government and the GAM guerrillas (*photo by William Nessen*)

immediately established strong support bases in the urban areas of Aceh Besar, North and East Aceh, which soon expanded to encompass parts of Pidie, South and West Aceh. By June 1999, the Medan-based *Waspada* newspaper reported that 56 per cent of Acehnese wanted a referendum on independence, while only 25.3 per cent preferred broad autonomy within the Indonesian Republic.[26] Even 500 sub-district level ulama, who had potentially stood to benefit from the implementation of Law No. 44/1999, convened a two-day meeting about Aceh's future in September 1999 to vote on whether "to stay with or separate from the Republic of Indonesia"[27] (see Fig. 18).

There were also detractors of Law No. 44/1999 within the provincial government. Many regional representatives did not see the law as a serious solution to the conflict and felt that their recommendations had been marginalised by Jakarta during the drafting process. Also, the law itself — which had been hurriedly prepared during the build-up to East Timor's referendum on independence — was incomplete and required several supporting regulations to enable its implementation. Aceh's then Governor, Syamsuddin Mahmud, was particularly "disappointed" by the legislation, which he saw as "a kind of statement about Aceh's special status ... [but] not really special autonomy".[28] Previously, in February 1999, Mahmud had articulated his considerably higher expectations of autonomy in a proposal that called for Aceh to retain 90 per cent of its natural resource revenue (and contribute only ten per cent to Jakarta), implement *Syari'ah*, create a separate provincial judicial system (with recourse for appeals to the national Supreme Court) and establish independent international relations, enter into cooperative agreements with, and request aid from foreign governments. According to Mahmud, these major concessions were warranted because the "government has yet to prove [its promise] of wide-ranging autonomy. It is something which is non-existent .... The name 'special region of Aceh' is merely that, a name."[29]

When Abdurrahman Wahid's government came to power in October 1999, few efforts were made to promote or implement Law No. 44/1999. Instead, the increasing frequency of demonstrations and organised strikes by SIRA and GAM — after Wahid indicated in November 1999 that Aceh would be allowed to hold an East-Timor style referendum — invoked panic amongst government and military leaders, which led to further security operations in the province. These operations, which were conducted in the absence of any clear political policy directives until the government brokered an internationally facilitated peace agreement with GAM in May 2000, were marked by a similar pattern of human rights violations against civilians that had weakened previous counter-insurgency campaigns in Aceh.

It was not until 19 December 2000 that Wahid paid a presidential visit to Banda Aceh to formally pronounce the implementation of *Syari'ah* in Aceh in accordance with Law No. 44/1999. By that stage, however, there was widespread public cynicism that Wahid's Aceh visit was less about enforcing *Syari'ah* than it was an attempt to divert outside attention away from military plans to launch a full-scale offensive against GAM, as the government's peace accord with the separatists verged on collapse.[30] This local scepticism was reinforced by the fact that the provincial government had already issued five regional regulations several months previously about banning alcoholic drinks, preparing a *Syari'ah* framework, promoting Islamic education, organising *adat* in accordance with Islamic law and allowing the Acehnese to manage their own religious, educational and cultural affairs.[31] Prior to Wahid's visit, GAM and SIRA had described Jakarta's emphasis on *Syari'ah* as an attempt to stereotype the Acehnese as Islamic "extremists"; one GAM spokesman, Amni Marzuki, even claimed that "The Indonesian government wants to make us look like Afghanistan."[32] It is unlikely that this was the government's intention, however, as most state leaders had already acknowledged that centre-periphery imbalances and human rights violations were at the heart of Aceh's contemporary conflict. Significantly, Wahid used his Aceh trip to apologise for his inability to solve these problems, stating that "If I were not a Muslim, I would probably have killed myself."[33]

As Aceh's security situation worsened, the government began to look toward a more "comprehensive" solution to Aceh's conflict that included the development of broader special autonomy legislation. In his chapter, McGibbon points out that the main impetus for this legislative initiative came from a small Jakarta-based coalition of Acehnese political reformers. Indeed, it was this group that presented the most inclusive special autonomy bill to the House of Representatives (DPR) on 17 January 2001 in a move to create "space for Acehnese society, including GAM, to solve the Aceh problem together".[34] As a result of the Acehnese delegation's submission, the DPR approved the inauguration of a 50-member "Special Committee for the Special Autonomy Draft of Aceh" to adopt and review the Acehnese bill in consultation with Acehnese political, community and business leaders.[35] The Home Affairs Department, under the auspices of the national government, also produced a special autonomy draft that envisaged some, but far fewer alterations to Aceh's pre-existing institutional, power and revenue-sharing arrangements with Jakarta. Although the final special autonomy package, which was passed on 19 July 2001 as Law No. 18 of 2001, contained elements of both drafts, it was largely based on the DPR draft and indicated that the national government had made some considerable concessions.

The NAD Law

Formally changing Aceh's name to Nanggroe Aceh Darussalam (*lit.* State of Aceh, Abode of Happiness), the so-called "NAD" law signified an important development in Jakarta's political Aceh strategy. Due to be implemented from 1 January 2002, Law No. 18/2001 was ratified by Wahid's successor, President Megawati Sukarnoputri, on 9 August 2001, and sought to provide a viable alternative to secession by granting the province unprecedented powers of self-governance and control over its natural resources.

If handled properly, Aceh stood to derive substantial financial benefits from the implementation of the NAD law. One of Jakarta's most generous concessions was its allocation of 70 per cent of Aceh's oil and natural gas mining revenue to the province for eight years in after-tax proceeds, after which time these profit-sharing arrangements were to be reduced to grant Aceh 50 per cent of its total oil and gas revenue. Chapter IV of the law further entitled Aceh to an increased portion of its shared tax income and natural resource revenue in the sectors of lands and building, personal income, general mining and fisheries and forestry, as well as the right to receive foreign loans after first notifying the national government.[36] As a safeguarding mechanism to ensure that Aceh's extra revenue would be used to "improve the welfare of the community", Chapter IV, Article 7(2) stipulated that "at least 30 per cent" of those revenues be "allocated to finance education in the Province of Nanggroe Aceh Darussalam".

The NAD law also expanded on the original *Daerah Istimewa* formula and Law No. 44/1999 by allowing Aceh to enforce aspects of Islamic law and to establish a *Syari'ah* court for Muslims that would be "free from the influence of any party" within Aceh.[37] Another significant provision that aimed to demonstrate Jakarta's confidence in Aceh's ability to "self-govern in accordance with national life" granted the Acehnese the right to directly elect their regional representatives "for 5 (five) years through an honest and fair, democratic, free confidential election".[38] On local governance, the NAD law returned to the provincial government the political, administrative and economic powers that had been devolved to district administrations through Laws No. 22 and 25 of 1999.[39]

The legislation also envisaged several new Acehnese institutions, the most symbolically important of which was a *Wali Nanggroe* (Head/ Guardian of State) to embody "the preservation of tradition and habitual culture" and to serve as a "unifier of society" but with no direct government role, like the Sultan of the Special Province of Yogyakarta.[40] The *Wali Nanggroe* was to be chosen by a council of respected Acehnese community leaders called a *Tuha Nanggroe* (State Elders). The decision to create this institution stemmed from a protracted debate during the drafting process about whether efforts should be made to accommodate GAM in the NAD law. Whereas Abdurrahman Wahid had argued that "there is no relationship between the [Aceh] conflict and the implementation of the specialities of the Aceh Darussalam [law]", most Acehnese legislators who were involved in the drafting process believed that special autonomy would fail without GAM's support.[41] Therefore, when the Acehnese

Fig. 19 GAM guerrillas on guard outside largest-ever meeting of GAM commanders, North Aceh, 4 January 2003 (*photo by William Nessen*)

delegation presented their special autonomy bill to the DPR, they nominated Hasan di Tiro as Aceh's first *Wali Nanggroe*. As one Acehnese Member of Parliament (MP), Teuku Syaiful Ahmad, explained, "he [Tiro] is the symbol of resistance against the central government. How could we ask GAM to surrender if we didn't give them any positions at all?"[42] While the government had agreed to the *Wali Nanggroe* provision, it refused to grant the honorary position to Tiro, who was already referred to by that title by his GAM followers. Another proposal by the former Acehnese IAIN Rector, Professor Safwan Idris, which was also rejected by Jakarta, was that GAM fighters be incorporated into a provincial police force, since "they already have uniforms, weapons and experience in security operations".[43] Instead, the only significant alteration to Aceh's pre-existing security arrangements with Jakarta was that the governor became responsible under the NAD law for coordinating security policies with, and appointing the regional police chief, who was obliged to report to the governor[44] (see Fig. 19).

Despite numerous concessions to Aceh, the implementation of the NAD law was impeded by several obstacles. The greatest problem was ongoing security operations in the province. Even before the imposition of martial law in Aceh on 18 May 2003 — when further decentralisation was postponed — security operations had formed an integral part of the Megawati administration's dual-track Aceh approach, which aimed to convince GAM to accept special autonomy through a series of internationally facilitated peace talks on one hand, while forcibly disarming the separatists on the other. It soon became apparent, however, that the government's main objective was to eliminate GAM as a precursor to peace. This heavy reliance on force to resolve Aceh's problems can be partly explained by the government's changing approach to decentralisation. Whereas the Habibie and Wahid administrations emphasised special autonomy as a comprehensive political solution to Aceh's conflict, there were two dominant perceptions about the NAD law within Megawati's government which indicated its declining importance as a policy priority. The first main view was that as the Acehnese had been awarded a fair opportunity to manage themselves with unprecedented control over their natural resources, Jakarta could disavow further responsibility for the decentralisation process. The second common perception was that the Acehnese would abuse their increased self-governing powers to continue struggling for eventual secession.

There was some truth in this second viewpoint as both GAM and SIRA rejected special autonomy as a compromise to Acehnese independence, and there was a widespread lack of grassroots support for the NAD law. Many Acehnese were deeply sceptical that the NAD law would produce any material benefits, judging from the government's previous broken promises about special autonomy. As the majority of Acehnese were not invited to participate in the development of the so-called "people's initiative approach" to special autonomy, public awareness about the content of the NAD law was also low.[45] This failure to publicise the legislation created additional risks that elements of Acehnese society would reject, ignore or become confused by the law, and that security forces personnel and local militant groups would take the task of interpreting and enforcing the legislation into their own hands.[46] Nor did the law respond to the main Acehnese demand for retribution and compensation for human rights violations. As the Acehnese co-founder of *Kontras* (National Commission for Missing Persons and Victims of Violence), Munir, explained:

> … the government's offer of the Nanggroe Aceh Darussalam special autonomy law failed to take into account what the Acehnese people really need. Special autonomy is only a shift of authority from the Minister of Home Affairs to the governor, but not the power itself.[47]

The rapid transferral of state power and authority to the provincial government also exacerbated pre-existing systemic problems. Much of Aceh's infrastructure had been destroyed by the conflict and provincial authorities conceded that they lacked control over about 80 per cent of the province.[48] In many areas there were no operable courts. Throughout Aceh, labyrinthine networks of illegal and semi-legal business relations were established among state officials, security forces personnel and GAM members. Not only did this dysfunctional system make it impossible to deliver most of the increased benefits and services that Acehnese society was supposed to receive through the implementation of the NAD law, but it also deepened the prevalent feeling of public mistrust toward the Indonesian state.

Aceh's leadership crisis presented a particular obstacle to the implementation of the NAD law. The Golkar-dominated provincial government was deeply unpopular and was widely seen as corrupt. In his chapter, McGibbon explains how Aceh's Governor, Abdullah Puteh, became the most prominent symbol of this corrupt political culture through his expanding business interests and personal involvement in several controversial "vanity" projects. The eradication of corruption was made extremely difficult by the inexperience of Acehnese politicians in managing increased budgets, the lack of institutional mechanisms to ensure governmental transparency and accountability and the various systemic obstacles associated with Aceh's war economy. In January 2003, a coalition of Acehnese NGOs drew national attention to this situation by urging Jakarta to reject an offer of US$400 million in foreign development aid because "the Aceh administration cannot even manage its provincial budget, let alone that much money".[49] The NGOs' allegations were supported by two separate Indonesian studies, which found that instead of emerging as one of Indonesia's wealthiest provinces after the implementation of the NAD law, Aceh was instead ranked "the most corrupt".[50] In April 2004, an Acehnese sociologist, Ahmad Humam Hamid, identified corruption as Aceh's most serious problem, stating that "during the 2002–2004 period, some Rp. 20 trillion (US$2.3 billion) has been channelled to Aceh, but the use of the funds is not clear".[51]

Another difficulty concerning the implementation of the NAD was that it was not a complete document and required several supporting *qanun,* or regional regulations.[52] According to Chapter I, Article 1(8) and Chapter III, Article 3(1) of the NAD law, the provincial government, as "the authority in the framework of implementing special autonomy", was responsible for formulating and enforcing these *qanun* after obtaining national government approval. There was no legal avenue through which Acehnese society could participate in the development of *qanun*, however, and there was strong public scepticism about the political will of state authorities to pass certain regulations, such as those that were necessary to prepare the province for holding direct local elections.

Of the *qanun* that were introduced shortly after the introduction of the NAD law, the most controversial were those concerning the implementation of aspects of *Syari'ah*. Although many Acehnese had initially welcomed the formal introduction of Islamic law, the Puteh government was soon criticised for reducing *Syari'ah* to a political commodity and for failing to apply the law to respond to the dominant Acehnese demand for justice for human rights abuses. Following the introduction of the Islamic dress code (*Wajib Tutup Aurat*) in early 2002, Acehnese women's organisations expressed fear that the provincial administration's emphasis on wearing the *jilbab* (Islamic women's headdress) would lead to increased acts of violence against them. Whilst most Acehnese women saw the enforcement of *Syari'ah* as being consistent with Aceh's Islamic values and culture, they resented the government's role in creating a negative public image of Islamic law that was based more on oppression than on the attainment of social justice. Although Aceh's provincial police force was initially made responsible for enforcing Islamic law, a separate, green- and white-uniformed *Syari'ah* police force (called *Wilayatul Hisbah*) was eventually established in Banda Aceh to impose Islamic dress, and other *qanun* about *Syari'ah* such as the banning of gambling and alcohol consumption, and the provision of separate services for men and women in beauty salons and hotels to uphold moral conduct.[53]

The provincial government's decision to employ a lashing executioner (*algojo hukuman cambuk*) through *Qanun* No. 11 of 2002 also reinforced rather than reduced the prevalent climate of fear in Aceh. Due to be implemented from the start of Ramadhan in November 2002, this *qanun* made the lashing executioner responsible for publicly caning those who propagated un-Islamic beliefs, sold or consumed food and beverages during the fasting month, disturbed or prevented others from worshipping and Muslims who failed to attend prayers for three consecutive Fridays without an acceptable reason.[54] Unlike the introduction of the Islamic dress code, however, there were few outspoken critics of the caning *qanun*, with the notable exception of one IAIN law lecturer, Dr. H. A. Hamid Sorong, who called on the Puteh government to refrain from tarnishing the political image of *Syari'ah* by using the law to perpetuate the cycle of violence in Aceh.[55]

Nor was Acehnese hope for justice for human rights abuses met by the inauguration of a provincial *Mahkamah Syari'ah* (Islamic court system) in March 2003, as excesses by security forces personnel continued to fall under the jurisdiction of military tribunals or the national court system. Although the *Mahkamah Syari'ah*, which was established in March 2003 through Presidential Instruction No. 11 of 2003, was authorised to decide on civil, material and criminal cases for Muslims according to *qishas* (punishment equal to the crime committed), the provincial and national governments decided that for the short term, the court would only resolve minor offences such as the sale and consumption of alcohol, and gradually expand its jurisdiction to settle more serious crimes such as adultery and murder after becoming more established.[56] According to Governor Puteh, this decision aimed to reassure Acehnese society that *Syari'ah* would be "implemented in a moderate way and gradually. We want to build a cool image of Islam in Aceh."[57] The authority of the *Mahkamah Syari'ah* was mainly limited, however, by a lack of clarity about what form Islamic law in Aceh should take, as only a few *qanun* had been passed at the time of the court's inauguration. This ambiguity was compounded by Chapter XII (Articles 25 and 26) of the NAD law, which required *Syari'ah* to be implemented in accordance with the national legal system and for appeal cases to be directed to the Indonesian Supreme Court. These provisions cast doubt over the extent to which the *Mahkamah Syari'ah* would be allowed to develop separately from the national legal system and whether its decisions would be upheld by the Supreme Court.[58]

Other provisions in the NAD law were either delayed or mismanaged. The requirement in Chapter IV, Article 7(2) that the provincial government must allocate 30 per cent of its natural resource revenue to improve education was not enforced for almost two years after the introduction of the law, and Acehnese school attendance rates continued to fall well below national attendance levels due to a combination of the escalating conflict and misallocated state funding.[59] In September 2002, public outcry followed a report by the Banda Aceh-based *Serambi Indonesia* newspaper that the Puteh administration had deposited Aceh's unspent annual education budget in a regional bank account.[60] By May 2003, when martial law was introduced, hundreds of schools had been burnt down and at least 135 teachers had become victims of violence, depriving tens of thousands of Acehnese children of education.[61] The following

year, however, the national government issued an encouraging report
that most of the incinerated schools had been rebuilt by Indonesian
soldiers.[62] Also, while critics continued to attack the Puteh government
for mismanaging Aceh's education budget, there were some positive
reports that at least part of the funds had been released to provide
scholarships for Acehnese school and tertiary students.[63]

No steps were immediately taken to prepare Aceh for holding direct
local elections in accordance with Chapter VIII of the NAD law. Instead,
the controversial provision gave rise to a protracted debate about the
nature of an Acehnese election and whether GAM would be allowed to
participate in the political process. Although Law No. 18/2001 clearly
stipulated the direct election of Acehnese governors, district heads and
mayors, the provision became highly politicised and misinterpreted by
both GAM and national government leaders during a series of internationally facilitated peace talks that were held between the two sides
in February, May and December of 2002. On 9 December 2002, when
both sides signed a "Cessation of Hostilities [Framework] Agreement"
(CoHA), they agreed that "on the basis of accepting the NAD law as
a starting point" to hold "a democratic all-inclusive dialogue involving
all elements of Acehnese society" that would lead to the election of a
democratic government in Aceh, Indonesia.[64] It soon became apparent,
however, that both parties continued to adopt vastly different interpretations of what an Acehnese election would entail, with GAM leaders
arguing that a separate Aceh election would determine the government
of an independent Acehnese state, while Jakarta maintained that the
Acehnese would only be allowed to vote in national elections.[65]

In May 2003, when the Megawati government unilaterally withdrew
from the CoHA and declared a state of military emergency in Aceh,
special autonomy effectively became meaningless. Placing the TNI in
charge of most aspects of Aceh's civilian administration, emergency rule
was accompanied by the launch of *Operasi Terpadu* (Integrated Operation).
Unlike previous Aceh security operations in the post-Suharto era, Jakarta
made no attempt to justify the military emergency by positioning it
within a broader political framework, and the sole long-term objective
of the "integrated" operation was to eliminate GAM.

Despite the relative weakness of Aceh's civilian leadership compared
with the Indonesian military, the provincial government continued to
pass *qanun* in accordance with the NAD law. Most of these new bylaws
focused on aspects of Syari'ah, such as the banning of *Khalwat* (close
proximity between an unrelated male and female), the distribution of

zakat (alms) and the organisation of Acehnese culture and customary law (*adat*) in accordance with Islam. While these *qanun* generated little controversy within Aceh's climate of fear, they failed to meet local expectations about justice. Aceh's human rights situation had sharply deteriorated during the year of martial law, and reports that emerged from the province about unlawful killings, arbitrary arrests, torture and widespread internal displacement were reminiscent of the late New Order. GAM, SIRA and other Acehnese groups and individuals also continued to oppose the special autonomy legislation in its entirety for offering too little, too late.

With the downgrading of Aceh's status from martial law to civil emergency in May 2004 came renewed concerns about the provincial administration's abuse of its special autonomy powers and resources. Although Governor Abdullah Puteh was suspended from duty on 20 July 2004 through Presidential Instruction No. 2 of 2004 and subsequently sentenced to ten years imprisonment for corruption, he was later confined to city arrest in Jakarta for "health reasons". Meanwhile, the more complex systemic problems of poor governmental accountability and transparency in Aceh's state institutions remained largely unaddressed. Under a more efficient provincial government, the redistribution of Aceh's natural resource wealth may have gradually reduced support for GAM by generating employment opportunities and improving access to public services and facilities. Instead, the massive injection of resource revenue into Aceh only exacerbated pre-existing tensions between Acehnese society and the provincial government.

While the introduction of a long awaited *qanun* on 9 March 2004 about holding direct elections for Acehnese governors, regents and mayors initially seemed promising, it was introduced at a time when Acehnese civil society was at its weakest. SIRA, the humanitarian NGOs and liberated press that had briefly flourished after the fall of Suharto had been militarily repressed, along with their leaders.[66] Most Acehnese were either unaware of their civil and political rights, or were too afraid to exercise them. Nor were there any legal mechanisms to encourage GAM to participate in the electoral process by transforming its militant struggle into a political campaign. Instead, after the year of martial law, the TNI — as the most powerful authority in the province — was well positioned to run candidates in local elections. Within this environment it seemed improbable that direct local elections would follow democratic procedure or lay the foundations for legitimate political leadership. The unrelenting and unrestrained application of state violence and the absence of any viable political alternative to secession also created fertile conditions for the birth to a new generation of GAM fighters, and hence, another phase in the Aceh conflict.

Postscript

On 26 December 2004, when Aceh was struck by a massive earthquake and tsunami, it seemed that no aspect of Acehnese life would ever return to normal. The devastation wrought by the waves was incalculable, and entire towns were swept into the Indian Ocean. In the immediate aftermath of the tsunami, the overwhelming scale of death and destruction made it hard to fathom how things could get any worse in Aceh. But they did.

At first, the magnitude of the Aceh disaster triggered an immediate change in approach by Jakarta and GAM toward the conflict. GAM called for a cease-fire to facilitate the enormous task of recovering corpses. Jakarta lifted its ban on foreigners from entering the province to allow for the distribution of international aid. The TNI, which had also suffered massive losses in the tsunami, soon reverted to a dual-track approach that comprised aid distribution and reconstruction efforts along Aceh's battered coastline on one hand, and ongoing counter-insurgency operations against GAM on the other.

Despite the disturbingly rapid return to security operations, GAM and Indonesian government leaders began to explore the unique opportunity presented by the tsunami to find a negotiated solution to the conflict. For the first half of 2005, both sides met for a new series of internationally facilitated peace talks in Helsinki. It was during these talks that GAM made a remarkable concession by agreeing for the first time not to bring its independence agenda to the negotiating table. GAM also agreed to discuss "self-governance" within the Indonesian Republic as an alternative to special autonomy.

Although, at the time of writing (June 2005), Jakarta has rejected GAM's demand for self-governance, the future of the NAD law remains uncertain. With much of Aceh's state infrastructure destroyed by the tsunami, the TNI has once again stepped in to fill the provincial power vacuum. The direct local elections that have scheduled for June 2005 in most other parts of the archipelago have been indefinitely postponed in Aceh. Syari'ah has continued to be discriminatively imposed as an instrument of repression against marginalised groups such as the poor, women and Aceh's non-Islamic minority. In June 2005, 27 civilians in

Bireuen regency were convicted of moral offences such as gambling and sexual misconduct, and sentenced to public lashings if they were unable to pay the alternative fine.[67] The TNI, meanwhile, has been assigned the important role of safeguarding the post-tsunami reconstruction and rehabilitation process from security disturbances by GAM. This effectively means that the capacity of civilian institutions to govern in Aceh will continue to be constrained by the interests and priorities of the Indonesian military. Any civilian administration's authority in Aceh will remain dependent on the TNI's unrestrained power. As reconstruction work has hardly begun in Aceh, the TNI is unlikely to leave any time soon.

Notes

1   This belief was reinforced by President Sukarno's inaugural Independence Day speech on 17 August 1945, when he recognised Aceh's "*Daerah Modal*" role during the revolution and described the Acehnese as national heroes. S.H. Hardi, *Daerah Istimewa Aceh: Latar Belakang Politik dan Masa Depannya* (Jakarta: PT Cita Panca Serangkai, 1993), p. xx.

2   Nazaruddin Sjamsuddin, *The Republican Revolt: A Study of the Acehnese Rebellion* (Singapore: Institute of Southeast Asian Studies, 1985), pp. 34–42.

3   Hardi, *Daerah Istimewa Aceh*, pp.114–8; Eric Eugene Morris, *Islam and Politics in Aceh. A Study of Center-Periphery Relations in Indonesia* (PhD Thesis, Cornell University, 1983), pp. 168–70.

4   Hardi, *Daerah Istimewa Aceh*, p. 132.

5   Sjamsuddin, *The Republican Revolt*, pp. 265, 329; Tim Kell, *The Roots of Acehnese Rebellion, 1989–1992* (New York, Ithaca: Cornell Modern Indonesia Project, 1995), pp. 11–2; Morris, *Islam and Politics*, pp. 214–39.

6   Morris, *Islam and Politics*, pp. 232–3.

7   At that time, Hasan Saleh was supported by approximately three-quarters of the then active Acehnese Darul Islam army. Ibid., pp. 230–3.

8   The "Jakarta Charter" was proposed in 1945 by Islamic leaders as a preamble to the Indonesian Constitution. It was subsequently blocked by the secular nationalist majority in government, but remained a contentious constitutional issue that Islamic parties attempted to revive under later governments.

9   Morris, *Islam and Politics*, p. 240, citing "Pernjataan Wali Negara/ Panglima Tentera dan Territorium Tgk. Tjhik di Tiro Tentera Islam Indonesia" (1 September 1961).

10   Sjamsuddin, *The Republican Revolt*, p. 310; Nazaruddin Sjamsuddin, "Issues and Politics of Regionalism in Indonesia: Evaluating the Acehnese Experience", in *Armed Separatism in Southeast Asia*, ed. Lim Joo-Jock and Vani. S. (Singapore: Institute of Southeast Asian Studies, 1984), p. 125.

11   Kell, *The Roots of Acehnese Rebellion,* pp. 13–28.
12   Morris, *Islam and Politics,* p. 260.
13   Ibid., pp. 270–6.
14   Teungku A. Hamid and Darwis A. Soelaiman, *Perbandingan Sekolah-Sekolah Umum dan Sekolah-Sekolah Agama di Propinsi Daerah Istimewa Atjeh* (Banda Aceh: Badan Perentjanaan Pembangunan Atjeh, 1971), pp. 1–10.
15   Husni, dk, "Pelaksanaan Otonomi Daerah Tingkat II Dalam Mewujudkan Otonomi Nyata Dan Bertanggung Jawab Di Kotamadya Banda Aceh", *Mon Mata,* no. 27 (September 1997): 12–26; Sjamsuddin, "Issues and Politics of Regionalism …", p. 126.
16   Kell, *The Roots of Acehnese Rebellion,* pp. 59–60.
17   Jimly Asshidiqie, Erman Radjagukguk, Ahmad Watik Pratiknya and Umar Juoro, *Reform in Indonesia: Vision and Achievements of B. J. Habibie.* Volume 2. *Legal and Socio-Culture* (Jakarta: PT Raja Grafindo Persada, December 1999), pp. 69–70.
18   Hadi Setia Tunggal, comp., *Undang-Undang Nomor 22 Tahun 1999 Tentang Pemerintah Daerah,* p. iii; Hadi Setia Tunggal, comp., *Undang-Undang Republik Indonesia Nomor 25 Tahun 1999 Tentang Perimbangan Keuangan Antara Pemerintah Pusat dan Daerah* (Jakarta: Harvarindo, 2000), pp. iii–vii.
19   Hadi Setia Tunggal, comp., *Undang-Undang Republik Indonesia Nomor 44 Tahun 1999 Tentang Penyelenggaraan Keistimewaan Propinsi Daerah Istimewa Aceh* (Jakarta: Harvarindo, 2000), pp. 5–6.
20   Ibid., pp. 1–2, Chapter I (10), (11); Chapter II, Article 3(1) and (2).
21   Ibid., Chapter III, Article 3(d) and 5(1), (2).
22   Ibid., Chapter III, Article 1 (2), Article III (6), Article 4.
23   "Rakyat Lebih Mendengar Mahasiswa dan LSM Ketimbang Para Pejabat dan Ulama", *Kontras,* 11 August 1999.
24   M. Yusuf Daud (Secretary General of the Free Acheh Movement in Europe), "Autonomy for Aceh is Just a shot in the Air", Press Statement, 27 September 1999.
25   "Timtim bisa Lepas jika tak Mampu Ikut Irama", *Serambi Indonesia,* 5 February 1999.
26   "Hasil Lengkap Jajak Pendapat Waspada: 56% Referendum Dan 25.3% Otonomi Luas", *Waspada,* 7 June 1999.
27   "Ulama Tuntut Referendum", *Serambi Indonesia,* 16 September 1999.
28   Interview, Syamsuddin Mahmud, South Jakarta, 20 November 2001.
29   "Aceh Needs Humanitarian Approach: Governor", *The Jakarta Post,* 12 July 1999.
30   Michelle Ann Miller, "The Life and Death of Aceh's Peace Process", *Inside Indonesia,* No. 75 (July–September 2003), pp. 29–30.
31   "'Kado' Presiden bukan permintaan rakyat Aceh", *Serambi Indonesia,* 18 December 2000; Arif Zulkifli and J. Kamal Farza, "Cure or Cancer?", *Tempo,* 19–25 December 2000, p. 20.

32 Tomi Soetjipto, "Interview: Islamic Law to Soothe Aceh", *Reuters*, 11 December 2000.

33 "Give Peace a Chance", *Asiaweek*, 12 January 2001, p.14.

34 "Otonomi Khusus Provinsi DI Aceh, Lain RUU NAD, Lain RUU OKNAD", *Kompas*, 17 January 2001.

35 "House approves committee for Aceh bill", *The Indonesian Observer*, 1 March 2001.

36 *Undang Undang Republik Indonesia Nomor 18 Tahun 2001 Tentang Otonomi Khusus Bagi Provinsi Daerah Istimewa Aceh Sebagai Provinsi Nanggroe Aceh Darussalam*, Chapter IV, Articles 4 and 5.

37 Ibid., Chapter 1, Article 1(7) and Chapter XII.

38 Interview with Dr Ahmad Farhan Hamid (Acehnese member of national parliament), Jakarta, 29 October 2002; Ibid., Chapter VII, Article 15(1) and Article 12(1), and Chapter IX, Articles 17 and 18.

39 Ibid., Chapter VIII, Article 11.

40 Ibid., Chapter VII, Article 10(1).

41 Interview with Abdurrahman Wahid, Jakarta, 23 October 2002.

42 Aulia Andri, Fitri and GB, "Aceh Special Autonomy Bill Handed to The House", *Detikworld*, 10 January 2001.

43 Interview with Prof. Safwan Idris (Rector, IAIN), Banda Aceh, 15 September 2000.

44 NAD law, Chapter X, Article 21(3), (6).

45 "Most Moderate Autonomy Law Draft Specially for Aceh", *Kompas*, 19 April 2001.

46 Michelle Ann Miller, "The Nanggroe Aceh Darussalam Law: A Serious Response to Acehnese Separatism?", *Asian Ethnicity* 5, 3 (October 2004): 342.

47 "Megawati urged to become more concrete on Aceh issues", *The Jakarta Post*, 4 September 2001.

48 Miller, "The Nanggroe Aceh Darussalam Law", pp. 342–3.

49 "Acehnese ask government to reject aid", *The Jakarta Post*, 23 January 2003.

50 These national corruption reports were produced in early 2003 by the Centre for Research and Education of Central Banking (PSPK) in Bank Indonesia, and the Economics Faculty of the Padjajaran University (*FE Unpad*). "Korupsi di Aceh, Penduduk Miskin Meningkat", *Sinar Harapan*, 31 March 2003.

51 Nani Farida, "KPK seeks to quiz Puteh on graft cases", *The Jakarta Post*, 21 April 2004.

52 Miller, "The Nanggroe Aceh Darussalam Law", p. 342.

53 Ditangkap, Waria Protes "Kami Diurusi, Korupsi Tidak", *Acehkita.com*, 2 August 2004.

54 *Qanun Provinsi Nanggroe Aceh Darussalam Nomor 11 Tahun 2002 Tentang Pelaksanaan Syariat Islam Bidang Aqidah, Ibadah dan Syi'ar Islam* (14 October

2002), Chapter 8, Articles 20–22; "Selama Ramadhan. Makan Siang Hari, Dihukum Cambuk", *Serambi Indonesia*, 18 October 2002.

[55] "Pakar Hukum Islam IAIN: Syariat Islam Jangan Jadikan Proyek Politik", *Serambi Indonesia*, 29 October 2002.

[56] Miller, "The Nanggroe Aceh Darussalam Law", p. 345.

[57] "Aceh initiates 'moderate' *Syari'ah* court", *The Jakarta Post*, 5 March 2003.

[58] Arskal Salim, "Epilogue. Shariá in Indonesia's Current Transition: An Update", in *Shariá and Politics in Modern Indonesia*, ed. Arskal Salim and Azyumardi Azra (Singapore: Institute of Southeast Asian Studies, 2004), pp. 227–8.

[59] World Bank, "Promoting Peaceful Development in Aceh", An informal background paper prepared for the Preparatory Conference on Peace and Reconstruction in Aceh in Tokyo, Japan (3 December 2002), pp. 5–6.

[60] "Rp 351 Milyar Dana Pendidikan Mengendap", *Serambi Indonesia*, 5 September 2002.

[61] Miller, "The Life and Death of Aceh's Peace Process", p. 29.

[62] "Aceh numbers don't add up", *Laksamana.net*, 6 May 2004.

[63] "Diknas NAD Bantah Ada Korupsi", *Acehkita.com*, 30 August 2004.

[64] *Cessation of Hostilities Framework Agreement Between Government of the Republic of Indonesia and the Free Acheh Movement*, 9 December 2002.

[65] Miller, "The Nanggroe Aceh Darussalam Law", pp. 350–1.

[66] Miller, "Elusive Truth", *Inside Indonesia*, No. 81 (January–March 2005): 10.

[67] "27 Pelanggar Syariat Islam akan Dicambuk di Bireuen", Media Indonesia Online, 13 June 2005.

15

Local Leadership and the Aceh Conflict

Rodd McGibbon

Recent accounts of the Aceh conflict have focused on the secessionist challenge that the Free Aceh Movement (GAM) has posed to the Indonesian government.[1] These accounts have highlighted how the repressive policies of the Suharto regime bred widespread resentment and a sense of injustice in Aceh that resulted in the emergence of GAM. The central government's exploitation of the province's resource base and its repressive security policies have clearly fuelled much of the separatist discontent of recent decades. Contemporary accounts of Aceh's political troubles such as Geoffrey Robinson's and Rizal Sukma's provide a compelling explanation of how local grievances have resulted from Jakarta's misrule and given rise to an alienated local population.[2]

But this is only part of the story. To add another layer of complexity to our understanding of the conflict, this chapter shifts the analysis from a grievance-based approach to a focus on local politics and leadership. It argues that recent accounts, particularly media reporting, have tended to pit Aceh against Jakarta in what is often regarded as a simple vertical conflict between centre and region. In doing so, the importance of local factors in explaining the contemporary conflict has been largely obscured. In contrast, this chapter will examine the evolution of local political elites and their role in integrating Aceh into the Indonesian state.

This local perspective on the conflict departs from a grievance-based account in several ways. To begin with, it rejects a key assumption of recent analysis and reporting, according to which the Aceh conflict is viewed as having recent origins in the New Order regime's misgoverning of the province. In contrast, this chapter adopts a broader historical perspective. In fact, the Aceh conflict can be understood in terms of a more enduring problem — how colonial and post-colonial authorities have sought to integrate Aceh into the state by governing indirectly through local elites. This chapter shows that a key to understanding the Aceh conflict is the failure of successive local elites, and their Jakarta-based patrons, to establish leadership claims over local politics. This has not only created a vacuum in political authority and legitimacy but also weakened the integrative institutions that bind Aceh to the state.

This focus on local politics and leadership also leads to different policy implications from a purely grievance-based approach. Robinson's account of the Aceh conflict is instructive here in arguing that the Habibie government's recognition of local grievances augured well for a resolution of the conflict. But five years later and this resolution was still proving elusive, belying Robinson's optimistic expectations. In adopting a grievance-based explanation, Robinson had good reason to be guardedly optimistic. Jakarta quickly offered the province wide-ranging concessions through special status and special autonomy laws. These concessions included provision for Aceh to implement Islamic law as well as the reallocation of lucrative gas and oil revenues and other sources of income to the province.

In spite of these concessions, however, the conflict persisted. Jakarta's adoption of coercive measures to quell rising separatist sentiment no doubt offset some of the goodwill that may have been generated by the wide-ranging concessions it was offering. But this does not fully explain why new policy initiatives had little impact on the conflict. An alternative explanation is required.

In examining local elements of the conflict, I show how the failures of local governance and the vacuum of local authority in post-Suharto Aceh were a major element in Jakarta's faltering efforts to resolve the conflict. In particular, the central government backed local leaders who enjoy little legitimacy and who failed to translate Jakarta's concessions into widespread benefits to the Acehnese community. In other words, the government's strategy of addressing the province's grievances through concessions foundered, at least partly, on its reliance on segments of the local political elite that were unable to garner community support. Furthermore, the local factions supported by Jakarta ultimately offered little support to the government's attempts to resolve the conflict.

This kind of analysis has taken on added urgency following the tsunami of 26 December 2004 that unleashed wide-scale devastation and loss of life along Aceh's western coastline. The humanitarian response that followed from both outside Indonesia and from ordinary Indonesians was remarkable. Volunteers from across the archipelago flowed into Aceh to help their national brethren, often taking on some of the most unwelcome tasks of corpse removal and cleanup. This display of solidarity raised hopes that the ties that once bound Aceh to Indonesia might again be reconnected.

The signing of a memorandum of understanding in Helsinki on 15 August 2005 between GAM and the Indonesian Government represented the most promising move toward peace since the conflict began in the mid-1970s. Early implementation of the MOU demonstrated that both sides were serious about peace, unlike previous initiatives. But hopes for a sustainable peace will only be realised if both the recovery effort and the implementation of the MOU result in the renewal of local leadership. Without the full participation of Acehnese in reconstruction, particularly through engaging local leaders, the tsunami response is unlikely to result in a sustainable resolution to the conflict. The enormity of the task of rebuilding the province will require that local governments assume full responsibility for the recovery effort, to be supported, but not overwhelmed or superseded, by Jakarta and the international community. Similarly, the MOU must eventuate in a political resolution of the conflict and the emergence of popular candidates for office. This will no doubt be a tricky process with government officials remaining suspicious that GAM will use local elections to re-ignite calls for independence.

To understand the background to the contemporary peace initiative, this chapter focuses on understanding the struggles among local leadership groups since Indonesia's political transition in 1998. It shows how various leadership groups have responded to changing political circum-stances, outlining the shifting alliances of technocrats, religious leaders, political reformers and counter elites after the fall of the Suharto regime. Before doing so, however, it is necessary to briefly examine the historical evolution of the main leadership groups in Aceh. The first part of this chapter examines how the colonial and post-colonial authorities have sought to integrate Aceh into the state through often troubled relations with segments of the local elite. Subsequent sections examine the rise and decline of the technocrats, before I turn to Jakarta's local alliances prior to the tsunami.

I define the Acehnese elite as those members of the upper echelons of the provincial legislature and government and their main political advisors. The analysis focuses on the provincial level. While this definition may be criticised for being too narrow, it is deliberately so for two reasons. Firstly, an institutional definition has the merit of focusing attention on who wields state power. Secondly, by focusing on formal power-holders the analysis is able to chart the rise and fall of various sections of the elite in terms of their proximity to government in a single narrative that avoids becoming unwieldy.

Local Power and Indirect Rule in Aceh

As earlier chapters in this volume have shown, a strong Acehnese political identity was shaped by the emergence of an expansionist trading state in the seventeenth and eighteenth centuries based upon a dynastic sultanate. Both in court politics and among the Sultan's local subjects, Acehnese identity was expressed through a common adherence to Islam and its powerful symbols. If the state and religion helped create a strong sense of being Acehnese, war also deepened Aceh's political identity. The expanding colonial empire of the Dutch East Indies encountered stiff Acehnese resistance in the late nineteenth century, particularly from the *ulama,* or Islamic teachers, who declared the struggle a *perang sabil* or holy war against the foreign infidels. As Reid shows elsewhere in this volume, Aceh was unlike most other regions in the East Indies in the sense that a distinctly Acehnese political identity was formed by an indigenous pre-colonial state in the form of the sultanate. In other areas, ethno-political identity was formed much later through the colonial state and the emergence of the nationalist movement.

The famous Dutch orientalist, Snouck Hurgronje, advised colonial authorities to adopt a strategy of cultivating the local aristocratic elite or *ulèëbalang* as the best way to bring Aceh under control. He also counselled military force against the *ulama* whose notions of the *ummat* (the Islamic community) and unwavering opposition to outside domination militated against Dutch colonial rule in the territory. In contrast, the *ulèëbalang,* who had grown rich through the pepper trade, were seen as potential collaborators whose interests centred on the maintenance of their own personal fiefdoms.[3] The dual strategy proposed by Hurgronje ultimately proved successful. Through a prolonged and costly war, Dutch control was finally imposed from the late nineteenth century through the indirect rule of the *ulèëbalang* who were given a relative free hand in their respective regions. The practice of ruling indirectly through a local elite maintaining local custom (*adat*) was common throughout the Dutch East Indies. It was a particularly crucial strategy in Aceh where the pacification of the fiercely independent Acehnese hinged on cultivating a collaborationist class of officials as an alternative to the popular *ulama* and their strident anti-colonialism.

World War II and the Japanese occupation, however, were to bring about the end of colonial rule in Indonesia in which Aceh played a crucial role as a stronghold of nationalist resistance. In the immediate post-war years in Aceh, the *ulama* mobilised traditional Islamic students and youth groups to eliminate the *uleebalang* as tensions heightened following growing competition between the two groups for power.[4] With key *uleebalang* leaders having fled or been killed, the *ulama* became the unrivalled leadership group and took over local government when independence was achieved. While the *ulama* sought to create a just society based upon Islamic precepts, Jakarta's nationalist elite tended to be dominated by Western-educated leaders who harboured deep reservations about what they saw as the "fanatical" brand of Islam in Aceh.

The chasm between Acehnese and national leaders led a popular rebellion under the venerated religious leader Daud Beureu'eh, as described in Chapters 8 and 9.

The rebellion was eventually quelled by Jakarta which offered special status to the region to manage local affairs in the areas of religion, customary law and education. The promise to grant Aceh special status and autonomy, necessary to quelling this rebellion, remained unfulfilled due to Jakarta's suspicion of the loyalty of the *ulama* and fear of their ability to mobilise popular support. The national government feared that surrendering autonomy to Aceh's popular *ulama* would undermine the secular nationalist underpinnings of the state. Thus, while the colonial state had been able to rule indirectly through the *uleebalang*, Indonesia's newly independent government was far less willing to forge a local alliance with the ascendant *ulama*. Indonesia's secular nationalist elite were opposed to the *ulama*'s commitment to achieving Islamic ideals. Although the *ulama* did not take up arms again, Jakarta's refusal to honour its agreement resulted in an uneasy integration of Aceh into the post-colonial state.

The growing turmoil in national politics in the mid-1960s, however, provided a new opportunity for Aceh's leadership to struggle for the goal of special status. The rise of the Indonesian Communist Party (PKI) provoked an anti-communist pogrom and bloodletting across Indonesia in 1965 following an attempted coup that involved the killing of top military commanders. Through their opposition to the PKI, the *ulama* and Islamic youth groups in Aceh were able to forge a local alliance with military forces. But this alliance was merely tactical for the military and, as events would transpire, did not foreshadow a more enduring convergence between local Acehnese leaders and the central government.

The events that surrounded the anti-PKI campaign raised expectations in Aceh that the new military-backed government known as the New Order would accommodate the aspirations of the Acehnese. Once again, Acehnese religious leaders and youth groups pressed Jakarta to grant special status to the province. In 1968, the provincial government responded to these demands by issuing a provincial regulation on implementation of elements of Islamic law.[5] But the New Order regime was no more accommodating to Aceh's Islamic aspirations than previous governments. The 1968 provincial regulation failed to get the necessary approval from the central government after objections from the Ministries of Religion and Home Affairs.[6] The military detention of Islamic student protestors in 1970 further signalled the end of the temporary alliance between the military and Islamic elements.[7] The clampdown by the security forces indicated that Islamic agitation would not be permissible under the New Order. It also dashed the hope of realizing special status for Aceh or of the formation of an anti-communist alliance between the new regime in Jakarta and Aceh's religious leadership.

Fostering a New Elite: The Technocrats under the New Order

The government's essentially hostile posture towards the *ulama*'s Islamic agenda represented a dilemma for the newly installed regime in Jakarta. Considering the region's strong sense of political identity, the central government risked provoking another rebellion if it could not secure support from local elites through which it was to govern Aceh. Neither of the two traditional leadership groups, however, represented viable local partners as the *ulama* were ideologically incompatible with the new regime, and the *ulèëbalang* had largely been eliminated as a cohesive political force in the 1940s.

It was to be an entirely different institution — the state universities — that would provide Jakarta with a channel to govern Aceh.[8] The state universities were established in the late 1950s and early 1960s and they soon produced an emerging group of intellectuals and students who would became a major political force in Acehnese politics with the backing of the central government. The rise of this group can be discerned as early as the anti-communist pogroms of 1965–6 in which it was not only the *ulama* who allied with the military but also students and intellectuals. The memoirs of Ibrahim Hasan[9], a Rector of Aceh's main state university and Governor during the late 1980s and 1990s, recounts how the military trained and armed battalions of student paramilitaries on campus. He claims that the movement to paralyse the PKI proceeded with amazing intensity on Acehnese campuses where the purge "was more spirited than in other areas".[10] In demonstrating their anti-communist credentials, local academics and their student protégés had shown their solidarity with the new regime in Jakarta. With Aceh lacking the landed gentry owing to the elimination of the *ulèëbalang*, the technocrats represented a natural local partner for Jakarta to counter the influence of the *ulama*.[11]

It was under the governorship of Muzakir Walad, a local businessman appointed in 1968, that the leading group of intellectuals and professionals became increasingly influential in the provincial government. Beginning from this period, academics and bureaucrats began to work together as the main local power holders in the province. These arrangements set in place an informal alliance between the universities, the bureaucracy and the military that was to be the dominant ruling coalition in Aceh throughout the New Order. During this period there was extensive exchange between the bureaucracy and the universities. A succession of governors had served as the rectors of the main state university of Syiah Kuala (*Unsyiah*) including Ibrahim Madjid, Ibrahim Hasan and Syamsuddin Mahmud — an arrangement that reflected the symbiotic relationship that developed between provincial government and university. Additionally the technocrats were supported by Acehnese business interests in Medan and Jakarta. Pro-development technocrats Walad and Hasan, for instance, had been appointed governors following lobbying efforts by Acehnese businessmen.[12]

A more important base for technocratic authority, however, was the relationship between the technocrats and their patrons in the central government. Some of Aceh's most prominent technocrats had been students of the prominent group of economists, known as the Berkeley Mafia, who had become the architects of New Order economic policy-making.[13] These strong patron-client relations resulted not only in regular exchange between the local bureaucracy and the universities within Aceh, but a circulation of Acehnese technocrats in the central bureaucracy. Acehnese served in the national government as ministers or as senior bureaucrats, and were also prominent in business and the armed forces. Bustanil Arifin, who had grown up in Aceh and was one of the few real insiders of the Suharto regime, was perhaps the most influential patron for Acehnese leaders. Bustanil's influence with Suharto is credited with preventing the military from dominating the local bureaucracy — as they had in other regions — through promoting Acehnese candidates for governor and district heads (*bupatis*).[14]

Supported by their Jakarta-based patrons, the technocrats rose to power, making Aceh perhaps the only region in Indonesia where the bureaucracy was staffed from top to bottom by local civilians. Indeed, the Acehnese dominance of the local bureaucracy and their high level of participation in the central government were unusual for Indonesia's highly centralised system in which governors, district heads and other senior officials were often brought in from outside the region. The New Order regime's strategy of governing the region through local elite paralleled the way in which the Dutch had ruled through the *ulèëbalang*. This historical parallel was not lost on one local official who described the technocrats as the "new *ulèëbalang*".[15]

These parallels with colonial policy went further than fostering the technocrats as the new *ulèëbalang*; they were also evident in the New Order regime's efforts to neutralise the *ulama* as a political force. By imposing tight political control over local leaders, the Suharto regime severely circumscribed the political space once enjoyed by the *ulama*. Post-revolutionary politics in Indonesia had been characterised by high level of political participation, and spanning nationalist, Islamic and communist constituencies. On coming to power, however, the New Order regime moved to curb political participation and to put an end to the kind of ideological mobilisation that Sukarno had encouraged. Government officials viewed expressions of religious and ethnic identity as a "primordial" threat to the state that had to be suppressed. In place of religious and ethnic politics, the Suharto regime promoted *Pancasila* as the sole ideology of the state.[16]

With military repression putting constraints on the exercise of political speech, the New Order was able to impose strong restrictions on Islamic discourse. By the early 1970s, the government had eliminated the multi-party system, allowing just two opposition parties that the Government could control more easily.[17] The forced amalgamation of Islamic parties into the United Development Party (PPP) weakened the main political channels through which Islamic aspirations could be expressed. The Government's own party, Golkar, was made up of so-called functional groups intended to transcend traditional ideological and social divisions in a union of corporatist interests that eschewed the divisive ideologies of religion and ethnicity.[18]

While repression and political control were key elements of the new authoritarian system, the regime also built an elaborate system of patronage and sanctions that bound provincial and local elites to the centre and ensured local compliance to the regime. This system imposed heavy costs on those *ulama* who opposed the government through excluding them from material benefits of development, while providing access to state resources for those who supported the regime.

It was not surprising that most *ulama* in Aceh chose to accommodate to the new regime.[19] The government sought to co-opt the more pragmatic *ulama* by appointing them to the religious bureaucracy. The Islamic Scholars' Council, the MUI, became not only an important vehicle for the government to co-opt senior *ulama*, but also a key channel for mobilising support for official development programmes. Legislative positions with the political parties, particularly PPP, also provided an institutional means of co-opting religious leaders. For many rural *ulama*, the *dayah* or boarding schools remained the most important institution. While some *ulama* retreated from public life to their *dayah*, many accepted the need to accommodate themselves to local officials and accepted small-scale patronage in return for supporting government policies.

Development and the Technocratic Agenda

The technocrats' main objective was centred on breaking what they saw as Aceh's isolation in economic and political terms.[20] This agenda was consistent with the focus of the new regime in Jakarta on development and modernisation. The technocrats promoted large-scale development programs both in agricultural and industrial sectors.[21] These policies resulted in the development of an industrial belt across the east and north coast into Aceh Besar, Banda Aceh and Sabang, dominated by the large liquefied natural gas plant operated by the US giant Exxon-Mobil in Lhokseumawe.[22]

The technocrats' mantra of *membangun daerah* (developing the region) differed markedly from the *ulama*'s preoccupation with creating an Islamic society. Under technocrats' rule, attempts to implement special status including Islamic law were abandoned. The technocrats dismissed the Islamic agenda as too "exclusive" and countered the charge that they were "secularists" by claiming that "to be a good Muslim does not mean that one has to become an Arab".[23]

Ibrahim Hasan, the quintessential Acehnese technocrat, and Governor for two terms from 1986–93, was arguably the most dynamic advocate of the New Order's modernising policies. His energy and single-mindedness were perhaps only matched by the praise and controversy that his policies provoked in equal measure. According to Hasan, Aceh had been excluded from the benefits of economic development and was isolated economically, culturally and politically not just from Jakarta but also from the outside world. The only way of breaking that isolation was to integrate more into the national economy to reap the benefits of development.

Hasan's main goal was to capture as many resources as possible from the centre to develop Acehnese agriculture and industry. But central government officials were too powerful and too wedded to the centralised political economy of the New Order for Acehnese to win concessions over revenue sharing. Thus, under Hasan, the technocrats based their strategy on maximising Aceh's development budget. Rather than swimming against the relentless tide of centralisation, the technocrats argued that Aceh should integrate more deeply into the national economy through supporting the modernising agenda of the New Order regime. For Hasan, a Golkar insider, this strategy not only involved economic integration but also implied that Aceh must politically align itself with the regime. To this end, Hasan fiercely promoted Golkar's political agenda, putting the full weight of the provincial government behind efforts to ensure a Golkar victory in the elections. According to Hasan, the victory of PPP in the 1982 general election in Aceh was a "fatal defeat" not just for Golkar but also for Aceh.[24] The PPP victory was a sign that Aceh was going its own way, and that the technocrats were losing popular support under the ineffective and unpopular leadership of Hadi Thayeb, a former diplomat. Hasan claimed that a further loss in 1987 would undermine development in the province by eroding Jakarta's commitment to funding the province. The problem for the technocrats was that Golkar had traditionally failed to resonate with Acehnese voters, while PPP had won considerable popularity through campaigning on the *keistimewaan* (special status) theme and using Islamic symbols.

In response, Golkar shifted its strategy in Aceh in the 1987 election to pre-empt PPP's Islamic politics by campaigning "through the window of religion".[25] Hasan's aim was to counter the widespread perception of Golkar as an alien force. Hence, Golkar's campaigns in 1987 and 1992 sought to mobilise the *ulama* throughout the province, while Hasan and other Golkar officials also sought to woo the old elements of the Darul Islam/TII, including Daud Beureu'eh.[26] Hasan's heavy-handed promotion of Golkar produced results. In the 1987 elections, Golkar achieved a victory for the first time in Aceh garnering 52 per cent of the vote. In 1992, in an oppressive climate owing to the military's counter-insurgency campaign, Golkar increased its vote to 60 per cent winning every district for the first time. Golkar's political hegemony was now complete. The government party was no doubt aided not only by the security climate in the province but also by the government's increasingly sophisticated methods of dispensing state patronage to those who supported it.[27]

The Legitimacy Deficit: Technocrats and *Ulama* in the Late New Order

The technocrats' claims to local leadership derived less from popular grassroots support than from their own technical expertise and their links to the central government. Unlike the *ulama,* the technocrats did not have a mass powerbase.[28] While not entirely divorced from their social roots (many came from rural *ulama* families), Aceh's new governing elite were cut off from Acehnese society by their Western education and upward accountability to Jakarta rather than to a mass base in Aceh.

Measured against their own goals, however, the performance of the technocrats met with some success. A major improvement in the region's infrastructure had been achieved with road and bridge construction programmes and major irrigation projects. Industrialisation along the North and East coast had occurred, a process that spurred rapid economic growth of the Acehnese economy.[29] Aceh had also integrated into the national and global economy.[30] Economic integration was paralleled in the political sphere by Aceh's close integration in the New Order regime, evidenced in the ways Acehnese occupied key posts in the central government, the military and business in disproportionate numbers to the province's small population. The province was also host to a series of national and international conferences designed to enhance Aceh's "national and global interactions".[31] Thus, by the mid-1990s, one could have concluded that the technocrats' vision of "breaking Aceh's isolation" was being realised.

But the costs of these policies were high. Local officials had jettisoned Aceh's fierce sense of independence to become enthusiastic participants in the centralised political economy of the New Order. By participating in a military dominated regime, Acehnese officials were in no position to refuse to support the military's operations against GAM from the late

1980s. Whatever personal revulsion they may have shared towards security operations, the technocrats became identified with a campaign that involved the deliberate use of terror by the military against the Acehnese population.[32] In the face of their widely-perceived complicity in military operations, the technocrats were easily discredited by their opponents as collaborators.

Furthermore, the economic development that the technocrats presided over provoked considerable local opposition. The rise of GAM can partly be attributed to the rapid socio-economic change brought about by industrialisation and the uneven impacts it had.[33] GAM found ready recruits in those same regions where industrialisation had occurred. Pidie, in addition to the districts of North Aceh and East Aceh, became GAM strongholds. The new industries in these areas resulted in rising levels of prosperity, at least for officials and for those employed there, and provided enormous revenues for the national budget. But these industries also stood out in otherwise poor regions that remained plagued by poverty, representing a glaring sign of the uneven impacts of technocrat policies. According to a 1993 survey by the Bureau of Statistics, only 10 per cent of villages had electricity in the industrialised districts along the north and east coast, while in the Lhokseumawe industrial zone only 20 per cent of the population had running water.[34]

One of the major problems with the region's economic development was the enclave nature of resource extraction industries.[35] The government had been unable to develop the kind of linkages between the new industrial belt along the coast and the agricultural regions of the hinterland.[36] At the same time, the rapid economic growth of these regions had attracted migrants from other parts of Indonesia, particularly Java. Thus, in the midst of an economic boom heralded by the provincial government, Acehnese continued to live in poverty while outsiders were capitalizing on the new economic opportunities resulting from greater exploitation of Aceh's natural resources. The influx of migrants into the province in the 1980s and 1990s provoked widespread local disaffection and the charge from GAM that Jakarta was intent on a policy of "Javanisation".[37]

An additional source of grievance was related to the ways in which the massive gas and oil revenues from Aceh's resource projects were collected by the central government, with very little allocated back to the region. The resentment this situation created extended well beyond GAM and its supporters and was evident among much of the Acehnese elite. The integration of Aceh into the national and global economy resulted in a web of economic interactions involving central ministries, international business and the military that simply bypassed local interests and channelled revenues out of Aceh.[38]

While provincial officials resented this injustice, they were widely viewed as the agents of these policies and the instrument of Jakarta's rule in the province. These perceptions eroded the efforts these officials made to press their claims to local leadership. As Kell argues, the technocrats were unable to establish their hegemony over the province.[39] In fact, they became an increasingly easy target for critics who pointed out that Jakarta's exploitation of the province's natural resources was fuelling separatist conflict. Furthermore, Ibrahim Hasan's push to ensure the electoral dominance of Golkar in the province provoked considerable opposition.[40] Morris' Ph.D. research identifies how a new generation of professionals and intellectuals emerged in Aceh in the 1970s and 1980s, and developed a strong critique of the technocrats as having sold out to Golkar and the regime.[41]

It was not just elements of the middle class that questioned the legitimacy of the technocrats. Many *ulama* also challenged their claims to local leadership. Again, the policy of "Golkarisation" provoked a strong reaction, particularly from PPP-linked *ulama*. The central government's continued refusal to honour "special status" remained a source of contention, at least in the early years of the New Order. During this period, the strong votes garnered by PPP represented a protest against the New Order, reflecting the existence of a limited symbolic space for resistance. The Golkarisation of the province, however, closed off this space and resulted in a further loss of political autonomy in Aceh. The coercion and political engineering that marked New Order rule provoked a sense of widespread revulsion toward the government.

The Golkarisation of the province also coincided with the re-emergence of GAM in the late 1980s, after it appeared that the movement had been all but extinguished a decade earlier. GAM's re-emergence in the late 1980s was at least partly triggered by the narrowing political space in Aceh and growing opposition to the political tactics of the government.

Other more independent *ulama* also criticised the technocrats. The "charismatic" *ulama*, Tgk. Bantaqiah of West Aceh, proved to be a major irritant to the provincial government.[42] The iconoclastic *ulama* strongly campaigned against Golkar, claiming that the government was seeking to introduce secularist tendencies into the province. The government attempted to co-opt him by funding a new boarding school complex for his followers, but he proudly maintained his autonomy, provoking continuing suspicion from the government. Other *ulama* criticised the technocrats' policies for abandoning the religious ideals that had defined Acehnese identity. As Hasan later complained, "intellectuals at the University of Syiah Kuala were slandered and accused of being secular and *bi'dah* (introducing impure innovations) ... by a small group of traditional thinkers who reject our critical and rational thinking".[43]

The provincial government was also plagued by allegations of corruption. Hasan himself fended off allegations of corruption when he was a senior official overseeing the free port at Sabang. Presiding over increased budgets for development, some provincial officials had reportedly accumulated large amounts of private wealth. However carefully the technocrats cultivated their local Islamic image, they constantly faced questions over personal integrity and the charge that they were merely implementing the secular designs of Jakarta. Furthermore, the technocrats' carefully groomed reputation for religious piety was tarnished by continual attacks from their opponents citing the emergence of brothels and bars near the industrial zone.[44]

While these criticisms reduced any legitimacy the technocrats may have gained from their pro-development policies, the *ulama* were in no position to capitalise on these attacks. The New Order regime and its whole political apparatus made Islamic opposition too costly. By the end of the New Order, the *ulama* had not only experienced a decline in their political cohesiveness but a fundamental transformation of their social base. This latter development was related to the emergence of a new social stratum of professionals and businesspeople from the late 1970s as a result of the regime's policy of rapid modernisation. This new middle class swelled following the expansion of government employment and the growth of large upstream industries and development projects.[45] As local leaders, the *ulama* were often the best-positioned to educate their children in modern tertiary institutions, which they increasingly did.[46] Thus, many of the *ulama* offspring became graduates from state universities, the very bastions of technocratic influence. Attaining tertiary qualifications, however, did not just result in social advancement but also expanded the worldview of these new recruits to Aceh's middle class.

The consequence of these processes was to erode the social basis upon which the *ulama* constituted a coherent political force in Aceh and to blur traditional ideological and political divisions. In the late colonial period Aceh, the *ulama* represented a force for social transformation and for the introduction of new ideas into the province. Under the All-Aceh

Ulama Association (PUSA), the *ulama* were the main advocates for modernisation and ridding the province of "feudal" influences. By the 1940s, they were leading a social revolution across the province. By the 1970s, however, the technocrats had essentially usurped the role of the *ulama* as the main agents of change.[47] By the time the New Order regime collapsed in 1998, the *ulama* had become a fragmented and deeply conservative political force. Most had been accommodated within what Morris refers to as the "institutional pockets" of the New Order.[48] Urban *ulama* were accommodated in positions in the MUI, the IAIN (the State Islamic University) and as teachers in the *madrasahs*. The *ulama* in the villages in the meantime focused attention on their respective *dayah*.[49] The urban *ulama* especially became key spokesmen for the regime with the MUI issuing *fatwa* supporting government policies and sanctioning local leaders that were opposed to the government. The insidious impact of the New Order system of rewards and patronage deeply compromised the *ulama* in Aceh and eliminated the independence they once possessed.[50] The strong ideological position on special status and Islamic law that the *ulama* articulated in the 1950s and 60s waned throughout the New Order period. From the latter part of the 1980s, the *ulama*'s "demands with regards to Islam became increasingly muted".[51]

The Decline of Technocrats and the Rise of Counter-Elites

Ibrahim Hasan's governorship ended with his appointment to the cabinet in 1993, with another technocrat, Syamsuddin Mahmud, appointed as the new governor. With Hasan's departure, however, the energy that had marked the technocratic vision faded. Syamsuddin was an experienced bureaucrat with strong academic credentials and was highly regarded for his personal integrity. But he lacked the drive and political ambition of Hasan. The tenure of Pak Syam, as he was affectionately known, recorded few achievements.[52] By its second term, Syamsuddin's administration had been overtaken by national events. After months of protests led by students across the country, Suharto was forced to resign in May 1998, handing power to his trusted vice-president B.J. Habibie. Habibie's rise to the presidency and the survival of other old officials was greeted by student protestors with calls for the elimination of remnants of the New Order.

In Aceh, protestors added a local orientation to these demands by highlighting the history of repression in the province. Encouraged by the unshackling of the local media, Acehnese leaders and activists began to expose many of the human rights violations that had occurred under the

New Order. In doing so, Islamic leaders, student activists and the media also targeted the participation of the technocrats in the New Order regime. In particular, the role of Ibrahim Hasan was spotlighted. A popular book written by a Jakarta-based Acehnese activist and local journalists charged Hasan with responsibility for military operations.[53] Many blamed Hasan not just for standing idly by as the military targeted Acehnese citizens, but for being behind the request for military intervention in the first place.[54] During the height of these allegations, Hasan was physically attacked by an irate student protestor. "I feel alienated from the people I love", Hasan has recalled, adding that "I've lost the right to live in Aceh and step foot on Aceh soil."[55]

With their standing tarnished by charges of complicity in past military abuses, the technocrats' fortunes were also undermined by the lack of support that Governor Syamsuddin Mahmud enjoyed within the central government. Syamsuddin was not counted as a political ally of the new President B.J. Habibie who had opposed Syamsuddin's bid for governor in the 1990s in favour of his own candidate.[56] With the election of Abdurrahman Wahid to the presidency in late 1999, Syamsuddin's relations with the central government broke down altogether and he was replaced by an interim governor, Ramli Ridwan.[57]

The environment unfolding in the province from 1998 onwards also militated against continued technocrat influence. The lifting of political controls over civil society resulted in a dramatic rise in political activity, particularly by an array of student groups. The military had all but retreated, as calls for them to withdraw from the province gathered momentum. It was a period of extraordinary ferment in civil society. Not surprisingly, this environment was ill-suited to the technocrats who owed their political success to the central government patronage which had sheltered them from popular pressures. They were essentially a product of the New Order and its whole apparatus of political demobilisation. The characteristics that had served them well during the New Order period were now a liability. Hence, the technocrats' lack of a mass base, a characteristic that had made them attractive local clients under the Suharto regime, now sidelined them in a period of intense political mobilisation. With the loss of credibility and public confidence in the main political institutions at this time, a vacuum in political authority resulted.

In this vacuum, an array of student groups and GAM took the political initiative. Students spanning from the Islamic right to the radical left mobilised for what they saw as a common objective, demanding a referendum for the province. The main student grouping to emerge, SIRA, comprised individuals and organisations covering the full spectrum of political opinion but united in their opposition to Jakarta. Unlike the technocrats, student and rebel leaders had rapidly developed a mass following from 1998, with their respective political strategies relying on the ability to mobilise support as political space opened up. GAM experienced a dramatic expansion in its base as it campaigned across the province. Proclaiming themselves as "liberators" who would ensure Acehnese taking control of their own land again, GAM leaders were able to recruit new followers throughout Aceh, extending their popular support from Pidie, North and East Aceh to virtually the whole province.

Student leaders also went on the political offensive after 1998 as a civil protest movement emerged demanding a referendum to determine the political status of the province. While university students were at the vanguard of the movement, calls for a referendum involved a popular front of religious leaders, traditional Muslim students (*santri*) and intellectuals. By November 1999, it appeared that the momentum for a referendum was unstoppable as the provincial capital of Banda Aceh was brought to standstill by hundreds of thousands of people in the largest rally ever seen in Aceh.

As events rapidly unfolded, the provincial government appeared paralyzed. Syamsuddin had kept his channels of communication open with the students. Lacking strong patrons in Jakarta, Syamsuddin made tentative moves toward supporting the students' demands. Some leaders claimed that the Governor had given his tacit support for demands for a referendum.[58] Syamsuddin clearly took a permissive attitude to students' political activities, evidenced in the freedom with which students made preparations for mass rallies. The Governor also sent a team to Stockholm to open up back-channel communications with GAM's exiled leadership.[59] But this was a period when Acehnese were demanding immediate action, fanned by students and GAM led agitation. As the Governor's overtures were largely rejected, the provincial government appeared increasingly irrelevant. Student and GAM leaders dismissed the technocrats as collaborators with Jakarta who had sold out Aceh's interests.

With political events moving at remarkable speed, GAM and the student movement rapidly mobilised popular support, forcing the government to give concessions. Thus, in 2000 the government of Abdurrahman Wahid sought to solve the conflict through involving an international NGO, the Henry Dunant Centre, as a facilitator in a dialogue between the government and GAM. The involvement of an international party represented a notable victory for GAM in establishing their claims to legitimacy. No matter how much they wanted to avoid the impression, the Indonesian government was essentially recognising GAM as having some legitimacy as least as a dialogue partner by their agreement to negotiate with their leadership. At least this was the way that GAM promoted the dialogue process locally.

Islamic Law and the *Ulama*

If the technocrats had become an anachronism in this environment of intense political mobilisation, many wondered what role the *ulama* might be able to play. In response to the threat of disintegration, the Habibie government grasped for a political solution to the rapidly deteriorating situation in Aceh. The government supported the initiative of Parliament members and its advisory team on Aceh to discuss new initiatives, including drafting a new law recognising the special status of Aceh was drafted.[60] The real impetus driving this process came from PPP politicians in the DPR who advocated the new law as a way of implementing the offer of special status contained in the 1959 resolution to the Darul Islam movement.[61] The thinking behind this initiative was spelt out in the law's elucidation in which it was noted that the roots of Aceh's contemporary conflict derived from the central government's refusal to honour the terms of the Darul Islam settlement. Law 44/1999 incorporated the key elements of the old special status offer, recognising Aceh's autonomy in religious affairs, education and local customary law (*adat*). In the area of religious affairs, provision was made for the implementation of Islamic law for Muslims. An additional concession was also extended to Aceh's religious leadership through mandating the establishment of an independent council of *ulamas* to provide input into provincial policies.

Desperate to find a solution to the rising tensions in Aceh, the central government and military (TNI) put their support behind the bill. The military — traditionally opposed to Aceh's Islamic demands — did not voice the usual secular nationalist fears that debates over Islamic law had traditionally provoked. On the contrary, the Military/Police parliamentary faction argued that special status had not been "optimally implemented" and called for a "deepening" and "sharpening" of the draft law.[62] Support from such an unexpected quarter reflected the extent to which national leaders were prepared to offer wide-ranging concessions to restive regions following growing fears that the country was unravelling.

A widespread belief emerged within official circles that if Aceh was given the right to implement Islamic law, discontent with Jakarta would fade, eroding GAM's popular base.[63] In debates over Aceh since 1998 central government officials remained strong supporters for Islamic law, tending to view it as the key to resolving the Aceh conflict. Prominent military officers, for instance, publicly supported the implementation of Islamic law in the province as a key initiative in addressing local grievances.[64]

The central government was also supportive of efforts to draft the special autonomy law, discussed in more detail below, which included provision for the establishment of Islamic courts. At the same time, implementation of the special status law resulted in the establishment of an Islamic Law Division (*Dinas Syariat*) within the provincial government with a separate budget and staffing. In June 2001, 180 *ulama* from across the province met to form the *Ulama* Consultative Council or MPU out of the old MUI. While this appeared little more than a name change, the MPU was intended to fulfil the role of being a genuinely independent council of *Ulama* as envisaged under the law. Addressing public scepticism about its formation, the new MPU chairman claimed that it would be "an independent *ulama* institution that sides with the interests of the people and the community of believers, and in carrying out its tasks, is on the same level as the government".[65] Following the establishment of the MPU, Islamic leaders and senior officials declared that the conflict should be resolved through an Islamic (*Islamiyah*) approach in which the MPU would have an important role.[66]

The implementation of Islamic law, however, did not garner the universal support that the government anticipated. The continuing religiosity of the Acehnese meant that few rejected Islamic law. But many local leaders, including some prominent *ulama*, argued that Islamic law had effectively been implemented in the everyday practices of the Acehnese people.[67] Others supported the implementation of Islamic law but only as part of an overall settlement that posited human rights, revenue-sharing and/or independence as more pressing priorities. GAM spokesmen and student leaders went further by suggesting that Islamic law was merely a ruse by Jakarta to stigmatise the province as "fanatical". Perhaps the most common response was to question the seriousness of both the central and provincial governments in implementing Islamic Law. Critics, including religious scholars from the State Islamic University, charged that Islamic Law was the product of a political deal that Jakarta had forged with provincial elites — a deal which had turned Islam into a "political commodity".[68] They claimed that accommodationist *ulama* and officials within the province's religious bureaucracy were pressing for Islamic law because it would provide them with increased government budgets and opportunities for rent seeking.

In light of such ambivalence, it was unsurprising that the offer of Islamic law provided no respite to the escalating conflict in Aceh, reflecting the government's misplaced strategy. In seeing the conflict through the lens of Islam, officials were adopting an anachronistic understanding of the Aceh conflict in terms of the political dynamics of the 1950s when the *ulama* represented the undisputed leaders of the Acehnese people and Islamic law was the core political demand. But the *ulama,* either because they were discredited or politically vulnerable, no longer represented the main advocate for Islamic politics as they had in the 1950s and 1960s. In fact, it was GAM and student groups that used Islamic symbols with the most success following the end of the New Order. As popular rallies were held throughout 1999, spokesmen from student groups such as the *Taliban* recalled the glory days of Iskandar Muda and recited the *Hikayat Perang Sabil.*[69] GAM also made use of Islamic symbolism to recruit throughout the province, mounting a remarkable "*dakwah*" (preaching) campaign that combined religious and political messages in local mosques.[70] The new emerging forces of GAM and the student movement were appealing to two different but equally alienated constituencies, with GAM's support base primarily rural, while the students were concentrated in mainly urban areas. In using Islamic symbols and messages to appeal to these constituencies, however, GAM and mainstream student leaders were making basic ethno-nationalist demands centring on a referendum and independence respectively. They were not pursuing the religious goal of an Islamic state.

The emasculation of the *ulama* as an independent political force in Aceh was underscored by the *ulama*'s aborted attempt to re-engage politically during 1999 and 2000. As with other elements of the civil society, a group of the leading *ulama* took advantage of the new political openness to establish the Association of Traditional Acehnese Ulama or HUDA in 1999 which immediately became active. Much of the impetus to revitalise the political leadership of the *ulama* came from the *Taliban* student group.[71] Community pressure on HUDA to play a more active political role grew as the security situation deteriorated in Aceh throughout 1999. As student agitation and GAM's rapid expansion eventually provoked a repressive response from the security forces, attention turned to the *ulama* with the prospect that they might reassert their claims to local leadership. In response to these expectations, HUDA made a foray into politics. In coalition with student groups, HUDA leaders became the main force behind preparations for the Aceh People's Congress (KRA). This was a major step for the *ulama*, whose inherently conservative nature was translated under the oppressive conditions of the New Order into a kind of political quietism. In an about-face reflecting the ferment of the times, the *ulama* had now thrust themselves into the treacherous politics of mass mobilisation.

They were soon challenged, however, in this new role. As planning for the KRA raised public expectations, the organisers were forced to deny that a declaration of Acehnese independence was being mooted. Opposition to the Congress and to the HUDA's emerging political role originated from several quarters. The provincial government was "highly suspicious" of these efforts according to one of the *ulama* organisers.[72] GAM leaders were also opposed to the event.[73] GAM had been building a strong rural support base and its leaders were not only deeply critical of what they claimed was HUDA's pro-government stance, but saw them as potential rivals for leadership. According to one prominent GAM negotiator, while the *ulama* "have a spiritual role, the Acehnese concept does not posit them with a political role".[74] GAM's attitude toward the *ulama* in fact reflected its broader suspicion of civil society attempting to play an independent role. If GAM saw the *ulama* as unwelcome rivals, many *ulama* also had a deep antipathy towards GAM leaders whom they claimed were stoking up unrealistic expectations in the community that would only result in further suffering of the Acehnese people at the hands of the security forces.

The pressure on HUDA further intensified with opposition to the Congress also coming from the security forces.[75] To make matters worse, splits began to emerge in the student movement — the force that had been instrumental in persuading the *ulama* to play a more active role — with militant groups opposing the KRA. Against a climate of growing intimidation and pressure from all sides, HUDA decided to withdraw from the organising committee of KRA. In the face of the hostility that their re-emergence on the political stage provoked, "the *ulama* from this point on chose to stay quiet and withdrew themselves", as one office-holder of HUDA later recalled.[76] Another HUDA representative explained that the *ulama* were just too exposed: "we only possess religious beliefs while the other sides that oppose us carry guns". Many *ulama*, he explained, lived in remote, isolated communities where they could be intimidated by both sides with impunity. Given their vulnerability in this conflict environment, the *ulama's* withdrawal from the KRA signalled a more general political retreat and dashed hopes that they would once again play a significant public role.

A previous incident that had highlighted the sense of vulnerability of the *ulama* was the massacre of Tgk. Bantaqiah and 56 of his followers by the military in his remote boarding school complex on 23 July 1999.[77] Some of the victims were executed after having received injuries from the initial massacre. The military claimed that Bantaqiah was involved in cultivating marijuana and suspected him of links to GAM, claims that have never been independently verified. The massacre sent shockwaves through Aceh, provoking outrage and fear in equal measure. Bantaqiah had been one of the few *ulama* to remain genuinely independent in Aceh. He had refused to compromise with the New Order and as such stood out as defiantly independent amid the pool of deeply compromised local leaders who had accommodated themselves to power holders in the past. Whatever the motivations for the military to perpetrate such an outrage, the massacre sent a clear signal to the *ulama* that independence carried fatal risks. It also indicated that political engagement was dangerous not just for the *ulama*, but also their followers. The flawed efforts to prosecute the soldiers responsible for the massacre, including the disappearance of the key witness and defendant in the case, only reinforced the *ulama's* sense of vulnerability and the impunity with which they could become targets of violence.

Special Autonomy and the Political Reform Group

The above analysis suggests that the *ulama* were in no position by 2000 to reprise the political leadership role they had played in the past — underlining the misplaced preoccupation the central government had with religious aspects of the conflict. With neither the *ulama* nor the technocrats representing credible local partners, the central government confronted a serious vacuum in local authority that was being exploited by GAM and student leaders. GAM became increasingly active over large swathes of the countryside throughout 1999, while a massive civil protest movement soon emerged in Aceh's main towns, provoking fear from Jakarta's political leaders that the country was disintegrating. For the first time in the contemporary resistance, GAM was linking up with mass elements within civil society. This was a major threat not just to Jakarta but to local business and government elites in Aceh.

As events were threatening to overtake them, a small group of Acehnese agitated the central government to grant the province wide-ranging autonomy. Following a decree in November 1999 on special autonomy from the People's Consultative Assembly (MPR), Indonesia's highest legislative body, local efforts were made to formulate a draft bill. The main impetus for these efforts came from a small group of Acehnese legislators led by National Mandate Party politician Farhan Hamid. This loose coalition of like-minded Acehnese emerged to champion special autonomy, consisting of NGO activists, intellectuals, former officials, businessmen and newly-elected legislators based in Jakarta.

It is difficult to trace the lineage of this group. They are best seen as a somewhat nebulous political force arising from social changes that resulted in the expansion of a middle class during the New Order. Some were in fact from *ulama* families, including Farhan who was the son of an *ulama* prominent during the 1940s. These reformers in fact shared a common understanding with the *ulama* from previous generations that Aceh should hold a special and distinct place in the state and that its autonomy should be protected. On the other hand, the political reformers were educated in the same universities as the technocrats, whom they saw as their seniors. They shared the same rationalist orientation and developmental ideals as the technocrats. But they also represented a reaction to the unaccountable government that had emerged under the technocrats. They wanted to eliminate the centralism that had characterised Jakarta's relations with Aceh and demanded control over natural resources. They also wanted a wholesale reform of governance that would revitalise the local administration. Their goal was to introduce accountability and transparency in policy-making by instituting local democracy. These ideas, classically middle-class, provided the main impetus for the process of drafting the law on special autonomy.

The key elements of the draft produced by the political reform group were local control of Aceh's natural resources, local control over the security forces and provision for direct local elections and local parties. The emphasis on local democracy was based upon the need for a rejuvenation of local government in the territory. According to the reformers, a revitalisation of local government could be achieved by making officials accountable through direct elections. The establishment of a democratic local government was critical not only for ensuring the effective provision of service delivery which had broken down, but for finding a resolution to the escalating conflict in Aceh. Without an effective and accountable local government, they argued, Jakarta could never regain the confidence of the Acehnese and a negotiated settlement could never be implemented. But, as subsequent events were to show, the reformers would remain in a marginal position. Like the technocrats before them, they were largely detached from the rest of Acehnese society and remained relatively powerless without central government patronage.

The other major impetus for drafting special autonomy law came from the provincial DPRD in Banda Aceh, which had become dominated by Islamic parties. The main draft produced by the DPRD included provision for Islamic law and for the establishment of Islamic courts. By September 2000, after sustained consultations, these two separate drafts were consolidated into a single bill that the Acehnese submitted to the DPR for consideration. After months of deliberation, the bill was finally passed in August 2001 as Law 18/2001 on Special Autonomy for *Nanggroe Aceh Darussalam* (NAD). The Law is discussed in more detail in Michelle Miller's contribution to this volume. It included generous revenue sharing arrangements, recognition of local symbols and provision for direct elections of the governor and *bupatis* (district heads). Islamic law remained a key element, although appeals were to be heard by the country's secular Supreme Court. Not surprisingly, in promoting the law, the central government tended to reduce special autonomy to a concession to the Acehnese to implement Islamic law.[78]

Local Government in Crisis

In November 2000, Abdullah Puteh, an Acehnese who had spent many years as a politically connected businessman in Jakarta was elected Governor.[79] Puteh was the Chairperson for a national association of businesses that sent Indonesian guest workers abroad, an industry viewed with some disfavour and plagued by scandals. Puteh had also been Suharto's appointment to the International Labour Organisation. He was a loyal Golkar figure who, like many ambitious politicians under the New Order, held office in the regime's youth organisation, the KNPI and in one of Golkar's main affiliates, MGKRI. Puteh's election as governor reflected a more general pattern across Indonesia. As Michael Malley has shown, the removal or resignation of many New Order officials in the regions following widespread calls for reform did not result in new reformers taking over.[80] On the contrary, it was the next generation of New Order bureaucrats and politically connected businessmen that tended to become the new heads of districts and provinces.

Puteh's tenure as governor was controversial from the very beginning. Even his indirect election by the provincial DPRD (the mechanism for electing governors under new political laws in Indonesia) was plagued by allegations of corruption.[81] Nevertheless, early in his tenure, it seemed that Puteh might build a broadly based government that would invite intellectuals and reformers into the government. He appointed a number of academics from *Unsyiah* as key advisors in the time-honoured tradition of technocrat governments in Aceh.

It was not long, however, before tensions arose between these advisors and Puteh. It quickly became apparent that Puteh was not going to pursue a reformist agenda, with patronage politics becoming the hallmark of his government instead. In response, several well-known advisors, who had also been key figures in drafting the special autonomy law, withdrew from the government.[82] This falling out had a broader significance as it marked an end to the symbiotic relationship between the provincial government and Aceh's state universities. That relationship had provided the ideological ballast for Aceh's governing elite since the 1960s.[83] With this arrangement now ended, the support base for Puteh's administration contracted considerably.

The intellectuals' withdrawal from the Puteh Government resulted in growing opposition centring on a loose coalition of academics, legislators and NGOs with a shared commitment to political reform.[84] A notable development in this coalition was the emergence of several corruption watchdogs in the province, Samak and Sorak which were active in documenting allegations of corruption in the local government and a number of high profile cases. Within the DPRD itself, a small group of likeminded legislators joined forces in what became known as Caucus 21, opposing the DPRD leadership and its alleged collusion with the Puteh Government.[85]

The continuing conflict between GAM and the security forces, however, sheltered the provincial government from public accountability, providing the conditions under which corruption could flourish. The deliberate targeting of civilian non-combatants by both GAM and the security forces, including the high-profile killings of DPRD members and the rectors of Aceh's two major universities, had major implications for local governance. Not only did it narrow the scope of civil society to function independently as a check on abuses of power and corruption within government, but also it meant that reform-minded critics had few avenues to participate in the public debate for fear of becoming targets.

Furthermore, the escalating violence resulted in the emergence of a conflict economy in which key interests that benefited from perpetrating the conflict became increasingly entrenched. While the military and GAM were gaining financially from the conflict, government officials also took advantage of the situation, using the escalating violence as justification for their own non-delivery of services or for their failure to implement development projects. At the same time, special autonomy funds and routine government allocations continued to be disbursed to the province. This combination of the allocation of large revenues to the province, escalating violence and an absence of checks on the government provided the conditions under which corruption became entrenched.

In this conflict economy, the political regime that emerged was kleptocratic in nature; thus, public funds could not be accounted for when a breakdown of public services occurred and development projects were abandoned. While the technocrats had themselves been accused of corruption, they had, in contrast, explicitly tied their legitimacy to performance, particularly to their ability to modernise the province. Under the Puteh administration a series of corruption cases soon emerged while the administration was criticised for inaction to address issues of poverty and development. Several "vanity" projects directly associated with the Governor attracted particularly adverse comment. Critics questioned the introduction of a fast boat service from Banda Aceh to Sabang, the establishment of a provincial airline and the purchase of a helicopter to transport the Governor throughout the province. [86] While the provincial airline eventually went bankrupt and the fast boat project was plagued by accusations of corruption, it was the helicopter purchase that raised the most controversy.[87] The *Far Eastern Economic Review* even aired allegations that the purchase of the helicopter was four times more expensive than market rates.[88] A leading daily newspaper in the region, the *Asian Wall Street Journal* also highlighted widespread corruption within the local government in Aceh.[89] Critics claimed that these projects were designed to divert attention away from the Government's failure to meet basic development needs.

In the first years of office, however, these scandals plagued the Puteh government without engulfing it. The advisors who had withdrawn from the provincial government returned to the campus and NGO work, becoming politically isolated in the process. In fact, the political reform group generally had little influence in either the DPRD or the central government.

The crucial alliance that Puteh forged to counter popular pressure was with the leadership of the DPRD, who resisted repeated demands to call the governor to account for allegations of poor performance and corruption. The DPRD chairman was a veteran PPP politician and his close relations with Puteh were interpreted as reflecting an alliance of

New Order elements to resist demands for reform. The DPRD had the actual power to unseat the Governor by rejecting his accountability report. Rather than using this power to provide effective oversight and improve the quality of governance, however, DPRD members made demands on the executive for their own material benefits. The relationship that developed between the DPRD and the provincial government was described as one of "collusion" by critics.[90] One of the most controversial examples of the alleged collusion between Puteh and the DPRD was the scheme approved by the provincial government in 2003 to provide "free grants" for each DPRD member amounting to around US$8,000 per person. On the timing that suggested a political payoff, the scheme was introduced in the lead-up to Puteh's accountability report to the DPRD.[91] Following a public outcry, the government was forced to reclassify the grants as "emergency credit" to divert public criticism.[92]

These dynamics were not just distinct to Aceh, but were common throughout Indonesia. The proportional electoral system and the lack of consolidation of political parties conspired to subvert the function of democratic accountability that local assemblies were supposed to perform. Central party boards determined the selection of candidates for DPRDs, with voters selecting not candidates but parties. Decades of patrimonial rule had conditioned both voters and party cadres. Becoming a candidate for political office was identified less with its representative function and more with a redistributive one, i.e. in providing access to state resources for their respective supporters. Given these expectations, legislative members had little reason to develop distinct policy or ideological platforms. Unburdened by policy parameters set by the parties and with little downward accountability to voters, DPRD members were free to engage in deal-making with the executive based on their material interests. In Aceh, these trends were exacerbated by the fact that the escalating conflict between GAM and security forces undermined the functioning of an independent civil society and media to provide necessary checks and balances on local government power.

Jakarta's Faltering Alliances

As we have seen above, the failure of special status to quell the escalating violence in Aceh originated from a misplaced emphasis on Islam as the core grievance fuelling the conflict. With the special status initiative having little effect, the government's strategy subsequently turned to adopting special autonomy and dialogue with GAM through international facilitators. This accommodationist strategy came under pressure from within the central government almost as soon as it had been devised.[93] The military and other hardliners wanted to use military force against GAM, whom they accused of using the respite in hostilities to step up the agitation for independence. While the strategy of accommodation was formulated in an *ad hoc* fashion, two interlocking objectives could be discerned: one was that the concessions offered through special autonomy would provide concrete benefits to local communities and thus generate renewed confidence in the state; the other centred on the prospect that the dialogue facilitated by the international NGO, the HDC, would achieve a political settlement between GAM and the government.

This strategy faced some formidable obstacles, however, not least the opposition of powerful interests to negotiating with GAM. For this strategy to be successful, therefore, it would require full support of all levels of the civilian government. But the government's strategy ran into trouble on two fronts: firstly, there was a distinct lack of coordination and support among national government institutions, reflecting the policy struggles taking place; secondly, and of most relevance to the present argument, the local government not only failed to take a leading role in advocating special autonomy and dialogue, but in some cases actively undermined Jakarta's initiatives.

This was clear in the provincial government's foot-dragging on special autonomy, despite strong advocacy from political reformers for timely implementation. While the provincial government and DPRD moved to pass the necessary budget bills, other implementing regulations languished in the DPRD. Throughout 2002, local government bureaus and non-governmental organisations drafted a variety of *qanuns* — as the implementing regulations for special autonomy were known by. Despite mounting criticisms against it, the DPRD failed to review or even schedule a debate for many of the *qanuns*, except the implementation of Islamic law, as discussed above.

The provision most subject to controversy was the direct elections of local government heads, namely the *bupatis* and the governor.[94] The draft *qanun* had been consolidated from bills prepared by two separate civil society coalitions with substantial input from key legislators in the DPRD. But the DPRD leadership refused to review the *qanun*, offering a variety of justifications in an attempt to prolong the process. In particular, direct elections of *bupatis* and the governor would have directly threatened the consensual deal-making that had resulted in old elites retaining power in Aceh, subjecting political candidates to competition from more popular grassroots leaders. It was not until mid-2004, when local elections for district heads were on the verge of being introduced nationally, that the DPRD finally passed the *qanun*.

As implementation of the law stalled, critics condemned the provincial government's performance. In May 2002, two well-known government critics Otto Syamsuddin and Farhan Hamid declared that the province had utterly failed in providing government accountable to the Acehnese.[95] An accompanying editorial in *Serambi Indonesia*, Aceh's major newspaper, appeared with the headline "The Rottenness of the Autonomy Era".[96] These critics highlighted not only the provincial government's failure to implement special autonomy, but also the corruption that had plagued the Puteh administration.

Thus not only had the provincial government hampered the full implementation of special autonomy, it had also misused autonomy funds going to the province intended to assuage local discontent. In fact, the large disbursement of special autonomy funds had few discernible benefits for local communities. The misuse of these funds meant that the development dividend intended to be an outcome of special autonomy failed to materialise. Academics and watchdog groups expressed growing concern that corruption was resulting in a massive misuse of the special autonomy funds.[97] They proposed that a trust fund be set up to manage special autonomy revenue and to set aside a proportion of the revenue for future when conditions allowed development programmes to be properly managed by a more accountable administration.[98] They argued that, under the law, gas and oil revenues were to be phased out starting within eight years, the same timeframe that existing natural gas reserves would be largely depleted. Thus, Aceh had a small window of opportunity to invest the special autonomy funds wisely. But the autonomy funds represented too lucrative a source of funds for the provincial administration, which refused to act upon the academics' advice.

In the face of continuing corruption and escalating conflict, Puteh's opponents in Aceh and Jakarta petitioned the central government to remove him. This pressure intensified as the dialogue process between GAM and the government faltered with the lack of support from the local government in the dialogue process becoming increasingly clear.

The Cessation of Hostilities Agreement (CoHA) had been signed by GAM and the Indonesia Government in December 2002 in a last-ditch effort to find a solution to the conflict (see Fig. 20). The agreement, backed by the international community, sought to put in place a framework for guaranteeing security through a series of confidence-

Fig. 20 Local Aceh (NAD) Government poster on display in Banda Aceh, celebrating the cease-fire agreement (CoHA) of 9 December 2002 (*courtesy Rodd McGibbon*)

building measures. Supporting measures were also planned by the government and donors to improve the humanitarian situation and to launch community development programs throughout the province. This support for "social reconstruction" was intended to deliver a "peace dividend" for Aceh's long-suffering community in order to build public support for resolving the conflict.[99]

Provincial and local governments in Aceh, however, failed to take a leading role in supporting the CoHA. In a visit to the province in early 2003, foreign diplomats who travelled throughout the territory reported a surprising lack of engagement by local officials in the peace process.[100] Local *bupatis* failed to launch significant development initiatives to support the CoHA. Speculation arose that the *bupatis* did not want to be identified with a process that they saw had little chance of success. Meanwhile, representatives of the international NGO facilitating the process complained that the provincial government had done little to provide education on the CoHA or to promote it publicly in other ways.[101]

An even more damning indictment of the Puteh administration emerged with mounting public speculation that local officials had siphoned off funds intended for social reconstruction.[102] In response to deep-seated concerns about the integrity of the local government, the central government established several teams to "supervise" the province, but this achieved little in improving the effectiveness of local government.[103] Yusuf Kalla, the Coordinating Minister for Social Affairs, and Susilo Bambang Yudhoyono, Coordinating Minister for Politics and Security, took the lead in the government's attempts to support dialogue with humanitarian and development initiatives, but soon expressed misgivings over what the provincial government had achieved with the enormous revenues flowing into the province. Kalla and other senior officials made repeated visits to the province to try to reverse the situation as the CoHA was breaking down. Similarly, non-governmental watchdog groups exposed numerous examples of what they called "fictive projects" in which funds had been allocated and spent for programmes that had never been implemented.

Amid these mounting attacks,[104] however, key elements within the central government rejected demands that Puteh be dismissed. The Governor appeared to have support from the powerful Ministry of Home Affairs, his own Golkar faction in the National Parliament and from President Megawati herself. Both the Home Affairs Minister, Hari Sabarno, and Golkar and DPR Chairman, Akbar Tanjung, had publicly put their support behind the embattled governor by dismissing calls for sacking him.[105] Meanwhile, Megawati's failure to act upon demands for Puteh's removal heightened speculation among Acehnese intellectuals that Puteh was being "protected" by Taufik Kiemas, Megawati's powerful husband who had developed a reputation for building a vast array of business contacts in the regions.

In light of these political alliances, Jakarta was essentially supporting elements of the local elite that neither enjoyed legitimacy nor had a commitment to resolving the conflict. There appeared to be a major disconnection between Jakarta's policies on autonomy and dialogue and its support for kleptocratic local elite whose interests were antithetical to these initiatives. This seeming contradiction probably reflected Megawati's own ambivalence regarding special autonomy and dialogue. It certainly demonstrated that Jakarta was opting to govern the province through New Order-style patron-client networks, instead of improving local governance to establish necessary supporting framework for implementing autonomy and dialogue initiatives.

It was hardly surprising, therefore, that within months of the CoHA being signed, the agreement rapidly unravelled. Of course the hardening ideological divisions between GAM and the government were the most direct cause for the deteriorating security position in early 2003.[106] But a major contributing factor was also the local government's lack of commitment to supporting the CoHA and faltering social reconstruction efforts. The weakness of the civilian government reinforced the widespread notion that dialogue must be abandoned in favour of more coercive measures. In May 2003, the government finally announced the imposition of martial law, abandoning the dialogue with GAM altogether.

The adoption of martial law indicated that Jakarta had failed to cultivate local elites with the necessary popular legitimacy to govern the province. In resorting to martial law, Jakarta essentially emasculated any authority wielded by local power-holders. Under the new arrangements, the military had wide-ranging powers: not only could it detain and interrogate people at will, the entire civilian administration was subordinate to the Military Administrator, effectively curtailing the governor's powers.

Political Change, Cataclysmic Events, New Opportunities?

While Puteh initially accommodated himself to the new realities,[107] even the military had realised it required a local administration with at least some credibility to hand power to when martial law was lifted.[108] Thus, during the early months of 2004, the martial law Administrator initiated and became directly involved in summoning high ranking provincial officials and subjecting them to interrogation as corruption suspects. The impunity with which corrupt officials had acted in the past was suddenly challenged. In April, Puteh was officially declared a suspect by the anti-corruption commission, provoking further pressure on Jakarta to remove the governor from office. His position seemed ever more tenuous as the media, apparently encouraged by leaks from the military, raised questions about Puteh's links to GAM.[109]

Backed by presidential patronage, however, Puteh was able to resist growing pressure on him to step down. In her final months as President, Megawati issued an official instruction that lent support to Puteh's efforts to remain in office. A public statement from several prominent *ulama* who criticised NGOs and other reform-minded elements for seeking Puteh's dismissal showed how easily local power-holders could co-opt the *ulama* to buttress their own political position.[110]

But Puteh's fate was sealed by the political defeat of his Jakarta-based patrons and the election of Susilo Bambang Yudhoyono and

Yusuf Kalla as President and Vice-President in the 2004 elections. With a new national leadership now in place, the anti-corruption commission moved to prosecute Puteh during the last quarter of 2004. He was subsequently found guilty of corruption charges by the anti-corruption court and received a ten-year gaol term. The deputy governor, Azwar Abubakar, who had endured strained relations with Puteh and enjoyed a far less tarnished reputation, took over as acting governor. The institution of a new administration in Jakarta with the main proponents for dialogue and negotiations at its helm renewed hope that talks with GAM might re-start.

These and other events were over in December 2004 when an earthquake and tsunami wiped out 10 per cent of Aceh's villages and destroyed many of its urban settlements. Banda Aceh's urban elite was especially devastated by the disaster: in particular the provincial government sustained heavy damages, while many coastal district governments were destroyed altogether.

Confronting destruction on such an enormous scale, the central government immediately welcomed support from foreign militaries and humanitarian workers from across the world. Thousands of ordinary Indonesian citizens also descended upon Aceh in a display of national solidarity not seen since Indonesia's revolutionary war for independence.

Tragic as they were, the cataclysmic events of 26 December held out new possibilities for transforming the situation on the ground in Aceh. Certainly the response from ordinary Indonesians to the tsunami initially created a reservoir of goodwill. The signing of the MOU between the government and GAM involved GAM accepting Indonesian sovereignty in return for amnesties, a reduction in the security forces and other concessions. While the tsunami had an important psychological impact on the antagonists, GAM's battle fatigue and the advent of a new administration in Jakarta were more important factors in the signing of the MOU.

In the early months after the tsunami, central government agencies took a lead role in recovery as provincial and district governments in Aceh were still reeling from the blow dealt them by the tsunami. The Agency for the Rehabilitation and Reconstruction of Aceh and Nias (BRR) was established as a cabinet level agency in mid-2005 to oversee the rebuilding of the province headed by the widely-respected former minister Kuntoro Mangkusubroto. This engagement in Aceh's reconstruction represented a new opportunity for Jakarta not only to restore local confidence in Indonesian rule, but to fashion a new relationship with

development-minded Acehnese officials through assisting local governments to take on increasing responsibilities in this process.

Of course, the opposite also remained a possibility — the large
amounts of funds being distributed for reconstruction were a lucrative
source of rent-seeking and cronyism by both local and national interests.
Claims in the media that local officials and businessmen were involved
in marking up IDP numbers and cutting corners on building barracks
for IDPs was an example of the former.[111] The push by national
conglomerates to influence city planning to win unfair advantages in the
awarding of building contracts an example of the latter.[112]

Arguably the most profound impact of the tsunami was the way it
opened up the province to the international community. Recognising
that it did not have the capacity to address the disaster alone, the
Indonesian government facilitated the entry of foreign military personnel,
humanitarian workers and journalists into Aceh as the world's spotlight
turned to Aceh's plight. This was a dramatic reversal for a province that
had been effectively closed off to foreigners since 2003. In May 2005,
the government further downgraded Aceh's security status, effectively
lifting the repressive restrictions on political expression and freedom of
movement in the province.

It was still unclear what long-term implications the presence of
international aid workers and media (over 350 international NGOs were
registered with the United Nations) would have for the conflict and
transforming the local environment. The "internationalisation" of the
province did not immediately spur separatist demands as Jakarta
feared. Quite the contrary, the deployment of international aid workers
was accompanied by reiterations of support for Indonesian sovereignty.
Furthermore, relief efforts enabled foreign governments and other
international agencies to strengthen their cooperation with the Indonesian
government and to strengthen official channels, including with the
TNI. It was unclear whether such harmonious relations would outlive
the transition from relief to reconstruction and long-term development.
Strains could possibly emerge as development agencies address long-
term issues that may challenge vested interests and press for full access
to Aceh, including in traditional conflict areas.

The one consequence immediately clear after the tsunami, however,
was that presence that so many aid workers and monitors made it
difficult for potential spoilers to go unnoticed, boasting implementation
of the MOU. The other consequence was that international engagement
was accompanied by greater demands for transparency, accountability

and local participation in planning and executing reconstruction. Foreign governments, UN agencies and international NGOs needed to demonstrate to their constituencies that the large public donations committed to Aceh were going to be used transparently. The access of the media to the province increased pressure on local and national authorities to ensure that reconstruction funds would not be used corruptly. The central government, with support from the World Bank and other donors, engaged in a variety of initiatives to establish systems to monitor activities and track financial flows.

Demands for greater accountability are likely to shape not only the reconstruction process but the contest over local leadership in the years to come. Whether internationalisation results in a more credible governing elite with popular legitimacy, however, is altogether unclear. At the very least, the opening up of the province to domestic and international scrutiny has introduced a new dynamic in the struggle for greater transparency and popular participation in Aceh. On the other hand, the large sums of money flowing into Aceh for reconstruction also represent a powerful incentive for vested interests to subvert transparency in decision-making. Likewise, the institution of direct elections for local government heads, including governor and vice-governor, from mid-2006 is a new, and as yet unclear, factor in the contest over local leadership.

Conclusion

In seeking to deepen our understanding of the Aceh conflict, it is necessary to take into account the evolution of local political elites and the ongoing search for credible leadership in the province. Acehnese discontent is not only focused on Jakarta's misrule of the province, but on an unresponsive and unaccountable local government and its failure to guarantee basic rights of its people. "The Aceh conflict", therefore, involves a more complex set of issues than the usual characterisation of it as a simple vertical conflict between centre and region. As this chapter has shown, the conflict is also related to longstanding local political rivalries and mass dissatisfaction with the ruling elite, which adds another layer to our understanding of contemporary Aceh.

In fact, the contemporary conflict can be understood in terms of a longer history in which colonial and post-colonial authorities have sought to integrate Aceh into the state through often troubled relations with segments of the local elite. The dilemma that post-independence

Indonesian leaders have shared with the Dutch before them has been to cultivate a local elite committed to central rule but at the same time able to command support among the fiercely independent Acehnese.

After more than a century of intense struggles and local rivalries, however, this objective remains as elusive as ever. Leadership in Aceh continues to be highly contested: none of the main leadership groups have been able to establish a stable hegemony over local politics. The only elements to do so were the *ulama* in the 1950s. Due to the intervention of the central government, however, the *ulama's* aspirations to local leadership were thwarted by Jakarta's opposition to their Islamic agenda and by its cultivation of a new technocratic elite. While the technocrats proved to be effective local clients for three decades, they ultimately lacked popular legitimacy. As a creation of the New Order they essentially disappeared with the regime that had fostered them. In the post-Suharto era, the escalation of armed conflict and the changing nature of Acehnese society militated against the *ulama* reviving their political role. With the decline of these leadership groups, there has been a vacuum of authority in the province that counter-elite groups such as GAM and the student movement have exploited to encourage resistance against central rule.

In the absence of a credible local elite through which it could govern the province, Jakarta has relied on using coercion and building patronage networks with local clients. This has resulted in human rights abuses, wide-scale corruption and lack of accountability, all of which have deepened Acehnese alienation from the state. In the post-Suharto era, the government's initial attempts to formulate a political solution through key initiatives have largely been eclipsed by a resort to coercion and to patrimonial patterns of political control.

The events of 26 December 2004, however, offered new opportunities to transform the situation on the ground in Aceh. But such an outcome was by no means assured. Certainly, the opening of the province to foreign aid workers and the media introduced a powerful new force for transparency and accountability. Similarly, direct elections for local government heads due in mid-2006 offered the possibility that candidates with popular legitimacy may emerge and lead to the formation of a local administration that supports, rather than impedes, peace efforts. The institution of a new national government under President Yudhoyono and Vice-President Kalla resulted in the best chance for peace since the conflict flared in the mid-1970s with the Helsinki MOU.

But while new political realities in Aceh contain the seeds for change and renewal, many obstacles remain. Reconstruction may offer the possibility of renewing local leadership and promoting accountable government. But the flow of resources into the province has also multiplied the incentives for those who had benefited from a lack of accountability to seek to further entrench themselves. Which scenario becomes reality will be determined by whether reconstruction and the implementation of the Helsinki agreement can address the decades-long search for credible local leadership — a leadership central to resolving the Aceh conflict.

Notes

[1] This chapter is based upon independent research conducted by the author and funded by the United States Institute for Peace. It does not represent the views of any official institution. I would like to acknowledge comments by David DiGiovanna, Greg Fealy and Jamie Davidson on an earlier draft.

[2] G. Robinson, "Rawan is as Rawan Does: The Origins of Disorder in New Order Aceh", *Indonesia*, no. 66 (1998): 127–56. R. Sukma, "The Acehnese Rebellion: Secessionist Movement in Post-Suharto Indonesia", in *Non-Traditional Security Issues in Southeast Asia*, ed. Andrew Tan and Kenneth Boutin (Singapore: Select Publishing, 2001).

[3] Anthony Reid, *The Blood of the People: Revolution and the End of Traditional Rule in Northern Sumatra* (Kuala Lumpur: Oxford University Press, 1979), p. 15.

[4] E. Morris, "Aceh: Social Revolution and the Islamic Vision", in *Regional Dynamics of the Indonesian Revolution: Unity from Diversity*, ed. Audrey Kahin (Honolulu: University of Hawaii Press, 1985).

[5] Kaoy Syah and Lukman Hakiem, *Keistimewaan Aceh Dalam Lintasan Sejarah: Proses Pembentukan UU No. 44/1999* (Jakarta: Pengurus Besar Al-Jami'iyatul Washliyah, 2000), pp. 33–6.

[6] Eric E. Morris, *Islam and Politics in Aceh: A Study of Center-Periphery Relations in Indonesia* (PhD thesis, Cornell University, 1983), pp. 273, 276.

[7] Ibid., p. 249.

[8] The role of the universities, both University of Syiah Kuala and the State Islamic University in developing a new class of intellectuals, which countered the influence of the *ulama*, is examined in Alfian, "The Ulama in Acehnese Society: A Preliminary Observation", *Kertas Karya* (Working Paper) No. 7 (Banda Aceh, Aceh Darussalam: Pusat Latihan Penelitian Ilmu-Ilmu Sosial Aceh, 1975).

[9] Ibrahim Hasan, *Namaku Ibrahim Hasan: Menebah Tangtangan Zaman* (Jakarta: Yayasan Malem Putra, 2003).

[10] Ibid., p. 130.

[11] Morris, *Islam and Politics in Aceh*.

12 Hasan, *Namaku Ibrahim Hasan*, p. 194. These business interests were seeking new economic opportunities that required accommodating themselves to the new regime in Jakarta. They probably saw the technocrats as the best way to defend their commercial interests while promoting a stable government in Aceh that had common goals with the new regime. Some of these businessmen were from old *ulèëbalang* families who had resettled in Jakarta and Medan following the social revolution in Aceh. (Interview with Kaoy Syah Banda Aceh, 5 July 2002.)

13 Hasan was an assistant at the University of Indonesia for the prominent economist and later minister Muhammad Sadli in 1960, while a previous governor Madjid Ibrahim had a close relationship with the most senior economic policy-maker in Indonesia, Widjojo Nitisastro.

14 Hasan, *Namaku Ibrahim Hasan*, for instance, describes how Bustanil persuaded Suharto against appointing non-Acehnese to the governorship following strong pressure from the military and its commander Benny Moerdani.

15 Cited in Morris, *Islam and Politics in Aceh*.

16 *Pancasila*, a Sanskrit compound formulated by Sukarno to denote the five principles, was the state ideology that was subsequently promoted by Suharto. The five principles related to: belief in one god; mutual help; the unity of Indonesia; democracy through consensus and consultation; and social justice for all.

17 The Islamic parties were forced to amalgamate into the United Development Party (PPP) while the secular nationalist and Christian parties were forced to join the Indonesian Democracy Party or PDI.

18 To ensure Golkar's electoral victory, all government officials were bound by the principle of "mono-loyalty" to Golkar. The bureaucrats who ran the election were also tasked with securing a victory for the Golkar party, which enjoyed the benefits of government facilities and organisation to campaign.

19 Morris, *Islam and Politics in Aceh*, p. 286.

20 The formulation Ibrahim Hasan used in defining his main policy objective was to "to break the pattern of Aceh's isolation" (Hasan, *Namaku Ibrahim Hasan,* p. 255). See also Morris, *Islam and Politics in Aceh*, p. 261.

21 Dayan Dawood and Sjafrizal, "Aceh: The LNG Boom and Enclave Development", in *Unity and Diversity: Regional Economic Development in Indonesia since 1970,* ed. Hal Hill (Singapore: Oxford University Press, 1989).

22 Ibid.

23 Hasan, *Namaku Ibrahim Hasan*, p. 448.

24 Ibid., p. 176.

25 Ibid.

26 Ibid., pp. 217–28.

27 Not only was Hasan rewarded with another term in office, many of the *bupatis* who ensured Golkar's victory in traditionally PPP areas also had

their terms extended. In the previous elections, the Golkar's win in 1987 was also rewarded by the central government by increasing the province's development budget by 750 per cent. Hasan, *Namaku Ibrahim Hasan*, p. 287.

[28] An analysis that emphasises the isolation of the technocrats from mainstream Acehnese society and the strong rural support base of the *ulama* is S. Schlegel, "Technocrats in a Muslim Society: Symbolic Community in Aceh", in *What is Modern Indonesian Culture*, ed. Gloria Davis, Southeast Asia Series No. 52 (Madison, Wisconsin: Centre for International Studies, Ohio University, 1979). The latter is also a strong theme in Alfian, "The Ulama in Acehnese Society".

[29] Hall Hill, ed., *Unity and Diversity: Regional Economic Development in Indonesia since 1970* (Singapore: Oxford University Press, 1989), pp. 108–10.

[30] See analyses in Hall Hill, ed., *Indonesia's New Order: The Dynamics of Socio-Economic Transformation* (Sydney: Allen and Unwin, 1994). Christine Drake, *National Integration in Indonesia: Patterns and Policies* (Honolulu: University of Hawaii Press, 1989).

[31] Hasan, *Namaku Ibrahim Hasan*, p. 255.

[32] Amnesty International, *'Shock Therapy' Restoring Order in Aceh, 1989–1993* (London: Amnesty International, 1993).

[33] T. Kell, *The Roots of the Acehnese Rebellion 1989–1992* (Ithaca, New York: Cornell Modern Indonesian Project, 1995), p. 16.

[34] *Tempo*, 10 December 2000. Kell, *The Roots of the Acehnese Rebellion 1989–1992*, p. 17.

[35] Dawood and Sjafrizal, "Aceh: The LNG Boom and Enclave Development".

[36] Kell, *The Roots of the Acehnese Rebellion 1989–1992*, p. 22.

[37] Ibid., p. 25. The population in districts that had launched major new industrial projects increased by 50 per cent during the years 1974–87. In three sub-districts closest to the production areas, there was a 300 per cent population increase during the same period. In 1992, almost one quarter of the population of Aceh lived in the Industrial Zone. *Tempo*, 10 December 2000.

[38] Kell, *The Roots of the Acehnese Rebellion 1989–1992*, p. 27. Ibrahim Hasan himself conceded that the Acehnese had not enjoyed the gas revenues they were entitled to. He claimed that in 1993 the central government transferred revenues to Aceh totalling Rp 500 billion to Aceh, amounting to less than 10 per cent of total value of Acehnese exports at around US$26 million. Hasan, *Namaku Ibrahim Hasan*, p. 286.

[39] Kell, *The Roots of the Acehnese Rebellion 1989–1992*, p. 60.

[40] Hasan himself concedes that there was "a group that had a real phobia about Golkar's political organisation which was equated with introducing secularist tendencies in the veranda of Mecca". Hasan, *Namaku Ibrahim Hasan*, p. 256.

[41]   Morris, *Islam and Politics in Aceh,* p. 267.

[42]   For sympathetic portraits of Tgk. Bantaqiah incident, see Dyah Rahmany P., *Matinya Bantaqiah: Menguak Tragedi Beoutong Ateuh* (Cordova, Banda Aceh: Institute for Civil Society Empowerment, 2001). Amran Zamzami, *Tragedi Anak Bangsa: Pembantaian Teungku Bantaqiah dan Santri-Santrinya* (Jakarta: PT. Bina Rena Pariwara, 2001).

[43]   Hasan, *Namaku Ibrahim Hasan,* pp. 153–5. The technocrats were particularly subject to criticism over what some *ulama* claimed was the rise in *maksiat* (sinful) practices in the province. Some *ulamas* claimed that the rapid urbanisation and industrialisation promoted by the technocrats had resulted in a rise in gambling and prostitution. For these *ulama,* the provincial government's permissive attitude was evidence of a lack of moral and ethical leadership in the province.

[44]   Kell, *The Roots of the Acehnese Rebellion 1989–1992,* p. 56.

[45]   Ibid., p. 45.

[46]   Ibid., p. 48.

[47]   According to Kaoy Syah the transformation in the political attitudes of the *ulama* can be traced back to when PUSA took power and moved into politics in the 1950s, essentially vacating the educational field to the more traditional and conservative *ulama.* As a result the *madrasahs,* which had been the wellspring of reformist energy, did not flourish as they had before. Interview with Kaoy Syah, Banda Aceh.

[48]   Morris, *Islam and Politics in Aceh,* p. 284.

[49]   Kell, *The Roots of the Acehnese Rebellion 1989–1992,* p. 48.

[50]   The government provided loyal *ulama* with support to their *Dayah* and to carry out *haji* visits in return for their support during the elections in 1987. See Hasan, *Namaku Ibrahim Hasan,* p. 280.

[51]   Kell, *The Roots of the Acehnese Rebellion 1989–1992,* p. 48.

[52]   While PPP activist Kaoy Syah and Lukman Hakiem are not the most objective in commenting on the technocrats' performance, they have mounted a powerful critique against Syamsuddin's term as governor. To illustrate their point they show how three of the declared objectives of the Syamsuddin administration ended in failure: namely the building of a railway along the north and east coast, which was not finished, the return of Sabang's Freeport status, which was only designated as "integrated economic area" (*Kapet*); and finally, on special status initiatives, all Syamsuddin had to show for his efforts was the establishment of a model general high school in Aceh. Kaoy Syah and Lukman Hakiem, *Keistimewaan Aceh Dalam Lintasan Sejarah,* p. 51.

[53]   Sayed Mudhahar Hamid Al-Chaidar and Yarmen Dinamika, *Aceh Bersimbah Darah: Menungkap Status Daerah Operasi Militer di Aceh 1989–1998* (Jakarta: Pustaka Al-Kaustar, 1999).

[54]   Ibid. See also H.M. Kaoy Syah and Lukman Hakiem, *Keistimewaan Aceh*

Dalam Lintasan Sejarah. Hasan's refutation of these claims is in Hasan, *Namaku Ibrahim Hasan.*

55   Hasan, *Namaku Ibrahim Hasan,* p. 442.

56   Kell, *The Roots of the Acehnese Rebellion 1989–1992,* p. 37.

57   Reports suggested that Abdurrahman had been angered by Syamsuddin's lacklustre performance as governor, while others cited his opposition to the *ulama* who had been unable to obtain provincial approval to organise political activities.

58   Interview with Muhammad Nazar, Chairman of Presidium Council for Aceh Referendum Centre (SIRA), Banda Aceh, 17 December 2002.

59   Sulaiman, *Aceh Merdeka: Ideologi, Kepemimpinan dan Gerakan* (Jakarta: Pustaka al Kausar, 2000).

60   Kaoy Syah and Hakiem, *Keistimewaan Aceh Dalam Lintasan Sejarah,* p. 56.

61   Ismail Metareum. "Kata Pengantar: Pelaksanaan Hukum Islam untuk Peningkatan Kemaslahatan Masyarakat dan Kejayaan Islam", in *Keistimewaan Aceh Dalam Lintasan Sejarah,* ed. Kaoy Syah and Hakiem (Jakarta: Pengurus Besar Al-Jami'iyatul Washliyah, 2000).

62   ABRI Faction, "ABRI Dukung Penuh" [Final Response of the Military faction in the Indonesian National Parliament to the bill on Special Status for Aceh], in Kaoy Syah and Lukman Hakiem, *Keistimewaan Aceh Dalam Lintasan Sejarah,* p. 83.

63   Interview with a senior official from the Ministry of Home Affairs, Jakarta, 3 October 2003.

64   Military officers have for the last several years at least been prominent advocates for Islamic law to be applied in Aceh. See books written by former Chief of Staff of the Aceh Military Command, Syarifudin Tippe, *El-Hurr: Nurani untuk Aceh* (Jakarta: Yayasan Ulul Arham, 2001); and Syarifudin Tippe, *Aceh di Persimpangan Jalan* (Jakarta: Pustaka Cidesindo, 2000). Recently the head of the North Aceh Military Command publicly supported a greater effort for implementing Islamic law. See *Serambi Indonesia,* 4 May 2004.

65   *Waspada,* 28 June 2001.

66   See comments by Muhammadiyah Chairman Imam Syuda' and caretaker governor Ramli Ridwan in *Serambi Indonesia,* 29 June 2000.

67   Interview, Banda Aceh, 10 April 2003.

68   Interview with Acehnese Muslim intellectuals, in Banda Aceh, 12 April 2003 and Jakarta, 28 July 2004.

69   E. Aspinall, "Whither Aceh", *Inside Indonesia,* no. 62 (April–June 2000).

70   Interview with the Acehnese sociologist and activist Otto Syamsuddin who witnessed this campaign in several villages, Jakarta, 26 June 2002.

71   Interview with office-holders in HUDA, Banda Aceh, 5 February 2002.

72   Interview, Banda Aceh, 2002.

73 Syamsuddin was opposed to the *ulama* and reportedly refused to provide government approval to HUDA to organise political events.

74 Interview with Tk. Kamarruzaman, Banda Aceh, 10 April 2003.

75 Interview, Banda Aceh, 5 February 2002.

76 Ibid.

77 For carefully documented accounts of the incident See Dyah Rahmany P., *Matinya Bantaqiah*; and Amran Zamzami, *Tragedi Anak Bangsa*.

78 One curious omission in either the draft or the final law was reference to human rights. A provision had in fact appeared in some of the earliest drafts but this merely invoked language from the Universal Declaration of Human Rights. In later drafts even this provision was omitted. This was a curious omission considering that some advocates of special autonomy have also previously been well known for their criticisms of the military's human rights record. In the face of this gap, it was difficult not to conclude that the reformist elite promoting the bill were chiefly preoccupied with self-government of which they would be the main beneficiaries. But, in failing to address human rights, supporters of the law were providing at best only a partial answer to resolving the Aceh conflict. In the absence of human rights grievances being addressed in some way, it was difficult to see how the conflict in Aceh could be resolved and popular discontent with Jakarta blunted.

79 For a profile of Abdullah Puteh, see "Daftar Hitam buat Puteh", *Forum Keadilan*, no. 24, 26 November 2001. See also a copy of his curriculum vitae on the provincial government website <http://www.nad.go.id/biodata/eksekutif/gub.html> [3 October 2004].

80 M. Malley, "New Rules, Old Structures and the Limits of Democratic Decentralisation", in *Local Power and Politics in Indonesia: Decentralisation and Democratisation,* ed. Edward Aspinall and Greg Fealy (Singapore: Institute of Southeast Asian Studies, 2003).

81 In an interview with the new governor, the magazine *Tempo* (27 August–2 September 2002) questioned him about accusations that he "bought his way" into the governorship. The former businessmen responded by saying that "I don't have anything with which to pay members and they can't be brought", referring to DPRD members who were being accused publicly of large-scale corruption.

82 The falling out with Puteh was reportedly triggered by his visit to China at the same time that peace negotiations had reached a critical period. Tensions had been growing between Puteh and his advisors over the latter's plans to establish state companies operated by the provincial government. The advisors were opposed to the idea on the basis that corruption and rent-seeking would result. One even criticised the Governor's purchase of the helicopter in public, further straining relations. Interview, Banda Aceh, 5 July 2002.

83 This is not to say that there was a complete rupture between the provincial government and the universities. In fact, there was still significant exchange and the government still used academics for expert advice. But the symbiotic relationship between university and government had now ended, with academics no longer being the main recruiting ground for the government and not enjoying the privileged access they once had. The ending of this relationship has also been reinforced by a growing coalition between younger academics and the new reform movement.

84 The conflict between the government and its critics in fact escalated over time. By late 2003, the South Jakarta district court had ruled for Puteh in a libel suit he had launched against Farhan Hamid, the main advocate for special autonomy. See "Gugat Abdullah Puteh Dikabulkan", *Tempo Interaktif*, 16 December 2003.

85 The driving force behind this group was M. Nasir Djamil, who became the most popular and well-known government critic among the political reformers.

86 The DPRD commission handling the case of the purchase of the speed boat estimated that the mark-up totalled Rp 6 billion or about US$700,000. *Serambi Indonesia*, 25 January 2003.

87 Even the *bupati* of West Aceh publicly criticised the helicopter purchase "Bupati Pertanyakan Pengadaan Heli NAD". *Serambi*, Rabu, 28 August 2002.

88 *Far Eastern Economic Review*, 9 October 2003, p. 20.

89 *Asian Wall Street Journal*, Mapes 2003.

90 Interview with J. Kamal Farza, Jakarta, 7 August 2003.

91 For a summary of this controversy see *Kontras*, no. 243, 28 May 2003.

92 A dissenting member of the provincial assembly, M. Nasir Djamil, rejected the "grant", claiming DPRD had "no right to accept the money". *Serambi Indonesia*, 7 April 2003.

93 I have addressed this in more detail in *Secessionist Challenges in Aceh and Papua: Is Special Autonomy the Solution?* East-West Centre Policy Studies Series No. 10 (Washington DC: East West Centre, 2004).

94 An excellent summary of the process can be found in "AKU Kalahkan Qanun Pilsung", *Kontras*, no. 227 (29 January–4 February 2003).

95 *Serambi Indonesia*, 29 May 2002. These criticisms only intensified. In a later missive Farhan Hamid made a scathing attack on Puteh, claiming that "corruption had become the new style in Aceh". "Korupsi, 'Jalan Hidup Baru' di Aceh", *Gatra*, 6 March 2003.

96 *Serambi Indonesia*, 29 May 2002.

97 See for instance, J. Kamal Farza, "Catatan Akhir Tahun Samak: 2002, Tahun Korupsi Aceh", *Kontras*, no. 223 (1–7 January 2003).

98 The issue was discussed in some detail at a workshop that brought together key advocates of special autonomy in Aceh and Papua. *Denpasar,* 21 May 2002.

99 This approach was outlined in the World Bank, "Promoting Peaceful Development in Aceh: An Informal Background Paper", prepared for the Preparatory Conference on Peace and Reconstruction in Aceh (Tokyo: The World Bank, 2002).

100 Confidential communication with the author, Jakarta, 13 March 2003.

101 Interview with HDC representative, Jakarta, 15 July 2003. For criticisms from local reformers towards the government's failure in promoting the CoHA see "Socialisasi COHA Bersama-sama", *Serambi Indonesia,* 17 April 2003.

102 See for instance "Proyek Kemanusiaan yang Keropos", *Koran Tempo,* 11 February 2003.

103 In the lead up to planning for martial law, for instance, Yusuf Kalla set up a team to monitor all humanitarian funds going to Aceh. "Awasi Penyaluran Dana Kemanusiaan Aceh", *Kompas,* 13 May 2003.

104 See for instance "Korupsi di Aceh, Penduduk Miskin Meningkat", *Sinar Harapan,* 31 March 2003.

105 They claimed that Jakarta did not have the authority to replace the governor except in the case of proven criminality. "Usul Pencopotan Gubernur NAD Tak Relevan", *Suara Karya,* 27 April 2003.

106 E. Aspinall and H. Crouch, *The Aceh Peace Process: Why it Failed.* East-West Centre Policy Studies Series No. 1(Washington D.C.: East West Centre, 2004).

107 Even before the cessation of hostilities agreement was signed, Puteh told *Tempo Magazine* (27 August–2 September 2002) "if the goal from the outset is to protect the public, the more troops the better". As Martial Law was being implemented, Puteh put his support behind military attempts to purge the local bureaucracy of alleged "GAM elements". *Serambi,* 10 June 2003.

108 Speculation that the military's opposition to Puteh may have also been related to the visit of the government's Monitoring Team in March 2004. The Monitoring Team met with a range of stakeholders and issued public statements that substantial funds already allocated to the province from the central government could not be accounted for. In response Puteh claimed that provincial authorities had been allocated only 6.6 trillion, with the remaining funds going to agencies outside of his control. Puteh's statement essentially implicated the security forces and other national agencies in the TMT's investigation that found unaccountable expenditures of budget funds for Aceh.

109 These links are examined in "TNI Selidiki Kaitan Puteh dan GAM", *Tempo Interaktif,* 7 September 2004.

110 "50 Ulama Minta Penangguhan Penahanan Puteh", *Suara Merdeka*, 5 February 2005.

111 "Ada Indikasi Korupsi Pembangunan Barak", *Kompas*, 26 February 2005.

112 "Cetak Biru Meulaboh Akan Diserahkan ke Artha Graha", *Kompas*, 28 January 2005.

Bibliography

Books and Journal Articles

Abduh. *Djihad*. Bandung: Penerbit Peladjar, 1968.

Abdurrauf, T.S. *Mir'at At-Tullab*. Banda Atjeh: Universitas Sjiah Kuala, 1971.

Abraham, Meera. *Two Tamil Merchant Guilds of South India*. New Delhi: Manohar, 1988.

ABRI Faction. "ABRI Dukung Penuh" [Final Response of the Military faction in the Indonesian National Parliament to the bill on Special Status for Aceh] in *Keistimewaan Aceh Dalam Lintasan Sejarah: Proses Pembentukan UU No. 44/ 1999*, ed. Kaoy Syah and Lukman Hakiem. Jakarta: Pengurus Besar Al-Jami'iyatul Washliyah, 2000.

Aceh Dalam Angka Seri 1985–1996. Banda Aceh: Kerjasama Kantor Statistik dengan Bappeda Prop. DI Aceh, 1996.

Al-Attas, S.M. Naguib. *Some Aspects of Sufism as Understood and Practised among the Malays*. Singapore: Malaysian Sociological Research Institute, 1963.

————. *The Oldest Known Malay Manuscript: A 16th Century Malay Translation of the 'Aqa'id of al-Nasafi*. Kuala Lumpur: University of Malaya, 1988.

Al-Chaidar, Sayed Mudhahar Hamid and Yarmen Dinamika. *Aceh Bersimbah Darah: Menungkap Status Daerah Operasi Militer di Aceh 1989–1998* [Aceh Bathed in Blood: Considering the Status of the Aceh DOM, 1989–98]. 4th edition. Jakarta: Pustaka Al-Kaustar, 1999.

Alfian, Teuku Ibrahim. "The Ulama in Acehnese Society: A Preliminary Observation", *Kertas Karya* No. 7 (Working Paper No. 7). Pusat Latihan Penelitian Ilmu–Ilmu Sosial Aceh, Aceh Darussalam, Banda Aceh, 1975.

————. *Perang di Jalan Allah: Aceh 1873–1912* [War in the Way of God]. Jakarta: Pustaka Sinar Harapan, 1987.

————. *Wajah Aceh dalam Lintasan Sejarah* [The Face of Aceh in the Eye of History]. Banda Aceh: The Documentation and Information Center of Acheh, 1999.

————, *et al.* ed. *The Dutch Colonial War in Acheh*. Third edition. Banda Aceh: The Documentation and Information Center of Acheh, 1999.

Ali Haji ibn Ahmad, Raja. *Tuhfat al-Nafis* [The Precious Gift], trans. V. Matheson and B.W. Andaya. Kuala Lumpur: Oxford University Press, 1982.

Amirul Hadi. *Islam and State in Sumatra: A Study of Seventeenth-Century Aceh*. Leiden: Brill, 2004.

Amnesty International. *'Shock Therapy' Restoring Order in Aceh, 1989–1993*. London, 1993.

_____. *Briefing on the Current Human Rights Situation in Indonesia*. 21 January 2001.

_____. *Briefing on the Deteriorating Human Rights Situation in Aceh for Participants in the ASEAN Regional Forum*. July 2001.

Anderson, John. *Acheen and the Ports on the North and East Coasts of Sumatra*. Kuala Lumpur: Oxford in Asia Historical Reprints, 1970.

Arasaratnam, S. *Merchants, Companies and Commerce on the Coromandel Coast 1650–1740*. Delhi: Oxford University Press, 1986.

Ardika, I.W. and Peter Bellwood. "Sembiran: The Beginnings of Indian Contact with Bali", *Antiquity* 65, 247 (1985): 221–32.

Arif, Abdullah. *Disekitar Peristiwa Pengchianat Tjoembok* (Kutaradja, 1946), translated by Anthony Reid as "The Affair of the Tjoembok Traitors", *Review of Indonesian and Malayan Affairs* 4/5 (1970–71): 36–57.

Aspinall, Edward. "Whither Aceh", *Inside Indonesia* 62 (April–June 2000).

_____. "Modernity, History and Ethnicity: Indonesian and Acehnese Nationalism in Conflict", *Review of Indonesian and Malaysian Affairs (RIMA)* 36, 1 (2002): 3–33.

_____. "Modernity, History and Ethnicity: Indonesian and Acehnese Nationalism in Conflict", in *Autonomy and Disintegration in Indonesia*, ed. Damien Kingsbury and Harry Aveling. New York; London: RoutledgeCurzon, 2003, pp. 128–47.

_____. "Sovereignty, the Successor State and Universal Human Rights: History and the International Structuring of Acehnese Nationalism", *Indonesia* 73 (April 2002): 1–24.

_____. "History and Separatism in Aceh: Ethnic Atavism Versus Civic Voluntarism?", in *Political Fragmentation in Southeast Asia: Alternative nations in the Making*, ed. Vivienne Wee. Hong Kong: Routledge, 2004.

Aspinall, Edward, and Mark T. Berger, "The Break-up of Indonesia? Nationalism and the Contradictions of Modernity in Post-Cold War Southeast Asia", *Third World Quarterly: Journal of Emerging Areas* 22, no. 6 (2001): 1003–24.

Aspinall, Edward, and H. Crouch. *The Aceh Peace Process: Why it Failed*. Policy Studies, No. 1. Washington DC: East West Center, 2003.

Asshidiqie, Jimly, Erman Radjagukguk, Ahmad Watik Pratiknya and Umar Juoro. *Reform in Indonesia: Vision and Achievements of B.J. Habibie. Volume 2. Legal and Socio-Culture*. Jakarta: PT Raja Grafindo Persada, 1999.

Azra, Azyumardi. *The Transmission of Islamic Reformism to Indonesia: Networks of Middle Eastern and Malay-Indonesian 'Ulama' in the Seventeenth and Eighteenth Centuries*. Australia: Allen & Unwin for Asian Studies Association of Australia, 2002.

Bantasyam, Saifuddin. "Peran Media dalam Proses Damai di Aceh" [The Role of the Media in the Aceh Peace Process], paper presented in International Seminar on

Conflict and Media Analysis and Conflict De-escalating Radio Programming in Indonesia organized by Conflict Studies Network, UNESCO Local Radio Network, International Media Support and Finnish Embassy at Parahyangan Catholic University Bandung 6–14 April 2003.

Barber, Richard, ed. *Aceh: The Untold Story.* Bangkok: Asian Forum for Human Rights and Development, 2000.

Barros, João de *Da Asia.* Lisbon 1773, reprinted Lisbon: Sam Carlos, 1973.

Barter, Shane. *Neither Wolf, nor Lamb: Embracing Civil Society in the Aceh Conflict.* Bangkok: Forum-Asia, 2004.

Bastin, John. "The Changing Balance of the Early Southeast Asian Pepper Trade", *Papers on Southeast Asian Subjects* No. 1. Kuala Lumpur: Department of History, University of Malaya, 1960.

Baylis, John, James Wirtz, Elliot Cohen and Colin S. Gray. *Strategy in the Contemporary World: An Introduction to Strategic Studies.* Oxford: Oxford University Press, 2002.

Bellin, Eva. "Contingent Democrats: Industrialists, Labor and Democratization in Late-Developing Countries", *World Politics* 52 (January 2000): 175–205.

_____. *Stalled Democracy: Capital, Labor, and the Paradox of State-Sponsored Development.* Ithaca and London: Cornell University Press, 2002.

Bennett, George. *Wanderings in New South Wales, Batavia, Pedir Coast, Singapore and China.* 2 vols. London: Richard Bentley, 1834.

Berkeley, Bill. *The Graves are Not yet Full: Race, Tribe, and Power in the Heart of Africa.* New York: Basic Books, 2001.

Bertrand, Jacques. *Nationalism and Ethnic Conflict in Indonesia.* Cambridge: Cambridge University Press, 2004.

Bodemar, Staffan. "Conflict in Aceh, Indonesia: Background, Current Situation and Future Prospects", Unpublished Paper, March 2004.

Booth, Anne. "Can Indonesia Survive as a Unitary State?", *Indonesia Circle* 58 (1992): 15–41.

Bouchon, Geneviève. "Les premiers voyages portugais à Pasai et à Pegou (1512–1520)", *Archipel* 18 (1979) : 127–57.

Bowen, John R. *Sumatran Politics and Poetics: Gayo History, 1900–1989.* New Haven: Yale University Press, 1991.

_____. *Muslims through Discourse: Religion and Ritual in Gayo Society.* Princeton: Princeton University Press, 1993.

Boxer, C.R. "The Acehnese Attack on Malacca in 1629, as Described in Contemporary Portuguese Sources", in *Malayan and Indonesian Studies: Essays Presented to Sir Richard Winstedt on His Eighty-fifth Birthday*, ed. J. Bastin and R. Roolvink. Oxford: Clarendon Press, 1964.

_____. "A Note on Portuguese Reactions to the Revival of the Red Sea Spice Trade and the Rise of Aceh, 1540–1600," *JSEAH* 10, no. 3 (1969).

Brakel, L.F. "State and Statecraft in 17th Century Aceh", in *Pre-colonial State Systems in Southeast Asia: the Malay Peninsula, Sumatra, Bali-Lombok, South*

Celebes. Monographs of the Malaysian Branch of the Royal Asiatic Society No. 6, ed. Anthony Reid and Lance Castles. Kuala Lumpur: MBRAS, 1975, pp. 56–66.

Bronson, Ben, M.Suhadi Basoeki and J. Wisseman. *Laporan Penelitian Arkeologi di Sumatra.* Jakarta: Pusat Penelitian Arkeologi Nasional, 1977.

Brown, C.C., trans. "Sejarah Melayu or 'Malay Annals'", *JMBRAS* 25, no. 2/3 (1952).

Bulbeck, David. "Indigenous Traditions and Exogenous Influences in the Early History of Peninsular Malaysia", in *Southeast Asia from Prehistory to History,* ed. Ian Glover and Peter Bellwood. London and New York: Routledge Curzon, 2004, pp. 314–36.

Bulbeck, David, Anthony Reid, Tan Lay Cheng and Wu Yiqi. *Southeast Asian Exports since the 14th Century: Cloves, Pepper, Coffee and Sugar.* Singapore: Institute of Southeast Asian Studies, 1998.

Christie, Clive J. *A Modern History of Southeast Asia: Decolonization, Nationalism and Separatism.* London: Tauris Academic Studies, 1996.

Christie, Jan Wisseman. "The Medieval Tamil-language Inscriptions in Southeast Asia and China", *Journal of Southeast Asian Studies* 2 (1998): 239–68.

Clapham, Christopher, ed. *African Guerrillas.* Bloomington: Indiana University Press, 1998.

Collins, James. "Chamic, Malay and Acehnese: The Malay World and the Malayic Languages", in *Le Campa et le Monde Malais. Actes de la conference Internationale surle Campa et le Monde Malais.* Kuala Lumpur: Nur Niaga, 1991.

Colmey, J. and D. Liebhold, "Suharto, Inc", *Time,* 24 May 1999.

Conboy, Ken. *Kopassus: Inside Indonesia's Special Forces.* Jakarta: Equinox Publishing, 2003.

Cowan, H.K.J. *De "Hikajat Malem Dagang".* The Hague: 1937.

_____. "Acehnese Dialects in Connection with Chamic Migrations", in *VICAL 2: Western Austronesian and Contact Languages: Papers of the Fifth Congress on Austronesian Linguistics,* part I, ed. Ray Harlow. Auckland: Linguistics Society of New Zealand, 1991.

Crone, D. "Military Regimes in Indonesia and Thailand", in *Civil Military Interaction in Asia and Africa,* ed. Charles Kennedy and David Louscher. Leiden; New York: E.J. Brill, 1991.

Croo, M.H. due. *De Maréchaussée in Atjeh.* Maastricht: Leiter Nypels, 1943.

Dampier, William. *Voyages and Discoveries,* ed. C. Wilkinson. London: Argonaut Press, 1931.

Davies, M. Unpublished open source intelligence assessment of TNI and Polri troop numbers in Aceh, August 2003.

Dawood, Dayan and Sjafrizal. "Aceh: The LNG Boom and Enclave Development", in *Unity and Diversity: Regional Economic Development in Indonesia since 1970,* ed. Hal Hill. Singapore: Oxford University Press, 1989.

Das Gupta, Arun. "Aceh in Indonesian Trade and Politics: 1600–1641". PhD dissertation, Cornell University, 1962.

Dijk, Cees van. *Rebellion under the Banner of Islam: the Darul Islam in Indonesia.* The Hague: Martinus Nijhoff, 1981.

Djajadiningrat, H. "Critisch Overzicht Van de in Maleische Werken vervatte gegevens over de Geschiedenis van het Soeltanaat Van Atjeh" [Critical Review of the Data in Malay Works about the History of the Sultanate of Aceh], *BKI* 65 (1911): 135–265.

Djamil, Joenoes. *Riwajat Barisan F (Fudjiwara Kikan) di Atjeh.* 1943; reissued in Banda Aceh: Diperbanyak oleh Pusat Latihan Penelitian Ilmu-Ilmu Sosial, Aceh, 1975.

Down To Earth. "Timor-Timur: Peluang basi masa depan berkelanjutan", *Down to Earth* No. 42, August 1999.

Drakard, Jane. *A Kingdom of Words: Language and Power in Sumatra.* Kuala Lumpur: Oxford University Press, 1999.

Drake, Christine. *National Integration in Indonesia: Patterns and Policies.* Honolulu: University of Hawaii Press, 1989.

Drewes, G.W.J. *Directions for Travelers on the Mystic Path.* The Hague: Martinus Nijhoff, 1977.

————. *Hikajat Potjut Muhamat: An Achehnese Epic.* The Hague: Martinus Nijhoff, 1979.

————. "New Light on the Coming of Islam to Indonesia", in *The Propagation of Islam in the Indonesian-Malay Archipelago*, ed. Alijah Gordon. Kuala Lumpur: Malaysian Sociological Research Institute, 2001, pp. 125–55.

————. trans. and ed. *Two Achehnese Poems: Hikajat Ranto and Hikajat Teungku Di Meuke.* The Hague: Martinus Nijhoff, 1980.

Drewes, G.W.J. and L.F. Brakel. *The Poems of Hamzah Fansuri.* Dordrecht: Foris Publications, 1986.

Durie, Mark. *A Grammar of Acehnese on the Basis of a Dialect of North Aceh.* Leiden: Foris for KITLV, 1985.

————. "Proto-Chamic and Acehnese mid Vowels: Towards Proto-Aceh-Chamic", *BSOAS* 53, no. 1 (1990): 100–4.

————. "Framing the Acehnese Text: Language Choice and Discourse Structures in Aceh", *Oceanic Linguistics* 35, no. 1 (June 1996).

Dyah Rahmani P. *Matinya Bantaqiah: Menguak Tragedi Beutong Ateuh* [The Death of Bantaqiah: Revealing the Tragedy of Beutong Ateuh]. Banda Aceh: Cordova, Institute for Civil Society Empowerment, 2001.

East Timor Action Network (ETAN). *West Timor Press Summaries.* New York: ETAN, 7 August 2001.

————. *West Timor Press Summaries.* New York: ETAN, 24 January 2002.

Eaton, Richard. *Sufis of Bijapur, 1300–1700: Social Roles of Sufis in Medieval India.* Princeton: Princeton University Press, 1978.

Eda, Fikar W. and S. Satya Dharma, eds. *Sebuah Kesaksian: Aceh Menggugat.* Jakarta: Pustaka Sinar Harapan, 1999.

Ellis, Joseph. *Founding Brothers: The Revolutionary Generation.* New York; Toronto: Random House, 2000.

Elson, R. *Suharto: A Political Biography.* Cambridge: Cambridge University Press, 2001.

Evans, G. "Indonesia's Military Culture Has to be Reformed", *International Herald Tribune,* 24 July 2001.

Fabiola Desy Unidjaja. "TNI Nothing More than Mercenaries: Analysts", *The Jakarta Post,* 17 March 2003.

Farcau, B. *The Transition to Democracy in Latin America.* Westport, Connecticut; London: Praeger, 1996.

Farida, Nani. "Aceh Governor Ready for Corruption Investigation", *The Jakarta Post,* 16 April 2004.

Farooqi, Naimur Rahman. "Mughal-Ottoman Relations: A Study of Political and Diplomatic Relations between Mughal India and the Ottoman Empire, 1556–1748". PhD dissertation, University of Wisconsin, 1986.

Fearon, James D. and David D. Laitin, "Ethnicity, Insurgency, and Civil War", *American Political Science Review* 97, no. 1 (February 2003).

Feith, Herb, "Dynamics of Guided Democracy", in *Indonesia,* ed. Ruth McVey. New Haven: Human Relations Area Files, 1963.

Foster, Sir William, ed. *The Voyages of James Lancaster to Brazil and the East Indies 1591–1603.* London: Hakluyt, 1940.

Fujiwara, Iwaichi. *F-kikan.* Tokyo: Hara Shobo, 1966.

Gelanggang, A.H. *Rahasia Pemberontakan Atjeh dan Kegagalan Politik Mr. S.M. Amin* [The Secret of the Aceh Rebellion and the Failure of the Policy of Mr S.M. Amin]. Kutaradja: Pustaka Murnihati, 1956.

Global Ministries of the Uniting Protestant Churches in the Netherlands (UPCN) and ICCO, "Towards Financial Transparency and Democratic Accountability of the Indonesian Military", Discussion Paper, The Hague, 2002.

Gould, James. "Sumatra–America's Pepperpot 1784–1873", *Essex Institute Historical Collections* 92 (1956): 100–4.

Guillot, Claude, ed. *Histoire de Barus: Le site de Lobu Tua,* Vol. II. *Étude archeologique et documents.* Paris: Cahiers d'Archipel, 2003.

Hadiz, Vedi R. "Reorganizing Political Power in Indonesia: A Reconsideration of so-called 'Democratic Transitions'", *The Pacific Review* 16, 4 (2003): 591–611.

Hamid, Teungku A. and Darwis A. Soelaiman. *Perbandingan Sekolah-Sekolah Umum dan Sekolah-Sekolah Agama di Propinsi Daerah Istimewa Atjeh.* Banda Aceh: Badan Perentjanaan Pembangunan Atjeh, 1971.

Hamka. *Kenang-Kenangan Hidup* [My Autobiography]. Kuala Lumpur: Antara, 1966.

Hardi, S.H. *Daerah Istimewa Aceh: Latar Belakang Politik dan Masa Depannya.* Jakarta: PT Cita Panca Serangkai, 1993.

Hasan, Ibrahim. *Namaku Ibrahim Hasan: Menebah Tantangan Zaman* [My Name is Ibrahim Hasan: Beating the Challenge of History]. Jakarta: Yayasan Malem Putra, 2003.

He Baogang. "Democratization and the National Identity Question in East Asia", in *New Challenges for Development and Modernization: Hongkong and the Asia-Pacific Region in the New Millenium*, ed. Yeung Yue Man. Hong Kong: Chinese University of Hong Kong Press, 2002, pp. 245–73.

Hefner, Robert W. "Introduction: Multiculturalism and Citizenship in Malaysia, Singapore and Indonesia", in *The Politics of Multiculturalism: Pluralism and Citizenship in Malaysia, Singapore, and Malaysia*, ed. Robert W. Hefner. Honolulu: University of Hawaii Press, 2001.

––––––––––. *Civil Islam: Muslims and Democratization in Indonesia*. Princeton, NJ: Princeton University Press, 2000.

Hill, A.H., trans. "Hikayat Raja–Raja Pasai", *JMBRAS* 33, no. 2 (1961).

Hill, Hal, ed. *Unity and Diversity: Regional Economic Development in Indonesia since 1970*. Singapore: OUP, 1989.

––––––––––, ed. *Indonesia's New Order: The Dynamics of Socio-Economic Transformation*. Sydney: Allen and Unwin, 1994.

Honna, Jun. *Military Politics and Democratisation in Indonesia*. London: Routledge Curzon, 2003.

Human Rights Watch (HRW). *World Report 2003: Asia: Indonesia* <http://www.hrw.org>.

––––––––––. *Indonesia: Why is Aceh Exploding*, 1999 <http://www.hrw.org/campaigns/indonesia/aceh0827.htm>.

––––––––––. *Indonesia: The War in Aceh* 13, no. 4 (August 2002).

––––––––––. *Indonesia: Accountability for Human Rights Violations in Aceh* 14, no. 1 (C). New York, 2002.

––––––––––. *Aceh under Martial Law: Inside the Secret War* 15, no. 10 (December 2003).

––––––––––. "Living in Fear: Child Soldiers and the Tamil Tigers in Sri Lanka" <http://hrw.org/reports/2004/srilanka1104/>.

Huntington, Samuel. *The Third Wave: Democratization in the Late 20th Century*. Norman, Oklahoma: University of Oklahoma Press, 1991.

Husni, dk, "Pelaksanaan Otonomi Daerah Tingkat II Dalam Mewujudkan Otonomi Nyata Dan Bertanggung Jawab Di Kotamadya Banda Aceh", *Mon Mata*, no. 27 (September 1997): 12–26.

Indonesian Legal Aid Foundation. *Human Rights Defenders and Humanitarian Workers under Aceh Martial Law*. Report No. 6, September 2003.

The International Campaign to Ban Landmines, Annual Landmine Monitor Reports <www.icbl.org/lm>.

International Crisis Group (ICG), "Indonesia: Keeping the Military under Control", *ICG Asia Report* 9, 5 September 2000.

––––––––––. "Aceh: Escalating Tension", *ICG Asia Briefing* 4, 7 December 2000.

––––––––––. "Aceh: Why Military Force Won't Bring Lasting Peace", *ICG Asia Report* 17, 12 June 2001.

_____. "Aceh: Can Autonomy Stem the Conflict", *ICG Asia Report* 18, 12 June 2001.

_____. "Indonesia: Next Steps in Military Reform", *ICG Asia Report* 24, 11 October 2001.

_____. "Aceh: A Slim Chance for Peace", *ICG Asia Briefing* 14, 27 March 2002.

_____. "Aceh: A Fragile Peace", *ICG Asia Report* 47, 9 May 2003.

_____. "Aceh: Why the Military Option Still Won't Work", *ICG Indonesia Briefing*, 9 May 2003.

_____. "Aceh: How to Lose Win Hearts and Minds", *ICG Indonesia Briefing*, 23 July 2003.

Iskandar, T., ed. *De Hikajat Atjeh*. The Hague: KITLV, 1958.

_____. "Nuru'd-din ar-Raniri Pengarang Abad ke-17", *Dewan Bahasa* 8, no. 10 (1964): 436–41.

_____. ed. *Bustanu's-salatin: bab II, fasal 13*. Kuala Lumpur: Dewan Bahasa dan Pustaka, 1966.

Ito, Takeshi. "Why Did Nuruddin ar-Raniri Leave Aceh in 1054 AH?", *BKI* 134 (1978): 489–91.

_____. "The World of the Adat Aceh: A Historical Study of the Sultanate of Aceh", Unpublished doctoral dissertation, Australian National University, 1984.

Johns, A.H. "Shams al-Din al-Samatrani", in *The Encyclopaedia of Islam,* 2nd ed. Vol. IX. Leiden: E.J. Brill, 1997, pp. 296–7.

Jongejans, J. *Land en Volk Van Atjeh: Vroeger en Nu*. Kutaraja-S'Gravenhage: NV Barns, 1938.

Kahin, Audrey R. *Rebellion to Integration: West Sumatra and the Indonesian Polity 1926–1998*. Amsterdam: Amsterdam University Press, 1999.

Kahin, Audrey R. and George McT. Kahin. *Subversion as Foreign Policy*. New York: The New Press, 1995.

Kammen, D. and S. Chandra. *A Tour of Duty: Changing Patterns of Military Politics in Indonesia in the 1990s*. Ithaca: Cornell Modern Indonesian Project, Cornell University Press, 1999.

Kaoy Syah and Lukman Hakiem. *Keistimewaan Aceh Dalam Lintasan Sejarah: Proses Pembentukan UU No. 44/1999* [The Special-ness of Aceh in the Eye of History: the Process of Creating Law No. 44 of 1999]. Jakarta: Pengurus Besar Al-Jami'iyatul Washliyah, 2000.

Kathirithamby-Wells, J. *The British West Sumatran Presidency (1760–85): Problems of Early Colonial Enterprise*. Kuala Lumpur: University of Malaya Press, 1977.

Kell, Timothy. *The Roots of Acehnese Rebellion 1989–1992*. Ithaca-New York: Cornell University Press, 1995.

Kementerian Penerangan, Bagian Dokumentasi, *Kronik Kementerian Penerangan No. 20, Sekitar Peristiwa Daud Beureuéh III*, Djakarta, 1955.

Kennedy, Raymond. "The Ethnology of the Greater Sunda Islands", Unpublished Ph.D. Dissertation, Yale University, 1935.

Kern, R.A. "Onderzoek Atjeh-moorden", Report to the Governor General in Batavia, 16 December 1921, *Kernpapieren* No. H 797/559. Leiden: KITLV.

_____. "The Propagation of Islām in the Indonesian-Malay Archipelago", in *The Propagation of Islām in the Indonesian-Malay Archipelago*, ed. Alijah Gordon. Kuala Lumpur: Malaysian Sociological Research Institute, 2001.

Kielstra, E.B. *Beschrijving van den Atjeh-oorlog*, 3 vols. The Hague: 1883–5.

Khor, Neil. *Glimpses of Old Penang*. Petaling Jaya: Star Publications, 2002.

Kingsbury, D. *Power Politics and the Indonesian Military*. London and New York: RoutledgeCurzon, 2003.

_____. "The Political Economy of East Timor Border Relations", *Southeast Asia Research* 11, no. 3 (November 2003).

Kielstra, E.B. *Beschrijving van den Atjèh-oorlog*, 3 vols. The Hague: 1883–5.

Klerck, E.S. de. *De Atjèh-oorlog*. The Hague: Nijhoff, 1912.

Komando Tentara dan Territorium I Bukit Barisan, *Memorandum Tentang Peristiwa Pemberontakan DI-TII di Atjeh*. Medan: Pertjetakan Madju, n.d.

Kreemer J. *Atjèh*, 2 vols. Leiden: Brill, 1922.

Krucq, K.C. "Beschrijving der kanonnen afkomstig uit Atjeh, thans in het Koninklijk Militair Invalidenhuis Bronbeek", *TBG* 81.

Laffan, Michael Francis. *Islamic Nationhood and Colonial Indonesia: The Umma Below the Winds*. London: RoutledgeCurzon, 2003.

Lancaster, James. *The voyage of Sir James Lancaster to Brazil and the East Indies, 1591–1603*, ed. Sir William Foster. London: Hakluyt Society, 1940.

Langan, K.F.H. van. "De inrichting van het Atjehsche Staatsbestuur onder het Sultanaat", *Bijdragen tot de Taal-, Land- en Volkenkunde van Nederlandsch-Indie* (*BKI*) 37 (1888): 382–471.

Latham, Ronald, trans. *The Travels of Marco Polo*. Harmondsworth: Penguin Books, 1958.

Lebar, Frank M., ed. *Ethnic Groups of Insular Southeast Asia*, Vol. I: *Indonesia, Andaman Islands and Madagascar*. New Haven: Human Relations Area Files, 1972.

Lee, Kam Hing. "The Shipping Lists of Dutch Melaka: A Source for the Study of Coastal Trade and Shipping in the Malay Peninsula during the Seventeenth and Eighteenth Centuries", in *Kapal dan Harta Karam: Ships and Sunken Treasure*, ed. Muhammad Y. Hashim. Kuala Lumpur: Persatuan Muzium Malaysia, 1986, pp. 53–76.

_____. "Pepper and the Revival of Aceh", in *Indonesian Heritage Series,* vol. 3: *Early Modern History,* ed. Anthony Reid. Singapore: Archipelago Press, 1999.

_____. *The Sultanate of Aceh: Relations with the British, 1760–1824*. Kuala Lumpur: Oxford University Press, 1995.

Lee, Kam Hing and Ahmat Adam. "Raffles and the Order of the Golden Sword", *Journal of the Malaysian Branch of the Royal Asiatic Society* (hereafter *JMBRAS*) 63, 2 (1990): 77–89.

Lev, Daniel. *The Transition to Guided Democracy*. Ithaca: Cornell Modern Indonesia Project, 1966.

Lewis, Dianne. *Jan Compagnie in the Straits of Malacca 1641–1795.* Athens, Ohio: Ohio University Monographs in International Studies, 1995.

Linz, Juan, J. and Alfred Stephan. *Problems of Democratic Transition and Consolidation: Southern Europe, South America, and Post-Communist Europe.* Baltimore: The John Hopkins University Press, 1996.

Locher-Scholten, Elsberth. *Sumatran Sultanate and Colonial State: Jambi and the Rise of Dutch Imperialism, 1830–1907.* Ithaca: Cornell Southeast Asia Program, 2004.

Lockyer, Charles. *An Account of the Trade in India.* London: S. Crouch, 1711.

Lombard, Denys. *Le Sultanat d'Atjèh au temps d'Iskandar Muda 1607–1636.* Paris: Ecole Française d'Extrême Orient, 1967.

Lowry, R. *The Armed Forces of Indonesia.* Sydney: Allen and Unwin, 1996.

Luttwak, Edward. *A Dictionary of Modern War.* London: Penguin Press, 1971.

McBeth, John. "Bitter Memories", *Far Eastern Economic Review,* 16 September 1999.

————. "The Army's Dirty Business", *Far Eastern Economic Review,* 7 November 2002.

McBeth, John and Michael Vatikiotis. "An About-Turn on the Military", *Far Eastern Economic Review,* 25 April 2002.

McCullough, David. *John Adams.* New York: Simon and Schuster, 2001.

McCulloch, L. *Trifungsi: The Role of the Indonesian Military in Business.* Bonn: Bonn International Centre for Conversion, 2000.

————. "Trifungsi: The Role of the Indonesian Military in Business", in *The Military as an Economic Actor,* ed. J. Brommelhorster and W. Paes. New York: Palgrave Macmillan, 2003.

————. "Greed: The Silent Force of the Conflict in Aceh", <http://www.preventconflict.org/portal/main/greed.pdf>, 2003.

McGibbon, Rodd. *Secessionist Challenges in Aceh and Papua: Is Special Autonomy the Solution?* East-West Center Policy Studies Series No. 10. Washington DC: East West Center, 2004.

McKinnon, E. Edwards. "Kota Cina: Its Context and Meaning in the Trade of Southeast Asia in the Twelfth and Fourteenth Centuries". PhD dissertation, Cornell University, 1984.

————. "Beyond Serandib: A Note on Lambri at the Northern Tip of Aceh", *Indonesia* 46 (1988): 103–21.

————. "Ceramic Recoveries (Surface Finds) at Lambaro, Aceh", *Journal of East West Maritime Relations* 2 (1992): 63–73.

————. "Ceramic Surface Finds from Siberaya, Kec. Tigapanah, Tanah Karo, Sumatera Utara", *HKI Newsletter* 22, 6 (November/December 1995).

————. "Ceramic Finds from Landfall sites at Krueng Raya, Kabupaten Aceh Besar", *HKI Newsletter* (1996).

————. "Medieval Tamil Involvement in Northern Sumatra, c11–14: The Gold and Resin Trade", *JMBRAS* 69, no. 1.

McRae, Dave. "A Discourse on Separatists", *Indonesia,* no. 74 (2002): 37–58.

Madale, Nagasara T. "The Future of the MNLF as a Separatist Movement", in *Armed Separatism in South East Asia*, ed. Lim Joo-Jock and S. Vani. Singapore: Institute of Southeast Asian Studies, 1984, pp. 176–89.

Magalhães, B. de. *East Timor: Indonesian Occupation and Genocide*. Oporto: Oporto University, 1992.

Malley, M. "New Rules, Old Structures and the Limits of Democratic Decentralisation", in *Local Power and Politics in Indonesia: Decentralisation and Democratisation*, ed. Edward Aspinall and Greg Fealy. Singapore: Institute of Southeast Asian Studies, 2003.

Mapes, T. "Indonesian Corruption, Wealth May Keep Aceh Rebellion Alive", *The Wall Street Journal*, 3 October 2003.

Marks, Harry. "The First Contest for Singapore, 1819–1824", *VKI* 27 (1959): 252–62.

Maududi, Abul 'A'la. *Toward Understanding Islam*. Nairobi: The Islamic Foundation, 1973.

Maxwell, W.G. and W.S. Gibson, eds. *Treaties and Engagements Affecting the Malay States and Borneo*. London: Truscott, 1924.

Meilink-Roelofsz, M.A.P. *Asian Trade and European Influence in the Indonesian Archipelago between about 1500 and about 1630*. The Hague: M. Nijhoff, 1962.

Mercado, Elisio R. "Culture Economics and Revolt in Mindano: The Origins of MNLF and Politics of Moro", in *Armed Separatism in South East Asia*, ed. Lim Joo-Jock and S. Vani. Singapore: Institute of Southeast Asian Studies, 1984, pp. 151–75.

Metareum, Ismail Hasan. "Kata Pengantar: Pelaksanaan Hukum Islam untuk Peningkatan Kemaslahatan Masyarakat dan Kejayaan Islam" [Introduction: The Implementation of Islamic Law for the Improvement of Society and the Glory of Islam], in *Keistimewaan Aceh*, ed. Kaoy Syah and Hakiem.

Mietzner, Marcus. "Business as Usual? The Indonesian Armed Forces and Local Politics in the Post-Soeharto Era", in *Local Power and Politics in Indonesia: Decentralization and Democratization*, ed. Edward Aspinall and Greg Fealy. Singapore: Institute of Southeast Asian Studies, 2003.

Miller, J. Innes. *The Spice Trade of the Roman Empire 29 B.C.–A.D. 641*. Oxford: Oxford University Press, 1979.

Miller, Michelle Ann. "The Nanggroe Aceh Darussalam Law: A Serious Response to Acehnese Separatism?", *Asian Ethnicity* 5, 3 (October 2004): 333–52.

Miller, Roland E. *Mappila Muslims of Kerala: A Study in Islamic Trends*. New Delhi: Orient Longman, 1976.

Mills, J.V.G. *Ma Huan: Ying-yai Shen-lan, "The Overall Survey of the Ocean's Shores" [1433]*. Cambridge: Cambridge University Press for the Haklyut Society, 1970.

Mohamad Sabil, T. *Hikajat Soeltan Atjeh Marhoem (Soeltan Iskandar Moeda)*. Batavia, 1932.

Mohammad Said, H. *Aceh Sepanjang Abad*. 2nd ed. Medan: Waspada, 1981.

Morris, Eric Eugene. *Islam and Politics in Aceh: A Study of Center-Periphery Relations in Indonesia*. PhD thesis, Cornell University. Ithaca: Cornell University, 1983.

———. "Aceh: Social Revolution and the Islamic Vision", in *Regional Dynamics of the Indonesian Revolution: Unity from Diversity*, ed. Kahin, A. Honolulu: University of Hawaii Press, 1985.

Munir. "The Stagnation of Reforms in the Indonesian Armed Forces", *INFID*, 2003.

Murphy, D. "Indonesia — Cosy Relations", *Far Eastern Economic Review*, 9 March 2000.

Nasution, A.H. *Fundamentals of Guerilla Warfare*. 2nd ed. Jakarta: Seruling Masa, 1970.

Nasution, M. Yunan. *Djihad*. Jakarta: Publicita, 1970.

Nessen, William. "Villagers Describe Atrocities: Indonesia Moves Against Guerrillas", *The Boston Globe*, 18 April 2001.

Niemann, G.K. "Bijdrage tot de kennis der verhouding van het Tjam tot de talen van Indonesie", *BKI* 40 (1891): 27–44.

Nik Hasan Shuhaimi Nik Abd. Rahman and Othman Mohd. Yatim. *Warisan Lembah Bujang*. Bangi: Ikatan Ahli Arkeologi Malaysia, Universiti Kebangsaan Malaysia, 1992.

Obbink, H. Th. *De Heilige Oorlog volgens den Koran*. Leiden: E.J. Brill, 1901.

Oxfam. *Overview of the Coffee Sector in Timor Leste*. London: Oxfam, January 2003.

Peters, Rudolph. *Islam and Colonialism: The Doctrine of Jihad in Modern History*. Den Haag: Mouton, 1979.

Philip, G. *The Military in South American Politics*. London: Croom Helm, 1985.

Piekaar, A.J. *Atjeh en De Oorlog met Japan*. S'Gravenhage-Bandung: W. Van Hoeve, 1949.

Pinto, Fernão Mendes. *The Travels of Mendez Pinto*, trans. Rebecca Catz. Chicago: University of Chicago Press, 1989.

Pires, Tomé. *The Suma Oriental of Tomé Pires*, ed A. Cortesão. Cambridge: Hakluyt, 1944.

Pour, J. *Benny Moerdani: Profil Prajurit Negarawan*. Jakarta: Yayasan Kejuangan Panglima Besar Surdiman, 1993.

Propinsi Sumatera Utara [North Sumatra Province]. Jakarta: Kempen RI, 1954.

Rabasa, Angel and John Haseman. *The Military and Democracy in Indonesia*. Santa Monica: RAND's National Security Research Division, 2002.

Raffles, Sophia, ed. *Memoir of the Life and Public Services of Sir Thomas Stamford Raffles*, by his widow. London: James Duncan, 1835.

Raffles, Thomas Stamford. "Raffles and the Indian Archipelago", *Journal of the Indian Archipelago and East Asia* (1856).

Raniri, Nuru'd-din ar-. *Bustanu's-Salatin, Bab II, Fasal 13*, ed. T. Iskandar. Kuala Lumpur: Dewan Bahasa dan Pustaka, 1966.

Raphael, Ray. *A People's History of the American Revolution: How Common People Shaped the Fight for Independence*. New York: The New Press, 2001.

Reid, Anthony. *The Contest for North Sumatra: Atjeh, the Netherlands and Britain, 1858–1898.* Kuala Lumpur: University of Malaya Press; New York: Oxford University, 1969.

————. "Indonesian Diplomacy: A Documentary Study of Atjehnese Foreign Policy in the Reign of Sultan Mahmud, 1870–4", *JMBRAS* 42, pt. 2 (1969): 74–114.

————. *The Blood of the People: Revolution and the End of Traditional Rule in Northern Sumatra.* Kuala Lumpur: Oxford University Press, 1979.

————. *Southeast Asia in the Age of Commerce 1450–1680. Volume One: The Lands below the Winds.* New Haven and London: Yale University Press, 1988.

————. *Southeast Asia in the Age of Commerce 1450–1680. Volume Two: Expansion and Crisis.* New Haven and London: Yale University Press, 1993.

————, ed. *Witnesses to Sumatra: A Travellers' Anthology.* Kuala Lumpur: Oxford University Press, 1995.

————. *The Last Stand of Asian Autonomies: Response to Modernity in the Diverse States of Southeast Asia and Korea, 1750–1900.* New York: St. Martin's Press, 1997.

————. ed. *Indonesian Heritage Series,* vol. 3: *Early Modern History.* Singapore: Archipelago Press, 1999.

————. "Aceh and Indonesia: a Stormy Marriage", *Prosea Research Paper* 42, Taipei: Academia Sinica, 2001.

————. "War, Peace and the Burden of History in Aceh", *Working Paper Series* No. 1, Asia Research Institute, National University of Singapore, June 2003.

————. *An Indonesian Frontier: Acehnese and other Histories of Sumatra.* Singapore: Singapore University Press, 2004.

Reid, Anthony and Lance Castles, eds. *Pre-colonial State Systems in Southeast Asia: The Malay, Peninsula, Sumatra, Bali-Lombok, South Celebes. Monographs of the Malaysian Branch of the Royal Asiatic Society No. 6.* Kuala Lumpur: MBRAS, 1975.

Retnosari, Ulyati. "Song as the Resistance Language against Domination: A Case Study on 'Hikayat Perang Sabil' in Aceh and 'Oh freedom' in the Black American Society", Unpublished M.A. thesis, Gadjah Mada University, 2004.

Ricklefs, M.C. *A History of Modern Indonesia since c.1300.* 2nd ed. Basingstoke: Macmillan, 1993.

Riddell, P.G. *Transferring a Tradition: 'Abd al-Ra'uf al-Singkili's Rendering into Malay of the Jalalayn Commentary.* Berkeley, CA: Centres for South and Southeast Asian Studies, University of California, 1990.

Robinson, Geoffrey. "Rawan is as Rawan Does: The Origins of Disorder in New Order Aceh", *Indonesia,* no. 66 (October 1998): 127–56.

————. "Rawan is as Rawan Does: The Origins of Disorder in New Order Aceh", in *Violence and the State in Suharto's Indonesia,* ed. Benedict R.O'G. Anderson. Ithaca, NY: Southeast Asia Program Publications, Cornell University, 2001.

Rooney, Dawn F. *Betel Chewing Traditions in South-east Asia.* Kuala Lumpur: Oxford University Press, 1993.

Ross, Michael. "Resources and Rebellion in Aceh, Indonesia", Yale World Bank Project on "The Economics of Political Violence", Unpublished manuscript, 5 June 2003.

Rubin, A.P. *The International Personality of the Malay Peninsula: A Study of the International Law of Imperialism.* Kuala Lumpur: University of Malaya Press, 1974.

Rutherford, D. "Waiting for the End in Biak", in *Violence and the State in Suharto's Indonesia,* ed. B. Anderson. Ithaca: Cornell University Press, 2001.

Saleh, Hasan. *Revolusi Islam di Indonesia.* Darussalam: Pustaka Djihad, 1956.

————. *Mengapa Aceh Bergolak.* Jakarta: Pustaka Utama Grafiti, 1992.

Salim, Arskal. "Epilogue. Shariá in Indonesia's Current Transition: An Update", in *Shariá and Politics in Modern Indonesia,* ed. Arskal Salim and Azyumardi Azra. Singapore: Institute of Southeast Asian Studies, 2004, pp. 213–32.

Santos Alves, Jorge Manuel dos. *O Dominio do Norte de Samatra: A historia dos sultanatos de Samudera-Pacem e de Achém, e das suas relações com os Portugueses (1500–1580)* [The Control of North Sumatra: a history of the sultanates of Samudra-Pasai and Aceh, and of their relations with the Portuguese (1500–1580)]. Lisbon: Sociedade Historica da Independência de Portugal, 1999, pp. 80–1.

————. "The Foreign Trader's Management in the Sultanates of the Straits of Malacca", in *From the Mediterranean to the China Sea,* ed. Claude Guillot, Denys Lombard and Roderich Ptak. Wiesbaden: Harrassowitz, 1998, pp. 131–42.

Santos Alves, Jorge M. dos and P-Y Manguin. *O Roteiro das Cousas do Achem de D. João Ribeiro Gaio.* Lisbon: Comissão Nacional para as Comemorações dos Descobrimentos Portugueses, 1997.

Sastri, K.A. Nilakanta. *History of Śrivijaya.* Madras: University of Madras, 1949.

Schlegel, S. "Technocrats in a Muslim Society: Symbolic Community in Aceh", in *What is Modern Indonesian Culture,* ed. Gloria Davis. Southeast Asia Series No. 52, Center for International Studies. Madison, Wisconsin: Ohio University, 1979.

Schulze, Kirsten E. "The Struggle for an Independent Aceh: The Ideology, Capacity, and Strategy of GAM", *Studies in Conflict and Terrorism* 26, 4 (July–August 2003).

————. "The Other Side to Aceh's Rebels", *Asia Times,* 22 July 2003.

————. *The Free Aceh Movement (GAM): Anatomy of a Separatist Organization.* Policy Studies 2. Washington DC: East West Center, 2004.

————. "Not a Romantic Movement", *Inside Indonesia,* January–March 2005.

SEAP Indonesia, No. 73. Ithaca: Cornell University Southeast Asia Program Publications, 2000.

Shellabear, W.G. "An Account of Some of the Oldest Malay MSS Now Extant", *JSBRAS* 31 (1898):107–51.

_____, ed. *Sejarah Melayu* (The Malay Annals) (1909). 10th printing. Singapore: Malay Publishing House, 1961.

Siapno, Jacqueline. *Gender, Islam, Nationalism and State in Aceh: The Paradox of Power, Cooptation and Resistance.* London: RoutledgeCurzon, 2002.

Siegel, James. *The Rope of God.* Berkeley: University of California Press, 1969.

_____. *Shadow and Sound: The Historical Thought of a Sumatran People.* Chicago: University of Chicago Press, 1979.

Singh, Bilveer. *Civil-military Relations in Democratising Indonesia: The Potentials and Limits to Change.* Canberra: Strategic Defence Studies Centre, Australian National University, 2001.

Sjamsuddin, Nazarudin. "Issues and Politics of Regionalism in Indonesia: Evaluating the Acehnese Experience", in *Armed Separatism in Southeast Asia*, ed. Lim Joo-Jock and S. Vani. Singapore: Institute of Southeast Asian Studies, 1984, pp. 111–28.

_____. *The Republican Revolt: A Study of the Acehnese Rebellion.* Singapore: Institute of Southeast Asian Studies, 1985.

_____. *Integrasi Politik di Indonesia.* Jakarta: PT Gramedia, 1989.

Smith, Anthony L. "Aceh: Democratic Times, Authoritarian Solutions", *New Zealand Journal of Asian Studies* 4, 2 (December 2002).

_____. "Conflict in Aceh: The Consequences of a Broken Social Contract", *Harvard Asia Quarterly* 6,1 (Winter 2002): 47–55.

Smith, Vincent. *The Oxford History of India.* 3rd ed. Oxford: Oxford University Press, 1958.

Snouck, C. Hurgronje. *Mekka in the Latter Part of the 19th Century*, trans. J. Monahan. The Hague: 1889.

_____. *The Acehnese*, trans. A.W.S. O'Sullivan, 2 vols. Leiden/London: E.J. Brill, 1906.

Steinberg, David J., *et al. In Search of Southeast Asia: A Modern History.* Kuala Lumpur: Oxford University Press, 1971.

Stepan, A. "The New Professionalism of Internal Warfare and Military Role Expansion", in *Armies and Politics in Latin America*, ed. A. Lowenthal. New York, London: Jolmes and Meier Publishers, 1976.

Sukma, Rizal. "The Acehnese Rebellion: Secessionist Movement in Post-Soeharto Indonesia", in *Non-Traditional Security Issues in Southeast Asia*, ed. Andrew T.H. Tan and J.D. Kenneth Boutin. Singapore: Select Publishing, 2001.

_____. "Aceh in Post Suharto Indonesia: Protracted Conflict amid Democratization", in *Autonomy and Disintegration in Indonesia*, ed. Damien Kingsburry and Harry Aveling. London: RoutledgeCurzon, 2003, pp. 152–65.

_____. *Security Operations in Aceh: Goals, Consequences, and Lessons.* Policy Paper 3. Washington DC: East-West Center, 2004.

Sulaiman, M. Isa. *Sejarah Aceh: Sebuah Gugatan Terhadap Tradis (1942–1962)* [History of Aceh: Intergroup Conflict of Aceh 1942–1962]. Jakarta: Pustaka Sinar Harapan, 1997.

_____. *Aceh Merdeka: Ideologi, Kepemimpinan dan Gerakan* [The Free Aceh Movement: Its Ideology, Leadership and Struggle]. Jakarta: Pustaka al Kausar, 2000.

Suryadinata, Leo. Evi Nurvidya Arifin and Aris Ananta. *Indonesia's Population: Ethnicity and Religion in a Changing Political Landscape.* Singapore: Institute of Southeast Asian Studies, 2003.

Talsya, Tk. Alibasjah. *Sedjarah dan Dokumen-Dokumen Pemberontakan di Atjeh.* Djakarta: Penerbit Kesuma, n.d..

Tapol. *East Timor Under the Indonesian Jackboot.* Tapol, the Indonesian Human Rights Campaign, Occasional report No. 26, October 1998.

_____. *The TNI's Dirty War in East Timor,* 17 June 1999.

Tarling, Nicholas. "British Policy in the Malay Peninsula and Archipelago, 1824–1871", *JMBRAS* 30, pt. 3 (1957).

_____. *Anglo-Dutch Rivalry in the Malay World, 1780–1824.* Cambridge: Cambridge University Press, 1962.

_____, ed. *The Cambridge History of Southeast Asia.* Vol. 1. Cambridge: Cambridge University Press, 1992.

Tarrow, Sidney, *et al., Power in Movements: Social Movements, Collective Action and Politics.* Cambridge: Cambridge University Press, 1994.

Tesoro, J. "Voting for the Future", *Asiaweek* 10 (September 1999).

Thurgood, Graham. *From Ancient Cham to Modern Dialects: Two Thousand Years of Language Contact and Change.* Honolulu: University of Hawaii Press, 1999.

Tibbets, G.R. *A Study of the Arab Texts Containing Material on South-East Asia.* Oriental Translation Fund, New Series Vol. XLIV. London: E.J. Brill, published for the Royal Asiatic Society, London, 1979.

Tippe, Syarifudin. *Aceh di Persimpangan Jalan.* Jakarta: Pustaka Cidesindo, 2000.

_____. *El-Hurr: Nurani untuk Aceh.* Jakarta: Yayasan Ulul Arham, 2001.

Tiro, Tengku Hasan M. di. *Demokrasi Untuk Indonesia* [Democracy for Indonesia]. Aceh: Penerbit Seulawah, 1958.

_____. *The Political Future of Malay Archipelago.* New York: January 1965.

_____. *Atjeh Bak Mata Donja* [Aceh according to the World Vision]. New York: 15 March 1968.

_____. *One Hundred Years Anniversary of the Battle of Bandar Aceh, April 1873– April 1973.* New York: Institute of Aceh in America, 1973.

_____. *The Price of Freedom: The Unfinished Diary of Tengku Hasan di Tiro.* State of Acheh-Sumatra: Ministry of Education and Information, 1982.

_____. *The Case and the Cause of the National Liberation Front of Acheh Sumatra.* London: NLFAS, 1985.

Tocqueville, Alexis de. *Old Regime and the French Revolution.* New York: Doubleday, 1955.

Trimingham, J.S. *The Sufi Orders in Islam.* Oxford: OUP, 1971.

Tunggal, Hadi Setia, comp. *Undang-Undang Nomor 22 Tahun 1999 Tentang Pemerintah Daerah* (Harvarindo, Jakarta, 2000).

————, comp. *Undang-Undang Republik Indonesia Nomor 25 Tahun 1999 Tentang Perimbangan Keuangan Antara Pemerintah Pusat dan Daerah* (Harvarindo, Jakarta, 2000).

————, comp. *Undang-Undang Republik Indonesia Nomor 44 Tahun 1999 Tentang Penyelenggaraan Keistimewaan Propinsi Daerah Istimewa Aceh* (Harvarindo, Jakarta, 2000).

————, comp. *Undang Undang Republik Indonesia Nomor 18 Tahun 2001 Tentang Otonomi Khusus Bagi Provinsi Daerah Istimewa Aceh Sebagai Provinsi Nanggroe Aceh Darussalam.*

Vakily, A. "Sufism, Power Politics and Reform: Al-Raniri's Opposition to Hamzah al-Fansuri's Teachings Reconsidered", *Studia Islamika* 4, 1 (1997): 113–35.

Veer, Paul van't. *De Atjeh-oorlog.* Amsterdam: Arbeiderspers, 1969.

Veltman, T.J. "Nota over de geschiedenis van het landschap Pidië", *TBG* 58 (1919): 15–157.

Vliet, Jeremias van. "Description of the Kingdom of Siam" [1636], trans. L.F. van Ravenswaay, *Journal of the Siam Society* 7, no. 1 (1910): 43–6.

Volkstelling 1930. deel IV *Inheemsche Bevolking van Sumatra.* Batavia: Department Van Economische Zaken, 1934.

Voorhoeve, P. "Bajan Tadjalli", *TBG* 23, 1 (1952): 87–115.

————. "Short Note: Nuruddin ar-Raniri", *BKI* 115 (1959): 90–1.

————, comp. *Catalogue of Acehnese Manuscripts in the Library of Leiden University and other collections outside Aceh,* trans. and ed. M. Durie. Leiden: Leiden University Library, 1994.

Walker, M.J. and S. Santoso. "Romano-Indian Rouletted Pottery in Indonesia", *Mankind,* no. 11 (1977): 39–45.

————. "Romano-Indian Rouletted Pottery in Indonesia", *Asian Perspectives* 20, no. 2 (1977): 228–35.

Wap, J.J.F. *De Gezantschap van den Sultan van Achin, Anno 1602, aan Prins Maurits van Nassau en de Oud-Nederlandsche Republiek.* Rotterdam: H. Nigh, 1862.

Webster, Anthony. *Gentlemen Capitalists: British imperialism in South East Asia, 1770–1890.* London; New York: Tauris Academic Studies, 1998.

Weiss, S. "Indonesia: The Military Can Shape up if Washington Helps", *International Herald Tribune,* 20 August 2001.

Wicki, J., ed. *Documenta Indica* VII. MHSI 89. Rome, 1962.

Widjanarko, Tulus and Asep S. Sambodja, eds. *Aceh Merdeka Dalam Perdebatan.* Jakarta: Cita Putra Bangsa, 1999.

Widjojo, A. "Indonesia's Changing Security Structure and its Implications for US Policy", address to United States-Indonesia Society, Washington DC, 21 February 2002.

Winstedt, R.O. "Some Malay Mystics, Heretical and Orthodox", *JMBRAS* 1 (1923): 313–8.

World Bank, The, "Promoting Peaceful Development in Aceh: An Informal Background Paper", prepared for the Preparatory Conference on Peace and Reconstruction in Aceh, Tokyo, 2002.

Wolters, O.W. *The Fall of Śrivijaya in Malay History.* Kuala Lumpur: OUP, 1970.

Woltring, J., ed. *Bescheiden Betreffende de Buitenlandse Politiek van Nederland. Tweede Periode, 1871–98*, I. The Hague, 1962.

Wurtzburg, C.E. *Raffles of the Eastern Isles.* London: Hodder and Stoughton, 1954.

Wyatt, David, ed. *The Crystal Sands: The Chronicles of Nagara Sri Dharrmaraja*, Ithaca: Cornell University Southeast Asia Program, 1975.

Yamin, K., "Indonesian Forces' Corruption Exposed", *Asia Times On-line*, 14 October 2002.

Young, R.J. *The English East India Company and Trade on the West Coast of Sumatra, 1730–1760.* PhD thesis, University of Pennsylvania, 1970.

Zainol, Salina Hj. "Hubungan perdangan antara Aceh, Sumatera Ttimur dan Pulau Pinang, 1819–1871", Unpublished MA thesis, University of Malaya, 1995.

Zamzami, Amran. *Tragedi Anak Bangsa: Pembantaian Teungku Bantaqiah dan Santri-Santrinya.* Jakarta: PT. Bina Rena Pariwara, 2001.

Zentgraaff, H.C. *Atjeh.* Batavia: De Unie, 1938.

Newspapers and Magazines

Abadi
Aneta
Antara
Bijaksana
Fikiran Rakyat
Gamma
Inside Indonesia
Kayhan International
Kengpo
Kompas
Kontras
Media Indonesia Online
Peristiwa
Republika
Semangat Merdeka
Serambi Indonesia.
Sinar Deli
Tapol Bulletin
Tegas
Tempo
Waspada
The Economist. "Still Waiting for Wahid", *The Economist*, 25–31 March 2000.

The Jakarta Post. "No Way to Oecussi through West Timor", *TheJakartaPost.com*, 31 May 2002.

————. "Blame Game over the Aceh Problem", 7 July 2004.

Gatra. "Penyulundupan: Manikmati Kencing Solar", 10 February 2001.

Republika. "Mbak Tutut Invites East Timorese Citizen in Portugal", trans. Carmel Budiardjo, *Republika*, 12 January 1994.

Time Asia Magazine, "Aceh: A Losing Battle", 21 June 2004.

Official Documents, Typescript and Stencilled Sources

Aceh Dalam Angka Seri 1985–1996 [Aceh in Figures]. Banda Aceh: Kerjasama Kantor Statistik dengan Bappeda Prop. DI Aceh, 1996. A Joint Statement of the *Ulamas* of Aceh, dated 15 May 1948.

Al Khalidy, M. Wali. *Tiang Selamat bagi segala lapisan Pemerintah dan rakya* [The Happiness Pillar for the Whole Government and People]. Labuhan Haji: 9 Rabiul Awal 1377.

Beureueh, Daud. *Keterangan Politik* [Political Statement]. Aceh: 21 September 1959.

————. *Menyambut Nisfu Syakban 1373 H* [Appeal on the Occasion of Anniversary of Nisyfu Syakban 1954]. Mardhatillah: 5 April 1954.

————. *Seruan Dakwah* [Religious Proselytizing]. Medan Jihad: 15 April 1954.

————. *Bekerjasama dengan musyrik untuk menghancurkan Islam adalah musyrik* [To Ally with the Polytheism to Destroy Islam Means the Infidels]. Mardhatillah: 1959.

Buitenlandse Zaken Dossier Atjeh.

Cessation of Hostilities Framework Agreement Between Government of the Republic of Indonesia and the Free Acheh Movement, 9 December 2002.

Coordinating Ministry for Political and Security Affairs. *Keputusan Presiden Republik Indonesia Nomor 28 Tahun 2003 tentang Pernyataan Keadaan Bahaya dengan Tingkatan Keadaan Darurat Militer di Provinsi Nanggroe Aceh Darussalam* [Presidential Decree No. 23/2003 on the Declaration of a State of Emergency with the Status of Martial Law in Nanggroe Aceh Darussalam Province] in <www.polkam.go.id> [20 April 2004].

Decree of Premier of Republic of Indonesia dated 26 May 1959 No I/Misi/1959.

Draft Treaty of Alliance, enclosed in Studer to Davis 4 October 1873, US Consular Despatches, Singapore, reproduced in Reid, "Indonesian Diplomacy", pp. 97–100.

File of M. Harun Mahmud's case No 83/1978/T, B. Aceh: 1979.

File of Tgk Nurdin Amin's case No 5/1980/T, B. Aceh: 1980.

File of A. Wahab Umar Tiro's case No 47/14/1979/T, B. Aceh: 1980.

Hikayat Perang Sabil (HPS), Ms. Cod. Leiden University Library.

Local Regulation of Aceh Residency No 1/1946, Kutaraja: 24 June 1946 regarding the *ulëëbalang's* property.

Local Regulation of Special Province of Aceh No 1/1966 regarding the formation the Council of the Ulama.

Madras Public Department Consultations, Range 240, vol. 36, British Library.

Memorandum of transfer of governor position, Governor Nyak Adam Kamil on 7 July 1967.

Ministry of Foreign Affairs. "Joint Understanding on Humanitarian Pause for Aceh", 2003 <www.deplu.go.id> [3 July 2003].

Minutes of the working committee of The Aceh Council 1946–1947.

Minutes of the *Peperda* Meeting with the local prominent figures in Kutaraja on 16 March 1958.

Perjuangan Aceh Merdeka [Struggle of the Free Aceh Movement]. Wilayah Berdaulat: 14 August 1977.

Propinsi Sumetera Utara [Province of North Sumatra]. Jakarta: Kempen RI, 1954.

Qanun Provinsi Nanggroe Aceh Darussalam Nomor 11 Tahun 2002 Tentang Pelaksanaan Syariat Islam Bidang Aqidah, Ibadah dan Syi'ar Islam (14 October 2002).

Raffles-Minto Collection. The British Library.

Straits Settlements Factory Record. The India Office Records, the British Library.

Sumatra Factory Record. The India Office Records, the British Library.

Volkstelling 1930. Inhemsche Bevolking van Sumatra, deel IV, Batavia: Department Van Economische Zaken, 1934.

Index

'Abd al-Ra'uf bin Ali al-Fansuri al-Singkili, 43, 45–6, 48

Abdullah, Zaini, 147, 184, 261–2, 279

Abdussamad, Syaikh, 114–5

ABRI, *see* TNI

Abu al-Kahyr ibn Shakyh ibn Hajar, 48, 57

Abu Bakar, Said, 105, 128

Aceh Besar, 6, 8, 10, 12, 22, 28, 30–1, 73–4, 82, 88, 98–9, 105, 126, 158, 213, 250–1, 257, 299, 323

Aceh-Dutch war, *see* Dutch, Aceh war

Aceh Darussalam (dynasty), 10, 13, 38–9, 115

Aceh Merdeka (*AM*), 177, 179, 183–93, 256; *see also* GAM; nationalism; separatism

Aceh People's Congress (KRA), 334–5

activism/activists, 104–6, 118, 139, 150, 165, 167–71, 188, 193, 254, 283, 287, 329, 354; human rights, 161, 165, 169–70, 177, 191, 198, 253, 284; NGO, 139, 165, 286, 337; PUSA, 105–6, 127, 132, 143–4; student, 118, 139, 167, 329

adat, 5, 9, 12, 43, 60, 294, 296, 300, 309; *hukum*, 43, 47; *see also* law, customary

administrations, 82, 105, 132, 136, 189, 201–1, 211, 231, 293, 296–7, 304, 329, 347; colonial, 101, 103; local/provincial, 134, 152–3, 192, 296–7, 302, 305–9, 311, 337, 339–40, 343–6, 350, 354; pre-colonial, 40; *see also* bureaucracy; government

Afghanistan, 190, 301

agriculture, 6–7, 74–5, 123, 125–6, 140, 206, 212, 323, 326; *see also* plantations

Aidit, Syed Hussein, Penang merchant, 87, 90

Al-Attas, Syed M. Naguib, 40, 44–5

al-Hamid, Muhammad, 45, 48

Al Khalidy, Mudawali, 130, 136

al-Kurani, Ibrahim, 46, 48

al-Nasafi, Creed of, 44–5

al-Raniri, Nur al-Din, 10, 38–9, 41–2, 45, 48; *see also Bustan al-Salatin*

al-Rijal, Sayf, 42, 45

Ali, Hasan, 132, 143, 145, 156

Ambon, 115, 160, 174; *see also* Maluku

Amnesty International, 235, 254

Anglo-French wars, 74, 84–5

Annapoorny incident, 85–6

anti-foreign sentiment, 6, 13, 57, 62, 81, 101, 105, 110, 318

Arab, 5, 7, 23–4, 36, 38–9, 42, 44–6, 48–9, 55, 62, 87, 98, 113, 117, 323; traders, 10, 23, 28, 31, 35–6, 58–9, 61, 63; world, 5, 53, 55

Arabic, 10, 20, 32, 36, 71, 197

Arif, Teuku Nyak, 107, 117, 127

Arifin, Bustanil, 321, 352

armed forces, *see* TNI

Aru, 33, 41, 56

ASNLF, *see* GAM

atrocities, *see* civilian(s), violence against; human rights, abuses; violence

Austronesian (language family), 5, 7
authoritarian(ism), 58, 121, 166, 208,
    272, 275, 277–8, 297–8, 322
authority: civilian, 200, 202, 219,
    276, 152; colonial, 91, 317–8;
    foreign, 55, 91, 114–5; Indonesian
    national, 15, 79, 90, 107, 139,
    238, 293, 295–6, 304–6, 311,
    349, 358; local/provincial, 130,
    132, 135, 203, 293, 297, 305,
    316, 336, 349; military, 139,
    254, 283–5, 287, 309; religious,
    41–3, 47, 107, *see also ulama*;
    ulèëbalang, 9, 100, 106; *see also*
    leadership; power
autonomy, 9, 17, 90, 121–2, 126,
    128, 130, 145–6, 153, 163, 167,
    203, 208, 219, 243, 245–6, 259–
    60, 262, 264–5, 277, 281–2,
    292–4, 296–8, 319, 327, 332,
    343, 345; legislation, 203, 246,
    260, 264, 277, 281–2, 287, 296–
    310, 316, 332–3, 337–9, 342–3,
    356; "special", 16, 141, 194, 196,
    210–2, 246, 259–60, 264, 281,
    287, 292–4, 297–8, 300–5, 308–
    10, 316, 319–20, 323–4, 327,
    329, 332–3, 336–9, 341–3, 345,
    354–8; *see also* decentralisation;
    law, autonomy; NAD

Baitturrahman mosque, 42, 44, 132
Bali, 2, 23, 52
Banda Aceh, 1, 6, 10, 20, 25, 27, 61,
    81–3, 85, 87, 97, 100, 112, 118,
    129, 164, 167, 197, 214, 217, 231
bangsa, 159–60, 168, 174; *see also*
    suku bangsa
Bantaqiah, Tgk, 327, 336; massacre
    of, 163, 277, 335, 354, 356
Barus, 25, 28, 31, 35, 44, 78, 82, 86
Batak, 6, 8, 12, 159–61, 168, 174,
    see also Karo-Batak

Batavia, 2, 13, 61, 65, 69, 72, 96–7,
    102, 111, 114, 122
Belawan, 29, 124, 134, 146, 228
Bengal, 30, 32, 53, 59, 68, 78, 83,
    86, 94; Bay of, 22–3, 84
Bengkulen, 4, 62, 73, 77–8, 84,
    87–8
betelnut, 5, 61, 73, 75–7; *see also*
    plantations; trade/traders
Beureu'eh, Daud, 13, 104–6, 117,
    127–33, 137–8, 142–5, 147,
    153–4, 159–61, 181, 183–5,
    294–5, 319, 324; *see also*
    Darul Islam
Bireuen, 231, 239, 250, 258, 311
Brimob, 173, 248, 254; *see also* police
British, 13, 19, 40, 52, 58–63, 65–7,
    70, 72, 74–5, 77–81, 83–92, 96–8,
    100, 103, 114, 182; as colonial
    power, 52, 60, 62, 65–6, 72, 88,
    103, 114; interest in Aceh, 62,
    70, 83–4, 88, 92; settlements, 4,
    62, 65–6, 72, 78, 97, 100; trade/
    traders, 61, 63, 74, 84, 86–8, 90,
    92; *see also* English East India
    Company; London Treaty, Anglo-
    Dutch (1824)
Buddhism, 26, 33, 35–6
bughat, 131, 136, 140
Bugis, 12, 42, 72–3, 76, 78
Bulog, 207, 222
bupati, 153, 156, 215, 248, 321,
    338, 342, 344, 352, 357
bureaucracy, 123, 135, 137, 140, 192,
    274, 284, 287, 321–2, 333, 358
bureaucrats, 125, 135, 153, 321, 329,
    338, 352; *see also* technocrats
Burma, 29, 32–3, 72, 90, 94
Bustan al-Salatin, 38, 53, 60

Calcutta, 84–5, 87–8
Canning, Capt. John, 86, 89, 93–4
cash crops, *see* agriculture; plantations

cease-fire, 16, 155, 196, 247, 259, 299, 310, 344; *see also* CoHA; peace process

Central Aceh, 3, 126, 163, 184, 217, 235–6, 239, 248, 250

centralisation, 16, 40, 100, 134, 151, 181, 245, 260, 286, 295, 321, 324–5, 337

centre-periphery relations, 16, 121–2, 134, 170, 187, 295, 297, 301, 315, 322–3, 349

ceramics, 23, 27, 29, 33

Champa, 7–8, 10, 54

Cham (language), 5, 7–8, 10, 19

China, 7, 10, 22, 27–9, 31, 33, 36, 53–6, 65, 74, 84, 90, 356; trade with, 7, 24, 27–8, 31, 33, 55, 84

Chinese, 5–6, 10–12, 20, 24, 31, 33–4, 59, 129, 189, 218; migrants, 5, 123; trade/traders, 5, 7, 24, 27–8, 59, 84

Christianity, 6, 23–4, 30, 36, 140, 352

Chulias (Tamil Muslims), 7, 61, 63, 73, 75–6, 81, 85, 89, 91

CIA, 182, 189–90

civil defence groups, *see* militias

civil servants, 228, 230, 257, 265

civil society, 161, 200, 209, 260, 274–7, 283, 286–8, 309, 330, 334–6, 339, 341–2

civil war, 10, 62, 76, 79, 81, 85, 87–9, 91, 161

civilian(s), 15, 152, 165, 193, 198, 208, 210, 227–8, 231, 245, 247, 251, 255–7, 263, 275, 280, 288–9, 300, 310, 321; authority, 200, 202, 219, 276; control, 208, 219, 278; infrastructure, 248–9, 265, 311; leadership, 182, 192, 249–50, 263–4, 274, 276, 278–82, 287, 308; violence against, 151–2, 156–8, 160, 162–6, 168, 171, 191, 214, 226,

229, 234, 244, 257–8, 261, 265, 339

see also human rights, abuses; violence

coffee, 5, 102, 125, 212, 215, 217; *see also* plantations; trade/traders

CoHA, 16, 155, 210–1, 227, 238, 241, 243–4, 259, 269, 282–3, 286, 288, 308, 343–6, 358; *see also* cease-fire; peace process

Cola kingdom (India), 24

colonialism, 10, 14, 52, 72, 96, 101–3, 122–3, 126, 139, 143, 146, 175, 179–80, 185, 239, 293, 316–9, 322, 328, 349; British, 52, 60, 62, 65–6, 72, 88, 103, 114; Dutch, 2, 4, 6, 9, 13, 52, 61, 63–5, 72, 74, 77–8, 88–90, 92, 96–107, 110–5, 117–8, 122–3, 127–8, 135–6, 139, 143–4, 154, 160–2, 169, 180–1, 318–9, 322, 328, legacy of, 96, 122, 169; Javanese/Indonesian, 118, 135, 149, 160–1, 168–9, 230, 233–5

Cold War, 152, 242–3

communism, 154, 189, 319, 322, *see also* PKI; anti-, 6, 166, 182, 189, 319–20

Coombes, Capt. J., 88, 95

copra, 5, 124, 142; *see also* plantations; trade/traders

corruption, 204, 211–2, 214, 218–20, 222, 287, 293, 305, 309, 313, 327, 339–40, 343, 345–7, 349–50, 356–7

Cot Jeumpa incident, 158, 161–2, 164, 166

Cot Trieng siege, 282

Crisis Management Initiative (CMI), 287, 289; *see also* Helsinki peace talks

culture, 22, 29, 31–3, 77, 140–1, 200, 202, 264, 293; Acehnese,

32–3, 134, 190, 242, 246, 260, 297–8, 300, 302, 305–6, 309; Indonesian, 232; Javanese, 12, 32, 134; military, 199, 213

Cumbok, Mohammad Daud, 106, 127, 143

Cumbok War, 127, 129

customary law, *see adat*; law, customary

Cut Nyak Dien, 101, 249

Darul Islam, 115, 122, 124–5, 129, 131, 133, 136, 139, 142–3, 145, 147, 151–6, 159–61, 163, 165, 168, 172, 174, 177, 179–81, 294–5, 298, 311, 324, 332; leaders, 122, 131, 133, 151, 154, 156, 159, 161, 168, 180–1, 183–4, 186

Daud, Ishak, 191, 193, 250

Daya, 8, 39

dayah, 113, 136, 140, 232, 323, 329, 354; *see also madrasah*; schools, Islamic

decentralisation, 264, 292, 297, 304; *see also* autonomy; NAD

Deli, 29, 33, 39, 41, 53, 55, 60, 63

democracy/democratisation, 3, 15, 17, 102, 131, 136–7, 141, 208, 210, 272–86, 288–9, 292, 302, 308–9, 337, 341, 352

Djuly, Jacoub, 181, 183–5, 192, 195–6

DOM period, 16, 150, 163, 165, 167, 169, 172, 175, 187, 193, 209, 213, 244, 257, 259, 276; *see also Operasi Jaring Merah*

DPR (National Parliament), 281, 301, 303, 332, 338, 345

DPRD (Regional Assembly), 337–42, 356–7

drugs, 207, 212–4, 223; marijuana, 165, 213–4, 336

Dutch, 2, 8, 14, 16, 38, 40, 52, 54–5, 58–68, 71–2, 74, 76–8, 88–90, 92, 96–107, 110–8, 111, 122–3, 126–9, 135–6, 140, 143–4, 154, 160–2, 167, 171, 174, 180–3, 185–7, 195, 204, 239, 293–4, 318, 322, 349; Aceh policy, 98, 101–2, 123; Aceh war, 14, 16, 27, 55, 96–100, 110–5, 117–8, 126, 140, 160–1, 181, 318; colonialism/occupation, 2, 4, 6, 9, 13, 52, 61, 63–5, 72, 74, 77–8, 88–90, 92, 96–107, 110–5, 117–8, 122–3, 127–8, 135–6, 139, 143–4, 154, 160–2, 169, 180–1, 318–9, 322, 328; conquest, 52, 64–5, 96, 98, 100, 104; East India Company (VOC), 40, 61–2, 90; invasion, 12, 66–7, 76, 97–8

earthquake, 1, 3–4, 10, 310, 347; *see also* tsunami

earthenware, 22, 26, 29, 33

East Aceh, 122–4, 128, 144, 146, 183, 188, 227, 229, 233, 238–9, 248, 250, 258, 299, 326, 331

East Timor, 15, 166, 206, 208, 211, 217–8, 226, 237–9, 245, 263, 275, 277–9, 283, 292, 298–300; independence, 237, 278, 299; referendum, 237–8, 275, 277–9, 299–300

economy, 2, 9, 15, 121–5, 136, 139, 152, 157, 171, 179, 186, 188–90, 199–202, 206, 208, 211–2, 218–20, 230, 245–8, 259–60, 264, 273–7, 281, 288–9, 293, 295, 297, 321, 323–6, 339–40, 351–2, 354; colonial era, 73, 75, 82–4, 90–2, 96, 100, 102; crisis, 121, 202, 297; exploitation, 15, 122, 139, 264, 288, 315, 326–7;

global, 123–4, 139, 325–6; infrastructure, 122, 124; local/provincial, 90, 124, 126, 128, 134, 211, 233, 248, 293, 295, 297, 302, 305, 325–6, 339–40, 351–2, 354; national, 122–3, 125, 199, 202, 212, 323–4; policies, 123–4, 126, 179, 321; pre-colonial, 23, 33, 36

education, 5, 110, 124, 128, 133, 186, 188, 201–2, 205, 228–33, 248–9, 251, 294, 296–8, 300, 302, 307–8, 319, 325, 332, 344, 354; colonial era, 103–4, 106, 123; *see also* schools

Egypt, 56–7, 65, 104

elections, 104, 107, 187, 208, 239, 272, 275, 277–8, 284–6, 324, 327, 337–8, 341–2, 352, 354; 1999 general, 238, 275, 277, 283, 288; 1999 presidential, 277–8, 330; 2004 general, 284–6; 2004 presidential, 285, 347; local, 286–7, 302, 306, 308–10, 337–8, 342, 349–50

elites, 5, 9, 19, 96, 192, 201, 275, 289, 317, 320, 329, 336, 349–50, 356; Acehnese, 1, 14, 68, 98, 106, 122, 132, 134, 140–1, 181, 260, 295, 315–8, 320, 322, 325–6, 333, 339, 342, 345–7, 349–50; national, 131, 145, 158, 319

emergency rule, 16, 139, 181, 232, 284, 308–9; *see also* martial law

employment, 5, 81, 136, 139, 233, 248, 309, 326, 328

English, *see* British

English East India Company, 40, 62–3, 80, 84

ethnic/ethnicity, 5, 10, 28, 32, 131, 136, 159–62, 166, 174, 208, 218, 226, 235–6, 244, 265;

Acehnese, 5, 136, 140, 142, 151, 153, 159–63, 168, 170–1, 235–6, 244, 265; *see also bangsa*; *suku bangsa*; nationalism/nationalists, Acehnese ethno-

Europe, 4, 10, 59, 62–3, 67, 72, 75, 81, 84–5, 88–9, 96, 98–9, 125, 181–2, 237; powers, 12, 14, 40, 52, 58, 60, 63–4, 66–7, 97; trade/traders, 12, 23, 60, 63

European Union (EU), 215, 239–40, 259, 291

Exxon Mobil Oil Indonesia (EMOI), 125, 192, 207, 211, 213, 215–6, 233–4, 295, 323; *see also* oil

Fansuri, Hamzah, 44–6, 48

fatwa, 42, 47, 130, 136, 143, 329

federalism, 122, 132–3, 181, 245, 286, 294

feudalism, 102–3, 122, 126, 328

Finland, *see* Helsinki peace talks

fishing industry, 212, 216–7, 302

foreign: advisors, 32, 83, 86–7, 91, 242; powers, 72, 91, 135; relations with, 14, 24, 53–6, 58, 60–4, 66–7, 96; traders, 26, 28, 42, 61, 75, 77, 82–3, 91–2

Forrest, Captain Thomas, 80–1

France, 13, 40, 58, 60–2, 64–5, 72, 74, 78, 84–5, 88, 91, 97, 182; traders, 61, 64, 84

Front Pemuda Aceh, 161–3, 165, 167

GAM, 13, 15–6, 18, 118, 121–2, 133, 135–6, 139–41, 147–9, 151–2, 154–6, 161, 164–5, 168–9, 172, 177–8, 180, 182–3, 186, 191–4, 196–8, 209–11, 214, 217, 225–65 *passim*, 274, 277–9, 281–4, 287–8, 290–3, 297–305, 308–11, 315, 325–7, 330–6, 339, 341–3, 346–7, 350,

358; government, 185, 231;
ideology, 138, 152, 168, 231,
237, 242–3, 249; leadership, 118,
121, 133, 135, 147, 182, 191,
193, 211, 226, 236, 243, 249–52,
259, 261, 265, 298, 330–1, 335;
legitimacy of, 177–9, 184–5,
239–40, 260, 262, 331;
proclamation of independence,
138, 185; symbolism, 135, 147,
303; support base/sympathisers,
138–9, 149, 158, 162, 177, 179,
185, 189, 190–2, 209–10, 225,
235–6, 242, 245, 249, 251,
255–8, 309, 326, 330–2, 334–5
Gayo (ethnic group), 3–4, 8, 33,
123, 136, 142, 235–6
Gelanggang, A.H, 156–8, 160–1, 163
Geneva peace talks, 239–41, 260, 279
Geudong, 22, 33, 37
Ghauth, Muhammad, Aceh envoy,
64–5, 71
Golkar, 222, 257, 305, 322, 324,
327, 338, 345, 352–3
Government: and Acehnese society,
17, 150–1, 161–2, 170, 292,
319, 350; central, 17, 121, 124,
128, 130, 132–3, 134–5, 139–41,
150, 152–4, 158, 161–3, 209,
277, 286, 297, 297, 303, 315–6,
319–21, 325–7, 330, 332–3,
336–8, 340–1, 343, 345, 347,
349–50, 353, 358; civil, 15, 99,
229–31, 272, 278–80, 308, 342,
346; colonial, 97, 99–101, 105,
114, 118, 122, 139, 154, 175;
foreign, 63, 65–7, 78, 81, 83–8,
190, 226, 239, 241, 261, 265;
GAM, 185, 231; local/provincial,
127–8, 130, 133–4, 137, 139,
144, 187, 215, 230, 247–8, 260,
287, 293–4, 296, 298–300, 302,
305–9, 316–9, 321, 324, 326–7,

331, 333, 335, 337–50, 354,
356–7; self-, 17, 194, 294, 301–2,
304, 310, 356; Sumatran, 128, 144
Gujarat, 30–1, 33, 41, 53, 57,
59–61, 63

Habibie, B. J., President of Indonesia
(1988–9), xxxii, 209, 237, 259,
275–8, 280, 288, 297–8, 304,
316, 329–30, 332
hadiths, 46, 104, 154
Hamid, Farhan, 336, 343, 357
Hardi, Vice Premier, 133
Hasan, Husaini, 147, 184
Hasan, Ibrahim, Aceh Governor, 125,
320–1, 323, 327, 329, 352–3
Hasan Krueng Kale, Tgk., 117, 145
Hasbi, Muchtar, 184, 188
Hatta, Mohammad (Indonesian Vice-
President), 118, 128–9, 144, 152,
185; and Sukarno, 118, 144
health, 201–2, 205, 211, 248, 279, 309
Helsinki peace talks, 17, 287, 310,
350
Henry Dunant Centre (HDC), 239,
241, 279, 282–4, 331, 342; *see
also* cease-fire; peace process
hikayat, 61, 111–3, 115, 117
Hikayat Aceh, 10, 53–4
Hikayta Malem Dagang, 60, 111
Hikayat Meukota Alam, 55
Hikayat Muhammad Hanafiyah, 113
Hikayat Perang Sabil (HPS), 99,
111–8, 334
Hikayat Potjut Muhamat, 79
Hikayat Raja-Raja Pasai, 52–3, 110
Hindu/Hinduism, 6, 10, 29–30, 33,
36, 60, 68, 154
Holland, *see* Dutch
holy war, 14, 99–100, 106, 108–11,
113–8, 127, 130, 135, 141, 144,
152, 318; *see also jihad*; *perang
sabil*

HUDA, 334–5, 356
human rights, 163, 200, 237, 243,
    245, 257, 272–3, 285, 309, 333,
    356; abuses, 149, 167–70, 179,
    201, 209, 211, 226, 238, 245,
    257–8, 260, 276–8, 285–6, 289,
    292, 298, 300–1, 304, 306–7,
    329, 350; activism, 161, 165,
    169–70, 177, 191, 198, 253,
    284; groups/organisations, 163,
    169, 193, 198, 216, 237–8, 244–5,
    253, 255, 298; investigations,
    159, 163, 169, 241, 245, 257,
    276, 297
Human Rights Watch, 257–8
Humanitarian Pause, 237, 247, 259,
    279–80, 290; *see also* cease-fire;
    peace process

IAIN, 132, 296, 303, 306, 328
Ibrahimy, Nur El, 127–8
ICRC, 229, 245
identity, 9–10, 12–3, 30, 33, 38–9,
    46, 49, 136, 149, 151–2, 159–62,
    166, 170, 242, 294, 317–8, 320,
    322, 327; Acehnese, 9, 12–3, 30,
    33, 39, 46, 136, 151–2, 159,
    242, 294, 317–8, 327;
    Indonesian, 22; Islamic, 42, 49
identity cards, 217, 228, 257, 285
ideology, 15, 56, 108, 115, 118,
    138–40, 152, 161, 167–8, 171–2,
    183, 185, 232, 294–5, 320, 322,
    328–9, 339, 341, 346, 352;
    GAM, 138, 152, 168, 231, 237,
    242–3, 249; Indonesian state,
    294, 322, 352
Idi, 117, 144
Idi Rayeuk, 95, 258
immigrants, *see* migrants;
    transmigrants
independence, 9, 15, 17–8, 124,
    127, 139, 146; Acehnese, 13, 30,

61–2, 66, 68, 72, 90, 96–7, 101,
    149, 194, 211, 226, 239–40,
    247, 293, 304, 335; East
    Timorese, 237, 278, 299; GAM
    proclamation of, 138, 185;
    Indonesian, 106, 110, 117–8,
    124, 127, 144, 162, 169, 181,
    228, 286, 293, 319, 349;
    movement, *see* GAM; Moro
India, 5–7, 12, 14, 22–4, 27–33, 36,
    44–6, 48–9, 53, 55–7, 59, 61–2,
    65, 74–5, 81, 83–4, 86, 90–1,
    96, 98, 114, 120; trade/traders,
    6–7, 10, 23–4, 26–8, 30–2, 76
Indian Ocean, 3, 13–4, 22–4, 32,
    56–8, 68, 74, 84, 91, 96, 194,
    310
Indochina, 7, 33
Indrapuri, Tgk. Ahmad Hasballah,
    117, 128
industry, 5, 91, 124, 204, 233–4,
    295, 323, 325–6, 328, 338, 353–
    4; *see also* drugs; fishing industry;
    logging; oil
infidels, 57, 110–1, 115–7, 119, 294,
    318; *see also kafir*
infrastructure, 1, 122, 156, 184, 210,
    229, 233, 248, 293, 305, 310,
    325; civilian, 248–9, 265, 311;
    economic, 122, 124; GAM, 265
Inong Bale, 228, 254
Inpres, see Presidential Instruction
Internally Displaced Persons (IDPs),
    255, 309, 348; *see also* refugees
international community, 2, 15, 17,
    200, 226, 229, 238–41, 243–4,
    259, 262, 279, 317, 343, 348
International Crisis Group (ICG),
    203, 219, 232, 236, 274, 280
Iskandar Muda, Sultan of Aceh
    (1607–36), 36, 40–4, 53–5,
    59–61, 111, 334
Iskandar Thani, Sultan of Aceh

(1636–41), 5, 38, 41–2, 45, 53, 60–1

Islam, 2, 5, 9–10, 12, 14, 16, 30–3, 39–40, 42–9, 55–8, 61, 68, 99, 101, 104, 106, 109–11, 114, 116, 120, 123, 127–8, 131, 133, 135, 140–1, 144, 147, 151–5, 159, 161–2, 169, 171, 174, 179, 190, 237, 242, 278, 293–6, 298, 300, 306–7, 309–11, 318–20, 322–4, 328–30, 332–4, 338, 341, 350, 352, *see also* Muslim(s); alliances/networks, 55–7, 152; early influences, 30, 36; groups/ organisations, 162, 169, 278; law, 9, 42–3, 46–7, 50, 130, 152–4, 159, 173, 294–5, 298, 300, 302, 306–7, 316, 319, 323, 329, 332–4, 338, 342, 355; scholars/ teachers, 8, 44, 47–8, 115, 122, 318, 322, 333, *see also ulama*; schools, 9, 44–6, 48, 99, 103–4, 106, 113, 126–7, 130, 132, 232, 277, 296, 323, 327, 335, *see also dayah*; *madrasah*; state, 42, 130, 148, 151, 153–4, 159, 294–5, 334; symbolism, 318, 324, 334

Islamicisation, 5–7, 19, 30, 32, 39, 48

Jakarta Charter, 294, 311

Japan/Japanese, 3, 29, 124, 233, 259, 291, 314; occupation, 105–8, 110, 117, 127, 143, 318

Java, 2, 5–6, 13–4, 23, 31, 33, 52–3, 56, 83–5, 88, 90, 104, 117, 136, 149, 180–1, 275, 290, 293, 295, 326; West, 151, 294

Javanese, 5, 12, 28, 30–2, 35, 37–8, 49, 53, 59–60, 98, 103, 118, 123, 134, 136, 147, 161, 174, 181, 229–30, 232–6, 238, 244, 265, 290; colonialism, 118, 149,

230, 233–5; culture, 12, 32, 134; migrants, 229, 234–5, 238, 265, 326

jawi, 32, 197

Jews, 30, 62, 111, 116, 179

jihad, 14, 109–11, 113, 120, 141, 154; *see also* holy war; *perang sabil*

Johor, 40–1, 53, 60

Joint Security Committee (JSC), 210, 239, 241, 291; *see also* CoHA

journalists, 2, 159, 177, 214, 221, 228–9, 244, 265, 287, 329, 348

Kadaram, 25, 35*; see also* Kedah

kafir, 151, 154, 173, 294; *see also* infidels

Kalla, Yusuf, 255, 345, 347, 350, 358

Karo-Batak, 5, 28–9, 33

Kartosuwiryo, S.M., 130, 151; *see also* Darul Islam

Kedah, 23, 25, 32, 35, 41, 53, 60, 77

Kerala, India, 23–4, 30, 68

Keumala, temporary Aceh capital, 99, 101

kings, 8, 10, 25, 32, 36, 39–40, 53–6, 60, 63–4, 68, 70, 79, 116; Acehnese, 8, 19, 39–40, 49, 55–6, 60, 63, 81, 111; *see also* sultans

kinship, 9, 12

Kliet, Abu, 177, 182–3

Kodam, 132, 216, 231, 247, 280; Iskandar Muda 132, 216, 231, 247, 284; *see also* TNI, territorial command system

Köhler, Maj. Gen. J.H.R, 97, 111

Komnas HAM (National Human Rights Commission), 245, 285

Kontras, 216, 255, 257, 271, 304

Kopassandha, 247, 249

Kopassus, 247, 253

Kostrad, 175, 245, 278, 280–1

Kota Cina, 28–9

KRA, *see* Aceh People's Congress (KRA)

Krueng Raya, 20, 22, 24, 27, 29, 31, 36

KTP, *see* identity cards

Kuala Lumpur, 145, 189

Kutakarang, Tgk Chik, 5, 115

Kuta Lubhok, 30, 36

Kutaradja, 31, 100, 129, 132–3, 143–5, 161; *see also* Banda Aceh

Lamreh, 20, 27; Krueng, 36

Lamri, 7, 20, 24–5, 31, 36

Lancaster, James, 40, 58–9

Langsa, 124, 129, 231, 239, 284

language, 5, 7–8, 12, 19, 25, 61, 84, 109–10, 136, 159, 178, 356; Acehnese, 3, 5, 7–8, 53, 61, 114–5, 155; Arabic, 10, 20, 32, 36, 71, 197; Dutch, 8; English, 3, 15, 17, 51, 63, 174, 178, 189; French, 84; Indonesian, 3, 5; Malay, 8, 10, 25, 35, 44–5, 48, 58, 60–1, 63, 69, 71; Mon-Khmer, 7, 19; Tamil, 25, 28–9

law, 15, 58, 67, 78, 87, 102, 106, 113, 124, 128–9, 131–4, 136, 140, 144, 164, 191, 200–1, 203–5, 208–11, 216, 218–9, 225–6, 230, 239, 246–7, 257, 259, 261–2, 265, 274, 277, 280, 284, 287; autonomy, 203, 246, 260, 264, 277, 281–2, 287, 296–310, 316, 332–3, 337–9, 342–3, 356, *see also* NAD*;* customary, 43, 47, 60, 294, 296–7, 319, 332, *see also adat;* international, 257, 261–2; Islamic, 9, 42–3, 46–7, 50, 130, 152–4, 159, 173, 294–5, 298, 300, 302, 306–7, 316, 319, 323, 329, 332–4, 338, 342, 355; martial, *see* martial law; No.44/ 1999, 292, 297–300, 302, 332; No.18/2001, 281, 292, 301, 338, *see also* NAD; pre-colonial, 42; rule of, 200, 220, 246, 248, 272, 274

leadership, 118, 128, 140–2, 158, 162, 179; Acehnese, 17, 100, 102, 105, 107, 128–9, 140–2, 152, 156, 180, 189, 293, 296, 301–2, 305, 308–9, 315–22, 324–31, 333–4, 336, 339–40, 342, 349–51; civilian, 182, 184, 187, 192, 249–50, 263–4, 274, 276, 278–82, 287, 308–9, 333–4; Darul Islam, 122, 131, 133, 151, 154, 156, 159, 161, 168, 180–1, 183–4, 186; GAM, 121, 147, 182, 191, 193, 211, 226, 236, 243, 249–52, 259, 261, 265, 298, 330–1, 335; national, 107, 152, 169, 181, 183, 185, 211, 262, 276, 288, 293, 308, 310, 319, 332, 336, 347, 349; military, 160, 187, 276, 279–83, 287, 300; religious, 104, 114, 117, 126, 130, 136, 138, 162, 184, 294, 311, 317, 319–20, 323, 329, 331–4, 354, see also *ulama*; resistance, 99, 114, 126, 130–3, 151, 153–4, 156, 159, 161, 167–8, 181, 183–4, 294, 309, 330; royal, 42; student, 118, 330–1, 333–4, 336

Lebai Dappah, 74–5, 78, 82, 87

legislators, 302, 337, 339; Acehnese, 231, 336, 339, 342

legitimacy, 220, 234, 239–40, 309, 316, 325, 327–8, 340, 345–6, 349–50; of GAM, 177–9, 184–5, 239–40, 260, 262, 331; of Indonesian state, 220, 262, 316

Lhok Cut, 22, 29–30

Lhok Jok, 229, 233

Lhoknga, 217, 253
Lhokseumawe, 22, 33, 86–7, 90,
    147, 154, 179, 183, 188–9, 207,
    231, 233, 247, 254, 295, 323,
    326; industrial zone, 295, 234,
    326, 328, 353; *see also* PT Arun
    NGL; Exxon Mobil Oil Indonesia
    (EMOI); oil
Libya, 138, 141, 179, 190, 193, 226,
    236–7
literature, 2, 14, 39, 43, 54, 149, 156
logging, 125, 142, 164, 207, 211–2,
    215, 217, 222
London Treaty, Anglo-Dutch (1824),
    52, 72, 74, 89–90, 96–7
LSM, *see* Non-governmental
    Organisations (NGOs)

Madjid, Ibrahim, Aceh Governor,
    321, 352
madrasah, 127–8, 130, 296, 329,
    354; *see also dayah*; schools,
    Islamic
Mahkamah Syariah, 128, 307
Mahmud, Amir Rasyid, 182–3
Mahmud, Malik, 182–4, 186, 188–91,
    193, 226, 240–1, 261–2
Mahmud, Syamsuddin, Aceh
    Governor, 299–300, 321, 329–31,
    354–6
Mahmud, Tuanku, 114, 117
Majapahit, 31–2, 37, 53; *see also*
    Negarakrtagama
Malabar, 53, 59, 74
Malacca Straits, *see* Melaka Straits
Malay, 6, 32, 47–9, 60, 64, 76, 91;
    archipelago, 76, 88–9; language,
    8, 10, 12, 25, 35, 44–5, 48, 58,
    60–1, 63, 69, 71; people, 42, 49,
    60; Peninsula, 19, 41, 44, 77, 91,
    124, 131–2, 142; scholars, 38,
    46; states, 60, 76, 91; world,
    39–40, 43, 48–9, 64–5, 88

Malaya, 105, 182
Malaysia, 52, 74, 91, 138, 141,
    148–9, 187, 190, 193, 237, 249,
    252, 258, 261–2
Maluku, 56, 262; *see also* Ambon
Manaf, Muzakkir, 250, 253
martial law, 187, 209–10, 212, 217,
    228, 231–3, 244, 247, 250–1,
    254, 257, 261–2, 264–5, 275,
    277, 280, 283–8, 304, 307, 309,
    346, 358; *see also Operasi Terpadu*
Marzuki, Amni bin, 240–1, 250
Masyumi, 129, 145, 187
Mecca, 39, 42, 45, 47–50, 55–7, 64,
    84, 101, 104, 116, 296; Sheriff
    of, 42, 47; *see also Serambi*
    Mekkah
Medan, 6, 106, 122, 124–5, 128–9,
    138, 144, 147, 152, 157, 162,
    164, 180, 213, 215–6, 228, 247,
    261, 286, 299, 321, 352
media, 158, 161–2, 166, 168–9,
    209, 211, 232, 244, 285–6, 315,
    329, 341, 345–6, 348–50;
    foreign/international, 2, 238, 340;
    print, 129, 152, 158, 181, 234,
    286, 299, 307, 340, 343;
    television, 166, 257
Medina, 45–6, 50, 55
Melaka, 8, 12, 30–1, 39–41, 52–3,
    55, 62, 77, 88, 110–1, 113;
    chronicle, 8, 113; Portuguese,
    39–41, 56–7, 110–1
Melaka Straits, 26, 34, 47, 52–3, 61,
    73–4, 76, 84, 90–1, 111, 228,
    244, 252
merchants, 6, 23, 30–1, 42, 47, 53,
    57, 63, 68, 76, 82–3, 85–7, 90–2;
    Arab, 10, 23, 28, 31, 35–6,
    58–9, 61, 63; Chinese, 5, 7, 24,
    27–8, 59, 84; European, 12, 23,
    60, 63; foreign, 26, 28, 42, 61,
    75, 77, 82–3, 91–2; French, 61,

64, 84; Indian, 6–7, 10, 23–4,
26–8, 30–2, 76; Penang, 5, 97–8,
100; Tamil, 7, 26, 28–30; *see also*
trade
meunasah, 9, 113
migrants, 6, 8, 41, 123, 326;
Acehnese, 74, 77, 92; Chinese, 5,
123; Javanese, 229, 234–5, 238,
265, 326; *see also* transmigrants
militias, 127–8, 136, 139, 143, 147,
206, 211, 217, 223, 235, 238–9,
248, 263, 287
military, *see* TNI
Minangkabau, 9, 12, 28, 30, 42, 45,
63, 104, 160–1, 168, 174
Moro, 122, 140, 148
MPR, 336
Mukims, 6, 30, 81, 95, 126–7
Munir, 284, 304
Muslim(s), 12, 14, 36, 39, 47, 53–4,
56–7, 66, 101, 109, 114–7, 120,
130, 135, 140, 153–4, 193,
294–6, 301–2, 306–7, 323,
331–2; Malayo-, 14, 140;
national liberation movements,
242–3, 265; non-, 57–8, 110,
293, 295; non-Acehnese, 7, 10,
44, 57, 68; traders, 30–1, 68;
see also Islam
MUI, 322, 328–9, 333
Muzakkar, Kahar, 131, 145

NAD, 281, 284–5, 301–8, 310, 338,
344; *see also* law, No.18/2001
Nahdlatul Ulama, 278
Nanggala operations, 244, 247–9,
252; *see also* security, operations
Nanggroe Aceh Darussalam, *see* NAD
Nasihat al-Muslimin, 114–5
Natal, 78, 86–7, 91
nation, 66, 110, 131, 174; Acehnese,
135, 151, 159, 170, 185, 232;
Indonesian, 160–1, 275, 282, 295

nation-state, 169, 272
nationalism, 150, 161, 171, 242–3,
265, 318; Acehnese, ethno-, 8,
12–3, 68, 121–2, 131, 136, 139,
140, 149, 152, 158, 160–1,
166–70, 174, 177–8, 183–5,
237, 242, 311, 318, 334;
Indonesian, 96, 104–5, 141, 154,
166, 169, 176, 185, 220, 242,
251, 275, 280, 285, 287–8, 293,
311, 319, 322, 332, 352
natural resources, 121–2, 124–5,
129, 134, 151, 170, 206–7,
211–3, 233, 277, 326–7; control
over, 300–2, 304, 307, 309, 337;
exploitation of, 121–2, 125,
134–5, 151, 234, 277, 326–7
Nazar, Muhammad, 254, 283; *see also*
SIRA
Negara Aceh Sumatra, 135
Negara Bagian Aceh (NBA), 131–2,
145, 181–2, 294
Negara Islam Indonesia (NII), 131–2,
145, 151, 182, 295
Negarakrtagama, 31, 37
Netherlands, *see* Dutch
New Order government, 6, 13, 121,
125–6, 134, 139, 150, 156, 166,
171, 177–80, 187, 189–91, 208,
220, 225, 244, 275, 281, 295–8,
309, 315, 319–25, 327–30, 334,
336–8, 340, 345, 350; collapse
of, 125, 166, 187, 297; policies,
134, 141, 179, 186, 245, 259,
296–7, 315, 321, 323, 325–9;
post- era, 151, 166, 175–6, 190,
192, 209, 257–60, 264, 273,
288, 292, 297, 308, 316, 350; *see
also* Suharto
Nias, 4, 347
Nisan (tombstones), 30, 32, 36
Non-governmental Organisations
(NGOs), 15, 139, 163, 169, 216,

238–9, 244, 253–5, 257, 285, 298, 305, 309, 339–40, 347; activists, 139, 165, 286, 337; international, 163, 254, 284, 331, 342, 344, 349

oil, 122, 124–5, 128, 134, 207, 211–3, 233–4, 295, 302, 316, 326, 343; *see also* PT Arun NGL; Exxon Mobil Oil Indonesia (EMOI); Pertamina
OKPH, 245–9, 251–2, 254, 257, 264; *see also* security, operations
Operasi Jaring Merah, xxxii, 244, 248–9, 251–2, 255–7, 263–4; *see also* DOM period
Operasi Terpadu, 245, 247–52, 254–5, 257–8, 261–4, 308
Ottoman, 14, 40, 47, 54, 56–7, 64, 66–7; *see also* Turkey

Padang, 4, 62, 73, 77–8, 160
Padang Lawas, 25, 28, 30
Palembang, 19, 25, 29, 114
palm oil, 91, 125, 142, 164, 212, 215; *see also* plantations; trade
Pancasila, 134, 160, 165, 248, 322, 352
Paneuk, Daud, 184, 188–9
Panglima Laut, 78, 82–3
Panglima Polem, 61, 101, 114
Panglima Sagis, 79, 81–2, 86, 88, 127
Pannai, 25, 28
Papua, 207, 216, 222, 262, 273, 278, 292
parties, 169, 187, 189, 243, 274–5, 277, 285–8, 319, 322–3, 336–8, 341, 352; Islamic, 104, 311, 322, 338, 352; local, 337; opposition, 322
Pasai, 7–8, 10–1, 20, 32, 37, 39, 53, 58, 68, 110; Krueng, 37

patronage, 9–10, 53, 61, 82, 104, 204–5, 316, 321–4, 329–31, 337, 339, 346–7
patron-client relations, 123, 206, 321, 345, 350
pax Neerlandica, 96
PDI, 352
PDIP, 275, 288
peace process, xxxii, xxxiii, 15–7, 153, 210–1, 226, 237–8, 240–3, 246–7, 250–1, 259–60, 262, 264–5, 274, 282–3, 300, 304, 308, 310, 344, 356; *see also* cease-fire; CoHA
Penang, 25, 62–3, 65–6, 73, 75–7, 79, 81, 83–91, 96, 98, 100, 105; traders, 5, 97–8, 100
pepper, 5, 8, 26, 41, 55–6, 58–62, 64–5, 73–9, 82, 84, 89–91, 95, 124, 318; *see also* plantations; trade
Perak, Malaysia, 40, 53, 60
Persia, 5, 23, 10, 36, 44, 55
Pertamina, 124–5, 146, 207, 234; *see also* oil
perang sabil, 109, 115–7, 119, 185, 318; *see also* *Hikayat Perang Sabil*; holy war
pesantren, 130; see also dayah; madrasah; schools, Islamic
Pesindo, 106, 127
Philippines, 122, 140, 182, 241
Pidie, 3, 6–8, 10, 39, 73, 75, 77, 82–3, 86, 99, 101, 104, 106–8, 118, 123–4, 126–7, 130, 144, 156, 184, 186, 188–9, 227, 238, 247, 299, 326, 331
piracy/pirates, 58, 77–9, 83, 87–8, 91, 207, 228, 244
PKI, 145, 187, 189, 319–20; *see also* communism
plantations, 5, 73–5, 79, 90, 123, 125, 128, 130, 164, 212, 215–7, 235; *see also* agriculture

police, 113, 133, 153, 156–7, 164,
172–3, 184, 192–4, 200, 211,
213–5, 217, 219, 225, 227, 236,
247, 253–4, 258, 261–3, 279,
303, 306, 332; *see also* Brimob
policies 2, 12, 189, 207, 237, 239,
273, 332, 337, 341–2, 352;
colonial, 66, 98, 101–2, 105,
122–3, 322; GAM, 238; national,
124, 126, 131–2, 162–3, 169,
201, 210–1, 244–5, 273, 277–8,
280–1, 288, 296–7, 300, 303,
316, 323, 345, 352; New Order,
134, 141, 179, 186, 245, 259,
296–7, 315, 321, 323, 325–9;
royal, 40–1, 60
population, 5, 12, 18, 41, 131, 140,
161; Aceh, 1, 4–7, 10, 18, 31,
33, 73, 86, 90, 102–3, 123, 126,
155–8, 160, 163–5, 187, 212,
218, 226–9, 233, 238, 241–2,
244, 247–8, 255–7, 263, 315,
325–6, 353
Portugal/Portuguese, 10–12, 20, 32,
36, 39–41, 47, 53, 55–60, 68,
111, 113, 218; Melaka, 39–41,
56–7, 110–1
pottery, *see* ceramics; earthenware
poverty, 124, 126, 157, 212–3, 264,
295, 326, 340
power: local/provincial, 9, 128,
231, 254, 294, 296–8, 301–2,
304, 309, 317–8, 321, 325,
336–7, 339–42, 346–7, 354;
military, 201, 204, 210, 230,
283, 309, 311 royal, 12, 41–2,
45, 54, 56, 59–63, 72, 79–83,
86, 92, 135; *ulèëbalang*, 9, 12,
62, 73, 79, 87–8, 92, 100;
Western, 52, 72, 74, 82, 84–5,
88–91, 97
power vacuum, 106, 310, 316, 330,
336, 350

PPP, 257, 322–4, 327, 332, 340,
352, 354
Prawiranegara, Sjafruddin, 128–9,
132, 144, 181–2, 293
Presidential Instruction, 307, 309;
No. 4/2001, 210, 235
protection business, 205, 207, 213,
215–6; *see also* TNI, business
PRRI/Permesta rebellion, 182–3,
187, 190
PT Arun NGL, 125, 135, 215, 233–4
Pulot Leupung-Cot Jeumpa affair, *see*
Cot Jeumpa incident
PUSA, 105–6, 122, 124, 127–9,
132, 142–4, 186, 328, 354;
activists, 105–6, 127, 132, 143–4
Puteh, Abdullah, Aceh Governor,
xxxiii, 211, 231, 257, 287, 338–41,
343–7, 356–8

Qaddafi, Colonel Muammar, 179, 190
qanun, 305–9, 342
Qur'an, 109–11, 113–5, 117, 132,
143–4, 154

Raffles, Stamford, 4, 19, 63, 79, 81,
83, 85, 87–9, 96
rajas, 10, 12, 38, 41, 59, 76, 81–2, 114
Rasyid, "Pawang", 184–5, 188–9
referendum movement, 118, 165–9,
193, 198, 209, 237, 253–4, 260,
275, 277, 279, 283, 288, 298–300,
330–1, 334; *see also* SIRA
reform, 9, 44–6, 48, 102, 156, 280,
282, 292, 297, 336–40; era, 121,
193, 292, 297; group, 336–8,
340, 342, 345, 347, 356–8;
Islamic, 44–6, 48, 354; security
sector, 199–201, 218–20, 280,
282
refugees, 10, 149, 217, 238, 245,
249, 258, 283, 290; *see also*
Internally Displaced Persons (IDPs)

regionalism, 152–3, 169, 181, 189, 294; *see also* nationalism, separatism

religion, 2, 5, 9–10, 26, 33, 41–5, 47, 54–5, 58, 86, 99–100, 106, 111, 113–5, 117, 122, 126–8, 130, 132–3, 135–6, 139–41, 143, 151–2, 154, 159, 161, 183, 185, 190, 232, 242, 251, 294–8, 300, 317–20, 322–4, 327–8, 331–6; and Acehnese, 9, 43–5, 104, 113, 115, 117, 122–3, 135, 153–4, 169, 294–6, 298, 300, 333–4

Republic of Indonesia, 106–7, 110, 127, 143, 151, 154, 159, 180–1, 203, 209, 218–9, 226, 232, 241, 243, 257, 260, 293–4, 299, 310

Republik Persatuan Indonesia, see RPI

Riau, 76, 88, 91, 121

Rimba, Tgk. Abdullah Ujung, 134–5

RPI, 132–3, 135, 182

rubber, 5, 91, 102, 123–5, 142, 212, 215; *see also* plantations; trade

rulers, 11–2, 24, 42–3, 47, 54, 57–9, 66, 68, 76–7, 79, 81–3, 86–7, 89, 91–2, 110; Acehnese, 42–3, 47, 54, 57–8, 74, 76, 79, 81–4, 86–7, 89–92, 99–100, 102, 115; *see also* kings; rajas; sultans

Rum, Sultan, 54–5

Ryacudu, Lt. Gen. Ryamizard, 246, 254, 280–1

Sabang, 67, 100, 134, 250, 257, 323, 328, 340, 354; as free port, 100, 134, 328, 354

Sabarno, Hari, 345

Said, Mohammad, 32, 36

Saiful Alam Shah, claimant to Aceh throne, 87–8

Said, Teuku Ali, 129, 250

Saleh, Hasan, 133, 139, 147, 154, 156–7, 173, 197, 294, 311

Samudera Pasai, 30–3, 37, 58, 110

Samudra-Pase, Yusuf Ali, 249–50

Sastroamijoyo, Ali, 158

scholars, 35, 45–8, 114, 149–50, 177–8, 186, 190–1; Acehnese, 44–5, 47–8, 115, 177, 322, 333; Islamic, 8, 44, 47–8, 115, 122, 322, 333, *see also ulama*; Malay, 38, 46

schools, 103–4, 134, 181, 191, 296, 307–8, 354; burnings of, 231–3, 244, 261, 307–8; Islamic, 9, 44–6, 48, 99, 103–4, 106, 113, 126–7, 130, 132, 232, 277, 296, 323, 327, 335; *see also dayah; madrasah*

security, 58, 89, 91, 96, 126, 130, 137, 139, 165, 174, 179, 199–201, 208, 216, 220, 233–4, 238, 247–9, 264, 278, 280–3, 285–7, 289, 297, 301, 303, 311, 324, 334, 343, 345–6, 348; approach, 163, 200–1, 244–5, 262, 272, 287, 289, 297, 303, 315; human, 276, 286; national, 165–6, 220, 276; operations, 147, 157–8, 163, 165, 170, 181, 206, 210–2, 216, 225–6, 228, 233, 235, 244–52, 254–8, 260, 262–5, 273–4, 276, 280, 284, 288, 292, 298, 300, 303–4, 308, 310, 325, 329; *see also* TNI

Selangor, 76–7

self-determination, 118, 135, 151, 167, 184, 239

self-image (Acehnese), 13–4, 46, 55

self-governance/government, 17, 194, 294, 301–2, 304, 310, 356

separatism/separatists, 3, 13, 15, 121, 131–2, 135, 139, 151, 156, 170–1, 207, 209, 214, 219, 244–5, 254, 260, 262, 272–3,

275, 278–9, 283, 289, 292, 300, 304, 315–6, 327, 346, 348; *see also* nationalism

Serambi Mekkah, 2, 38–9, 46–7, 49, 56

Shams al-Din al-Sumatra'i, 42, 44–6, 48

Siam, 14, 44, 53–4, 58–60, 72

Simeulue, 4, 142, 215

Simpang KKA massacre, 163, 166

Singapore, 62, 66–7, 73, 88–92, 96–8, 147, 182–3, 189, 218, 237

Singkil, 45, 63, 74–5, 77–9, 82, 86

SIRA, 167–8, 170, 209–10, 254, 283, 298, 300, 304, 309, 330

Sjamsuddin, Nazaruddin, 3, 159, 161, 163, 166, 182

Sjamsoedin, Maj. Gen. Sjafrie, 248, 280, 287

social revolution, 9, 107, 122, 152, 186, 328, 352; *see also* PUSA

South Aceh, 126, 182, 248, 250, 299

Southeast Asia, 2, 14, 22–4, 27–9, 39, 46, 56, 58, 61–2, 72, 75–6, 84, 90, 99, 110, 182, 193

sovereignty,14, 17, 66, 87, 97, 125, 239; Acehnese, 71, 135, 167, 177–8, 183, 185, 194, 275, 283, 289; Indonesian, 129, 262, 293, 348; royal, 12, 42, 86

Soviet Union, 189–90

special autonomy, see autonomy, special

Special Region of Aceh, 133–4, 292, 297, 300

Sri Lanka, 3–4, 26–7, 29, 33

Srivijaya, 24, 35

SSR, *see* reform, security sector

State: Acehnese, 12–3, 39–40, 42, 45, 47, 72, 82, 89, 135, 145, 167, 308, 131, 135–6, 138, 140, 185, 209, 211, 226, 231, 242, 290, 294, 301–2, 308, 317–8; apparatus, 157, 160, 274, 293,

310; federated, 122, 129, 133, 135, 140, 294; institutions, 132, 169, 207, 229, 296, 309, 316, 320–1; intra- conflict, 273–4, 279; Islamic, 42, 130, 148, 151, 153–4, 159, 294–5, 334; -less, 12, 96; power, 274, 276, 295–7, 305, 317; port-, 8, 10, 86; "Successor", 135–6; unitary, 131, 277, 280–2, 286, 288; violence, 151–2, 156, 161–4, 166, 168, 170–1, 309

stoneware, 22, 27, 29, 33, 35

students, 25, 45, 104, 106, 118, 162, 166–7, 189, 209, 254–5, 275, 277, 283–4, 296, 298, 308, 318, 320–1, 329–31, 333–6, 350; activists, 118, 139, 167, 329; groups/organisations, 167–9, 209, 254, 298, 330, 334; leaders, 118, 330–1, 333–4, 336

Subianto, Col. Prabowo, 175

Sudarsono, Juwono, 202–3, 221

Sufis, 45–6, 48, *see also* tarekat

Shattariyya Order, 46, 48; *see also* Islam; Muslim(s)

Snouk Hurgronje, Christian, 2–3, 5–6, 9, 38–9, 101, 318

Suharto, President of Indonesia (1967–98), 6, 13, 16, 150–1, 163, 171, 177, 187, 189, 193, 196, 201, 204, 218, 221, 275–6, 278, 281, 295, 315, 321–2, 330, 338, 352, *see also* New Order government; fall of, 3, 118, 139, 149, 180, 193–4, 202, 225–6, 237, 243–5, 249, 253, 264, 272, 309, 317, 329; post-era, 151, 166, 175–6, 190, 192, 209, 257–9, 264, 273, 288, 292, 297, 308, 316, 350

Sukarno, President of Indonesia (1945–67), 131, 143–4, 187,

196, 294, 311, 322, 352; and Hatta, 118, 144; government, 186–7, 189, 294

Sukarnoputri, Megawati, 208, 210–1, 275, 280–2, 284–5, 288; as president (2001–4), 208, 210–1, 288, 301, 304, 308, 345, 347; as vice-president (1999–2001), 208, 280, 288

suku bangsa, 160, 174

Sulawesi, 76, 182

Sultan Ala'ad-din Ahmad Syah (1727–35), 72, 76

Sultan Ala'ad-din Jehan Syah (1735–60), 79–80

Sultan Alau'd-Din Ri'ayat Shah al-Kahar (1537?–71), 39–40, 47, 54, 56–7, 110–1

Sultan Ala u'd-din Ri'ayat Syah Sayyid al-Mukammil (1589–1604), 40, 44, 58

Sultan Ala'ud-din Mansur Syah (Tuanku Ibrahim, regent from 1838, r. 1857–70), 5, 8, 63–6, 70–1, 76, 90, 95

Sultan Ali Mughayat Syah (1515–30), 10, 12, 39

Sultan Jauhar Alam (contested 1790–1823), 81–3, 85–91

Sultan Mahmud Syah (1870–4), 80, 82

Sultan Muhammad Daud Syah (1874–1903), 99, 101–2, 106, 112, 115, 135

Sultan Muhammad Syah (1823–38), 84, 90

Sultan Perumudal Perumal, of Pasai, 53, 68

Sultana 'Inayat Shah Zakiyat al-Din Shah (1678–88), 42, 46

Sultana Kamalat Shah (1688–99), 42, 47

Sultana Taj al-'Alam Safiyat al-Din Shah (1641–75), 41–2, 46, 61

sultanate, 12, 36, 52, 56–8, 62, 68, 91–2; Aceh, 12, 14, 30–3, 41–2, 44–5, 48, 50, 56, 72, 79, 85, 92, 96, 98, 111, 123, 136, 139, 147, 242, 318

sultans, 8, 11–2, 31–2, 36–7, 40–1, 53–7, 62–8, 82, 302; Acehnese, 5, 9–11, 38–48, 53–9, 61–7, 72, 74–7, 79–90, 95–6, 98–9, 101–2, 110–2, 115, 118, 135, 318

Sumatra, 3–5, 7–12, 22–6, 28–9, 31–3, 36–7, 39, 41, 47, 52–3, 55, 62, 66, 73, 75, 77, 79, 83, 96–7, 103, 105, 117, 128, 134, 144, 182, 293; East, 122–3, 129, 144, 155; government, 128, 144; North, 22, 39, 52, 73, 124, 129, 144–5, 157, 168, 213, 228, 236, 247, 273, 286, 293; West, 9, 44–5, 61, 104, 195

Suparman, Lt. Gen. Djadja, 278

Sutarto, Gen. Endriartono, 212, 251, 285, 291

Sutowo, Maj. Gen. Ibnu, 124

Suwarya, Maj. Gen. Endang, 251, 254

Sweden, 139, 249–50, 252, 261–2, 298, 331

Syafi'ie, Abdullah, 184, 188–9, 231, 249–50, 278

syahbandar, 76, 97

Syari'ah, *see* law, Islamic

Syiah Kuala University, 296, 321, 327, 338, 351

Syaikh Abbas, *see* Kutakarang, Tgk Chik

symbolism, 12, 99, 101, 136, 228, 302, 305; Acehnese, 154, 318, 327, 338; GAM, 135, 147, 303; Islamic, 318, 324, 334

Takengon, 144, 156, 239, 241

Tamiang, 90, 122, 142, 250, 255

Tamil, 6–7, 23–6, 28–31, 35–7;
    language, 25, 28–9; traders, 7,
    24, 26, 28–30, 35–6, *see also*
    Chulias
Tapanuli, 78–9, 129, 144
Tapus, 78–9, 86
tarekat, 130, 136; *see also* Shattariyya
technocrats, 260, 295, 317, 320–32,
    336–8, 340, 350, 352–4
Thailand, 14, 29, 33, 72, 90, 182,
    227, 240, 252, 261–2; *see also*
    Siam
Tiba, Teungku Sofyan Ibrahim, 197,
    240, 250
timber, *see* logging
Tiro, Sheikh Saman, Teungku Chik
    di, 99–101, 106, 108, 114, 117,
    126
Tiro, T.M. Hasan di, 101, 104, 118,
    121–2, 126–9, 131–40, 143,
    145–7, 179–81, 185–6, 195–6,
    198, 226, 261, 266, 268, 303
TNI, 1–2, 5, 15–6, 121–2, 130,
    132–3, 136, 138–8, 147, 149–59,
    156–7, 162–6, 168–72, 178,
    181, 187, 191–4, 198–221, 223,
    225–9, 232–9, 241–60, 262–5,
    272–89, 291, 293, 297–8, 300,
    304–5, 307–11, 318–22, 324–6,
    329–30, 332, 334–5, 337, 339,
    341, 346–8, 355–6, 358; Aceh
    operations, 147, 157–8, 163,
    165, 170, 181, 206, 210–2, 216,
    225–6, 228, 233, 235, 244–52,
    254–8, 260, 262–5, 273–4, 276,
    280, 284, 288, 292, 298, 300,
    303–4, 308, 310, 325, 329; Aceh
    strategy, 225, 242, 244, 247–8,
    252, 258, 261–5, 274, 324;
    atrocities, *see* civilian(s), violence
    against; human rights, abuses;
    violence, state; budget, 165, 199,
    201–4, 209, 212, 218–21, 286;

business, 15, 164–5, 199–201,
    203–9, 211–21, 223, 305;
    capacity, 155, 201, 203–4,
    218–9, 251, 262–3; territorial
    command system, 205, 216, 231,
    262
Total People's Defence doctrine, 248
trade/traders, 5–8, 10, 12, 22–9,
    31–3, 35–6, 38, 49, 53, 55–6,
    58–66, 74–9, 81–92, 96–8, 100,
    124, 128, 132, 134, 139, 204,
    207, 212–3, 215, 223, 318; Arab,
    10, 23, 28, 31, 35–6, 55, 58–9,
    61, 63; British, 61, 63, 74, 84,
    86–8, 90, 92; Chinese, 5, 7, 24,
    27–8, 59, 84; European, 12, 23,
    60, 63; foreign, 26, 28, 42, 61,
    75, 77, 82–3, 91–2; French, 61,
    64, 84; Indian, 6–7, 10, 23–4,
    26–8, 30–2, 76; Muslim, 30–1,
    68; Penang, 5, 75, 85, 87, 90–1,
    97–8, 100; pre-colonial, 22–4,
    27; Tamil, 7, 24, 26, 28–30,
    35–6; *see also* merchants
traditions, 5, 20, 43, 46, 55, 61, 76,
    82, 103, 106, 118, 128, 133–4,
    140, 193, 200, 298, 302, 338;
    see also culture
transmigrants, 5, 229, 234–5, 238;
    see also migrants, Javanese
tsunami, 1, 3–4, 17, 185, 194, 197,
    287–9, 310–1, 316–7, 347–8
Tuanku, Raja, 81–2, 114
Turkey, 3, 5, 13–4, 40, 47, 53–7, 61,
    63–9, 71, 97–8, 110

ulama, 5, 9, 53, 57–8, 63, 99, 101,
    104–7, 115, 117, 122, 126, 130,
    132–6, 140, 143, 152–3, 163,
    184–5, 187, 191, 294–6, 298–9,
    318–20, 322–5, 327–9, 332–7,
    347, 350–1, 353–6; council, 135,
    298

ulèëbalang, 5, 9, 12, 37, 61–2, 73–4, 76, 78–82, 86–92, 95, 98–108, 117, 123–4, 126–30, 135, 143, 152, 318–20, 322, 352

Uleelheue, 31, 100

Uma, Teuku, 100–1

ummat, 132, 160, 174, 318; *see also* Islam; Muslim(s)

United Kingdom, *see* British

United Nations (UN), 131, 135, 146, 162, 167, 181, 237, 239–41, 244–5, 262, 275, 279, 348–9

United States of America (USA), 63, 67, 72, 75, 78, 88, 91, 97, 147, 167, 181–2, 189, 213, 233–4, 237, 239–40, 259, 291, 351

Vietnam, 7, 29, 33, 72, 182, 227

violence, 2, 6, 46–7, 108, 127, 139, 149–53, 156–66, 159, 168, 170–1, 178–9, 186–7, 200, 207, 210, 229, 235, 238, 243, 259–63, 280, 287, 289–90, 294, 304, 306–7, 309, 336, 339–41; moratorium on, 238, 240; state, 151–2, 156, 161–4, 166, 168, 170–1, 309; *see also* civilian(s), violence against; human rights, abuses

VOC, *see* Dutch, East India Company

Wahid, Abdul, 115–6

Wahid, Abdurrahman, President of Indonesia (1999–2001), 201, 208, 210, 239, 259–60, 275, 278–80, 288, 300–2, 304, 330–1

Wali Nanggroe, 302–3

West Aceh, 100, 105, 126, 177, 180, 182, 188, 235, 250–1, 299, 327, 357

Wiranto, General, 259, 276, 278

Wirayuda, Hassan, 255, 259, 279, 282

women, 9, 41–3, 47, 113–6, 127, 175, 228, 252, 254, 257, 285, 299, 306, 308, 310

Yamani, Sheikh Muhammad, 48, 57

Yogyakarta, 128–9, 162, 181, 204, 273, 302

youth, 63, 99, 106, 127, 138, 159, 162–3, 166–8, 170, 184, 194, 275, 318–9, 338; groups/organisations, 161, 167–8, 318–9, 338

Yudhoyono, Susilo Bambang, President of Indonesia (since 2004), 259, 282, 285, 287–8, 345, 347, 250

Yusuf, Maj. Gen. Djali, 251, 291

zakat, 296, 309